"The island seems rocky and inhospitable until one has landed. Everything changes then, and it would be difficult to find another such place or island with so much diversified scenery in so small a compass—both beautiful and picturesque: a woods in which one can become lost, little valleys, miniature ravines, a marsh for the Sora to hide in, a pond for the sandpiper, cliffs for grand views, and beautiful rocks for some artists to daub with paint."

John W. Dewis, M.D.
September 1918

Blue Jay, Sep 25, 2014. © Bill Thompson.

The Birds of Monhegan

Brett M. Ewald

The Birds of Monhegan
Copyright © 2023 Brett M. Ewald

ISBN: 978-1-954517-54-7

All rights reserved. No part of this book may be reproduced in any form or by any electronic or mechanical means, including information storage and retrieval systems, without permission in writing from the author, except by a reviewer, who may quote brief passages in review.

Design by Brett M. Ewald and Shane Ewald
Cover art by Karl Bardon
Monhegan Trail Map by Monhegan Associates, Inc.
Boundary and Birding Maps by Shane Ewald
Back cover photo by Luke Seitz

First Edition: May 2023

Indie Author Books
12 High Street, Thomaston, Maine
www.indieauthorbooks.com

Printed in the United States of America

0 9 8 7 6 5 4 3 2 1

www.BirdsofMonhegan.com

For Sheryl,
> the sun that warms my heart
> the wind that lifts my soul
> the rock that keeps me strong
> the tide that carries me on

Least Flycatcher, May 16, 2011. © Geoff Dennis.

CONTENTS

FOREWORD by Davis Finch 9
PREFACE & ACKNOWLEDGEMENTS 11
INTRODUCTION 13
ISLAND HISTORY 15
    Birding History 16
    The Present and Future of Birding 19
MAKING THE MOST OF YOUR BIRDING 21
    Habitats 21
    Weather and Birds 23
    Birding Seasonality and Locations 27
        The Village and the Meadow 28
        Lobster Cove/Point 31
        The Ice Pond 32
        Lighthouse Hill and the Ballfield 34
        The Headlands 34
            Black Head 35
            White Head 35
            Burnt Head and Underhill Trail 36
        Cathedral Woods 36
        The Coniferous North 36
        Manana 37
        Monhegan's Islets 38
        Ferry Crossings 39
    Visitor Services and Accommodations 39
INTRODUCTION TO SPECIES ACCOUNTS 41
    Period Covered 41
    Geographic Boundaries 41
    Sources of Data 42
        Source Abbreviations and Acronyms 43
        List of Observers/Contributors 44
    Defining a Record 48
    Species Account Format 49
        Status 49
        Occurrence 50
        Historical/Regional 62
SPECIES ACCOUNTS 65
HYPOTHETICALS 267
REFERENCES 269
ANNOTATED CHECKLIST OF MONHEGAN BIRDS 275
INDEX OF SPECIES ACCOUNTS BY COMMON NAME 283

View from White Head to the northeast toward Black Head. © Brett M. Ewald.

FOREWORD

In just the few decades since about 1960, Monhegan Island has become an ornithological legend, some would say a miracle, visited by an almost unimaginable array of rare birds and by a rapidly increasing number of sophisticated ornithotourists, both skillful birdwatchers and gifted photographers.

Such a visitor is Brett Ewald, whose illuminating account herein tells the whole story: all the birds, every species, even all the individuals of the scarcer ones, the observers, the dates, and the many minor yet fabled localities such as obscure gardens in little-known backyards, or particular stacks of lobster traps, or a certain humble but hallowed clothesline, each site forever sanctified by some astonishing avian rarity still bright in memory. Brett's skill interpreting and summarizing so great a body of information is wondrous: his book reads like a vast revelation, recounting the past and on occasion foretelling the future. This is in every sense an auspicious volume.

But this beautiful island offers so much in addition to the birds, as landscape painters discovered as early as the 19th century: its mighty headlands are the highest in the northeastern United States, with views out to sea as far as Matinicus Rock. Monhegan's Lighthouse Hill and eminences around the village afford prospects southwestward to historic Seguin Island and the mainland, with Pemaquid Point's distant, faintly blinking light, while on the northeastern horizon stand, like a little family, the delicate and remote Camden Hills, forever seeming about to vanish.

And Monhegan's seasons as well touch the heart: timid spring with its secular, late-blooming lilacs, and the ever-poignant arrière-saison after summer ends and the asters begin to fade, and so too the frail blooms of Scarlet Pimpernel among the rocks of Lobster Point. Then autumn, with empty hotel rooms and unaccustomed silence, or the hiss of leafless, wind-shaken thickets or the plangent, lonely tones of a faraway bellbuoy. And winter, perhaps the season that's best experienced in a museum: Rockwell Kent's stark and snowy landscapes are beautiful beyond words, and deeply moving.

What good fortune it is to hold the island in an unending, spiritual embrace, and to revisit its every corner in fact, in memory, or in art. What good fortune, as well, to know "Munhiggin's" residents: admirably strong all of them, and unfailingly kind and welcoming.

Davis Finch
September 2022

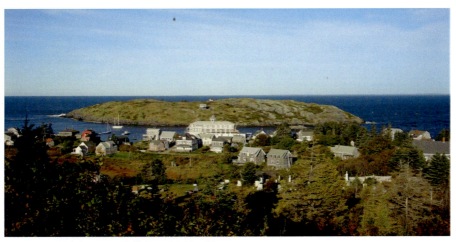

View from Lighthouse Hill. © Brett M. Ewald.

Vesper Sparrow, Oct 2, 2021. © Luke Seitz.

PREFACE & ACKNOWLEDGEMENTS

It's hard to believe that more than twenty years have passed since my wife Sheryl and I first set foot upon Monhegan—a day-trip stopover while on our way Downeast to lead a birding tour for puffins and songbirds. Four hours. Only four hours in June of 2001 to explore Monhegan. Four hours to take in the rugged beauty and charming setting, and of course, its birds. Four too-short hours! But despite this short duration, just like so many others before and since, we were captured in Monhegan's trap.

That first visit would be followed by many others during fall migration over the next two decades, experiencing the birds, places, and people that have made Monhegan one of the top birding destinations in North America. It was too-brief immersions in salty breezes, fantastic sunsets, and innumerable encounters with birds....or in some cases memorable near misses, such as a Virginia's Warbler *by ten minutes* with the ferry waiting for us to board it. It was the excitement of stepping off the *Laura B.* or *Elizabeth Ann* into the expectations of what might be. It was chats with Tom and Josephine Martin across the breadth of their seed- and bird-infested yard, a must-stop on every pass through the village. It was the contentment of seawatching with White Head at our backs and the ocean far below, with shearwaters skimming by, gannets plunge-diving, and whale blows breaking the water's surface. It was regularly scanning for newly arrived drop-ins at the peaceful Ice Pond or the frenetic pace of a morning fallout, with birds all around and overhead, flashes of color and bursts of sound. It was the diversity and close-up views of warblers, many at eye level in the village's apple trees and lilacs. It was the never-ending delight of a Winter Wren's song and searches for fairies in Cathedral Woods. It was a Merlin repeatedly catching dragonflies over our heads at the Ballfield, while Peregrine Falcons kited in the breezes over Manana. It was the blooming flowers and associated butterflies that fluttered by. It was seeing the island from a different perspective on an around-the-island excursion on *Balmy Days*, with seals hauled out on the outer islets and Bald Eagles surveying their domain. It was taking a break from birding to savor a pizza from the Novelty (migrating birds love pizza breath) and settling in for a serene island night at Shining Sails, with dreams of what the morning would bring. It was overseeing it all from the sweeping vantage of the historic lighthouse, a connection between the past and present. It was a delightful little reprint available from the Monhegan Library, "*The Birds of Monhegan, A Fall Migration Census from 1918,*" encapsulating the same sense of discovery and wonder. It would lead to a desire to know more about the history and the current status of birds on the island—and the idea for *The Birds of Monhegan* book was hatched.

While getting the book into your hands has been a long journey—over 15 years—and though the ease of access to sightings has improved greatly over that period, it was the early support I received that helped initiate and sustain the project. I cannot thank the following enough for this needed impetus. Tom Martin (1921–2016) had an impact on the island's birders that cannot be overstated, through his direct interaction, bird feeding and photography over 50 years, visiting spring and fall. Although my interactions with him were infrequent, they were memorable, and a discussion of the book led to his sharing his personal handwritten notes right out of his well-used field guide. His enthusiasm about the island and its birds deserves our deepest appreciation. Tony Vazzano's support and sharing of many trip sightings were critical, and so too was the extensive review prepared by Jody Despres of *Maine Birdlife, Maine Bird Notes* and other journals and reports. Geoff Dennis generously shared sightings, photos and anecdotes and put me in touch with long-time Monhegan birder Jack Skelton and his sightings and experiences. Other early contributors of sightings, locations and checklists included Helen Bailey, Janice Doppler, Mike Emmons, Richard Duddy, Wendy Howes, Marie Jordan, Maeve Kim, Blake Mathys, Steve Nanz, John Puschock, Robert A. Quinn (New Hampshire Audubon), Bob Schutsky (including the Magnificent Frigatebird illustration by Doris Hough), Luke Seitz, Marie Louise St. Onge, Dena Temple, Joan Thompson, Frederick Thurber, Bill Townsend and Kathy Van Der Aue. Further sightings and clarifications of past reports were provided by Louis Bevier, Laura Blutstein, Jackie Boegel, Donna Cundy, Charles Duncan (who also made me aware of the early photo of Monhegan birders in Lucia Miller's book), Davis Finch, Noah Gibb, Eleanor Goldberg, Monica Grabin, Doug Hitchcox, Wendy Howes, Kathie Krause, Rob Lambert, Kristen Lindquist, Derek Lovitch (including many trip reports, blog posts and personal notes),

Tom Magarian (intensive birding in 2010 & 2011), Delia Mohlie, Howie Nielsen, Blair Nikula, Joe Scott, Bill Sheehan, Scott Surner, Jeremiah Trimble, and Jeff Wells (extensive personal notes and trip lists). Others provided sightings that proved invaluable, notably residents Jackie Boegel, Willard Boynton, Donna Cundy and Doug Hitchcox. Finally, I want to thank all the birders I've never met who took the time to report what they had seen, whether an article in the *Journal of the Maine Ornithological Society* in 1908 or eBird in 2022—you've helped us all to understand the magic of Monhegan's birds a little bit better.

I must thank the Monhegan Historical and Cultural Museum (an incredible island resource), in particular Jennifer Pye for her time and talents: she generously shared many historical checklists and correspondence from 1899 to the 2000s. Rebecca FitzPatrick and Monhegan Associates, Inc. gave permission to use their long-established trail map and work tirelessly to maintain and improve the island's habitat—they deserve every birder's appreciation and acknowledgement. Warmest thanks to the Miller/Taylor family, especially granddaughter Lele Miller Barkhausen and Henry, for sharing with us the legacy of Warner and Clarkie Taylor through original checklists and correspondence, as well as for their hospitality and stories of the island. Richard Farrell kindly provided permission to share the checklists of his mother Isabel Farrell and Joseph Van Os his banding results. Laura Kennedy Blandford provided insight and reports of the Deepwater Offshore Wind Turbine Site Surveys and Paul Adamus and Adrienne Leppold granted permission to use the *Maine Atlas of Breeding Birds* and Maine Bird Atlas data, respectively. Chris DeSorbo provided information and insight into the Biodiversity Research Institute raptor studies and Peregrine Falcon tracking, Kathy Klimkiewicz and Matt Rogosky assisted with Bird Banding Lab information and William Livingston shared his findings regarding the island's vegetation. Eva Matthews Lark from Hog Island Audubon Camp, Juanita Roushdy from Friends of Hog Island, and Meghan Kelly from History IT deserve thanks for providing and granting permission to use fabulous historical photos from the 1930s, as do Nan Nelson and the Nelson family for allowing inclusion of the Fall Migration Census cover, and Jennifer Bogo and National Audubon Society for use of the August 1968 *Audubon Field Notes* cover. Barbara Vickery and Scott Weidensaul were supportive and kind enough to grant permission to highlight Monhegan's part in Peter Vickery's *Birds of Maine*, while Louis Bevier advised regarding the Official List of Maine Birds. Louis Bevier, Derek Lovitch and Jeremiah Trimble provided insights and comments regarding early drafts, while I need to acknowledge Scott Weidensaul and Jeff Wells for reading the manuscript and providing testimonials. Davis Finch was a source of island information, edits, inspiration, and pleasant conversation throughout much of the later development of the book, and thoughtfully provided the Foreword. Thanks to Karen Thompson for kindly copy editing and providing suggestions regarding the text and format. *The Birds of Monhegan* has been brought to life by the beautiful original cover artwork by Karl Bardon and the incredible photos provided by an array of generous photographers to each of whom I am most grateful, most notably Geoff Dennis, Doug Hitchcox, Luke Seitz, Bill Thompson and Jeremiah Trimble, and also Louis Bevier, Jessica Bishop, Laura Blutstein, Donna Cundy, Adam Dudley, Charles Duncan, Cory Elowe, Ken Feustel, Marshall Iliff, Kyle Jones, Sebastian Jones, Fyn Kynd, Tom Magarian, Kent McFarland, Lukas Musher, Don Reimer, Scott Surner and Bobby Wilcox.

Our time on the island has been enriched by the companionship and generous sharing of experiences of many others through the years: Laura Blutstein, Don and Ann Cowley, Charles Duncan, Davis Finch, Nancy Frass, David Gulick, Bob and Sally Kendall, Kristen Lindquist, Derek and Jeannette Lovitch, Al and Linda Maley, Jane and Steve Mirick, Gayle Moore, Bryan Pfeiffer, Sallie and Tom Potter, Don and Sherry Reimer, Diane and Michael Thibault, Bill Thompson, Tony and Susan Vazzano, and others whose names I never knew or escape me now. I'd also like to thank the many tour participants I shared time with as part of memorable Lakeshore Nature Tours and NJ Audubon Eco-Travel trips on Monhegan. The hospitality provided by John and Winnie Murdock ensured we were always comfortable and ready for the next birding adventure.

Lastly, family has played an important part in the journey. My parents, Ralph and Margaret, provide continuous support of my interests and endeavors, along with Shane Ewald, Shawn and Stacey Ewald, Julie and Hristo Doichev, and Jim and Janine Hogan, including enabling the design and printing. I am lifted by the spirit of my late brother, Jeff—the true definition of a Big Brother. Most importantly, I couldn't have done this without my wife, Sheryl, whose love, support, patience and sharing of adventures provide such joy and meaning to my life.

So, check out what has been and prepare for what might show up next. Let me know what you come up with, or better yet, show it to me on Monhegan!

INTRODUCTION

Wolcott W. Ellsworth said it well in 1912 in his *Brief Description of the 'Sentinel of New England' for All Who Appreciate the Beautiful and the Picturesque*, stating that Monhegan is "the most famous island of this part of the coast. Today it is the delight of the weary worker, and an inspiration to artists. Whoever visits Monhegan desires to return".

So, what is it that has inspired, amazed, charmed, overwhelmed and fulfilled residents and visitors to its shores? It's not an imposing island by size, only 1.7 miles long and 0.7 miles wide, totaling 433 acres, but it surely does make up for it in what it offers to the eyes, ears, and soul. Any trip to this Midcoast Maine island starts with a boat ride, as the nearest mainland is Port Clyde, some 12 nautical miles distant. The voyage provides views of the coastal islands and then the open ocean before passing by islets and pulling into Monhegan's safe harbor, enabled by the largely uninhabited 25-acre island of Manana snuggled up next door. The lighthouse maintains its obvious perch overlooking the western side of Monhegan, signaling for two hundred years that safety and resources are to be found. Leaving the wharf behind, one is greeted by a small year-round island community with comfortable inns, B&Bs, seaside rentals, restaurants, cafes, and a brewery in season, sustained by a small general store, post office, and lobstering. You've stepped back a little in time and encounter a slower pace, with electricity a recent amenity for some and still no streetlights, with the few vehicles present owned by residents and mainly used on the gravel roads for deliveries and hauling luggage to visitor accommodations. The roads quickly become trails (measuring ~17 miles on the island!) that provide access to the two-thirds of the island that remain in a natural state, due to the foresight, commitment, and work of the Monhegan Associates. You can't help but enjoy the serenity of the spruce-fir forest or the Ice Pond, the expanse and variety provided by the nine-acre freshwater marshy meadow, or the VIEWS, whether the distant mainland from Lighthouse Hill, the lapping ocean at rocky Lobster Cove, or the incredible vistas from the headlands on the east side of the island, the highest cliffs on the U.S. Eastern Seaboard, reaching 160' at Black Head and White Head. And while you're taking a picture, make sure you're not stepping in front of an artist's easel with a masterpiece in the works!

Seawatching at Whitehead. © Brett M. Ewald.

Of course, for those like me, it has mostly been the birds. For over a century, it has been the birds, to the point that it is now legendary for the abundance, diversity and rarity of many that have graced its shores. This book is an attempt to provide a record of the **what** and **how many** of birds on Monhegan, an official record of occurrence.

Currently an amazing 336 species have been recorded on or from Monhegan, with another 19 on the hypothetical list; this is almost as many as some states. As of December 31, 2022, the Maine state list stood at 470 (Maine Bird Records Committee). Monhegan has contributed at least 15 first records for the state, and many more second or third records, with four species being recorded only on Monhegan, including all four records of Virginia's Warbler. The other three species are Gray Flycatcher, Cassin's Vireo, and Shiny Cowbird. Other first state records were Calliope Hummingbird, Bridled Tern, Swallow-tailed Kite, Say's Phoebe, Bell's Vireo, Varied Thrush, Black-throated Sparrow, Lark Sparrow, Brewer's Sparrow, Townsend's Warbler, and Hermit Warbler.

Some birders come for the regularity with which vagrants are encountered, for example, ten records of White-winged Dove, 44 of Western Kingbird, three of Townsend's Solitaire, five of Lark Bunting, 20 of Yellow-throated Warbler, and many records of the normally uncommon Clay-colored Sparrow and Lark Sparrow. Others come for the sheer volume of birds that can be encountered, with some eye-opening daily totals recorded for many species, for example 15,000 Common Eiders, 10,000 Great Shearwaters, 600 Sharp-shinned Hawks, 110 Merlins, 345 Red-eyed Vireos, 800 Golden-crowned Kinglets, 800 Swainson's Thrushes, 300 White-winged Crossbills, 5,000+ Dark-eyed Juncos, 3,000+ White-crowned Sparrows, 200 Common Yellowthroats, 353 Magnolia Warblers, 1,900 Yellow-rumped Warblers, and 225 Rose-breasted Grosbeaks. An astounding fallout of 776+ *Empidonax* flycatchers noted on May 30, 2013 consisted mainly of Alder and Willow Flycatchers—see The *Empidonax* Fallout on page 158.

This is just a sampling of the many amazing birding observations from this historic bump of land off Midcoast Maine, shaped like the back of a whale or the nave of a ship, depending on your perspective. It is this abundance and diversity that paint the picture of Monhegan's birdlife, a palette as rich as almost any other location in Eastern North America.

Wood Duck, Oct 4, 2020. © Luke Seitz.

ISLAND HISTORY

Monhegan's known history goes back centuries and is rooted in the fog of myth, legends, and unclear references stretching back millennia. This is all covered and scrutinized in detail in a number of historical publications, notably Charles Francis Jenney's *The Fortunate Island of Monhegan* (1922) and Ida Sedgwick Proper's aptly named *Monhegan, The Cradle of New England* (1930—the source of said title as observed and proclaimed by the Hon. Charles Levi Woodbury in his *Pemaquid and Monhegan* address to the Hyde Park Historical Society in 1891) and enhanced by Ruth Grant Faller's *Monhegan: Her Houses and Her People, 1780–2000* (2001). While it is not my intent to replay the human history of the island, early colonization and more importantly, habitat changes brought on by humans, have affected the birdlife living there and passing by (see the Reference section for additional informative sources).

Despite four known Native American sites dating back ~4000 years (Miller, 2005) and physical remnants in the form of projectile points still being found, much about their presence on Monhegan remains unknown. The name is apparently derived from Monchiggon, Algonquian for "out-to-sea island" and the island was also called Monahigan or Monhiggon, among other names. We do know that Samoset, who played an important role in the early years of the Plymouth settlement in Massachusetts, was an Abenaki tribal leader (Sagamore or "Lord") on Monhegan in the early 1600s and learned English from visiting sailors and fishermen. European recorded history dates back to the 1550s and the island was undoubtedly visited by various explorers. According to the Spanish, it was already "inhabited" by the British in 1558, and there were known visits by Martin Pring in 1603, Samuel de Champlain in 1604, the George Waymouth (or Weymouth) Expedition in 1605 (the first officially documented landing occurring on May 18) and Captain John Smith in 1614 (Proper, 1930).

The combination of a safe harbor (~2,000' long, 500'–900' wide and 18'–90' deep; Pope, 1916), fresh water, and proximity to the mainland made it the perfect staging area for exploration and preparation of local resources for return shipment. The subsequent establishment of a British fishing camp, principally for drying cod, brought the first real development to Monhegan. In 1674, John Dolling became the first inn-holder on the island, with a license for "houses of public entertainment" and sale of beer, wine and liquor (Jenney, 1922). The island did not escape being caught up in the territorial disputes of the British and French, resulting in the abandonment of the settlement in 1689 during the French and Indian Wars. After political maneuverings placed Monhegan in the hands of a Massachusetts citizen, Nicholas Davidson, it resumed its place as a commercial fishing destination and underwent substantial settling in the first half of the 1700s. Passing through a couple of owners, the island eventually became the possession of Henry Trefethren in 1777 and underwent true colonization after the family moved there in 1781. Joined through marriage to the Starlings and Horns (sometimes written as Hornes), the three families divided the island in 1807. These lineages continue on the island today; one need only stroll through the island's cemetery to witness the memorials to those who have gone before. The population had grown to 43 by 1810 and 68 by 1820, surprisingly only one shy of the census population of 69 in 2010 (Wikipedia, 2021)

The settlement became more formalized with the construction of the first lighthouse in 1824, just four years after Maine's statehood, and Monhegan's official designation as a plantation in 1839 (a form of local self-government in town-sized areas with a small population). The first library was established in 1845, a fog bell station was constructed on Manana in 1855, and a post office opened in 1858. By the middle of the 19th century, much of the island had been cleared of trees, apart from the Cathedral Woods area, for timber to be used in the building of boats and dwellings as well as to provide more acreage for agriculture. Along with a population increase (reaching a peak of 145 in 1870) came livestock and crops, chief of which were potatoes. Sheep were the most common livestock, reaching hundreds of individuals, with a few cows and oxen also present. By the end of the century, these practices were dwindling due to the impracticality of growing crops and controversy over livestock practices (Harris, 2014–15).

While fishing has remained a dominant industry, with a transition from cod and mackerel to lobster by the early 1900s, tourism has also played an important role in the island's sustainability. By the second half of the 19th century, the beauty of Monhegan was already attracting wealthy visitors, as well as early members of an artist colony which became firmly established by 1890. These included members of the New York School of Art and Pennsylvania Academy of the Fine Arts, such as Robert Henri, Edward Hopper and Rockwell Kent, and the island hosted a celebrated art exhibition in 1914. Perhaps the best-known artists to reside on the island have been Andrew Wyeth and his son Jamie, who maintains a residence to this day.

General tourism continued to grow in the early 20th century, with the addition of four hotels by 1915 (Pope, 1916) as well as summer homes and plans for many more, with project names such as Prospect Hill and Surf Side. This development caught the attention of Thomas Edison's son, Theodore, a regular visitor and admirer of the island since 1908. From the 1920's to the 1940s, he purchased as many plots of land as became available to preserve the natural state of the island, including the forests and headlands. In 1954, he donated these lands to a new organization of which he was a founder, Monhegan Associates, Inc., dedicated to conserving the lands for all in an undeveloped state (Edison, 1976), as stated in its bylaws:

> …to preserve for posterity the natural wild beauty, biotic communities, and desirable natural, artificial, and historic features of the so-called 'wild lands' portions of Monhegan Island, Maine, and its environs.

This act had the single, largest impact on the future of Monhegan's habitats and affected the quality of life of its residents and visitors, ultimately protecting the roughly two-thirds of the island (380 acres) outside of the village. Acquisition of land continues today. The maintained trails throughout are essential to hiking, general access, and of course, birding. This century also brought improvements to living and comfort, such as water supply, limited electricity, and telephone service.

Today, Monhegan's magic continues to inspire, and the daily population is a varied mix of year-round residents, seasonals, short-term renters, and day-trippers, escalating from the core of lobstering families in the winter (~60 individuals) to the main economic industry of tourism reaching hundreds per day in the summer peak. Artists continue to embrace the island, through residents and seasonals who occupy studios, often open to visitors at set times, and visiting individuals (sometimes taking part in week-long classes) who capture the essence of Monhegan on canvas and in other forms, available at several galleries and shops. Businesses have adapted or emerged to meet the changing desires of visitors, such as a coffee roaster, chocolate boutique, and brewery, and Monhegan remains a frequent subject in popular literature, such as National Geographic. And birders flock to the island, mainly in spring and fall.

BIRDING HISTORY

It was James Rosier, the historian of the Waymouth expedition, who made **the first known bird "observations" on Monhegan**, coming ashore for a short time on May 18, 1605 with Captain George Waymouth and eleven other men. He noted "very great egge shelles bigger than goose egges" about the remnants of a fire, possibly those of Great Auks or cranes but remaining unidentified, and more generally observed that "much fowl of divers kinds breed upon the shore and rocks" (Rosier, 1887 [Reprint of]; Jenney, 1922; Palmer 1949; Morey, 2005; Vickery, 2020).[1]

It would be more than three hundred years before another known reference to Monhegan's birds would appear in print with the publication of Francis Allen's *An Ornithological Reconnaissance of Monhegan* in 1908. His comment "Monhegan, as I suppose most Maine ornithologists know," however, suggests it was already well known as a bird study destination, assisted, no doubt, by the previously mentioned burgeoning tourist and artist industry

---

[1] The designation of Monhegan as a location of large egg shells is inferred by the ship's route and subsequent sightings related by Rosier, but not explicitly stated. It has been overlooked or not addressed by many historians, resulting in differing interpretations or conclusions. Palmer (1949) supported the egg observations as being on Monhegan but inconclusive as to species, while Vickery (2020) presents conflicting information under the Sandhill Crane and Great Auk accounts.

and associated accommodations and amenities to attract visitors. This is supported by a report to Washington D.C. in 1894 by lightkeeper William Stanley (undoubtedly a government report), addressing the abundance of birds around the lighthouse and stating that "Some nights they will appear in thousands" (*AFN* 14[1]: 10), as well as the earliest known checklist from Monhegan, a listing of 31 bird species recorded by Mrs. M. E. Hartwell in **1899**![2] This is followed by a list compiled in Aug 1908 by Charles F. Jenney and E. C. Jenney of bird species recorded by them 1900–1908 that were not included on Allen's list. Second-hand information gathered by Allen while there indicated an abundance of birds during migration, particularly autumn, a foreshadowing of birding as we presently know it. His observation that Monhegan is "small enough to make a detailed and comprehensive study of its bird-fauna both comparatively easy and very profitable" is followed by an appeal to other observers to publish their sightings for the benefit of New England ornithologists. It must have worked, as C. J. Maynard published his *Notes on Birds, Butterflies, Etc., Observed on Monhegan Island Maine* (from July 1909, arriving from Boston by train and steamer after an invitation by the Hon. Chas. F. Jenney). This is the same Charles F. Jenney who compiled the Monhegan bird sightings of Bertrand H. Wentworth as *The Fall Migration of 1918 at Monhegan Island, Maine*, published along with *A Visit to Monhegan Island, Maine, September 1918* by John W. Dewis, M.D. in C. J. Maynard's *Records of Walks and Talks with Nature* (Vol. 11). This group of amateur ornithologists, along with Professor John "Warner" Taylor, Clara Taylor, Mrs. Edwin C. Jenney, William Fuller (1914 Checklist) and Mrs. C. H. Gleason (1916 Checklist), would form the apparent core group of this early Monhegan birding heyday (Wentworth and Warner Taylor were noted landscape photographers).[3] Warner Taylor kept daily notes on sightings and observations of daily life during his time there 1915–1919 (spanning Jul 29–Sep 14), and coupled with subsequent bird observations (he visited and maintained a residence into the 1950s), culminated in the 1939 Summer Bird Census article, as published in the Monhegan Press.[2] While C. F. Jenney intended to publish his own bird sightings, his records have not come to light. The lack of winter records comes as no surprise, considering the harsh weather conditions and lack of visitor amenities.

Amateur ornithologists on Monhegan, 1917. *Front Row:* Miss Ordway, Mrs. C. H. Gleason. *Back Row:* Judge Charles Francis Jenney, Miss Cheeney, Bertrand Wentworth, Carl Winn, Mr. Cheeney, Miss Monroe, Mr. Warner Taylor. Photographer unknown—photo courtesy the Monhegan Historical and Cultural Museum Association.

---

[2] Information accessed through the archives of the Monhegan Historical and Cultural Museum Association.
[3] The awareness of birds on Maine's offshore islands and the developing ornithological efforts on Monhegan were assuredly enhanced by the extensive sightings in the late 1890s-early 1900s from nearby Seguin Island (visible to the southwest from Lobster Cove on a clear day). These were published by lighthouse keeper Herbert Spinney in *Maine Sportsman* and *The Journal of the Maine Ornithological Society*, which Spinney served as president.

The first known bird banding occurred as early as 1930, when Dr. Olin Sewall Pettingill, Jr. banded gulls at Duck Rock on June 29, but further known banding would not occur until 1960. Insights into island life and the birdlife present were imparted by island resident Josephine Townsend in letters to Mrs. Edwin C. Jenney in Jan 1934 and Jan and Mar 1939, providing rare winter and early spring bird observations and mentioning resources available, such as field guides, to birders at that time.[2] More detailed birding reports were to follow, commencing with a Christmas Bird Count on Dec 29, 1940. Sporadic yearlong sightings, extensive in certain years, by or compiled by island resident and Island Inn owner Isabel Farrell 1944–1946, 1948–1961, and 1967, along with six summer checklists from 1954 and 1955 collected by the Monhegan Museum (covering the period Jun 11–Sep 2), greatly aid in our understanding of presence/seasonality.[2] Some of the contributors of the 1954–55 checklists, namely Albert and Eva Schnitzer, would return in fall for three years, 1960–1962, to band songbirds as part of Operation Recovery (Schnitzer, 1963). Sightings by Helene Tetrault, Richard L. Plunkett, Rita White, Christopher M. Packard and others in the 1960s made it into the pages of the *Maine Field Naturalist* and *Audubon Field Notes*. Extensive banding of juvenile gulls was carried out in the summers of 1965, 1967, and 1969. Based on observations throughout the 1960s, the Monhegan Historical and Cultural Museum Association, formerly the Monhegan Museum, published a checklist of summer birds in 1970: *Birds of Monhegan Island, Maine; Also Manana, Nearby Islets, and Surrounding Waters. July and August Observations.*

Hog Island Audubon Camp, the celebrated educational institution in Mid-Coast Maine, first accepted campers in 1936 and has been leading birding trips and ornithology classes to Monhegan since at least 1938, led early on by well-known ornithologists Allan Cruickshank, Alexander Sprunt, Jr. and Roger Tory Peterson, and continues today through the efforts and talents of many notable birders and naturalists (National Audubon Society, 2021b).

Hog Island Audubon Camp at Lobster Cove, circa 1938. Photographer unknown—courtesy Friends of Hog Island Digital Archive.

The "Monhegan Audubon Club" listens to Allen Cruickshank imitate birds, circa 1941. Photo by Helen Cruickshank—courtesy Friends of Hog Island Digital Archive.

First arriving from Manhattan in 1954, Tom Martin and his wife Irene (and years later Josephine) spent a month on the island in spring and fall each year, continuing until the mid-2010s. Although Tom was initially focused on photography rather than birds, his pictures of rarities on the island ultimately caught the attention of an editor at *Audubon Field Notes* (later *American Birds*). This would result in a cover photo of Clay-colored Sparrow on the Aug 1968 issue (Vol. 22, No. 4), adding credibility and exposure to Monhegan's reputation and resulting in the inclusion of Tom's photos in other birding publications and guides. Many of Tom's photos can still be seen in digital format at the Monhegan Museum of Art and History, as well as short videos of Tom himself. While he didn't keep daily or even seasonal checklists, his notations of rarities in his field guide dating back to the mid-1960s were critical for documentation, particularly until the mid-1970s, when there was an increase in sightings by other birders. His presence and prolific bird feeding at their rental property near Fish Beach were even more important to the many birders who appreciated the sightings and birding banter while making their way through the village.

---

[2] Information accessed through the archives of the Monhegan Historical and Cultural Museum Association.

Tom Martin using a custom camera set-up to take macro photos of a Northern Parula. Photographer unknown—courtesy Monhegan Historical and Cultural Museum Association.

Macro photo of a Northern Flicker wing, highlighting the feather patterns. Photo by Tom Martin (1933-2016)—courtesy Monhegan Historical and Cultural Museum Association.

Another long-time visitor, John "Jack" Skelton, first spent time on Monhegan in 1933. He intermittently visited the island through the years, becoming a "serious" birder in 1976 and spending the third week of May on Monhegan for nearly the next 25 years. He kept notecards containing FOY (first of year) sightings, many of which occurred for him on Monhegan.

Starting in the mid 1970s, Denny Abbott, Davis Finch, Will Russell and Peter Vickery, along with Charles Duncan, Wendy Howes, Jan and Liz Pierson, Margery Plymire, Allison and Jeff Wells and others in the mid 1980s, would expand our knowledge of Monhegan's birds tremendously—the advent of what could be termed the modern era of Monhegan birding. A census of coastal waterbird breeding colonies, including four of the islands surrounding Monhegan, was conducted by the Maine Cooperative Wildlife Research Unit 1976–1977 (Korschgen, 1979). The *Maine Atlas of Breeding Birds* was compiled 1978–1983 and included reports from Monhegan (Adamus, 1987). 1978 would also see the first Christmas Bird Count on Monhegan since 1941; this was the start of fourteen consecutive counts followed by intermittent counts since 1994 (National Audubon Society, 2020). As word continued to spread regarding the rarities and abundance of birds on the island, the number of birders increased dramatically during spring and fall (including trips by Maine Audubon, other birding groups and professional tours) and sighting reports to the Maine Rare Bird Alert and published sources, such as *Maine Bird Life*, *Maine Bird Notes*, and *Guillemot*, increased significantly in the 1980s and 1990s. Along with the increase in birders came limited, intermittent songbird banding operations 1980–1991 and 2002.

Birding continued to flourish into the twenty-first century, with the eBird database of Cornell's Lab of Ornithology making tracking and storing sightings easier and more convenient than ever, giving a truer picture of the number of both birders and birds present. The last decade has seen a consistently high level of eBird checklist submissions during the spring and fall migration periods, with just a smattering from winter and summer, and now involves hundreds of observers and over 7,000 checklists (eBird, 2023). Professional birding companies took advantage of this sustained interest in Monhegan's birds and the possibilities that existed for further discoveries, with expanded opportunities offered by multiple companies.

In the fall of 2010, the Biodiversity Research Institute conducted a standardized hawkwatch and raptor banding, both diurnal and nocturnal, to document presence and Monhegan's stopover value, in part to assess risks posed by a proposed wind power facility (DeSorbo et al., 2012). Similarly, radar studies involving bird and bat presence and movements (impossible to separate on radar) were conducted Jul 2010–Jul 2011(Mizrahi et al., 2013) and acoustic monitoring of nocturnal bird migration was undertaken in fall 2011 to assess passage at a location near a proposed offshore deepwater wind energy test site approximately 5 km to the southwest of the island (Holberton & Wright, 2012). While on the island to conduct the radar studies, Tom Magarian provided a wealth of additional sightings, most importantly consistent reports from the summer and late fall to early spring periods. Finally, a Maine Bird Atlas project commenced in 2018, with observations from Monhegan contributing to its ultimate completion in 2022 and subsequent results (eBird Maine Bird Atlas, 2023).

THE PRESENT AND FUTURE OF BIRDING

Today, birding Monhegan is more popular than ever, with reservations for accommodation needed well in advance during the peak migration periods of May and Sep/early Oct. Rarities, especially first state or island records, continue to impress: in Sep of 2020, MacGillivray's Warbler and Black-throated Gray Warbler were new for the island and fifth and sixth records, respectively, for Maine. Many groups and professional tours can be seen taking advantage of the variety and close views, and the sharing of information is an important component of making the most of a visit. Photography has become widespread and no doubt Tom Martin would have appreciated the efforts taken to enjoy, share, and document sightings through this medium. While there is a paucity of sightings from outside the migration periods, several residents, among them Willard "Billy" Boynton, Donna Cundy and Doug Hitchcox, and occasional visitors provide much needed information during the summer (breeding) and winter seasons.

As mentioned, despite Monhegan's history, popularity and volume of reports, we still have much to learn about birds on and around the island—and you can be part of it. Undoubtedly, the largest gaps in our knowledge occur during winter and to a lesser extent summer. To illustrate the disproportionate coverage across months and seasons: **86%** of complete checklists (5,068) submitted to eBird prior to Feb 2023 (eBird, 2023) occurred during May, Sep & Oct (30%, 43%, and 13%, respectively), the "summer" months of Jun, Jul & Aug accounted for 10% (fairly evenly distributed), and the "winter" months of Dec, Jan & Feb accounted for <2% as a whole, mostly centered around the Christmas Bird Count period in late Dec–early Jan. There is even one week without any checklists submitted (Jan 8–14), while Feb was the least birded month with only nine checklists submitted. Even the "shoulder" spring and fall months of Mar, Apr and Nov only accounted for <3% (~1% each), reflecting the impact of less showy migration (few colorful songbirds, such as warblers, while waterbirds and sparrows are more numerous) and lack of visitor amenities, such as the closure of accommodations and eateries.

In the broader scheme of bird populations, the recovery of some groups, such as ducks (none listed in Warner Taylor's 1915–1919 sightings), shorebirds, seabirds, and wading birds from decimating market hunting and the millinery trade in the 1800s and early 1900s (paralleled by a switch from guns to binoculars by professional and amateur ornithologists) and raptors from DDT poisoning in the mid-20th century is remarkable and easy to observe. In the case of seabirds, the loss was so extreme that they were almost completely "eaten off" the outer islands of New England, with two major shooting campaigns (~1876 & 1896) eliminating almost all except the diminutive storm-petrels (Drury, 1974). This recovery is now overshadowed by the loss of 2.9 billion birds in North America since the 1970s (Rosenberg et al., 2019). This reduction is alarming and screams for better understanding of bird biology, movements, and conservation needs. Closer to home, the significant declines of many species (especially landbirds) are noted extensively in *The Birds of Maine* (Vickery et al., 2020) and mentioned in the Species Accounts here when appropriate.

It should be noted that a currently proposed demonstration project of one wind turbine—initially proposed as two—to be located ~two miles to the south of the island off Lobster Cove and within the Monhegan Island Lobster Conservation Area, brought about the initiation since 2010 of the various radar studies, acoustic monitoring, marine transects and migration studies (hawkwatch and raptor banding) that are cited in the species account section. The current timeline places a completed turbine at this location in 2023.

So, if after reading this book, you realize you have sightings that may contribute further to our understanding of birds on Monhegan, please reach out directly (brett.ewald90@gmail.com) with what you've seen. In particular, there are many breeding and winter species for which we have very few specific records, only a general understanding of their presence. Better yet, enjoy your first or a return trip to Monhegan and let me know what you find, no matter what time of year. Who knows, you may even make Monhegan birding history!

MAKING THE MOST OF YOUR BIRDING

Unless you're fortunate enough to be a resident of Monhegan, knowing where to look and under what conditions, as well as what resources are available, can help you make the most of your limited birding time.

HABITATS

One reason Monhegan attracts and holds a wide range of bird species is its mix of habitats, including fresh water, in an isolated small space. Early on, explorers took advantage of these resources and Rosier, upon first landing in 1605, noted Monhegan as "woody," with fir, birch, oak, and beech trees all along the shore, and gooseberries, strawberries, wild peas, and wild roses as well (Jenney, 1922). This was largely changed by the subsequent harvesting of trees for development and shipbuilding throughout the 17th and 18th centuries, resulting in the almost complete removal of mature trees (except for an area centered around Cathedral Woods and inland to the north). Much of the cleared land was cultivated or transformed into pastures for livestock in the 19th century.

Souvenir view of Monhegan from 1907, showng the extensive cleared areas in the central portion of the island (Horn's Hill in the background on the right).

Regrowth of vegetation after the cessation of many of these agricultural practices and a reduction in the amount of shipbuilding and other needs for native timber changed the landscape once again in the late 1800s and early 1900s. This process was also facilitated by a severe fire "that devastated the eastern end of the island during the late summer and fall of 1900"; a large tract of woods was destroyed and a peat bog in the center of the island burned underground for weeks (Cook, 1901). By the time Francis Allen visited in 1908, the interior was mostly a rather low growth of red and white spruce and balsam fir and swampy areas full of alders. He also noted a mix of scattered deciduous trees, such as birch, ash, and maple, and grassy pasture lands—formerly for sheep, whose fleece would inadvertently trap and spread seeds, including those of introduced plant species, to remote areas of the island (Cook, 1901). Blooming chickweed was present behind the eastern headlands and on the western slopes, with cherry and serviceberry along the edges and various shrubs and vines along the shore. The revegetation progressed, most notably in the wilder tracts to the north and east, to the point that Warner Taylor commented in 1939 that Monhegan was limited in bird species to be found (in comparison to the mainland) by the "**absence of farm lands** (*emphasis added*) and the scarcity of trees other than spruce." The preservation of natural areas afforded to two-thirds of the island (380 acres) by Monhegan Associates by 1954 allowed for a healthy return to natural processes and succession. In 1966, Monhegan Island was designated a National Natural Landmark for its coastal and island flora and *The Wildflowers of Monhegan, Maine, Including Nearby Islets,* compiled by Laurence Cooper, was published by the Monhegan Museum for the Monhegan Associates in 1981. A significant deer population was introduced in the 1950s as a source of food through hunting, then removed in the 1990s to eliminate a Lyme Disease epidemic brought on by deer ticks. Unfortunately, this came too late to undo the proliferation of invasive Japanese Barberry, first detected in 1971, in areas of extensive browsing that then expanded across the island. A control program was begun in 2003 to remove barberry and other less common invasive species.

Today, Monhegan's plant life is diverse and includes 14 tree species, 175+ wildflowers and herbs, 19 shrubs, 8 ferns, and other grass and sedge species (Miller, 2005–list compiled by Livingston and Dyer, 2003; Harris, 2014–15). An extensive list with many descriptions, including invasive species, can be found in the *Monhegan Nature Guide* by Lillian Harris (2014–15), including an updated Full List of Monhegan Wildflowers. A large portion of the "wildlands", the area of the island preserved by Monhegan Associates, can generally be characterized as coniferous forest (mainly spruces), lorded over by the old-growth Red Spruces in Cathedral Woods and reaching an extreme density in some areas, such as along the Red Ribbon Trail. The White Spruces that first repopulated the abandoned fields and cleared areas are nearing the end of their expected life spans and are susceptible to disease and parasites, most notably Eastern Dwarf Mistletoe and its associated "witch's brooms", and

A Merlin perched on a dead White Spruce overlooks the effects of dwarf mistletoe. © Brett M. Ewald

many dead or dying trees can be seen throughout the island. The later-developing Red Spruces are replacing them, as are balsam fir and deciduous species such as maple and birch. Wet swampy areas remain, containing both softwoods and hardwoods, with alders predominating, particularly in undeveloped areas near the Meadow and to the southeast towards Burnt Head—an area last cleared in the second half of the 20th century. Low growing shrubs and early successional trees, such as Rugosa Rose, Creeping Juniper (locally known as Trailing Yew) and serviceberries are scattered throughout, and an incredible assortment of wildflowers, lichens and mosses proliferate in appropriate micro-habitats. Livingston and Dyer categorized the Monhegan Associate lands in 2003 as 82% forested (310 acres), consisting of mature spruce, early successional forest, maturing mixed forest, immature mixedwood forest, and immature softwood forest, reflecting the impacts of historical land use (see Table 1).

Table 1. Forest types, acres involved, and historical status of Monhegan Associates, Inc. (MA) lands as categorized by Livingston and Dyer in 2003 (Miller, 2005).

Forest Type	Acres	% MA Lands	1873	1922	2003	Notes
Mature Spruce	103	27%	forested	forested	forested	earliest/never cleared
Early Successional	84	22%	cleared	cleared	forested	later former pastures
Maturing Mixed	65	17%	cleared	forested	forested	early former fields and pastures
Immature Mixedwood	46	12%	forested	cleared	forested	briefly cleared late 1800s–early 1900s for pastures
Immature Softwood	15	4%	?	?	forested	between Black Head and Green Point; uncertain history

The 18% non-forested area of Monhegan Associates land (70 acres) includes meadows, wetlands, and rocky headland areas. While the two-acre Ice Pond provides open freshwater with a limited mudflat at the northeastern end (dependent upon water level), the nine-acre Meadow (primary village water source) is full of reeds and grasses, and a small but notable grassy meadow or marsh area is found opposite Lobster Cove. The forested wetland of Long Swamp is populated by Red Maple and a variety of shrubs. There are also two unnamed and largely inaccessible seasonal streams, one draining Long Swamp to the east and the other in the southern portion of the island.

In the village itself and associated roads and residences (113 acres) grow many planted apple trees and lilacs that are a magnet for migrating birds, along with scattered conifers and deciduous trees, flower and vegetable gardens, and lawns. Of course, the island is outlined by rocky shores and towering cliffs, accompanied closely by Manana's predominantly low, heath-like vegetation, including cranberries, and the rocky low-lying islets. And surrounding it all is a saltwater harbor and open ocean, providing a habitat all its own and distant views; the nearest sizeable island is 5.6 miles to the north (Allen Island) and nearest mainland point is Port Clyde, 10.0 miles to the north-northeast.

WEATHER AND BIRDS

As everywhere, weather has an effect on much of what we do, and particularly on a remote island. There are some broad generalizations we can use to characterize the various components of weather, such as temperature, cloud cover, fog, wind, severe storms, and tides on Monhegan; these are examined in great detail in Alan Faller's *The Weather and Climate of Monhegan* (2003). Temperature is moderated by the surrounding waters, with average summer highs in the upper 60°s F and winter highs in the low 30°s F. While the winter months are generally the cloudiest and Jun–Oct the least cloudy, the summer months through Sep are the most likely to bring foggy conditions. Wind speed is opposite of the temperature scale, with the highest in the winter months, averaging ~20 mph, and lowest in the summer months, averaging ~10 mph. Wind direction is harder to characterize but dominated by north to northwest winds in the winter, south/southwest to southwest in the summer, and a mix of the two patterns in the spring and fall months. Despite major oceanic storms potentially impacting Monhegan an average of every 3–4 years since 1851, most of these have diminished in strength and impact by the time they pass by the island. Few have ever produced hurricane force winds on the island, but nonetheless, some have resulted in damage to property and habitat. Hurricane Bob in August 1991 was one of the few to pass very close by and had official maximum winds of 60 mph. Although not far from the world-famous tides in the Bay of Fundy, as high as 52', Monhegan's average range is ~9'.

Weather plays an incredibly important role throughout the year in the lives of birds on the island, in a myriad of ways. This may range from breeding adults and chicks dealing with the heat of summer to late fall migrants or winter visitors being forced to endure or move on due to freezing or harsh conditions, often worsening as winter progresses. An extreme situation developed in late winter of 1933–34, as a substantial covering of ice formed around the shoreline, hindering the feeding of gulls and crows, and freezing "Devil Divers" in the ice, with many perishing "all along the shore" (MJT personal correspondence).[2] It is unclear which species was involved, as Bufflehead and Pied-billed Grebe, both historically referred to by that quaint name, are unlikely candidates; other species of grebe, loon, or Black Guillemot seem more likely.

Weather is most evident, however, in how it affects the arrival, duration of stay and onward movement of birds during migration. Passing systems are one of the drivers of migration, with certain conditions resulting in a pronounced abundance and/or large diversity of species on the island, sometimes producing what is termed a "fallout" (the holy grail of birders), a result of a large landbird migratory event coupled with isolation from resources or unfavorable weather inhibiting continued migration. Monhegan's isolation, within a main migratory corridor, where landbirds can be negatively positioned over open water and seeking respite, results in the island becoming a "fallout" destination and migrant "trap." Additionally, its small size acts as a concentrating factor. In general, the effects of weather on waterbirds is less evident, and poorly understood.

---

[2] Information accessed through the archives of the Monhegan Historical and Cultural Museum Association.

In the spring, optimal conditions occur with the passage of a low pressure system to the north of Monhegan, with an associated warm front producing warmer temperatures and southerly breezes (southwest most favorable) that "bring" the birds along with it. Local westerly breezes that "push" birds offshore and/or inclement weather that inhibits continued migration, such as rain in the late night/early morning hours, may lead to a "fallout," as Monhegan becomes their literal "island in a storm," providing exhausted migrants a much-needed place to rest and refuel. This may take several days, and you will notice among the species accounts that migrating individuals or flocks may linger for several days or more in both spring and fall.

Two notable examples of spring fallouts occurred on May 30, 2013 and May 26, 2016. On the earlier date, the local weather station at Owl's Head on the mainland recorded a high of 54°F and E/SSE winds on the 29th changing to 82°F and WSW/SW winds on the 30th (Weather Underground, 2021). As described by R. and M. Lambert, massive numbers of birds arrived throughout the day and "several hundred birds per minute could be seen flying away from the island" (eBird, 2017). This was the day of an extraordinary *Empidonax* flycatcher movement involving over 700 individuals, including record high counts for Alder and Willow Flycatchers—see highlighted text on page 158). The day also produced the record high counts of Red-eyed Vireo (345) and Magnolia Warbler (353).

In the later example, the local weather changed from a high of 60°F and variable/S/W winds on May 25th to 72°F and W/SSW wind on the 26th. Peter Vickery, birding with Lars Jonsson and Bill Sheehan, described it as the largest spring fallout he ever experienced. Birding on Horn's Hill, they observed "**thousands of birds flying north at dawn,**" the flight heavy until ~5:30 a.m. and then diminishing until over by 6:00 a.m. Afterwards, the birds settled in the trees and bushes and were "literally everywhere" and it was **easy to see eight species of warbler in a single tree** (eBird, 2017). This historic day produced at least twenty species of warblers, among many other songbirds, and included high counts of 100 Red-eyed Vireos, 250 Cedar Waxwings, 160 American Redstarts, 180 Magnolia Warblers, 180 Yellow Warblers, 240 Blackpoll Warblers; thousands of other warblers and passerines went unidentified, mostly in the first ninety minutes of the day (eBird, 2017).

Geoff Dennis's journal notes from May 25, 2000 relate another exciting experience with a fallout, following three days of rain and winds from the north and east.

> Low overcast with light north wind in AM. Wind shifted to the east by 8 AM. By 9 AM, a thunderstorm and heavy rain again! Once again, I went out birding in the rain, but this time in thunder and lightning. On my way back from Lobster Cove in pouring rain and thunder, birds began appearing on the roadside – birds that weren't there earlier. Thunderstorms finally ended around 1 PM and birds began to appear everywhere, especially on Swim Beach and Fish Beach. Birds at beaches looked to be feeding on sand fleas and other insects. Wind had shifted to the west. Got a picture of a Mourning Warbler at Swim Beach after it crossed the road in front of me. Finally at Swim Beach, I sat on a large log and began shooting. With my feet I rolled the wrack line to expose sand fleas which the wind carried up the beach like a chum line. Birds began working my way feeding on the insects. A male Blackburnian startled me when it landed on my index finger working the shutter button while I had the camera to my face. An adult male Redstart stood on the sand at my knee, less than a foot away. Also, a Black-throated Green and Alder Flycatcher did the same, as if waiting for me to roll the rockweed. Occasionally, a Tree Swallow gave an alarm call, sending the Redstart, Alder, and Black-throated Green under my folded legs for cover. Six to eight Empids appeared, along with Pewee, 2 Black-throated Greens, 4 Redstarts, Canada, Wilson's, Yellow, Yellow-rump, 2 male and 1 female Chestnut-sideds, 2 male and 1 female Blackburnians. Emily joined me with more film. One male Blackburnian hopped on her knee and she was unable to photograph it because it was too close for her point and shoot camera.

Opposite Page: FALLOUT AT THE BEACH. Clockwise: Famished warblers at your feet—Bay-breasted, Yellow, Black-throated Blue, Black-and-white, Black-throated Green (top to bottom); Black-throated Blue Warbler and American Redstart; 3 Yellows, 1 Black-throated Green Warbler and 1 American Redstart; Hand-feeding a hungry Bay-breasted Warbler; A Black-throated Green Warbler seeking cover; Exhausted and wet Northern Parula and Hooded Warbler hiding in the rocks; American Redstart on floating vegetation; Black-throated Blue Warbler feeding. All photos © Geoff Dennis.

In the fall, the optimal conditions for a fallout occur with the passage of a low pressure system to the north and an associated cold front, producing cooler temperatures and northerly breezes (northwest most favorable). The same caveats apply in regard to westerly breezes and inclement weather as in the spring. The wind direction component is supported by the nocturnal acoustic monitoring in fall 2010, when the majority of nights with a higher passage rate (≥10 calls) corresponded with winds in the west–north range (Hoberton & Wright, 2012).

A noteworthy example of a fall fallout occurred on Sep 25, 2009. The local weather conditions changed from a high of 70°F and WSW/NW winds on the 24th to 57°F and WNW/NNE winds on the 25th. Luke Seitz's report of "at least a couple thousand birds" consisted of pre-dawn listening, birds coming in off the water at Lobster Cove in the early morning and birds "everywhere" to the north afterward, with warblers streaming overhead. High counts noted were 140 Red-eyed Vireos, 70 Swainson's Thrushes, 200 Savannah Sparrows, 80 Black-and-white Warblers, 35 Nashville Warblers, 180 Northern Parulas, 150 Magnolia Warblers, 400 Yellow-rumped Warblers, 85 Black-throated Green Warblers and 1,000 unidentified warblers; at least twenty species of warblers were present on this day.

Of course, there are many factors that influence the number and diversity of birds present at any given time, and forecasting a major event can be tricky at best. For those hoping to time a visit "just right," technology is providing short-term options to predict or interpret movement. Learning to understand bird activity signatures on NEXRAD weather radar can inform one as to what is happening in the moment, while the Cornell Laboratory of Ornithology's Birdcast (birdcast.info) provides three-day forecasts, as well as live migration maps and other tools. But remember, it doesn't take a major event at Monhegan to make it a magical day.

Hurricanes and tropical storms with origins in the southern Atlantic Ocean are also a source of excitement for birders in the summer and fall, potentially bringing species caught up within or pushed in front of the system, particularly seabirds that are rarely seen in northern waters. While these systems often produce strong winds and precipitation that make birding difficult, the rewards can be more than worth the effort. Examples of storm-borne rarities include a Bridled Tern on Aug 22, 1991 (first Maine record), two days after the passage of Hurricane Bob, and a Magnificent Frigatebird on Sep 26, 2003 (second Monhegan record), after Hurricane Isabel passed inland the previous week.

From the original sketch by Doris Hough—the Magnificent Frigatebird at Lobster Cove on Sep 26, 2003—as part of a Bird Treks tour. Courtesy Bob Schutsky.

BIRDING SEASONALITY AND LOCATIONS

The timing of your visit to Monhegan may depend on what species you most want to see. Even within the migration periods of spring and fall there is much variation in occurrence within bird families and individual species. Generally speaking, waterbird migration, excepting southern visitors such as shearwaters, is early in the spring and later in the fall, commencing for some in Feb and continuing as late as Dec–Jan, a pattern followed by blackbirds and sparrows in Mar/Apr & Oct/Nov and warblers and other songbirds in May/early Jun & Aug/Sep. The truth is that migration never really ends. The summer months are characterized by limited diversity but a heightened level of individual activity, as breeders perform courtship, nest building, and the rearing of young. Winter is also limited in diversity but provides shifting species due to weather and food availability and the possibility of rare or sought-after species. No matter what time of year you choose, your visit will be rewarding and memorable.

Deciding where to bird on a trip to Monhegan may depend on the length of your stay or the time of year you visit. Fortunately, anywhere on the island can be productive, but obviously, the more time you can spend in different habitats, the better your chance of encountering a greater diversity of species. A day trip generally provides ~four hours on the island and can be exciting, but will only permit a limited experience, while an overnight stay will provide a much better sense of what Monhegan offers (and who doesn't want to spend a night on an island?). Since a significant majority of birders visit during migration, most of the following locations are described with spring and fall in mind. As in all things birding, you never know what you will find, and each visit provides a different exciting experience.

It is recommended that day-trippers spend their time birding the village, including the Ice Pond and Lighthouse Hill, then continue to White Head or Burnt Head for the spectacular views, and finally following the Lobster Cove trail to the cove itself and the point beyond. Completing this route in limited time will require a steady pace. A stay of just a couple of days should enable a visitor to bird at most of the habitats outlined here, although you'll probably find that even a week on Monhegan won't sate your desire to remain; with seventeen miles of trails, there is plenty to explore. Plan your birding, depending on the local conditions, to take advantage of songbird arrival/movement in the morning and leave visiting the headlands (for seawatching with the sun at your back) and forested areas (with associated resident birds and lack of migrants) for the afternoons. As might be expected, given Monhegan's position along the coast, the general movement of birds over the island during migration is southwest to northeast in the spring and the reverse in the fall, supported by the early comments of lightkeeper William Stanley in 1894—"during the fall migration the birds come from the east. The course they take leaving is WSW" (*AFN* 14[1]: 10)—and radar work conducted in 2010–2011(Mizrahi et al., 2013). And while birds may appear "everywhere" during a fallout, certain areas, such as Green Point, Lobster Cove, Horn's Hill, or the open area behind the school, may position you better to witness the phenomenon. Return visits to your favorite spots, time permitting, are likely to turn up different species, and especially recommended for some locations where new migrants tend to arrive, such as the Ice Pond or Meadow.

The simple fact is that birds can be seen anywhere on the island, from the moment you step off the ferry to the time you depart, as well as from the boat itself while in the harbor and as you pass the islets (we've had Whimbrel fly over while waiting on the upper deck to cast off).

Trail numbers in the following sections follow those used on the official Monhegan Associates Trail Map (see inside front cover).

➢ THE VILLAGE AND THE MEADOW

It is often surprising to first-time visitors that some of the best birding occurs right along the gravel roads of the village, especially from the stretch of Black Head Rd. adjacent to the Ice Pond south along Main St. (sometimes known as Monhegan Ave.), passing the Meadow and continuing along Lobster Cove Rd. to its southern terminus. Birds can be found anywhere along this stretch, just stop at suitable habitat or when you see them. Along Black Head Rd, it is worth checking the feeders at the house just north of Ice Pond Rd. Farther south, the apple trees at the library and the vegetation behind it often attract warblers and vireos, and a side jaunt along the western portion of Tribler Rd. can produce more of the same. Be sure to search along the edge of the Meadow here and into the community garden between the road and the back of the library; Blue Grosbeaks have shown up here on several occasions. At the foot of Wharf Hill Rd, check the dense trees and shrubs in front of the Winter Works shop, as well as the stand of cherry and Horse Chestnut trees on the south side of the road for warblers, vireos, orioles, and more. A shrubby patch at the top of Wharf Hill Rd, across from the Island Inn and next to the Sterling House, has hosted Cassin's Vireo (first and only state record), MacGillivray's Warbler (only Monhegan record) and Black-throated Gray Warbler (only Monhegan record and on the same day as the MacGillivray's!!).

Farther along Main St., the Meadow opens up to the east, presenting nine acres of marsh/wading bird possibility, including ducks, shorebirds, rails (one record of Yellow Rail), and herons (including both records of Least Bittern). Search the Meadow edges in particular for sparrows, Bobolinks, Rusty Blackbirds and Dickcissels, while listening for Soras and Virginia Rails within. Dusk can be productive for the liftoff of roosting herons or bitterns initiating migration or changing position on the island, moving sometimes between the Meadow and the Ice Pond. Another excellent vantage for the Meadow is from the pumphouse area at the back northeast corner, accessed from the end of Tribler Rd. or the western end of the Alder Trail. Be sure to check the trees and shrubs near the end of the road as you descend to the level of the marsh. This area often has the largest visible expanse of the limited open water in the Meadow.

The extensive freshwater Meadow as viewed from Lighthouse Hill. © Brett M. Ewald.

Tall spruces surrounding the Meadow provide perches for woodpeckers or hunting raptors, notably Merlins. Check the utility wires stretching the length of the Meadow for kingbirds, including the occasional Western.

Anywhere in the course of your wanderings through town, don't forget to pay attention to the birds that may be overhead, especially early in the morning, when flocks of Cedar Waxwings or Bobolinks may be audible, along with the occasional Dickcissel giving its "raspberry" call. As things warm up, raptors become more evident and can be seen moving through, notably Ospreys, Northern Harriers, Sharp-shinned Hawks, and falcons; those lingering can be seen passing back and forth over the island as they determine the next phase of their journey or patrol for their next meal. Likewise, Monhegan being an artist's colony, be sure to appreciate the many pieces of sculptural art in yards and on buildings.

Roadside art. © Brett M. Ewald

Mike Stiler fish scultpture. © Brett M. Ewald

Continuing south along Main St. past homes and yards, search the clumps of lilacs and any apple trees along the road for warblers; Northern Parulas and Yellow Warblers seem especially noticeable in these environs and often provide close views. Many of the apple trees are completely ringed with small holes, a sure sign that Yellow-bellied Sapsuckers have been present in numbers over many years. Two of the three sand and gravel beaches on the island (the other is at Lobster Cove) are situated along the harbor end of their signature lanes: Swim Beach and Fish Beach. Both are worth checking for resting shorebirds or a view of waterfowl, gulls or guillemots in the harbor, especially in late fall–early spring. The beaches themselves are known to host tired or hungry warblers under fallout conditions in the spring, feeding on sand fleas and invertebrates found amongst the gravel and washed-up seaweed, seemingly unmindful of people near them.

Fish Beach and the harbor, with a rock breakwater on the left. © Brett M. Ewald.

An apple tree rife with sapsucker holes and an attendant Yellow-bellied Sapsucker. © Luke Seitz.

For decades, Tom and Josephine Martin fed birds from their raised former fish house, located just north of Fish Beach Lane with Fish & Maine on the corner, and across from the general store. Seed scattered on the ground and even in lobster traps provided food and shelter for many sparrows, blackbirds (including the only record of Shiny Cowbird in the state), and even warblers, such as Mourning.

Another spot to view the Meadow is from its southwest corner, along the left side of the Monhegan House. Present here is a shrubby treeline that may contain Lincoln's, Swamp, Song, and other species of sparrows, or provide a perch for an Eastern Kingbird or Northern Mockingbird.

A stroll down Wharton Ave., opposite the church, provides several vantages to view the harbor and notably its rocky shore, where many gulls and eiders roost. Search among them for less-common species, such as Iceland Gull or Lesser Black-backed Gull. A dense thicket along a swale a short distance down the road may hold the odd wren, thrasher or sparrow. The cul-de-sac at the end provides open views of the southern harbor out to the ocean and Manana, with many gulls and the occasional falcon riding the wind currents along its ridgetop or sloping southern face.

Gulls roosting on the rocks along the harbor's edge, as viewed from the southern end of Wharton Ave. © Brett M. Ewald

As previously mentioned, Monhegan's protected harbor provides sanctuary for a wide variety of waterbirds, including the ever-present Mallards, and can be viewed from many locations along the shore, as well as from arriving or departing ferries. Non-breeding waterfowl occasionally show up, including goldeneyes, Long-tailed Ducks, mergansers, grebes and loons, sometimes only as flyovers evaluating the stopover potential.

Horn's Hill provides another beautiful vantage point from which to view areas to the west and north, including the Meadow from above. This is another location where large movements of landbirds may occasionally be observed overhead in the early hours soon after dawn. Much of this area is residential, with numerous pockets of shrubby habitat.

Lobster Cove Rd. has several areas of thick scrub, perfect for wrens, catbirds, sparrows, and cardinals, and sometimes hosting Common Yellowthroats and Magnolia and Prairie Warblers. Check the spruces scattered along the road for boreal species such as Cape May and Bay-breasted Warblers, as well as kinglets, nuthatches, or irruptive crossbills. Just south and east of the Trailing Yew, the Cundy property maintains feeders abutting a hedgerow, and Donna Cundy graciously permits birders access in season, with the platform feeders and orange halves ablaze with the colors of orioles (Baltimore and Orchard), tanagers (Scarlet and Summer), Indigo Buntings, Rose-breasted Grosbeaks and others in the spring, and less vibrant visitors in the fall, such as chickadees and Purple Finches. The feeders have even hosted a Black-headed Grosbeak and Painted Bunting at the same time. (Please respect the property and consider a donation to alleviate expenses incurred in feeding the birds). The dense undergrowth surrounding the western end of the Underhill Trail (#3) is suitable for Black-throated

A Monhegan welcome. © Brett M. Ewald

Blue Warbler, Northern Waterthrush, and even the rare Connecticut Warbler. The dead or dying spruces beyond to the east provide conspicuous perches for roving flickers and songbirds and patrolling raptors to rest or assess the surroundings. Lobster Cove Rd. ends where the footpath to the cove itself starts (see following section).

Taking Mooring Chain Rd. to the west brings you to a scrubby swale crossed by a gravelled bridge (formerly wooden) providing a view of the northern end. After checking this area, follow Ocean Ave. south as it curves around the edge of the swale; this has often been a productive area for the uncommon Yellow-breasted Chat (hence the bridge is sometimes called the "chat bridge" by birders). Seed that is sometimes scattered along the road just past the south end of the swale often attracts a Lark Sparrow or Clay-colored Sparrow, along with more common Song and Chipping Sparrows. Once the road swings back southward, a stand of spruces may be alive with foraging chickadees, juncos, White-throated Sparrows and Black-throated Green and Yellow-rumped Warblers.

The start (western end) of the Underhill Trail. © Brett M. Ewald

At this point, you may choose to cut across an unnamed/unnumbered trail to Lobster Cove, overgrown at the west end, or retrace your steps to Lobster Cove Rd. If you proceed, beware poison ivy in spots along the edge of the trail, something to always be cautious of when birding off-road.

➢ LOBSTER COVE / LOBSTER POINT

Lobster Cove Trail appropriately begins at the southern terminus of Lobster Cove Rd. The apple trees and spruces on opposite sides near the start often hold warblers, while much of the trail is enclosed by shrubby thickets harboring yellowthroats, catbirds, and occasionally a Yellow-breasted Chat. The trail opens up to a sweeping view of the cove, rocky Lobster Point with the scattered wreckage of the tugboat D. T. Sheridan, which ran aground in 1948, and the ocean beyond. This is a particularly good vantage, especially at dawn, to watch for birds leaving the island in migration or coming in to Monhegan's food and shelter for the day. The nocturnal acoustic monitoring in Fall 2010 highlighted Lobster Cove as a migration departure point, mainly warblers and sparrows, in the first few hours after sunset (suggesting a concentration point) and arriving at or near dawn (Holberton & Wright, 2012). Descend and follow the trail around the gravel beach of

Lobster Cove at low tide (on the right) with Lobster Point beyond, the marsh/meadow on the left, and the wreck of the D. T. Sheridan in the distance. © Brett M. Ewald.

the cove, looking closely for shorebirds, such as Least Sandpipers, and pipits in the dried seaweed at the wrack line, or Spotted Sandpipers on the rocks. This is another beach where exhausted warblers are sometimes found foraging on the ground, particularly in the spring. Immediately to the east is a small but important and unique habitat on the island – a grassy, marsh-like area, sometimes frequented by Marsh and Sedge Wrens, Savannah and Swamp Sparrows, Bobolinks and even the occasional Nelson's Sparrow.

Climb through the rocks to a prominent position and settle in for some seawatching from Lobster Point. Black Guillemots and Common Eiders are often right offshore, Northern Gannets are regular (sometimes in large numbers), and the range of possible waterbirds is extensive and includes all three scoters, Harlequin Duck, cormorants, phalaropes, terns, loons, Atlantic Puffin, Razorbill, Pomarine and Parasitic Jaegers, Wilson's Storm-petrels, shearwaters, and many gulls.

➢ THE ICE POND

Appropriately named, as it was the source of cooling ice for the island's businesses and residents as late as the early 1970s, the Ice Pond is a must stop for any birder. As small as it is, it has featured many memorable sightings over the years. It is the most likely place for any dabbling ducks to appear, sometimes joining the numerous Mallards, some of which readily accept a handout, and less common American Black Ducks. Both Yellow-crowned and Black-crowned Night-Herons are known to frequent the edges of the pond, particularly the back end, and often remain for multiple days, even weeks. One or more Belted Kingfishers often rest on the wires extending across the water, and Sora has been seen probing the edges. Exposed mud flats towards the back are one of the best places to look for shorebirds such as yellowlegs or Solitary Sandpiper. As the pond itself only takes a couple of minutes to check, it is worth a stop each time one passes through the area.

The Ice Pond. © Brett M. Ewald

Flocks of songbirds are often seen moving through the trees along Ice Pond Rd. as you approach the pond from Black Head Rd., sometimes flitting along the pond's edge or crossing into the trees surrounding the open area to the west, the former site of the ice house for storing the cut product—the remains of a Boreal Owl were found inside this building in 2008, the only known record for Monhegan. It's worth stationing yourself here to see what will turn up, from warblers to vireos to flycatchers and more; this general area has hosted many rarities. Cross the wooden bridge to follow the ongoing residential trail, known as Mucky Lane, paying particular attention to the low and thick alders and shrubs hiding the wet slough that the bridge traverses, and maybe you'll spy a waterthrush or other skulking warblers. Farther along the trail you'll have the opportunity to gaze upon Nigh Duck and the distant Duck Rocks for gulls, cormorants, a visiting Bald Eagle or passing seabirds.

A stroll down Sterling Cove Rd. brings you to a narrow, obscure trail on the left that ultimately passes by the schoolhouse and returns you to Main St. The first part is dense and uneven, emerging into stunted growth among rocks and grasses. Be sure to check the dense trail margins for Magnolia Warbler and Rose-breasted Grosbeak and the open area for sparrows, or Cedar Waxwings passing overhead. A few feeders are often suspended next to the schoolhouse and seed may be scattered.

Opposite Page: LOBSTER TRAPS AT A MIGRANT TRAP. Clockwise: Black-and-white Warbler, Yellow Warbler and Black-throated Blue Warbler; Chipping Sparrow; Mourning Warbler; Common Yellowthroat; White-crowned Sparrow; Lincoln's Sparrow; Mourning Dove on a nest; Blue Grosbeak. All photos © Geoff Dennis.

➤ LIGHTHOUSE HILL AND THE BALLFIELD

Reaching the top of Lighthouse Hill (by following Lighthouse Hill Rd., of course) and the structure it is named for requires some exertion to overcome the elevation gain. Be sure to keep searching whenever you stop to catch your breath and maybe you'll be rewarded with scolding Black-capped Chickadees, gleaning Red-eyed Vireos, a probing Yellow-bellied Sapsucker, or a self-effacing Yellow-throated Vireo. Once you've reached the plateau, follow the trail up to the Lighthouse itself and associated outbuildings. The view to the west alone is worth the climb, a sweeping vista over the cemetery, Meadow and village, the imposing Island Inn, the harbor, Manana and onward over calming waters to the distant mainland. Try not to be lulled into a sense of complacency, as raptors may be passing above or below; this can also be a good location to get a sense of general bird movement or to witness Common Nighthawks at dusk. If time allows, visit the Monhegan Museum in the Keeper's House, a treasure trove of island history and artifacts, including birding information and many of Tom Martin's photos. The Gallery building often houses an art exhibit, showcasing another reason many have been attracted to Monhegan's charm.

Lighthouse Hill from the harbor, with the cemetery below left and the Fish House in the middle foreground (positioned behind the breakwater and hidden Fish Beach). © Brett M. Ewald

Past the Verizon tower and the scrubby habitat surrounding it is the open, sparsely grassed area known as the Ballfield. Be alert when approaching, as seed is sometimes scattered by birders in a cut-through area just off the gravel road entrance and a variety of sparrows may gather, including Lark and Clay-colored. The field itself may attract American Pipits or Horned Larks, while the edges may host sparrows, including Vesper, an occasional Olive-sided Flycatcher on a snag, Ruby-crowned Kinglets and a variety of other thicket-loving songbirds. Check around the garbage dumpsters on the south side for sparrows using them as cover from the Northern Harriers, Sharp-shinned Hawks, and falcons passing overhead. The trail to White Head, which starts on the east side of the Ballfield, is covered in the Headlands section.

➤ THE HEADLANDS

The three main cliff-top vantage points on the east side of the island offer incredible views of rocky ledges and seemingly endless ocean. One can imagine looking for fishing vessels, friend or foe, arriving from Europe in historical times. These are the highest headlands on the entire Eastern Seaboard of the U.S., topping off at 160' (Black Head and White Head) and 140' (Burnt Head).[4] Each has its own unique feel and opportunities, as do the very different trails and habitats traversed to reach them. White Head and Burnt Head are shorter and easier treks than Black Head, something to bear in mind if time is a factor. All three are optimal locations to seawatch for gannets, gulls, shearwaters (mainly Great, but also Sooty, Cory's, and Manx) and jaegers over the open water and Common Eiders (and the occasional King Eider), Black Guillemots, Herring and Great Black-backed Gulls and both Double-crested and Great Cormorants in the surf below. Gulls and cormorants can also be quite evident on the rocky ledges all along the cliffs and shoreline. Raptors, especially all three falcons,

---

[4] A note on names: the headland names are spelled in different ways on maps and in print, sometimes with the first part separated from the "head" portion (Black Head, White Head, Burnt Head) and sometimes both ways in the same publication (Burnt Head most often separated), with no clear indication of which spelling is correct. They have been standardized here as separate words—Black Head, White Head, Burnt Head.

can be seen passing by in search of prey. Whales, or at least their spouts, can often be seen in the distance with persistent scanning; Minke, Fin, and Humpback Whales are the most likely. The Matinicus Archipelago, with its twin lighthouse towers and similar isolated geography, emerges from the haze 20 miles to the east.

- BLACK HEAD

Northernmost of the headlands, Black Head is also the most remote and is accessed through the coniferous forest that covers much of the land protected by Monhegan Associates. Black Head Trail (#10) is basically an extension of the road beyond the northern limit of houses (on the western shore near Deadman's Cove). It's an uneven trail that leads through stands of spruce, deciduous swales, and ultimately involves clambering over and around a rocky ravine to reach your goal. A trail map is indispensable for remote areas,

Black Head. © Brett M. Ewald

but the trails are not always obvious in some of the rocky, uneven sections. While landbirds are fewer and less diverse, this area contains species that are less likely to be seen in the more developed areas. Winter Wrens can be found in the blowdowns and Golden-crowned Kinglets in the crowns of the spruces, with Brown Creepers working the trunks in between. Watch and listen for crossbills and Pine Siskins in the spruces and Olive-sided Flycatcher on exposed snags around clearings. The few patches of deciduous trees should be searched for vireos and warblers such as Blackburnian and Black-throated Blue, while White-throated Sparrows may appear anywhere. Listen for Common Ravens as they call overhead. Arrival at the overlook provides all the possibilities mentioned in the Headlands section above, and the likely presence of Dark-eyed Juncos and Yellow-rumped Warblers in the stunted growth around you.

- WHITE HEAD

The White Head Trail (#7) begins on the east side of the Ballfield. It first passes through an area of thick deciduous scrub where Red-eyed Vireos and warblers are often found. Emerging under an open spruce canopy, look for skulking thrushes, Winter Wrens, and sparrows. Once past the entrance of the Long Swamp Trail on the left, you'll climb through Bayberry with scattered Mountain Ashes, a favorite of Cedar Waxwings when the fruits are ripe. The trail opens onto one of the best vantage points on the island, a place to rest

Seawatching at White Head. © Brett M. Ewald.

your back against a rock while seawatching to your heart's content. Carefully check the rocks and cliff edges below for nesting Double-crested Cormorants—young still on nests as late as mid Sep in 2019. The large rocks below to the north are among the best places to see perched Great Cormorants.

- BURNT HEAD AND UNDERHILL TRAIL

Burnt Head can be easily accessed from two trails, and combining them for a loop hike is an enjoyable way to cover the area. Burnt Head Trail (#4) extends from Burnt Head Rd. and traverses an early successional mix of deciduous scrub and spruces. Be on the lookout for catbirds, Blue Jays, Song Sparrows, Common Yellowthroats and Palm Warblers. Once you reach the cliffs, several areas provide excellent vantage points for seawatching; Black Guillemots are often diving for food directly below. A return on the Underhill Trail (#3) passes through additional early successional habitat, becoming more mature and dense on the western end approaching Lobster Cove Rd. This trail has hosted two of the island's three records of Bell's Vireo. The species mix may change along with the habitat, and include Baltimore Orioles, Northern Waterthrushes and Magnolia and Black-and-white Warblers, or maybe even the aforementioned Connecticut Warbler.

Burnt Head on the left, with White Head and Black Head (farthest) on the right. © Brett M. Ewald.

➤ CATHEDRAL WOODS

Cathedral Woods is renowned as the only old-growth forest on Monhegan, having survived the harvesting in the 18th and 19th centuries largely due to its wet nature. The trail crosses several small and picturesque bridges and remains a magical place today. Tall spruces, draped in usnea over a lush carpet of mosses, form a natural cathedral, while whimsical and sometimes controversial fairy houses dot many areas of the trail (#11). For birders, while the diversity of species is low, the area can harbor both crossbills and Pine Siskins during irruption years and at least two of the six records of Black-backed Woodpecker occurred here. Red-breasted Nuthatches and Golden-crowned Kinglets call conspicuously from the treetops and Dark-eyed Juncos, White-throated Sparrows and thrushes sometimes skulk through the open understory.

The most productive way to bird Cathedral Woods is to combine it with a trek to Black Head, by cutting across Maple Trail (#16), or White Head, by cutting across Long Swamp Trail (#12). Maple Trail gets its name from the larger percentage of deciduous trees present, principally maples and birches, than in much of the coniferous north, potentially holding a different mix of species, including vireos and warblers. Long Swamp Trail passes through and along a narrow but extensive wet area that continues from Cathedral Woods. Surprisingly, the only record of Wood Duck breeding on Monhegan occurred here, apparently taking advantage of a muskrat's damming of the water's flow (beaver generally do not occur on the island).

➤ THE CONIFEROUS NORTH

Many of the trails in the "remote" northern portion of the island traverse spruce and fir forest contained by a rocky shoreline topped by windswept and scrubby growth. Some sections, particularly along the Cliff Trail (#1) include difficult terrain, from uneven tree roots to rocky outcroppings with steep inclines. The birdlife likely to be encountered is similar to that outlined for Black Head Trail – nuthatches, kinglets, Black-capped Chickadees, creepers, Northern Flickers, irruptive crossbills (potentially nesting during years when the cone crop is heavy), and other woodland species. Green Point, as the first land a southbound bird will encounter, is a desirable spot to observe at dawn after a night's migration in the fall. Pebble Beach is noted for its field of smooth sea-worn rocks, with both Harbor and Gray Seals present in the water or on the nearby Seal Ledges.

➢ MANANA

So near and yet so far.... Accessed by hiring a dinghy owner to take you over, Manana Island is largely unbirded, except from a distance, and there are only a couple of Manana-specific checklists known. While it is largely predominated by rocks and low-growing cranberries, there are several damp areas and ravines containing shrubs and trees, including spruces, and a spring that provides water. The scarcity of suitable habitat for many species can have a concentrating effect on migrants, and the island is likely to contain many of the same species present on Monhegan itself, and more of certain species preferring its rugged landscape. The rocky outcroppings along the top provide perfect perches for falcons, Bald Eagles, and Common Ravens, and gulls are often coasting in the breezes over its slopes or resting on its shoreline. Largely inconspicuous, Black Guillemots nest in burrows situated among rocks above the high tide line. Manana is close enough that several exciting finds have been made by viewers from Monhegan, including Sandhill Crane, Say's Phoebe and Loggerhead Shrike. Short-eared Owls have twice been seen over it and Snowy Owls are known to perch there during the winter. Other obvious occupants on the island are a generous handful of goats and a couple of sheep. Although the Coast Guard's Fog Signal Station and tram ramp are still present and intact, and the house partially built by a hermit who lived on the island from 1930–1975 is currently being remodeled, human occupancy is uncertain.

The dense spruce forest along the Evergreen Trail (#15). © Brett M. Ewald.

Manana Island, with Smutty Nose Island in the foreground, as seen while approaching the harbor/wharf. © Brett M. Ewald.

➢ MONHEGAN'S ISLETS

The small islands residing close by Monhegan provide peaceful roosting, nesting and stopover habitat for many eiders, gulls, cormorants, terns, shorebirds, guillemots, and raptors looking to avoid the commotion, predators, or inappropriate habitat present on Monhegan. Great Cormorants, Lesser Black-backed Gulls, Purple Sandpipers, and Bald Eagles are some of the less common species, but there are many more possibilities. These islands provide sanctuary for many nesting Common Eiders, Herring and Great Black-backed Gulls and Double-crested Cormorants (see banding results in the species accounts), and perhaps secretive Black Guillemots and Leach's Storm-Petrels as well. The names of the various islands can be confusing, as some are similar or have changed over the years. Smutty Nose Island, nestled up to Manana and providing some of the protection afforded by Monhegan's harbor, is the most easily viewed from ferries enter to disembark and embark passengers or from any point in the wharf area. Nigh Duck (also called Inner Duck Rock) is easily viewed from western points such as Sterling Cove Rd. and Mucky Lane. Eastern Duck Rock is the largest of the offshore islets, similar in size to Smutty Nose, and has a number of smaller, unnamed rocks clustered about it. The two islands farther west and most distant are collectively known as the Outer Rocks or Duck Rocks (sometimes Outer Duck Rocks or even Western Duck Rock and Middle Duck Rock), but most often without differentiating the two. As a micro-habitat, these rocks have hosted Red Knot and many of the Ruddy Turnstone records for "Monhegan."

Top: Eastern Duck Rock. Bottom: Nigh Duck, with the Duck Rocks beyond and the mainland in the distance, as seen from behind the school. © Brett M. Ewald..

While approaching ferries usually provide closer views of the outer islets before entering the harbor from the north, departing ferries often head south out of the harbor and pass the islets at a greater distance or not at all, in the case of ferries headed west to New Harbor or Boothbay Harbor. The best way to view and bird them is an around-the-island boat ride on *Balmy Days*, often offered for walk-ons at 2 PM (conditions permitting) during the spring-fall tourist season; these trips also provide a different perspective of the eastern headlands and overall sense of Monhegan's size and topography.

➢ FERRY CROSSINGS

The boat trip to or from the island presents an opportunity to view seabirds of the open ocean that may be difficult to see from shore, notably scoters, loons, gulls, terns, shearwaters, Northern Fulmars, phalaropes and alcids (puffins, Razorbills, and murres), depending on season. As the subject of this publication is species recorded on the island or within the Monhegan Island Lobster Conservation Area, sightings from the ferries are not included unless specified as within this perimeter.

Elizabeth Ann bringing the next group of potential birders to Monhegan. © Brett M. Ewald.

Located between Swim Beach and Fish Beach along Main St., the Rope Shed is a source of all manner of island information and upcoming events. © Brett M. Ewald.

VISITOR SERVICES AND ACCOMMODATIONS

As already mentioned, planning ahead is critical in making the most of a birding adventure to Monhegan, including proper apparel and footwear. Please remember that vehicles are not transported to Monhegan, it is walking only. Based on a tourism economy, most businesses are not open in the off-season (mid Oct–Apr). A full listing of the ferry options, currently arriving from Port Clyde, New Harbor, and Boothbay Harbor, and where you can stay, eat, shop and learn (including the Monhegan Museum and library) and important general visitor information can be found at **www.monheganwelcome.com**. There is presently one general store in operation and there is no bank, but ATMs are available. Electricity is not available in some establishments and there are no streetlights either, so pack a flashlight for night excursions; camping and littering are not allowed, and smoking is ONLY permitted within the village. Restrooms are limited to one public option (donations requested) apart from those of accommodations and restaurants that you are patronizing.

An official Visitor's Guide to Monhegan Island Maine booklet is available at the various ferry terminals and highlights the "rules of the road," important safety and planning information, and establishments and businesses currently open. A listing of artists in residence on the island and their open studio hours is also usually available.

For birders, especially first-time visitors, the official **Monhegan Associates Trail Map** (see inside front cover) is a critical document to determine where you are and where you hope to be. Maps can be picked up at many of the locations listed above for a small fee. The importance of the Monhegan Associates (www.MonheganAssociates.org) and their role, largely volunteer, in preserving and maintaining the trails and undeveloped portions of the island can't be overstated.

A Monhegan Birds WhatsApp Bird Alert has been created to share sightings on the island in a timely fashion. All are welcome to join and participate, whether to take advantage of real-time observations by others or to inform others of your exciting finds. To join, download WhatsApp onto your phone and contact the author at brett.ewald90@gmail.com to provide your phone number to add you to the group. After that, you'll be able to text out and receive sightings while on the island, or receive other's sightings whether there or elsewhere—if you want and can bear to know what you're missing!

Northern Parula, May 22, 2018. © Jeremiah Trimble.

SPECIES ACCOUNT INTRODUCTION

PERIOD COVERED

While Monhegan has a "birding" history that stretches over four centuries, since Rosier's mention of various fowl and eggs from 1605, specific bird records are only known from a yearly checklist from 1899 onward, with increased interest and further observations, including published reports, over the next two decades and continuing through the 20th century. Special attention has been paid to these historical and little-known efforts through the 1970 Checklist (see Occurrence section), after which access through published reports, bird alerts, and eBird made sightings more widely known. The designated cutoff date for inclusion was Feb 28, 2023, basically concluding with the end of the winter 2022–2023 season; the last complete checklist submitted on Nov 13, 2022, with only incidental sighting reported thereafter (eBird, 2023).

GEOGRAPHIC BOUNDARY

The intent of this publication is to include any sightings **within the Monhegan Island Lobster Conservation Area** (MILCA), as **observed from land on Monhegan or the surrounding islands**, including Manana, Smutty Nose, Nigh Duck, Eastern Duck Rock, and the Duck Rocks, or **from a vessel that is passing through these waters,** most notably the around-the-island voyages often provided during tourist seasons by Hardy Boat Cruises on *Balmy Days* and arriving/departing ferries. MILCA is the official geographic area within which Monhegan's lobster fishery exclusively operates Oct 1–Jun 30 (the only U.S. lobster fishery with a closed season). This area is simply defined as being **two nautical miles (2.3 statute miles) distant from Monhegan on the east, north, and west sides of the island, expanding to three nautical miles (3.5 miles) from the southwest to southeast** (see map below).

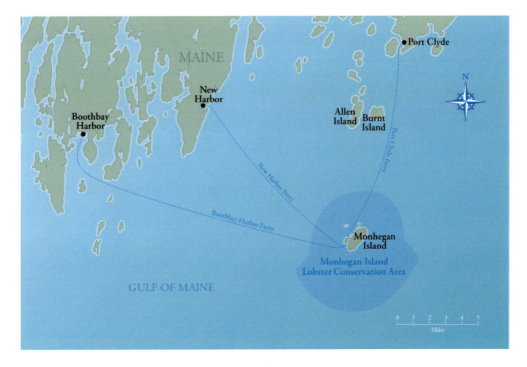

The boundary in terms of latitude and longitude coordinates for specific purposes is: "Beginning at a point located at latitude 43°45'09" north and longitude 069°22'16" west that is 2 nautical miles southwesterly of the nearest shore of Monhegan Island; in a southwesterly direction to latitude 43°44'28" north and longitude 069°23'37" west at a point on the three-nautical-mile line around the southern end of Monhegan Island to latitude 43°44'94" (*sic—should apparently be 04"*) north and longitude 069°14'26" west; then in a somewhat northerly direction to latitude 43°45'8" north and longitude 069°15'3" west, to a point that is 2 nautical miles from the nearest shore of Monhegan Island; then following a line that is 2 nautical miles from the nearest shore of Monhegan Island and that continues around the northern end of Monhegan Island to the point of beginning." This legal designation is found in the Maine Revised Statutes of the Maine Legislature – Title 12: Conservation, Part 9: Marine Resources, Subpart 2: Licensing; Chapter 619: Lobster and Crab Fishing Licenses, Subchapter 5: Monhegan Lobster Conservation Area.

Every effort has been made to maintain this standard, but confusion arises from the many checklists in which sightings included both the ferry crossings to/from Monhegan and time spent on the island, in which case there is often no way to know the location of specific sightings. In these cases, most sightings of waterbirds, such as waterfowl, shorebirds, waders, jaegers, gulls, terns, loons, grebes, alcids, shearwaters, have been **excluded**, unless an acceptable location is specified, whereas landbird and raptor sightings a have generally been **included**, as the chance of these occurring during the crossing are slight. This situation has most often happened when a birder travels to Monhegan in the morning and birds in the afternoon or birds in the morning and departs the island in the afternoon. There are also many instances of day-tripping, e.g. taking a morning ferry to Monhegan, spending ~four hours on the island, then returning to the mainland in the afternoon. There are even several instances in which birders, upon hearing of a rarity on Monhegan, took a ferry over, quickly located the sought-after bird, and returned almost immediately on the same boat they arrived on. Some checklists have been submitted or reported with only the on-island birding or hiking distance recorded, while accompanying notes show that a crossing was also involved, but its distance not reported. It is possible and disconcerting that other checklists or sources may have included water-crossing sightings without announcing that fact or other supporting details, but without certain knowledge or a sighting arousing suspicion, they may have been included here unknown. All these various factors have been taken into account to present the most accurate account possible.

SOURCES OF DATA

A wide variety of sources have been meticulously searched for sightings and observations relevant to the birdlife of Monhegan. These sources include both print and online publications, databases, unpublished reports, triplists, individual checklists and personal notes, letters and checklists gathered over the past twenty years. The following sources that are marked with an asterisk (*) are covered in detail in the Occurrence and Historical/Regional sections of the Species Account Format (titles summarized or abbreviated in some instances for use in the Species Accounts).

For distribution and status on a national or regional level beyond Maine, the Cornell Lab of Ornithology's *Birds of the World Online* (2020) was consulted, along with *The Sibley Guide to Birds* (Sibley, 2000), *Field Guide to the Birds of North America* (Dunn and Alderfer, 2011), *A Birder's Guide to Eastern Massachusetts* (Bird Observer, 1994), *Bull's Birds of New York State* (Levine, 1998) and *The Birds of New Jersey* (Boyle, 2011).

Many Maine sources were perused, some dating back to the 1800s, including the following: *Catalogue of the Birds of Maine* by C. H. Hitchcock (1862; no specific mention of Monhegan), *Birds of Maine* by Everett Smith (1883; no specific mention of Monhegan), *Birds of Maine* by Ora Willis Knight (1908; no specific mention of Monhegan, but some Lincoln County reports), *Maine Birds** by Ralph Palmer (1949), *Summer Birds of Lincoln County Maine** by Allan Cruickshank (1950), *Annotated Checklist of Maine Birds* by Peter Vickery (1978), *Birds of Maine** by Peter Vickery et al. (2020), and the Maine Bird Records Committee's Official List of Maine Birds* (2022).

Ornithological journals, national and local, provided many records and included *Auk, Bird-Banding, Bird-Lore, Bird Observer, Audubon Field Notes, American Birds, Field Notes, North American Birds, EBBA News, Records* of *Walks and Talks with Nature* by C. J. Maynard (1909 Notes*), *Journal of Maine Ornithological Society* (1900–1908 Reconnaissance & Supplements*), *The Maine Naturalist, Maine Field Observer, Maine Field Naturalist, The Guillemot, Maine Birdlife,* and *Maine Bird Notes*. An excellent Chronology of Maine Bird Record Publications is provided in *Birds of Maine* (Vickery et al., 2020: 41).

Targeted studies consulted included National Audubon Society's Christmas Bird Count*, two atlases of Maine birds (*Maine Atlas of Breeding Birds** [Adamus, 1987] and Maine Bird Atlas* [ongoing]), coastal waterbird breeding surveys (Coastal Waterbird Colonies*), various gull, raptor and songbird banding operations (results from the USGS Bird Banding Lab and Biodiversity Research Institute—see the Occurrence section of the Species Account Format for a breakdown and details*), a one-season standardized hawkwatch (Biodiversity Research Institute 2010 Fall Hawkwatch*) and boat-based surveys off the southern end of the island 2011–2014 (Deepwater Offshore Wind Test Site Surveys*).

Other valuable sources included the Maine Audubon Rare Bird Alert, Maine-Birds listserve, personal journals and correspondence of Warner Taylor (1915–1919 Taylor Journals*–courtesy Lele Miller and the Miller-Taylor family), published checklists and articles (Monhegan Press) and personal correspondence accessed through the archives of the Monhegan Historical and Cultural Museum Association (1900–1908 Supplements*, 1914 & 1916 Checklists*, 1934 & 1939 personal correspondence from Josephine Townsend to Mrs. Edwin C. Jenney, 1944–1967 Farrell Records*, 1954 & 1955 Summer Records*, 1970 Summer Checklist*), personal notes from Tom Martin (Monhegan checklist with handwritten notes in the margins, acquired in 2005 and possibly including sightings as early as 1954, with 1964 as the earliest listed date), highlights and numerous triplists from Jeff Wells, Tony Vazanno and Geoff Dennis, observations from the files of Jody Despres, seasonal presence notes from Jack Skelton, multiple triplists from Wendy Howes, Bird Treks tour checklists from Bob Schutsky, personal observations by Tom Magarian, the Maine Birding Field Notes blog and triplists by Derek Lovitch, triplists from Kristen Lindquist, and the My Life On Monhegan Facebook page posts of Donna Cundy.

Of course, the heart and soul of the records involved is the abundant sightings, from common to rare, reported by hundreds of visiting birders and birding groups, including societies and professional tours. It need hardly be said that the Cornell Lab of Ornithology's eBird database has proven to be an incredibly rich resource, with historical Monhegan records stretching as far back as the late 1970s, a noted increase in reports in the 2000s, and consistently high levels of checklists from ~2009–present, now totaling over 7,000 checklists submitted, mostly during migration seasons (eBird, 2023). Lastly, but personally most important, the data has relied on the generosity of individuals, reaching out directly with their observations and experiences (please see acknowledgements in the preface).

I have noted source data errors, omissions, clarifications and editorial remarks in *italics* where appropriate in the Format and Species Accounts, not to highlight the discrepancies but to correct the historical dataset.

ACCOUNT ABBREVIATIONS & ACRONYMS

AB - American Birds
ACMB - Annotated Checklist of Maine Birds
AFN - Audubon Field Notes
BBL - USGS Bird Banding Laboratory
BL - Bird-Lore
BO - Bird Observer
BRI - Biodiversity Research Institute
CBC - Christmas Bird Count
cw - count week (CBC)
CWC - Coastal Waterbird Colonies: Maine
DOWTS - Deep Offshore Wind Test Site
et al. - and others (more than three in this case)
fide - according to
FN - Field Notes
G - Guillemot

ind(s). - individual(s)
MABB - Maine Atlas of Breeding Birds
MARBA - Maine Rare Bird Alert
MASS - Maine Aerial Seabird Survey
MB - Maine Birdlife
MBA - Maine Bird Atlas (ongoing)
MBN - Maine Bird Notes
ME-BRC - Maine Bird Records Committee
MFO - Maine Field Observer
MN - The Maine Naturalist
mob - many observers
NAB - North American Birds
OLMB - Official List of Maine Birds
WB - Wilson Bulletin
w/e - week ending

LIST OF OBSERVERS/CONTRIBUTORS

Every effort has been made to provide the original observer(s) or reporter for every record listed; if not available, a source has been provided. Abbreviations have been used to simplify/shorten the text, arranged alphabetically by **last name** for individuals or **first name** of organizations. Following these abbreviations are observers who provided significant sightings that aren't directly cited in the publication or were part of a larger group of observers (four or more, designated as et al.). Please forgive any errors or omissions.

DAb - Denny Abbott
SA - Steve Abbott
BA - Benjamin Abrahams
NA - Nathaniel Abrahams
DA - Don Adams
JAi - Janet Aiken
BAk - Bob Ake
JAl - Jonathan Alderfer
JA - John Alexander
FA - Francis Allen
TAn - Trina Anderson
GA - Gary Annibal
CA - Connie Arness
MA - Mr. Arnold
MSA - Mrs. Arnold
TAr - Tom Arter
TA - Tom Aversa
BAv - Belinda Avey
AMB - Aaron M. Bagg
HB - Helen Bailey
IB - Ilze Balodis
MBa - Marygrace Barber
BBa - Bruce Barker
WBk - Weston Barker
BBy - Ben Barkley
SBa - Susan Barnard
SB - Scott Barnes
?Ba - Barnes
WBs - Walt Barrows
WBa - William Batsford
DB - David Beattie
MBe - M. Beck
TBe - Timothy Becker
PBe - Paul Beerman
KB - Kris Benarcik
BBn - Betty Bengston
PBn - Peter Bengston
SBe - Seth Benz
AB - Ami Bergstrom
EAB - E. Alexander Bergstrom
MEAB - Mrs. E. A. Bergstrom
PBm - Peter Bergstrom
RB - Rick Bergstrom
?Be - Bernstein
JBy - Jim Berry
JBe - John Berry
TB - Trish Berube

LB - Louis Bevier
JBi - Jessica Bishop
LKB - Laura Kennedy Blandford
BBl - Bill Blauvelt
JBl - Julie Blue
LBl - Laura Blutstein
BBo - Bonnie Bochan
JB - Jackie Boegel
MjB - Mary Jane Boland
BBc - Benjamin Bolduc
CB - CK Borg
WBo - Willard Boynton
LBt - Lisa Brackett
MaB - Martin Brazeau
LBr - Lysle Brinker
MBr - Mary Brogan
WBr - Will Broussard
GBr - Greg Brown
MB - Mary Brown
PB - Phil Brown
JBu - Jim Buccheri
CBu - Carl Buchheister
FGB - F. G. Buckley
PAB - P. A. Buckley
NB - Nancy Buis
LBu - Lloyd Bunten
?Bu - Burrell
MBu - Malcolm Burson
GB - Greg Butcher
BCa - Bartram B. Cadbury
JCa - Joseph Cadbury
CC - Courtney Cameron
MC - Matthew Cameron
OC - Oscar Canino
PCa - Peter Capobianco
LC - Laura Carberry
GC - Greg Carter
BC - Brendan Casey
CCh - C. Charles
RFC - R. F. Cheney
JCh - Jeff Cherry
BCl - Benjamin Clock
DCl - Dennis Clutter
LCo - L. Coates
RCo - R. Coates
MCo - Mich Coker
ACe - Ana Cole

BCo - Bruce Cole
JCe - Jason Cole
JC - Jeremy Coleman
JCo - Jennifer Commons
CAS - Conn. Audubon Society
PC - Paul Corcoran
KC - Kevin Couture
CCo - Colleen Cowdery
RC - Ruth Cranmer
PCr - Peter Cross
BCr - Bob Crowley
AC - Allan Cruickshank
MAC - Mrs. A. Cruickshank
DC - Donna Cundy
MCu - Mason Currier
PCu - Palmer Curtis
ED - Ellie Davis
LD - Lloyd Davis
SDa - Seth Davis
TD - Todd Day
CDe - Carol Decker
SD - Shawn Decker
BD - Benjamin Delewski
PD - Phillip DeMaynadier
MD - Mathias Deming
GD - Geoff Dennis
JD - Jody Despres
JDe - John Dewis
KD - Kathryn Dia
LDi - Lois Diane
VD - Vineeta Dixit
CDo - Chris Dobbins
ID - Ian Doherty
RDo - Ryan Doherty
PDe - Paul Donahue
DD - Dan Donaldson
PDo - Paul Dorien
AD - Alexei Douhovnikoff
TDo - Travis Dow
RD - Randall Downer
RDu - Richard Duddy
TDu - T. Duddy
CDu - Chris Duffy
CDD - Charlie Duncan
CDd - Chris Dunford
DDd - David Dunford
DDF - Dana Duxbury-Fox

RE - Rich Eakin
LE - Linda Eastman
NE - Nancy Eckhardt
PE - Philip Edmundson
CE - Charles Eldermire
HE - Hap Ellis
REl - Robin Ellwood
CEl - Cory Elowe
KE - Kirk Elwell
RPE - Ruth P. Emery
JE - Jennifer Esten
CEs - Chuck Estes
BEv - Bruce Evans
TEv - Toni Evans
BME - Brett Ewald
SE - Sheryl Ewald
NFa - Norm Famous
IF - Isabel Farrell
JF - Josh Fecteau
ShF - Shea Fee
RF - Rob Fergus
BF - Bob Ferris
KFe - Ken Feustel
SFe - Suzy Feustel
DF - Davis Finch
KF - Kristen Finkbeiner
JFi - Joe Fischer
EF - Edward Flanders
NF - N. Flynn
JFo - Jess Foley
TFo - Tom Foley
PF - Patricia Folsom
MF - Michael Foster
PFr - Paul Frank
TF - Tucker Frank
CF - Clara Fuller
LF - Linda Fuller
WF - William Fuller
DFu - David Funke
JG - Jay Gamble
KG - Kay Gammons
DGa - Dustin Gardner
DGi - Dan Gardoqui
MGa - Mark Garland
RG - Richard Garrigus
NG - Noah Gibb
AG - Andrew Gilbert
JGi - Jane Gillette
MCG - Mrs. C. H. Gleason
EG - Eleanor Goldberg
TG - Tracy Goupil
SG - Seamus Gourley
BGr - Bill Grabin
MGr - Monica Grabin

MWG - Mrs. W. B. D. Gray
BG - Bill Gruenbaum
LG - Laura Guerard
CG - Carlos Guindon
DG - David Gulick
JGw - John Gwynne
NHa - Nathan Hall
SH - Scott Hall
CFH - Carl F. Hamann
MCFH - Mrs. Carl F. Hamann
LHa - Linda Hamp
HBC - Hampshire Bird Club
BHa - Bill Hancock
FH - Frederic Hareau
LH - Lynn Harper
BHn - Brian Harrington
RHa - Ronald Harrower
SHa - Sage Harrower
MEH - Mrs. M. E. Hartwell
NHn - Nolan Hayden
TH - Tim Healy
RHe - Rick Heil
PHe - Pat Heirs
DHe - Don Heitzmann
DHr - Don Herriott
LHe - Lynne Hertzog
DHt - Dawn Hewitt
KH - Kristina Hick
SHi - Sibley Higginbotham
JHi - Jason Hill
DHi - David Hilton
CHi - Christopher Hinkle
BHi - Barbara Hitchcock
AH - Alex Hitchcox
DH - Doug Hitchcox
PH - Paul Hitchcox
HIAC - Hog Is. Audubon Camp
LHo - Lewis Holmes
FHo - Fleur Hopper
NH - Nancy Houlihan
JHo - Jeffrey House
WH - Wendy Howes
MHo - Michael Howland
RH - Rich Hoyer
MH - Margi Huber
BH - Bill Hunt
SHu - Shane Hunt
CH - Charles Huntington
JH - John Hutchison
CHy - Casey Hynes
EH - Eric Hynes
AI - Angela Iannicelli
KI - Kathie Iannicelli
MI - Marshall Iliff

JJ - Jalna Jaeger
KJ - Ken Janes
GJ - Gary Jarvis
EJ - Edward Jenkins
CFJ - Charles F. Jenney
ECJ - Edwin C. Jenney
MCFJ - Mrs. C. F. Jenney
TJe - Tony Jerome
MJe - Mary Jewett
AJ - Andy Johnson
MJ - Molly Johnson
TJ - Tom Johnson
CJ - Caroline Jones
FJ - Florentine Jones
KJo - Kyle Jones
RJ - Robert Jones
SJ - Sebastian Jones
LJ - Lars Jonsson
BJ - Brenda Jordan
MJo - Marie Jordan
LK - Logan Kahle
JKa - James Kalat
AK - Amanda Kallenbach
JKe - John Keator
AKe - Allan R. Keith
SK - Seth Kellogg
JKy - Jerry Kelly
KK - K. Kemper
CK - Chris Kenaley
OK - Oen Kennedy
IKi - Iris Kilpatrick
JK - John Kitsteiner
WK - Will Kostick
KKl - Ken Klapper
ELK - E. Leroy Knight
MK - Meagan Krieger
IK - Isaac Kruger
TK - Tyler Krul
FK - Fyn Kynd
DLa - D. Ladd
ML - Maggie Lambert
RL - Robby Lambert
AL - Andy Lantz
CL - Clint Lapierre
CLa - Constance Lapite
EL - Eva Matthews Lark
VL - Vern Laux
PL - Paula Laverty
JLa - John Lazzaro
MLe - Michele Ledue
MLn - Margaret Lehmann
SLe - Stan Lequire
MLi - M. Libby
KLi - Kyle Lima

JLi - Jeremy Linden
KL - Kristen Lindquist
HL - Hilda Livingstone
NLo - Nancy Loomis
JLo - John Lorenc
SL - Stephanie Lovell
DL - Derek Lovitch
JL - Jeannette Lovitch
MLu - Marjorie Ludwig
NL - Nicholas Lund
RM - Richard MacDonald
MMa - Molly MacInnis
WM - Dr. William C. Mackie
GMa - Gail Mackiernan
LMa - Lisa Madry
TMag - Tom Magarian
DMa - Dean Mahlstedt
MAS - Maine Audubon Society
DM - Don Mairs
AMy - Alfred Maley
LMy - Linda Maley
JMa - Jonathan Manchester
FM - Frank Mantlik
mob - many observers
TM - Travis Marceron
CMa - Carol Mardeusz
FMa - Frank Marenghi
IM - Irene Martin
JMar - Josephine Martin
TMar - Tom Martin
BM - Becky Marvil
RMa - Robert Mayer
CJM - C. J. Maynard
JM - Jonathan Mays
TMz - Travis Mazerall
SMc - Sheila McCarthy
BMc - Beth McCullough
AM - Amy McDonald
KM - Kent McFarland
RMc - Robert McKenzie
PMc - Peggy McLeod
SMn - Steve McMullin
TMe - Tova Mellen
MM - Marcia Merithew
HM - Holly Merker
LMe - Loren Merrill
TSM - Tara Stewart Merrill
MMe - Mandy Metrano
RMi - Robert Milardo
PM - Paul Miliotis
JMi - John Miller
VM - Valerie Miller
SM - Stephen Mirick
CMi - Clotilde Misfud

SMa - Shai Mitra
DMo - Delia Mohlie
TMo - Ted Mohlie
EM - Eric Monaco
GM - Graham Montgomery
AMo - Alison Moore
LMo - Lily Morello
MMJ - Minot C. Morse, Jr.
CM - Clark Moseley
BMo - B. Moser
LM - Lena Moser
PMo - Pat Moynahan
JMu - James Muchmore
BMu - Bella Munoz
EAM - E. A. Munroe
JMy - John Murphy
LiM - Lin Murphy
CMu - Christine Murray
BMa - Brendan Murtha
LMu - Lukas Musher
AN - Andy Naber
EN - Eric Nguyen
WN - William Nichols
HN - Howie Nielsen
BN - Blair Nikula
CN - Charlie Nims
JNo - Joanne Normandin
JN - John Nove
DN - David Nyzio
EO - Evan Obercian
RO - Robert O'Connell
JO - Jeffrey Offermann
BO - Brian Olsen
AO - Ana Paula Oxom
MO - Miklos Oyler
SPa - Sally Pachulski
CP - Christopher M. Packard
RPa - Ralph Palmer
BPa - Bruce Panowski
GPa - Geoffrey Parks
AP - Alexander Patia
HP - Helen Patton
DPJ - David Peake-Jones
APe - Andrea Perko
MPe - Mike Perko
WP - William Perro
NP - Nate Peterson
RTP - Roger Tory Peterson
BP - Bryan Pfeiffer
KP - Kit Pfeiffer
MP - Maxine Pichon
EP - Elizabeth Pierson
JP - Jan Pierson
TP - Troy Ploger

RLP - Richard L. Plunkett
MPl - Margery Plymire
SP - Steve Pollock
LP - Linda Powell
GP - Gail Presley
RP - Robert Prol
DP - Diane Prosser
JPy - Jenn Pye
RQ - Robert Quinn
JRa - Jose Ramirez
KR - Kathleen Rawdon
ER - Edward Raynor
LR - Liz Redding
MRe - Mike Redmond
DR - Don Reimer
PR - Peter Reman
MRi - Maureen Ridge
WRi - Wendy Rigazio
CR - Chris Rimmer
MRo - Michael Rizzo
TR - Tal Roberts
RR - Rob Robinson
JR - Jordan Roderick
CRo - Chris Rohrer
FNR - F. N. Rolf
MFNR - Mrs. F. N. Rolf
PR - Pamela Rollinger
JRo - Jeanne Rollins
MR - Michael Root
TRo - Tina Rosier
ERo - Elsie Rowe
SRe - Sheila Rowe
TRe - Thomas Rowe
KRu - Katie Rubright
NR - Nancy Russ
WR - Will Russell
ASa - Alexa Sarussi
JSt - John Schaust
CS - Connie Schlotterbeck
ASc - Anita Schmidt
KS - Kathryn Schneider
AS - Albert Schnitzer
ES - Eva Schnitzer
MS - Margie Schoeller
JSl - John Scholl
GSc - Greg Schrader
NSc - Nicole Schrader
KSc - Kai Schraml
BSc - Bob Schutsky
JSc - Joe Scott
HS - Heidi Seitz
LS - Luke Seitz
NS - Nathaniel Sharp
WJS - William Sheehan

RSh - Rosanne Sherry
JSw - James Sherwonit
JSh - Joseph Shetler
JS - Jack Skelton
DSk - Dennis Skillman
JSo - Jackie Sones
JSm - Jan Smith
LSm - Laurel Smith
RSm - Robert Smith
LSo - Leslie Smoot
ESo - Eric Sorenson
GSo - Graham Sorenson
RS - Rob Speirs
BSq - Billy Squid
WSq - Willy Squid
LSt - Leslie Starr
GS - Gene Stauffer
RSt - Rick Steber
ASt - Ava Steenstrup
DSt - David Stejskal
JSs - Joanne Stevens
TS - Tara Stewart
BSt - Bob Stymeist
DS - Doug Suitor
JSu - Jack Sullivan
MSu - Margo Sullivan
SS - Scott Surner
SSu - Scott Sutcliffe
SSr - Sherman Suter
JSn - Janet Swanson
DT - Dan Tankersley
CTa - Clara Taylor
WT - Warner Taylor
HT - Helene Tetrault
ATh - AW Thayer
Ray Adams
Cindy Baisden
Shane Barker
Teri Bergin
Bruce Black
Ginny Bishop
Rosalie Borzik
Jo Ann Bowes
Nancy Bradfield
Lois Bryman
Emile Carter
? Conkey
Susan Coppola
Zekiel Cornell
Nancy Dickinson
Kathy Donahue
Ann Edison
Dave Flynn
Jane Gantt

BTh - Brendan Thomas
BTn - Bill Thompson
JTh - Jaden Thompson
FT - Fred Tilly
RT - Robert Timberlake
ST - Stuart Tingley
CT - Charlie Todd
AT - Anne Townsend
BT - Bill Townsend
JAT - J. A. Townsend
MJT - Mrs. J. A. Townsend
JT - Jeremiah Trimble
DTu - Dave Tucker
JTu - Joe Turner
AV - Ariana Van Den Akker
KV - Kathleen Van Der Aue
BVD - Benjamin Van Doren
TV - Tony Vazzano
AV - A. Vial
BSV - B. Vickery
PDV - Peter Vickery
MV - Margaret Viens
NV - Nancy Vogt
SWa - Sidney Wade
AW - Alison Wagner
JWa - Judy Walker
SWk - Steve Walker
SWh - Stella Walsh
EW - Erin Walter
GWa - Greg Ward
SW - Susan Ware
IW - Isabel Wasson
MWa - Maili Waters
VW - Val Watson
DW - Drew Weber
Stephen Gantt
Valerie Gebert
Brian Genge
Carol Greenstone
B. Gwynn
Erich Hetzel
Janice Hetzel
Claudine King
Josh Lincoln
Diane Losier
Mary Ann Lunniss
Teri Martine
Eric Masterson
Sarah Mazerall
Jennifer McKown
Ryan Merrill
Kim Nelson
Robert Norton
Deborah Peale

MW - Magill Weber
MWe - Mary Weber
AWe - Allison Wells
JVW - Jeff Wells
BHW - Bertrand H. Wentworth
KW - Kristin Wentzell
SWe - Steve Weston
WW - Warren Whaley
NW - Nathaniel Wheelwright
CW - C. Whittle
BWx - Billy Wilcox
TW - The Wildlab
JWi - Judith Williams
GW - Gabriel Willow
MWi - Martin Wilson
SWi - Stu Wilson
BW - Ben Winger
BWi - Bradford Winn
MWo - Maureen Wolter
PW - Paul Wolter
KWo - Kate Wong
CWo - Charles Wood
LW - Linda Woodward
SWr - Sharalee Wrigley
JWy - John Wyatt
KY - Keenan Yakola
MY - Margaretta Yarborough
LY - Laurie Yntema
SY - W. Scott Young
JY - John C. Yrizarry
SZ - Sara Zagorski
KZ - Karen Zeleznik
JZ - Janice Zepko
LZ - Lachlan Ziegler
MZ - Marian Zimmerman
Rob Peale
Tom Perls
Carolyn Ragan
Lea Ramirez
Suzannah Reed
Michael Reidy
Barbara Retzlaff
P. Richards
Mrs. William Riddle
Ryan Schain
Stephen Shunk
George Silver
Michael Smith
Kathy Stagl
Shelley Vermilion
Rita White
Janet Winslow
Will Wright

DEFINING A RECORD

While the concept of "what is a record?" may seem straightforward, this isn't always the case and it bears some clarification for these purposes. For Monhegan Island, a record is customarily **the total reported on a daily checklist,** the most common form of reporting for this location. This may involve scattered, unassociated individuals having no connection or interaction whatsoever, and differs from a more generally used approach whereby each individual or flock is considered a record, although this aspect of presence is sometimes addressed in the Occurrence discussion in the species account. This means that for two separately submitted checklists from the same day, with different observers but a duplicate certain species, the highest checklist total is the record considered here for that day, even though it is likely that the two checklists don't replicate all the same individuals and the total on the island for that day may actually be higher. However, as discussed further in the data source section for Christmas Bird Counts, different party sightings are combined to form a single CBC record since different parties cover different sectors of the count circle. Records marked as "during" a certain time period were observed at some point within the extreme dates, possibly more than one day, but timing is uncertain and most often results from triplists without specific daily sightings.

When an individual bird does linger on the island for more than one day, the record for that individual "extends" until it is no longer reported (i.e., a single record may cover multiple days/weeks). This is most important when considering a rare species or a sighting during an unexpected season. In these cases, when no other individual of a species is expected, the record continues even though there are gaps in reporting (days without reports followed by re-sightings), until the individual is no longer present. For less rare species, but still not "common", when multiple individuals are generally possible, a sighting is considered a separate record if there is even a one-day gap in reporting, unless details or observer comments suggest otherwise; in some cases, a specific individual may be tracked due to plumage features. When additional individuals of a species are reported on days subsequent to an existing record, it is considered a new or additional record. For common species with multiple individuals present at any one time, individual length of stay cannot be determined and totals on consecutive days are considered separate records. In rare cases where the exact same total is reported on consecutive days, such as 40 individuals on three consecutive days for a species, this is considered a lingering group or flock and considered a single record. Due to the subjective nature of perceiving the actual number of records in some cases, a few species with limited historical/seasonal records, such as the Night-Herons, are listed with +/- next to the record count, since some records may involve repeat individuals or new arrivals so that an accurate, exact total is likely to be speculative.

The validity of records is a matter of the utmost importance, and every effort has been made to corroborate sightings and sources and investigate questionable reports. As a rule, the determination of the Maine Bird Records Committee (ME-RBC) has been followed for state review species except, of course, in cases where a review has not yet occurred; in these instances, the observer(s) and details provided are taken into account.

Birding sustenance from the Novelty. © Brett M. Ewald.

SPECIES ACCOUNT FORMAT

The Species Accounts present the 336 species documented within the MILCA and follow the names and taxonomic order as presented in the American Ornithological Society's 7th Edition of the *Checklist of North and Middle American Birds*, through the 62nd supplement (Chesser et al., 2021). An additional nineteen species are listed as hypothetical, with brief notes on occurrence and details; while possibly correct, they lack adequate documentation or clarity of location for inclusion.

STATUS

A concise representation of the level of presence, indicating relative abundance, frequency of occurrence, seasonality, and breeding, if applicable.

ABUNDANCE/FREQUENCY TERMS

Please keep in mind that the abundance terms generally apply to the number to be expected during a thorough search in a peak migration, summer, or winter period; numbers may vary greatly from day to day, notably during migration periods. It should also be noted that even though a species may occur irregularly, a single flock can change its status on a seasonal basis (i.e., uncommon to fairly common), depending on the size of the flock, particularly in flocking species such as waterfowl.

- Abundant - 100+ per day.
- Common - 25–100 per day.
- Fairly Common - 5–25 per day.
- Uncommon - 1–5 per day.
- Scarce - 1–5 per season.
- Rare - more than 10 historical records, but not annual.
- Very Rare - 2–10 historical records.
- Accidental - 1 record ever.

SEASONALITY

For most species, presence has been addressed by season using the following terms. It should be understood that seasonal terms do not follow a set calendar period (i.e. spring does not necessarily = March, April, May) but vary by species based on movements, breeding, or winter range, and may encompass four months or more or as little as one month (i.e. spring migration for many species continues well into June and is addressed in the occurrence section). Due to the overwhelming high percentage of visitation by birders in spring and fall, the associated migrations have been listed first in the species status. Keep in mind that for a limited number of seabirds that breed in the Southern Hemisphere (shearwaters and Wilson's Storm-Petrel), summer/early fall sightings are during the non-breeding, wandering portion of their biological year.

- Migrant - a species of passage which occurs in spring and/or fall, but does not breed at Monhegan; listed as spring migrant and/or fall migrant. Post-breeding dispersal is considered as fall migration for these purposes.
- Visitor - a non-breeding species which occurs as a temporary visitor; listed as summer visitor or winter visitor.
- Resident - a species that breeds at Monhegan; may occur as summer resident or permanent resident.
- Vagrant - a species whose normal migration route (including post-breeding dispersal), breeding range, or winter range does not include or pass by Monhegan.

OCCURRENCE

A presentation of records, based on seasonality (except for species that are permanent residents only), that indicates historical presence, length of seasonal presence, peak abundance periods, maximum counts and seasonal presence by year, spring 2013–winter 2022/23.

In general, for those species with fewer than 50 historical records, the total number of records is provided first, followed by a breakdown by season in parentheses, as appropriate, followed by the date when the species was first recorded. For those species with more than 50 records, but fewer than 25 in any particular season, the number of records is provided at the start of that particular season's occurrence statement, followed by the number of years (of that season) over which the records occurred. For those species with only a handful of records within a season (generally six or fewer), all of the records are listed. First records for Maine appear in red; for select "rare" species other early records are noted, such as second or third state records.

The order of seasons in this section is chronological, starting with spring. For species with a range of presence within a season, the outside dates are given; for those species with a continuing presence into the following season and an unclear seasonal transition, such as spring migration continuing past the start of local breeding, the cut-off or transition dates for seasonal record inclusion are indicated. A schedule of specific dates for each species has been determined, based on general duration of migrations, breeding or visitor presence; this schedule follows intervals of one third/one half month (i.e., seasonal starting/ending dates may be May 31/June 1, June 10/11, 15/16, or 20/21, generalized on occasion as early [the first ten days of the month], mid [the middle ten days of the month], or late [the last ten(+/-) days of the month]. For migrant species, this is followed by the peak period of presence/movement .

Maximum counts are provided by season if applicable, except in the case of permanent resident only species, where a single set of yearly maximum counts is listed. A minimum of three maximum counts (numerical total) is listed, sometimes involving multiple records for a certain total, with date and observer(s) provided for each record; for some records a publication/source is provided. Records from the Maine Rare Bird Alert are often listed as week ending = w/e (occurring at some time during the previous week but without an exact date—sometimes listed as week of), with the compilers of that alert listed (i.e., fide KG). Christmas Bird Count totals may have involved more than one report but are included here as one record (i.e., 21 Common Goldeneyes in 1978–14 by PDV, 7 by a second party). Records with more than three observers may be listed with et al. or mob (many observers) after the initial reporter. The **highest ever single day record/count** is highlighted in bold text, unless a species has only occurred as single daily individuals.

This section concludes with a Ten-Year summary of occurrence by season, indicating the number of years spring 2013–winter 2022/23 the species was recorded (not the number of records during those years). The limiting effects of the Covid pandemic on travel to Monhegan resulted in fewer than normal reports in 2020 and 2021, most notably in May for both years (few reports at all in spring 2020 and only two before Jun 1 in spring 2021), causing a numerical distortion on the Ten-Year summaries that needs to be taken into account.

In an effort to compress the text, names of months have been shortened to only the first three letters and the period (.) has been left off the monthly abbreviations, maxima (max) and average (avg). To avoid confusion with observer name abbreviations, state names have not been shortened to the two-letter designation, but instead a longer abbreviation or spelled out in full.

This is followed by a listing of status, specific records, summary and/or discussion as included in the following historical Monhegan censuses, research projects, articles and checklists (abbreviations in parentheses). The *Birds of Monhegan Island* checklist by Peter Vickery, published in 2013, has not been included in this section due to its recent publication.

Maine Atlas of Breeding Birds (MABB) & **Maine Bird Atlas (MBA)** - two separate bird atlases with a focus on breeding have been undertaken in Maine, one completed covering 1978–1983 (Adamus, 1987) and one nearing completion with 2018–2022 data available (compiling sightings from throughout the year, not just breeding; eBird Maine Bird Atlas, 2023); species labeled as confirmed, probable, and possible. The *MABB* produced 42 confirmed, 9 probable and 33 possible breeding species (84 total) on Monhegan. The MBA produced 41 confirmed, 10 probable and 26 possible breeding species (77 total); reports outside the safe dates have been excluded, unless clear evidence was observed, and the results presented here are not official. No direct comparison is being attempted due to the incomplete status of the MBA.

- Confirmed = definitive evidence of breeding such as nest with young, nest with eggs, adult carrying fecal sac, adult feeding young, adult carrying food, recently fledged young, occupied nest, used nest, distraction display, nest building, carrying nesting material, or physiological evidence on a bird in hand.
- Probable = suggestive but inconclusive evidence such as woodpecker or wren nest building (possible dummy nests), agitated behavior, adult visiting probable nest site, courtship, display, or copulation, territorial defense, pair in suitable habitat, multiple singing birds (seven+) or a singing bird spanning seven days.
- Possible = present in appropriate habitat during breeding season including a singing bird.

Unfortunately, there are no sighting records available for the *MABB*, as atlasers were only required to submit the level of breeding observed for each species, and further details are not known to be available. For this reason, these observations, without date or observer, are not included in the summary of records or only mentioned in a general sense, unless a particular observation is the only known occurrence during the summer season for a species.

Coastal Waterbird Colonies: Maine (CWC) - a census of waterbird breeding colonies conducted by the Maine Cooperative Wildlife Research Unit in the "rocky, island-bound coastal region" of Maine in 1976 and 1977, as part of a larger study extending from the southern border of Virginia to the Maine–Canada border (Korschgen, 1979). Waterbirds consisted of gulls, terns, alcids, eiders, cormorants, storm-petrels, herons and egrets. Surveys were conducted in the nesting season (May 23–Jul 19 in 1977) by aerial photography and visitation by boat, with efforts in 1976 considered an experimental period only and 1977 data presented as baseline information; a total of 353 colony sites was surveyed within Maine, containing 100,813 pairs of nineteen species. Counts of nests or adults were made for each species present, with most sites containing more than one species.

Waterbird colonies were noted on four of Monhegan's surrounding islands, but surprisingly not on Manana or Monhegan itself, where nesting has been noted in recent years. The following results concern five species and indicate the number of nesting pairs observed:

- Eastern Duck Rock: 25 Common Eiders, 6 Black Guillemots, 45 Herring Gulls, 37 Great Black-backed Gulls, 20 Double-crested Cormorants.
- Nigh Duck (listed as Inner Duck Rock): 25 Common Eiders, 16 Herring Gulls, 9 Great Black-backed Gulls.
- Smutty Nose: 1 Great Black-backed Gulls.
- Duck Rocks: 5 Great Black-backed Gulls.

Christmas Bird Count (CBC) - conducted 26 years since Dec 1940; the CBC year is dated according to Jan counts (i.e. the Dec 1940 tally is officially part of the 1941 CBC). Monhegan CBCs occurred on the following dates with the accompanying results and observers (National Audubon Society, 2018, 2020):

- Dec 29, 1940: 23 species, 484 inds.; JAT.
- Dec 28, 1978: 40 species, 1,319 inds.; DAb, DF, TMar, CMi, RPa, PDV.
- Dec 22, 1979: 49 species, 1,152 inds.; DAb, DF, CMi, PDV.
- Dec 30, 1980: 48 species + 7 cw*, 898 inds.; Dab, BF, DF, CMi, PDV.
- Dec 29, 1981: 45 species + 6 cw, 1,702 inds.; DF, CMi, JRo, PDV.
- Dec 28, 1982: 46 species, 1,910 inds.; CDD, DGa, JRo, PDV.

- Dec 29, 1983: 46 species + 4 cw, 1,251 inds.; TAr, CDD, LH, JRo, PDV, JVW.
- Dec 27, 1984: 40 species + 1 cw, 1,236 inds.; PCu, CDD, BHi, JRo, PDV, JVW, SWe.
- Jan 3, 1986: 43 species + 7 cw, 1,216 inds.; IB, CDD, BHi, PDV, JVW.
- Jan 1, 1987: 38 species + 3 cw, 2,253 inds.; IB, CDD.
- Dec 27, 1987: 44 species + 2 cw, 2,100 inds.; IB, PDe, CDD, BHi, PDV.
- Dec 22, 1988: 43 species, 2,127 inds.; IB, CDD, PDV, JVW.
- Dec 21, 1989: 48 species + 6 cw, 2,380 inds.; IB, CDD, PDV.
- Jan 1, 1991: 44 species + 2 cw, 746 inds.; CDD, PDV.
- Jan 1, 1992: 46 species + 1 cw, 1,935 inds.; PDe, CDD, PDV.
- Dec 27, 1994: 46 species, 1,786 inds.; CDD, PDV.
- Jan 2, 1997: 39 species, 691 inds.; DM, PDV.
- Jan 4, 2007: 54 species + 7 cw, 2,043 inds.; CDD, DF, PDV.
- Jan 3, 2008: 45 species + 7 cw, 573 inds.; DF, PDV.
- Jan 5, 2010: 47 species + 3 cw, 752 inds.; CDD, DF, WJS, PDV.
- Jan 5, 2012: 43 species + 4 cw, 625 inds.; DH, PM.
- Jan 3, 2013: 53 species + 5 cw, 619 inds.; CDD, DH, PM, WN, PDV.
- Jan 3, 2015: 40 species + 1 cw, 355 inds.; DH, FK, WN.
- Jan 5, 2016: 48 species + 7 cw, 494 inds.; DH, FK, KLi, RO.
- Jan 2, 2020: 38 species, 439 inds.; DH.
- Jan 3, 2021: 40 species, 643 inds.; DH.

*cw = count week (species not recorded on the CBC date but present within the periods three days prior or three days after).

Species average = 43.7.
Average number of individuals = 1,220.3.
Total number of species = 119 + 2 count week only; one hybrid (Mallard x American Black Duck).

The species-specific results are presented in the following format: years recorded (percentage of 26 counts) + count weeks, first CBC recorded, max count and year recorded, average count total.

CBC totals have been considered one record for these purposes, regardless if more than one party was involved in conducting the count and no one participant observed all the individuals. It is possible that count week birds may not have been on or very near Monhegan, as the count circle has a diameter of fifteen miles and birds, such as waterfowl and seabirds, may have been seen from a ferry crossing outside the distance guideline used in this publication. For this reason, a record may appear as part of the CBC summary but not in the presentation of records above it.

The Dec 28, 1982 and Dec 29, 1983 CBCs are apparently erroneously recorded as Dec 27, 1982 and Dec 27, 1983 in both the National Audubon Society CBC historical records and associated count summaries in American Birds (PDV's personal notes, fide BSV). For an unknown reason, the 1941 CBC count results have been recently removed from the CBC database (since Nov 2018), and the historical database now starts with the 1979 count. Wilson's Snipe, Winter Wren and Eastern Towhee were each removed in recent decades from a larger species complex and records before the "split" appear in the CBC database as Wilson's/Common Snipe, Pacific/Winter Wren and Spotted/Eastern Towhee, while recent records appear under the current species name. The general use of the term Crow, Chickadee and Grackle to indicate the expected species at the time of the 1941 count, had been listed in the CBC database as crow sp., chickadee sp. and grackle sp.; they are included here as American Crow, Black-capped Chickadee and Common Grackle. The 15 Goldfinches counted in 1941 did not even appear in the 2018 version of the database, but are included here as American Goldfinch (Townsend, 1941).

1899 Checklist – an unpublished list of 31 bird species identified by Mrs. M. E. Hartwell in 1899.[2] They are broken down into Order and Family and include alternate specific names. These are the first species-specific sightings known for Monhegan Island, but contain no specific dates.

Table 2. Species recorded on Monhegan in 1899 by Mrs. M. E. Hartwell.

Yellow-billed Cuckoo	Black-capped Chickadee	Dark-eyed Junco
Semipalmated Sandpiper	Red-breasted Nuthatch	Vesper Sparrow
Herring Gull	American Robin	Song Sparrow
Sharp-shinned Hawk	Cedar Waxwing	Black-and-white Warbler
Eastern Kingbird	Pine Grosbeak	Common Yellowthroat
Least Flycatcher	Red Crossbill	American Redstart
Eastern Phoebe	White-winged Crossbill	Blackburnian Warbler
American Crow	Pine Siskin	Yellow Warbler
Tree Swallow	American Goldfinch	Canada Warbler
Barn Swallow	Chipping Sparrow	
Cliff Swallow	Fox Sparrow	

1900–1908 Reconnaissance & Supplements - a combination of the careful observations made by Frances Allen during May 30–Jun 6, 1908 (with additional notes on habitat and other wildlife), published as *An Ornithological Reconnaissance of Monhegan Island* (Allen, 1908a), an unpublished list of species seen by C. F. Jenney and E. C. Jenney Aug 12, 1900 (earliest dated sighting)–Aug 1908, compiled in Aug 1908 and intentionally including only bird species additional to Allen's list, and an unpublished checklist of birds seen by Dr. William C. Mackie on a brief visit Jul 31–Aug 2, 1908.[2] A combined total of 78 species was recorded.

A total of 39 species was recorded by Allen, with dates and details provided for some observations; May 31 is noted as the earliest specific date for a sighting. He remarks that the island was "fairly well populated" with birds, but not a large number of species, and that most summer residents should have arrived by Jun 6, therefore the list shows "practically the entire breeding population." He allows that a few species were probably migrants and that one season can only be regarded as a "preliminary" list of summer birds. He was "glad" there were no House ("English") Sparrows on Monhegan, "as yet," but surprised at the total lack of thrushes, White-throated Sparrow and Northern Parula, and only one Yellow-rumped ("Myrtle") Warbler. Allen also noted that Monhegan's small size allowed for a "detailed and comprehensive study" to be completed easily and profitably and that other attempts, past and future, should be published for the benefit of New England ornithologists. Remarks to him while there suggested that birds were abundant during migrations, particularly in fall.

A total of 51 species was included on the Jenneys' list, 38 of which were additional to Allen's, four erroneously included as being new, and nine specifically noted as reported by Allen but not observed by the Jenneys. Specific dates, month or season of the year are given for 18 of the additional species, one is only specified to year, and one species Black-billed Cuckoo, also reported by Allen, is listed as seen in a year additional to 1908.

A total of 27 species was recorded by Mackie. Spotted Sandpiper was the only species not already reported by Allen or the Jenneys.

1909 Notes – observations by C. J. Maynard, Charles F. Jenney, Mrs. C. F. Jenney, and Edwin C. Jenney during a Jul 1–7, 1909 trip, published as *Notes on Birds, Butterflies, Etc., Observed on Monhegan Island, Maine* (Maynard, 1909). The amount of time they spent on Monhegan is unclear, as they left Boston late on Jul 1 by train, continued by steamer early the next morning to Bath for a stop, then by steamer to Boothbay Harbor and onward to Monhegan, and probably did not arrive until late afternoon on Jul 2, and possibly didn't even bird until Jul 3. They apparently left on Jul 6, as Northern Gannets were noted flying toward the island from ~two miles away, likely seen from the return trip to the mainland. Regardless, they recorded observations from the various stages of their trip, including the steamer ride over, and distinctly noted 29 species on Monhegan (excluding

---

[2] Information accessed through the archives of the Monhegan Historical and Cultural Museum Association.

the aforementioned Northern Gannets), providing many details or observations regarding behavior, but few exact dates. Most surprising is the presence of a Black Vulture; an "old fisherman" who saw it told C. F. Jenney that a similar bird with a red head (undoubtedly a Turkey Vulture) had been present "some years ago" (see species accounts for more details).

1914 & 1916 Checklists – unpublished checklists of birds seen by William Fuller during Jul 31–Aug 5, 1914 and Mrs. C. H. Gleason during Aug 16–Sep 16, 1916.[2] A combined total of 109 species was recorded.

Fuller reported 32 species, listing/adding new species by date. This checklist is incomplete, as the header indicates it was a Jul 31–Aug 28 triplist, but the final addition is on Aug 5 and the following pages are missing at this time. Three species—Herring Gull, Common Tern and Wilson's Storm-Petrel—have not been included here, as they are possibly ferry sightings, being the first listings on the checklist. Also, Fish Crow, a hypothetical species, is listed with a question mark next to it.

Gleason reported 105 species. Rarities include Western Sandpiper (the only report for Monhegan and considered hypothetical for these purposes), Arctic Three-toed Woodpecker (Black-backed Woodpecker), Red-headed Woodpecker and 'Sharp-tailed Sparrow'. This checklist was provided to the Monhegan Museum by Hannah Whittier and Larry Cooper at separate times (the Cooper list only contained the first 95 species).

1915–1919 Taylor Journals - records retrieved from the personal journals of Warner Taylor, a professor, noted photographer, and amateur ornithologist who spent time on Monhegan 1913–1950s (generally in late summer and early fall). His journal entries include variable daily lists 1915–1918 of species seen with occasional specific numbers, bird walk locations and general weather conditions and a full daily checklist for 1919 with detailed notes on weather, walk location and duration of observation period.[5]

The top portion of the extensive, handwritten, original Warner Taylor checklist for the period Sep 1-14, 1919.[5]

A total of 118 bird species was recorded. The highest single-day species total was 70 on Sep 10, 1916. Especially notable is the inclusion of Leach's Storm-Petrels, Ruffed Grouse and American Three-toed Woodpecker and the lack of waterfowl (only Brant and Red-breasted Merganser) and certain raptors (no Bald Eagle or Peregrine Falcon). Companions during his bird walks to various parts of the island included CFJ (with his 55X spotting scope), MCFJ, BHW, Miss Monroe, MG, Mrs. Allen, and his wife Clara Taylor (Clarkie–CTa); *sightings from 1916 and 1918 may overlap with sightings by Mrs. C. H. Gleason (see 1914 & 1916 Checklists above) and Charles F. Jenney (see 1918 Fall Migration Census below)*. While a destination is often given for a walk, such as Lobster Cove or Green Point, rarely is an exact location given for a specific sighting. An afternoon outing to Eastern Duck Rock with Clarkie on Sep 8, 1917 is the only known specific birding trip to this locality, yielding ten species, including 300

---

[2] Information accessed through the archives of the Monhegan Historical and Cultural Museum Association.
[5] Courtesy of Lele Miller and the Miller-Taylor family.

Red-necked Phalaropes just offshore. Taylor once mentions whistling to attract songbirds, having successfully "collected" two Black-capped Chickadees, two Northern Parulas and four Black-throated Green Warblers about himself. The recent publication of E. H. Eaton's *Birds of New York* (1910, 1914) and comparisons of bird sightings with CFJ are also discussed (CFJ's bird list over six weeks in 1916 was 84 species). See *1939 Summer Census* for another Taylor contribution.

Journal entries also provide insight into the daily life of a visitor on the island, including meeting the boat, fishing, lobster dinner engagements, dances, croquet, bridge tournaments and other card games. They also reveal the ups and downs of the permanent residents, from large mackerel harvests to dealing with a wagon/pedestrian accident, a drowning, and the sinking of the barge David Wallace (Aug 9, 1915).

Table 3. Summary of Warner Taylor's observations during 1915–1919.

	1915	1916	1917	1918	1919
Period Covered	Aug 9–Sep 12	Aug 19–Sep 10	Jul 29–Sep 13	?–Aug 4 & 8	Sep 1–14
Days With Observations	14	13	14	2+	9
Species Recorded	56	95	63	37	71

1918 Fall Migration Census - a reprint, with a foreword, by the Monhegan Memorial Library containing both an article by John W. Dewis, M.D. (*A Visit to Monhegan Island, Maine, September 1918*) and a compilation by Charles F. Jenney (*The Fall Migration of 1918 at Monhegan Island, Maine, from Letters of Bertrand H. Wentworth of Gardiner, Maine*)—both originally published in *Records of Walks and Talks with Nature* (1919). A combined total of 110 species was reported.

Records are generally presented in the species accounts by observer (Dewis and then Wentworth if recorded during both periods), in the following format: observer, dates observed (number of individuals seen each date when available), additional comments.

The Monhegan Library booklet that helped inspire this project. Cover design by Elise Macy Nelson (1898-1980).

- Dewis recorded 71 species during Sep 4–12, 1918, with no observations on Sep 13 due to driving rain, and departure on Sep 14). Observations were made at all times with Judge Charles F. Jenney and at times with Professor Warner Taylor and Bertrand H. Wentworth; identification was always corroborated by at least one of these other observers. Weather conditions were provided for each day.

   Additional remarks addressed the usual methods to reach Monhegan, including a steamer from Boothbay or Thomaston to Port Clyde and across. Dewis commented that the island is like a "ship turned upside down" upon first appearance and was called "La Nef" (Ship Island) by Champlain in 1604. While the island seemed "rocky and inhospitable" from the water, everything changes once .you've landed, and "it would be difficult to find another place or island with so much diversified scenery in so small a compas—both beautiful and picturesque: a woods in which one can become lost, little valleys, miniature ravines, a marsh for the Sora to hide in, a pond for the sandpiper, cliffs for grand views, and beautiful rocks for some artists to daub with paint." He finished by saying that Monhegan is surely "a Mecca for the bird student."

   The lighthouse keeper, Mr. Corbett, reported no dead birds around the station on the morning of Sep 9, after a wet and rainy night, although one came within the cage and a number flew around the light; birds are sometimes killed at the station on wet and foggy nights. CFJ and BHW noted that birds "do not come out much" the day after migration, instead resting under cover and avoiding the hawks that are after them.

- Wentworth recorded 85 species (excluding a Bewick's Wren which he himself questioned) over nineteen days during Sep 29–Oct 25 (no observations on Sep 30, Oct 2–3, 5, 10–11, 14 & 18). The number of species seen on these nineteen days ranged from a low of 15 on Oct 1 to a high of 38 on Oct 17. Although remaining on the island until Nov 2, he noted few birds due to a busy schedule and fog and rain Oct 26–31. CFJ commented that while the notes from BHW were in the form of letters not meant for publication but for inclusion in his records of Monhegan birds, the level of migration and the lateness of the season deemed the sightings worthy of special note. He used the words of the correspondence when possible and numbers present when provided. It should be noted that BHW was present on the island with Dewis for some of his observations, but left the island for eight days, returning on Sep 29, during which time a Miss Gleason reported a notable flight (no details available). Weather conditions and systems are addressed during the period of observations.

Wentworth began to take two-hour walks on Oct 6 when a "notable flight" was under way, with a "very high wave" on the 8th. He had never before encountered so many sparrows, to the point that he ceased trying to identify them, because of their restless behavior and difficult identification, to concentrate on other species present. His time was limited, such that he did not go far afield or give attention to "shore birds." Each walk during this "sparrow wave" produced twenty to thirty species, declining on the 9th due to their departure. He noted his first Red-headed Woodpecker on the 11th, although he was too busy for other observations. Birds remained scarce until a northwest gale on Oct 15 produced a movement of American Robins and other thrushes, Purple Finches and juncos, continuing through the 17th. The passage of another front produced a "migration wave of the first order" on the 19th, with the largest numbers accounted for by Song Sparrow, Dark-eyed Juncos and Hermit Thrushes, along with high numbers of American Robins. Another wave of the first order occurred on the 24th ("one of the finest days of the season") and cleared out by the 25th, the largest contrast in numbers he had ever known.

Wentworth made several other comments relating to his observations and identification. His records should not be compared to the earlier Dewis/Jenney observations with regard to waterbirds, as he "did not try to cover that part of the field." He did not feel certain regarding identifying hawks, his "glasses" not being strong enough; he remarked that hawks were not as common as in September and the decline coincided with the departure of Northern Flickers. "The usual uncertainty holds as to Least and Alder Flycatchers." Wentworth stated that CFJ would have found many more species of sparrows, as he (BHW) "throws up" his hands when it comes to sparrows in October, suggesting that one may not be sure of identification without "taking" (collecting) them, and that it seemed he was seeing all of those pictured on Plate 81 of Eaton's *Birds of New York* at Lobster Cove on October 8 "on the sea-weed, in the nearby marsh, and the sandy path between." An amusing anecdote relates his struggling to identify a "Yellow" Palm Warbler that was not wagging its tail, only to discover it didn't have a tail and that Mrs. Davis had just rescued it from her cat.

1939 Summer Census - a contribution by Prof. Warner Taylor to the Monhegan Press (1939) listing birds observed on Monhegan during the summer months, considered July and August, noting 85 species (*despite the title itself stating 91*) as regular, uncommon or rare/accidental residents (denotes breeders on or near Monhegan) or visitors.[2] He allows for the fact that some of the latter, such as the shorebirds and winter finches, may be migrants or sporadic visitors, while ignoring that early fall movements of warblers; likewise raptors, except the Osprey, are considered fall migrants arriving after the middle of August. Certain species were noted as "at sea" or on the Outer Rocks. The extent of the records considered in this census is unclear. According to an editor's note, the intent of the article was to contribute to the "current interest in Monhegan's natural assets."

While WT's note that Monhegan "is not especially rich in summer birdlife" may be subjective, his comment that it being an island "has probably little bearing on the number and variety of species" is certainly questionable, considering what we now know about Maine's birds. He points out the lack of certain habitats, such as farmland, fresh water, mainland shrubbery and tree diversity as limiting factors, while stating that the island's "only" advantage is as an observation point for waterbirds. He also made note of a September 12 afternoon from several years earlier on which he recorded 72 land birds, most of them strangers in July and August.

---

[2] Information accessed through the archives of the Monhegan Historical and Cultural Museum Association.

1944–1967 Farrell Records - a compilation by island resident Isabel Farrell (owner of the Island Inn from the early 1950s–1967) of sightings at various times of year from 1944–1967.[2] A total of 203 species was reported on these checklists. The sightings are broken down into checklists by month for 1944–1959 and 1960–61 (no sightings from 1947) and by day for Apr 2–24 & Jun 1–8, 1967.

- 1944: 2 species during Apr, Oct.
- 1945: 4 species during May, Sep–Oct.
- 1946: 8 species during Jan, Mar–Apr, Oct.
- 1948: 15 species during May, Dec.
- 1949: 58 species during Jan–May, Aug–Dec.
- 1950: 69 species during Jan–Jun, Sep–Dec.
- 1951: 55 species during Jan–Jun, Sep–Dec.
- 1952: 29 species during Feb–Apr, Aug, Oct–Nov.
- 1953: 25 species during Aug–Sep.
- 1954: 76 species during Jun–Sep.
- 1955: 99 species during Apr, Jun–Aug.
- 1956: 26 species during May.
- 1957: 29 species during Jun–Aug.
- 1958: 57 species during May–Oct.
- 1959: 124 species during Mar–Sep.
- 1960: 144 species during Apr–Sep.
- 1961: 84 species during Apr–May.
- 1967: 49 species during Apr 2–24, Jun 1–8.

While apparently a compilation of sightings by Isabel Farrell herself, there are a limited number of sightings by other birders, listed as "Other sightings" at the end of the 1944–1959 checklist or with special notations for 1967. Some are listed with an observer's name, with only first or last names given for some: Barnes (1959), Bernstein (1967), Burrell, Conkey, Cord, Ann Edison, Elsie Rowe and Rita (White–1967). Select sightings were also reported by other birders in the 1954 & 1955 Summer Records (see following section).

Special notations were made for several species. Iceland Gull was listed as "infrequent winter records—no date," therefore without enough information for inclusion. A Northern Shrike reported in Jun 1954 has been excluded based on timing and probably refers to a Loggerhead Shrike present in Jul 1954 (as reported in the 1954 & 1955 Summer Records–see below). Lapland Longspur, reported in Jun 1954, was listed as Longspur with a "?" and therefore excluded here. Yellow-headed Blackbird was noted as "Seen several times in May??" and a "?" between Aug & Sep with "also Edison" (*presumably Ann, fide Richard Farrell pers. comm.*), again, not enough details for inclusion. The comment "Feeding tray 'Parkers'—several seasons" is written on the line for Dickcissel but may have an arrow pointing to the Aug 1959 listing of Indigo Bunting and so is disregarded for lack of clarity.

---

[2] Information accessed through the archives of the Monhegan Historical and Cultural Museum Association.

1954 & 1955 Summer Records – six unpublished checklists from various observers during separate visits to the island during the summers of 1954 (three) and 1955 (three).[2] A total of 100 species was reported on these checklists (see discussion below for comments and exclusions).

- 46 species during Jun 19–25, 1954; Eva and Albert Schnitzer.
- 46 species during Jun 27–Jul 4, 1954; Mr. and Mrs. F. N. Rolf.
- 42 species during Jul 10–16, 1954; Mr. and Mrs. E. Alexander Bergstrom.
- 44 species during Jun 11–15, 1955; Mr. and Mrs. Carl F. Hamann from Aurora, OH.
- 23 species during Jun 30–Jul 5, 1955; Mr. and Mrs. Arnold from Wilmington, DE.
- 83 species during Aug 21–Sep 3, 1955; Mr. and Mrs. E. Alexander Bergstrom, accompanied at various times by Mrs. Isabel Wasson, Margaret Lehmann, Mrs. William Riddle and Nancy Bradfield.

Remarkable was the Carolina Wren record (Jul 10–16, 1954 checklist), the first known record for Monhegan (see species account for further details). Fish Crow (Jun 19–25, 1954 checklist) is included on the hypothetical list, as the identifications are considered questionable. Wilson's Storm-Petrel is excluded from the species account for being seen from a boat, both Acadian Flycatcher and Worm-eating Warbler are excluded for being of "doubtful certainty" by the compiler (see species accounts for further details), Common Redpoll, Pine Grosbeak and Lapland Longspur are excluded for being listed with a question mark, and Yellow Rail is excuded because the description given of its vocalizations doesn't match the species' call. "Tern" was listed on the Jun 19–25, 1954 checklist, with illegible notes next to the listing that may have specified the species.

Mr. and Mrs. Bergstrom made special notes for their 1955 visit, finding 83 species on or from Monhegan, and an additional five seen from the mail boat ferry ride between Monhegan and Port Clyde; including the others of their party, totals of 88 and 94 species were observed, respectively (the additional species not included in the Bergstrom list). Age, sex and abundance data were provided for some species. They reported general weather conditions, indicating an abnormally dry season with no rain at all from recent Hurricane Diane, to the point of a "water crisis," and ten days of fog before their arrival. Winds shifting from southerly to northerly on Aug 23 provided "some suggestion of daytime migration in a series of Eastern Kingbirds moving north over the spruce tops at the south end of the island." A switch from southwest to northwest winds on Aug 28 brought a small but obvious wave of migrants, amounting to 53 species seen. Sep 2 saw "some indications of a wave, especially vireos." Their stated impression was that "any sharp cold wave with NW wind at this season should bring a wave of migrants, with relative lulls between."

The Bergstroms also made efforts to track down records of earlier bird observations, among them the 1918 Dewis and Wentworth reports. They had conversations with Warner Taylor and Morris Shulman, an artist from New York who apparently observed birds on Monhegan for many years *(unknown in any official sense)*, mentioning that both were willing to recount experiences but neither had written notes. They also mentioned Josephine Townsend as an active birder who lived on Monhegan before WWII, and an indirect report of a collection of bird skins or mounts made on the island "many years ago" by Mr. Cabot, apparently still in the possession of the family, but the matter was not investigated further.

1970 Summer Checklist - a compilation of July and August observations on Monhegan, Manana, nearby islets and surrounding waters from the previous ten years by "competent observers" (Monhegan Museum, 1970).[2] It is a list of permanent residents, regular breeders, summer residents of uncertain breeding status and to a lesser extent irregular or erratic breeders (crossbills, Pine Siskin), non-breeders from nearby breeding areas (Leach's Storm-Petrel, Common and Arctic Terns), summering non-breeders (White-winged Scoter, Common Loon, Red-throated Loon, Northern Gannet, Great Cormorant; often old, injured, or immature birds), summer visitors (shearwaters, Wilson's Storm-Petrel), post-breeding dispersal of nearby breeders (Wood Duck, Hooded Merganser, Belted Kingfisher), northward post-breeding dispersal before southward migration (Little Blue Heron and Snowy Egret), migrants (notably shorebirds as early as the beginning of July or more general migration in late August), and rare, casual, and accidental visitors (very few reports or outside of typical range,

---

[2] Information accessed through the archives of the Monhegan Historical and Cultural Museum Association.

such as Western Tanager, Lark Sparrow, Harris's Sparrow, White-crowned Sparrow (Gambel's subspecies), and Yellow-headed Blackbird). The list includes a total of 148 species.

- 55 species are marked as having been known to breed in the area.
- 6 species are marked as summer residents and possible breeders.
- 34 species are highlighted as expected to be found in suitable habitat on at least 75% of half-day trips.

The checklist introduction states that the breeding species are the same as on the adjacent mainland, but fewer in number, and that Monhegan, like other small coastal islands, is noted for spring and fall migrations, when Western strays can be expected. It is strictly a list of species, without supporting dates or details; there are some species listed for which there are no known records in July or August, such as Long-tailed Duck and the Gambel's White-crowned Sparrow, indicating a gap in our knowledge of sightings in the 1960s.

Banding - banding operations have been irregularly conducted on Monhegan and the surrounding islands as far back as 1930, focusing on gulls, raptors and songbirds (see breakdown below). The banding results are generally presented in the following format: total number banded over number of seasons involved, peak seasonal total and season/year, maximum daily total.

Gull Banding - conducted four years (1930 on Duck Rock, 1965, 1967 & 1969 at unknown location[s]) involving Herring Gull and Great Black-backed Gull chicks; Dr. Olin Sewall Pettingill, Jr. was the bander in 1930 and Ian Drury, Jr. was the bander in the 1960s (USGS Bird Banding Laboratory, 2005).

- Summer 1930: 19 inds., all Herring Gulls on Jun 29, 1930.
- Summer 1965: 380 inds. of two species over two days, Jun 29 & Jul 8, max 324 on Jun 29.
- Summer 1967: 105 inds. of two species over six days, Jul 4–Aug 4, max 32 on Jul 23.
- Summer 1969: 147 inds. of two species on Jul 23.

Raptor Banding - part of a study in the fall of 2010 (in conjunction with a hawkwatch–see 2010 Fall Hawkwatch below), conducted by the Biodiversity Research Institute to determine stopover/migration presence of diurnal and nocturnal raptors on Monhegan (DeSorbo et al., 2012). Raptor banding took place at a station on Manana. Owl banding took place at a station in Cathedral Woods.

- Diurnal raptors: 25 inds. of three species (17 Peregrine Falcons, 6 Merlins, 2 American Kestrels) during Sep 18–Oct 18.
- Nocturnal raptors: 18 Northern Saw-whet Owls over thirteen nights, Oct 4–23, max 6 on Oct 23.

The details of timing, age/sex, recoveries of 3 Northern Saw-whet Owls, recaptures (length of stay) and satellite tracking of 2 transmitter-tagged Peregrine Falcons can be found in the species accounts.

Operation Recovery - songbird banding conducted over three years, 1960–1962, by Albert and Eva Schnitzer, mainly in the Meadow (*from photos, appearing to concentrate on the southwest portion*) and to a lesser extent on the Cundy property, capturing 2,672 inds. of 70 species (Schnitzer, 1963). Nets were set up in the Meadow by trampling marsh grasses and a net lane extended 200' into the wet meadow. A net beneath a large tree at the Meadow's edge produced woodpeckers, kinglets, creepers and vireos. Operation Recovery was the name given to an Atlantic coastal netting project, started in 1955, focused on recoveries of birds banded farther to the north in the fall, with large-scale banding at coastal concentration points (Baird et al., 1958).

- Fall 1960: 1,159 inds. of 57 species (includes 3 *Empidonax* sp.) over twenty-one days, Sep 19–Oct 10, max 181 on Oct 10.
- Fall 1961: 755 inds. of 45 species (includes 1 *Empidonax* sp.) over six days, Oct 4–Oct 9, max 236 on Oct 8.
- Fall 1962: 758 inds. of 40 species (includes 4 *Empidonax* sp.) over ten days, Sep 24–Oct 10, max 171 on Oct 2.

E. Alexander Bergstrom made several interesting anecdotal observations in the early 1960s regarding Operation Recovery on Monhegan, such as banding only being possible after the "rush of summer visitors leaves in early Sep," thereby missing Aug specialties like Lark Sparrow and migrants arriving from the east/northeast on the east side of the island (possibly from Nova Scotia or returning to land after drifting over the ocean on northwesterly winds) and feeding as they work their way westward on the island, then departing westerly toward the mainland (1961 & 1964). Albert Schnitzer noted only one return (a retrapping of an ind. at the same site) in the three years of Operation Recovery, that being a Black-capped Chickadee that was probably a local resident and observed at a feeder. He highlighted the possibility that no two yearly migration routes of an ind. banded on Monhegan are alike and therefore will not bring the bird back to the island (1963). Schnitzer also remarked that while he could only guess at the number of migrants that pass Monhegan, it must certainly be "at least in the dozens of millions" and that competent observers with binoculars could provide "truer figures than netters." It would be exciting to see the results of a fall count the Schnitzers conducted in 1957, in which Cedar Waxwing was their most common bird (Schnitzer, 1962), but unfortunately the location of this data is unknown (possibly included in the 1944–1967 Farrell Records).

There are several discrepancies between the BBL dataset (USGS Bird Banding Laboratory, 2005) and the published summary by Schnitzer (1963). There are 3 Empidonax sp. and 13 Red-eyed Vireos missing from the 1960 BBL data (included here), while Schnitzer's published totals for Dark-eyed Junco (listed as Slate-colored Junco) should be 225 (listed as 226) and Chipping Sparrow should be 8 (listed as 9). Three Song Sparrows banded on Sep 21, 1960 were erroneously entered into the BBL database as Sep 21, 1961. In the published results for 1961, the correct total for Myrtle (Yellow-rumped) Warbler should be 261 (listed as 262), while the total for Western Palm Warbler should be 16 (listed as 15). In the published results for 1962, 5 Empidonax sp. are included in the BBL data as 4 Least Flycatchers (included here as 4 Empidonax sp). Single Baltimore Orioles and Common Yellowthroats in the database as banded on Sep 23, 1962 are probably meant to be Sep 24, 1962, as the banding operation didn't start until that date. There are also 1 Least Sandpiper, 17 Savannah Sparrows, 2 Song Sparrows and 1 Lincoln's Sparrow banded on Sep 15, 1962 included for Monhegan, but there is no indication of who may have banded these birds and since the lack of mention in the literature suggests that these could be erroneous, they are not included here.

Misc. Songbird Banding - highly variable efforts conducted during 1980–1991 by Joseph A. Van Os, 1984–91 by Margery R. Plymire and 2002 by June M. Ficker (studying ticks on birds), broken down by season (USGS Bird Banding Laboratory, 2005).

- Fall 1980: 13 inds. of nine species over two days, Sep 13 & Oct 3, max 9 on Oct 3.
- Fall 1981: 916 inds. of 59 species over twenty days, Aug 24–Sep 20, max 114 on Sep 3.
- Spring 1984: 264 inds. of 48 species over nine days, May 9–Jun 7, max 70 on May 11.
- Fall 1984: 58 inds. of 28 species over five days, Sep 24–Oct 6, max 30 on Sep 25.
- Spring 1985: 176 inds. of 30 species over four days, May 17–20, max 103 on May 20.
- Fall 1985: 17 inds. of eight species over two days, Sep 23–24, max 16 on Sep 23.
- Spring 1989: 79 inds. of 18 species over three days, May 15–17, max 43 on May 16.
- Fall 1989: 21 inds. of five species over two days, Oct 25–26, max 14 on Oct 26.
- Spring 1990: 22 inds. of ten species over two days, May 17 & 29, max 21 on May 29.
- Summer 1991: 13 inds. of seven species over four days, Jun 20–Jul 17, max 6 on Jul 16.
- Fall 1991: 38 inds. of ten species over 21 days, Aug 7–Oct 5, max 4 on Aug 14.
- Spring 2002: 36 inds. of 17 species over two days, May 22–23, max 25 on May 22.

2010 Fall Hawkwatch - conducted by BRI in the fall of 2010 at two locations, Manana Island and near Lobster Cove, to quantify presence and establish stopover value on offshore islands for migratory raptors, as well as assess risks posed to wildlife by proposed wind power facilities (DeSorbo et al., 2012). Presented in species accounts as total counted (breakdown by location [Lob=Lobster Cove, Man=Manana]), days present, period present, max. count and date.

Overall, 807 inds. of nine species (includes an unidentified buteo) were recorded over 28 days, Sep 15–Oct 18, max 112 on Sep 20. Counters included Fred Tilly, Jeff Johnson, Al Hinde, Jeremiah Trimble and Ken Wright.

- Lobster Cove: 428 inds. of seven species (no Northern Goshawk) over nine days, Sep 15–23, max 112 on Sep 20.
- Manana: 372 inds. of eight species over nineteen days, Sep 25–Oct 18, max 102 on Oct 2.

Table 4. Species breakdown of Biodiversity Research Institute hawkwatch in Fall 2010 (DeSorbo et al., 2012).

Species	Count
Osprey	74
Northern Harrier	78
Sharp-shinned Hawk	53
Northern Goshawk	1
Bald Eagle	3
American Kestrel	64
Merlin	393
Peregrine Falcon	139
Unidentified Buteo	1
Unidentified Falcon	1
Total	807

This is the first and only known standardized raptor migration count on the offshore islands of Maine. The study focused on raptors departing the island and the results do not reflect the flight patterns of foraging (lingering) inds. The observation site was moved from near Lobster Cove to a high point on Manana to improve visibility. All raptors recorded had a westerly component to their flight direction, with 87% within the southwest–west range, presumably orienting toward other offshore islands or the mainland in continuing their migration. Seventy-five percent of the birds passed to the north and west (30% and 45%, respectively), indicating that actively migrating raptors will be most evident from the village and west-side vantages, including Lobster Cove, rather than from the eastern headlands. Eighty-eight percent of the migrants were observed passing at heights ≤200', potentially putting them within the sweep range of most wind turbine rotors.

DOWTS (Deepwater Offshore Wind Test Site) Surveys 2011–2014 - conducted by Lubird Kennedy Environmental Services for the University of Maine's Advanced Structures and Composites Center to establish baseline presence of birds, principally seabirds, and other wildlife (seals, whales, fishes, porpoises, turtles, etc.) in the proposed location of an offshore wind test turbine platform. This resulted in five published reports covering Sep–Nov 2011 (Kennedy & Holberton, 2012) Jun–Aug 2012 (Kennedy, 2012b), Apr–Jun 2013 (Kennedy, 2013a), Jul–Dec 2013 (Kennedy, 2013c) and Dec 2013–May 2014 (Kennedy, 2014a). Presented in species accounts as overall number recorded, days recorded (percentage of days recorded), date range, max count and date.

Observations were recorded from a boat traversing set transects during various times of the year, within a designated 7.5 square mile "Monhegan Test Site" that is centered on a point at N 43.719° W 69.333° (approximately 2.5 miles distant and almost directly south of the island). Two sets of surveys, each consisting of three parallel north-to-south transects, 2,000m long and 900m apart, were conducted within the Test Site each time: a "Control Quadrant" survey just west of immediately south of the island at a distance of approximately 1.4–2.5 miles (completely within the Monhegan Island Lobster Conservation Area [MILCA]), and a "Test Quadrant" survey immediately south and slightly east of the Control Quadrant, that fell partly within the MILCA and partly outside its boundary. To ensure accuracy of inclusion, **only** the Control Quadrant observations and specific sightings from the Test Quadrant that were clearly marked as occurring within the MILCA (approximately the northern third of the Test Quadrant) are included and addressed in the species accounts. These are the only known standardized boat-based, open-water bird surveys conducted in Monhegan Island Lobster Conservation waters.

Overall, 3,667 inds. of twenty-eight species were recorded over sixty days in the Control Quadrant (some inds. identified only as scoter, duck, shorebird, phalarope, large gull, small gull, tern, cormorant, alcid or hawk). Breakdown by bird type is 12 geese, 312 ducks, 7 grebes, 18 shorebirds, 2 jaegers, 122 alcids, 835 gulls, 44 terns,

36 loons, 197 storm-petrels, 270 shearwaters, 210 gannets, 1,589 cormorants, 1 heron, 1 hawk, and 1 raven. Double-crested Cormorant was the most abundant species (1,567), while Herring Gull was the most regularly observed and the only species to be recorded each day.

- 2011: 1,856 inds. of thirteen species over six days, Sep 22–Nov 16, max 1,548 on Sep 27.
- 2012: 502 inds. of fourteen species over ten days, Jun 23–Aug 29, max 152 on Jun 26.
- 2013: 1,100 inds. of twenty species over thirty-one days, Apr 21–Dec 31, 119 on Nov 16.
- 2014: 209 inds. of fourteen species over thirteen days, Jan 16–May 13.

The number of individuals, species, gender and age when possible, flight direction and height above water were recorded for each observation. Behavioral information was also noted as sitting on the water, a type of flying, or a type of feeding, as well as any relation to working lobster boats within the quadrant to record activities and habitat use in assessing potential turbine site risks. A special focus was given to bird species of conservation concern, including Common Murre, Razorbill, Atlantic Puffin, Laughing Gull and Great Shearwater. The adjacent Test Quadrant produced 2,684 inds. of twenty-eight species, with Black Scoter (2), unidentified hummingbird (1), Dovekie (3), Manx Shearwater (3) and Merlin (1) the only species not recorded in the Control Quadrant.

In general, the survey concluded that due to their low height of flight, below the sweep of the turbine blades, the inds. or species observed were not at high risk to be involved in direct turbine strikes. The likeliest impacts would probably result from birds being attracted to use the turbine platform for resting or staging, and the potential foraging opportunities presented, mainly to the large gull species, by enhanced fish habitat under and around the platform.

The Occurrence section is concluded by observational and anecdotal information that varies by species and elaborates on status, occurrence and behavior. General areas addressed include historical status change, large movements and their duration, exceptional seasons, confusion regarding records, regional presence and origin of vagrants, seasonal boundaries and overlapping seasonality, periods of underreporting, length of stay on the island, location(s), breeding data, flock size, nocturnal flight calls/records, vocalizations, behavior, age and sex data when available, and interesting or unusual observations.

Information regarding subspecific and hybrid observations is presented in a separate paragraph, as well as "lumped" observations, such as "Traill's" Flycatcher (Alder or Willow Flycatcher).

HISTORICAL/REGIONAL

A concise presentation of Monhegan sightings and information in major Maine ornithological resources in chronological order by author's or compiler's name, extending from 1949–2020, as well as additional Maine records of certain rare species to provide a broader context (OLMB, see below).

Palmer - *Maine Birds* by Ralph S. Palmer (1949). An historical review of the bird life of Maine, the first in over forty years (*Birds of Maine* by Knight in 1908). A thorough presentation of seasonal status, ecology, and remarks regarding food, behavior, etc. The total of 349 species includes "authentic birds of the state," established introduced, extirpated, extinct, and fossil records and excludes introductions not established or needing human aid and hypotheticals. Many species include records or mention of Monhegan, as noted.

Cruickshank - *Summer Birds of Lincoln County, Maine* by Allan Cruickshank (1950). A detailed, annotated county list for June, July and August based on the birding efforts of the author and Carl Buchheister, Joseph Cadbury, Roger Tory Peterson and others over the previous ten years. Contains seasonal status, including some specific records, and remarks concerning migration outside June–August (mainly fall) and habitat. A total of 255 species is treated, with many including records or mention of Monhegan.

Vickery - *Birds of Maine* by Peter D. Vickery with managing editors Barbara S. Vickery and Scott Weidensaul and coauthors Charles D. Duncan, William J. Sheehan and Jeff Wells (2020). A comprehensive work on all things birds in Maine, covering distribution, history, status and conservation needs, and species accounts. The species accounts feature seasonal and global status, distribution and remarks, followed by a summary of records by season. The total of 464 species includes 285 regularly occurring, with 217 of these as breeders, 30 as primarily winter residents, and 38 as migrants only. Many species include records or mention of Monhegan, as noted.

An island specific sidebar by Jeremiah Trimble marks Monhegan's special place in Maine's ornithology. In it, he highlights its beauty, landscape, Tom Martin's contributions, location, benefits to birds, weather conditions affecting bird presence, habitat, and diversity, abundance and rarity of birds seen, truly marking Monhegan as a migration hotspot.

OLMB - Official List of Maine Birds, as compiled by the Maine Bird Records Committee (2022). An online checklist that contains 470 species as of December 31, 2022 and presented through the Eleventh Report of the Maine Bird Records Committee (Persons et al., 2022). Provides links for select rare species to a listing of state reports, broken down into Accepted, Unaccepted, and Not Yet Reviewed. For those select rarities that have been recorded on Monhegan, a summary is provided here of the additional state records. Unaccepted records will generally not appear here, unless noted as such, although reports of these sightings may still be present on eBird or in other sources.

Red Crossbill, May 22, 2018. © Luke Seitz.

Peregrine Falcon, Sep 24, 2022, Burnt Head. © Brett M. Ewald.

SPECIES ACCOUNTS

SNOW GOOSE
Anser caerulescens

Status: Accidental spring and rare fall migrant, very rare winter visitor.

Occurrence: Fourteen records (1 spring, 11 fall, 2 winter). Spring record: 3 on Apr 3–4, 1967 (IF). Fall records over eleven years since Oct 11, 1987, span Sep 22–Nov 21; fall max: **220** on Oct 3, 1998 (JT), 50 on Oct 4, 1992 (LB), 30 on Oct 11, 1987 (JVW), 20 on Oct 13, 2014 (BBy et al.). Winter records: 5 on Jan 2–4, 2013 (CBC Jan 3–DH et al.), 1 on Dec 14, 2022–Jan 12, 2023 (DC, JPy). Ten-Year: F-3, W-1.

- CBC: one year (4%), 5 on Jan 3, 2013, avg 0.2.
- 1944–1967 Farrell Records: 3 on Apr 3–4, 1967 (2 adults, 1 immature)

The 30 seen in Oct 1987 were observed flying south. 1989 was the only year with multiple records (singles on Sep 28 and Oct 7)—perhaps it was the same ind., but no notes indicate so. An adult was noted on a rock at the Seal Ledges on two consecutive days during Sep 24–26, 2008 (BSc), the 20 reported on Oct 13, 2014 were seen over the ocean from Lobster Cove, while 10 on Sep 22, 2018 were a single flock flying west over the harbor. An adult was present on Manana Nov 19–21, 2021 (DC). The spring and winter records constitute the only other multi-day sighting; the Apr 1967 inds. were noted as staying overnight, while the Jan 2013 ind. was marked as continuing on Jan 3, so of unknown arrival date, but flying into the Meadow from the south. Only one blue morph ind. has been recorded, an overwintering adult present from Dec 14, 2022 (DC) until at least Jan 12, 2023 (JPy). Two other fall inds. were identified as adults, while the spring inds. were identified as 2 adults and 1 immature and the winter inds. were identified as 1 adult and 4 immatures.

BRANT
Branta bernicla

Status: Very rare spring and fall migrant.

Occurrence: Twelve records (6 spring, 5 fall, 1 unknown)—all except 1916 and 1952 records (see below) and an undated record in 1976 (TMar personal notes) since 2009. Spring dates span Mar 16–May 28 (all except two records May 15 or later): unreported number during Mar 1952 (IF), 1 on May 21–24, 2009 (GD, DS et al.), **7** on Mar 16, 2010 (DC), **7** on May 15–16, 2011 (TMag, LS, GD), 1 on May 15, 2018 (DC), 1 on May 28–29, 2018 (PMo et al.). Fall dates span Aug 21 (possibly as early as Aug 16)–Nov 7: 1 on Aug 21–Sep 10, 1916 (WT, MCG), 2 on Oct 12, 2009 (JM), 1 on Oct 9, 2010 (TMag), 1 on Nov 7, 2010 (TMag), 1 on Sep 20, 2016 (PBn, BBn). Ten-Year: SP-1, F-1.

- 1914 & 1916 Checklists: included 1916.
- 1915–1919 Taylor Journals: 1916–recorded seven days Aug 21–Sep 10 (1 on Aug 21 & 25, unreported number Aug 22, 30, 31, Sep 6, 10). *Likely a single ind. responsible for all records, based on rarity.*
- 1944–1967 Farrell Records: 1952–Mar.

The reports by MCG & WT in 1916 likely involve the same ind. and counted as one record of 1 for these purposes. Location provided for four of the records: the May 2009 ind. was observed eating sea lettuce at Swim Beach and was "surprisingly tame" (DF), the Oct 2009 pair was flying over the harbor, the 7 Mar 2010 inds. were in the harbor, and the two-day record in Sep 2016 was seen on the north end of Nigh Duck Island. Without further details, it is impossible to tell if the two records in Fall 2010 were the same ind. It is surprising that there are so few records for a species that is sometimes common as an offshore migrant in Maine, including historically.

Brant, May 15, 2011. © Geoff Dennis.

CANADA GOOSE
Branta canadensis

Status: Uncommon spring and fairly common to common fall migrant, rare summer and winter visitor.

Occurrence: Record from Apr 1950 is earliest known (IF). Lack of winter/early spring coverage complicates understanding—spring migration probably underway by late February (earliest recorded Mar 6), peaks Apr, continues into early Jun; spring max: 30 on Apr 10, 2011 (TMag), 12 on Apr 12, 2014 (DOWTS–LKB), 9 on Apr 7, 2020 (DC), 6 on May 31, 2011 (DH). Ten summer records over seven years (four in 2014) since 2012, scattered throughout; max 2 on Jun 22, 2019, six records of singles, the remaining three are an unreported number. Fall migration underway in early Sep, peaks last week Sep–mid Nov, and continues into early Dec; fall max: **318** on Oct 2, 2017 (LS), 160 on Oct 9, 2010 (TMag) and Oct 8, 2011 (JM), 155 on Oct 27, 2012 (JP). Twelve winter records over eleven years since 1981, most associated with CBC period, latest Jan 26; winter max: 171 on Dec 29, 1981 (CBC–PDV), 38 on Jan 5, 2018 (DC), 25 on Dec 19, 2021 (DC), 5 on Dec 21, 1989 (CBC–PDV). Ten-Year: SP-10, SU-5, F-10, W-3.

- CBC: six years (23%) plus one count week, first on Dec 29, 1981, max 171 on Dec 29, 1981, avg 28.8.
- 1944-1967 Farrell Records: 1950–Apr; 1951–Apr; 1960–Apr.
- 1970 Summer Checklist: included.
- DOWTS Surveys 2011–2014: 12 on Apr 12, 2014 (1.7%).

Although extirpated from Maine in the 1800s, reintroduction in the 1960s (earliest known record on Monhegan in 1950) has increased the population to record levels in the state (Vickery et al., 2020). Undoubtedly underreported during spring migration on Monhegan; early winter records may be lingering birds or late migrants due to warm weather/non-freezing conditions. While many are noted as flyover flocks or singles (65 is the max. reported as one flock), including the flock from the DOWTS, others have been observed landing in the Meadow, singles or doubles at the Ice Pond, Swim Beach and in the harbor. One lingering group of 19 in 2010 was noted as being seen each day Oct 29–31 (possibly as early as Oct 11; unreported number) and alighting in the Meadow (LS, MI, JT); a group of 18 were observed heading to the mainland on Oct 31 (same inds.?). There is a report of 1 shot at the northern end of island on Oct 10, 2010 (JM).

WOOD DUCK
Aix sponsa

Status: Rare to scarce spring and scarce fall migrant, very rare summer visitor or resident, accidental winter visitor.

Occurrence: Spring dates span Apr 4–Jun 4, with no apparent peak period; spring max: **16** on Jun 3, 2020 (JT, LS), 10 on May 27, 2014 (JT), 9 on May 17, 2019 (DPJ), 7 on May 26, 2014 (JT) & May 23, 2022 (JT, LS, MWa). Three summer records: unreported number during w/e Jul 6, 2005 (fide SP, KG; MARBA), 1 on Jul 14–15, 2021 (BTh), 1 on Jul 7, 2022 (LS, MW); the only breeding record, involving an adult w/young on May 28, 2018 (CG, CDu), falls into the spring period for these purposes. Fall dates span Aug 25–Nov 15, with the peak mid Oct–mid Nov; fall max: 14 on Oct 2, 2003 (JT), 12 on Oct 4, 2020 (LMu, BBc), 10 on Oct 13, 2014 (LS et al.), 8 on Oct 10, 2014 (JT). One winter record: female on Nov 28–Dec 26, 2018 (DC). Ten-Year: SP-8, SU-2, F-10, W-1.

- 1944–1967 Farrell Records: 1960–Sep.
- 1970 Summer Checklist: included, noted as local post-breeding dispersal from nearby areas.

The largest noted flock size of 16 (the overall max count) occurred in flight over the Meadow and was seen several times. Multi-day stays are common, with presumably the same birds staying over one week on occasion. Most often seen at the Ice Pond or Meadow or a combination of both, although an unusual sighting occurred in the outlet stream to Swim Beach (LS); flyovers reported from various locations, including the harbor, Manana, and in off the water at dawn. The highly unexpected record on May 28, 2018 (noted above) of an adult calling in a duckling on a "beaver pond" along Long Swamp Trail not only confirms breeding (not included in MBA), but is somewhat early for a fledgling in Maine; there are only the three true summer records known for Monhegan. The unusual 2018 winter record involved a female "hanging out" and coming to seed scattered across from the general store on Nov 26 and noted as still present on Dec 26 (location unknown–DC). One fall ind. was noted pushing an apple around the Ice Pond and nibbling on it (KL). While males have outnumbered females on the island (more than 2:1), pairs have often been identified as an adult male and adult female; there has only been one fall report of an immature male.

Historical/Regional:

- Vickery: cites 10 on Oct 13, 2014 (LS et al.) as an offshore record (WJS in Vickery et al., 2020).

Wood Duck, Ice Pond, Oct 3, 2020. © Luke Seitz

BLUE-WINGED TEAL
Spatula discors

Status: Rare spring and fall migrant, very rare summer visitor and possible breeder.

Occurrence: Spring records span Apr 4–w/e Jun 12, with no apparent peak; spring max: 3 on May 5, 2010 (NL), 2 on many dates (5 reported as May 17, 1997 is for a two-day trip list). Three summer records, all from 2022 and probably involving the same ind(s)., possibly breeding (see discussion, below): 1 on Jul 5, 2022 (DH), 1 or 2 on Jul 25–26, 2022 (noted as continuing–DL, JL), 2 on Aug 14, 2022 (LS, MWa). Fall records span Aug 23–Nov 26, with only one record after Oct 12 (see Palmer, below), with no apparent peak; fall max: **11** on Sep 14, 1980 (PDV), 5 on Sep 7, 1986 (PDV), 4 on Sep 27, 2010 (DH, AW). Ten-Year: SP-4, SU-1, F-7.

- MBA: probable.
- 1944–1967 Farrell Records: 1950–May; 1960–Sep.
- 1970 Summer Checklist: included.

Similar in occurrence and habits to Wood Duck, with long-staying inds. occurring, such as two reported on five days over the period Apr 14–May 3, 2011, a female reported five days over the period Sep 17–25, 2012 (and possibly until Oct 11), two inds. observed each day Sep 14–22, 2014, a male in the Meadow nineteen days over the period May 16–Jun 7, 2021 (every day May 16–Jun 1) and joined by a female on May 18 and 28–29 (possibly breeding) and a female in the Meadow nine days over the period Sep 13–30, 2021. A pair, first noted at the Ice Pond on May 18, 2022 (*possibly the same pair as May 2021?*–Michael, Anu)

was observed at the Meadow most days until at least Jun 1; breeding suggested by copulation on May 23, 2022 (JT, LS, MWa), apparent continued presence into Jul, and a female and juvenile at the Ice Pond on Aug 14–15 (LS, MWa). Most sightings occur at the Ice Pond, Meadow (or a combination of both) or as flyovers (including one with a White-winged Scoter).

Historical/Regional:
- Palmer: one killed on Nov 26, 1917.

Blue-winged Teal, Ice Pond, Sep 22, 2014. © Bill Thompson.

NORTHERN SHOVELER
Anas clypeata

Status: Accidental spring and fall migrant.

Occurrence: Two records (1 spring, 1 fall) since first recorded in 2017. Spring record: **3** (2 male, 1 female) on Apr 7–8, 2017 (only 1 male seen on Apr 7–DC [ph], JB, LBt). Fall record: 1 immature male on Oct 1–2, 2019 (DH et al.). Ten-Year: SP-1, F-1.

The Apr 2017 observations occurred in the Meadow behind the general store and are considered one record, despite only 1 male reported/photographed on the 7th (the other two likely overlooked/not visible during incidental observation), with all 3 present on the 8th. The Oct 2019 ind. was at the Ice Pond.

Northern Shoveler - immature male, Ice Pond, Oct 1, 2019. © Luke Seitz.

GADWALL
Mareca strapera

Status: Accidental fall migrant.

Occurrence: One record: **3** (2 females and one male) on Nov 10, 2022 (LS, MWa). Ten-Year: F-1.

Observed flying southward past Manana.

EURASIAN WIGEON
Mareca penelope

Status: Very rare fall vagrant.

Occurrence: Two records: male on Oct 11, 2010 (JT), male Oct 7–14, 2012 (JT, DH; ph.).

The Oct 2010 ind. was observed flying south over the harbor. The Oct 2012 ind., a molting male, was first observed with a Blue-winged Teal in the Meadow late in the day on Oct 7 (DH, JT) and was also seen there on Oct 8, 11, 12, & 14.

Eurasian Wigeon, Oct 8, 2012. © Jeremiah Trimble.

AMERICAN WIGEON
Mareca americana

Status: Accidental spring and very rare fall migrant.

Occurrence: Five records (1 spring, 4 fall) since 1983. Spring record: 1 on Mar 10–22, 2017 (DC). Fall records: female on Dec 29, 1983 (PDV), 1 on Oct 7, 1984 (SS), **2** on Sep 19, 2008 (LS), 1 female on Sep 20, 2020 (EJ et al.). Ten-Year: SP-1, F-1.

- CBC: one year (4%), max 1 on Dec 29, 1983, avg 0.0.

The Dec 1983 ind. was in the harbor on the CBC and could be considered a winter visitor. The pair in 2008 (male and female) were on the Ice Pond. The Mar 2017 ind. was only noted on the 10th (harbor) and 22nd, but considered the same ind. due to rarity. The Sep 2020 ind. was in the Ice Pond.

MALLARD
Anas platyrhynchos

Status: Fairly common permanent resident, uncommon spring and fairly common fall migrant, fairly common winter visitor.

Occurrence: Noticeably present throughout the year, pattern of seasonal movements complicated by residents; fairly consistent peak numbers (lowest in spring, but underreported). Affected by spring thaw, migration mostly occurs in Mar and Apr; spring max: 13 on Mar 19, 2022 (KL), 10 on Mar 5, 2012 (DH), 9 on Mar 20, 2022 (KL), 8 on May 5, 2018 (DC). Breeding obvious and numbers augmented by late May with the arrival of young (earliest May 14), two or three broods possible (latest ducklings Aug 9); summer max: **55** on May 23, 2013 (JH); 24 on Aug 29, 2007 (DL) & May 15, 2022 (LS, MWa), 23 on May 27, 2018 (EN, ATh), May 14, 2022 (LS, MWa) & May 17, 2022 (LS, MWa). Fall migration occurring mid Sep through Nov (or later), with a peak in late Sep; fall max: 50 on Sep 22, 2009 (BG), Sep 24, 2009 (BG) & Sep 20, 2020 (LMu, BBc, JMu), 45 on Nov 6, 2020 (FK, DH), 40 on Sep 22, 2006 (CE), Sep 25, 2007 (JSc), Sep 29–Oct 1, 2007 (DL) & Sep 28, 2019 (BM et al.), Oct 3, 2020 (LMu, BBc) & Sep 26, 2021 (ID). Winter numbers affected by freeze-up, therefore highest early in the season; winter max: 35 on Jan 3, 2021 (DH), 33 on Jan 4, 2007 (CBC–PDV et al.), 30 on Jan 2, 1997 (CBC–PDV, DM) & Jan 2, 2021 (DH), 29 on Jan 2, 2020 (CBC–DH), 21 on Feb 7, 2018 (DC). Ten-Year: SP-8, SU-10, F-10, W-6.

- *MABB*: confirmed; MBA: confirmed.
- CBC: 25 years (96%; all but 1941), max 35 on Jan 3, 2021, avg 13.8.
- 1900–1908 Reconnaissance & Supplements: 1 killed by an island resident in 1905 and mounted (CFJ, ECJ–*unclear if only the specimen was observed*).
- 1970 Summer Checklist: included.
- Songbird Banding: 1 on Sep 11, 1981.

Although the first breeding in Maine didn't occur until 1949, it is now the most common duck in the state (Vickery et al., 2020). Understanding the presence and movements of Mallards on Monhegan is confusing, mostly due to the difficulty of separating migrants from resident birds, some of which appear to be semi-domestic (irregularly fed at the Ice Pond or coming into bird feeders/scattered seed in town, e.g. 20 coming to feed at the Cundy residence on Jan 31, 2022 after a snow storm [DC]). It is compounded by their commonness, as many reports do not include the number (marked as "X"), and the seasonal lack of reports in winter and early spring. In general,

Monarch hitching a ride on a Mallard, Ice Pond, Sep 30, 2017. © Bill Thompson.

numbers in Maine have slowly increased over the past 100 years (note almost all the max dates since 2007). While the highest total recorded (55 on May 23) is included as a summer max, it is possible it includes late migrants, as spring migration is usually over by early May. Mating noted at the Ice Pond as early as Apr 6 and ducklings are usually present by the last week of May (earliest May 14). Ducklings are most often observed at the Ice Pond or in the Meadow with an adult female, sometimes as late as mid Aug; max 11 reported on May 30, 2013 (RL, ML). Mallards will often move around over the course of the day, and in addition to the aforementioned favorite haunts of the Ice Pond and Meadow (usually near the pump house in the back), they are often noted in the harbor (particularly at Swim Beach) and feeding among the rocks and seaweed at Lobster Cove.

AMERICAN BLACK DUCK
Anas rubripes

Status: Uncommon spring and uncommon to fairly common fall migrant, uncommon summer visitor/resident, fairly common winter visitor; *possible permanent resident*.

Occurrence: Spring migration reports scattered throughout Mar and Apr, mostly completed by early May; spring max: 9 on Mar 21, 2012 (T Mag), 6 on May 7, 1985 (PDV) & Apr 7, 2013 (DH), 5 on Apr 5–6, 2012 (DH) & Apr 5, 2013 (DH). Summer patterns uncertain and underreported, listed as possible on *MABB* and seven reports of young (2011, two in 2021, four in 2022–see below); summer max: 8 on May 20 & 22, 2022 (female with 7 young–BGr, RMi), 7 on Jun 16, 2011 (female with 6 young–CDd & DDd) & May 26, 2021 (LP), 6 on May 29, 2010 (KR), July 5, 2015 (SY) & May 24 & 26, 2022 (BTn). Fall migration begins with regional post-breeding dispersal in early Aug, peaks with northerly migrants in late Sep–Oct, and continues into mid Dec; fall max: 10 on Sep 21, 2007 (LS), Sep 21–22, 2012 (MW), Aug 31, 2014 (Jho) & Sep 18, 2020 (LMu, BBc, JMu), 9 on Oct 7, 1989 (SS), Oct 8, 2017 (BSq, WSq) & Nov 3, 2010 (TMag), 8 on Sep 26, 2001 (JT), Oct 29, 2010 (TMag), Oct 31, 2010 (TMag) & Oct 1, 2020 (LMu, BBc). As with Mallard, winter numbers affected by freeze-up and highest early in season; winter max: **60** on Jan 3, 2008 (CBC–PDV, DF), 39 on Dec 22, 1979 (CBC–PDV et al.), 34 on Jan 25, 2013 (DH). Ten-Year: SP-3, SU-10, F-10, W-6.

- *MABB*: possible; MBA: confirmed.
- CBC: 26 years (100%), max 60 on Jan 3, 2008, avg 20.7.
- 1944–1967 Farrell Records: 1954–Jun & Jul; 1955–Aug.
- 1954 & 1955 Summer Records: 1954–included June 27–July 4.
- 1970 Summer Checklist: known to breed in the area.

While designated as a summer visitor and breeder, it is likely that American Black Duck is an uncommon permanent resident, associating with and possibly breeding with Mallard—the matter needs further clarification. Seven reports involve ducklings (recently fledged young) since 2011, provide highest max counts. The female and 6 young on Jun 16, 2011 (CDd, DDd) were feeding on sea lettuce at Lobster Cove. The 7 on May 26, 2021 (LP) and 5 on Jun 7, 2021 (CDD, LBl) are marked as recently fledged young, confirming breeding for MBA; likely but unclear if adult[s] present and possibility of hybrid offspring with Mallard exists (see below). The four reports of young in 2022 span May 20–26 (4–8 inds.) and likely involve the same family group. An additional report of female with 9 ducklings on May 20, 2015 (TK) was listed as 1 American Black Duck, but possibly a summer max count. No indication of largest single flock size; the 39 recorded on Dec 22, 1979 involved two separate groups. Reported most often from the Ice Pond, often associating with Mallards; other locations include the harbor (sometimes larger flocks), Lobster Cove, the Meadow, and the eastern shoreline near Gull Cove and below Burnt Head.

Hybrids of American Black Duck x Mallard, although undoubtedly present, had been overlooked until recently, as all official records are since 2004. Regularly reported since (multiple records per year), occurring throughout the year (usually singles or doubles); the max of 10 was a family group on May 23, 2015 (JT, BN, JO) and there have been reports of 6, 4 (two reports), and 3 (three reports)—all in the fall. Four inds. have been identified as males, but none as certain females. One hybrid male was with 7 American Black Ducks on the Ice Pond, the most favored location. One ind. was at the Hitchcox feeders on the 2013 CBC (DH).

American Black Duck, Sep 17, 2021. © Bill Thompson.

NORTHERN PINTAIL
Anas acuta

Status: Very rare fall migrant, accidental winter visitor.

Occurrence: Nine records (8 fall, 1 winter) since 1984. Fall records (four records in 2010) within the short span of Sep 23–Oct 11: 1 on Sep 28, 1984 (PDV), 1 on Sep 23, 2010 (SM), 1 on Sep 26, 2010 (SZ et al.), 1 on Oct 3, 2010 (LS, DL), 1 on Oct 11, 2010 (JT et al.), **4** on Oct 4, 2016 (JT, JO), female on Oct 2, 2017 (DL), 2 on Oct 9, 2021 (JT, LS). Winter record: 2 males on Jan 13–22, 2022 (DC, MT). Ten-Year: F-3, W-1.

Six of the fall records involved flybys, the other two lack details; Sep 1984 ind. flying past Monhegan, Oct 3, 2010 ind. off White Head with a flock of Double-crested Cormorants, Oct 11, 2010 flyover with migrating flock of Canada Geese, 2016 group flying north over Nigh Duck, disappearing into Deadman's Cove, Oct 2021 inds. flying south beyond Manana. Despite four records of singles in 2010, the circumstances don't suggest repeat inds. The sole winter record involved two males frequenting the small outlet stream to Swim Beach from the Meadow, sometimes associating with Mallards, reported Jan 13 (fide DC), 20 (DC) & 22 (MT).

GREEN-WINGED TEAL
Anas crecca

Status: Rare spring and scarce to uncommon fall migrant, very rare winter visitor.

Occurrence: Thirteen spring records over ten years since 1950 (all but one since 1985), spanning Mar 5–May 24, with two records each in 1997, 2011, 2012; spring max: 2 on May 7, 1985 (PDV), May 13–14, 1997 (PDV), Apr 6, 2011 (TMag) & May 3, 2011 (TMag). Fall migration spans Sep 4–mid Dec, peaks late Sep–early Nov; fall max: **13** on Oct 4, 2020 (JT, LS, BBy), 12 on Oct 7, 2005 (MI, AM), 9 on Nov 10, 2018 (DH, FK), 6 on Sep 30, 2007 (DL) & Oct 4, 2019 (JT, LS, AO). Six winter records, generally centered around CBC: unreported number during Dec 18–24, 1989 (CBC count week), 2 on Dec 24–Jan 1, 2011 (seen three days, possibly same two inds. seen earlier in fall, see below–TMag), 1 on Jan 19, 2011 (DC), 1 on Jan 5, 2012 (CBC–PDV et al.), 1 on Jan 5–6, 2016 (CBC Jan 5–DH et al.), overwintering female prior to Jan 3–Feb 21, 2021 (DH, DC). Ten-Year: SP-5, F-10, W-2.

- CBC: 3 years (12%) plus one count week, max 1 on Jan 5, 2012, Jan 5, 2016 & Jan 3, 2021, avg 0.1.
- 1944–1967 Farrell Records: 1950–Apr.
- 1970 Summer Checklist: included.

It is debatable whether late Dec/early Jan records should be considered late fall migrants or winter visitors; lingering birds may lean towards the latter, but there are only two records after CBC until early Mar; the Mar 5, 2012 record is actually marked as presumably the same ind. as CBC (lack of coverage complicates understanding). An ind. in spring 2017 was noted on Mar 10 as mingling with Mallards eating cracked corn put out by the general store for a few days (DC). Like the 2017 ind., a female present on the Jan 3, 2021 CBC (noted as having been present for 1.5 weeks already) mingled with Mallards coming to feed by the general store, as well as spending time in the harbor and present until at least Feb 21 (only reported Jan 3, 22, 31, Feb 21). Other long-staying inds. included possibly the same 2 inds. reported over nine days Sep 22–Jan 1, 2011 (one present Jan 1, considered a separate record here), but not definitive and the Jan 5–6, 2016 record (single) noted as seen throughout early winter by residents (DH–*perhaps the same ind. reported in winter 2016, 2017 and 2021?*) Most often reported from the Ice Pond and Meadow, sometimes associating with Mallards/American Black Ducks, also in the harbor, the cove at Nigh Duck, and off Bald Head; flyby records noted at Lobster Cove, with 5 Common Eiders off the west side of the island, and with a flock of scoters and scaup. The max count of 13 on Oct 4, 2020 included a flock of 12 offshore and 1 in the Meadow. Few records indicate age/sex, with almost all involving females/female types, with only one for adult male.

Green-winged Teal, Sep 21, 2011. © Luke Seitz.

REDHEAD
Aythya americana

Status: Accidental fall migrant.

Occurrence: One record: **2** (adult male and immature) on Sep 29, 1998 (WBo).

RING-NECKED DUCK
Aythya collaris

Status: Very rare spring and fall migrant.

Occurrence: Six records (4 spring, 2 fall) since 1995. Spring records: unreported number on Apr 29, 1995 (TMar), adult male on May 26, 2013 (LS et al.), adult male on May 6–14, 2016 (DHi, DC et al.), adult male on Mar 31, 2017 (DC). Fall records: female on Oct 2–14, 2019 (DC, LS et al.–see below), **2** at Burnt Head on Oct 5, 2019. Ten-Year: SP-3, F-1.

The male in May 2013 was seen leaving the Meadow and flying out over the harbor. The May 2016 record involved sightings at the Ice Pond on May 6, 7, 12, 13, 14. The female in 2019 was first observed at Lobster Cove on Oct 2 and later flew to the east side of the Meadow near the pump house, where it was also observed on Oct 3, 10, 11, 12, 13, 14 (considered same ind. due to site fidelity despite gap in appearance. The Oct 5, 2019 record involved a flyby pair at Burnt Head, heading toward town, never relocated.

Ring-necked Duck - female, Meadow, Oct 13, 2019. © Bill Thompson.

GREATER SCAUP
Aythya marila

Status: Accidental spring and very rare fall migrant, accidental winter visitor.

Occurrence: Six records (1 spring, 4 fall, 1 winter) —all but a 1947 record since 2008. Spring record: unreported number during Mar 1947 (fide IF). Fall records: **8** on Oct 31, 2010 (MI, JT, LS), 1 on Nov 6, 2016 (DH, LB, FK), 1 on Sep 25, 2017 (JT), 1 on Oct 8, 2019 (EJ). Winter record: 1 female on Jan 4, 2008 (PDV, DF, DAb). Ten-Year: F-3.

- CBC: 1 count week in 2008; seen day after the count on Jan. 4.
- 1944–1967 Farrell Records: 1949–Mar.

Four of the five records involved flybys (no details in 2017): over the harbor in 2008, with scoters and one Green-winged Teal in 2010, from Lobster Cove in 2016, and between Manana and Monhegan in 2019. The 2008 record was the only one identified to sex.

KING EIDER
Somateria spectabilis

Status: Accidental spring and very rare fall migrant, very rare winter visitor.

Occurrence: Six records (1 spring, 3 fall, 2 winter) since 1978. Spring record: unreported number during the period May 22–25, 1998 (TV–trip report). Fall records: female on Sep 24, 1993 (PDV), 1 on Sep 26, 2000 (JT), female on Sep 27–Oct 13, 2019 (NS, JHi, mob). Winter records: immature male on Dec. 27–29, 1978 (CBC–PDV), **6** (1 immature male, 5 female) on Jan 2, 1997 (CBC–PDV, DM). Ten-Year: F-1.

- CBC: 2 years (8%; 1979, 1997), max 6 on Jan 2, 1997, avg 2.7.

The Dec 1978 ind. was seen each of the three days on the east side of the island. The group in 1997 was located off Burnt Head/White Head, staying together and not associating with Common Eiders. The female in 2019, first reported from Lobster Cove, apparently spent all its time between the southern end of the harbor and Lobster Cove, often associating with Common Eiders.

Historical/Regional:

- Vickery: cites 1997 CBC count as highest winter record (WJS in Vickery et al., 2020).

COMMON EIDER
Somateria mollissima

Status: Common permanent resident, common spring and abundant fall migrant, abundant winter visitor.

Occurrence: Noticeably present throughout the year along the shoreline and adjacent islands, but understanding incomplete due to inconsistent reporting or undocumented numbers. Winter visitors departing through Mar and Apr, supplemented by migrants from farther south into early May; spring max: 200 on May 25, 1987 (JVW), Apr 7, 2013 (DH) & May 6, 1985 (PDV), 120 on Apr 18, 2012 (DH, PMo), 114 on Apr 10, 2011 (TMag). Breeding occurs along the rocky shores of Monhegan and surrounding islands, with ducklings present by mid Jun; summer max: 200 on May 29, 1983 (PDV), May 13, 2011 (DH) & Aug 1, 2012 (RMc, MWi), 165 on May 27, 2014 (JT) & May 28, 2019 (JT, JO), 150 on Jul 19, 1984 (PDV), May 28, 2013 (KL), May 31, 2014 (JT), & May 22, 2016 (PDV). Post breeding dispersal/gathering results in large congregations by mid Sep–early Oct, with migration continuing into early Dec; fall max: **15,000** on Sep 26–28, 2000 (JT), 8,000 on Sep 26, 2005 (JT), 5,000 on Sep 25, 2000 (JT) & Sep 19, 2005 (SM), 2,500 on Oct 5, 1978 (PDV) & Oct

King Eider (top) and Common Eider (bottom), Harbor, Oct 6, 2019. © Adam Dudley.

11, 1987 (JVW). Winter population arrives by early Dec, with records mostly centered around the CBC due to coverage; winter max: 1,420 on Dec 21, 1989 (CBC–PDV, CDD, IB), 1,309 on Jan 1, 1987 (CBC), 529 on Dec 29, 1981 (CBC–PDV et al.). Ten-Year: SP-8, SU-10, F-10, W-4.

- *MABB*: confirmed; MBA: confirmed.
- CWC: Eastern Duck Rock–25 pairs, Inner Duck Rock–25 pairs.
- CBC: 25 years (96%; all but 1941), max 1,420 on Dec. 21, 1989 (PDV, CDD, IB), avg 255.5.
- 1900–1908 Reconnaissance & Supplements: unreported number on Oct 12, 1907 (CFJ, ECJ).
- 1944–1967 Farrell Records: 1948–Dec; 1949–Mar; 1950–Feb, Mar, Oct; 1951–Feb, Oct; 1952–Mar, Oct, Nov; 1955–Aug; 1959–May, Jul; 1960–Apr, Aug, Sep.
- 1954 & 1955 Summer Records: 1955–max 37 together at White Head on Aug 28.
- 1970 Summer Checklist: highlighted and known to breed in area.
- DOWTS Surveys 2011–2014: 248 over thirteen days (21.7%), all seasons, max 99 on Nov 16, 2013; an additional 93 over six days, Mar 25–Apr 27 & Oct 29–Nov 21, reported in the northern end of the Test Quadrant and included here, including flocks of 40 and 35 resting on the water on Nov 16, 2011 & Nov 21, 2013, respectively.

Understanding its level of presence is complicated by seasonal underreporting (especially Jan–Apr after CBC), inclusion of birds seen from the ferries while crossing, and many records marked X or even omitted. The total of 15,000 recorded three days in Sep 2000 is remarkable. The spring max of 200 in Apr 2013 involved many passing north in pairs and occasionally larger groups (DH). The simple fact is that Common Eiders can be seen almost anywhere in the marine environment, with rafts (sometimes 100+) occurring off Lobster Cove, any of the eastern headlands, around the Seal Ledges, and even in the harbor. Nesting begins on the rocky shoreline of Monhegan and the nearby islands in May (occupied nests noted May 27, 2018–MW), with the first ducklings sighted by mid June and females with young reported throughout the summer (many separate groups on June 13, 2014, each with ducklings–MP; four juveniles with a female as late as Aug 22, 2020–GWa, Mho). It is well known that the adult males leave after mating (line of 18 molting males in flight on Jul 13, 2017–FM; group of 11 females and 1 immature male on Jul 17, 2016–DH). The females raise the young by themselves, with cooperative mothering resulting in groups of ducklings with several females, known as crèches (5 hens with 12 ducklings during Jun 22–25, 2018–KL). It is hard to believe that Common Eider was almost extirpated as a breeder in the state in the early 1900s. The return of males in Sep, coupled with the post-breeding groups of females and immatures, results in the high early fall numbers: a report of 600 males that "must have just arrived from offshore" on Sep 17, 1984 (PDV) may have involved birds seen from the ferry, but illustrates the seasonal movements.

Many records identified to the expected subspecies *S. m. dresseri*, with no records of the northern breeder *S. m. borealis* for Monhegan.

Historical/Regional:

- Vickery: cites Sep 2000 record (JT) as second highest count (WJS in Vickery et al., 2020).

HARLEQUIN DUCK
Histrionicus histrionicus

Status: Very rare spring and rare fall migrant, very rare winter visitor.

Occurrence: Twenty-six records (8 spring, 11 fall, 7 winter) since 1982. Spring records span Mar 24–May 24: 5 on May 21–24, 2003 (possibly until the 26th [trip report]–BCr, RSm, RQ), 2 on May 7, 2007 (KW), 2 on May 9, 2008 (BD), 1 on May 18, 2010 (GD), 1 on Apr 29, 2011 (TMag), 2 on Apr 5, 2012 (DH), 5 on Apr 9, 2019 (JB), 1 on Mar 24, 2021 (KL). Fall records span Oct 3–Nov 12: 1 on Oct 30, 2010 (JT, LS, MI), 4 on Nov 4, 2010 (GD), 1 on Oct 20, 2013 (SSu), 1 on Oct 21, 2017 (JP), 1 on Oct 22, 2017 (JP), 3 on Nov 8, 2020 (FK, DH), 1 on Nov 12, 2020 (JT, LS), **7** on Oct 9, 2021 (JT, LS), 1 on Oct 10, 2021 DH), 1 on Oct 3–4, 2022 (LMu), 2 on Nov 5, 2022 (DH). Winter records, all associated with CBC period, span Dec 22–Jan 5: 1 on Dec 27–28, 1982 (PDV), 2 on Jan 2–3, 1986 (PDV), 5 on Dec 22, 1988 (PDV), 1 on Jan 1, 1991 (PDV), 1 on Jan 2, 1997 (PDV), 2 on Jan 4–5, 2016 (DH et al.), 1 on Jan 2, 2020 (DH). Ten-Year: SP-2, F-4, W-2.

- CBC: 6 years (23%), first on Dec 27, 1982, max 5 on Dec 22, 1988, avg 0.5.

Only five seasons with multiple records—two each in Fall 2010, Fall 2017 (male and female; unexpectedly on consecutive days), Fall 2020 (possibly a lingering bird–three day gap), Fall 2021 (possibly a lingering bird, but consecutive days at a wholly different location–see below) and Fall 2022. Winter status incomplete, accentuated by the CBC records. Details provided for sixteen of the records: female off Lobster Cove in Dec 1982, 5 adult males at Lobster Cove in May 2003, immature male at the south end of the harbor in May 2010, female off Bald Head in Oct 2010, adult male, immature male & 2 females at the south end of the harbor in Nov 2010, adult male and female off Gull Rock in Apr 2012, probable juvenile on the SE side in Oct 2013, male near White Head on Oct 21, 2017, female along southwest shore on Oct 22, 2017, 3 adult males and 2 females/juveniles swimming off Lobster Cove in Apr 2019, adult male off Lobster Cove in Jan 2020, 2 adult males and a female off Lobster Cove on Nov 8, 2020, flyby adult male at Lobster Cove in Mar 2021, 7 inds. seen near the western Outer Duck, while an adult male was at Lobster Cove the following day, female off Lobster Cove in Oct 2022.. Interestingly Squeaker Cove is named after the male Harlequin's high squeaky whistle.

Harlequin Duck, May 18, 2010. © Geoff Dennis.

SURF SCOTER
Melanitta perspicillata

Status: Rare to scarce spring and uncommon to fairly common fall migrant, very rare summer and rare to scarce winter visitor.

Occurrence: Spring dates span Apr 4–May 30; spring max: 19 on Apr 27, 2013 (DOWTS–LKB), 15 on Apr 4, 2012 (DH), 9 on May 27, 2017 (JT, LS, CL) & May 20, 2022 (JT, LS, MWa), 7 on May 21, 2022 (JT, LS, MWa). Two summer records: adult male on Aug 6, 2013 (TR), 1 on Jul 18–20, 2019 (JT). Fall migration dates span Aug 26–early Dec., with a peak mid–late Sep–late Oct; fall max: **400** on Sep 26, 2005 (JT), 293 on Oct 8, 2018 (LS), 278 on Oct 9, 2015 (JT, JO), 107 on Oct 9, 2021 (JT, LS). Winter records all associated with CBC period; winter max: 6 on Dec 21, 1989 (CBC–PDV), 4 on Jan 3, 2013 (CBC–PDV, CDD, WN), 3 on Dec 27, 1994 (CBC). Ten-Year: SP-9, SU-2, F-10.

- CBC: 5 years (19%) plus four count weeks, first on Dec 30, 1980, max 6 on Dec 21, 1989, avg 2.8.
- 1944–1967 Farrell Records: 1960–Aug.
- 1970 Summer Checklist: included.
- DOWTS Surveys 2011–2014: 29 over three days (5%), Apr and Oct–Nov, max 19 on Apr 27, 2013; an additional 2 on Nov 5, 2013 were observed in the northern end of the Test Quadrant and are included here.

Most often seen migrating by Monhegan, with Lobster Cove and Burnt Head favorite locations; the high count of 278 on Oct 9, 2015 involved flocks moving south (JT, JO). Similar to Common Eider in that this species is often encountered near the mainland, inshore islands, or even offshore waters on the ferry rides—every effort has been made to avoid inclusion of such sightings. This species' status also suffers from lack of reports during the winter/early spring period. The adult male in Aug 2013 was off Duck Rocks (TR). Another male was in the harbor on May 30, 2017 (LB).

Historical/Regional:

- Vickery: cites record of 40 on Sep 26, 1994 (PDV et al.; Tamara Enz in Vickery et al., 2020).

WHITE-WINGED SCOTER
Melanitta fusca

Status: Scarce to uncommon spring and uncommon to fairly common fall migrant, accidental summer visitor, scarce (*presumably uncommon*) winter visitor.

Occurrence: Spring dates span May 1–Jun 8, undoubtedly overlooked in Apr, peak occurring second half of May; spring max: 89 on May 28, 2019 (LS), 45 on May 28, 2017 (LB), 30 on May 21, 2017 (JVW). One summer record: Aug 1, 2012 (MWi). Fall migration Aug 27–early Dec, peak late Sep–late Oct; fall max: **153** on Oct 9, 2021 (JT, LS), 87 on Oct 9, 2015 (JT, JO), 60 on Oct 1, 1998 (JT), Oct 20, 2010 (TMag) & Oct 22, 2011 (MI, DH, PM). Almost all winter records associated with CBC period; winter max: 4 on Dec 21, 1989 (CBC–PDV) and Jan 3, 2015 (CBC–DH, FK, WN), 3 on Dec 27, 1994 (CBC–PDV), Dec 27, 2004 (PDV, CDD), and Jan 4, 2007 (CBC). Ten-Year: SP-9, F-10, W-3.

- CBC: 12 years (46%) plus two count weeks, first on Dec 28, 1978, max 4 on Dec 21, 1989 & Jan 3, 2015, avg 1.1.
- 1900–1908 Reconnaissance & Supplements: included in Jenney supplement.
- 1918 Fall Migration Census: Wentworth–Oct 18.
- 1939 Summer Census: included as rare or accidental.
- 1944-1967 Farrell Records: 1950–Nov.

- 1970 Summer Checklist: included, noted as summering non-breeder, south of normal range.
- DOWTS Surveys 2011–2014: 14 over five days (8.3%; all in 2013), Sep 17–Dec 7, max 4 on Oct 10 & Dec 7, 2013; an additional 8 on Oct 10, 2013 reported in the northern end of the Test Quadrant and included here.

As with the other scoters, our understanding is incomplete due to a lack of coverage mid Jan–Apr and compromised by reports from travel to/from the island. Since they tend to pass by the island, intentional seawatching is often required to detect their presence. Lobster Cove is a favorite reporting vantage, with small flocks passing by, while the north end of the island, Burnt Head, and White Head are also productive locations. The max spring flight of 89 on May 28, 2019 was composed of migrants passing offshore. There have been several reports of inds. flying past the harbor, including 2 males on Sep 25, 2014 (TH, DM, LB). A flyby male accompanied by a Blue-winged Teal was reported on Oct 3, 2016 (JO).

BLACK SCOTER
Melanitta americana

Status: Scarce to fairly common spring and uncommon to fairly common fall migrant, very rare summer and rare to scarce winter visitor.

Occurrence: Spring dates span Mar 14–Jun 7, reports scattered and undoubtedly underreported in early spring; spring max: 31 on May 27, 2014 (JT), 30 on May 31, 2011 (DH), 19 on May 27, 2014 (BN), 18 on May 6, 1985 (PDV). Two summer records: 3 on Jul 2, 2019 (DL, JL), 1 on July 2, 2021 (DH). Fall dates span Sep 13–mid Dec, peak late Sep–mid Nov; fall max: **127** on Oct 9, 2015 (JT, JO), 60 on Sep 28, 2001 (JT), 56 on Oct 9 & 10, 2010 (JT), 44 on Oct 11, 2015 (JT). Twelve winter records over eleven years since 1979, all but two associated with CBC period; winter max: 21 on Jan 3, 2021 (CBC–DH), 7 on Jan 2, 2021 (DH), 5 on Jan 2, 2020 (CBC–DH), 4 on Dec. 22, 2018 (DC). Ten-Year: SP-6, SU-2, F-10, W-3.

- CBC: 8 years (31%) plus 1 count week, first on Dec 22, 1979, max 21 on Jan 3, 2021, avg 1.4.
- 1900–1908 Reconnaissance & Supplements: included in Jenney supplement as American Scoter.
- 1970 Summer Checklist: included. Listed as Common Scoter.

Similar status concerns as other scoters, i.e., seasonal underreporting and ferry crossing reports, most obvious in the low number of winter records. The adult male present on Jul 2, 2021 near the south end of Manana is perhaps the same ind. lingering the last part of May–Jun 7 in the south harbor area. Sometimes noted as flyby flocks, with Lobster Cove a favorite observation site, along with Burnt Head and White Head. The species also mixes with Surf Scoter, White-winged Scoter, and Common Eider; nine males and two females were flybys with 3 Surf Scoters on Oct 11, 2010 (JM). Other minimal sex data available included 1 male and 7 females off Nigh Duck on Apr 4, 2018 (DC), 2 males and 1 female off Pebble Beach on Jul 2, 2019 (DL, JL) and three other reports of 2 males. An unusual flock of 28 was noted in the harbor on May 27, 2014 (JT).

Historical/Regional:

- Vickery: cites the 127 on Oct 9, 2015 record (JT, JO) as an early seasonal occurrence (Tamara Enz in Vickery et al., 2020).

LONG-TAILED DUCK
Clangula hyemalis

Status: Uncommon to fairly common spring and fall migrant, fairly common winter visitor.

Occurrence: Spring migration underway by late Feb–May 31, peak early Mar–mid Apr; spring max: 15+ on Mar 21, 2022 (KL), 15 on Mar 8 & 9, 2011 (TMag), 12 on Mar 7, 2011 (TMag), 10+ on Mar 20, 2022 (KL), 10 on Mar 6, 2011 (TMag). Fall migration dates span Oct 7–mid Dec, numbers increasing by early Nov and continues through Dec.; fall maxima: **100** on Nov 6, 2010 (TMag), 46 on Nov 10, 2022 (LS, MWa), 23 on Nov 11, 2022 (LS, MWa), 21 on Nov 13, 2022 (LS, MWa). Winter visitors gather by late Dec; winter maxima: 45 on Dec 27, 1994 (CBC–PDV) and Dec 27, 2004 (PDV), 35 on Dec 27, 1984 (CBC–PDV), 32 on Jan 1, 1991 (CBC–PDV). Ten-Year: SP-7, F-9, W-6.

- CBC: 26 years (100%), max 45 on Dec 27, 1994 (PDV), avg 17.0.
- 1944–1967 Farrell Records: 1950–Nov. Listed as Old-squaw.
- 1970 Summer Checklist: included as Old Squaw.
- DOWTS Surveys 2011–2014: 1 on March 25, 2014 (1.7%).

It is not easy to determine clear migration and wintering parameters. The fall max of 100 is well above any other sighting and occurred during a seawatch at Burnt Head (TMag). Due to shifting flocks and lack of sighting details, it is also hard to distinguish the continuing presence of inds./flocks;

1 ind. at Lobster Cove noted as continuing on May 25, 2017 (BBa), while the two-day spring max of 15 was in the harbor (as were the 15+ on Mar 21, 2022). Most often reported from Lobster Cove and/or as flybys, but several reports from the harbor. The 10+ observed on Mar 20, 2022 were off Pebble Beach.

Long-tailed Duck, May 21, 2019. © Geoff Dennis.

BUFFLEHEAD
Bucephala albeola

Status: Accidental spring and very rare fall migrant, rare to fairly common winter visitor.

Occurrence: Twenty-nine records (1 spring, 2 fall, 26 winter). Spring record: female on Mar 17, 2019 (JB). Fall records: unreported number during Oct 1950 (IF), female on Oct 30, 2010 (MI, JT). Winter records span Dec 21–Feb 18, most associated with the CBC period, only seven records since 1992; winter max: **73** on Dec 30, 1980 (CBC–PDV), 36 on Dec 22, 1979 (CBC–PDV), 30 on Dec 28, 1978 (CBC–PDV). Ten-Year: SP-1, W-2.

- CBC: 17 years (65%), first on Dec 28, 1978, max 73 on Dec 30, 1980, avg 11.9.
- 1944–1967 Farrell Records: 1950–Oct.

Underreported late fall–early spring, except the CBC period. The Fall 2010 record from Lobster Cove, Mar 2019 in the harbor and Jan 2–3, 2021 (CBC Jan 3–DH) female in the harbor are the only reports that include location; 6 reported on Jan 4, 2007 (CBC), 2 on Jan 3, 2008 (CBC), 6 on Feb 18, 2011 (TMag) and the aforementioned female in Jan 2021 are the only other records since 1992. It is surprising that the three max counts are three of the four earliest records (the other is 2 on Dec. 21, 1979). Majority of records involve 5 or more inds.; only singles on Dec 29, 1983 (PDV), Oct 30, 2010 (JT, MI), Mar 17, 2019 (DC), Jan 2–3, 2021 (DH) & Jan 31, 2022 (DC) and 2 on Dec 21, 1979 (PDV) & Jan 3, 2008 (CBC) involve fewer individuals.

COMMON GOLDENEYE
Bucephala clangula

Status: Very rare spring and accidental fall migrant, scarce winter visitor.

Occurrence: Twenty-five records (4 spring, 1 fall, 21 winter) since first reported in Feb 1950. Spring records: unreported number during Mar 1950 (IF), Mar 22–Apr 6, 2011 (TMag–see below), Apr 2, 2015 (DC), female on Mar 18, 2022 (KL). Fall record: adult male on Sep 26, 1998 (BSc). Winter records over twenty years since 1950, almost all associated with CBC period, span Dec 21–Feb 18 (1950 record during Feb); winter max: **14** on Dec. 28, 1978 (CBC–PDV), 8 on Dec 27, 1984 (PDV), 5 on Dec 21, 1989 (CBC–PDV). Ten-Year: SP-2, W-2.

- CBC: recorded 13 years (50%) plus two count week, first on Dec. 28, 1978, max. of 21 on Dec. 28, 1978, avg. 1.9.
- 1944–1967 Farrell Records: 1950–Feb, Mar. Listed as American Golden-eye.

As with other sea ducks, sometimes recorded on ferry crossings causing concern regarding the appropriateness of reports, and underreported through the winter/early spring months. The 1950 records, occurring during Feb and Mar, considered two records due to rarity (one falling in winter, one in spring), although the possibility of lingering inds. exists. Only six winter records outside the CBC count period: unreported number during Feb 1950 (IF), 2 on Feb 18, 2011 (TMag), 1 on Jan 26, 2013 (DH), 1 on Feb 3, 2019 (DC) & 1 immature male on Jan 19, 2022 (DC), immature male & female on Feb 13, 2022 (DC). The most common location has been the harbor (five records), including the single female on Jan. 26, 2013, noted as possibly being the same ind. from the Jan. 3, 2013 CBC (DH); a single ind. was observed in the harbor on four dates spanning Mar 22–Apr 6, 2011 and is considered the same bird (TMag). The Sep 1998 record was at Lobster Cove with Common Eiders and Surf Scoters (BSc). The Mar 2022 ind. was at Lobster Cove.

BARROW'S GOLDENEYE
Bucephala islandica

Status: Very rare winter visitor.

Occurrence: Two records: female on Dec 29, 1981 (CBC–DF, CMi), female on Dec 26, 2010 (TMag).

- CBC: one year (4%): 1 on Dec 29, 1981, avg 0.0.

The Dec 1981 ind. was observed in the harbor.

HOODED MERGANSER
Lophodytes cucullatus

Status: Very rare spring migrant.

Occurrence: Three records: 1 on May 25, 1990, 1 on Mar 25, 2011 (TMag), female on May 14, 2022 (LS, MWa, HL). Ten-Year: SP-1.

- 1970 Summer Checklist: included, noted as local post-breeding dispersal from nearby areas.

As an uncommon spring migrant and breeder and common fall migrant on the mainland, it is surprising that there are only three known occurrences, although included on the 1970 checklist. The May 2022 ind. was in the Meadow.

COMMON MERGANSER
Mergus merganser

Status: Very rare spring and fall migrant, very rare winter visitor.

Occurrence: Nine records (2 spring, 3 fall, 4 winter) since Oct 15, 1907, span Sep 23–May 27. Spring records: 1 on Mar 8, 2011 (TMag), 1 on May 27, 2014 (JT, BN). Fall records: unreported number on Oct 15, 1907 (CFJ, ECJ), 1 on Oct 31, 2010 (MI, LS, JT), 20 on Sep 23, 2012 (DL, SB, CW). Winter records: 6 on Dec 29, 1940 (CBC), **22** on Dec 27, 1984 (CBC–PDV), 17 on Dec 21, 1989 (CBC–PDV), 18 on Jan 1, 1991 (CBC–PDV). Ten-Year: SP-1.

- CBC: four years (15%), first on Dec 29, 1940, max 22 on Dec 27, 1984, avg 2.4.
- 1900–1908 Reconnaissance & Supplements: unreported number on Oct 15, 1907 (CFJ, ECJ). Listed as American Merganser-sheldrake.

Only two records provided details: a female on Oct 31, 2010 was flying south over the harbor with a probable Red-breasted Merganser, and a female on May 27, 2014 was seen alighting in a cove on the western side of the island.

RED-BREASTED MERGANSER
Mergus serrator

Status: Uncommon spring and fall migrant, uncommon to fairly common winter visitor.

Occurrence: Spring migration underway early Mar–June 6; spring max: 11 on Mar 21, 2012 (TMag), 9 on Apr 6, 2011 (TMag), 7 on May 20, 2011 (DL, NH). Fall dates span Aug 12–mid Dec, increase in mid Oct that continues through Nov; fall maxima: 16 on Oct 25, 2021 (SJ), 10 on Nov 3, 2010 (TMag) & Nov 22, 2011 (DH), 8 on Oct 31, 2010 (TMag), 5 on Oct 29, 2010 (LS, MI, JT). Most winter records associated with CBC period; winter max: **24** on Jan 3, 1986 (CBC–PDV), 18 on Dec 29, 1983 (CBC–PDV), 16 on Dec 22, 1979 (CBC–PDV) and Dec 28, 1982 (CBC–PDV). Ten-Year: SP-8, F-7, W-8.

- CBC: 25 years (96%; all except 2020), max 24 on Jan 3, 1986, avg 10.4.
- 1900–1908 Reconnaissance & Supplements: one pair on June 1, 1908 (FA).
- 1915–1919 Taylor Journals: 2 on Aug 12, 16, Sep 8, 1917. Seen from Green Point on both Aug dates and Eastern Duck Rock on Sep 8.
- 1944–1967 Farrell Records: 1949–Dec; 1950–Apr; 1951–Feb, Oct; 1961–Apr.
- 1970 Summer Checklist: included.

This is another duck species that is often encountered on ferry crossings, confusing report locations, and underreported in winter/early spring. The latest spring record involved a female first noted off White Head on Jun 1, 2021 (RS) and last reported in the schoolyard on Jun 6 (JFo) after tourists rescued it from being stuck in a ditch (*sick/injured?*). Also interesting were 2 lingering inds. in Aug/Sep 1917 at Green Point and Eastern Duck Rock (see Taylor Journals above), as all other records occurred after Sep 21. The scattering of reports indicating sex were split between male and female, and included 2 males displaying in the harbor on Jan. 25, 2013 (DH) and a female on Nigh Duck. Sometimes reported as flybys, particularly from Lobster Cove, but also noted by the Duck Rocks and twice from White Head.

RUFFED GROUSE
Bonasa umbellus

Status: Very rare fall visitor.

Occurrence: Three records: unreported number on Sep 10, 1916 (WT, CTa), unreported number during Aug 1959 (BU), unreported number on unknown date during 1954–2005 (TMar).

- 1915–1919 Taylor Journals: unreported number on Sep 10, 1916.
- 1944–1967 Farrell Records: 1959–Aug (BU).

No details provided for any record, but the 1916 & 1959 records suggest fall dispersal/migration. The 1916 record occurred on the "best day" for WT on Monhegan – a day when he and CTa found 70 species. The report of unknown date from TMar's personal notes would have occurred at some point between his first arrival in 1954 and 2005, most likely May or Sep (separating from 1959 record).

RING-NECKED PHEASANT
Phasianus colchicus

Status: Uncommon permanent resident, introduced.

Occurrence: Reports scattered throughout the year, lowest numbers generally in summer; year maxima: **40** on Sep 22, 2005 (HN), 36 on May 20, 2022 (JT, LS, MWa), 31 on May 16, 2022 (LS, MWa), 24 on May 20, 2021 (JT, LS), 20 on May 18, 2022 (LHo), Sep 25, 2022 (HN) & Oct 2, 2022 (LMu, BBo), 19 on Oct 4, 2020 (JT, LS, BBy), 18 on Sep 27–28, 2020 (DL) & Oct 5, 2020 (JT, LS, BBy) & May 24, 2021 (JT et al.). Ten-Year: 10.

- *MABB*: confirmed; MBA: confirmed.
- CBC: 20 years (77%) plus one count week, first on Dec 28, 1978, max 15 on Jan 4, 2007, avg 5.8.
- 1939 Summer Census: regular summer resident.
- 1944–1967 Farrell Records: 1949–May; 1951–Oct; 1952–Feb; 1954–Jun, Jul, Aug; 1955–Jun, Aug; 1959–May, Jun; 1960–Apr, May, Aug, Sep; 1961–Apr.
- 1954 & 1955 Summer Records: included on five of the checklists (all but Jun 30–Jul 5, 1955); 1+ on Aug 26, 1955 (MLn).
- 1970 Summer Checklist: marked as known to breed in area.

Population apparently remains fairly stable and low in numbers, although noticeable increase past several years due to successful breeding (see max counts); survivability enhanced by limited predators on offshore islands (Vickery et al., 2020). The max of 40 on Sep 22, 2005 was the day after a release of captive bred-birds (HN); other max counts all involve family groups. It is unclear how many releases have been made since the first ones occurred in the late 1930s (see Palmer, below), but their presence on the 1939, 1944–67, 1954–55, and 1970 checklists and records indicate a continuing presence. An article in the Monhegan Press on Jul 2, 1938 indicated a request by the State Conservation Department to aid in protecting the "recently stocked" pheasants that had "multiplied greatly during the past year" (indicating a possible 1937 release); broods numbering as many as 14 chicks were seen "during the first months of the year." Efforts by MJT to prevent the declaration of an open season on Monhegan by the State in Fall 1938 were apparently too late, but enough of a bluff/confusion that islanders did not hunt them; as of Jan 1939, numbers were low and not multiplying fast, possibly due to hawks and cats getting some of the young ones (MJT). Breeding often obvious by late May with the appearance of family groups, most often adult females with recently hatched young, illustrated by an unreported number of chicks on May 8, 2006 (KL), 1 adult male and 2 adult females with 6 chicks on May 18, 2021 (JO) and an adult female with 12 young on May 18, 2022 (LHo). Older juveniles reported through the summer months, such as two family groups involving 2 adult females and 13 juveniles on July 27, 2020 (GBr), while grown young are obvious into Oct. Reports from throughout the island, including in lawns and gardens, at/on feeders, in the Meadow, at the Ice Pond, forest near Pulpit Rock, Lobster Cove, and even on the roof of a studio. Outside of family groups, males are reported and obvious much more regularly than females, and often heard but not seen—males extremely vocal Apr–Nov, including a male in display flight giving call on Nov 5, 2016 (JF, DH).

Historical/Regional:
- Palmer: introduced in late 1930s, followed by breeding.
- Cruickshank: a few pairs nest.
- Vickery: mentions releases, chicks in May 2006 (KL) and max count of 40 in Sep 2005 (HN; Richard V. Joyce in Vickery et al., 2020).

Ring-necked Pheasant, May 14, 2011. © Geoff Dennis.

PIED-BILLED GREBE
Podilymbus podiceps

Status: Accidental spring and rare fall migrant.

Occurrence: Twelve records (1 spring, 11 fall) since 1916. Spring record: unreported number during Mar 1950 (IF). Fall records over ten years, span Aug 25 (possibly as early as Aug 16)–Oct 26, all single birds: 1 on Aug 25–Sep 6, 1916 (WT, MCG), Sep 10–Oct 1, 1982 (PDV, WH), Sep 28, 1984 (PDV), Oct 11, 1987 (JVW), Oct 3, 1997 (JT), Oct 1 *or* 2, 1988 (trip report–WH), Sep 26–28, 2000 (JT), Sep 19–20, 2005 (BME, SE, SM), Sep 15, 2010 (EH), Oct 26, 2010 (TMag), Aug 30–31, 2011 (SW).

- 1914 & 1916 Checklists: included 1916.

- 1915–1919 Taylor Journals: 1 on Aug 25–Sep 6, 1916 (reported Aug 25, 26, 30, 31, Sep 3, 4, 6).
- 1939 Summer Census: rare or accidental (*1 record, likely the 1916 ind.*).
- 1944–1967 Farrell Records: 1950–Mar.
- 1970 Summer Checklist: included (*possibly based on the 1939 Census?*).

The reports by MCG & WT in 1916 likely involve the same ind. and count as one record of 1 for these purposes; almost certainly the one record referred to by WT in his 1939 Census. 2010 is the only year with more than one record; as the period between sightings was routinely birded, it is likely it was a different ind. The long-staying ind. in 1982 was reported Sep 10, 11, 12, 13, 29, 30; with a lack of coverage and the same observer for all the reports, it is being considered the same ind. The Oct 1987 ind. was at the Ice Pond. The 2005 ind. was at the Ice Pond on Sep 19 and near Swim Beach on Sep 20. The Sep 15, 2010 ind. was in the harbor.

Historical/Regional:
- Vickery: uncommon in Sep–Oct (PDV in Vickery et al., 2020).

HORNED GREBE
Podiceps auritus

Status: Accidental spring and very rare fall migrant, rare winter visitor.

Occurrence: Eighteen records (1 spring, 6 fall, 11 winter) since first recorded on Dec 22, 1979 (CBC–PDV). Spring record: 1 during May 16–20, 2004 period (trip report–TV). Fall dates span Sep 13–Dec 3, with a concentration late Sep–mid Oct, all since 2003: 2 on Sep 29, 2003 (JT, TV), 4 on Sep 13, 2007 (RF), 1 on Dec 3, 2010 (TMag), 1 on Oct 24, 2012 (JP), 2 on Oct 6, 2014 (JT et al.), 1 on Oct 3, 2018 (GB, LF). Winter records all occurring on CBC, spanning Dec 22–Jan 3; winter max: **6** on Dec 29, 1983 (PDV), 2 on Dec 27, 1984 (PDV) & Jan 3, 2013 (WN et al.). Ten-Year: F-2.

- CBC: 11 years (42%), first on Dec 22, 1979, max 6 on Dec 29, 1983, avg 0.8.

Undoubtedly underreported during the winter/early spring period; it is hard to believe there have been so few records. This is another species with reports mixed with ferry crossings, limiting inclusion. *The eBird report of 13 on the 1980 CBC (Dec 22, 1979) appears to be in error and may have been Red-necked Grebe, as the official CBC total is 1.* The 2 reported on Oct 6, 2014 were early-morning flybys at Lobster Cove (JT et al.)

RED-NECKED GREBE
Podiceps grisegena

Status: Rare to scarce spring and scarce fall migrant, accidental summer and rare to scarce (*presumably uncommon*) winter visitor.

Occurrence: Thirteen spring records but undoubtedly underreported (eleven records in 2011), dates span Mar 6–May 14; spring max: 6 on Apr 3, 2011 (TMag) & Apr 27, 2013 (DOWTS–LKB), 3 on Apr 14, 2011 (TMag), 2 on Mar 8, 2011 (TMag), Mar 15, 2011 (TMag), & May 2, 2011 (TMag). One summer record: 1 on Jul 26, 2012 (LKB). Fall migration spans Aug 26–late Nov, peak late Sep–early Nov; fall max: 8 on Aug 26, 2010 (early and exceptional–TMag), 6 on Sep 21, 2005 (DL), 3 on Sep 25, 2002 (JT), 2 on many dates. Almost all winter reports associated with CBC period; winter max: **18** on Jan 1, 1992 (CBC–PDV) & Jan 3, 2013 (CBC), 13 on Dec 22, 1979 (CBC) and Dec 30, 1980 (CBC–PDV), 11 on Dec 27, 1987 (CBC–PDV et al.). Ten-Year: SP-2, F-7, W-5.

- CBC: 20 years (77%) plus one count week, first on Dec 28, 1978, max 18 on Jan 1, 1992 & Jan 3, 2013, avg 4.4.
- DOWTS Surveys 2011–2014: 7 over two days (3.3%), Jul 26, 2012 & max 6 on Apr 27, 2013.

The fact that almost all the spring records occur in 2011 (one record in May 2017), the year with consistent coverage by TMag, highlights the underreporting in other years, not only in spring, but late fall and winter as well (excepting CBC period). CBC results indicate the possibility of a status of uncommon in winter. Understanding also complicated by reports including "ferry birds", unusable for this purpose. Combination of flybys and birds on the water reported; noted locations include Lobster Cove (including the max fall flight of a flyby flock of 8 heading northeast and the second max count of 6 heading north), below the headlands, and harbor. The only summer record was an offshore flyby as part of the DOWTS surveys (LKB). Without more details, length of stay by inds. is unclear.

ROCK PIGEON
Columba livia

Status: Very rare spring and fall visitor, very rare summer and winter visitor.

Occurrence: Twenty-four records (10 spring, 8 fall, 3 summer, 3 winter) since first known record in 1984 (although included on 1970 Summer Checklist). Spring records span Apr 6–May 30 (possibly May 31 as part of a trip report May 29–31) over ten years since 1987; all singles (five records) or undetermined number. Summer records: 1 on Jul 19, 1984 (PDV), 4 on Jun 3, 2005 (JVW), 1 on Aug 6–7, 2012 (DL). Fall dates span Sep 14–Oct 7 over eight years since 1993; fall max: **10** on Oct 2, 2005 (JT), 7 on Sep 22, 2005 (JT, SM), 6 on Oct 1, 2010 (DL), 5 on Sep 30, 2005 (JT), Oct 5, 2005 (MI, AM) & Sep 21, 2007 (LS). Winter records, all associated with CBC period: 1 on Jan 1, 2007 (CBC–PDV), 1 on Jan 3, 2008 (CBC–PDV), 1 on Dec 31, 1990 (PDV). Ten-Year: SP-1, F-1.

- CBC: 2 years (8%) and one count week, max 1 on Jan 1 2007 & Jan 3, 2008, avg 0.1.
- 1970 Summer Checklist: included.

A species without migratory tendencies, any Monhegan sighting represents wandering or dispersal. With almost no details provided, all reports within a season have been considered a single record, despite shifting numbers or gaps over the course of the reports (considered as encountering only part of the flock if below the max., rather than additional inds. joining those already present). The 4 seen on Jun 3, 2005 are possibly continuing from a May 16–23 trip report of unreported number. Single ind. records have lingered as long as eleven days (May 12–22, 1997, with sightings on May 12, 13, 14, & 22). Three records have involved continuing small flocks: 4 on Sep 22–24, 2004, up to 10 over fourteen days Sep 19–Oct 7, 2005 (variable numbers from 2–10, with 3 on Sep 19 and 2 on Oct 7—see max counts above), up to 5 over thirteen days Sep 14–29, 2007 (variable numbers from 1–5 inds., with 1 on Sep 14 & Sep 29 and the 5 on Sep 21 the only day above 2). Location provided for only two records: 1 flying around the west side of the island (May 21, 2018) and 1 flyby near the school in the early morning (Oct 3, 2019).

BAND-TAILED PIGEON
Patagioenas fasciata

Status: Very rare fall vagrant.

Occurrence: Two records: 1 on Sep 19, 1990 (LBu; *MBN* 4[3]: 25), 1 on Sep 25, 1994 (PDV et al.; *MBN* 8[1]: 8). Second and third Maine records; 1990 not yet reviewed, 1994 accepted by ME-BRC #1994–004.

The Sep 1990 ind. was observed for about five minutes while perched in a dead tree (*MBN* 4[3]: 25). The Sep 1994 ind. was watched by 11 observers for at least six minutes, perched in a dead spruce before dropping into a thicket (*MBN* 8[1]: 8).

Historical/Regional:

- Vickery: cites 1990 and 1994 (*erroneously listed as Sep 24*) records (PDV in Vickery et al., 2020).

- OLMB: the first and only other Maine record was on Apr 25–May 2, 1980 on Southport Island, Lincoln Co. (accepted).

EURASIAN COLLARED-DOVE
Streptopelia decaocto

Status: Accidental summer vagrant.

Occurrence: One record: 1 on May 27–Jul 2, 2019 (JT, KL, DL, JL, mob). Second Maine record; accepted by ME-BRC #2019–021 (many photos). Ten-Year: SP-1.

Reported May 27–31, June 8–12, 23, 29, & 30 and Jul 2. Remained along Lobster Cove Rd. in the vicinity of the Brewery, including feeding at the Hill Studio feeder on May 28, singing persistently throughout its stay (first discovered by vocalization and noted in every eBird report). The accepted record extends only to Jun 23; sightings (non-eBird) continued into early Jul.

Historical/Regional:

- OLMB: three additional state records—two accepted (May 28, 2013 at Falmouth, Cumberland Co. and May 14, 2020 at Pemaquid Point, Lincoln Co.) and one not yet reviewed (Jun 4–5, 2006 in Kennebunk, York Co).

Eurasian Collared-Dove, May 30, 2019. © Jeremiah Trimble

WHITE-WINGED DOVE
Zenaida asiatica

Status: Very rare spring and fall vagrant.

Occurrence: Ten records (7 spring, 3 fall) since first recorded in 1982, all singles. Spring records span May 16–Jun 14: May 30–31, 2003 (LB, HN), May 21–w/e May 30, 2008 (GD, fide EH et al. & KL, PD on May 24; MARBA), May 16–20, 2010 (DH, EH, JSs, GD),

White-winged Dove, May 20, 2010. © Geoff Dennis.

May 31–Jun 1, 2011 (DH, GW, TMag), Jun 14, 2013 (DH), May 16–17, 2015 (BBl et al.) & May 24–31, 2019 (JT, mob). Fall records: Sep 20–Oct 6, 1982 (DF, PDV, TMar; *AB* 37[2]: 157), Sep 23–Oct 10, 1983 (RHe, JSm, PDV; *MB* 5[4]: 46, *AB* 38[2]: 177), Oct 2, 1997 (fide PDV, *FN* 52: 31). Ten-Year: SP-3.

Increased presence is reflected by records throughout Maine and the Northeast; forty documented Maine records since first in Dec 1973 (Vickery et al., 2020). Seven of the Monhegan records have involved multiple-day stays, the longest being twenty-one days in 1983. Consecutive records in Fall 1982 and 1983 (the earliest records) raises the possibility of a returning ind.; molting adult reported Sep 23, 27, 28, 29, 30, & Oct 1, 1983 (apparently predated by a cat, with feathers found near the Trailing Yew–PDV). Species always reported from town areas (no details for 1997). Often observed in spruce trees, but also at feeders in 2003 (Wharton Ave.), 2011 (near the Ice Pond), 2015 (near the Ice Pond) and 2019 (suet at Donna Cundy's). The May 2008 ind. was singing across Lobster Cove Rd. from the Cundy residence and the 2019 ind. was calling and singing around the Cundy residence on multiple days and singing from Horn's Hill on May 31.

Historical/Regional:

- Vickery: cites Sep 1982, Sep–Oct 1983 (has last date as Oct 10), Oct 1997, & May 2003 records (PDV in Vickery et al., 2020).

MOURNING DOVE
Zenaida macroura

Status: Fairly common permanent resident, spring and fall migrant of unclear magnitude.

Occurrence: Noticeably present throughout the year, numbers highest in fall, lowest in winter; year max: **56** on Aug 15, 2022 (LS, MWa), 50 on Sep 26, 2018 (TA) & Oct 3, 2018 (GB, LF), 46 on Nov 10, 2020 (LS, JT), 45 on Sep 29, 2020 (WR), Sep 26, 2021 (ID) & Oct 9, 2022 (SJ), 40 on Oct 5, 2020 (TMz), Nov 9, 2020 (FK, DH), Jul 15, 2021 (BTh), Sep 25, 2021 (ID), Sep 29, 2021 (CDD, LBl), Oct 7, 2021 (TA, DN), Oct 12, 2021 (BWx), Sep 7, 2022 (RH), Sep 10, 2022 (RH) & Oct 3, 2022 (BBc, LMu), 38 on Oct 24, 2022 (ShF). Ten-Year: 10.

- *MABB*: possible; MBA: confirmed.
- CBC: 22 years (85%), first on Dec 28, 1978, max 27 on Jan 3, 2008, avg 7.1.
- 1914 & 1916 Checklists: included 1916.
- 1915–1919 Taylor Journals: 4 on Sep 6, 1916, 1 on Sep 4, 1919.
- 1918 Fall Migration Census: Wentworth–Oct 8 (3), 16 (1), 29.
- 1944–1967 Farrell Records: 1950–Mar, Apr, Oct; 1951–Oct; 1952–Mar; 1958–Sep; 1959–Aug; 1960–Apr, May, Aug, Sep; 1961–May; 1967–Apr 7, 8.
- 1970 Summer Checklist: has been a summer resident and possible breeder.

Species whose occurrence has increased in Maine since the early 1900s; note that max counts are all since 2018. As a partial migrant, the presence of migrants is masked by residents, making it difficult to quantify, but most evident in the fall. Often obvious around town and nearby trail areas, sometimes perched conspicuously in dead spruces or coming to feeders (interestingly, frozen baked beans put out as food for doves in winter 1938–39–MJT); absent from the dense coniferous portions of the island. Its general commonness and ever-present nature lead to indifference in reporting, both numbers and details. The max count of 56 on Aug 15, 2022 was a mix of adults and juveniles. Very limited specific breeding information available; one juvenile was observed with an adult on Jun 13, 2013 (DH), a recently fledged young was observed on Jul 3, 2018 (DH), an adult was carrying nesting material on Jun 5, 2021 (FTu) and a adult with juvenile on Jun 25, 2022 (KL).

Historical/Regional:
- Vickery: cites 25 on May 25, 1987 (ST) as exceptionally high number in summer (BSV in Vickery et al., 2020).

YELLOW-BILLED CUCKOO
Coccyzus americanus

Status: Rare spring and scarce fall migrant, very rare summer visitor.

Occurrence: Twenty-two spring records over thirteen years since 1994, span Apr 26–Jun 8; spring max: 4 on June 4, 2020 (JT, LS), 2 on May 19, 2018 (JT) & Jun 2, 2021 (JT, LS). Two summer records: 1 during w/e Jun 16, 2006–w/e Aug 4, 2006 (fide JWa, KG, LS, LW; MARBA), 1 on Aug 11, 2020 (JPi). Fall dates span Sep 5–Oct 24 since first recorded in 1946, peak last ten days of Sep–mid Oct; fall max: **5** on Sep 15, 1964 (RLP; *AFN* 19[1]: 11) & Oct 7, 2020 (JT, LS, BBy), 4 on Sep 22–23, 1991 (PDV) & Oct 10, 2011 (DH), 3 on Sep 29, 1983 (PDV), Sep 21, 1991 (PDV), Sep 22, 2007 (LS), Oct 3, 2011 (DH), Oct 7, 2011 (JM), Oct 11, 2011 (DH) & Oct 9, 2020 (JT, LS, HS). Ten-Year: SP-8, SU-1, F-9.

- 1899 Checklist: included.
- 1944–1967 Farrell Records: 1946–Oct.
- Banding: 2 total over two seasons (Fall 1961, Fall 1980), max 1 on Oct 9, 1961 & Oct 3, 1980.

Near the northern edge of its breeding range, its presence and the increase in recent records doubtless reflect range expansion to the north and east in the second half of the last century (Hughes, J. M., 2020). Although stated by Vickery (see below) to be sometimes resident on Monhegan through summer, it is not included in *MABB* or MBA, and the only summer records involve a presumed same ind. (no details provided in MARBA) through much of summer 2006, possibly first reported w/e May 26, and a calling ind. near Burnt Head in Aug 2020. The Sep 1964 max count occurred right after the passage of Hurricane Dora and the species was noted as widespread. Several of the higher migration counts (only 3 or 4 inds.) evoked comments of being conservative, with birds seen throughout the day or "all over the island," supporting the propensity for inds. to move around; the max spring count of 4 was noted as "seen and calling around the island" (JT, LS). Tendency to remain solitary, even when multiple inds. are on the island, although 2 were observed together on at least two occasions. Migrants have lingered for several days on occasion, possibly longer, but it is difficult to be certain. Reported from many areas around town, in scrub, apple trees and spruces, often first detected in flight; multiple reports from Lobster Cove and near the Ice Pond, where one ind. was heard calling on Sep 25 & 27, 2018 (SBa, AK).

Historical/Regional:
- Palmer: only a handful of records for May, although sometimes a summer resident.
- Vickery: cites Apr 26, 1998 (WBo–*FN* 52: 306) record as early and 4 on Sep 22–23, 1991 (PDV) as a high count; sometimes resident through summer (PDV in Vickery et al., 2020).

Yellow-billed Cuckoo, Sep 25, 2021. © Bill Thompson

BLACK-BILLED CUCKOO
Coccyzus erythropthalmus

Status: Scarce spring and fall migrant, rare summer visitor and possible resident (has bred).

Occurrence: One of the later spring migrants, dates span May 14–mid Jun; spring max: **7** on May 21, 2022 (LS), 5 on May 22, 2022 (JT, LS, MWa), 4–5 on May 23, 2022 (DL), 4 on May 20, 2022 (JT, LS, MWa) & May 27, 2022 (CHi), 3 on May 26, 2016 (JT, JO, BN), & May 23–25, 2022 (JBi et al.). Thirteen summer records over eleven years since 1907 (two each in 1915 & 1954), including nesting in 1938 (see discussion below) and confirmed status in *MABB*; summer max: 3 on Aug 11, 1915 (six of the summer records are of an unreported number). Fall dates span late Aug–Oct 19; fall max: 3 on Oct 7, 1961 (banded), Oct 5, 2020 (JT, LS, BBy) & Oct 8, 2020 (JT, LS), 2 on Sep 8, 1980 (PDV), Sep 14, 1981, Sep 27, 2010 (EH), Oct 3, 2010 (LS, TMag, NH) & Oct 10, 2015 (JT, DH, JO). Ten-Year: SP-8, SU-2, F-9.

- *MABB*: confirmed.
- 1900–1908 Reconnaissance & Supplements: one heard singing on Jun 4–6, 1908 (FA); unreported number during summer 1907 & summer 1908 (CFJ, ECJ); unreported number during Jul 31–Aug 2, 1908 (WM).
- 1909 Notes: rather common, several seen and more heard in thickets bordering woodlands.
- 1914 & 1916 Checklists: unreported number on Aug 2, 1914; included 1916.
- 1915–1919 Taylor Journals: 1 on Aug 10, 3 on Aug 11, 1915; 2 on Aug 26, 1916; 1 on Sep 4, 1919.
- 1918 Fall Migration Census: Wentworth–Oct 7.
- 1939 Summer Census: regular summer resident.
- 1944–1967 Farrell Records: 1954–Jun, Jul; 1955–Aug; 1957–Aug; 1958–Sep; 1959–Jun, Aug; 1960–Jun, Aug, Sep.
- 1954 & 1955 Summer Records: 1954–heard during Jun 19-25 & Jul 15; 1955–single birds on Aug 27, 28, 29, Sep 1, 2 (IW), noted as in different spots (except for Sep 2).
- 1970 Summer Checklist: known to breed in the area.
- Banding: 5 over three seasons (Fall 1960, Fall 1961, Fall 1981), peak 3 in Fall 1961, max 3 on Oct 7, 1961.

Formerly more common, this species has decreased significantly in North America over the past century, especially through the 1980s and 1990s (Hughes, J. M., 2020), supported by comparing recent and historical Monhegan records, particularly summer (Jun & Aug Farrell records of unspecified day not included as summer records due to overlap with spring and fall). An exception is the notable influx in spring 2022, producing most of the max counts (certainly involving lingering inds.). Surely underreported at all seasons, due to its secretive nature. Few details provided, but reported from many of the usual birding locations, including along Black Head Rd. and Trail and twice at the north end of the island. Reported nesting on/near Lighthouse Hill in early Jul 1918 (Monhegan Press, 1938b); a juvenile near the Ice Pond on Jul 28, 2021 (TMe) is notable. Heard calling on multiple occasions, spring and fall.

Historical/Regional:

- Palmer: cites Taylor's 1939 census as indicating nesting.
- Vickery: spring and fall high counts never more than 2 (*see max counts above*; PDV in Vickery et al., 2020).

Black-billed Cuckoo, May 22, 2022. © Luke Seitz.

COMMON NIGHTHAWK
Chordeiles minor

Status: Scarce spring and rare to scarce fall migrant (sometimes fairly common).

Occurrence: A late spring migrant, dates span May 14–Jun 10, peak the last week of May; spring max: **25** on May 30, 2013 (RL, ML), 7 on May 23, 2022 (JT, LS, MWa), 3 on May 29, 2004 (JVW). Early fall migrant, dates span Jul 18–Oct 9, peak the first half of Sep (no doubt underreported in Aug); fall maxima: **25** on Sep 9, 2017 (JCo), 20 on Sep 5, 1983 (PDV) & Sep 10, 1983 (PDV), 14 on Sep 8, 1985 (PDV). Ten-Year: SP-9, F-8.

- 1900–1908 Reconnaissance & Supplements: 1 seen on Jun 1, 1908 near Green Point (FA). Listed as Nighthawk.
- 1914 & 1916 Checklists: included 1916.
- 1915–1919 Taylor Journals: 1915–Aug 21 (4), Sep 2, 5, 12 (1); 1916–Aug 22, 26, Sep 6, 10; 1917–Sep 8 (1); 1919–Sep 4 (1), 5 (1), 13 (2), 14 (2).
- 1918 Fall Migration Census: Dewis: 1 on Sep 7. Listed as Night Hawk.
- 1944–1967 Farrell Records: 1951–May; 1955–Jun, Aug; 1957–Aug; 1959–May, Aug; 1960–Aug.

- 1954 & 1955 Summer Records: 1955–included Jun 11–15, Aug 23 (1) 24 (1 on horizontal spruce branch about fourteen feet high at edge of clearing), 28 (1), Sep 2 (11–MLn); all noted as diurnal sightings.
- 1970 Summer Checklist: included.

Surprisingly high number of recent max counts, especially spring, despite an 80–90% population drop since the early 1900s (Vickery et al., 2020). The 25 seen on May 30, 2013 are far more than any other spring count and more reminiscent of fall movements, when nighthawks commonly migrate in loose groups or "bands". Many nighthawks head south in Aug, when there are few birders on Monhegan. High counts tend to be one-day events (or at least greatly diminished on following days), arguing against lingering birds, although several inds. have appeared to remain a couple of days, but it is impossible to be certain. Most often seen at dusk as flybys or hunting for insects over the Meadow, but also reported over Lighthouse Hill; possible at any time of day, such as the 20 (largest single flock reported) at mid-day, part of the max count May 30, 2013. One ind. was observed foraging for fireflies over the Meadow from a nearby lichen-covered rock (May 20, 2012–PW). Often calling in flight, but also heard from daytime roosting sites, such as the spruces behind Donna Cundy's and near the Brewery, and along the Red Ribbon Trail. An odd roosting site was the stone wall near Lobster Cove on May 19, 1996 (TW).

Common Nighthawk, Sep 18, 2014. © Bill Thompson.

CHUCK-WILL'S-WIDOW
Antrostomus carolinensis

Status: Very rare spring vagrant.

Occurrence: Two records: 1 on May 23, 1991 (fide LBr), 1 on May 20, 1998 (TMar personal notes). The 1991 record is listed on the OLMB but not yet reviewed, the 1998 record is not listed.

Vagrant from the south (nearest breeding Long Island, NY and NJ). The May 1991 ind. was unseen but vocalizing (recorded by an unnamed source and confirmed by LBr and JVW).

Historical/Regional:

- Vickery: cites May 1991 record (PDV in Vickery et al., 2020).
- OLMB: twenty-two additional state records—eight accepted and fourteen not yet reviewed, all since 1974.

EASTERN WHIP-POOR-WILL
Antrostomus vociferus

Status: Very rare spring and accidental fall migrant, *presumably overlooked*.

Occurrence: Seven records (6 spring, 1 fall) since 1949. Spring records: unreported number during May 1949 (IF), unreported number during May 1950 (IF), unreported number during May–Jun 1959 (IF), 1 during May 18–25, 1996 (GD), 1 on Jun 1, 2004 (WBo), 1 on May 23–24, 2022 (DL et al.). Fall record: 1 on Sep 5–7, 1980 (PDV). Ten-Year: SP-1.

- 1944-1967 Farrell Records: 1949–May; 1950, May, Jun; 1959–May, Jun.
- 1970 Summer Checklist: included as Whip-poor-will.

Due to its secretive and nocturnal habits and scattered breeding presence in Maine, it is likely that this species is overlooked as a migrant on Monhegan; its population decline may foretell fewer future records. The May & Jun reports from 1959 considered one record due to rarity; possibility of more than one ind. and first summer record. The Jun 2004 ind. was heard calling. The Sep 1980 ind. was seen at dusk in front of Tribler Cottage for three consecutive nights. The May 2022 ind. was heard calling on two consecutive nights on Horn's Hill.

Historical/Regional:

- Vickery: cites Sep 1980 and Jun 2004 records (PDV in Vickery et al., 2020).

CHIMNEY SWIFT
Chaetura pelagica

Status: Scarce to uncommon spring and rare fall migrant, very rare summer visitor.

Occurrence: Spring dates span May 5–Jun 5, no particular peak; spring max: 20 on May 28, 1983 (ST), 13 on May 24, 2019 (JT, CL, TJe), 9 on May 14, 2017 (JT), 8 on May 30, 1983 (PDV), May 27, 1989 (SS) & May 5, 2017 (DH). Four summer records since 1954 (three from 1954 & 1955), but included on 1939 checklist: unreported number Jun 19–25, 1954 (AS, ES), unreported number during Jun 27–Jul 4, 1954 (FNR, MFNR), unreported number during Jun 11–15, 1955 (CFH, MCFH), 1 on Jun 26, 2021 (KL). Early fall migrant, dates span Jul 30–Oct 2, peak first half of Sep (underreported in Aug); fall max: **50** on Sep 1, 1919, 21 on Oct 2, 2004 (JT), 5 on Sep 24, 2007 (JSc), 4 on Sep 6, 1985 (PDV). Ten-Year: SP-9, SU-1, F-2.

- 1915–1919 Taylor Journals: 1916–Aug 26 (2), 31, Sep 4, 10; 1919–Sep 1 (50).
- 1918 Fall Migration Census: Dewis–Sep 4 (2), 11 (1).
- 1939 Summer Census: uncommon summer visitor.
- 1944–1967 Farrell Records: 1954–Jun, Jul; 1955–Jun, Aug; 1956–May; 1959–May, Jun, Aug; 1960–May, Aug; 1961–May; 1967–Jun 2 (3), 3 (3), 4 (4), 5 (3).
- 1954 & 1955 Summer Records: 1954–included Jun 19-25 and Jun 27-Jul 4; 1955–included Jun 11–15, Aug 26 (2–IW et al.), 28 (2+), 29 (6), 30 (1).
- 1970 Summer Checklist: included.

The Farrell records from 1954 & 1955 are likely the same inds. as reported in the 1954 & 1955 Summer Records and considered as such here. Few details available. A single flock of 9, a high count from May 14, 2017, was repeatedly attempting to enter a chimney behind the Trailing Yew (JT). Single reports of inds. over the Meadow and Ice Pond. Scarcity of suitable chimneys may explain lack of recent summer records. Many of this species migrate in Aug, a time when few birders visit Monhegan.

Historical/Regional:
- Vickery: cites 20 on May 28, 1983 (ST), 8 on May 30, 1983 (PDV) & 3 on May 30, 2014 as late spring records and six records from late Sep/early Oct as late fall records, including max count and latest date of Oct 2 (PDV in Vickery et al., 2020).

RUBY-THROATED HUMMINGBIRD
Archilochus colubris

Status: Uncommon spring and fall migrant, rare summer visitor and possible breeder.

Occurrence: Spring dates span May 5–mid Jun, peak mid–late May; spring max: **30** on May 25, 1983 (ST; AB 37[5]: 845), 12 on May 30, 2013 (RL, ML) & May 25, 2019 (TG), 10 on May 25, 1986 (JVW) & May 26, 1996 (SS), May 21, 2011 (JH) & May 27, 2012 (RL). Twenty summer records over twelve years (three in 2020, four in 2021), all but the first three since 2000 (undetermined number during the Jun 27–Jul 4, 1954 period [see checklist below], unknown date confirmed in *MABB*, unreported number during Jul 1960 [IF], scattered mid Jun–end of Jul; summer max: 2 on Jul 22, 2008 (PF), Jul 17, 2016 (DH), Jul 19, 2021 (HIAC et al.) & Jul 3, 2022 (DH). Fall dates span early Aug–Oct 8, peak the first three weeks of Sep; fall max: 25 on Sep 17, 2013 (PDV et al.), 18 on Sep 6, 1985 (PDV), 13 on Sep 13, 1980 (PDV). Ten-Year: SP-10, SU-6, F-10.

- *MABB*: confirmed; MBA: possible.
- 1900–1908 Reconnaissance & Supplements: included as Ruby-throated Humming-bird in Jenney supplement, unreported number during Jul 31–Aug 2, 1908 (WM–considered a fall record for these purposes).
- 1914 & 1916 Checklists: included as Humming Bird 1916.
- 1915–1919 Taylor Journals: 1915–Aug 15 (2), 16 (1), Sep 2 (1), 5 (1), 12 (1); 1916–Aug 30, Sep 3, 4, 6 (5), 10; 1917–Sep 5 (1); 1919–Sep 4 (2), 5 (3), 13 (1), 14 (1). Listed as Hummingbird.
- 1918 Fall Migration Census: Dewis–15: Sep 7 (9–one adult male, 8 immature/female), 8 (4), 10 (1), 12 (1); Wentworth–1 on Sep 29.
- 1939 Summer Census: regular summer visitor.
- 1944–1967 Farrell Records: 1948–May; 1951–May; 1953–Aug; 1954–Jul, Aug; 1955–Aug; 1958–Sep; 1959–May, Aug; 1960–Jul, Aug, Sep; 1961–May.
- 1954 & 1955 Summer Records: 1954–included Jun 27-Jul 4; 1955–Aug 24 (1), 28 (3+), 29 (12+–MLn), 30 (1).
- 1970 Summer Checklist: marked as having been a summer resident and possible breeder.

Generally scattered throughout the usual town/trail birding areas, including feeders on occasion (notably at Hitchcox and Cundy residences), while largely absent from the spruce-dominated portions of the island. Prevalent at patches of Jewelweed and also noted feeding at sapsucker holes drilled in apple trees.

MBA status based on an ind. in appropriate habitat on Jul 2, 2021 (DH).

Historical/Regional:

- Vickery: cites 30 on May 25, 1983 (ST) and 12 on May 30, 2013 (ML, RL) as high spring counts and 25 on Sep 17, 2013 (PDV) as high fall count (C. Scott Weidensaul in Vickery et al., 2020).

Ruby-throated Hummingbird, Sep 20, 2020. © Bill Thompson.

CALLIOPE HUMMINGBIRD
Selasphorus calliope

Status: Accidental fall vagrant.

Occurrence: One record: hatch-year male on Oct 6, 2005 (MI, AM; *NAB* 60: 38). First Maine record; accepted by ME-BRC #2005–003 (photos by MI).

Present for only two hours in the morning, it was feeding on scarlet salvia in front of the Monhegan House (DF).

Historical/Regional:

- Vickery: cites 2005 sighting as first Maine record (PDV in Vickery et al., 2020).
- OLMB: two additional state records—one accepted (Oct 23–Nov 1, 2008 at Blue Hill, Hancock Co.) and one not yet reviewed (Oct 6, 2007 in New Harbor, Lincoln Co.).

Calliope Hummingbird, Oct 6, 2005. © Marshall Iliff.

RUFOUS HUMMINGBIRD
Selasphorus rufus

Status: Accidental fall vagrant.

Occurrence: One record: adult male on Oct 4–6, 2012 (DH, LD, WN); specific identification confirmed by photos (DH, WN). Not yet reviewed by the ME-BRC.

Discovered by DH coming to feeder in Hitchcox yard, making frequent visits over three days.

An immature *Selasphorus* hummingbird (Rufous or Allen's) was reported on Sep 15, 1980 (PDV), but details noted did not allow specific identification.

Historical/Regional:

- OLMB: seventeen additional state records— eight accepted and nine not yet reviewed (earliest in 1957); four more records accepted as Rufous/Allen's Hummingbird.

Rufous Hummingbird, Oct 5, 2012. © Doug Hitchcox.

VIRGINIA RAIL
Rallus limicola

Status: Rare spring and fall migrant, very rare summer visitor and possible breeder.

Occurrence: Spring records over fourteen years since 1986, span Apr 18–early Jun, peak second half of May; spring max: **7** on May 18, 2022 (LS, MWa), May 23, 2022 (JT, LS, MWa), 5 on May 28–29, 2014 (JT), May 18, 2021 (JT et al.) & May 22, 2022 (DTu), 4 on May 24, 2014 (JT), May 20, 2022 (JT, LS, MWa) & May 27, 2022 (CHi). Five summer records since 2019, no confirmed breeding: 1 on Jun 11–12, 2019 (DH), 1 on Jun 12, 2020 (DH), 1 on Jun 16, 2021 (CDd), 1 on Jul 2, 2021 (DH, CEs), 1 on Jun 12, 2022 (MY). Twenty-three fall records over thirteen years since 1962, span Sep 10–Nov 12, peak late Sep–mid

Virginia Rail, Meadow, Oct 24, 2021. © Sebastian Jones.

Oct; fall max: 2 on Oct 21 & 22, 2011 (JT, DH, PM, MI), Sep 26, 2014 (BTn), Sep 21, 2020 (GSc, NSc), Oct 4, 2020 (JT, LS, BBy), Oct 2, 2021 (JT, LS), Oct 6, 2021 (JT, LS) & Oct 23–25, 2021 (SJ, CJ). Ten-Year: SP-9, SU-4, F-6.

- MBA: probable.
- 1970 Summer Checklist: included

The secretive nature of rails makes it very difficult to determine their seasonality, quantity, and length of stay, with heard only records predominating, and underreporting certainly the norm. Spring of 2014, 2021 & 2022 were exceptional, involving all of the max counts, probably involving some of the same inds. and seemingly indicating birds lingering for multiple days and possibly extended periods (gaps of over three days between reports are considered as separate records, although it is very likely inds. were overlooked); reported every day from May 22–30 in 2014, varying from 1–5 inds., every day May 16–Jun 1 in 2021, varying from 1–5 inds. and every day May 13–Jun 1, 2022, varying from 1–7 inds. In fact, most of the spring and fall records involved multiple days, often three or four days and likely more, but possibility of departing inds./new arrivals. Two inds. in appropriate habitat on Jun 8, 2019 and May 31, 2021 (among other reports of multiple inds. those years) were the basis for the probable status on the MBA. The consistent presence of multiple inds. in recent spring seasons and reports of singles lingering into summer suggests breeding birds, but lacking certainty and underscored by the inability to determine true number of inds. present, the unclear duration of spring migration and lack of summer coverage, despite increased attention for MBA. Almost all records providing location were from the Meadow, more often heard calling than seen; the only exception is a bird in the marshy meadow at Lobster Cove, heard on Sep 28, 2007 (BSc). Sightings at the Meadow were noted near the pump house, in the outlet stream to Swim Beach, once in flight overhead and dropping in, and once in a garden near the road in response to a tape recording (feeding in view for about ten minutes–PW).

Historical/Regional:

- Vickery: cites 2 on Apr 18, 2012 (DH) as early spring and 2 on Oct 22, 2011 as latest fall (DH et al.; PDV in Vickery et al., 2020).

CORN CRAKE
Crex crex

Status: Accidental fall vagrant.

Occurrence: One record: 1 on Oct 5, 2014 (DH). Second Maine record; accepted by ME-BRC #2014–016 (photos by DH). Ten-Year: F-1.

Encountered in the front yard of a house at the west end of Bates Lane (near the school). The bird was seen briefly while making passes across the back of the mowed lawn (DH).

Historical/Regional:

- Vickery: cites 2014 record (PDV in Vickery et al., 2020).
- OLMB: first and only other Maine record was a specimen taken Oct 14, 1889 in Falmouth, Cumberland Co. (not yet reviewed, specimen verified), one of two present and taken, the second not preserved.

Corn Crake, Oct 5, 2014. © Doug Hitchcox.

SORA
Porzana carolina

Status: Rare to scarce spring and fall migrant, very rare summer visitor.

Occurrence: Spring records all recent, occurring over fourteen years since 1997, including annually since 2013, span May 4–Jun 9, peak second half of May; spring max: **4** on May 25–28, 2016 (JE) & May 18, 2021 (JT et al.), 3 on May 21, 2016 (JT, JO), May 23, 2016 (JT, JO, BN), May 28, 2019 & Jun 4, 2021 (JFo). Three recent summer records: 1 on Jun 17, 2018 (BEv, TEv), 1 on Jul 3, 2018 (DH), 1 on Jun 15, 2021 (JFo). Despite slightly more reports than spring, most fall records are of single birds (multiples only in 2020 & 2021) over twenty-one years since 1918, span Sep 1–Oct 22, peak late Sep–early Oct; fall max: **4** on Sep 29, 2020 (WR), 3 on Sep 10, 2020 (SMn), Sep 30, 2020 (DH) & Oct 5, 2020 (JT, LS, BBy), 2 on Sep 28 2020 (JLo), Oct 1–2, 2020 (WR, DH, KSc), Oct 4, 2020 (DH) & Sep 24, 2021 (GP). Ten-Year: SP-10, SU-2, F-7.

- *MABB*: possible; MBA: possible.
- 1915–1919 Taylor Journals: 1919–Sep 1 (1), 13 (1). Listed as Sora Rail.
- 1918 Fall Migration Census: Dewis–Sep 12 (1 caught by a cat, dead); Wentworth–Oct 20 (1 near old dam [*Ice Pond*]), Oct 22 (1)
- Banding: 2 total over one season–1 on Aug 27, 1981 & Aug 30, 1981.

Similar to Virginia Rail in pattern of occurrence and detectability; certainly overlooked, and difficult/impossible to determine number of inds. or length of stay. More consistent daily reporting over the past ten years has undoubtedly increased our understanding of presence (note all max counts since 2016). Spring 2016, Fall 2020 and Spring 2021 were exceptional, involving almost all of the max counts, probably involving some of the same inds. and supporting the view that birds linger for multiple days and possibly extended periods (gaps of over three days between reports are considered as separate records, although it is probable that inds. were overlooked); inds. were reported every day May 19–30, 2016, varying from 1–4 inds., on fifteen days over Sep 20–Oct 9, 2020, varying from 1–4 inds. and every day May 15–Jun 4, 2021, varying from 1–4 inds. In fact, most of the records in spring and fall involved multiple days, often three or four days, and up to ten days in Fall 2012 (Sep 18–27), twenty-one days in Spring 2015 (May 10–30), sixteen days in Spring 2017 (May 15–30) and thirty-two days in Spring/Summer 2021 (May 15–Jun 15); the possibility of departing inds./new arrivals must be considered. Summer records in 2018 (likely the same ind.), possible status in *MABB* and possible status in MBA (2 calling birds in Meadow on Jun 1, 2021) suggest the possibility of breeding, and the Meadow is certainly appropriate habitat. Most often reported from the Meadow, predominantly heard only and sometimes calling throughout the day, but observed from the pump house area and several times at the outlet to Swim Beach along Main St.; also seen several times at the Ice Pond, once a juv. from the bridge over the swale on Mooring Chain Rd. (known as the chat bridge–LS) and even 3(!) in a mudhole between the Post Office and Starling House on Sep 10, 2020 (SMn). A juvenile persisted along the edge of the Ice Pond during drought conditions Sep 21–24, 2016, providing close views for many observers (BME, FMa, mob). Interesting that several records involve cats: a dead ind. acquired from a cat in 1918, one rescued from a cat that was playing with it on Oct 3, 2013, after which the Sora ran and then flew back into the Meadow (BSt), and one flushed by a cat across Main St. from Pierce Cottage on Oct 8, 2020 (TMz) that landed in the middle of the Meadow.

Historical/Regional:

- Palmer: cites Dewis and Wentworth 1918 records.
- Vickery: cites three late May records as late spring migrants, four first-half Sep records as early fall and Oct 12, 2015 (LS) as late fall for island (PDV in Vickery et al., 2020).

Sora, Meadow, May 14, 2015. © Geoff Dennis.

COMMON GALLINULE
Gallinula galeata

Status: Accidental spring and very rare fall migrant.

Occurrence: Seven records (1 spring, 6 fall) since 1960. Spring record: unreported number during Apr–May, 1960 (fide IF). Fall records, all except one from 1983, span Sep 3–Oct 2: adult on Sep 3–6, 1983 (reported each day–PDV), juvenile Sep 9–12, 1983 (PDV), a **second** juvenile joined the first on Sep 10 (both at the Ice Pond–PDV), adult on Sep 16–18, 1983 (JVW, NFa, PFr; *G* 12[5]:42), 1 on Sep 23, 1983 (DF), 1 on Oct 2, 1993 (BN et al.; *AB* 48[1]: 38).

- 1944–1967 Farrell Records: 1960–Apr, May. Listed as Florida Gallinule.

Without specific dates and due to rarity, the Apr and May 1960 reports considered one record. It is interesting that five of the six fall records occurred in 1983; while the two juveniles were noted at the Ice Pond on Sep 10; it is possible that the Sep 23, 1983 ind. was a repeat of an earlier record and was also seen at the Ice Pond, but based on the earlier changeover, four-day gap, and lack of details it is considered separately here. The Oct 1993 ind. "stumbled across the road" (BN).

Historical/Regional:

- Vickery: ~10 records, including Oct 2, 1983 (BN), listed as late; undated observation of one departing the island to the south only to be pursued by ~80 gulls, then landing on the water and swimming back towards shore, ultimately flying back to land and into spruces (PDV; PDV in Vickery et al., 2020).

AMERICAN COOT
Fulica americana

Status: Accidental spring and very rare fall migrant.

Occurrence: Three records (1 spring, 2 fall) since 2011. Spring record: 1 on Apr 9–May 1, 2011 (reported eight days: Apr 9, 12, 16–17, 28–30, May 1–all reports TMag). Fall records: 1 on Oct 11, 2012 (DH), 1 on Oct 31, 2017 (KL). Ten-Year: F-1.

- 1970 Summer Checklist: included (listed under Geese and Ducks).

It is notable that all records are recent. The spring 2011 ind. was observed at the Ice Pond and despite gaps between reports, it was almost certainly the same ind. throughout. The Oct 2012 ind. was in the Meadow near the pump house and the Oct 2017 ind. was at the Ice Pond.

SANDHILL CRANE
Antigone canadensis

Status: Very rare spring migrant.

Occurrence: Three records: 1 on May 23, 2008 (DF, TMar), **3** on May 17, 2015 (DMo et al.; ph.), 1 on May 23–24, 2022 (LS, DL, DG, mob; ph.). Ten-Year: SP-1.

The May 2008 ind. was heard calling in flight over the Ice Pond before landing on Manana, where it was observed by TMar through a spotting scope (DF personal comm.). The May 2015 inds. were observed in the Meadow. The 2022 ind. was seen flying into the harbor and landing on the rocks below the Wharton Ave. cul-de-sac midday. In the evening it was noted in the Meadow, where it remained the next morning, before flying west toward the mainland. Although Sandhill Crane was considered by Palmer and Cruickshank as a possible identification for the large eggs found by Rosier on Monhegan in 1605 (also possibly/more likely Great Auk—see historical accounts below), the first modern Maine record didn't occur until 1961, and it remains uncommon in the state.

Historical/Regional:

- Palmer: lists Crane sp., not Sandhill in particular, as possibly recorded by James Rosier on Monhegan Island (and Allens Island) during the Waymouth voyage in 1605 ([Reprint] 1887: 103), as large egg shells (larger than goose) were discovered, Great Auk cannot be ruled out (*in fact, more likely*–see Vickery, below).
- Cruickshank: cites Rosier report from 1605 Waymouth voyage and references Palmer account.

- Vickery: references Rosier 1605 account ([Reprint] 1887: 103) as unclear and historically references Palmer discussion and suggests Great Auk most likely source of large egg shells on Monhegan Island and Allens Island (PDV in Vickery et al., 2020).

Sandhill Crane, May 23, 2022. © Bill Thompson.

AMERICAN OYSTERCATCHER
Haematopus palliatus

Status: Very rare spring and accidental fall migrant, accidental summer visitor.

Occurrence: Six records (4 spring, 1 summer, 1 fall) since 1995. Spring records: unreported number in 1995 (TMar), unreported number w/e May 22, 2001 (WBo), 1 on May 26, 2016 (JT et al.), **3** on Jun 3, 2020 (LS, JT). Summer record: 1 on July 3, 2020 (DH). Fall record: 1 on Aug 19, 2010. Ten-Year: SP-2, SU-1.

Increased presence in Maine due to range expansion since the late 1970s, and breeding since 1995, undoubtedly explain these recent Monhegan occurrences (Vickery et al., 2020). The Aug 2010 ind. was heard calling as it flew by to the south after sunset (TMag). The May 2016 ind. was originally observed flying north (calling) past Nigh Duck, then later returned south and disappeared behind Manana (JT, JO, BN). The Jun 2020 inds. were flying south through the harbor. The Jul 2020 ind. was heard flying north on the west side of the harbor.

BLACK-BELLIED PLOVER
Pluvialis squatarola

Status: Rare spring and scarce fall migrant.

Occurrence: Twenty-four spring records over twenty years since 1982, span the short period May 15–Jun 3; spring max: **6** on May 22, 2014 (MM), 4 on May 24, 1986 (SS), 3 on May 16, 2017 (RM). Fall dates span Aug 22–Oct 29, peak mid Sep–mid Oct; fall max: 5 on Oct 16, 2017 (DH), 4 on Oct 15, 2017 (DH), 3 on Sep 23, 2017 (BTn, JT) & Oct 5, 2018 (LS, JT). Ten-Year: SP-7, F-9.

- 1915–1919 Taylor Journals: 1 on Sep 1, 1919.
- 1939 Summer Census: uncommon summer visitor (*erroneously listed as Black-billed Plover*).
- 1944–1967 Farrell Records: 1955–Aug; 1957–Aug.
- 1954 & 1955 Summer Records: 1955–Aug 23 (1 at Lobster Cove), 25 (1 at Lobster Cove), 28.
- 1970 Summer Checklist: included.

Most often encountered as calling flyovers (including the max of 6 in May 2014) and therefore possible anywhere on the island. A 1955 ind. was noted at Lobster Cove twice in three days, an immature bird was observed (noted as very tame) at Lobster Cove Sep 18–21, 2012 (DH et al.), and a juvenile was on the south tip of Manana on Sep 23, 2017 (LB).

Black-bellied Plover, May 21, 2006. © Geoff Dennis.

AMERICAN GOLDEN-PLOVER
Pluvialis dominica

Status: Rare fall migrant.

Occurrence: Thirty-two records over eighteen years (six records in 2011) since first recorded on Sep 10, 1983 (PDV); dates span Jul 31–Oct 29, peak mid Sep–early Oct; fall max: **9** on Sep 28, 2000 (JT), 2 on Sep 20, 2016 (DT). Ten-Year: F-4.

The six records in 2011 involved single inds. on consecutive days Sep 21–25 & Sep 28, three noted as flyovers with no details for the others; perhaps (likely?) the same ind. but no specific evidence of a lingering bird. All nine records giving any details were flyovers (sometimes calling); one was noted as a juvenile, one accompanied by a Black-bellied Plover and one heard around the harbor.

KILLDEER
Charadrius vociferus

Status: Rare spring and rare to scarce fall migrant, very rare summer visitor and possible breeder, very rare winter visitor.

Occurrence: Spring dates span Mar 8–end of May (late migrants/non-breeders), slight peak late Mar–early Apr; spring max: 3 on May 23, 1997 (SS) and Apr 5, 2011 (TMag), 2 on May 13, 1988 (JVW) & Mar 26 & 31, 2015 (DC). Eight summer records scattered through the month of Jun over six years since 1967 (all but the 1967 record since 2009, but also noted in 1970 as having bred on Manana, but no details provided), all singles or unreported number (1967 record). Fall migration begins early Jul with post-breeding dispersal/gathering–Oct 14, peak early Sep–early Oct; fall max: **7** on Oct 11, 1987 (JVW), 3 on Sep 28, 1997 (SS) & Oct 3–4, 2020 (JT, LS, MW), 2 on Sep 22, 2003 (SS). Two winter records: unreported number during Dec 1949 (IF), 1 on Dec 23, 2016 (DC). Ten-Year: SP-8, SU-3, F-9, W-1.

- 1944–1967 Farrell Records: 1949–Dec; 1950–Mar; 1954–Jul; 1958–Aug; 1967–Apr 3 (1), Jun 1, 4.
- 1954 & 1955 Summer Records: 1 on Jul 12, 1954.
- 1970 Summer Checklist: highlighted and marked as known to breed in the area–Manana.

Certainly underreported during the peak of spring migration (late Mar/Apr) and likely in late fall when there are few birders around. The Jun 1 & 4, 1967 reports are considered one record due to rarity at this season. The Dec 2016 ind. was reported as "around for several days." The 3 inds. on Oct 4, 2020 were observed together. Few details provided throughout; five records of calling flyovers (once over the Meadow), one spring record beside the Meadow and two in the Meadow (one calling), one at Fish Beach and one over Smutty Nose.

SEMIPALMATED PLOVER
Charadrius semipalmatus

Status: Very rare spring and scarce fall migrant.

Occurrence: Eight spring records since 2011, span May 15–29: 8 on May 15, 2011 (DH), 1 on May 27, 2014 (JT), 1 on May 29, 2015 (JT, BN), 1 on May 26, 2018 (SS), 1 on May 19, 2019 (BTn), 1 on May 20, 2021 (JT, LS), 2 on May 16, 2022 (LS, MWa), 1 on May 23, 2022 (DGi, PB). Fall dates span Jul 18–Oct 14, peak mid Aug–late Sep; fall max: **17** on Sep 22, 2011 (LS, JT), 15 on Sep 18, 2020 (DH), 10 on Aug 14, 2010 (TMag), 9 on Sep 29, 2005 (JT). Ten-Year: SP-6, F-10.

- 1900–1908 Reconnaissance & Supplements: included in Jenney supplement as Ring-necked Plover.
- 1914 & 1916 Checklists: included 1916.
- 1915–1919 Taylor Journals: 1916–Aug 31 (1), Sep 10; 1917–Sep 8 (1 on Eastern Duck Rock).
- 1939 Summer Census: uncommon summer visitor.

Killdeer, Oct 4, 2021. © Jeremiah Trimble.

- 1944–1967 Farrell Records: 1953–Aug; 1955–Aug; 1960–Aug.
- 1954 & 1955 Summer Records: 1955–1 or 2 Aug 22–29, 1955, often heard in flight.
- 1970 Summer Checklist: included.

Certainly underreported late Jul/Aug due to lack of coverage at a time when fall migration is well underway for this species, highlighted by the eleven records in Jul/Aug 2010 (including 10 on Aug 14, 6 on Aug 20, and 7 on Aug 23), a season of consistent coverage by TMag. Many reports involve calling flyovers from scattered locations, including Lobster Cove, the Ice Pond, Ocean Ave., and the harbor; the high count of 15 on Sep 18, 2020 involved several flyover groups. Several records of inds. feeding at the beach area at Lobster Cove, one record from a beach along the harbor (Swim or Fish Beach), and 1 on Eastern Duck Rock on Sep 8, 1917 (WT, CTa). As expected with shorebirds, juveniles migrate after adults in fall and there are five records of juveniles (involving 7 inds.) the second half of Sep–early Oct; no inds. noted to age earlier in the season.

Semipalmated Plover, Sep 19, 2018. © Bill Thompson.

UPLAND SANDPIPER
Bartramia longicauda

Status: Very rare spring and fall migrant.

Occurrence: Six records (4 spring, 2 fall) since first recorded in 1981 (PDV), all singles. Spring records span May 5–28: May 5–6, 1984 (PDV), May 28, 1989 (AWe, JVW), May 21–23, 1997 (not seen on the 22nd– SS, LBr), May 21, 2011 (TMag, DL). Fall records: Sep 4, 1981 (PDV), Sep 5, 1983 (PDV).

- 1970 Summer Checklist: included. Listed as Upland Plover.

The May 1989 ind. was a flyover (JVW).

Historical/Regional:
- Vickery: cites 1989 and 1997 records as late spring migrants, both fall records illustrating casual status on outer islands (PDV & CDD in Vickery et al., 2020).

WHIMBREL
Numenius phaeopus

Status: Accidental spring and rare fall migrant.

Occurrence: Fifty-one records (1 spring, 50 fall) since 1907. Spring record: unreported number during Apr 1961 (fide IF). Fall records over twenty-six years since 1907 (all but two since 1980), span Jul 24–Sep 28, all but the Jul 24 record scattered after Aug 31 (a "summer" 1908 record likely a fall migrant–see below); fall max: **3** on Sep 13, 1981 (PDV) & Sep 16, 2015 (DG), 2 on Sep 17, 2015 (TJ et al.) & Sep 19, 2018 (BME, SE et al.). Ten-Year: F-8.

- 1900–1908 Reconnaissance & Supplements: unreported number Aug 31, 1907, unreported number summer 1908 (CFJ, ECJ–*a likely fall migrant observed in Jul/Aug and treated as such above, rather than the only summer record for this species*).
- 1944–1967 Farrell Records: 1961–Apr. Listed as Hudsonian Curlew.
- 1970 Summer Checklist: included.

Likely underreported in late Jul/Aug, a peak time for this species along the East coast. All fifteen records giving details involved flyovers, all but four of these records noted as calling. The two inds. on Sep 17, 2015 were juveniles seen over the island four times (TJ et al.); other locations given include Lobster Cove, town, and harbor; possible anywhere over the island.

HUDSONIAN GODWIT
Limosa haemastica

Status: Accidental fall migrant.

Occurrence: One record: adult on Sep 24, 2016 (FMa, EF; ph.). Ten-Year: F-1.

Discovered by FMa flying NW toward Manana, as seen from the Island Inn.

RUDDY TURNSTONE
Arenaria interpres

Status: Very rare spring and rare fall migrant.

Occurrence: Forty records (5 spring, 35 fall) since 1953. Spring records all single birds (one unreported number), span May 15–31: 1 on May 15, 2005 (HN),

1 on May 16, 2010 (DH, EH), unreported number during a May 29–31, 2010 trip report (LBl), 1 on May 30, 2013 (RL, ML), 1 on May 24, 2018 (LS, JT). Fall records over twenty-three years since 1953 (note status on 1939 Census below), scattered throughout Jul 22–Oct 17, peak mid Aug–mid Sep: fall max: **9** on Aug 13, 2015 (BA, TR), 8 on Aug 18, 2015 (TR), 5 on Aug 4, 2015 (AP) & Jul 26, 2022 (DL, JL), 4 on Sep 5, 1987 (PDV) & Aug 20, 2016 (BTh). Ten-Year: SP-2, F-9.

- 1939 Summer Census: included as uncommon summer visitor (Outer Rocks).
- 1944–1967 Farrell Records: 1953–Aug, Sep; 1954–Aug, Sep; 1955–Aug; 1958–Aug, Sep; 1960–Jul, Aug, Sep.
- 1954 & 1955 Summer Records: 1955–Aug 23–Sep 2 (1–3 present at Lobster Cove).
- 1970 Summer Checklist: included.

Fall 2015 was exceptional (note the max counts) as turnstones gathered and were observed those three separate days flying around the Duck Rocks and the Monhegan shoreline and on the rocks near the dock. While it is impossible to determine the actual number of inds. involved, it is counted as two records for this purpose (5 increasing to 9). The only other record of probable lingering inds. involved 1–3 at Lobster Cove over Aug 23–Sep 2, 1955 (EAB, MEAB). Records only indicating month considered separate records for these purposes (two in 1958 [Aug, Sep] and three in 1960 [Jul, Aug, Sep]). Locations provided for eight other records indicated the offshore islands, confusingly identified as Seal Island, Outer Duck islands, Duck Rocks, rocky ledges, and Duck Rock South, but apparently most refer to the Outer Duck Rocks, suggesting a unique micro-habitat preference, also noted in the 1939 Summer Census. An interesting record involved 2 inds, one of them leucistic,. at Lobster Cove on Sep 19, 2012 (DH).

RED KNOT
Calidris canutus

Status: Accidental spring and fall migrant.

Occurrence: Two records (1 spring, 1 fall) since 2000. Spring record: 1 on Jun 6, 2007 (KL). Fall record: 1 on Sep 24, 2000 (JT).

Both inds. were seen from ferries on the Outer Duck Rocks. A potential second fall record was observed and photographed at a distance on Sep 6, 2015, but the identification was not definitive.

SANDERLING
Calidris alba

Status: Rare fall migrant.

Occurrence: Nineteen records scattered over seventeen years since first recorded on Sep 2–3, 1916 (WT, CTa–only record prior to 1980), span Jul 31–Oct 2, with only two records before Sep 2; fall max: **8** on Sep 12, 1983 (PDV), 7 on Sep 17, 2018 (CDD, SSr), 6 on Sep 8, 1980 (PDV). Ten-Year: F-4.

- 1915–1919 Taylor Journals: unreported number (recorded as Sanderlings) on Sep 2–3, 1916 at Lobster Cove with Clarkie (CTa).
- 1939 Summer Census: uncommon summer visitor.
- 1944–1967 Farrell Records: 1960–Aug.

1983 and 2003 were the only years with two records. The only details provided involved the lingering Sanderlings at Lobster Cove in 1916, a single bird on Sep 24, 1993 in basic plumage at Lobster Cove (PDV), and a single flyby past Lobster Cove on Sep 15, 2021 (BME, BTn). An additional report of 3 inds. on Sep 17, 2018 going east past Pebble Beach (SSr) may have involved some of the 7 inds. also reported that day.

DUNLIN
Calidris alpina

Status: Accidental spring and very rare fall migrant.

Occurrence: Five records (1 spring, 4 fall) since first recorded in 1997. Spring record: **2** on May 27, 2014 (JT, BN). Fall records span short period Sep 26–Oct 5: **2** on Oct 2, 1997 (JT), 1 on Sep 26, 2002 (JT), 1 on Oct 2, 2003 (JT), 1 on Oct 5, 2019. Ten-Year: SP-1, F-1.

The spring 2014 record involved two birds in alternate plumage heading north with a flock of Short-billed Dowitchers, briefly landing on distant rocks before continuing north (JT). The Oct 2019 ind. was a calling flyover.

PURPLE SANDPIPER
Calidris maritima

Status: Rare spring and very rare fall migrant (*presumably scarce to uncommon*), accidental summer visitor, rare winter visitor (*presumably scarce to uncommon*).

Occurrence: Forty-three records (15 spring, 1 summer, 6 fall, 21 winter) since 1937; certainly underreported during expected periods of presence due to lack of coverage in late fall, winter and early spring. Spring records over twelve years since 1989, late spring only and span May 16–27; spring max: 100 on May 23, 2013 (FM), 20 on May 24, 1997 (SS), 15 on May 26, 1995 (SS), 9 on May 21, 2017 (JKe). Summer record: 1 on Jul 26, 2022 (DL, JL). Fall records: 3 on Aug 28, 1937 (AC), 1 on Aug 30, 1937 (AC), unreported number during Aug 1960 (fide IF), 28 on Nov 11, 2020 (JT, LS), 1 on Oct 7, 2021 (HN), 2 on Sep 13, 2022 (HIAC et al.). Winter records over twenty years since 1978, almost all records associated with CBC period, span Dec 5–Jan 26; fall max: **233** on Dec 22, 1979 (CBC–PDV), 42 on Jan 1, 1992 (CBC–PDV), 39 on Dec 30, 1980 (CBC–PDV). Ten-Year: SP-5, SU-1, F-3, W-3.

- CBC: 16 years (62%) plus two count weeks, first recorded on Dec 28, 1978, max 233 on Dec 22, 1979, avg 19.2.
- 1939 Summer Census: included as uncommon summer visitor on Outer Rocks.
- 1944–1967 Farrell Records: 1960–Aug.

Surprisingly, all three historic fall records (two from Aug 1937 [Cruickshank, 1938] and one from Aug 1960) occur in the earliest portion of an extended fall migration period, while the two recent records align more with regional records suggesting a peak in late fall almost completely overlooked on Monhegan (Vickery et al., 2020). While these Aug records may have involved non-breeding summer visitors, early migrants are more likely and possibly the reason for inclusion on the 1939 Summer Census. Surely underreported overall late fall–early spring, except the CBC period. The species' affinity for rocky shores and the ability to "disappear" there may also contribute to the low number of reports; better scrutiny of the Duck Rocks, Seal Ledges, Nigh Duck, etc., may yield results. The only summer record occurred on the Outer Duck Rocks. Oddly, and maybe because of their elusiveness, the only other locations provided are Lobster Cove (four records), Smutty Nose Island (one record), and Pebble Beach (one record).

Historical/Regional:
- Vickery: cites 2013 max count as a high offshore number (PDV & CDD in Vickery et al., 2020).

BAIRD'S SANDPIPER
Calidris bairdii

Status: Very rare fall migrant.

Occurrence: Two records: 1 on Aug 27, 1968 (PAB, FGB; *AFN* 23[3]: 457), juvenile on Sep 13, 2012 (DL; ph.). Ten-Year: F-1.

The Sep 2012 ind. was among the seaweed and rocks at Lobster Cove.

LEAST SANDPIPER
Calidris minutilla

Status: Rare spring and scarce fall migrant.

Occurrence: Twenty-five spring records over sixteen years since 1982 (including seven consecutive recent years 2013–2019), span May 11–31; spring max: 7 on May 11, 2015 (OC), 6 on May 23, 2022 (JT, LS, MWa), 4 on May 23, 2015 (mob), May 19, 2021 (JT, LS) & May 20, 2022 (JT et al.). An early fall migrant, dates span Jul 5–Oct 1, peak early Aug–mid Sep; fall max: **30** on Aug 11, 2010 (TMag), 10+ on Aug 23, 1955 (EAB, MEAB), 9 on Aug 29, 2007 (DL), 8 on Sep 4, 1983 (PDV). Ten-Year: SP-9, F-9.

- 1900–1908 Reconnaissance & Supplements: included in Jenney supplement.
- 1914–1916 Checklists: unreported number on Aug 1, 1914; included 1916.
- 1915–1919 Taylor Journals: 1915–Aug 9 (5); 1916–Aug 25 (1), 26, 30, 31, Sep 3, 4, 6, 10; 1917–Aug 5, 16, Sep 8 (1 on Eastern Duck Rock); 1919–Sep 13 (1).
- 1918 Fall Migration Census: Dewis–1 on Sep 6.
- 1939 Summer Census: regular summer visitor.
- 1944–1967 Farrell Records: 1954–Jul; 1955–Aug; 1957–Aug; 1958–Aug; 1959–Jul, Aug; 1960–Jul,

Purple Sandpiper, May 18, 2012. © Geoff Dennis.

Aug.

- 1954 & 1955 Summer Records: 1954–included Jul 10–16, noted as generally flyovers; 1955–Aug 23–Sep 2 at Lobster Cove (10+ on Aug 23 diminishing to 2 inds.).
- 1970 Summer Checklist: included.
- Banding: 1 on Sep 15, 1962.

Most spring records were the only report of the year and single day events; 2015 and 2022 were exceptions, with varying totals scattered over four days each year, including the max counts, with overlapping of inds. probable (considered three records in 2022 due to consecutive day reports). Consistent coverage during Jul/Aug would undoubtedly reveal a more extensive presence. Shifting numbers in the fall make it difficult to determine length of stay, but certainly several days on some occasions. Lobster Cove is the most reliable location to find them, often feeding among the drying seaweed, with several reports from the Ice Pond, one on the boardwalk in the Meadow, and even a record in 1916 of 1 on Eastern Duck Rock. Four records, involving 9 inds., from the second half of Sep were noted as juveniles. Interestingly, 3 on May 30, 2019 were nocturnal flight calls and noted as at least 3, while a single on Jul 18, 2019 was also noted as nocturnal (JT).

Least Sandpiper, Sep 17, 2018. © Bill Thompson.

WHITE-RUMPED SANDPIPER
Calidris fuscicollis

Status: Very rare fall migrant.

Occurrence: Three records: unreported number during Aug 1958 (IF), unreported number during Sep 1959 (IF), 1 on Oct 5, 2018 (LS, JT; ph.). Ten-Year: F-1.

- 1939 Summer Census: rare or accidental summer visitor.
- 1944–1967 Farrell Records: 1958–Aug; 1959–Sep.

The Oct 2018 ind. was a flyover with thirteen Pectoral Sandpipers; seen over the town and possibly disappearing into the Meadow, but not relocated. No details available for inclusion on the 1939 Census.

PECTORAL SANDPIPER
Calidris melanotos

Status: Accidental spring and rare fall migrant.

Occurrence: Twenty-one records (1 spring, 20 fall) since 1960. Spring record: 2 on May 22, 2019 (HN). Fall records over fifteen years since first recorded during Jul/Aug 1960 (fide IF), with all other records since 1982 and scattered throughout Aug 22–Oct 12; fall max: **13** on Oct 5, 2018 (LS, JT), 3 on Oct 12, 2014 (LS et al.), 2 on Sep 3, 2010 (TMag), Sep 17, 2014 (PDV, TJ, MJ), & Sep 25, 2016 (MV, BM). Ten-Year: SP-1, F-6.

- 1944–1967 Farrell Records: 1960–Jul, Aug.

The 1960 Farrell report considered one record here due to rarity. The May 2019 inds. were on rocks near the water's edge near the wreck of the D. T. Sheridan (HN). Two fall records involved calling flyovers, one around Lobster Cove, while another silent flyover also passed Lobster Cove. The group of 13 on Oct 5, 2018 was observed flying over town, accompanied by the only record of a White-rumped Sandpiper, and appeared to drop into the Meadow, but was not relocated. Three records of singles were the most in a year, occurring Sep 27, Oct 8, & 10–11, 2011 (no details provided to indicate same/different inds.).

SEMIPALMATED SANDPIPER
Calidris pusilla

Status: Very rare spring and rare to scarce fall migrant.

Occurrence: Fifty-three records (5 spring, 47 fall, 1 unknown) since first recorded in 1899. Spring records span May 20–31: 1 on May 24–26, 1986 (SS, JVW), 3 on May 31, 2011 (DH), 1 on May 20, 2012 (LC, PW, DHe), 1 on May 25, 2013 (DH, LS, DL), 1 on May 30, 2016 (MO). Fall records over twenty-six years since 1914 (all but the 1914 [one], 1916 [five], 1917 [one], 1954 [one], 1959 [two], and 1960 [two] records since 1985), span Jul 18–Oct 9; fall max: **10** on Sep 2, 1955 (EAB, MEAB), 6 on Aug 17, 2006, 3 on Jul 27, 2010 (TMag), Aug 11, 2010 (TMag), & Oct 9, 2014 (JT). Unknown date: unreported number in 1899 (MEH). Ten-Year: SP-2, F-10.

- 1899 Checklist: included.
- 1914 & 1916 Checklists: unreported number on

Aug 1, 1914; included 1916.
- 1915–1919 Taylor Journals: 1916–Aug 19, 21, Sep 3, 6, 10; 1917–Aug 5.
- 1944–1967 Farrell Records: 1954–Aug; 1955–Aug; 1959–Jul, Aug; 1960–Jul, Aug.
- 1954 & 1955 Summer Records: 1955–Aug 23–Sep 2 at Lobster Cove (increasing from 1 to 10 inds.).
- 1970 Summer Checklist: included.

Few details provided for records; locations included Lobster Cove (four times, including the increasing group at Lobster Cove in 1955, along with a group of Least Sandpipers, and another time with a Least Sandpiper and Semipalmated Plover), the Ice Pond, and Fish and Swim Beach (same ind.). One juv. was noted on Sep 20, 2008 (LS). Surprisingly, only five instances of reports on consecutive days; the only instance of more than two days involved one ind. increasing to 10 inds. at Lobster Cove over the period Aug 23–Sep 2, 1955 (IF).

Semipalmated Sandpiper, Sep 25, 2018. © Bill Thompson.

SHORT-BILLED DOWITCHER
Limnodromus griseus

Status: Rare spring and very rare fall migrant.

Occurrence: Eighteen records (12 spring, 6 fall) since first known record in 2002 (although included on 1970 Checklist). Spring records over eleven years since 2002, span short period May 14–31: spring max: **35** on May 28, 2005 (LBr), 11 on May 21, 2022 (LS, MWa, JT), 8 on May 15, 2011 (TMag), 6 on May 27, 2014 (JT, BN), 2 on May 30, 2004 (JVW). Fall migration early and doubtlessly underreported in Jul and Aug, dates span Jul 7–Sep 12: 1 on Jul 14, 2010 (TMag), 1 on Jul 20, 2010 (TMag), 1 on Jul 7, 2011 (TMag), 1 on Sep 12, 2012 (JSt), 1 on Jul 12, 2017 (FMa), 4 on Jul 19, 2019 (JT). Ten-Year: SP-5, F-2.

- 1970 Summer Checklist: included.

Note that three of the fall records occur in the years with more consistent "summer" coverage by TMag (2010 & 2011), highlighting its absence in other years; fall 2010 is the only season with two records. The max count of 35 in May 2005 were flyovers, the May 2007 ind. was a calling flyover above the harbor, the flock of 6 with two Dunlin in May 2014 were flyovers, a rare standing bird was on the east side of the Meadow near the pump house in May 2015 (BBa), the May 2021 ind. was observed flying into the Meadow on the 30th and viewed from the pumphouse on the 31st (MO, BTn) and the 11 on May 21, 2022 were flying west over Manana. Details from the fall are limited to a bird flushed and calling at Lobster Cove before heading southwest in Jul 2017 and 4 flyovers calling above Manana in Jul 2019.

Short-billed Dowitcher, May 31, 2021. © Bill Thompson.

AMERICAN WOODCOCK
Scolopax minor

Status: Rare spring and rare to scarce fall migrant, scarce summer resident.

Occurrence: Underreported due to its secretive nature and seasonal timing. One of the earliest migrants that breed; nineteen spring records over thirteen years since 1967, with migrating birds Mar 7–mid May becoming indistinguishable from residents; spring max: 4 on Mar 19, 2011 (TMag), 2 on Apr 16, 1967 (IF), May 2, 2018 (EL), Mar 22, 2021 (KL, DC) & May 14, 2022 (MBu, EG). Breeding underway by May (possibly even mid Apr, with earliest noted Apr 28, 2008 [fide EH, KG, SWh; MARBA]), although not confirmed in either atlas (May 16 has been used as the start of "summer" records); due to coverage, majority of records second half of May; summer max: **6** on May 27, 2019 (PMo, MS), 5 on May 22, 2022 (JLo), 4 on May 20, 2015 (MM) & May 22, 2016 (PMo, MS), 3 on May 16, 2015 (KL), May 24, 2016 (LM), May 26, 2016 (TW, KRu), May 18, 2018 (KL), May 22, 2018 (JT), May 26, 2018 (SS), & May 25, 2019

(JBl). Fall migration underway early Sep–Nov 12, peaks in Oct (presumably continuing through Nov); fall max: 3 on Oct 29, 2010 (MI, LS, JT) & Nov 10, 2020 (LS, JT), 2 on Oct 17, 1918 (BHW), Sep 11, 1981 (PDV), Oct 22, 2011 (DH et al.), Sep 19, 2013 (BTn), Oct 7, 2018 (LS), Oct 4, 2019 (JT, LS, AO), Nov 12, 2020 (JT, LS) & Oct 22, 2021 (SJ, CJ). Ten-Year: SP-7, SU-10, F-10.

- *MABB*: probable; MBA: probable.
- 1918 Fall Migration Census: Wentworth–2 on Oct 17.
- 1939 Summer Census: included as rare or accidental visitor. Listed as Woodcock.
- 1944–1967 Farrell Records: 1951–Oct; 1955–Jun, Jul, Aug; 1957–Jun; 1958–Jun; 1959–Jun; 1960–May, Jul, Aug; 1961–May; 1967–Apr 2 (1), 4 (1), 7 (1), 13, 16 (2), 18 (1), 20, 21, 22.
- 1954 & 1955 Summer Records: 1955–included Jun 11–15 & Jun 30–Jul 5, Aug 28 (1 along Gull Cove Trail in the early morning).
- 1970 Summer Checklist: included.

The timing of its migration places American Woodcock outside the main birding periods, leading to a lack of reports during peak movements; i.e., Apr reports only in 1967 (counted as three records due to gaps in reports and inability to discern lingering or breeding from migrant inds.) and only three reports in Nov (all in 2020). Coupled with its tendency to avoid detection when not displaying, it is certainly underreported throughout the entire period of its presence. Contrarily, the obvious nature of its courtship display leads to a focus of reports in May (including providing the probable status for the MBA), with dusk sightings frequently noted at the Ballfield, as well as from Lighthouse Hill, Horn's Hill and the field near the cemetery; and often involving aerial displays and "peent" calls. In one instance, two displaying males were observed with a third ind. sitting in the grass (May 26, 2016–TW). Breeding on Monhegan is proven by a dead juvenile on May 5, 1985 (PDV). High probability of repeat sighting of some displaying inds., particularly in recent years with increased reporting, but length of stay unknown; summer presence poorly understood after May, with no reports between Jun 12 and Aug 3. Fall records with details note a combination of flushed birds (road near the Ice Pond, Underhill Trail, near the school, from a bordering residence into the Meadow, and "in woods") and flyovers (several times along ridges at the edge of the Meadow), including one instance of an aerial display (Sep 20, 2017–BTn).

WILSON'S SNIPE
Gallinago delicata

Status: Rare spring and scarce to uncommon fall migrant, very rare winter visitor.

Occurrence: Thirteen spring records over nine years since 1960 (two in 1960, three in 2013, two in 2011), span during Apr (earliest specified Apr 30)–May 29;

Wilson's Snipe, Meadow, Jan 3, 2015. © Fyn Kynd.

spring max: 2 on May 7, 1985 (PDV), May 3, 2011 (TMag) & May 22, 2013 (JH). Fall dates span during Aug (earliest specified Sep 1)–Nov 15, peak mid Sep–late Oct; fall max: **12** on Oct 21, 2011 (MI et al.), 8 on Oct 11, 2014 (LS et al.) & Sep 28, 2015 (BTn), 6 on Oct 3, 2006 (PDV), Oct 22, 2012 (DH et al.) & Oct 7, 2012 (JT). Three winter records, all associated with the CBC period: 1 on Dec 20–22, 1988 (WBo, CBC–PDV, not reported on Dec 21), 1 on Jan 4, 2007 (CBC–PDV), 1 on Jan 3–4, 2015 (DH, FK, WN, CBC on Jan 4). Ten-Year: SP-3, F-10, W-1.

- CBC: 3 years (12%), first on Dec 22, 1988, max 1 on all three dates, avg 0.1.
- 1918 Fall Migration Census: Wentworth–1 on Oct 20 near the old dam (*Ice Pond*).
- 1944–1967 Farrell Records: 1960–Apr, May, Aug, Sep.

Undoubtedly missed during Apr, the regional peak timing for its spring migration. Inds. known to linger, including two of the winter records, but length of stay uncertain, especially given the number of inds. apparently observed departing during certain seasons. Often observed flying out of the Meadow at dusk, sometimes calling (including the max count of 12 and a flock of 8 on Sep 28, 2015–BTn), seen multiple times at the Ice Pond and Lobster Cove, and once each at the end of Sterling Cove Rd., Bates Lane, Wharton Ave. and the Ballfield.

Historical/Regional:

- Palmer: cites 1918 Wentworth record.
- Vickery: cites the 2007 and 2015 winter records (PDV & CDD in Vickery et al., 2020).

SPOTTED SANDPIPER
Actitis macularius

Status: Scarce to uncommon spring and fall migrant, accidental summer visitor and possible breeder.

Occurrence: Spring migration underway May 6–Jun 7, with most sightings the second half of May (most likely underreported in early May, only three records in early Jun [1908, 2020 & 2021]); spring max: **21** on May 20, 2022 (LS, MWa, JT), 6 on May 23, 1987 (SS), 5 on May 27 or 28, 2018 (KL) & May 18, 2021 (JT, LS, JO), 4 on May 22, 2013 (DH), May 27, 2014 (JT), May 24, 2015 (JT), May 26, 2016 (JE) & May 22, 2022 (JT, LS, MWa). Summer status unclear; despite its confirmed status as a breeder in *MABB* and noted inclusion on the 1970 Checklist, there is only one dated "summer" record: undetermined number during Jun 27–Jul 4, 1954 (EAB, MEAB–the other mid Jul 1954 record falls into the possible early fall migration period). Fall migration underway by second week of Jul–Oct 14, with an extended peak late Aug–early Oct; fall max: 6 on Aug 21, 2010 (TMag), 5 on Aug 9, 1915 (WT, CFJ) & Oct 1, 2005 (JT) & Sep 27, 2010 (ED), 4 on Sep 5, 1917 (WT), Aug 6, 2012 (DL), Sep 15, 2017 (RJ et al.), Jul 30, 2020 (GBr), Aug 4, 2021 (JCe) & Aug 14, 2022 (LS, MWa). Ten-Year: SP-10, F-10.

- *MABB*: confirmed; MBA: probable.
- 1900–1908 Reconnaissance & Supplements: 2 or 3 pairs seen during May 31–Jun 6, 1908 (FA); unreported number during Jul 31–Aug 2, 1908 (WM).
- 1914 & 1916 Checklists: unreported number on Jul 31, 1914, included 1916.
- 1915–1919 Taylor Journals: 1915–Aug 9 (5), Sep 2; 1916–Aug 22, 25 (1), Sep 10; 1917–Jul 29 (3), Aug 4, 16, Sep 5 (4), 8 (3 on Eastern Duck Rock); 1918–unknown date; 1919–Sep 4 (1), 5 (2), 14 (1).
- 1918 Fall Migration Census: Dewis–4 (1 on Sep 4, 6, 8 & 10).
- 1944–1967 Farrell Records: 1949–Sep; 1953–Sep; 1954–Jun, Jul; 1955–Jun, Jul, Aug; 1957–Aug; 1958–Aug; 1959–Jul, Aug; 1960–May, Jul, Aug; 1961–May.
- 1954 & 1955 Summer Records: 1954–included Jun 27-Jul 4 & Jul 10-16; 1955–included Jun 11–15, Jun 30–Jul 5 & Aug 22–Sep 2 (widely distributed around the island, up to 3 together).
- 1970 Summer Checklist: highlighted and marked as known to breed in area.

Probably underreported during the late spring–early fall period (Jun–Aug), and records from early Jun and mid Jul may actually involve residents, but no supporting evidence. The 2 or 3 pairs seen in 1908 (see above) seem to indicate breeding and a pair at Lobster Cove on May 30, 2019 (MI) was also suggestive. Three at the Ice Pond on May 28, 2021 resulted in inclusion in MBA (pair in suitable habitat), but were possibly migrants. Records only specified to the months of Jun or Jul in 1954, 1955, 1959, and 1960 considered likely late spring or early fall migrants. A noteworthy report of 11 on Sep 6, 1985 (PDV) included a ferry crossing and is therefore excluded from the max counts considered here. Inds. known to linger for several days. Most often reported from the Ice Pond or Lobster Cove, but possible anywhere along the shore/harbor, with sightings from Swim Beach, Fish Beach, Squeaker Cove, Deadman's Cove, Pebble Beach, the eastern cliffs, and a couple of times from the Meadow; 3 on Eastern Duck Rock on Sep 3, 1917 (WT, CTa).

Spotted Sandpiper, Sep 25, 2018. © Bill Thompson.

SOLITARY SANDPIPER
Tringa solitaria

Status: Rare spring and scarce fall migrant.

Occurrence: Thirty-one spring records over eighteen years since 1985, span Apr 8–May 30 (all but one May 5 or later); spring max: 6 on May 18, 2008 (GD), 3 on May 14, 2010 (DH, MLe) & May 7, 2017 (DH), 2 on May 23, 1997 (SS), May 5, 2010 (NL), & May 16, 2010 (EH). Fall dates span Jul 26–Oct 9, with a peak throughout Sep; fall max: **8** on Aug 31, 1916 (WT, CTa), 4 on Sep 23, 2018 (JSw, CAS) & Sep 16, 2021 (BTn), 3 on ten days, all since 2006. Ten-Year: SP-4, F-10.

- 1914 & 1916 Checklists: included 1916.
- 1915–1919 Taylor Journals: 1916–Aug 19, 31 (8), Sep 3, 4, 6; 1917–Sep 5 (1); 1919–Sep 11 (2), 13 (2).
- 1918 Fall Migration Census: Dewis–5 total, noted as "seen numbers of times at the Ice Pond;" Sep 7 (2), Sep 8 (2), Sep 10 (1).
- 1939 Summer Census: uncommon summer visitor.
- 1944–1967 Farrell Records: 1958–Aug; 1960–Aug, Sep.
- 1954 & 1955 Summer Records: 1955–Sep 1 (1 at Ice Pond–MLn).
- 1970 Summer Checklist: included.

Inds. known to linger for several days; most often reported from the Ice Pond, as illustrated by 3 seen there Sep 23 & 25, 2018 and 3 on Sep 13–16, 2021 (4 present on the 16th), and the spring max count of 6 together in May 2008. There are also multiple reports from the Meadow and one from Lobster Cove.

Historical/Regional:

- Palmer: migrant birds occasionally found in sheltered places on offshore islands, including Monhegan.
- Vickery: cites Apr 8, 1987 record as earliest for state (PDV & CDD in Vickery et al., 2020).

Solitary Sandpiper, Sep 21, 2018. © Bill Thompson.

LESSER YELLOWLEGS
Tringa flavipes

Status: Very rare spring and rare to scarce fall migrant.

Occurrence: Fifty-four records (9 spring, 45 fall) since 1955. Spring records over seven years since 1997, span May 15–27; spring max: 3 on May 18, 2015 (LC, DHe), 2 on May 15, 2011 (LS) & May 20, 2022 (JT, LS, MWa). Fall records over twenty years since 1955 (six records in 2018, seven in 2019, eight in 2021), span Jul 3–Sep 26; fall max: **12** on Sep 2, 1955 (MLn), 5 on Sep 14, 2019 (BTn), 2 on Aug 11, 2010 (TMag), Aug 16, 2018 (RG), Sep 18, 2018 (CDD, JAl, SSr), Sep 27, 2019 (CN, DDF), Jul 19, 2021 (HIAC et al.) & Aug 5, 2021 (JCe, ACe). Ten-Year: SP-4, F-8.

- 1944–1967 Farrell Records: 1955–Aug; 1959–Aug; 1960–Aug.
- 1954–1955 Summer Records: 1955–Sep 2 (12 flyovers–MLn).
- 1970 Summer Checklist: included.

More than half the fall records occurred over four years: five records Jul 27–Sep 10, 2010 (largely due to consistent coverage by TMag and indicative of underreporting early fall [Jul–Aug] during other years), six records Jul 3–Sep 28, 2018, seven records Jul 20–Sep 28, 2019 and eight records Jul 19–Sep 26, 2021. Only fourteen records with any details: eleven involving flyovers (eight calling, including one nocturnal migrant at 4:14 a.m. on Aug 29, 2022 [SG]), two at the Ice Pond and one at the Meadow. The high percentage of flyover records argues against lingering inds.; only three instances of reports from two consecutive days, but nothing to indicate continuing birds.

WILLET
Tringa semipalmata

Status: Rare spring and very rare fall migrant.

Occurrence: Thirty-five records (33 spring, 2 fall) since 1984. Spring records over eighteen years since 1984 (six in 2021, four in 2022) span Apr 29–Jun 7; spring max: **16** on May 29, 2017 (JT, LS, CL), 7 on May 20, 2022 (JT et al.), 6 on May 22, 2022 (DTu), 5 on May 16, 2011 (TMag), 4 on Apr 29, 2021 (DC). Fall records: 1 on Sep 30, 1997 (JT), 1 on Sep 23, 2017 (JSc, SMc, CN). Ten-Year: SP-7, F-1.

Although Willets recovered from market hunting in the late 1800/early 1900s and both subspecies are regular in Maine since the 1970s, the abundance and seasonal timing on Monhegan are both surprising and misleading when compared to the historical and more recent regional records (Vickery et al., 2020). It appears to be more common than formerly, but with a concentration in spring instead of fall. Maine reports show a yearly peak in mid Jul, no doubt underreported at this time on Monhegan. Often seen in flight and calling, arguing against lingering birds, but few details have been provided. Most are single day records, but several instances of consecutive day sightings (May 14–16, 2011, May 28–29, 2017 & May 22–23, 2021) involve variable numbers and since no details link inds., they are considered separate records here. There are records providing location from Lobster Cove, the harbor, and the Meadow. Three seen well offshore from Lobster Cove ultimately made their way into the harbor and landed there on May 31, 2022 (DL, JL).

Fifteen of the records (14 spring, 1 fall) have been identified as Eastern Willet (*T. s. semipalmata*), including the max. count of 16. Despite a limited presence in fall at coastal Maine sites, Western Willet (*T. s. inornata*) is yet to be detected on Monhegan.

Historical/Regional:
- Vickery: nearly annual since early 1990s (PDV & CDD in Vickery et al., 2020).

Willets, Harbor, May 20, 2022. © Laura Blutstein.

GREATER YELLOWLEGS
Tringa melanoleuca

Status: Scarce to uncommon spring and fall migrant.

Occurrence: Spring dates span Apr 17–Jun 14, peak the first three weeks of May; spring max: **35** on May 15, 2011 (TMag), 7 on May 15, 2021 (JT, LS, JO) & May 15, 2022 (LS, MWa), 6 on May 16, 2021 (JT, LS, JO), 4 on May 22, 2005 (JH) and May 22, 2013 (JH). Fall dates early and extensive, span Jul 4–Oct 29, peak early Sep–early Oct; fall max: 5 on Sep 19, 1987 (DSt), 4 on Oct 7, 2012 (JT), 3 on Sep 10, 1983 (PDV), Sep 8, 1985 (PDV), Sep 2, 2016 (JC), Sep. 20, 2018 (JAl, SSr), Jul 20, 2019 (JT), Sep 13, 2019 (LK) & Sep 15, 2021 (BHn et al.). Ten-Year: SP-10, F-10.

- 1900–1908 Reconnaissance & Supplements: unreported number on Aug 29, 1907 (CFJ, ECJ).
- 1914 & 1916 Checklists: included 1916.
- 1915–1919 Taylor Journals: 1916–Aug 31 (1), Sep 3.
- 1939 Summer Census: uncommon visitor.
- 1944–1967 Farrell Records: 1955–Aug; 1959–Aug; 1960–Aug.
- 1954 & 1955 Summer Records: 1955–1 or 2 in flight on Aug 22, 24, 29, Sep 1.
- 1970 Summer Checklist: included.

While several birds have been found in the Meadow and at the Ice Pond, and once at Fish Beach, many reports involve flyovers, usually calling, most commonly at Lobster Cove, but possible anywhere on the island or over Manana.

Greater Yellowlegs, May 14, 2015. © Geoff Dennis.

WILSON'S PHALAROPE
Phalaropus tricolor

Status: Accidental fall migrant.

Occurrence: One record: 1 on Sep 10, 1988 (RE, NH).

Discovered at the Ice Pond. Accidental in the state before 1960, now a regular spring and fall migrant.

RED-NECKED PHALAROPE
Phalaropus lobatus

Status: Rare (sometimes abundant by numbers) spring and fall migrant.

Occurrence: Forty-two records (20 spring, 21 fall, 1 unknown date) since first recorded during 1900–1908 (unknown date); historical records suggest an extensive presence in earlier years (see Monhegan checklists and Cruickshank below). Extremely variable spring records over eighteen years since 1978, span May 15–Jun 5; spring max: **5,000** on May 25, 1985 (SS), 2,000 on May 26, 1985 (SS), 800 on May 27, 1995 (SS), 400 on May 24, 1986 (SS), 75 on May 2, 1990 (JVW). Fall records over eighteen years since 1915, span Jul 19–Sep 29 (all but Jul 19 record occurred mid Aug or later); fall max: **3,000–5,000** during the last week of Aug 1937 (CBu, JCa, AC), 1,000 on Aug 16, 1917 (WT), 350 on Sep 8, 1917 (WT, CTa), 25 on Sep 4, 1918 (JDe), 12 on Jul 19, 2019 (JT), 5 on Sep 23, 2017 (JT). Unknown date: unreported number during 1900–Aug 1908 period (CFJ, ECJ). Ten-Year: SP-5, F-4.

- 1900–1908 Reconnaissance & Supplements: included in Jenney supplement as Northern Phalarope.
- 1914 & 1916 Checklists: included 1916. Listed as Northern Phalarope and Sea Goose.
- 1915–1919 Taylor Journals: 1915–Aug 16–17, 28, Sep 1; 1916–Sep 6; 1917–Aug 16 (1,000), Sep 8 (350 at Eastern Duck Rock w/CTa). Listed as Northern Phalaropes and phalaropes.
- 1918 Fall Migration Census: Dewis–Sep 4 (25–12 and two small flocks); a flying flock was also seen from the boat near the island when arriving on Sep 4; listed as Northern Phalarope.
- 1939 Summer Census: regular summer visitor at sea. Listed as Northern Phalarope.
- 1944–1967 Farrell Records: 1960–Jul, Sep. Listed as Northern Phalarope.
- 1970 Summer Checklist: included as Northern Phalarope.
- DOWTS Surveys 2011–2014: 1 on Sep 28, 2011 (1.7%).

Although easily overlooked without targeted observation, there are surprisingly few records for a species once known to stage by the millions during migration in the nearby Bay of Fundy/Passamaquoddy Bay. These numbers dropped drastically to virtually none between the 1970s and the present. Cruickshank noted reports of thousands by Monhegan (no details available except the report from 1937 [Cruickshank, 1938]); illustrated by the largest Monhegan numbers occurring 1995 or prior. The thousands reported in Aug 1937 were reported as "at least" 3,000–5000 off Monhegan in one spectacular flock, while the thousands over two days in 1985 were noted as "just off the island" on May 25 and off Lobster Cove on May 26, and highlight the disparity among records. There is a record of ~10,000 "around Monhegan" on Aug 22, 1972 (Sibley Higginbotham et al.; *AB* 27[1]: 27), but no details to pinpoint distance from the island for inclusion here. Presence on the water is typical, noted again from Lobster Cove (including flying around the weed line–JT), just past Nigh Duck and fifty feet from shore of Eastern Duck Rock (WT, CTa), also as a flyby from Nigh Duck. Inclusion on many checklists including ferry crossings not considered here as just as likely seen in transit away from Monhegan; other reports from fishing trips "off Monhegan" are likely >three miles offshore and are excluded here, but add additional information regarding status in nearby waters (see Vickery below).

Historical/Regional:

- Cruickshank: not unusual to see many thousands over the shoals around Monhegan in fall.
- Vickery: Monhegan is at the western edge of the area of most numerous occurrence along the coast; formerly 100–500 present off the island in late May, highest count in 2000s is 12 on May 20, 2011 (DH); lists 5,000 as high count; *reports seen while fishing "off Monhegan" of 1,500 on May 27, 1973 (MLi), 4 on May 7, 1981 (MLi) as early spring and 25 on July 18, 1960 (MFO 5:72) as early fall have been excluded from this account due to probability of distance offshore >Monhegan Lobster Conservation Area* (PDV & CDD in Vickery et al., 2020).

RED PHALAROPE
Phalaropus fulicarius

Status: Very rare spring and fall migrant.

Occurrence: Six records (3 spring, 3 fall) since first recorded in 1984. Spring records: **60+** on May 27, 1984 (BT; *AB* 38: 885), 1 on May 25–26, 1985 (SS),

2 on May 22, 2005 (JH). Fall records: 1 on Sep 27, 1987 (PDV), 1 on Aug 24, 1995 (DA), 8 on Sep 28, 2011 (DH).

- 1970 Summer Checklist: included.

The only details relate to the May 1985 record, a female that was with a large flock of Red-necked Phalaropes off Lobster Cove on May 26.

Historical/Regional:

- Vickery: small numbers regularly off Monhegan, cites >60 on May 27, 1984 (BT, *AB* 38: 885; PDV & CDD in Vickery et al., 2020).

POMARINE JAEGER
Stercorarius pomarinus

Status: Rare fall migrant, accidental summer and winter visitor.

Occurrence: Thirty-five records (1 summer, 33 fall, 1 winter) since 1985. Summer record: 1 on Jul 12, 2011 (TMag). Fall records over fifteen years since 1985 (4 records in 2011, 3 in 2003, 2014, 2016 & 2022), span Sep 8–Nov 23, peak late Sep–mid Oct; fall max: **15** on Sep 25, 2002 (JT), 8 on Sep 26, 2003 (SS), 5 on Oct 21, 2011 (MI, JT, PM). Winter record: 1 on Jan 3, 2013 (CBC–PDV, WN). Ten-Year: F-8, W-1.

- CBC: one year (4%), 1 on Jan 3, 2013, avg 0.0.
- DOWTS Surveys 2011–2014: 1 on Sep 22, 2011 (1.7%).

As early as 1916, Arthur Norton noted that the Pomarine Jaeger is "well known to all fishermen and distinguished by an obscene name" because of its harrying and parasitic behavior. Underreported due to its fleeting offshore tendencies, especially throughout its most expected period of presence (Aug–Oct), as well as a lack of coverage in late summer/early fall; a dedicated seawatch offers the best chance to encounter one. Several reports on checklists that also included ferry crossings to/from Monhegan have been excluded due to lack of location details. Generally seen as flybys from the eastern headlands or Lobster Point; watch for them chasing gulls or terns. An ind. reported from shore on Sep 22, 2011 is possibly the same ind. recorded on the DOWTS survey that day and is considered one record for these purposes. The max flight in 2012 involved inds. flying west past Lobster Cove, many of them adults (JT). Four observed on Nov 11, 2020 included 1 south of Manana and 3 off Duck Rock (including 1 dark ind.), all of them chasing Great Shearwaters at some point. Only 4 other fall inds. definitively identified to age, all adult light morphs in the fall, several other inds. noted as light or dark but without further clarification.

Historical/Regional

- Vickery: cites Jan 2013 report as only winter record for Monhegan (Jan–Mar; CDD in Vickery et al., 2020).

Pomarine/Parasitic Jaeger (unidentified jaeger): Due to the difficulty of separating Pomarine and Parasitic Jaegers, there have been an additional ten records identified as Pomarine/Parasitic over five years since 1998, including 4 on Sep 25, 2002 (the max count day for Pomarine) and a max of 8 on Sep 29, 2003 (JT).

PARASITIC JAEGER
Stercorarius parasiticus

Status: Very rare spring and rare fall migrant, very rare summer visitor.

Occurrence: Seventeen records (2 spring, 4 summer, 11 fall) since 1968 (all but the 1968 record since 2002). Spring records: unreported number on May 23, 2016 (JKe), 1 on May 26, 2017 (LS, CL, JT). Summer records: 2 on Jul 22, 1968 (JGw, fide RPE; *AFN* 225]: 588), 1 on Jul 12, 2011 (TMag), 1 on Jul 15, 2011 (TMag), 1 on Jul 26, 2021 (DCl). Fall records over seven years since 2002, span Aug 21–Nov 6: fall max: **3** on Sep 8, 2011 (DH, NL) & Oct 9, 2015 (JT, JO). Ten-Year: SP-2, SU-1, F-3.

Surprisingly, all records are recent, except the first in 1968. Similar to Pomarine Jaeger, it is underreported due to its pelagic tendencies, especially throughout its most expected period of presence (Aug–Oct), and additionally in late summer/early fall due to lack of coverage; a dedicated seawatch offers the best chance to encounter one. Just as likely to be seen outside the MILCA on a ferry crossing as from Monhegan, checklists including both areas have been excluded unless details provided. Most likely to be seen from the eastern headlands or Lobster Cove Point, chasing gulls or terns. A juvenile was observed chasing and being chased by a Peregrine Falcon on Sep 26, 2012 (BN, JT), while another ind. was chasing a Herring Gull and bathing on Oct 7, 2014 (JT).

Historical/Regional:

- Vickery: cites 2 on Oct 1, 2016 (mob) as late record under winter period (*this eBird sighting possibly includes a ferry crossing and is excluded from this account*; CDD in Vickery et al., 2020).

DOVEKIE
Alle alle

Status: Very rare spring and fall migrant, accidental summer and rare winter visitor.

Occurrence: Thirty records (2 spring, 1 summer, 6 fall, 21 winter) since 1940. Spring records: unreported number on Apr 1, 1997 (WBo, fide KG), 1 on Apr 15, 1997 (fide WBo). Summer record: undetermined number and date from listing in 1939 Summer Census (fide WT). Fall records: unreported number during Nov 1949 (IF), unreported number during Nov 1950 (IF), 3 on Oct 13–14, 1982 (PDV), 1 on Oct 12, 1984 (WBo), 1 on Oct 29, 2010 (JT), 1 on Nov 10, 2022 (LS, MWa). Winter records over twenty years since 1940, almost all associated with CBC, span Dec 14–Feb 8; winter max: **43** on Dec 28, 1982 (CBC–PDV), 20 on Dec 29, 1940 (CBC), 11 on Dec 27, 1987 (CBC–PDV). Ten-Year: F-1, W-3.

- CBC: 15 years (58%), first on Dec 29, 1940, max 43 on Dec 27, 1982 *(actually Dec. 28)*, avg 3.7.
- 1939 Summer Census: accidental summer visitor (one record).
- 1944–1967 Farrell Records: 1949–Nov; 1950–Nov; 1952–Feb.
- 1970 Summer Checklist: included.
- DWOTS: 1 on Jan 16, 2014 & 1 on Feb 8, 2014 were in the northern extreme of the Test Quadrant and therefore within the MILCA and included here; 1 on Feb 3, 2014 was observed in the southern portion of the Test Quadrant and outside the MILCA and not included here (no records from the Control Quadrant).

Undoubtedly underreported in late fall/winter due to lack of coverage. Nineteen noted from a ferry crossing on Oct 13, 1982 (surprisingly early), included "several" right in the harbor upon arrival and another from the island later in the afternoon; what were considered to be the same 3 were noted the following day from the island and listed as the same record. Several records of birds seen on the water from Lobster Cove included the CBC observations in 2020 & 2021. The two DOWTS records noted above were also observed on the water. Confusion regarding sightings from ferry crossings has resulted in exclusion of other records from this account. One example is a high count of 120 reported on Dec 27, 1982, which included a morning ferry crossing, which notes "all on the water, harbor south." Other excluded records reported from fishing trips as "off Monhegan" and likely outside the Monhegan Island Lobster Conservation Area add additional information regarding status in nearby waters (see Vickery below). Unclear why included on 1970 Summer Checklist, but perhaps this was based on the 1939 Census record.

Historical/Regional:

- Vickery: cites Oct 29, 2010 (JT) record as early for fall, discusses and lists many CBC records as outer edge of inshore waters, and confusingly lists unreported number on Apr 1, 1997 (WBo, fide KG) as latest spring and 1 on Apr 15, 1997 (fide WBo) as late winter. Includes offshore late fall and winter sightings (seen while fishing east and south) from late 1950s–1980s with 1–20 off island during Nov 1961 and 1–15 daily off island late 1962–Jan 25, 1963, when they suddenly disappeared (MLi–*these observations excluded here due to unknown distance from island and likely outside MILCA*; PDV in Vickery et al., 2020).

Dovekies, Lobster Cove, Jan 2, 2020. © Doug Hitchcox.

COMMON MURRE
Uria aalge

Status: Very rare spring and fall migrant, rare summer and very rare winter visitor.

Occurrence: Twenty-one records (2 spring, 13 summer, 3 fall, 4 winter) since 1987. Spring records: 1 on Feb 26, 2014 (DOWTS–LKB), 1 on Mar 18, 2014 (DOWTS–LKB). Summer records over seven years since 1988, span May 2–Jun 16; summer max: **4** on May 2, 2013 (DOWTS–LKB), 3 on May 20, 2016 (fide KL), 2 on Jul 10, 2013 (DOWTS–LKB). Fall records: 2 on Oct 5, 2018 (JT, LS), unreported number on Sep 25, 1998 (JWa), 1 on Oct 9, 2022 (SJ). Winter records: 1 on Dec 27–28, 1987 (CBC–PDV), 2 on Dec 27, 1994 (CBC–PDV), 1 during Jan 1–7, 2007 (CBC count week), 2 on Dec 27, 2004 (PDV). Ten-Year: SP-1, SU-6, F-2.

- CBC: 2 years (8%) plus one count week (2007): 1 on Dec 27, 1987, 2 on Dec 27, 1994, avg 0.1.
- DOWTS Surveys 2011–2014: 6 over three days (5%), Feb 26–May 2, max 4 on May 2, 2013; 2 on Jul 10, 2013 in the northern end of the Test Quadrant are also included here (1 on Apr 21,

2013 & 1 on Jul 3, 2013 were observed at the southern end of the Test Quadrant and not included here).

Possibly underreported throughout late fall–spring period (Oct–Apr) due to lack of coverage and the species' preference for offshore waters; with spring migration occurring mostly Mar–Apr, the records in May–Jun have been considered summer visitors, but movements are not fully understood. The species has recently bred in very small numbers as close as Matinicus Rock. Most likely to be either flybys or on the water; the only locations given are Lobster Cove, off Manana to the southwest, the DOWTS surveys and from ferries approaching the island. Only a couple of additional reports including ferry crossings excluded.

Historical/Regional:

- Vickery: cites six records from Monhegan and southwest since 1997, including Sep 25, 1998 (JWa); rare on coastal CBCs, cites 2 on Dec 27, 1994 as one of only three CBC sites with records of multiple inds. (PDV in Vickery et al., 2020).

THICK-BILLED MURRE
Uria lomvia

Status: Very rare spring migrant, very rare winter visitor.

Occurrence: Eight records (2 spring, 6 winter) over seven years since 1979. Spring records: 1 during May 19–24, 2002 (TV), 2 on Mar 12, 2018 (DC). Winter records span Dec 20 (trip list)–Feb 7: 1 on Dec 22, 1979 (CBC–PDV), 7 on Dec 29, 1982 (PDV), 4 on Jan 5, 1987 (PDV), unreported number during Dec 20–22, 1989 (CBC cw), **90** on Jan 4, 2007 (CBC), 3 (1) on Feb 6–7, 2009 (LS).

- CBC: 2 years (8%) plus two count weeks (1987, 1989): 1 on Dec 22, 1979, 90 on Jan 4, 2007, avg 3.5.

Possibly underreported Nov–Mar due to lack of coverage, despite Monhegan location within the species' winter range. The 7 reported on Dec 29, 1982 were all off Burnt Head, while the 3 on Feb 6, 2009 were on the water off Lobster Cove with Razorbills, with 1 remaining on Feb 7. Two checklists including ferry crossing were excluded (one in Dec, one in May).

Historical/Regional:

- Vickery: irregular on CBC, cites 90 on Jan 4, 2007 as exceptional (PDV in Vickery et al., 2020).

RAZORBILL
Alca torda

Status: Very rare (*presumably rare*) spring and rare (*presumably uncommon to common*) fall migrant of highly variable numbers, uncommon summer and very rare winter visitor.

Occurrence: Four spring records but plainly underreported (three records from DOWTS), all from 2013–2014: 1 on Apr 7, 2013 (DH), 2 on Apr 27, 2013 (DOWTS–LKB), 2 on May 2, 2013 (DOWTS–LKB), 3 on Mar 18, 2014 (DOWTS–LKB). Summer records span May 15–Jul 21, concentrated last three weeks of May–first week of Jun due to coverage; summer max: 40 on May 31, 2011 (DH), 8 on May 27, 2017 (JT, LS, CL), 7 on May 28, 2014 (JT). Fall migration extensive and very late, dates span Sep 10–mid Jan, peak late Dec; fall max: **745** on Jan 1, 1992 (CBC–PDV), 715 on Dec 27, 1994 (CBC–PDV) & Dec 27, 2004 (PDV), 541 on Dec 27, 1987 (CBC–PDV). Nine winter records over four years (seasons) since 2009, but very little coverage: 8 on Feb 6, 2009 (LS), 8 on Jan 25, 2013 (DH), 2 on Jan 26, 2013 (DH), 5 on Jan 27, 2013 (DH), 1 on Dec 31, 2013 (DOWTS–LKB), 2 on Jan 16, 2014, (DOWTS–LKB), 8 on Feb 3, 2014 (DOWTS–LKB), 2 on Feb 26, 2014 (DOWTS–LKB), 1 on Feb 24, 2022 (JCh). Ten-Year: SP-2, SU-10, F-7, W-2.

- CBC: 19 years (72%) plus two count weeks, first on Dec 22, 1979, max 745 on Jan 1, 1992, avg 106.9.
- DOWTS Surveys 2011–2014: 18 over nine days (15%), Nov 9–May 2, max 4 on Dec 31, 2013; 1 on Dec 31, 2013, 8 on Feb 3, 2014 & 1 on Feb 26, 2014 reported in the northern end of the Test Quadrant are also included here (1 on May 28, 2013, 3 on Dec 31, 2013, 1 on Feb 3, 2014 & 2 on Apr 12, 2014 were observed near or at the southern end of the Test Quadrant and not included here).

Population has increased since protection in the early 1900s, dramatically so in the last twenty years (Lavers et al., 2020); inception of breeding in Maine (1950s) and increase in nearby New Brunswick and Nova Scotia. Movements generally not well known; those in late fall–early spring are possibly instigated/affected by harsh weather. Certainly underreported during peak regional migration (Mar–Apr & Nov–Dec) due to lack of coverage, likewise winter period (mid Jan–end Feb); note records provided by DOWTS surveys. Early summer (May) sightings are likely related to the nearest breeding colony at Matinicus Rock (only Maine breeding site until 1970s [Korschgen, 1979]) and overlooked June–Aug; the max count of 40 on May 31, 2011 (DH) is exceptional and intriguing. Often encountered as flybys, especially at Lobster Cove, but other reports from points all around the island, including Pulpit Rock, White Head, Burnt Head and DOWTS surveys; also noted on the water at Lobster Cove and even in the harbor on one occasion. Multiple checklists including ferry crossing excluded due to indication of inds. away from Monhegan or lack of precise location.

Historical/Regional:

- Vickery: rare prior to 1990 in May–early Jun in SE Maine and since 2000 1–5 observed regularly off Monhegan, presumably non-breeding (cites 5 on May 21, 2000 (LBr, DLa); cites six records of singles off Monhegan during Sep as more recent fall records; discusses CBC results as indicative of winter increase since 1980 (PDV in Vickery et al., 2020).

Razorbill, May 24, 2019. © Scott Surner.

BLACK GUILLEMOT
Cepphus grylle

Status: Fairly common to common permanent resident.

Occurrence: Steady presence throughout the year, highest numbers in spring; year maxima: **276** on May 15, 2021 (JT, LS, JO), 179 on May 15, 2022 (LS, MWa), 174 on May 16, 2021 (JT, LS, JO), 120 on Jul 7, 2022 (LS, MWa), 115 on May 14, 2022 (LS, MWa), 110 on May 20, 2021 (JT, LS), 96 on May 17, 2022 (LS, MWa), 90 on May 28, 2012 (RL), 85 on May 8, 2022 (LS, MWa), 80 on May 16, 2010 (EH), 78 on May 28, 2014 (JT). Ten-Year: 10.

- *MABB*: confirmed; MBA: confirmed.
- CWC: Inner Duck Rock–12 pairs, Eastern Duck Rock–6 pairs.
- CBC: 25 years (96%; all but 1941), max 58 on Dec 28, 1978, avg 24.3.
- 1900–1908 Reconnaissance & Supplements: included in Jenney supplement as Guillemot – Sea Pigeon.
- 1915–1919 Taylor Journals: 1 on Sep 6, 1916.
- 1918 Fall Migration Census: Dewis–1 on Sep 10.
- 1944–1967 Farrell Records: 1951–May; 1954–Jun, Jul; 1955–Jun, Aug; 1958–Sep; 1959–Jun, Jul, Aug; 1960–Jul, Aug.
- 1954 & 1955 Summer Records: 1954–included Jun 27–Jul 4 & Jul 10–16; 1955–Aug 24 (1), 25 (2).
- 1970 Summer Checklist: highlighted and marked as known to breed in area.
- DOWTS Surveys 2011–2014: 5 over four days (6.7%), Apr 21–May 6 & Nov 16–Dec 7, max 2 on Apr 21, 2013.

After decimation due to hunting in late 1800s, the population steadily increased through at least the 1970s (Korschgen, 1979); note max counts are all of recent occurrence. Currently, generally distributed around Maine's islands and coastline resulting in inclusion on many checklists from ferries while crossing (excluded when known as such) and a high number of eBird records of unreported number. Often observed singly or in small, scattered groups, large gatherings in spring undoubtedly tied to commencement of breeding in May. 2021 & 2022 were exceptional for numbers around Manana, including the seven highest max counts; of the total of 276 on May 15, 2021 (observed on both ends of Manana), 178 were on the north end, as were 70+ of the 115 reported on May 14, 2022. Noted as flying into holes between the rocks on Manana as early as May 18, 2014 (JGi), carrying food into the rocks near Pulpit Rock on Jul 9, 2017 (DH), first juvenile of year in the harbor on Aug 11, 2010 (TMag) and still on Manana as late as Aug 16, 2015 (PBm). Confirmed breeding for the MBA with adults carrying food on Jul 2, 2021 (towards Nigh Duck–DH) and Jul 19, 2021 (MC). Probable close on the water anywhere around Monhegan, including in the harbor, and around any of the nearby islands/ledges; in addition to the max counts in May 2021, large gatherings also noted several other times on the north end of Manana, including a group of 60+ on Apr 19, 2012 (part of a day with 75–DH) and 34 on May 7, 2017 (DH); the 120 on Jul 7, 2022 were noted as mostly around "Manana and rocks" (LS, MWa).

Historical/Regional:

- Vickery: included Monhegan in Midcoast grouping of islands with CBCs that average 22–31 Black Guillemots per count (PDV in Vickery et al., 2020).

Black Guillemot, May 21, 2021. © Bill Thompson.

ATLANTIC PUFFIN
Fratercula arctica

Status: Rare fall migrant, rare to scarce (*presumably uncommon to fairly common*) summer and rare winter visitor.

Occurrence: Summer presence undoubtedly underreported, dates span May 14–Aug 14; summer max: **28** on Jul 7, 2022 (LS, MWa), 26 on Jul 19, 2019 (JT), 22 on Jul 15, 2010 (TMag), 16 on Jul 14, 2010 (TMag). Thirteen fall records over twelve years since 2002, dates span Sep 19–Nov 13; fall max: 3 on Oct 6, 2018 (JJ), 2 on Oct 9, 2015 (JT, JO). Eleven winter records over nine years since 1978, all but four associated with CBC period, span Dec 7–Jan 4; winter max: 6 on Dec 31, 2013 (DOWTS–LKB), 3 on Dec 29, 1981 (CBC–PDV), 2 on Dec 27, 1987 (CBC–PDV) & Feb 3, 2014 (DOWTS–LKB). Ten-Year: SU-9, F-7, W-2.

- CBC: 4 years (15%) plus three count weeks, first on Dec 28, 1978, max 3 on Dec 29, 1981, avg 0.3.
- 1970 Summer Checklist: included as Common Puffin.
- DOWTS Surveys 2011–2014: 20 over twelve days (20%), May 14–Aug 6 & Dec 7–31, max 6 on Dec 31, 2013; 1 on May 14, 2013 & 2 on Feb 3, 2014 reported in the northern end of the Test Quadrant are also included here.

At the southern limit of its breeding range and eliminated from Maine islands in the late 1800s by the market hunting, Atlantic Puffin has rebounded since the early 1900s, when the only breeding site was Matinicus Rock. It wasn't until the restoration efforts of Project Puffin, started in 1973 at Eastern Egg Rock, that other breeding colonies became successful; there are now five Maine colonies and over 1,000 pairs. The colony at Eastern Egg Rock, the closest to Monhegan at only 7.5 miles and now with 150 pairs (National Audubon Society, 2021a), is a probable source of many of the summer sightings as adults disperse to forage; puffins may travel up to 70 miles to feed (Wynne-Edwards, 1935: 336), so even the colony at Matinicus Rock (23.3 miles) is easily within range on a daily basis. Despite limited numbers, it is undoubtedly overlooked as a spring migrant (Mar–early May) and underreported in summer (especially) and fall (late Aug–Nov) due to lack of coverage and its offshore distribution requiring dedicated seawatching. There was a high number of summer records, including some max counts, in 2010 and 2011 when there were consistent reports by TMag. A possible status on the MBA was submitted with reports of 4 off Lobster Cove and 4 off the northern half of the island on Jul 19, 2021 (HIAC et al.), but these were most likely visitors from nearby colonies. With this species' movements, it's not surprising that many checklists from ferry crossings have stated sightings as such, resulting in exclusion, along with those where a location isn't given. Often reported as flybys past Lobster Cove, such as most of the max count of 28 on Jul 7, 2022 (including some on the water) and the 26 on Jul 19, 2019 in early morning (JT), but possible from anywhere on the shoreline (note DOWTS surveys); 1 was noted as close to shore off Black Head during Jul 1–2, 2019 (DL).

Historical/Regional:

- Vickery: cites 2 on Oct 9, 2015 (JT, JO) as south of breeding grounds by Oct–early Nov; 1–3 recorded on 33% of CBCs (PDV in Vickery et al., 2020).

BLACK-LEGGED KITTIWAKE
Rissa tridactyla

Status: Rare spring and scarce to fairly common irregular (*presumably regular*) fall migrant, common to abundant irregular (*presumably regular*) winter visitor.

Occurrence: Eleven spring records over eight years since 1983, span Apr 8–May 30, underreported in Mar and Apr; spring max: 10 on Apr 8, 2011 (TMag), 5 on Apr 14, 2011 (TMag), 3 on May 27, 1990 (JVW). Fall migration spans Aug 3–mid Dec, peak late Nov–mid Dec, numbers building towards winter levels, but underreported throughout late fall; fall max: 212 on Nov 12, 2022 (LS, MWa), 147 on Nov 11, 2020 (JT, LS), 81 on Nov 10, 2022 (LS, MWa), 52 on Dec 4, 2010 (TMag). Winter presence through end of Feb, peak late Dec–early Jan (supported by CBC period reports), underreported throughout rest of season; winter max: **858** on Dec 27, 1982 (CBC–PDV), 750 on Dec 22, 1988 (CBC–PDV), 459 on Jan 4, 2007 (CBC). Ten-Year: SP-3, F-6, W-4.

- CBC: 24 years (92%), first on Dec 29, 1978, max of 858 on Dec 27, 1982, avg 122.1.
- DOWTS Surveys 2011–2014: 7 over five days (8.3%), Nov 9–Feb 3, max 2 on Nov 9, 2011 & Nov 21, 2013; 1 on Jan 16, 2014 reported in northern end of Test Quadrant included here (4 in southern end on same day not included).

Many aspects of migration and winter movements remain unclear, including nomadic movements to pelagic feeding areas (Hatch et al., 2020). Monhegan status also uncertain due to high variability in daily numbers, lack of coverage during some prime periods, and lack of clarity in separating migrants/visitors in late fall/early spring; undoubtedly more common and regular than current records show. Many eBird records that included a ferry crossing and the likelihood of inds. seen away from the island have been excluded. Likely to be seen from any vantage offering a view of surrounding waters, particularly Lobster Cove and the eastern headlands; all 212 on Nov 12, 2022 were noted as heading southeast past the southern end of Manana. Although inds. easily identified as adult or immature, few details have been provided; the 147 on Nov 11, 2020, consisted almost entirely of adults (4–5 juv.) in a steady southbound movement (JT, LS).

IVORY GULL
Pagophila eburnea

Status: Accidental spring and winter vagrant.

Occurrence: Two records (1 spring, 1 winter) since first recorded in 1975. Spring record: 1 in May 1975 (TMar personal notes). Winter record: immature on Dec 30, 1986–Mar 4, 1987 (CDD [ph.], PDV, DF, mob). The 1986–87 record accepted by ME-BRC #1986–002, while the 1975 record is not listed.

- CBC: 1 year (4%), 1 on Jan 1, 1987, avg 0.0.

No details available for the 1975 record. The 1987 record was possibly seen on Dec 29, present daily Dec 30–Jan 4 and also reported on Jan 9, 21 & 26 and Feb 4, last reported by various observers on Mar 4 (*G* 16[2]: 14); noted moving from the harbor as far north as Pebble Beach and over to the west side of Manana.

A report of an immature on the Duck Rocks on May 14, 1997 (listed as May 13 in FN) was not accepted by the ME-RBC due to questionable identification (possibly an Iceland Gull), but was also recorded in TMar's personal notes without details and may have been the same ind. that spent the winter near Portland, last seen Mar 13 (*FN* 51[4]: 846).

A "new gull" present during the winter of 1933–34, "pure white about the size of a dove" might have been this species. Observed by MJT and several times by her father as he returned from lobstering, later correspondence indicated an identification as Ross's Gull, for which there are no records for Maine (MJT personal correspondence; information accessed through the archives of the Monhegan Historical and Cultural Museum Association).

Historical/Regional:

- Vickery: cites May 1997 as spring record and 1986/87 record as long-staying (PDV in Vickery et al., 2020).
- OLMB: eighteen additional state records—five accepted and thirteen not yet reviewed, earliest in 1880.

Ivory Gull, Dec 31, 1986. © Charles Duncan.

BONAPARTE'S GULL
Chroicocephalus philadelphia

Status: Rare spring and scarce fall migrant, very rare winter visitor.

Occurrence: Sixteen spring records over eleven years since 1985, span Apr 6–May 31; spring maxima: 4 on May 26, 1995 (SS), 2 on May 29, 2004 (JVW) & May 20, 2022 (LS, MWa), 1 or undetermined number all other records except a trip report of 6 during May 30–31, 2003 (HN). Extended fall dates span Jul 18–late Dec (possibly later, depending on freeze-up), peak late Sep–mid Dec; fall maxima: **40** on Dec 5, 2010 (TMag), 8 on Nov 7, 2010 (TMag) & Sep 27, 2014 (JBe), 6 on Sep 24, 2002 (JT) & Oct 2, 2009 (BC). Three winter records: 1 on Jan 4, 2010 (WJS), 1 on Jan 3, 2008 (CBC), 1 on Jan 25 & 26, 2013 (DH). Ten-Year: SP-5, F-10.

- CBC: 2 years (8%), 3 on Dec 21, 1989 & 1 on Jan 1, 2008, avg 0.2.
- 1944–1967 Farrell Records: 1955–Aug.
- DOWTS Surveys 2011–2014: 5 on three days (5%), Aug 25–Dec 7, max 3 on Nov 21, 2013; 2 on Nov 16, 2013 reported in northern end of Test Quadrant and included here.

Underreported in spring (pre-May) and late fall/early winter due to lack of observers, making status unclear or speculative. Many reports including ferry crossings excluded due to likelihood of sightings away from the island. Reports from late July considered early migrants, but summer visitors somewhat regular closer to mainland and possible. Migration period variable in late fall/early winter due to influence of harsh weather, blurring migrant versus visitor status at that time (Dec 31 migrant cutoff for these purposes). Few details available but reported several times as flybys; likely possible from any water view vantage, particularly Lobster Cove, the eastern headlands, and the harbor. The only noted lingering bird was the winter record Jan 25–26, 2013, a first-winter bird first noted off Fish Beach with Ring-billed Gulls and then from White Head the next day flying around the island (DH). A flock of 80 small gulls, presumed to be Bonaparte's, were observed flying past Lobster Cove on Sep 23, 2013 (FM).

BLACK-HEADED GULL
Chroicocephalus ridibundus

Status: Accidental fall migrant and very rare winter visitor.

Occurrence: Four records (1 fall, 3 winter) since first recorded in 1979. Fall record: adult on Oct 31, 2010 (MI). Winter records: first-winter on Dec 22, 1979 (CBC–PDV), **2** adults on Dec 21, 1989 (CBC–PDV), first-winter on Jan 5–6, 2016 (CBC–DH et al.). Ten-Year: W-1.

- CBC: two years (8%), 1 on Dec 22, 1979 & 2 on Dec 21, 1989, avg 0.1.

A casual visitor along the coast that is a rather recent addition to Maine's avifauna. The two separate inds. in 1989 were located in the harbor and offshore. The Oct 2010 ind. flew south close to the shoreline at Lobster Cove. The Jan 2016 ind. was foraging near the Fish Beach breakwater on Jan 5 and was in the harbor on the 6th.

Black-headed Gull, Jan 6, 2016. © Fyn Kynd.

LITTLE GULL
Hydrocoloeus minutus

Status: Accidental fall migrant.

Occurrence: One record: **2** on Sep 30, 2005 (JT).

Observed flying south past Nigh Duck and behind (west of) Manana.

LAUGHING GULL
Leucophaeus atricilla

Status: Uncommon to fairly common spring and fall migrant, uncommon to fairly common summer visitor.

Occurrence: An early migrant, spring dates span Apr 12–late May, when distinction between migrants and summer visitors is unclear, probably underreported in Apr/early May; spring max: **50** on May 29, 1989 (JVW), 30 on May 20, 2012 (NH), 24 on May 12, 2012 (RS). Scattered reports throughout summer period (May 21–Aug 10) with numbers possibly supplemented by post-fledging dispersal in late Jul–Aug; summer max: 45 on May 23, 2022 (JT, LS, MWa) & Jul 7, 2022 (LS, MWa), 42 on May 27, 2016 (JT, JO), 32 on May 29, 2014 (JT) & Jun 3, 2020 (JT, LS), 30 on

Jul 16, 2003 (JA) & May 28, 2019 (LS). Fall migration spans mid Aug–Oct 22, peak the last part of Aug–mid Sep; fall max: 48 on Aug 15, 2022 (LS, MWa), 45 on Aug 14, 2015 (DC), 42 on Sep 9, 2022 (MCo, RH, BMc), 40 on Sep 15, 2017 (ASt, CS), 35 on Aug 21, 2010 (TMag). Ten-Year: SP-9, SU-10, F-10.

- 1914 & 1916 Checklists: included 1916.
- 1915–1919 Taylor Journals: 1918–unknown date (prior to Aug 4).
- 1939 Summer Census: regular summer visitor.
- 1944–1967 Farrell Records: 1952–Aug; 1955–Aug; 1959–Aug.
- 1954 & 1955 Summer Records: 1955–Aug 26 (1), 28 (1), both in "spring" plumage.
- 1970 Summer Checklist: included.
- DOWTS Surveys 2011–2014: 56 over twenty days (33.7%), Apr 12–Aug 25, max 17 on Jun 16, 2013.

As a species increasing in number over the past fifty years and breeding again in Maine (Burger, 2020), it is no surprise that all of the max counts have occurred since 2003. The migration picture is complicated by overlapping periods with non-breeding summer visitors and northward dispersal after breeding as early as late Jul through Aug; poor understanding due to insufficient coverage in spring and summer, excepting May. Most often seen in the harbor, often perched on the rocks adjacent to Wharton Ave. (including the fall max count of 45) or on Smutty Nose, or on any of the other surrounding islands and ledges of Monhegan, particularly Lobster Cove. Appears occasionally at the Ice Pond and small flocks have been noted flying and calling over the Meadow. Probable anywhere between Monhegan and the mainland; many checklists that included ferry rides have been excluded. Almost all records providing identification to age have occurred in the fall, with 14 juveniles, 8 immatures, and 6 adults noted; 2 adults in summer are the only other inds. identified.

RING-BILLED GULL
Larus delawarensis

Status: Scarce to uncommon spring and uncommon fall migrant, very rare summer and rare to scarce (*presumably uncommon*) winter visitor.

Occurrence: Spring dates span Apr 5–early Jun, underreported in Apr and early May; spring max: 7 on May 14, 2010 (DH, MLe), 6 on May 22, 2013 (SK, JZ), 5 on May 24, 2018 (JH) & May 24, 2019 (PBe). Five summer records: unreported number during Jun 19–25, 1954 (AS, ES), unreported number during Jun 27–Jul 4, 1954 (FNR, MFNR), unreported number during Jun 30–Jul 5, 1955 (MA, MSA), 2 on Jun 21, 2011 (TMag), unreported number on Jun 21, 2013 (JKe), 1 on Jul 3, 2021 (DH). Fall migrants span early Aug–mid/late Dec, peak late Oct–mid Nov; fall max: **10** on Nov 12, 2011 (DH, PM), 8 on Sep 28, 2002 (JT), Oct 30, 2010 (MI, LS, JT), Oct 31, 2010 (MI, LS, JT) & Nov 11, 2018 (DH, FK), 6 on Sep 26, 1981 (PDV), Sep 25, 1993 (PDV), Oct 2, 2003 (JT), Sep 21, 2006 (CE), Sep 27, 2010 (EH), Oct 31, 2010 (TMag), Sep 23, 2013 (DH, PM) & Sep 26, 2013 (SM). Twenty-four +/- winter records over nineteen years since 1982, most associated with CBC period (only two records in late Jan and two in Feb, certainly underreported through winter); winter max: 8 on Jan 5, 2012 (CBC–DH, PM), 6 on Jan 5, 2010 (PDV), & Jan 25, 2013 (DH), 5 on Jan 3, 1986 (CBC). Ten-Year: SP-10, SU-2, F-10, W-4.

- CBC: 16 years (62%), first on Dec 27, 1982, max 8 on Jan 5, 2012, avg 1.6.
- 1918 Fall Migration Census: Dewis–1 young on Sep 10.
- 1954 & 1955 Summer Records: 1954–included Jun 19–25 & Jun 27–Jul 4; 1955–included Jun 30–Jul 5.
- 1970 Summer Checklist: included.

Another waterbird species for which a number of reports have been excluded due to checklists including a ferry crossing, making location uncertain; underreported in early spring and late fall into winter when coverage is lacking. Variable numbers on consecutive day reports make lingering information unclear and obscure clarity with respect to number of records. Often found around the harbor, notably the beaches and rocks adjacent to Wharton Ave., also reported from Lobster Cove and the Ice Pond. The high count of 8 on Oct 31, 2010 included at least 3 migrants flying south offshore (MI, JT, LS). The handful of reports including age information indicate a mix of immature and adult birds; a group of 4 on Fish Beach on Sep 23, 2013 were all juveniles (FM).

Ring-billed Gull, Sep 23, 2013. © Bill Thompson.

HERRING GULL
Larus argentatus

Status: Common to abundant permanent resident, common to abundant spring and abundant fall migrant, abundant winter visitor.

Occurrence: Possibly the most obvious and omnipresent species on/around the island. Noticeably present throughout the year along the shoreline, adjacent islands, and anywhere in the air or on the water; highest numbers in fall and lowest in late winter and summer, but understanding incomplete due to inconsistent reporting or undocumented numbers and lack of clarity between shifting populations (see below). Winter visitors depart through Mar and Apr into early May at least; spring max: 300 on Apr 19, 2012 (DH, PMo), 200 on Feb 20, 1987 (JVW), 160 on May 5, 2017 (DH), 120 on Apr 4, 2012 (DH) & Apr 8, 2013 (DH). Breeding occurs on cliffs/rocks on the east side of Monhegan, Eastern Duck Rock and Nigh Duck, with adults on eggs by late May; summer max: 650 on May 24, 2022 (JT, LS, MWa), 350 on Jul 19, 2021 (MCu), 300 on May 25, 1986 (JVW), May 24, 1987 (JVW) & May 29, 2004 (JVW), 269 on Jul 20, 2019 (JT), 250 on May 19, 2015 (BBa) & May 20, 2021 (JP). Post breeding dispersal/gathering through Aug and into Sep, peak migration mid Sep–mid Oct, continuing through Dec; fall max: **1,000** on Sep 21, 2007 (LS), 950 on Oct 11, 2010 (JT), 910 on Oct 9, 2010 (JT) & Oct 10, 2010 (JT), 700 on Sep 23, 2014 (BBa). Winter population arriving/continuing by early Jan, with coverage mostly centered around the CBC period, undoubtedly underreported after early Jan; winter max: 379 on Jan 1, 1992 (CBC–PDV), 275 on Jan 4, 2007 (CBC), 201 on Jan 3, 1986 (CBC–PDV). Ten-Year: SP-10, SU-10, F-10, W-7.

- *MABB*: confirmed; MBA: confirmed.
- CWC: Eastern Duck Rock–45 pairs, Inner Duck Rock (Nigh Duck)–16 pairs.
- CBC: 26 years (100%), peak 379 on Jan 1, 1992, avg 193.0.
- 1899 Checklist: included as American Herring Gull.
- 1900–1908 Reconnaissance & Supplements: constantly in small gatherings along shores, max of 16 adult and 2 immature on Jun 3, 1908, not breeding on the island (FA); unreported number during Jul 31–Aug 2, 1908 (WM).
- 1909 Notes: very abundant about the island; all but one were adults.
- 1914 & 1916 Checklists: included 1916.
- 1915–1919 Taylor Journals: 1915–Aug 9, 11, 28, 31, Sep 1, 5, 12; 1916–recorded all but one day (Sep 2); 1917–Jul 29, Aug 4, 16, Sep 5, 8; 1918–recorded before Aug 4 & Aug 28; 1919–recorded each day.
- 1918 Fall Migration Census: Dewis–large flocks daily (many each day). Wentworth–common.
- 1939 Summer Census: regular summer resident.
- 1944–1967 Farrell Records: 1948–Dec; 1949–Feb, Mar, Apr, May, Sep, Dec; 1950–Oct; 1952–Oct; 1954–Jun, Jul; 1955–Jun, Jul, Aug; 1957–Aug; 1958–Aug, Sep, Oct; 1959–Apr, May, Jun, Jul, Aug, Sep; 1960–Apr, May, Jun, Jul, Aug, Sep; 1961–Apr, May
- 1954 & 1955 Summer Records: 1954–included all three checklists; 1955–included all three checklists, noted as abundant Aug 22–Sep 2.
- 1970 Summer Checklist: highlighted and marked as known to breed in area.
- Banding: 492 total over four seasons, peak 297 in 1965, max 246 on June 29, 1965.
- DOWTS Surveys 2011–2014: 670 over sixty days (100%), year-long, max 52 on Aug 25, 2013.

Understanding its level of presence is complicated by seasonal underreporting (especially Jan–Apr after CBC), inclusion of birds on checklists seen from the ferries while crossing (excluded when known to be such), an extremely high number of eBird records marked X (over 25%!), or when overlooked due to its commonness or constantly shifting locations. If a concerted effort were made to establish its numbers, it is likely there would be much higher totals throughout the year. The large percentage of max counts being recent may actually reflect an increased effort to document numbers of all birds seen for eBird checklists, rather than an increase in population/presence. Also unclear what portion of summer residents leave the island, with dispersal starting shortly after breeding/fledging, and are replaced by northern visitors in winter. Undoubtedly present every winter, the Ten-Year count of only seven is a reflection of the lack of any coverage some years. The simple fact is that Herring Gulls are probably visible from anywhere on or around the island. Resting/roosting birds are commonplace on the rocky shores everywhere and notable on the surrounding islands, with large numbers often on the rocks adjacent to Wharton Ave., Gull Cove, Manana, Smutty Nose, Nigh Duck, and the Duck Rocks. Movements of birds from offshore or nearby feeding areas to roost sites around the harbor at dusk result in birds continuously streaming by. Frequently seen coming and going from the Ice Pond and bathing/preening while there. Groups often observed riding updrafts/kiting off the south end of Manana.

Nesting begins in May on the ledges of the eastern headlands, most obvious below White Head, and the nearby islands. Copulating birds and adults on nests (lined with grass) with eggs often reported by the last week in May (as early as May 19) and continuing at least into mid Jul, with three broods possible (Korschgen, 1979). The largest of the few reports of nests involved "dozens" of incubating Herring Gulls below White Head on May 19, 2015 (KP), 27 nests along the Cliff Trail between White Head and Black Head on Jun 16, 2018 (BEv, TEv) and 20+ near White Head on May 29, 2017 (LB), in addition to the CWC census below (no census has been performed since), and likely scattered throughout the cliffs. Additional report of nests on nearby islands involved two nests on Nigh Duck on Jun 18, 2018 (BEv, TEv) and occupied nests on Nigh Duck and Eastern Duck Rock on Jun 1, 2019 (MASS), but likely overlooked. Fledglings reported as early as Jun 16 and as late as Jul 19. Little effort has been made to characterize age distribution; notable reports include almost all adults for 100 inds. on Apr 6, 2013, 90% adults of 220 on May 27, 2015 (JT) and mostly immatures in a group of at least 50 following lobster boats—a common occurrence—on Oct 6, 2016 (RT).

Herring Gull with chicks, White Head, Jun 23, 2019. © Cory Elowe.

A recurring unique ind. with two green wing-tags marked 195 was reported over the course of at least seven years. Tagged at Revere Beach, MA on Mar 15, 2013 as part of a Mass Dept. of Conservation and Recreation gull study, first reported on Monhegan at Burnt Head on Apr 5–6, 2013 (DH). A distant bird reported with blue wing-tags on May 17, 2013 was probably this ind. Later reports include May 28, 2013 (DL, JL), Jun 14, 2013 in the harbor (DH), May 18, 2014 (DH), May 23, 2014 (BBa), Oct 3, 2014 (DH), May 22, 2015 (PMo, LE–tag number not noted), Sep 23, 2017 (LB), Sep 30, 2017 (KM), May 27, 2018 (MW), May 29, 2018 in harbor (DH), Oct 1, 2018 (DH) and June 11, 2019 (DH).

There are several other notable banding records/recoveries. One of the 19 chicks banded (#703367) by Dr. Olin Pettingill, Jr. at Duck Rock on Jun 29, 1930 was found dead at Long Pond, Plymouth, MA on Apr 25, 1940 (Cooke, M. T., 1942). A bird banded on Kent Island, New Brunswick, Canada on Aug 20, 1942 was found dead on Monhegan on Jul 25, 1948 (Paynter, Jr., R. A., 1949). One of the strangest banding-related events actually involved a bird never present at Monhegan. At one time the longevity record was thought to belong to a Herring Gull banded on Monhegan; another one of the 19 chicks banded by Dr. Pettingill, Jr. on Jun 29, 1930 (mentioned above) was apparently found dead on Jun 20, 1966 on the shore of Lake Michigan's Little Traverse Bay near Petoskey, MI, making the bird 36 years old and possibly the oldest known wild bird in the world at that time. This was reported as such ("an 'ancient' Herring Gull") in the newsletter of the Cornell University Lab of Ornithology, *Auk*, and *EBBA NEWS* before further examination revealed an error by the lab and an official retraction was published in 1974 (Jonkel and Pettingill). The dead gull was actually banded by Pettingill on the Beaver Islands in Lake Michigan on Jul 8, 1948—only 18 years old and many miles away!

An adult hybrid Great Black-backed x Herring Gull, also known as a Great Lakes Gull, was observed on Sep 24, 2021 (DL).

Historical/Regional:

- Vickery: cites 1,000 on Sep 21, 2007 (LS) as a high count (JVW in Vickery et al., 2020).

Herring Gull #195, Sep 30, 2017. © Kent McFarland.

ICELAND GULL
Larus glaucoides

Status: Rare spring and very rare fall migrant, rare to scarce winter visitor.

Occurrence: Sixteen spring records over eleven years since 1981 (three in 2021), span early Mar–May 31, with probability of lingering winter visitors in several instances; spring max: 3 on May 23, 1981 (JP, EP) & Mar 5, 2012 (DH), 2 on Apr 6, 2011 (TMag), Apr 9, 2011 (TMag) & Mar 6, 2012 (DH). Seven fall records over five years since 1981: immature on Sep 5–26, 1981 (PDV), adult on Sep 20, 2005 (BME, SE et al.), 1 on Nov 7, 2010 (TMag), 1 on Nov 20, 2010 (TMag), 3 on Nov 22, 2010 (TMag), juvenile on Oct 11, 2013 (MZ), juvenile/1st winter Nov 6–11, 2020 (FK, et al.). Winter records are concentrated in the CBC period and undoubtedly underreported through most of Jan and Feb; winter max: **11** on Jan 3, 2008 (CBC–PDV [*incorrectly entered as Jan 4 in eBird*]), 10 on Dec 30, 1980 (CBC–PDV), 7 on Dec 29, 1981 (CBC–PDV) & Dec 29, 1983 (CBC–PDV). Ten-Year: SP-4, F-3, W-7.

- CBC: 23 years (88%) plus 2 count weeks (only missing in 1941), first on Dec 22, 1979, max 11 on Jan 3, 2008, avg 3.0; recorded as Kumlien's Gull in 1980, 1981, 1982, 1 Thayer's Gull in 1989.
- 1944–1967 Farrell Records: "infrequent winter records"–no dates.
- 1970 Summer Checklist: included.

A species whose distribution patterns are not fully understood. Distinction between migrants/visitors confusing during late fall/early spring with status period cutoffs of Nov 30 and Feb 28/29 used for these purposes. Several checklists excluded due to inclusion of ferry crossing. Several instances of multiple-day stays, but lack of details for many records; the Sep 1981 ind. was reported on seven days over the 22 days it was noted as continuing in the harbor; an ind. first reported w/e May 19, 2006 was noted as continuing at Lobster Cove the next week and last seen at Fish Beach on May 27 (DF). One or two inds. reported on sixteen days between Mar 2 and Apr 23, 2011 (a season of consistent coverage by TMag) undoubtedly refer to lingering bird(s), and counted as two records for these purposes, but possibly more were involved and separation of inds. not possible without more information. Most likely to be found around the harbor (including the long-staying ind. in Sep 1981), sometimes feeding or roosting with other gulls, particularly Herring Gulls, on the rocks adjacent to Wharton Ave. Also seen at Lobster Cove on several occasions and Burnt Head and Pebble Beach once. An ind. was noted coming in to scraps thrown out on Apr 6, 2012 (DH). Breakdown of 59 inds. aged: 16 adult, 1 third-winter, 6 second-winter, 26 first-winter, 10 unknown immature.

At least half of the records have been identified as the expected Kumlien's subspecies (*L. g. kumlieni*), with many just noted to species level. There has been only one record of Thayer's Gull (*L. g. thayeri*— formerly species level 1973–2017): 1 first-winter on the Dec 22, 1988 CBC, along with 3 Kumlien's (PDV, *AB* 43[2]: 285); not listed on OLMB. There have been no reports of *L. g. glaucoides*.

Historical/Regional:

- Vickery: cites 1 on Sep 20, 2005 (BME) as an early fall record (JVW in Vickery et al., 2020).

Iceland Gull, May 18, 2016. © Geoff Dennis.

LESSER BLACK-BACKED GULL
Larus fuscus

Status: Very rare spring and scarce fall migrant, accidental winter visitor.

Occurrence: A recent addition to Monhegan's birds, first recorded on Sep 23, 1990 (BN et al.) and annual since 2007. Eight spring records over six years since 2015, span only May 18–Jun 2: first-summer on May 26, 2015 (JT, BN, JO), adult on May 26, 2017 (LS, CL, JT), third-year on May 25–27, 2018 (LS et al.), 1 on May 26, 2019 (JT, LS, JO), first-summer on Jun 2, 2020 (JT, LS), 1 on May 18, 2022 (LS, MWa), 2 on May 20, 2022 (JT, LS, MWa), 1 on May 23–24, 2022 (JT, LS, MWa). Fall dates span Sep 3–Nov 15, peak mid Sep–early Oct; fall max: **6** on Sep 22, 2022 (DL), 5 on Oct 2, 2003 (JT) & Oct 8, 2021 (JT), 4 on Sep 19, 2012 (JH), Sep 5, 2022 (MCo) & Sep 22, 2022 (SS). One winter record: 1 on Jan 2, 2011 (TMag). Ten-Year: SP-6, F-10.

Lesser Black-backed Gull, Sep 20, 2014. © Bill Thompson.

A European species now established in eastern North America (first Maine record in 1968, first breeding in 2006) and rapidly increasing in Greenland since first nesting in 1990, it is surprising how quickly it has become expected in fall. It has been recorded twenty-four of the thirty-three years since 1990, including each of the last fifteen; notable are the recent spring records, indicative of a developing annual migration pattern. The first record was an adult present at least Sep 23–24, 1990 in the harbor (BN, DF). Inds. known to linger for multiple days, up to four days for a specific ind. in 2004 (Sep 21–24), and probable that more are just not identified as continuing. Most often seen around the harbor area, particularly on the rocks adjacent to Wharton Ave., Smutty Nose, and Nigh Duck, and less often on the eastern side, at the Ice Pond or as a flyby at Lobster Cove; possible anywhere around the island or nearby islands. The max count of 6 in Sep 2022 were on roosting on Smutty Nose Island (5 adults, 1 juvenile). Often roosting and associating with Herring and Great Black-backed Gulls and together when more than one present. In addition to the age information for spring inds. and the fall max count noted above, fall birds of a specific age class are: 26 adult, 5 third-winter, 4 second-winter, 18 juvenile/first-winter, 1 immature.

GLAUCOUS GULL
Larus hyperboreus

Status: Very rare spring and fall migrant, rare winter visitor.

Occurrence: Twenty records (5 spring, 2 fall, 13 winter) since first recorded in 1978. Spring records over five years: second-year on May 27–29, 1994 (SS), 1 during May 15–25, 1996 (GD), second-year on May 20 (GD) & during May 23–28, 1999 (TV), 1 on May 24, 2006 (MJo), adult on April 6–7, 2013 (DH). Fall records: 1 on Sep 14, 1999 (WBo), first-winter on Sep 29, 2007 (BSc). Winter records over twelve years since Dec 1978, span Dec 22–Feb 20, ten during CBC period; winter maxima: **2** on Dec 22, 1979 (CBC–PDV) & Dec 29, 1981 (CBC–PDV). Ten-Year: SP-1, W-1.

- CBC: eight years (31%) plus two count weeks, first on Dec 28, 1978, max 2 on Dec 22, 1979 & Dec 29, 1981, avg 0.4.

The spring 2013 ind. spent its time around the harbor, including roosting with Herring Gulls, the fall 2007 ind. was a first-winter bird in the harbor, and single occurrences were noted for winter inds. in the harbor, a flyby at Lobster Cove, and a flyby at Deadman's Cove. While all three of the spring inds. lingered for multiple days (the 1999 ind. noted during two consecutive trip reports), all of the fall and winter records have been one-day events, most likely due in part to targeted CBC effort with lack of follow-up observations. Winter inds. identified to age include 4 adult, 3 immature, 1 first-winter.

Discrepancies/omissions exist with some CBC/eBird records: the Jan 3, 1986 record may actually be Jan 2 (records in eBird for both dates, but the Jan 2 record includes the ferry crossing and is excluded here), as the CBC has it for count week and not the CBC date; the Jan 4, 2015 record is missing from the CBC database as a count week record. eBird records for Jan 21, 1987 and Jan 4, 2008 are also excluded for including ferry crossings, but may have been seen at the island (particularly the 2008 record, as it was recorded on the CBC on Jan 3).

Historical/Regional:

- Vickery: cites 1 on May 29, 1994 (SS) & 1 on May 24, 2006 (MJo) records as late spring, 1 on Sep 14, 1999 (WBo) as early fall (JVW in Vickery et al., 2020).

Glaucous Gull, Jan 4, 2015. © Doug Hitchcox.

GREAT BLACK-BACKED GULL
Larus marinus

Status: Fairly common permanent resident, fairly common to common spring and common to abundant fall migrant, common to abundant winter visitor.

Occurrence: Plainly evident throughout the year, particularly along the shoreline and on adjacent islands; highest numbers in fall and lowest in early summer, but understanding incomplete due to inconsistent reporting or undocumented numbers and lack of clarity between shifting populations (see below). Winter visitors departing through Mar and Apr; spring max: 200 on May 24, 1987 (JVW), 155 on May 24, 2022 (JT, LS, MWa), 100 on May 26, 2013 (LS, KL). Breeds in small numbers, but few records/details available, with non-breeding inds. present; summer max: 78 on Jun 29, 1965 (banded), 55 on Jul 7, 2022 (LS, MWa), 50 on Jul 18, 2018 (TRo), 47 on Jul 7, 2017 (DH). Post breeding dispersal/gathering through Aug and into Sep, peak migration late Sep–mid Oct, continuing through Nov; fall max: **400** on Sep 24, 2015 (SM), 389 on Oct 8, 2021 (JT, LS), 380 on Oct 11, 2010 (JT), 345 on Sep 29, 2012 (JT, BN). Winter population arriving/continuing in Dec, with coverage mostly centered around the CBC period, underreported after early Jan; winter maxima: 305 on Dec 29, 1983 (CBC–PDV), 235 on Dec 22, 1988 (CBC–PDV), 203 on Dec 28, 1978 (CBC). Ten-Year: SP-9, SU-10, F-10, W-6.

- *MABB*: confirmed; MBA: confirmed.
- CWC: Eastern Duck Rock–37 pairs, Inner Duck Rock–9 pairs, Duck Rocks–5 pairs.
- CBC: 26 years (100%), max 305 on Dec 29, 1983, avg 70.8.
- 1900–1908 Reconnaissance & Supplements: included in Jenney supplement; unreported number during Jul 31–Aug 2 (WM). Listed as Black-backed Gull.
- 1914 & 1916 Checklists: included 1916.
- 1915–1919 Taylor Journals: 1915–Aug 17; 1916–Aug 19, 20, 21, 22, 25 (6), 30, 31, Sep 3, 4, 6, 10; 1917–Aug 4, 16 (3), Sep 5 (3), 8 (1); 1919–Sep 5 (2), 11 (5), 13 (4), 14 (3).
- 1918 Fall Migration Census: Dewis–41; Sep 4 (10), 5 (7), 7 (2), 8 (4), 9 (1), 10 (12), 11 (1), 12 (4). Wentworth–Oct 12 (noted by Jenney that it must have been overlooked other days, as it is common in fall).
- 1939 Summer Census: regular summer visitor.
- 1944–1967 Farrell Records: 1949–Mar, Apr, May; 1950–Apr; 1954–Jun, Jul; 1955–Jun, Jul, Aug; 1957–Aug; 1958–Aug, Sep; 1959–May, Jun, Jul, Aug, Sep; 1960–Apr, May, Jun, Jul, Aug, Sep; 1961–Apr, May.
- 1954 & 1955 Summer Records: 1954–included all three checklists; 1955–included all three checklists, noted as common Aug 22–Sep 2.
- 1970 Summer Checklist: highlighted and marked as known to breed in area.
- Banding: 159 total over three seasons, peak 83 in 1965, max 78 on June 29, 1965.
- DOWTS Surveys 2011–2014: 83 over twenty-nine days (48.3%), Apr 4–Nov 21, max 11 on Aug 29, 2012.

As is the case with Herring Gull, understanding Great Black-backed Gull's varying seasonal abundance is complicated by underreporting, especially Jan–Apr and summer, inclusion of birds on checklists seen from the ferries while crossing (excluded when known to be such), an extremely high number of eBird records marked X (over 30%!), or when overlooked due to its commonness or constantly shifting locations. Nearly extirpated by the millinery trade and eggers in the 1800s, it returned to Maine as a breeding bird in 1930 (see Palmer, below) and continued its population growth and range expansion through the 1990s, when the closure of many municipal landfills and the decline of marine fisheries precipitated a reduction in its numbers (Vickery et al., 2020). If a concerted effort were made to count the birds present on Monhegan, it is likely there would be higher totals throughout the year. Also, it is unclear what portion of summer residents leave the island, with dispersal starting shortly after breeding/fledging, and are replaced by northern visitors in winter. Undoubtedly present every winter, the Ten-Year count of only 6 is a reflection of the lack of any coverage some years, as is the lack of reports in Spring 2020 due to Covid. Resting/roosting birds are commonplace on the rocky shores everywhere and notably on the surrounding islands, with large numbers frequenting the rocks adjacent to Wharton Ave., Gull Cove, Manana, Smutty Nose, Nigh Duck, and the Duck Rocks. Birds move from nearby offshore feeding areas to roost sites around the harbor at dusk and are sometimes seen coming and going from the Ice Pond or bathing and preening while there. Inds. are regularly observed riding updrafts/kiting off the south end of Manana with Herring Gulls. Nesting may begin as early as late Apr, but the only records with details (in addition to the CWC census below) note three nests on Nigh Duck on Jun 16, 2011 (CDd, DDd) and occupied nests on Nigh Duck and Eastern Duck Rock on Jun 1, 2019 (MASS) and on Jun 12, 2020 (DH), a few chicks on Nigh Duck on Jul 17, 2016 (DH) and nest with young on Jun 2, 2021 (DH), and recently fledged young on Jul 3 & 4, 2018 (DH) and Jul 19, 2021 (HIAC et al.); breeding is apparently routinely overlooked.

An adult hybrid Great Black-backed x Herring Gull, also known as Great Lakes Gull, was observed on Sep 24, 2021 (DL).

Historical/Regional:

- Vickery: cites 400 on Sep 24, 2015 as a high fall count (JVW in Vickery et al., 2020).

Great Black-backed Gull, Oct 9, 2019. © Doug Hitchcox.

BRIDLED TERN
Onychoprion anaethetus

Status: Accidental summer vagrant.

Occurrence: One record: 1 on Aug 22, 1991 (THi; *AB* 46[1]: 64–photo included]. First Maine record; not yet reviewed by ME-BRC.

In the wake of Hurricane Bob, this ind. was found emaciated but alive (discovered and photographed by THi), dying shortly thereafter. It was one of a number of unexpected southern terns noted along the coast of New England in the week after the arrival of Hurricane Bob on Aug 19,1991.

Historical/Regional:

- Vickery: cites 1991 record (PDV in Vickery et al., 2020).
- OLMB: three additional state records—two accepted (June 19–July 22, 2006 at Outer Green Island, Cumberland Co. & Jul 6, 2017 at Machias Seal Island, Washington Co.) and one not yet reviewed (Jul 16, 2007 at Stratton Island, York Co.).

CASPIAN TERN
Hydroprogne caspia

Status: Very rare spring and rare fall migrant.

Occurrence: Twenty-five records (2 spring, 23 fall) since 1986. Spring records: 1 on May 21, 2011 (DL, NH), 1 on May 17, 2022 (LS, MWa). Fall records over nineteen years since 1986, span Sep 12 (possibly as early as Sep 10–trip report)–Oct 13; fall maxima: **6** on Sep 27, 2017 (JT), 4 on Sep 15, 2021 (BME, BTn), 3 on Sep 23, 2011 (WBa), 2 on twelve days. Ten-Year: SP-1, F-6.

Two records involved inds. lingering for several days; 2 inds. reported on Sep 22, 26 & Oct 2, 2004 may have been the same birds, but no confirming details provided, and an adult and begging juvenile were present Sep 26–27, 2007 (BSc, KL). Most often reported flying by Lobster Cove, sometimes patrolling back and forth, and also in the harbor and around Nigh Duck; frequently vocalizing. The May 2022 ind. was flying north past Manana. Those aged include four adults and two juveniles.

ROSEATE TERN
Sterna dougallii

Status: Very rare spring and fall migrant, very rare summer visitor.

Occurrence: Nine records (3 spring, 2 summer, 4 fall) since first recorded in 1954. Spring records: 1 on May 26, 1995 (SS), 1 on May 26, 2016 (JT, JO), 1 on May 20, 2021 (JT, LS). Summer records: 1 on Jun 23, 2017 (CCo), **3** on Jul 7, 2022 (LS, MWa). Fall records: unreported number during Jul 10–16, 1954 (EAB, MEAB), 1 on Jul 27, 2010 (TMag), 1 on Jul 18, 2019 (JT), 1–2 on Jul 25, 2022 (DL, JL). Ten-Year: SP-2, SU-2, F-2.

- 1944–1967 Farrell Records: 1954–Jul.
- 1954 & 1955 Summer Records: 1954–included Jul 10–16.

An uncommon breeder on only five coastal islands

in Maine, the closest being Eastern Egg Rock at 7.5 miles (Vickery et al., 2020). Note that all except the Jul 1954 record since 1995. The fall records (all in Jul) are considered post breeding/fledging dispersals instead of summer visitors, which can occur by mid Jul and into Aug, prior to actual southward migration. Only four records include location: the 2016 spring ind. was a flyby off Nigh Duck giving a short call, the summer 2017 ind. was also flying by Nigh Duck and the two Jul 2022 records (one summer, one fall) were observed off Lobster Cove.

COMMON TERN
Sterna hirundo

Status: Uncommon to fairly common spring and uncommon fall migrant, rare summer visitor.

Occurrence: Spring dates span May 12–early Jun, transitioning to summer visitors, peak last week of May; spring max: **50** on May 26, 1995 (SS), 44 on May 27, 2016 (JT, JO), 42 on May 25, 2018 (LS). Twenty-seven summer records over thirteen years since 1909 (1909 Notes as a single records and 1954 checklists as two, other twenty-four over ten years since 1995, with four in 2011, three in 2021, four in 2022) during Jun 11–Jul 10 summer period, certainly underreported due to lack of coverage; summer max: 41 on Jul 7, 2022 (LS, MWa), 9 on Jul 10, 2013 (DOWTS–LKB), 7 on Jul 9, 2010 (TMag) & Jul 3, 2022 (DH), 6 on Jun 28, 2017 (KC), 5 on Jul 8, 2011 (TMag) & Jul 8, 2018 (MMa). Fall migration spans post breeding/fledging dispersal underway by mid Jul–Oct 1, early peak mid Jul; fall max: 40 on Jul 19, 2021 (HIAC et al.), 35 on Jul 12, 2010 (TMag), 20 on Jul 12, 2011 (TMag), 19 on Jul 19, 2019 (JT). Ten-Year: SP-10, SU-6, F-9.

- *MABB*: confirmed.
- 1900–1908 Reconnaissance & Supplements: *Sterna sp.* listed as abundant; by calls were all Common (not able to identify by sight); not breeding (FA); unreported number during Jul 31–Aug 2, 1908 (WM).
- 1909 Notes: a few seen among the Arctic Terns.
- 1914 & 1916 Checklists: included 1916.
- 1915–1919 Taylor Journals: 1915–Aug 9 (3), 17, Sep 12 (2); 1916–Aug 19, 20, 21, 22, 25, 26, 30, 31, Sep 3, 4, 6, 10; 1917–Aug 4, 16; 1918–prior to Aug 4.
- 1939 Summer Census: regular summer visitor.
- 1944–1967 Farrell Records: 1954–Jun, Jul, Aug, Sep; 1958–Aug; 1959–Jul, Aug; 1960–Jul, Aug, Sep.
- 1954 & 1955 Summer Records: 1954–included Jun 27–Jul 4 & Jul 10–16 (tern listed on Jun 19–25 checklist, unclear which species).
- 1970 Summer Checklist: included, noted as a non-breeder that comes to feed from nearby breeding areas.
- DOWTS Surveys 2011–2014: 15 over four days (6.7%), Jun 26–Aug 6, max 5 on Aug 6, 2012 & Jul 10, 2013; 3 on Jun 26, 2013 and 4 on Jul 10, 2013 reported in northern end of Test Quadrant and included here (the 4 on Jul 10, 2013 in addition to 5 in Control Quadrant).

As a species that breeds in colonies on islands not too distant (such as Eastern Egg Rock and Metinic Island), it is undoubtedly underreported Jun–Aug due to lack of coverage, particularly when post breeding/fledging dispersal begins by mid Jul (Jul 11 used for the beginning of the fall migration period for these purposes). Confirmation for MBA of an adult carrying food and recently fledged young on Jul 19, 2021 (MCu, HIAC et al.). The early "fall" peak coincides with this dispersal. Lack of clarity for migration/summer classification, due in part to the possibility of late-arriving spring migrants and far-foraging birds/non-breeders from these nearby colonies. Generally heads south to coastal staging areas by Sep before true migration begins; a transoceanic migrant once departing the staging areas. A cluster of records from 2010 and 2011, a time of repeated reporting by TMag, illustrates a presumed higher status level; these records may involve some lingering/repeat inds., but variable numbers and/or gaps between reports. Likely to be observed during ferry crossings, the reason checklists with combined crossing/island birding excluded unless details indicate otherwise; possibility of wrongful inclusion from checklists without details where distance travelled is absent or incomplete. Few reports provide details; offshore flybys most likely, but also reported in the harbor. The majority of sightings by TMag during Jul & Aug in 2010 and 2011 occurred at Lobster Cove.

ARCTIC TERN
Sterna paradisaea

Status: Very rare spring and fall migrant, very rare summer visitor.

Occurrence: Twenty-five records (8 spring, 8 summer, 8 fall, 1 unknown date) since first recorded during 1900–1908, no doubt underreported due to lack of summer/early fall coverage. Spring records over eight years since 1987, span May 20–Jun 9; spring max: **4** on May 27, 2016 (JT, JO–four reported on eBird as May 31, 2003 is a two day total including May 30), 2 on May 21, 2012 (SBe). Summer records over six years since 1909: abundant during Jul 2–7, 1909 (CJM–unable to separate to date or quantity, so listed as one record, see below), 1 on Jun 27, 2011 (TMag), 2 on Jun 28, 2011 (TMag), 3 on Jul 2, 2011 (TMag), 2 on Jun 23, 2017 (CCo), 2 on Jul 9–10, 2018 (JK), 1 on Jul 6, 2020 (DH), 2 on Jul 7, 2022 (LS, MWa). Fall records over six years since during 1900–1908 (three in 2010), span last three weeks of Jul–Aug 12; fall max: **4** on Jul 17, 2010 (TMag) & Aug 12, 2010 (TMag), 3+ on Jul 25, 2022 (DL, JL), 2 on Jul 15, 2011 (TMag). Unknown date: unreported number during 1900–1908 (CFJ, ECJ). Ten-Year: SP-3, SU-4, F-3.

- 1900–1908 Reconnaissance & Supplements: included in Jenney supplement; unreported number during Jul 31–Aug 2, 1908, also notes a young ind. (WM).
- 1909 Notes: abundant in harbor and elsewhere, feeding on refuse from fish houses, calling.
- 1915–1919 Taylor Journals: 1915–Aug 17; 1916–Aug 30; 1917–Aug 4.
- 1939 Summer Census: regular summer visitor.
- 1970 Summer Checklist: included, noted as a non-breeder that comes to feed from nearby breeding areas.

Patterns of timing and distribution similar to Common Tern, although suffering a >40% decline since only 2008 (Vickery et al., 2020). As a species that breeds in limited numbers on islands as near as Eastern Egg Rock and Metinic Island, it is without doubt underreported Jun–Aug, particularly when post breeding/fledging dispersal begins by mid Jul (Jul 11 used for the beginning of the fall migration period for these purposes). Lack of clarity for migration or summer classification with so few records and possibility of late-arriving spring migrants and far-foraging birds or non-breeders from these nearby colonies; it is notable that there are no records Jun 10–22. A transoceanic migrant, Arctic Tern does not remain or pass along the coast for long after departure. The cluster of records from 2010 and 2011, a time of repeated reporting by Tom Magarian, illustrates a presumed higher status level; these records may involve some lingering/repeat inds. but there are gaps between reports and variable numbers. Most likely to be observed during ferry crossings, the reason checklists with combined crossing/island birding are excluded unless details indicate otherwise; possibility of wrongful inclusion from checklists without details where distance travelled is absent or incomplete. Other than the harbor location provided in the 1909 Notes, Lobster Cove is the only location noted, involving six of the seven 2010 and 2011 records and the two Jul 2022 records.

ROYAL TERN
Thalasseus maximus

Status: Accidental fall vagrant.

Occurrence: One record: 1 on Sep 27, 2009 (CDD).

Latest seasonal record for Maine. A coastal, southern species with a first state record in Sep 1960 (Vickery et al., 2020); nearest regular breeding is in Maryland.

Historical/Regional:

- Vickery: cites 2009 record as latest for state (PDV in Vickery et al., 2020).

BLACK SKIMMER
Rynchops niger

Status: Accidental spring and very rare fall vagrant.

Occurrence: Three records (1 spring, 2 fall) since 1984. Spring record: **6 or 7** on May 20, 1984 (TMar personal notes; *AB* 38[5]: 885). Fall records: 3 on Sep 24, 2010 (BN et al.), 1 on Oct 1, 2019 (JT, DL, et al.). Ten-Year: F-1.

A southern coastal species, nearest breeding is in Massachusetts; presence in Maine historically associated with hurricanes, but less so in recent decades (Vickery 2020). The May 1984 inds. were flybys. The Sep 2010 inds. were immatures on Nigh Duck. The 2019 ind. was observed flying north of Manana for some time and circling over Nigh Duck, before drifting northward out of sight.

RED-THROATED LOON
Gavia stellata

Status: Scarce to uncommon spring and fall migrant, accidental summer and very rare winter visitor.

Occurrence: Spring dates span Mar 8–Jun 5, peak late Apr–late May, but picture incomplete; spring max: 9 on May 16, 2010 (DH), 8 on Apr 29, 2011 (TMag) & May 21, 2011 (TMag), 7 on May 24, 2018 (JT), 5 on May 3, 2011 (TMag). One summer record: Jun 27–28, 2011 (TMag). Fall dates span Sep 23–mid Dec, peak late Sep–early Nov; fall max: **16** on Nov 13, 2022 (LS, MWa), 10 on Nov 10, 2022 (LS, MWa), 5 on Oct 29, 2010 (TMag), 4 on Sep 23, 2008 (JSc), Sep 27, 2010 (DH), Oct 30, 2010 (MI, LS, JT), Oct

22–23, 2011 (TMag) & Oct 13, 2014. Three winter records: unreported number during Feb 1949, 2 on Jan 5, 2012 (CBC–DH, PM), 3 on Jan 2, 2020 (CBC–DH). Ten-Year: SP-10, F-7, W-1.

- CBC: 2 years (8%) plus three count weeks (2007, 2013, 2016), first on Jan 5, 2012, max 3 on Jan 2, 2020, avg 0.2.
- 1944–1967 Farrell Records: 1949–Feb.
- 1970 Summer Checklist: included, noted as summering non-breeder, south of normal range.

It is notable that all max counts of this species occurred since 2008, with only singles reported before 2003, perhaps indicating an increase or a shift in migration pattern. This is another species that suffers from "location confusion", with many reports involving birds seen on ferry crossings, making it impossible to differentiate and include them; this is very prevalent in earlier (1980s) reports. Underreported in early spring and possibly through the winter; only winter report on CBC, with count week reports unclear as to distance from the island (possibly outside MILCA). *The eBird report of 17 on the 2010 CBC (Jan 5) appears to be in error and should have been Common Loon.* The one summer record is a consecutive day sighting, with presumed same ind., (details lacking). One ind. on May 27, 2014 reported in breeding plumage (full alternate–JT). Location data lacking, with several reports from Burnt Head, Lobster Cove, and one report from White Head.

PACIFIC LOON
Gavia pacifica

Status: Accidental spring and very rare fall migrant, very rare winter vagrant.

Occurrence: Eight records (1 spring, 3 fall, 5 winter) since 1981, all singles since 19. Spring record: adult on May 14, 2021 (JT, LS, JO). Fall records: Oct 1, 2018 (JT, RDo–accepted by ME-BRC #2018–038), adult on Oct 8, 2021 (JT, LS, MWa), Oct 9, 2022 (PDo, KL; ph.–accepted by ME-BRC #2022–035). Winter records span Dec 22–Feb. 8, four records occurring on CBC: Dec 29, 1981 (CBC–PDV), Dec 27, 1984 (CBC–CDD), Jan 3–4, 1986 (CBC–PDV, CDD et al.), Dec. 22, 1988 (CBC–PDV), Feb. 6–8, 2009 (LS). Ten-Year: SP-1, F-3.

- CBC: 4 years (15%), first on Dec 29, 1981, max 1 on all four dates, avg 0.2.

Almost annual in Maine since 1974, with first state record in 1947 (Vickery et al., 2020). May 2021 and Oct 2018 inds. in alternate (breeding) plumage; Oct 2022 ind. in basic (non-breeding) plumage. All winter records involve birds in basic plumage. Initial records (1981, 1984) occurred before split of subspecies into Pacific and Arctic Loon in 1985. Notes for the 1981 and 1988 records by PDV indicate an identification based on range with no known characters noted to separate from Arctic, but contradicted by the observation of dark upperparts extending to the waterline with no obvious flank patch (a known identification feature of Pacific Loon). Notable is the observation by PDV in 1986 (the third record) that it "may be the same ind. wintering in the area." The 1986 record was observed at Lobster Cove on count day (PDV, CDD) and resighted the next day with additional observers. The Feb. 2009 record is the only other multi-day report, observed on Feb. 6 & 8 off Lobster Cove with two Common Loons. The 1988 record was with four Common Loons. The 2018 record was observed flying west past Lobster Cove. The Oct 8, 2021 ind. was a southbound flyby. The Oct 2022 ind. was on the water off Pebble Beach. While the Oct 2018 and 2022 records were accepted and listed on the OLMB by the ME-BRC, none of the other records are listed (see below).

Historical/Regional:

- Vickery: notes as having multiple sightings (PDV in Vickery et al., 2020).
- OLMB: eleven other state records listed, but many not – ten accepted, one not yet reviewed.

Pacific Loon, May 14, 2021. © Jeremiah Trimble.

COMMON LOON
Gavia immer

Status: Fairly common spring and fall migrant, scarce summer visitor, uncommon to fairly common winter visitor.

Occurrence: Spring migration underway by late Mar–mid Jun, peaks late Apr–late May; spring max: 44 on May 27, 2016 (JT, JO), 21 on May 23, 2011 (TMag) and May 25, 2018 (LS), 20 on May 21, 2017. Summer reports of singles and doubles scattered throughout the late Jun to mid Aug period; summer max: 4 on Jul 3, 2013 (DOWTS–LKB). Fall migration/post-fledging dispersal underway by late Aug, peaks late Sep–early Nov, with migrants transitioning to winter visitors early Dec; fall max: **266** on Nov 13, 2022 (LS, MWa), 124 on Oct 8, 2021 (JT, LS, MWa), 53 on Oct 9, 2021 (JT, LS), 45 on Sep 29, 2005 (JT), 42 on Oct 3, 2017 (JT). Winter population arriving by mid Dec., with coverage mostly centered around the CBC period and providing the highest counts; winter max: 43 on Dec 27, 1984 (CBC–PDV), 28 on Dec 27, 1994 (CBC) and Dec 27, 2004 (PDV, CDD), 27 on Dec 22, 1979 (CBC–PDV) and Jan 3, 2013 (CBC). Ten-Year: SP-10, SU-8, F-10, W-6.

- CBC: 26 years (100%), max 27 on Jan 3, 2013, avg 15.5.
- 1900–1908 Reconnaissance & Supplements: 1 on Jun 1, 1908 (FA). Listed as Loon.
- 1914 & 1916 Checklists: included 1916.
- 1915–1919 Taylor Journals: 1 on Sep 13, 1919.
- 1918 Fall Migration Census: Wentworth–Oct 17 (heard), 24 (1 brought in), 25 (heard). Listed as Loon.
- 1944–1967 Farrell Records: 1944–Oct; 1950–Sep; 1954–Jun, Jul; 1959–May; 1960–Aug.
- 1954 & 1955 Summer Records: 1954–included Jun 27–Jul 4.
- 1970 Summer Checklist: included, noted as summering non-breeder, south of normal range.
- DOWTS Surveys 2011–2014: 36 over nineteen days (31.7%), May 2–Dec 7, max 5 on May 13, 2014.

Reports from many locations of birds on the water and in flight, with high-flying migrants occasionally noted, and many reports from Lobster Cove, the eastern cliffs, and the harbor. Often seen in small groups of 3–4 inds.; the largest single flock was 23 on Oct 22, 2011 (out of 26 reported–MI et al.). The max fall flights of 266 (at Lobster Point), 124 and 53 were composed of southbound migrants. Similar to Red-throated Loon in terms of "location confusion," with a much larger quantity of reports including ferry birds, eliminating consideration for the island. Underreported during the winter/early spring period. Limited reports as basic (non-breeding/immature) or alternate (breeding) plumage, sometimes both in a single report (in Apr and Sep), with alternate plumage noted as early as Apr 6 and as late as Sep 29. A group of 5 on Jun 13, 2013 appeared to be mostly immature birds retaining basic plumage (DH), an expected plumage for late migrating/non-breeding birds.

WILSON'S STORM-PETREL
Oceanites oceanicus

Status: Rare to uncommon (sometimes abundant) summer visitor.

Occurrence: Sixty-four records since 1900–1908 period, sixty records over eleven years since 2004 (annual 2007–2013, eleven records in 2010, twenty in 2011, nine in 2012). Irregular, with scattered reports of great variability in numbers from early summer to early fall, span Apr 25–Sep 21, peak mid Jun–mid Jul; max: **1,000** on Jun 14, 2011 (TMag), 800 on Jun 16, 2011, 530 on Jun 13, 2011 (TMag), 500 on Jun 15, 2011 (TMag), 336 on Jul 7, 2022 (MWa, LS), 300 on Jun 25, 2011 (TMag), 125 on Jul 23, 2010 (TMag). Ten-Year: SU-4.

- 1900–1908 Reconnaissance & Supplements: included in Jenney supplement as Stormy Petrel (CFJ, ECJ).
- 1915–1919 Taylor Journals: 1918–unreported number prior to Aug 4. Listed as Wilson's Petrel.
- 1939 Summer Census: regular summer visitor at sea. Listed as Wilson's Petrel.
- 1944–1967 Farrell Records: 1960–Jul.
- 1970 Summer Checklist: highlighted, noted as summer visitor that breeds in Southern Hemisphere. Listed as Wilson's Petrel.
- DOWTS Surveys 2011–2014: 197 over twelve days (20%), Jun 23–Aug 13, max 52 on Jun 26, 2012; an additional 37 over nine of the twelve days noted above were reported in the northern end of the Test Quadrant and included here (249 over thirteen days [max 114 on Jun 23, 2012] were reported in the southern end and not included here).

First known 'modern' record on Apr 25, 1981 (JP, LP) is the only one earlier than May 23. All dated records from only eleven years: 1981, 2004, annually 2007–2013, 2019–2022 (inclusion on historic checklists without specific dates). As with shearwaters, the majority of records were from 2010 (eleven spanning Jul 9–Aug 10), 2011 (twenty spanning Jun 13–Sep 10), and 2012 (nine spanning Jun 23–Sep 9), when consistent seawatching coverage was provided by TMag at Lobster Cove (including almost all the max counts) and the DOWTS surveys (2012). These efforts highlight the underreporting of this species in other years and the high daily totals possible with concerted effort. Few details provided with any records; a couple of other reports off Lobster Cove (including the 336 on Jul 7, 2022) and one off Burnt Head. Another species where inclusion with ferry crossing sightings eliminates some possible records.

LEACH'S STORM-PETREL
Oceanodroma leucorhoa

Status: Accidental spring and very rare fall migrant, very rare summer visitor.

Occurrence: Six records (1 spring, 3 summer, 2 fall) since 1915. Spring record: 1 on May 30, 2019 (MI, JT, RDo). Summer records: unreported number Aug 16–17, 1915 (WT, CFJ et al.), Jun 1954 (IF), Jul 1959 (IF). Fall records: 1 on Sep 4, 1916 (WT), 1 on Sep. 22, 2013 (FM). Ten-Year: SP-1, F-1.

- 1915–1919 Taylor Journals: 1915–Aug 16, 17; 1916–Sep 4 (1). Listed as Leach's Petrel.
- 1944–1967 Farrell Records: 1954–Jun; 1959–Jul.
- 1970 Summer Checklist: included, noted as a non-breeder that comes to feed from nearby breeding areas. Listed as Leach's Petrel.

Possibly overlooked as a spring and fall migrant, as well as a visitor in the summer, as they breed on islands to the east in Maine; its nocturnal movements during the breeding season obviously play a role. The 2019 record was a nocturnal vocalization near the harbor between 12:00–12:38 a.m. The 1915 record was observed through CFJ's 55x spotting scope and was possibly an ind. breeding at a nearby island or a dispersing non-breeder. The 2013 record was observed fairly close to shore off Lobster Cove. Four other "Monhegan" reports that include ferry crossings/incomplete information were excluded. Also included on Tom Martin's checklist, but no details given. Its inclusion on the 1970 Summer Checklist may be due to its "nearby" breeding status.

NORTHERN FULMAR
Fulmarus glacialis

Status: Accidental spring and rare fall migrant, accidental summer visitor.

Occurrence: Nineteen records (1 spring, 1 summer, 17 fall) since first recorded Sep 28, 2003. Spring record: 1 on May 25, 2018 (JT, LS). Summer record: 1 on Jul 2, 2011 (TMag). Fall records over ten years (two in 2003, four in 2017, five in 2020), span Sep 22–Nov 12; fall max: **181** on Nov 10, 2022 (LS, MWa), 49 on Oct 9, 2015 (JT, JO), 23 on Sep 30, 2020 (DH), 8 on Oct 4, 2017 (LS), Oct 8, 2020 (JT, LS) & Nov 11, 2020 (JT, LS), 6 on Nov 12, 2022 (LS, MWa). Ten-Year: SP-1, F-7.

- DOWTS Surveys 2011–2014: 1 on Sep 22, 2011 (1.7%; 1 reported on Nov 9, 2011 was in the southern end of the Test Quadrant and not included here).

The spring record was a light morph flying north. The 49 inds. recorded on Oct 9, 2015 consisted mostly of dark morph inds. (90%) moving south (majority seen north of Manana). The 23 inds. on Sep 30, 2020 occurred as part of a "massive tubenose flight" (mostly Great Shearwaters) just after the passage of a major storm with strong south winds; it involved southbound birds on the west side of the island, with 18 light and 5 dark morph inds. observed (DH). The 181 inds. flying south on Nov 10, 2022 were mostly light morph. Three other fall records noted morph, all light birds: 1 off Bald Head on Oct 21, 2011, 1 off Lobster Cove on Oct 13, 2014 & 2 on Oct 6, 2020 (JT, LS, BBy). Fall 2017 produced records on four days during Oct 1–7. Surprisingly, compared to recent Maine sightings during winter (eBird reports), not seen on any Monhegan CBC (or even ferry crossings at that time),

CORY'S SHEARWATER
Calonectris diomedea

Status: Rare to scarce summer/fall visitor.

Occurrence: Reports of this nomadic species, first known record on Jul 18, 1979 (unknown observer; *AB* 33[6]: 845–all other records since Sep 2005), are scattered throughout the mid-summer to mid-fall period, spanning Jun 23–Nov 10, with a peak late Sep–early Oct; max: **270** on Oct 2, 2016 (JT, JO), 105 on Oct 4, 2016 (CR), 80 on Sep 30, 2020 (WR), 39 on Oct 3, 2009 (SS), 36 on Sep 23, 2016 (FM), 25 on Sep 21, 2016 (BME et al.), 20 on Sep 29, 2009 (SS), 16 on Jul, 14, 2010 (TMag). Ten-Year: SU/F-7.

- DOWTS Surveys 2011–2014: 10 over four days (6.7%), Jun 23–Aug 6 in 2012, max 3 on Jun 23, 2012, Aug 1, 2012 & Aug 6, 2012. An additional 2 on Jul 18, 2012, 1 on Jul 26, 2012 & 2 on Aug 6, 2012 were reported in the northern end of the Test Quadrant and included here (an additional 5 on Jul 18, 2012 & 1 on Aug 6, 2012 were in the southern end of the Test Quadrant and not included here).

Although only one record is known prior to 2005, Cory's Shearwaters have been present every year since 2009, except 2013, 2018 & 2021). Underreported during the Jul–early Sep period, emphasized by eleven of twelve 'summer' records (Jul & Aug) occurring in 2010 & 2011 by TMag, mostly while seawatching from Lobster Cove, and on the DOWTS in 2012 (LKB); the exception is a record of 6 on Jul 25, 2022 at Lobster Cove (DL, JL). Records concentrated in years when loose migrating/feeding flocks provide multi-day/week events with variable daily totals; most noticeable in 2009 (reported seven days over Sep 23–Oct 3), 2010 (reported nine days over Jul 9–Sep 4), 2016 (reported twenty-three days over Sep 5–Oct 8, including every day Sep 20–Oct 8, except Sep 30) and 2020 (reported fourteen days over Sep 16–Oct 10). It is impossible to determine if these were repeat sightings or different inds. that were part of a larger movement. Most often reported from Lobster Cove, but also from White Head, once from Pulpit Rock and off Manana, varying from very close to shore to >2 miles offshore. Sometimes seen in the company of Great Shearwater. The peak flight of 270 involved a "good movement plus massive beehive" of feeding Cory's Shearwaters (JT, JO). The 80 on Sep 30, 2020 were part of a large southbound movement of seabirds (mostly Great Shearwaters), observed from Lobster Cove, after a major storm that produced strong south winds. Reports from Sep 21 & 23, 2016 pertain to a group resting/feeding off White Head, including over a pod of 40 Atlantic White-sided Dolphins (FM).

Cory's Shearwaters, Sep 22, 2020. © Bill Thompson.

SOOTY SHEARWATER

Ardenna grisea

Status: Rare to scarce (sometimes uncommon) summer/fall visitor.

Occurrence: Appears irregularly with scattered reports from early summer to mid-fall, spanning May 21–Nov 16; max: **36** on Jul 14, 2010 (TMag), 25 on Jul 9, 2010 (TMag), 15 on Sep 8, 2011 (DH, NL), 12 on Jun 13, 2011 (TMag) & Jun 25, 2011 (TMag). Ten-Year: SU/F-9.

- 1970 Summer Checklist: included, noted as summer visitor that breeds in Southern Hemisphere.
- DOWTS Surveys 2011–2014: 4 over four days (6.7%), Jul 10–Nov 16, max 1 on four days; an additional 1 on Sep 27, 2011 & 1 on Jul 10, 2013 were reported in the northern end of the Test Quadrant and included here.

Scattered records from the late 1960s—first known record 2 on Sep 7, 1967 (fide RPE; *AFN* 21[1]: 8)—through mid-2000s, recorded annually since 2008 (1–2 records per year), except 2013 and 2018. All records other than the max counts are of 8 inds. or fewer. Numerous summer records from 2010 (seven days over Jul 9–Aug 3) and 2011 (eight days over May 21–Jul 11) due to persistent seawatching by Tom Magarian; as is the case with Great Shearwater, undoubtedly underreported in summer as there are no other reports from Jun–Aug. Does not appear to linger or become involved in multi-day events as do Cory's and Great Shearwaters, although an ind. in 2016 was reported in the harbor on May 26 after apparently being seen at Lobster Cove and around the island the previous week (JT et al.) and was just outside the harbor on May 30 (PW, MWo). Numerous reports of this species from Lobster Cove, including the two max flights, and one report each from White Head, inside the Duck Rocks, and flying south past Manana; has been observed alighting on the water.

Historical/Regional:

- Vickery: 1 on May 26, 2016 (PDV) as early date (CDD in Vickery et al., 2020).

GREAT SHEARWATER

Ardenna gravis

Status: Uncommon to common (sometimes abundant) summer/fall visitor.

Occurrence: Similar to Cory's Shearwater, this nomadic species appears irregularly and in highly variable numbers from early summer–late fall, spanning May 26–Nov 16, with a peak early Sep–mid Oct; max: **10,000** on Sep 25, 2002 (JT), 2,170 on Sep 30, 2020 (DH), 2,000 on Sep 28, 2002 (JT), 1,410 on Sep 18, 2011 (LS), 1,072 on Oct 7, 2014 (JT et al.), 856 on Oct 8, 2014 (JT), 800 on Sep 23, 2002 (JT). Largest "summer" total is 100 on Jun 26, 2012 (DOWTS–LKB). Ten-Year: SU/F-10.

- 1970 Summer Checklist: included, noted as summer visitor that breeds in Southern Hemisphere. Listed as Greater Shearwater.
- DOWTS Surveys 2011-2014: 252 over fifteen days (25%), Jun 23–Nov 16, max 84 on Nov 9, 2011; an additional 72 over eleven days, Jun 23–Nov 16, were reported in the northern end of the Control Quadrant and included here.

(Notable were single flocks of 115 and 30 resting on the water in approximately the same location in the southern portion of the Test Quadrant on Oct 23 & Nov 5, 2013, respectively, and not included here).

Recorded as early as 1936 (see Cruickshank below) and also noted in 1965 (TMar personal notes), near annual since 1997 (no reports 2004). As with Cory's, multi-day/week events obvious some years, with possible redundancy of inds., as flocks feed and progress through the area. Modest passage in 2005, 2009, 2010 (including late push four days over Oct 20–Nov 8), 2012, 2016; exceptional passage in 2002 (every day Sep 23–28, including 800 on Sep 23, 10,000 on Sep 25, 2,000 on Sep 28), 2011 (ten days over Jun 13–Jul 12, including a peak of 55 on Jul 12, and twenty days over Aug 29–Nov 8, with peaks of 300 on Sep 8, 1,410 on Sep 18, 100 on Sep 21, 250 on Sep 23, 175 on Sep 28, 180 on Oct 21), and 2014 (five days over Oct 5–13, peaks of 1,072 on Oct 7, 856 on Oct 8). All 'summer' reports (Jun–late Aug) are from 2010 & 2011 (when there was extensive seawatching by TMag), 2012 & 2013 (DOWTS surveys) and 2020–2022. Most often reported from Lobster Cove, including the two max counts of 10,000 and 2,000 in 2002, but also from White Head, Burnt Head and a large flight from Gull Rock (1,410 heading north on Sep 18, 2011, with 435 in the last fifteen minutes at dusk–LS); also noted on the west side flying past Manana (from lawn chairs at Tribler Cottage–SM). The high number of 2,170 on Sep 30, 2020 was observed to the west from the school grounds and was part of a "massive tubenose movement" southbound just after the passage of a major storm with strong south winds (DH); 1,000 were noted passing Lobster Cove that same day (WR). A report of over 2,000 shearwaters on Sep 29, 2006, just after rain stopped, was noted as mostly Great Shearwaters (BN, fide KL), but without a specified count is not included in the max counts above. No pattern to direction of flight (noted N, S, W to E, etc.) and varying from near shore to distant, once noted as common on the east side of the island with none on the west; large flocks have also been observed resting on the water; sometimes associating with Cory's Shearwaters.

Historical/Regional:
- Cruickshank: latest record off Monhegan on Sep 4, 1936.
- Vickery: cites 1 off island on May 26, 2012 (PHe) and 1 off island on May 30, 2015 (JZ) as early records, 10,000 on Sep 25, 2002 (JT) as well above normal (CDD in Vickery et al., 2020).

MANX SHEARWATER
Puffinus puffinus

Status: Rare to scarce summer/fall visitor.

Occurrence: Thirty-nine records since first known occurrence on Sep 29, 1997 (JT), despite inclusion on 1970 Summer Checklist. Scattered reports over fourteen years span May 26–Nov 12, with a peak in mid-late Sep; max: **7** on Jun 25, 2011 (TMag) & Sep 18, 2011 (TMag), 5 on Sep 25, 2002 (JT), 4 on Sep 29, 1997 (JT), 3 on Sep 29, 2005 (JT) & Jul 25, 2022 (DL, JL). Ten-Year: SU/F-8.

- 1970 Summer Checklist: included, noted as rare, casual, or accidental visitor.
- DOWTS Surveys 2011–2014: None reported within the Control Quadrant; 2 flybys on Aug 3, 2013 were reported at the northern end of the Test Quadrant and included here (an additional 1 on Aug 20, 2013 was in the southern end of the Test Quadrant and not included here).

Notable as breeding since 2009 on Matinicus Rock, the only colony known in the U.S. (Vickery et al., 2020). As with other shearwater species, concentration of records in summers of 2010 (six) and 2011 (seven of eight) result from the consistent seawatching of TMag from Lobster Cove, with the other Jun–Aug records 2020–2022. Five records in 2005 (four singles, one of two inds.) all occurring Sep 18–29 (possibly repeat inds.?). Usually seen as flybys, with several reports from Lobster Cove, one each from White Head, Gull Rock, and off Nigh Duck. The Jul 2018 ind. was bathing off Lobster Cove (DL, JL). Noted as being among gannets and also associating with Great Shearwaters.

Historical/Regional:
- Vickery: cites 1 on May 26, 2016 (JT) and 1 on May 27, 2017 (JT, LS, CL) as recent, 1 on Oct 1, 2016 (JT, JO) and 2 on Oct 6, 2016 (LS, JT) as late; *listing of 14 seen intermittently Jul 1–30, 2017 should be Matinicus Rock* (CDD in Vickery et al., 2020).

MAGNIFICENT FRIGATEBIRD
Fregata magnificens

Status: Accidental spring and fall vagrant.

Occurrence: Two records (1 spring, 1 fall). Spring record: female soaring off Monhegan on May 21, 1978 (PDV et al.). Fall record: adult female on Sep 26, 2003 (BSc, TMar et al.). Third and sixth known Maine records, respectively; neither yet reviewed by ME-BRC.

The 2003 ind. was observed for ten minutes at Lobster Cove; reports from Gloucester and Marblehead, MA on Sep 27 may have been the same bird; possible connection with Hurricane Isabel the previous week, but no other reports (*NAB* 58[1]: 37).

Historical/Regional:

- Vickery: cites 1978 and 2003 records (Rachel L. Prestigiacomo in Vickery et al., 2020).
- OLMB: ten additional state records—three accepted and seven not yet reviewed, earliest "about" 1871.

NORTHERN GANNET
Morus bassanus

Status: Uncommon to fairly common spring and common to abundant fall migrant, uncommon summer and very rare (*presumably scarce*) winter visitor.

Occurrence: Spring dates Apr 4–mid Jun, peak late Apr–late May; spring max: 114 on Apr 29, 2011 (TMag), 75 on May 30, 2013 (RL, ML), 73 on May 20, 2015 (DL), 68 on May 18, 2021 (JT, LS, JO), 67 on May 19, 2021 (JT, LS, JO), 34 on May 23, 2011 (TMag). Irregular in summer with scattered reports throughout; summer max: 48 on Aug 7, 2010 (TMag), 39 on Jul 15, 2010 (TMag), 34 on Aug 14, 2022 (LS, MWa), 32 on Jul 20, 2019 (JT). Extended fall migration late Aug–mid Jan, peak early Sep–mid Nov; fall max: **550** on Sep 24, 2009 (LS), 500 on Sep 8, 2011 (DH, NL), 450 on Oct 8, 2010 (PC), 400 on Sep 26, 2001 (JT), Sep 15, 2010 (BP) & Oct 12, 2010 (JT). Three winter records: 1 on Jan 27, 2013 (DH), 1 during Jan 16–17, 2018 (KL), 1 first-winter on Jan 19, 2022 (DC). Ten-Year: SP-10, SU-8, F-10, W-2.

- CBC: 16 years (62%) plus two count weeks, first recorded on Dec 28, 1978, max 87 on Jan 3, 1986, avg 11.1.
- 1900–1908 Reconnaissance & Supplements: included in Jenney supplement as Gannet.
- 1944–1967 Farrell Records: 1949–Oct; 1951–Nov; 1955–Aug; 1960–Aug.
- 1954 & 1955 Summer Records: 1955–Aug 28 (4+ off White Head).
- 1970 Summer Checklist: included, noted as summering non-breeder, south of normal range. Listed as Gannet.
- DOWTS Surveys 2011–2014: 210 over thirty-five days (58.3%), Apr 21–Nov 21, max 18 on Aug 3, 2013; an additional 46 over twenty-four days, Apr 27–Nov 16, were reported in the northern end of the Test Quadrant and included here.

Reported from all points around the island's coast, especially Lobster Cove, White Head, and Burnt Head, but even passing through the harbor. The highest totals have sometimes involved birds surrounding the island, but also a gathering of 200 at Lobster Cove and 210 afloat off the east side; the summer max counts have all occurred at Lobster Cove. Feeding frenzies, involving plunge-diving, are not uncommon and have been noted on several occasions over Harbor Porpoises and once above a Minke Whale. Irregular and shifting, with little evidence to suggest the continued presence of a certain group for any length of time. The unusual occurrence of gannets perching on the Duck Rocks has been observed on two occasions—6 adults and subadults on the westernmost rocks on Sep 19, 1997 (PDV) and up to 7 adults roosting on the Duck Rocks and Nigh Duck over the extended period of Sep 10–Oct 3, 2017 (reported five days in varying numbers, and noted on Sep 10 as having been already present for much of late summer–JVW). All ages often reported together during migration, with a general trend of adults preceding immatures in spring (adults dominate in Apr, subadults & immatures in late May–Jun); inds. lingering into Jan are almost always adults (reports from CBC count period in 2013, 2015, 2016 involved only adults, as did one of the winter records). Despite several eBird comments from the CBC count period that gannets are regular in Jan, not rare or unusual, there remain only three records of single birds for the Jan 6–Apr 3 period; this is obviously due in part to the greatly reduced coverage at this season, but overall Maine reports suggest that the remainder of the late and extended fall migration wanes by mid Jan, when the species becomes uncommon at best. As Northern Gannets are often seen in passing and not easy to count, there are many reports with an undetermined number (x). Also, observed anywhere between the outer 'mainland' islands and Monhegan, many reports include ferry crossing sightings and are excluded from this account.

Northern Gannet, Sep 25, 2019. © Brett M. Ewald.

GREAT CORMORANT
Phalacrocorax carbo

Status: Uncommon spring and fairly common fall migrant, very rare summer visitor, fairly common to common winter visitor.

Occurrence: Spring migration underway early Mar–May 31, peak late Mar–mid Apr; spring max: 18 on Apr 7, 2013 (DH), 9 on Apr 4, 2012 (DH), 8 on Mar 24, 2011 (TMag) & Apr 8, 2013 (TMag). Twelve summer records over seven years since 1960 (two records in 2012 & 2020, four in 2021); summer max: 6+ during Jun 27–29, 2005 (DL, JL), 4 on Jul 16–17, 2018 (only 2 on the 17th–DL, JL). 2 on Jul 21, 2008 (SWi), Jul 31, 2012 (MWi), Jun 5, 2021 (TF) & Jun 1, 2022 (AN). Fall migration/post-fledging dispersal evident by late Aug (earliest Aug 18), peak mid Sep–mid Nov, continuing into Dec; fall max: 45 on Sep 26, 2000 (JT) & Sep 28, 2011 (SM), 35 on Sep 28, 2000 (JT), 33 on Nov 12, 2018 (DH, FK). Winter population arriving/in place by early Dec, with coverage mostly centered around the CBC; winter max: **107** on Dec 28, 1978 (CBC–PDV et al.), 63 on Dec 27, 1984 (CBC–PDV, JVW), 58 on Dec 28, 1982 (CBC–PDV). Ten-Year: SP-10, SU-4, F-10, W-6.

- CBC: 26 years (100%), max 107 on Dec 28, 1978, avg 24.6. Listed as European Cormorant on 1941 count.
- 1918 Fall Migration Census: Wentworth–there is a listing for "Cormorant," seen eight days, that may refer to this species or Double-crested Cormorant.
- 1944–1967 Farrell Records: 1959–Aug; 1960–Apr, Jul. Listed as European Cormorant.
- 1970 Summer Census: included, noted as summering non-breeder, south of normal range.

It is interesting that the max spring and fall counts have all occurred since 2000, while the top winter counts occurred 1984 or before. Individuals encountered on ferry crossings, including a number of high eBird totals, have been excluded. Reported from many outer vantage points around the island, most notably the ledges and cliffs on the east side, especially those below White Head; also recorded on Manana, Nigh Duck, the Duck Rocks, and the outer ledges. Often seen associating with Double-crested Cormorants on the rocks, water, and in flight, usually as singles or doubles mixed with passing groups; flybys are common, particularly during migration, and are the rule at Lobster Cove. Largest flocks include a group of 22 on the water off Black Head on Oct 30, 2010 (MI et al.) and a skein of 17 passing northward on Apr 7, 2013 (DH); a total of 28 on Nov 10, 2020 involved a couple of flyby groups of 10+ (LS, JT). Both adults and immatures reported throughout the species' presence.

Great Cormorant, May 25, 2021. © Bill Thompson.

DOUBLE-CRESTED CORMORANT
Phalacrocorax auritus

Status: Common to abundant spring and abundant fall migrant, common summer resident, very rare winter visitor.

Occurrence: Opposite seasonally to Great Cormorant, spring migration underway by early Apr. (earliest Mar 14), peak late Apr–mid May, transitioning to/supplementing summer residents by the end of the month into Jun; spring max: 316 on May 17, 2022 (LS, MWa), 250 on May 15, 2017 (RM) & May 21, 2022 (WBk, JTh), 225 on May 27, 2014 (JT), 200 on May 6, 1984 (PDV) & May 12, 1988 (JVW). Adults on nests by late May on the eastern cliffs and nearby rocky islands, particularly Nigh Duck; earliest reported May 15 (45 nests already on May 24, 2015); summer max: 275 on Jul 7, 2022 (LS, MWa), 250 on Jul 19, 2021 (MCu), 232 on Jul 29, 2020 (GBr), 220 on Jul 3, 2021 (DH), 200 on Aug 1, 2012 (RMc). Fall migration/post-breeding dispersal evident by late Aug, peak early Sep–late Oct, ending by late Nov; fall max: **3,587** on Oct 8, 2021 (JT, LS, MWa), 1,500 on Sep 27, 2011 (DOWTS–LKB), 1,100 on Sep 26, 2000 (JT), 1,030 on Sep 29, 2005 (JT), 1,000 on Sep 29, 2004 (BME et al.) & Sep 30, 2019 (DL, JL). Four winter records, all focused around CBC period: 1–2 on Dec 21–22, 1979 (2 on the 22nd–CBC-PDV), 1 on Dec 28, 1982 (CBC–PDV), undetermined number during Dec 31–Jan 6, 1986 (CBC count week), 1 on Jan 5, 2010 (CBC–PDV). Ten-Year: SP-10, SU-10, F-10.

- *MABB*: confirmed; MBA: confirmed.
- CWC: Eastern Duck Rock–20 pairs.
- CBC: 3 years (12%) plus one count week, first on Dec 28, 1978, max 2 on Dec 28, 1978, avg 0.2.
- 1900–1908 Reconnaissance & Supplements: one each on May 31, Jun 3, 4, 1908 flying along shore or perched on buoy (FA); included in Jenney supplement.
- 1914 & 1916 Checklists: included 1916 as Cormorant.
- 1915–1919 Taylor Journals: 1915–Aug 10 (1), 17, 31 (1), Sep 5, 12 (3); 1916–Aug 30 (15), 31 (1), Sep 3, 4, 6 (1); 1917–Aug 4, Sep 5 (17), 8 (3); 1918–prior to Aug 4, Aug 28; 1919–Sep 4 (2), 5 (7), 11 (3), 13 (7), 14 (4).
- 1918 Fall Migration Census: Dewis–116 (Sep 4 [12], 5 [8], 7 [51], 8 [14], 9 [11], 10 [8], 11 [6], 12 [6]; Wentworth–there is a listing for "Cormorant," seen eight days, that may refer to this species or Great Cormorant.
- 1939 Summer Census: regular summer visitor.
- 1944–1967 Farrell Records: 1952–Nov; 1954–Jun, Jul; 1955–Jun, Jul, Aug; 1957–Aug; 1958–Aug, Sep; 1959–Mar, May, Jun, Jul, Aug; 1960–Apr, May, Jun, Jul, Aug, Sep; 1961–Apr.
- 1954 & 1955 Summer Records: 1954–included all three checklists; 1955–included all three checklists, noted as abundant Aug 22–Sep 2.
- 1970 Summer Checklist: highlighted and marked as known to breed in area.
- DOWTS Surveys 2011–2014: 1,567 over nine days (15%), May 2–Oct 11, max 1500 on Sep 27, 2011; an additional 67 over three days, May 14, Sep 28 & Oct 11) were observed in the northern end of the Test Quadrant and included here.

The many recent max summer counts are probably due to increased reporting/scrutiny, especially for MBA. Seeming omnipresent for much of the year at all points around the shoreline of Monhegan and on Manana and the smaller islands. During migration, Double-crested Cormorants may be visible almost anywhere, with flocks of 100+ not uncommon in the fall, the largest reported being 480 on Oct 22, 2017 (JP); the max count of 3,587 on Oct 8, 2021 involved southbound flocks (mostly in a ninety-minute dedicated watch), while the 1,500 on Sep 27, 2011 was composed of two large flocks heading SW at a height of over 50m (DOWTS–LKB). A report of 3,000 cormorant species on Oct 10, 1983, noted as flocks of 100–500 passing by, doubtless referred entirely or mostly to this species. Often perched on the rocks or ledges of the cliffs on the east side (sometimes with Great Cormorant), the rocky islands, including those in the harbor, or feeding close to shore or farther out at sea. This species is common and often seen in passing, when not easy to count; there are hundreds of reports with an unreported number (X). Also observed anywhere between the outer 'mainland' islands and Monhegan, many reports include ferry crossing sightings and are excluded from this account. Perhaps underreported in the winter due to lack of coverage, but very rare to rare nonetheless. Almost no records indicating the age of inds. Overlapping of spring migration/breeding complicates understanding of the species' status the second half of May—high counts at this time are undoubtedly a mix of the two. Nesting observed from mid May (on nests on Nigh Duck as early as May 15, 2019 [DPJ]) to at least late Jul; other reports of nests on Nigh Duck (25 on Jun 16, 2011, 40 on Jun 18, 2018, 65 nests on May 30, 2019 [MI]) and a high of 80 nests on Jun 12, 2020 (DH) and Smutty Nose (45 nests on May 24, 2011), in addition to those in the CWC census below and lower numbers nesting on the headland cliffs and rocks (several occupied stick nests on Jun 4, 2020 (DR). 138 of the 149 inds. reported on Jun 18, 2018 were on Nigh Duck (DH). Exceptionally late breeding (possibly historically late) recorded in 2019, with chicks in nests noted on the cliffs below White Head on Sep 10, 2019 (five in one nest–HM) and continuing through at least Sep 27 (seven near-fledging chicks in three nests on Sep 23 & 27–BME, CR et al.).

Historical/Regional:

- Vickery: cites 250 off island on Sep 25, 1982 (DF) as notable record and 2,000 seen from ferry between island and Port Clyde on Sep 29, 1982 (DF; Richard V. Joyce in Vickery et al., 2020).

Double-crested Cormorants - adult (right) with fledglings at nests, White Head, Sep 23, 2019. © Brett M. Ewald.

AMERICAN BITTERN
Botaurus lentiginosus

Status: Rare spring and fall migrant.

Occurrence: Forty-eight records (14 spring, 34 fall) since 1916. Spring records, all single birds (three unreported number) over ten years since 1949 (all but the three in 1949 & 1961 since 1992), span Apr 24–May 29; four separate reports in 2017 (May 7, 10, 14, 27) only spring with multiple records. Fall records over twenty-four years since 1916 (twenty-five records since 1981, involving four years with multiple records [2005–three, 2006–two, 2007–two, 2010–three] with gaps of four to twelve days between reports), span Aug 23–week of Dec 10 (latest date since 1981 is Oct 10); fall max: **5** on Oct 5, 1918 (BHW), 2 on Sep 18, 2019 (DW). Ten-Year: SP-2, F-6.

American Bittern, Sep 20, 2010. © Geoff Dennis.

- 1914 & 1916 Checklists: included 1916.
- 1915–1919 Taylor Journals: 1917–Aug 23 (1 at Ice Pond); 1919–Sep 10 (1), 14 (1).
- 1918 Fall Migration Census: Wentworth–Oct 1 (1), 5 (at least 5), 12.
- 1939 Summer Census: uncommon summer visitor.
- 1944–1967 Farrell Records: 1949–Apr; 1961–Apr, May.

It is very possible that the years with multiple records involved lingering single inds. (not unusual for wading birds), but it is impossible to be sure and the are considered separate for these purposes. Closely associated reports Sep 20–23, 2010 (no sighting the 21st) and Sep 10 & 12, 2012 (JSt) considered the same ind. Difficult to detect, most obvious when flying (four records) or flushed (two records); locations noted as the Meadow (eight reports), Ice Pond (four reports), high over Manana early in the morning (one report–JT, LS) and the grassy area NW of Lobster Cove (one report).

Historical/Regional:

- Palmer: cites latest date as "the week of Dec 10, 1939 (Mrs. J. A. Townsend).

LEAST BITTERN
Ixobrychus exilis

Status: Very rare spring migrant.

Occurrence: Two records: male on May 26–27, 2017 (JT, LS, CL, mob), 1 on May 25, 2019 (JT, LS). Ten-Year: SP-2.

Least Bittern, Meadow, May 27, 2017. © Luke Seitz.

Despite its elusive nature, it is likely to occur again on the island, as it is an uncommon spring and fall migrant and breeder in the state. The 2017 ind. was seen leaving the Meadow and returning on the 26th, flying between the houses and over Main St. On the 27th, it was twice seen in flight over the Meadow (around 10:30 a.m. and 2 p.m.–WBo), as well as in the Meadow flying from shrubs to high cattails (EW). The 2019 ind. was heard calling in the Meadow.

GREAT BLUE HERON
Ardea herodias

Status: Scarce to uncommon spring and uncommon fall migrant, rare to scarce summer visitor and possible breeder, very rare winter visitor.

Occurrence: Spring migration underway Mar 14–early Jun, peak early May–late May; spring max: 19 on May 25, 2019 (RSm), 10 on May 10, 2011 (TMag) & May 21, 2016 (JO), 7 on May 30, 2017 (LB), 6 on Apr 3, 2015 (DC), May 28, 2016 (JO) & Mar 31, 2022 (DC, JBu). Summer records of singles scattered throughout, with breeding confirmed for *MABB* (no details); summer max: 3 on Jul 12, 2021 (BTh), 2 on Jul 26, 2019 (DP). Fall migration/dispersal evident mid Aug–late Nov, peak mid Sep–mid Oct; fall max: **46** on Oct 5, 2012 (CCh, video), 14 on Oct 11, 2014 (JT), 8 on Sep 26, 2000 (JT) & Sep 30, 2021 (LMu, BBc). Six winter records, almost all associated with CBC period: 1 on Dec 29, 1940 (CBC), 1 on Dec 22, 1979 (CBC–PDV), unreported number during CBC count week Jan 1–7, 2007, 1 on Jan 3, 2013 (CBC), 1 on Dec 13, 2014 (DC), 1 on Dec 26, 2021 (DC). Ten-Year: SP-10, SU-5, F-10, W-2.

- *MABB*: confirmed.
- CBC: 3 years (12%) plus one count week, first on Dec 29, 1940, max 1 each year, avg 0.1.
- 1914 & 1916 Checklists: unreported number on Aug 5, 1914; included 1916.
- 1915–1919 Taylor Journals: 1915–Aug 10 (1), 11 (1); 1916–Sep 6 (4), 10; 1917–Sep 6 (1); 1918–prior to Aug 4; 1919–Sep 13 (1), 14 (1).
- 1918 Fall Migration Census: Wentworth–Oct 12 (1).
- 1939 Summer Census: regular summer visitor.
- 1944–1967 Farrell Records: 1949–Mar, Oct; 1955–Apr, Aug; 1957–Aug; 1958–Aug, Sep; 1960–Apr, May, Aug, Sep; 1961–Apr, May.
- 1954 & 1955 Summer Records: 1955–Aug 20 (1 on Manana–MLn).
- 1970 Summer Checklist: included.
- DOWTS Surveys 2011–2014: 1 on Jul 26, 2012 (1.7%, flyover at approx. 40m).

Lack of coverage late fall–early spring affects understanding of status. Possible that CBC period reports should be considered late fall migrants; departure from Maine affected by freeze-up. When multiples recorded, often seen in small flocks of 2–4; the max fall count of 46 was a minimum counted from an amazing video captured by CCh (posted by DC) of a migratory group moving south behind/east of the Cundy property, with flybys, inds. departing from spruce trees, and others still perched on the tops of trees (likely more were present). A single flock of 10 landed briefly on Nigh Duck on May 26, 2016 (JT, JO). Migrants often noted as flyovers, particularly reports of multiples, from many locations; as a partially nocturnal migrant, several reports at dawn, including high at first light, and twice "squawks" at night. Sightings of birds perched in trees (including spruces) have come mostly from the Ice Pond and Meadow, but also Fish Beach, Lobster Cove, below White Head, on Manana and Smutty Nose, and even on a dinghy in the harbor; possible on any of the rocky islands or edges of Monhegan. Due to regular and shifting occurrence, impossible to determine how long inds. remain on the island.

GREAT EGRET
Ardea alba

Status: Very rare spring and fall migrant, very rare summer visitor.

Occurrence: Nine records (4 spring, 2 summer, 3 fall) since 2012, all singles. Spring records: May 27, 2015 (MjB et al.), May 24–26, 2017 (MJo, JS et al.), Jun 1, 2020 (JT, LS), May 15, 2021 (JT, LS, JO). Summer records, possibly post-breeding dispersal: Aug 7, 2012 (DH), Jul 26, 2022 (DL, JL). Fall records: Oct 31, 2017 (KL), Sep 28, 2019 (CR, CN, mob), Oct 31, 2021 (DC). Ten-Year: SP-4, SU-1, F-3.

The first record for the island in 2012 was flushed from the Ice Pond after only about fifteen minutes by a poodle going for a swim (DH). The May 2015 ind. was sighted shortly after dawn flying between Nigh Duck and the harbor and later was seen in the Meadow. The only multi-day record (May 2017) was observed flying east over the Meadow and by White Head on May 24th and perched in a tree on the east side of the Meadow on the 26th. The Oct 2017 ind. was seen at both the Meadow and the Ice Pond. The Sep 2019 ind. was observed flying over the harbor between Monhegan and Manana. The May 2021 ind. was observed flying into and out of the Meadow. The Oct 2021 ind. was in the Meadow.

Great Egret, Sep 28, 2019. © Doug Hitchcox.

SNOWY EGRET
Egretta thula

Status: Very rare spring and accidental fall visitor.

Occurrence: Eleven records (10 spring, 1 fall) since 1985. Spring records, all singles, over eight years during 1985–2019, span Apr 6–May 29: May 25, 1985 (SS), May 25, 1986 (JVW), May 13–15, 1997 (PDV, GD), May 21–23, 1997 (SS), May 29, 2004 (JVW), May 17, 2005 (GD, HN, TV), May 4, 2010 (NL), May 16, 2010 (EH), Apr 6, 2013 (DH), May 15, 2019 (KP). Fall record the only multi-bird report: **2** on Oct 25, 1988 (WBo). Ten-Year: SP-2.

- 1970 Summer Checklist: included, noted as southern breeder with northward post-breeding dispersal before southward fall migration.

It is possible that the two records each from 1997 & 2010 involve the same inds., despite separation of five and twelve days, respectively. The fall record is late for this species in the region; it is more likely as a post-breeding disperser in late summer/early fall. Location provided for only five of the records: May 15, 1997 ind. was at Lobster Cove (location unknown on the 13th and unreported on the 14th), May 17, 2005 ind. was at Lobster Cove, May 16, 2010 ind. was at Lobster Cove, Apr 6, 2013 ind. was at the Ice Pond (flushed once after thirty minutes but quickly returned—observed catching fish in the pond–DH) and the May 2019 ind. was on the rocks at water's edge below White Head, among dozens of incubating Herring Gulls.

Warner Taylor wrote an account of a possible Snowy Egret at the Ice Pond on Jul 30, 1927 (observed with his 24x Busch binoculars)—a potential first state record (account provided by Lele Miller, personal comm.). His separation from immature Little Blue Heron (itself a rarity) was mainly focused on the lack of dusky tips to the outer primaries, which was corroborated in photos by Cyril Nelson (present whereabouts of photos unknown); he also examined skins at a later date at the American Museum of Natural History with Frank M. Chapman, confirming the trait as a constant among the specimens present. Realizing the scientific significance of the sighting, he quickly obtained permission from the Maine State House at Augusta to collect the ind., which proved futile. Regarding statements by Forbush in the 'recent' *Birds of Massachusetts* (1925, p. 133), pertaining to the rarity and similarity of the two species, that "sight records can be accepted no more," Warner suggested a tempering or qualification, on occasion, of an observation made by a "constituted authority," something precluded by the finality of Forbush's statement. The omission of Snowy Egret in his 1939 Summer Census suggests Taylor pursued the acceptance of the identification no further. It would be another twenty-one years (1948) before the first official record of Snowy Egret occurred in Maine.

LITTLE BLUE HERON
Egretta caerulea

Status: Very rare spring and fall migrant, very rare summer visitor.

Occurrence: Fourteen records (4 spring, 3 summer, 5 fall, 2 undated) since 1946. Spring records: unreported number during Apr 1946 (fide IF), unreported number during May 1956 (fide IF), unreported number during Apr 1960 (IF), unreported number during May 1960 (IF). Summer records: two of unreported number and date from listing in 1939 Summer Census (possibly fall records of postbreeding dispersal), adult on Jun 30–Jul 2, 2021 (Carol ? fide DH, DH, CEs). Fall records: immature during Aug 1959 (fide IF), 1 on Aug 8–16, 1960 (IF; *AFN* 14[5]: 434), immature during Aug 1965 (fide CP; *AFN* 19[5]: 523), 1 on Nov 6, 1988 (WBo, JB; *AB* 43 [1]: 62), immature on Aug 16, 2018 (RG). Undated records: unreported number during 1997 (TMar), unreported number during 2005 (TMar). Ten-Year: SU-1, F-1.

- 1939 Summer Census: included as rare (2 records).
- 1944–1967 Farrell Records: 1946–Apr; 1956–May; 1959–Aug (1 immature); 1960–Apr, May, Aug.

Snowy Egret, May 17, 2005. © Geoff Dennis.

- 1970 Summer Checklist: included, noted as southern breeder with northward post-breeding dispersal before southward fall migration.

As with Snowy Egret, likely to be recorded as a late summer/early fall post-breeding disperser; this may be the case with the 1939 records, which don't specify when, even to year, that the records occurred; Aug records considered the fall period for these purposes. The undated 1997 and 2005 records would have occurred during the Martins' normal times on the island (May, Sep). The Aug 2018 ind. was an immature in the back of the Meadow near the pump house. The Jun/Jul 2021 record was first observed at the Ice Pond on Jun 30 and perched on Smutty Nose on Jul 2. No details provided for any of the other records.

Historical/Regional:

- Palmer: mentions records from 1939 Census.
- Cruickshank: reported to have occurred twice, but details unknown (probably the 1939 records).
- Vickery: cites Nov 6, 1988 (WBo, JB) record as one of only seven in Nov for state (Isaac Merson in Vickery et al., 2020).

TRICOLORED HERON
Egretta tricolor

Status: Very rare spring visitor.

Occurrence: Two records: 1 on May 20, 1997 (GD, TMar; ph.), 1 on Jun 3, 2020 (JT, LS; ph.). Ten-Year: SP-1.

An uncommon late spring–early fall southern visitor to Maine, including the coastal islands; likely to occur again. The May 1997 ind. was at the Ice Pond. The Jun 2020 ind. flew north through the harbor.

CATTLE EGRET
Bubulcus ibis

Status: Very rare spring visitor.

Occurrence: Three records since first recorded in 1983, span May 5–28: **4** in May 1983 (max was 4, exact first date undetermined but before May 19, with at least one continuing [see below]–PDV, TMar personal notes), 1 on May 5–7, 2015 (DC), 3 on May 7–28, 2017 (reported fifteen days, only 2 on May 28–DH, mob). Ten-Year: SP-2.

Tom Martin's personal notes indicate 4 inds. in May 1983, while eBird reports from that year indicate 1 adult present May 19–21, with notes that at least the one present for several days (and stated as "one adult remains" on May 20)—probably the max of 4 occurred before May 19, as the Martins usually arrived the 2nd week of May. The only location given was the Meadow on May 20. The 2015 record was seen on the

Stanley lawn near the church May 5 and close by at the Cundy property near the Trailing Yew on May 7 (DC). The long-staying trio in 2017 were seen almost daily after a gap from first report on May 7 to May 13. While usually reported together, reports of 1 or 2 birds indicate separation of the birds at times, with only 2 located on the last day of their stay. First seen in the Meadow, they had moved to the lawns around Tom Martin's and the North End Market (general store) on May 13/14, an area that they frequented for much of their stay (including near the Monhegan House), shifting to lawns near the Trailing Yew for the last two days; observed roosting on the edge of the Meadow on May 25 and flying out to roost on Nigh Duck at dusk on May 27.

Cattle Egret, May 27, 2017. © Luke Seitz.

GREEN HERON
Butorides virescens

Status: Scarce spring and very rare fall migrant.

Occurrence: Spring dates span Apr 24–June 9, peak late Apr–late May; spring maxima: **2** on many dates (3 possible on several occasions, but confusion with ferry crossing sightings, different observers, trip report eliminate certainty). A summer presence is only supported by the probable status in the *MABB*, but no date or details. Eight fall records span Aug 23–Oct 7: 1 on Aug 23, 1955 (MEAB, MLn, IW), unreported number during Sep 1960 (IF), 1 on Sep 26, 1981 (PDV), 1 on Sep 30, 1982, 1 on Oct 6–7, 1990, 1 on Sep 25–27, 2006 (BME, PF et al.), 1 on Sep 13, 2019 (JLo), **2** on Sep 28, 2019 (ESo). Ten-Year: SP-8, F-1.

- *MABB*: probable; MBA: possible.

- 1944–1967 Farrell Records: 1955–Aug; 1959–Jun; 1960–May, Sep; 1961–May.
- 1954 & 1955 Summer Records: 1955–Aug 23 (1 at Lobster Cove–MEAB, MLn, IW).
- 1970 Summer Checklist: included.

It is likely that inds. linger for multiple days (see fall records), possibly for extended periods, but difficult to be certain and determine length of stay or number of different inds. throughout a season; a single ind. in Spring 2022 is likely responsible for sightings ever day May 15–20 and 22–25, and possibly lingered until the latest spring record on Jun 9. The MBA designation as possible involves an ind. in appropriate habitat on May 28, 2021; possibly a late spring migrant. Almost always reported at the Ice Pond or the Meadow (note 1955 at Lobster Cove).

BLACK-CROWNED NIGHT-HERON
Nycticorax nycticorax

Status: Very rare spring and scarce fall migrant, very rare summer visitor.

Occurrence: Fifty-eight records +/- (9 spring, 5 summer, 44 fall +/-) since first recorded on Jun 2, 1908 (FA). Spring records over nine years, span during Apr (earliest specified Apr 28)–Jun 4. 1 on Jun 2–4, 1908 (FA), unreported number during Apr 1960 (fide IF), undetermined number on May 23, 1994, 1 on May 17, 2002 (GD), 1 on Apr 28, 2008 (fide EH, KG, SWh; MARBA), 1 on May 14, 2010 (DH, MLe), 1 on May 3–6, 2011 (TMag), 1 on May 15–17, 2021 (JT et al.), 1 on May 25, 2022 (DPJ, VD). Summer records: 1 during Jul 2–7, 1909 (CJM–see below), 2 on Aug 4, 1917 (WT), unreported number prior to Aug 4, 1918 (WT), juvenile on Jul 29, 2019 (ER), juvenile on Jul 28, 2020 (BO). Fall dates span during Aug (earliest specified Sep 2)–w/e Nov 11; fall max: **6** on Sep 28, 2012 (JT), 5 on Sep 11, 2019 (HM, SBe et al.), 4 on Sep 10, 1919 (WT) & Oct 7, 2012 (JT), 3 on Sep 21, 2012 (SM, DH, PM), Oct 4, 2012 (DH), Sep 2, 2016 & Sep 15, 2020 (JLo). Ten-Year: SP-2, SU-2, F-9.

- 1900–1908 Summer Reconnaissance & Supplements: 1 seen on June 2, 3 & 4, 1908 (FA).
- 1909 Notes: 1 seen in flight. Listed as Night Heron.
- 1915–1919 Taylor Journals: 1917–Aug 4 (2); 1918–prior to Aug 4; 1919–Sep 10 (4), 11 (1), 13 (1), 14 (1).
- 1939 Summer Census: included as accidental (1 record).
- 1944–1967 Farrell Records: 1960–Apr, Aug.

- 1970 Summer Checklist: included.

Known to linger for multiple days, up to a week or possibly longer. It is extemely difficult to interpret fall records and number of inds. actually involved due to inds. coming/going during the course of a season and gaps in reporting, possibly due to local movements or departure of inds., hence the +/- qualification for number of records. Without further details, the 1939 Summer record is likely an early fall migrant and considered as such for this account. All reports indicating location, except two, were from the Ice Pond, sometimes in the company of Yellow-crowned Night-Heron; the only exceptions were a juvenile on Jul 29, 2019 on rocks at the edge of the harbor and 1 on May 15, 2021 flying into the Meadow (Michael ? and Anu ?). Of seven inds. aged in the fall, 4 were adult, 3 juvenile. Heard calling on several occasions, including a nocturnal ind. at 7:36 p.m. on Sep 2, 2022 (SG).

Historical/Regional:

- Vickery: cites 6 on Sep 28, 2012 (JT) record as notable and 1 on Oct 28 & Nov 11, 2006 (fide JWa) as late (Isaac Merson & BSV in Vickery et al., 2020).

YELLOW-CROWNED NIGHT-HERON
Nyctanassa violacea

Status: Very rare spring and rare to scarce fall visitor, very rare summer visitor.

Occurrence: Forty-seven records +/- (4 spring, 7 summer, 36 fall +/-) since first recorded on Aug 13, 1916 (EAM–see historical below; third state record; *MN* 6[2]: 91). Four spring records over three years span Apr 15–May 30: 1 on Apr 15–16, 2000 (WBo), 1 during w/e May 18–26, 2000 (GD [May 19] & TV, HN et al. trip reports), 1 on May 11, 2002 (WBo), 1 on May 14–30, 2015 (EG, GD, mob). Summer records over six years: immature during Jul 1959 (IF), immature on Jul 17, 2016 at the Ice Pond (PH, DH), juvenile on Jul 22, 2019 on shoreline rocks (GPa), juvenile on Jul 24, 2020 (TB), 2 juveniles Jul 25–29, 2020 (TB, GBr), juvenile on Aug 6, 2021 (JCe), 1 on Jul 29, 2022 (TW). Fall records span Aug 13–Nov 26, with the majority of sightings early Sep–early Oct; fall max: **3** on Sep 11, 1982 (PDV), Sep 16, 1988 (PDV), Sep 14, 1991 (LBr et al.), Sep 17–21, 2015 (BTn), Sep 15, 2016 (BTn) & Sep 17–25, 2020 (JLo, mob). Ten-Year: SP-1, SU-5, F-7.

- 1914 & 1916 Checklists: included 1916.
- 1915–1919 Taylor Journals: 1916–Aug 26 (1), 30.
- 1944–1967 Farrell Records: 1958–Aug (1 immature); 1959–July (1 immature); 1960–Aug.
- 1970 Summer Checklist: included.

Dramatic increase in Maine since 1950 and nearly annual in the state since 1967 (Vickery et al., 2020). This is reflected in the recent increase (since 2016) in juvenile sightings on Monhegan during Jul/early Aug, and is likely the result of post-fledging dispersal from other locations. Two juveniles, first reported at the Ice Pond on Jul 25, 2020 (TB), were present at least through Jul 29 and reported from north of the dock, the Ice Pond, and Lobster Cove; possibly longer staying and part of the 3 lingering inds. in Sep–Oct (no reports in Aug/early Sep but lack of coverage). It is extremely difficult to interpret fall records and number of inds. actually involved due to inds. coming/going during the course of a season and gaps in reporting, possibly due to local movements or departure of inds., hence the +/- qualification for number of records. The 1916 record, with reports by MCG & WT and considered one record (Forbush, 1925; also Palmer & Cruickshank, below), is likely an early fall migrant/post-breeding dispersal and considered as such for this account; likewise, the reports from Aug 1959 and Aug 1960 are considered fall records. Known to linger for extensive periods, such as an immature Aug 28–Oct 2, 1975 (AKe, JY et al.; *AB* 30[1]: 30), the adult in spring 2015 (sixteen of seventeen days May 14–May 30), at least one immature, but up to three reported, in 2015 (sixteen days over Sep 3–24), and one immature in 2017 (fifteen days over Sep 13–Oct 9, but possibly as early as Sep 5), 1–2 juveniles in 2019 over eleven days Sep 12–Oct 12, and 1–3 juveniles over fourteen days Sep 17–Oct 5 (3 present Sep 17, 18, 20, 25, 27; one perished about Oct 1, 2 still present Oct 5). Fall max all within the short span of Sep. 11–25. Almost all sightings from the Ice Pond, standing along the shoreline or perched in trees above; an exception is the two immatures in fall 2013 (only report of two on Sep 9), which spent their time singly around the Meadow (never reported at the Ice Pond), including on the ground near the cemetery (FM) and in an apple tree near the road (BCl). Other reports not already mentioned include on the rocks at Lobster Cove, flying south out of the spruces at Lobster Cove at dusk, and flying out from near the Meadow at dusk and calling. Majority of fall sightings have been identified as juvenile/immature; only two adult reports known: the Spring 2015 record and 1 on Oct 7, 2016 (RT). Sometimes associating with Black-crowned Night-Heron.

Historical/Regional:

- Palmer: 1 on Aug 13, 26 & 27, 1916 (E. A. Munroe).
- Cruickshank: cites 1916 Munroe record.
- Vickery: included in list of sites with records of 3–4 inds. and as an offshore island with numerous reports late summer/fall, cites the Sep 1982, 1988, & 1991 records of 3 inds. as high counts and 1 on Sep 5–Oct 9, 2017 (mob) as recent (PDV in Vickery et al., 2020).

Yellow-crowned Night-Heron, Ice Pond, Sep 18, 2020. © Bill Thompson

GLOSSY IBIS
Plegadis falcinellus

Status: Very rare spring visitor.

Occurrence: Six records over six years since first recorded in May 1967: unreported number during May 1967 (TMar), **7** on May 11-15, 1971 (TMar), 1 on/about May 20, 1984 (PCr), unreported number the third week of May 1991 (JS), unreported number during May 1996 (TMar), 1 on May 26, 2018 (SS). Ten-Year: SP-1.

The May 2018 ind. was a flyover.

BLACK VULTURE
Coragyps atratus

Status: Accidental summer visitor.

Occurrence: One record: adult male on Jul 4–6, 1909 (CJM).

- 1909 Notes: 1 present Jul 4–6 (see details below).

First seen in flight around midday on Jul 4, over the village the morning of Jul 5 and over the southern end of the island later, and shot near the lighthouse on Jul 6 by someone who thought it was trying to catch his chickens; specimen presented to Charles Jenney and sex determined by dissection (see Palmer and Cruickshank, below).

Historical/Regional:

- Palmer: male shot on Jul 6, 1909 (Maynard).
- Cruickshank: cites Maynard record from Jul 6, 1909.

TURKEY VULTURE
Cathartes aura

Status: Very rare spring and accidental fall visitor, very rare summer visitor.

Occurrence: Fourteen records (10 spring, 3 summer, 1 fall) since 1984. Spring records: 1 on May 6, 1984 (PDV, BSV, CDD), 1 on May 25, 1996 (GD), 1 on May 19–20, 2002 (TMar), 2–**3** during spring 2008 (prior to May 26–KI, fide DF), 1 on Apr 14, 2011 (TMag), 1 on May 8, 2011 (PDV, JP, NW), 1 on May 15, 2013 (GD), 1 on Apr 23, 2108 (DC), 1 on Apr 23, 2018 (DC), 1 on May 18, 2018 (BTn, JVW). Summer records: 1 on Jun 19, 2011 (TMag), 1 on Jun 16, 2014 (JKa), 1 on Jul 7, 2022 (MWa, LS). Fall record: 1 on Oct 13–14, 2018 (TMz). Ten-Year: SP-3, SU-2, F-1.

- 1909 Notes: not recorded, but reference to an ind. seen years before (see discussion below).

Increasing in Maine since 1976, with first breeding in 1978 (Vickery et al., 2020). All but two Monhegan records since 2002; likely to be reported more often, as the species expands its range/numbers northward. The 2–3 inds. in spring 2008 were observed on several occasions prior to May 26 and were likely lingering inds., but are lacking further details. Three records in 2011 with long periods between (over three weeks), unlikely to be the same ind. An apparent record involves a bird shot, some years before the Black Vulture in 1909, that was similar but with a red head, as told by an old fisherman to CJM (Maynard, 1909). The May 1984 ind. was observed from the Ice Pond and later over the lighthouse. The May 1996 ind. flew northward over the harbor, the May 2002 & May 2013 inds. were flyovers, the Jun 2014 ind. was an adult gliding by and the May 2018 ind. was soaring around the lighthouse. The Jul 2022 ind. was first observed perched on the rocks near Lobster Cove and later on Manana.

Turkey Vulture, Jul 17, 2022. © Luke Seitz.

OSPREY
Pandion haliaetus

Status: Scarce to uncommon spring and uncommon fall migrant, rare summer visitor.

Occurrence: Spring dates Apr 4–mid Jun, peak early–late May; spring max: 8 on May 29, 1994 (SS), 6 on May 22, 2016 (JT, JO, BN) & May 25, 2019 (JT), 5 on Jun 2, 2020 (JT, LS) & May 19, 2021 (JT, LS, JO). Thirteen summer records over eleven years since 1917; summer max: 2 on Jul 7, 2018 (RD, PD). Fall migration spans early Aug–Oct 17, peak the month of Sep (especially late); fall max: exceptional **200** on Sep 25, 1981 (PDV), 80 on Sep 14, 1986 (PDV), 40 on Sep 25, 1986 (PDV), 20 on Sep 26, 1981 (PDV), Sep 16, 1984 (PDV) & Sep 28, 2002 (JT). Ten-Year: SP-10, SU-5, F-10.

- MBA: possible.
- 1900–1908 Reconnaissance & Supplements: 2 on Jun 5, 1908, singles at other times (FA). Listed as American Osprey.
- 1914 & 1916 Checklists: included 1916.
- 1915–1919 Taylor Journals: 1916–Sep 3 (1), 10; 1917–Jul 29 (1); 1919–Sep 1 (1), 4 (1), 5 (1), 13 (1), 14 (2). Listed as Fish Hawk.
- 1918 Fall Migration Census: Dewis–5 (1 on Sep 9, 4 on Sep 11); Wentworth–3 (1 on Oct 9, 2 on Oct 17).
- 1939 Summer Census: regular summer visitor.
- 1944–1967 Farrell Records: 1949–Sep; 1950–Sep, Oct; 1952–Oct; 1954–Jul, Aug, Sep; 1955–Aug; 1959–Aug; 1960–Aug, Sep.
- 1954 & 1955 Summer Records: 1954–Jul 12 (1); 1955–Aug 28 (1).
- 1970 Summer Checklist: included.
- 2010 Fall Hawkwatch: 74 total (35 Lob, 39 Man) over 21 days spanning Sep 16–Oct 14, max 15 on Sep 23.

Significant increase in state presence since late 1960s after recovery from DDT (Vickery et al., 2020). The max flight of 200 in Sep 1981, much higher than any other count, noted as "birds flew past Monhegan in a constant stream" (PDV) and was after a morning ferry ride to the island; a follow-up flight the next day produced an impressive 20. The two other highest counts, 80 and 40, also included ferry rides (in the morning and late afternoon, respectively), but are included as the vast majority, if not all, probably occurred on Monhegan or in nearshore waters. As is often the case, the best numbers occurred as part of more general raptor movements under conducive conditions and seen overhead or as flybys. MBA status based on inds. present and carrying food in appropriate habitat on Jul 7, 2018 (RD, PD). Possible anywhere on the island; noted soaring over Horn's Hill, Lighthouse Hill, the Meadow, Manana, and once calling near Lobster Cove.

Historical/Regional:

- Vickery: cites three fall max counts above as high counts for Monhegan (*date for max count of 200 should be Sep 25, 1981, not 1984*; PDV in Vickery et al., 2020).

Osprey, May 25, 2019. © Jeremiah Trimble.

SWALLOW-TAILED KITE
Elanoides forficatus

Status: Accidental spring vagrant.

Occurrence: One record: 1 on May 19–25, 1986 (TMar, IB, CDD, SS, mob; *AB* 40[3]: 443, *G* 15[3]: 23. First Maine record; not yet reviewed by ME-BRC.

On May 24, observed for three to four hours perched in a spruce tree at the edge of the Meadow and seen by 50+ birders (JVW).

Historical/Regional:

- Vickery: cites 1986 record as first for Maine (PDV in Vickery et al., 2020).
- OLMB: nine additional state records—seven accepted and two not yet reviewed.

GOLDEN EAGLE
Aquila chrysaetos

Status: Accidental winter visitor.

Occurrence: One record: 1 in Dec 1975 (Tom Martin's personal notes).

While unusual, the species is likely to be encountered again, as it is a rare but regular migrant/visitor in Maine late fall–early spring.

NORTHERN HARRIER
Circus hudsonius

Status: Scarce spring and uncommon to fairly common fall migrant, very rare winter visitor.

Occurrence: Spring records span Apr 6–Jun 8, with most sightings occurring in May; spring max: 4 on May 6, 1984 (PDV), 2 on May 22, 1997 (SS), May 5, 2010 (NL) & May 28, 2014 (BBa, BCo). Fall dates span Aug 19–Nov 16, peak mid Sep–early Oct, most gone by the end of Oct; fall max: **60** on Sep 25, 1986 (PDV), 40 on Sep 14, 1986 (PDV), 25 on Sep 25, 1987 (PDV). Three winter records: 1 on Dec 31, 1939 (MJT), immature/female on Jan 3, 2013 (CBC–DH, WN), 1 on Dec 28, 2017 (DC). Ten-Year: SP-6, F-10, W-1.

- CBC: 1 year (4%): 1 on Jan 3, 2013, avg 0.0.
- 1900–1908 Reconnaissance & Supplements: 1 on Aug 1, 1907 (CFJ, ECJ).
- 1914 & 1916 Checklists: included 1916.
- 1915–1919 Taylor Journals: 1915–Aug 27 (1), Sep 12 (1); 1916–Aug 20, Sep 3, 6 (3); 1917–Sep 5 (1); 1918–Aug 28; 1919–Sep 4 (3), 5 (1), 10 (1), 13 (2), 14 (1). Listed as Marsh Hawk.
- 1918 Fall Migration Census: Dewis–3 (1 on Sep 9, 10, 11); Wentworth–(Sep 29, Oct 21). Listed as Marsh Hawk.
- 1939 Summer Checklist: uncommon summer visitor. Listed as Marsh Hawk.
- 1944–1967 Farrell Records: 1949–Sep; 1951–Sep; 1953–Aug, Sep; 1955–Aug; 1959–Aug; 1960–Sep. Listed as Marsh Hawk.
- 1954 & 1955 Summer Records: 1955–Aug 27 (1–MEAB et al.), 28 (2), 1 (29), all "brown" (immature/female).
- 1970 Summer Checklist: included. Listed as Marsh Hawk.
- 2010 Fall Hawkwatch: 78 total (40 Lob, 38 Man) over fifteen days spanning Sep 17–Oct 14, max 14 on Sep 21.

As with Osprey, the max flights were part of reports that included ferry rides (late afternoon on Sep 14, 1986, morning on Sep 25, 1986, and morning on Sep. 25, 1987), but undoubtedly reflect the movement over the island/nearshore waters; to omit them would be an injustice to our understanding of the species on Monhegan. The fact that these highest counts all occurred in the 1980s may also reflect the species' overall decline. Possible overhead anywhere on the island, most often reported over Manana or from Lobster Cove as birds move past Monhegan, seen heading south or towards the mainland in fall; main flights a component of general raptor movements (some same max days as Osprey). Surprisingly, only five reports associated with the Meadow. Of 44 inds. identified to age/sex in the fall, there were 6 adult male, 7 adult female, 25 immature, and 6 immature/female type; six inds. identified in spring included 1 adult male and 5 females.

Historical/Regional:

- Palmer: cites Dewis and Wentworth 1918 records and only winter record on Dec 31, 1939 (Mrs. J. A. Townsend).
- Vickery: cites 60 on Sep 25, 1986 (PDV) as the high fall count; mentions Palmer's inclusion of Dec 1939 record as only winter report at that time (PDV in Vickery et al., 2020).

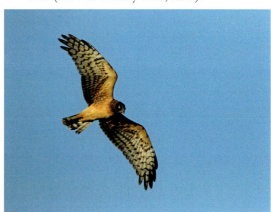

Northern Harrier, Oct 9, 2020. © Luke Seitz.

SHARP-SHINNED HAWK
Accipiter striatus

Status: Scarce spring and uncommon to fairly common fall migrant, very rare summer and winter visitor.

Occurrence: Spring migration Mar 9–early Jun, peak the first three weeks of May; spring max: 6 on May 16, 2010 (EH), 3 on May 6, 1984 (PDV) & May 12, 2012 (RS). Six summer records fall outside the normal migration window: 1 on Aug 9, 1915 (WT, CFJ), 1 on Jul 15, 2010 (TMag), 1 on Jun 16–17, 2021

(CDd, JFo), 1 on Jul 30, 2021 (NP), 1 on Jun 15, 2022 (IKi), 1 on Jul 26, 2022 (DL, JL). Fall migration mid Aug–late Nov, peak early Sep–early Oct; fall max: **600** on Sep 16, 1984 (PDV), 250 on Sep 14, 1986 (PDV), 180 on Sep 25, 1986. Ten winter records over nine years since 1983 (two in 2013), almost all associated with the CBC period, and none after Jan 27; winter max: 2 on Jan 3, 2013 (CBC, but official count is 1, see below–WN). Ten-Year: SP-10, SU-2, F-10, W-2.

- CBC: 6 years (23%) plus 2 count weeks, first recorded on Dec 29, 1983, max 1 on all dates (eBird report from Jan 3, 2013 indicates 2, but questioned by the compiler as possibly the same ind.), avg 0.3.
- 1899 Checklist: included.
- 1909 Notes: bones and feathers of a male found in the fissure of a rock on shore (ECJ).
- 1914 & 1916 Checklists: included 1916.
- 1915–1919 Taylor Journals: 1915–Aug 9 (1), Sep 12 (4); 1916–Sep 2 (1), 3 (1), 6 (1), 10; 1918–Aug 28; 1919–Sep 4 (2), 5 (2), 10 (3), 11 (3), 13 (5), 14 (5).
- 1918 Fall Migration Census: Dewis–26 (Sep 4, 8 [6], 9 [6], 10 [7], 11 [5], 12); Wentworth–Sep 29, Oct 7, 8, 13, 15.
- 1939 Summer Census: regular summer visitor.
- 1944–1967 Farrell Records: 1949–Sep, Oct, Nov.
- 1954 & 1955 Summer Records: 1955–Aug 26 (1–MEAB, MLn, IW), two others, considered possible male Cooper's Hawk, not included.
- 1970 Summer Checklist: included.
- Banding: 3 total over 2 seasons, peak 2 in Fall 1960 (1 each on Oct 8 & 9, as well as Oct 6, 1961).
- 2010 Fall Hawkwatch: 53 total (37 Lob, 16 Man) over twelve days spanning Sep 16–Oct 14, max 15 on Sep 18.

Probably underreported in late Mar–Apr, based on migration patterns on the mainland (only one spring record before Apr 18). Few reports of any quantity include details, but likely to be encountered anywhere on the island on flight days, sometimes hunting migrant songbirds; the massive flight on Sep 16, 1984 consisted mostly of birds flying south off Lobster Cove (all birds aged were immature). As was the case with Osprey on exactly the same dates, the next two highest flights involved reports that included ferry rides (late afternoon on Sep 14, 1986 and in the morning on Sep 25, 1986), but are included as the vast majority, if not all, probably occurred on Monhegan or in nearshore waters, once again indicating the concentration of raptor migration under conducive conditions. While it seems that inds. in the fall often circle back north when at the south end of the island, hesitant to cross open water, it is difficult to determine how long they may remain on the island. A number of the few winter birds remained for multiple days, sometimes stalking birds at feeders (such as those at the Hitchcox residence), as noted for 1 immature on Jan 2–3, 2013 and 1 adult male on Jan 25–27 2013 (also observed chasing crossbills over Cathedral Woods–DH et al.). Despite a smattering of adult sightings, the vast preponderance of aged birds are immatures, as evidenced by the max flight noted above, the 250 immatures of the second-highest total, and 40 immatures each on Sep 8 & 9, 1985 (PDV), supporting the accepted notion that immatures are more frequently "blown" off course and end up on islands or coastal peninsulas.

Historical/Regional:

- Palmer: largest number in fall seen along the coast, even out to Monhegan.
- Cruickshank: flocks of several dozen not unusual even out on Monhegan after brisk northwest wind in late Aug and Sep.
- Vickery: still regular into last week of May; cites >600 on Sep 16, 1984 (PDV) and 60 on Sep 19, 2013 (PDV) as high counts along coast (PDV in Vickery et al., 2020).

Sharp-shinned Hawk, Sep 24, 2015. © Bill Thompson.

COOPER'S HAWK
Accipiter cooperii

Status: Rare spring and scarce fall migrant, accidental winter visitor.

Occurrence: Fifteen spring records over eleven years since 1988 span Apr 5–w/e Jun 2, 2006 (latest definitive date May 28), with all but the Apr 5 record occurring in May, and eleven occurring in the second half of the month (likely underreported in Apr/early May); spring max: 2 on May 15, 2010 (DH, MLe). Fall dates span Aug 28–Nov 4, with most sightings occurring mid Sep–early Oct; fall max: **8** on Sep 22, 2008 (JM), 3 on Sep 13, 1919 (WT) & Sep 9–10, 2011 (DH, RP, NL), 2 on Sep 11, 1919 (WT), Sep 14, 1919 (WT), Sep 17–24, 2007 (also reported Sep 19 & 21–PF, LS, JSc) & Sep 24 & 27, 2014 (BBa). One winter record: 1 on Dec 25, 2010 (TMag). Ten-Year: SP-1, F-8.

- 1914 & 1916 Checklists: included 1916.
- 1915–1919 Taylor Journals: 1916–Sep 10; 1919–Sep 6 (1), 10 (1), 11 (2), 13 (3), 14 (2).
- 1939 Summer Census: regular summer visitor (*erroneously listed as Copper's Hawk*).
- 1944–1967 Farrell Records: 1949–Sep, Oct.

The regional timing of spring migration indicates underreporting in early spring. The only spring record to include a location was that of Apr 5, 2012: an adult stalking birds at feeders (DH); fall birds usually flyovers; reported several times over the Meadow or around town, but location rarely mentioned. The early Sep records from the Taylor Journals likely the listing as regular summer visitor on the 1939 Summer Census, and considered fall migrants here. It is certain that some inds. linger, but difficult to determine how often; several times noted as present for two or three days and notable that the max count of 3 was on two consecutive days and that all the records of 2 inds. involved multiple reports within a couple of days of each other. While none of these max totals was specifically marked as continuing, the circumstantial evidence is compelling for lingering birds and considered as such for these purposes. A continuing immature, Sep 18–25, 2020, is the longest staying ind. (JRa et al.). Many times observed chasing prey, including Mourning Dove, Northern Flicker, and European Starling, or simply perched. Only two spring records noted to age, both adult; large majority of fall records noted to age have been immature, as expected.

Historical/Regional:

- Vickery: cites 8 on Sep 22, 2008 (JM) as a high count (PDV in Vickery et al., 2020).

NORTHERN GOSHAWK
Accipiter gentilis

Status: Very rare fall migrant , very rare winter visitor.

Occurrence: Eight records (6 fall, 2 winter) since first recorded on Sep 11, 1981 (PDV), all singles. Fall records unexpectedly early (likely underreported later), span Sep 9–Oct 5: immature on Sep 11, 1981 (PDV), immature on Sep 9, 1983 (PDV), Oct 2–3, 1997 (JT), immature on Sep 22, 2008 (JM), Oct 5, 2010 (2010 Hawkwatch–FT). Winter records both associated with CBC period: Jan 4, 2007 (CBC), Jan 4, 2010 (WJS).

- CBC: 1 year (4%), 1 on Jan 4, 2007, avg 0.0.
- 2010 Fall Hawkwatch: 1 Total (Man), Oct 5.

Few details provided for such a rare and sought-after species; no locations or behaviors noted (the ind. recorded on the 2010 Hawkwatch was observed from Manana) and only the three fall inds. were identified to age: immature. It is surprising that there are no records in fall after early Oct, as the species is generally considered a late fall migrant in the East; early season records likely indicate dispersal of juveniles or non-breeders.

Historical/Regional:

- Vickery: cites Sep 9, 1983 (PDV), Sep 11, 1981 (PDV) & Sep 22, 2008 (JM) records as early dispersal of immatures (PDV in Vickery et al., 2020).

BALD EAGLE
Haliaeetus leucocephalus

Status: Scarce to uncommon spring and uncommon fall migrant, rare summer and winter visitor; has bred.

Occurrence: Bald Eagle numbers and movements are complicated; little variability between seasons, but lowest numbers in summer and certainly underreported in summer and winter. Spring migration underway by early Mar–late May; likely that inds. heading to breeding grounds in Mar and Apr supplemented by post-breeding dispersal of southern breeders in May; spring max: 5 on May 12, 2012 (RS) & May 23, 2019 (AK), 4 on May 10, 2014 (DC), 3 on ten days spanning Apr 6–May 27. Seventeen summer records over ten years since 2005 (four in 2019, three in 2021), span early Jun–early Aug but concentrated in June, likely made up of southern wanderers and non-breeders; summer max: 2 on June 23, 2019 (CEl), Jun 1–7, 2021 (GP, KB) & Aug 3, 2021 (LHa). Fall migration underway mid Aug–end of Nov, peak mid Sep–early Nov; fall max: **8** on Sep 25, 2013 (PB) & Nov 13, 2020 (LS, JT), 7 on Oct 8, 2012 (JT) & Oct 8, 2018 (LS), 6 on Oct 6, 2016 (TM). Thirty-one winter records over sixteen years (seasons) since 1981 (four records in 2005–2006 and five in 2006–2007 likely represent overwintering inds.), twelve associated with CBC period: winter max: 5 on Jan 4, 2010 (WJS), 4 on Jan 4, 2010 (CBC–PDV, WJS), 3 on Jan 3, 2013 (CBC–PDV et al.), Jan 26, 2013 (DH) & Jan 3, 2015 (CBC–DH, FK, WN). Ten-Year: SP-10, SU-7, F-10, W-6.

- CBC: 10 years (38%), plus one count week, first on Dec 27, 1994 (count week was 1981), max 4 on Jan 5, 2010, avg 1.0.
- 1939 Summer Census: uncommon summer visitor. Listed as Bald-headed Eagle.
- 2010 Fall Hawkwatch: 3 total (2 Lob, 1 Man) over three days spanning Sep 18–Oct 3, max 1 each day.

Decimated by contaminants to fewer than forty known Maine nests in the 1970s, had recovered to over 700 nests by 2018, with adults generally resident and immatures migratory (Vickery et al., 2020). The origins of Monhegan inds. are hard to know and may involve a combination of year-round Maine residents, short/long distance migrants, and post-breeding wanderers from the south; southern Bald Eagles breed much earlier in the year (Jan–Feb), with some, notably juveniles, wandering north to Maine or farther in late spring/summer. One tagged juvenile from NY was noted on Sep 6 or 7, 1986 (WH). Two adults at a nest along the shoreline at the northern end of the island (away from any trail) on May 14, 2004 (GD) constitute the only known direct evidence of breeding on the island. A pair apparently overwintered in 2005–2006 and 2006–2007 (*same inds.?*), with four records w/e Dec 29, 2005–w/e Mar 3, 2006 (joined by a third ind. in Feb–fide JWa et al.; MARBA) and five records w/e Dec 29, 2006–Mar 3, 2007 (noted as continuing in Feb–fide JWa, KG; MARBA). Bald Eagles are most often seen standing on any of the various islands surrounding Monhegan, including on top of Manana, or observed soaring over the harbor or Manana; likely in flight anywhere over the island. Noted several times from White Head, including a bird arriving over the ocean from the east (possibly from Matinicus Rock–PDV). "Pairs" of adults in fall reported from the Seal Rocks and Burnt Head (JM), and were once observed defending prey from an immature on Nigh Duck (FM). Other reported behavior include catching fish, being harassed by crows, and four adults hunting gulls at Gull Cove (RR). While it seems certain that inds. and pairs linger on/around the island, the length of stay is uncertain (possibly weeks) and inds. may move freely between Monhegan and inshore islands/mainland. The 85+ records noting age included all age classes (juvenile, immature, 2–3 years old, near adult, adult), with the large majority being adults.

Historical/Regional:

- Vickery: occasional to uncommon before 2000, cites 7 on Oct 8, 2012 (JT), 8 on Sep 25, 2013 (PB) and 5 on five dates as recent high counts (PDV in Vickery et al., 2020).

Bald Eagle adults at nest on northern end of island, May 14, 2004. © Geoff Dennis.

RED-SHOULDERED HAWK
Buteo lineatus

Status: Accidental spring and very rare fall migrant.

Occurrence: Three records (1 spring, 2 fall) since 1959. Spring record: 1 during May 24–26, 2008 (KL, PD). Fall records: unreported number during Aug 1959 (?Bu, fide IF), 1 during mid Sep in 1970s (HT).

- 1944–1967 Farrell Records: 1959–Aug.

Near northern edge of breeding range and in reduced numbers since mid 1900s. The May 2008 ind. was a flyover near the Meadow. Exact date/year unknown and no details available for the Sep 1970s ind.

BROAD-WINGED HAWK
Buteo platypterus

Status: Very rare spring and rare fall migrant.

Occurrence: Twenty records (4 spring, 16 fall) since first known record on Sep 6, 1919 (1–WT). Spring records: 1 on May 18, 2018 (KL), adult on May 27–28, 2021 (JBi, BTn), immature on May 23, 2022 (DL et al.), immature on Jun 1, 2022 (LHe et al.). Fall records over twelve years (three in 1919, two in 2009 & 2013), span Sep 6–Oct 11; fall max: **9** on Sep 17–20, 2013 (PDV et al.), 7 on Sep 25–27, 2013 (PDV, SB et al.), 2 on Sep 13, 1919 (WT), Sep 28, 1983 (DF) & Sep 16, 1984 (PDV, WH). Ten-Year: SP-3, F-4.

- 1915–1919 Taylor Journals: 1919–Sep 6 (1), 13 (2), 14 (1).
- 1939 Summer Census: uncommon summer visitor.
- 1970 Summer Checklist: included.

The two records from Fall 2013 are complicated and involve two "groups" separated by four days of no sightings (unlikely, but not impossible, to be overlooked in this peak birding season); coupled with the second group seen coming in off the ocean at White Head indicates the probability of different inds. The max count of 9 (2 adults, 7 immatures) was noted on the first day (Sep 17–PDV et al.) and followed up by a lingering adult over the lighthouse on Sep 19 (JKy) and one immature over the Ice Pond on Sep 20 (BTn). The second record first involved 6 inds. (1 adult, 5 immature) on Sep 25; reported separately, the 5 immatures were "kettling" over the ocean at White Head before drifting over the island (PB), later noted soaring over Horn's Hill (SM), while the adult was over the lighthouse (PDV, SWr); on Sep. 26 there were 6 immatures (possibly 7–8) soaring over Burnt Head in the morning (PDV, SB), shortly later over the Trailing Yew (PB), and later still were 4 over the Ice Pond (CDd); followed by at least two lingering birds on Sep. 27 (adult and immature reported). Impossible to be sure just how many Broad-winged Hawks were actually present on the island in 2013. There are only four other records with location details: a Sep 25–26, 2009 ind. was a juvenile high overhead on Lobster Cove Rd. (LS, DS), the May 2020 ind. was a flyover between the school and the Ice Pond both days, the May 2022 ind. was an immature over the Trailing Yew (DL) heading south, and a juvenile was soaring east of the Trailing Yew on Sep 25, 2022 (BME).

RED-TAILED HAWK
Buteo jamaicensis

Status: Accidental spring and very rare fall migrant, accidental summer visitor.

Occurrence: Nine records (1 spring, 1 summer, 7 fall) since 1916 with next record not until Sep 25, 1981 (PDV), all single birds or unreported number (three records). Spring record: Apr 6, 2013 (DH). Summer record: immature on Jun 15, 2020 (DH). Fall records occurring during the short span of during Aug (earliest specified Sep 12)–Sep 29: unreported number during Aug 16–Sep 16, 1916 (MCG), unreported number during Aug 1959 (?Bu, fide IF), unreported number during Aug 1960 (IF), adult dark morph on Sep. 25, 1981 (PDV), Sep 21–22, 1991 (PDV), Sep 12, 1992 (SMa), Sep 29, 2002 (JT). Ten-Year: SP-1, SU-1.

- 1914 & 1916 Checklists: included 1916.
- 1944–1967 Farrell Records: 1959–Aug; 1960–Aug.

It is remarkable, for a species with so few records, that the 1981 ind. was a dark morph adult ("entirely dark brown with a bright red tail"–PDV), most likely of the western subspecies *B. j. calurus*. The only spring record was being mobbed by American Crows over Ocean Ave. and made two passes over Lobster Cove shortly afterward (DH). The Jun 2020 record was being mobbed by blackbirds over the Meadow (DH).

Historical/Regional:

- Vickery: mentioned as occurring at Monhegan and Manana Island hawkwatches (Heidi Franklin in Vickery et al., 2020).

ROUGH-LEGGED HAWK
Buteo lagopus

Status: Very rare winter visitor.

Occurrence: Three records since first recorded in 1989, all associated with the CBC period: 1 on Dec 21, 1989 (CBC–PDV), 1 on Jan 1, 1991 (CBC–PDV), 3 on Jan 4, 2010 (WJS).

- CBC: 2 years (8%) plus one count week (see above), first on Dec 21, 1989, max 1 both years, avg 0.0.

No details provided for any records.

GREAT HORNED OWL
Bubo virginianus

Status: Very rare spring and fall visitor or possible breeder, accidental winter visitor.

Occurrence: Eleven records (2 spring, 8 fall, 1 winter) since first recorded in 1976, all singles. Spring records: Mar 12, 2018 (DC), May 17–19, 2019 (DR). Fall records over seven years, span Sep 2–Oct 29: 1 heard on Oct 2, 1976 (WR, fide DF), 1 heard during late Sep 1977 (DF), Oct 5, 2003 (WJS), Oct 29, 2010 (MI), male on Oct 3–12, 2017 (LS, GC), Sep 2, 2018 (DC), Oct 5, 2018 (LS, JT), Oct 7, 2021 (HN, TMz). Winter record: Dec 1, 2021 (DC). Ten-Year: SP-2, F-3, W-1.

- MBA: possible.

The Sep 1977 ind. was calling east of the Chadwick House. The Oct 2010 ind. flashed through the woods by the Lighthouse. The Oct 2017 ind. was calling repeatedly on Oct 3 (LS) and noted as continuing on Oct 12, reported multiple times (GC–not reported during the interim). The Mar 2018 (4 a.m.) and Sep 2, 2018 inds. were calling behind Donna Cundy's while the Oct 5, 2018 ind. was calling around 11 p.m. (location not provided); possibly/likely the same ind. The May 2019 ind. was a male hooting three consecutive nights—the first two 8–10 p.m. and around 4 a.m. on the third night; recorded as possible for the MBA (DR). Seven records over 2017–2021 support the possibility of a resident pair.

Historical/Regional:

- Vickery: few fall records, cites late Sep 1977 (DF) and Oct in 2003, 2010, 2017, 2018 (PDV in Vickery et al., 2020).

Great Horned Owl, Dec 21, 2021. © Donna Cundy.

SNOWY OWL
Bubo scandiacus

Status: Rare winter visitor.

Occurrence: Twenty-three records over ten+ years (winter seasons) since during 1900–1908 (fifteen since 1981), span during Oct (earliest definite Oct 30)–Mar 28: 2 during 1900–1908 (considered two separate records), unreported number during Jan 1946 (IF), unreported number during Oct 1949 (IF), 1 on Dec 29, 1981 (CBC–PDV), 1 on Dec 28, 1982 (PDV), 1 on Dec 31, 1990 (PDV), immature on Jan 1, 1992 (CBC–PDV), 1 during w/e Jan 4, 2008 (fide EH, SWh; MARBA), 1 on Nov 20, 2013 (fide DH, eBird), **3** on Dec 1, 2013 (fide DH; MARBA), 1 on Dec 3, 2013 (fide DC), 1 on Feb 22, 2014 (PH), 2 on Mar 11, 2014 (DC), 1 on Oct 30–Nov 5, 2014 (WBo, DC), 1 on Jan 3–14, 2015 (CBC Jan 3–DH, FK, WN, WBo), 1 on Jan 21, 2018 (DC), 1 during Feb 25–28, 2018 (fide DC), 1 on Mar 5, 2018 (DC), 1 on Mar 28–29, 2018 (DC, PR), 1 on Feb 7, 2021 (DC), 1 on Nov 20, 2021 (DC), 1 on Mar 5–7, 2022 (DC, JBu). Ten-Year: W-4.

- CBC: 4 years (15%), first on Dec 29, 1981, max 1 all four years, avg 0.2.
- 1900–1908 Reconnaissance & Supplements: 2 killed by an island resident and mounted (CFJ, ECJ–*unclear if only the specimens were observed*).
- 1944–1967 Farrell Records: 1946–Jan; 1949–Oct.

Since the species is prone to irruptions, typically involving 30–100 inds. statewide (Vickery et al., 2020), the 3 inds. in 2013 (widespread across Maine that year), second-hand reports of 3 in 2014 and the three records in 2018 are not surprising. It is highly likely that some were present during significant historical incursions, such as those that occurred in 1926–27, 1941–42, and other years (Gross, 1947). Most are one-day records, unusual for a species known to remain in one area for lengthy periods of time, highlighting the lack of coverage during the winter period; it is likely that 1 of the 3 on Dec 1, 2013 was the ind. reported on Nov 20, as well as the ind. being mobbed by crows at Gull Rock on Dec 3. Possibly only one ind. was present Oct 2014–Jan 2015; reports from only four days (Oct 30, Nov 5, Jan 3, Jan 14), considered two records due to rarity and closeness of first two dates and noted as continuing on Jan 14. Some inds., particularly the Oct/Nov and Mar records, could be considered fall/spring migrants, but considered winter visitors for this purpose due to their nomadic tendencies and lack of duration details. The Feb 2014 ind. was on a stump in the Meadow (reports from residents that 3 in total had been on the island, but no details). The Oct/Nov 2014 ind. was chased off by crows and jays on Lighthouse Hill on Oct 30 and seen near the Ice Pond on Nov 5. The Jan 2015 ind. was an apparent female, perched on Manana all day. Unclear if the multiple reports from winter 2018 involve one or more inds.; the Jan 2018 and Mar 28, 2018 inds. were both perched on a chimney, the late Feb ind. was observed eating a muskrat on a lawn and flying over the Meadow at dusk (fide DC) and the Mar 5, 2018 ind. was over Lobster Cove in the morning.

Historical/Regional:

- Vickery: cites 1 on Nov 5, 2014 as a recent record (PDV in Vickery et al., 2020).

Snowy Owl, Jan 21, 2018. © Donna Cundy.

BARRED OWL
Strix varia

Status: Very rare spring visitor.

Occurrence: Two records: 1 on May 20, 2013 (CB), 1 dead on Mar 9, 2014 (DC, ph.; MARBA). Ten-Year: SP-2.

The Mar 2014 ind. was found along the Alder Trail (#6) near the junction with the connector trail to the Gull Cove Trail (#5).

Historical/Regional:

- Vickery: "reported a few times" (HN, CB), including one dead (DC; PDV in Vickery et al., 2020).

SHORT-EARED OWL
Asio flammeus

Status: Very rare fall migrant, accidental winter visitor.

Occurrence: Five records (4 fall, 1 winter) since first recorded in 1987. Fall records: 1 on Oct 27, 1996 (DAb, SA), 1 on Sep 22, 2004 (LBu), 1 on Oct 29, 2010 (JT), 1 on Sep 29, 2017 (BTn, PE). Winter record: 1 on Dec 27–28, 1987 (CBC–PDV). Ten-Year: F-1.

- CBC: 1 year (4%), 1 on Dec 27, 1987, avg 0.0.

The 1987 ind. was flying high over the island on Dec 28. The Oct 2010 ind. was flying over Manana after sunset. The Sep 2017 ind. was seen heading towards Manana and then flying over it in the afternoon (around 4 p.m.).

Historical/Regional:

- Vickery: cites 1 on Oct 27, 1996 (DAb, SA), 1 on Sep 22, 2004 (LBu), 1 on Oct 29, 2010 (JT) & Sep 29, 2017 (PE, BTn) as observations well offshore (PDV in Vickery et al., 2020).

Short-eared Owl, Sep 29, 2017. © Bill Thompson.

BOREAL OWL
Aegolius funereus

Status: Accidental fall migrant.

Occurrence: One record: 1 dead on Jan 9, 2008 (DC, fide EH, SWh; MARBA–*listed as Jan 10 on Maine-Birds and in eBird as an historical checklist on Nov 11, 2008 and marked as being of questionable date*).

Probably overlooked as a winter visitor, particularly during incursion years, due to lack of coverage and secretive nature. The remains of the one record were discovered by a student inside the former Ice House across the road from the Ice Pond.

NORTHERN SAW-WHET OWL
Aegolius acadicus

Status: Accidental spring and rare (*presumably scarce to fairly common*) fall migrant.

Occurrence: Thirteen records (1 spring, 12 fall) since 1992. Spring record: 1 recently dead on Mar 22, 2021 (NV, fide KL). Fall records over five years since 1992 (nightly banding totals counted as one record each), span Sep 24–Nov 8: 1 on Sep 27, 1992 (PDV), 1 on Sep 24, 1993 (dead–PDV), 3 on Oct 12, 2010 (BRI banding, JT), 4 on Oct 13, 2010 (BRI banding), 1 on Oct 16, 2010 (BRI banding, TMag), 2 on Oct 17, 2010 (BRI banding, TMag), 1 on Oct 18, 2010 (BRI banding), 1 on Oct 21, 2020 (BRI banding), **6** on Oct 23, 2010 (BRI banding), 1 on Oct 29, 2010 (MI, LS, JT), 1 on Nov 8, 2020 (FK, DH), 1 on Oct 8, 2021 (JT, LS). Ten-Year: SP-1, F-2.

- 1939 Summer Census: rare summer resident. Listed as Acadian Owl.
- Banding: 18 total during Oct 12–23 (banding in operation thirteen days during Oct 4–24), max 6 on Oct 23 (see discussion below).

Possibly annual but overlooked on Monhegan, the migration of Northern Saw-whet Owls goes mostly undetected throughout much of their range (including the Northeast) without targeted searching/banding. The only spring record involved the intact remains of a recently deceased ind. in the yard of the house immediately north of the Monhegan House (fide KL). The BRI banding study in Cathedral Woods in Oct 2010 yielded the majority (seven) of the fall records. Results are as indicated above, with no owls banded on Oct 4, 6, 14, 19, 20 & 24 (Desorbo et al., 2012). The ind. on Oct 29 was located in Cathedral Woods near the former net lanes. Three foreign recoveries provide source and return information: two were banded in Quebec 13 & 34 days earlier, one was banded in NY in Oct 2009. There were two recaptures providing staging/lingering information: one bird banded on Oct 13 was recaptured on the 16th and one bird banded on Oct 17 was recaptured on the 18th. Fourteen banded inds. were identified to sex: 11 were female, 3 were male. All of the banded birds were aged: 16 hatch-year and 2 after-hatch-year. The Nov 2020 ind. responded to playback after 11 p.m. in the conifers along Black Head Rd. The Oct 2021 ind. was noted before dawn near Lobster Cove. Possibly an historic breeder, as reported by Palmer (see below), but no details/confirmation available.

Historical/Regional:

- Palmer: reported to nest.

BELTED KINGFISHER
Megaceryle alcyon

Status: Scarce spring and uncommon fall migrant.

Occurrence: Spring dates span Apr 3–June 5, peak mid Apr–mid May; spring max: 2 on eleven days since 1988, span Apr 6–Jun 3. Protracted fall dates span Jul 19–w/e Nov 11 (latest definite date Oct 28), peak early Sep–mid Oct; fall max: **10** on Sep 26, 2000 (JT), 9 on Sep 28, 2012 (JT, BN), 8 on Oct 11, 2014 (JT) & Oct 10, 2015 (JT, JO). Ten-Year: SP-10, F-10.

- 1900–1908 Reconnaissance & Supplements: 1 on Aug 26, 1903 (CFJ, ECJ).
- 1914 & 1916 Checklists: included 1916.
- 1915–1919 Taylor Journals: 1915–Aug 9 (1), 28 (1), Sep 12 (3); 1916–Aug 25 (1), Sep 6, 10; 1917–Aug 18 (1), Sep 5 (1); 1918–Aug 28; 1919–Sep 4 (1), 5 (1), 13 (2).
- 1918 Fall Migration Census: Dewis–1 on Sep 11; Wentworth–Oct 6, 12.
- 1944–1967 Farrell Records: 1945–Sep; 1949–Oct; 1950–Apr, May, Aug, Sep, Oct; 1951–Apr, May, Sep; 1954–Jun; 1957–Oct; 1958–Aug, Oct; 1959–May, Aug; 1960–Apr, May, Aug, Sep; 1961–Apr.
- 1970 Summer Checklist: included, noted as local post-breeding dispersal from nearby areas.

Jun 1960 report possibly a summer visitor, but considered a spring migrant for these purposes; likewise, an ind. on Jul 19, 2021 (BAv) likely a post-breeding dispersal and considered a fall record (next earliest fall record Aug 3). High percentage of records from the Ice Pond, with 6 reported at one time on Oct 10, 2015 (out of 8 that day–JT, JO); also reported from the Meadow on occasion and once at Lobster Cove. An anomaly was "many around all over the island" on Oct 11, 2014 (8 reported–LS et al.). Two inds. were migrating north past Manana far out over the water on May 23, 2022 (JT, LS, MWa). Undoubtedly linger for multiple days and extended periods on occasion, but difficult to be certain of specific inds. and turnover possible, as any kingfisher around is drawn to the limited appropriate habitat.

Belted Kingfisher, Oct 5, 2021. © Jeremiah Trimble.

RED-HEADED WOODPECKER
Melanerpes erythrocephalus

Status: Very rare spring and rare fall migrant.

Occurrence: Five spring records over four years 1980–1989 (one additional possibility of undetermined date in 1990–see below), span Apr 22–May 27: 1 on May 24–25, 1980 (JP et al.), unreported number May 26–27, 1987 (CH), 1 on Apr 22, 1989 (MAS), unreported number on May 26, 1989 (fide BT; *G* 18[2]: 27), 1 during May 18–25, 1996 (GD). Fall dates span Sep 11 (possibly earlier in 1916)–w/e Dec 1 since first reported in 1916; fall max: **5** on Sep 15, 1981 (HT; *AB* 36[2]: 154), 3 on Sep 23, 1983 (RHe, JSm), Sep 24, 1984 (MPl) & Sep 28, 1987 (PDV), 2 on seventeen days over ten years, span Sep 13–Oct 15. Ten-Year: F-8.

- 1914 & 1916 Checklists: included 1916.
- 1918 Fall Migration Census: Wentworth–Oct 11, 13, 16 (mentions it had been recorded two previous years; see Cruickshank, below).
- 1970 Summer Checklist: included.

There is one record of an undetermined date, May–mid July, 1990 (MAS), that is probably a spring record (not included here) or would be a potential first summer record. At least three distinct inds. present in fall of 1982, 1983, 1984, 1987 & 2011, with possibly more in 1977 & 1983 (see Vickery, below). Often lingers for multiple days, up to at least eight days for one ind. in 2011 and ten days for an adult in 2021 (Oct 2–11, joined by an immature Oct 4–6 near the Brewery–TA et al.). Similarily, an adult was present Sep 25–29, 2022 at the south end of the island, where an immature appeared on Sep 28 and lingered until at least Oct 8. The three juvs. in 2011 were separated by gaps of fifteen and six days (present Oct 21–22,

Nov 7–14 & Nov 21). The simultaneous presence of one adult and two juvs. in both fall 1984 and 1987 is presumably the reason that breeding was assumed (no details to support breeding, and no records for all of Maine in the *MABB*). Inds. tend to be long-staying in certain areas, with limited movement. Often found in spruces, both dead and alive, although once reported in apple trees. Multiple reports from Horn's Hill, Lobster Cove Rd. and opposite the north end of the Island Inn, and also at the Ice Pond, Hitchcox feeders, Lighthouse Hill Rd, the north end of the island, Trail #10 to Black Head, and along the White Head Trail. With a majority of fall records indicating the age of inds. (none in spring), the breakdown is 29 juvenile and 15 adult. Inds. have been heard calling on several instances in the fall.

Historical/Regional:

- Cruickshank: both county records from the island; early Sep 1916 (Mrs. Gleason) and 1919 (Jenney). Surprisingly, does not mention the Wentworth record in 1918 (unless it is a typographical error for the 1919 Jenney record).
- Vickery: nearly annual late Sep–early Oct 1976–1990, every one–four years subsequently; cites 4–5 over Sep 15–Oct 4, 1977 (DF et al.), 3–6 fall 1983 and 2 in 1981 as high counts (BSV in Vickery et al., 2020).

Red-headed Woodpecker, Oct 10, 2020. © Luke Seitz.

RED-BELLIED WOODPECKER
Melanerpes carolinus

Status: Rare to scarce spring and fall migrant, accidental summer and very rare winter visitor.

Occurrence: A fairly recent addition to the island's birdlife with the first record on May 28, 1989 (WH et al.), now almost annual in both spring and fall. Spring dates May 4–w/e Jun 12 (latest definitive date Jun 7), except for an overwintering ind. in 2012 recorded in Jan and Mar 5 onward and an ind. noted on Feb 28 & Mar 14, 2018 (see details below); spring max: **8** on May 12, 2012 (RS), 4 on May 25, 2012 (RL, JM) & May 25, 2021 (BTh), 3 on seven days. One summer record: 1 on Jun 27–Jul 2, 2021 (DC, DH). Fall dates span Aug 28–w/e Nov 26 (latest definite date Nov 23), peak late Sep–early Nov; fall max: 6 on Oct 4, 2020 (JT, LS, BBy), 5 on Oct 13, 2012 (DH) and Nov 9, 2022 (LS, MWa), 4 on Nov 9, 2011 (JM) & Oct 3, 2020 (WR). Five winter records: 1 on Jan 4–Apr 24, 2005 (DH, PM et al.), 1 on Jan 4–Apr 4, 2012 (DH–see below), 1 on Jan 3–26, 2013 (CBC–PDV et al.), female during Jan 16–17, 2018 (KL), 1 on Feb 28–Mar 14, 2018 (DC–see below). Ten-Year: SP-9, F-9, W-1.

- MBA: possible.
- CBC: 2 years (8%), max 1 on Jan 5, 2012 & Jan 3, 2013, avg 0.1.

Expansion as a breeder into southern Maine over recent decades (first state record in 1958, with first confirmed breeding in 1996), has led to its fairly regular appearance on the island, despite limited migratory tendencies. Notable influxes in Fall 2011, Spring 2012, Fall 2012, Fall 2014 and Fall 2020 involved multiple inds. over extended periods, with actual numbers hard to determine and details lacking for many reports; inds. often separate, although feeders (notably suet) are a gathering point. Inds. known to linger for weeks, with the winter records most obvious; a female in 2012 was observed on Jan 4 & 5, Mar 6, and Apr 4 and intermittently until at least Apr 24, first in town and then around the Ice Pond (DH et al.–noted as long-continuing and possibly the same bird from late-fall 2011, present until Nov 22), a male in 2013 was reported behind the Meadow on Jan 3 and relocated on Jan 26 at Shining Sails (DH), and an ind. in winter 2018 (likely continuing) was observed along Tribler Rd. during Jan 16–17 and at Donna Cundy's feeders on Feb 28 (eating suet) & Mar 14. The 2021 summer record involved reports on Jun 27 (male at Cundy feeders) & Jul 2, presumed to be the same ind. due to rarity in this season. Possible status on MBA related to several reports of inds. in appropriate habitat or singing in 2021 (span May 26–Jul 2). Reported at various locations around town, most often Lobster Cove Rd., near the Ice Pond, and feeders at the Hitchcox house. Heard calling on many occasions. The 34 inds. identified to sex are split almost evenly, with 18 males and 16 females.

Historical/Regional:

- Vickery: cites a female on May 28, 1989 (WH et al.) as first spring record for island (PDV in Vickery et al., 2020).

Red-bellied Woodpecker, Oct 14, 2019. © Bill Thompson.

YELLOW-BELLIED SAPSUCKER
Sphyrapicus varius

Status: Rare to scarce spring and fairly common to common fall migrant.

Occurrence: Spring dates span Apr 5–Jun 4, peak mid Apr–third week of May; spring max: 5 on May 14, 2021 (JT, LS, BBy), 4 on Apr 12, 2011 (TMag) & Apr 27, 2011 (TMag), 3 on May 19, 1983 (PDV), Apr 24, 2011 (TMag), Apr 26, 2011 (TMag) & May 22, 2013 (JH). Fall dates span Sep 10–Nov 12, peak late Sep–mid Oct; fall max: **246** on Oct 4, 2020 (JT, LS, BBy), 110 on Sep 26, 1981 (VL, PDV et al.; *AB* 36[2]: 154), 85 on Oct 8, 2011 (JM), 80 on Oct 12, 2009 (JM) & Sep 30, 2019 (DH). Ten-Year: SP-7, F-10.

- MBA: possible.
- 1914 & 1916 Checklists: included 1916.
- 1915–1919 Taylor Journals: 1916–Sep 10.
- 1918 Fall Migration Census: Wentworth–Oct 1, 4, 7, 8, 9 (increasing day by day), 12 (1), 17 (1), 19 (1).
- 1944–1967 Farrell Records: 1949–Oct; 1950–Apr, May, Oct; 1951–Apr, May, Oct; 1959–May; 1960–Apr, Sep; 1961–Apr; 1967–Apr 6 (1), 14 (1).
- 1970 Summer Checklist: included as Sapsucker.
- Banding: 22 total over five seasons, peak 9 in Fall 1961, max 4 on Oct 5, 1961.

Underreported in Apr, supported by the max counts occurring when TMag provided consistent spring coverage. Large fall movements sometimes multi-day events, especially in 2011 (five consecutive days of 35+ spanning Oct 7–11, including 85 on Oct 8) and 2012 (five consecutive days of 30+ spanning Oct 4–8, including high of 65 on Oct 8). These fallouts have been described as sapsuckers everywhere and the island "crawling with them" (WH). The max count of 246 on Oct 4, 2020 featured an "all day long" movement, often very high overhead, as well as "12–16 in some single apple trees and groups of 5+ together in the northern woods" (JT, LS, BBy), preceded/followed by counts of 40 and 31, respectively. As mentioned, these birds are particularly drawn to the many apple trees scattered around town, and described as being in every apple tree, some of which are seemingly completely full of sapsucker holes. Also reported from Horse Chestnut and spruce trees and feeding on Mountain Ash berries. Surprisingly few details for the number of sightings. Reported calling frequently and occasionally drumming. The 2021 MBA status of possible is the result of an ind. in appropriate habitat on May 28, 2021, likely a migrant. Most inds. identified to age/sex in fall have been noted as juveniles, such as 10 out of 12 on Sep 29, 2013, with the others an adult male and adult female (CDd), and 14 marked as almost all juveniles on Oct 6, 2019 (LK).

Historical/Regional:

- Vickery: regular in spring until the end of May; cites 1 on Sep 12, 1983 (PDV) and Sep 14, 1980 (PDV) as early, and 60–80 on Sep 30, 1978 (DF, PDV), >110 on Sep 26, 1981 (PDV), 80 on Oct 12, 2009 (JM), and 85 on Oct 8, 2011 (JM) as examples of numerous reports in fall (PDV in Vickery et al., 2020).

Yellow-bellied Sapsucker, May 15, 2012. © Geoff Dennis.

AMERICAN THREE-TOED WOODPECKER
Picoides dorsalis

Status: Accidental fall visitor.

Occurrence: One record: 1 in Oct 1969 (Tom Martin's personal notes).

- 1970 Summer Checklist: included.

Generally a nonmigratory resident of northern Maine, but known to disperse southward, with only a few records along the coast. No details available. Inclusion on 1970 checklist probably due to the 1969 record.

BLACK-BACKED WOODPECKER
Picoides arcticus

Status: Very rare fall and accidental winter visitor.

Occurrence: Eight records (7 fall, 1 winter) since 1916. Fall records over seven years, span Sep 10–Oct 31: 1 on Sep 10, 1916 (CTa, MCG), unreported number on Sep 26, 1956 (*WB* 71: 350), 1–**2** on Oct 4–8, 1974 (only 1 present Oct 5, 6 & 8–DF, WR et al.), 1 on Oct 31, 2000 (WBo, fide KG), 1 male on Sep 23, 2004 (SM, MI et al.), 1 on Sep 21, 2009 (fide EH, SWh; MARBA), 1 on Sep 27–Oct 9, 2020 (ASc et al., mob). Winter record: male on Dec 30–31, 1980 (CBC–PDV, DF). Ten-Year: F-1.

- CBC: 1 year (4 %), max 1 on Dec 30, 1980, avg 0.0.
- 1914 & 1916 Checklists: included 1916.
- 1915–1919 Taylor Journals: 1 on Sep 10, 1916 (CTa). Listed as Arctic Three-toed Woodpecker.
- 1939 Summer Census: accidental visitor (one record–*possibly the 1916 record*).
- 1970 Summer Checklist: included as Arctic Three-toed Woodpecker.

The 1956 record was part of a widespread invasion into the Northeastern U.S. of this species and American Three-toed Woodpecker over the fall 1956 and winter 1957 period, as reported in the 1959 *Wilson Bulletin* (West and Speirs, 1959). The Oct 1974 inds. were observed along Lobster Cove Rd. near the Trailing Yew by a WINGS tour, with both reported on Oct 4, but only 1 located on Oct 5, 6 (male) & 8 (unclear if 1 may have departed) and no reports on the 7th. Both the 1980 and 2004 records were in Cathedral Woods. The Sep/Oct 2020 ind., an apparent adult female, was noted feeding in dead spruces in the Red Ribbon Trail/Black Head Rd. area Sep 27 & Oct 1–6 and along Lobster Cove Rd. between Underhill Trail and the Brewery on Oct 9.

Historical/Regional:

- Cruickshank: 1 carefully studied in early Sep 1916 (Mrs. Gleason).
- Vickery: cites 2000 and 2004 fall records as examples of not being shy to cross water (Tamara Enz in Vickery et al., 2020).

Black-backed Woodpecker, Oct 4, 2020. © Luke Seitz.

DOWNY WOODPECKER
Dryobates pubescens

Status: Uncommon permanent resident, possibly supplemented by dispersal/migration.

Occurrence: Status complicated and confusing; a permanent resident known as a species to be partially migratory or wandering, but movements unclear. Reports from throughout the year, but concentrated spring and fall for the obvious reason of observer coverage; year max: **11** on Sep 17, 2015 (PDV et al.), 10 on Sep 22, 2016 (DT), 8 on Sep 21, 2007 (LS), Oct 1, 2007 (DL) & Sep 25–26, 2009 (WR, DH, NL, MLe). Ten-Year: 10.

- *MABB*: confirmed.
- CBC: recorded 15 years (58%) plus 2 count weeks, first on Dec 22, 1979, max 4 on Jan 5, 2010, avg 1.1.

- 1900–1908 Reconnaissance & Supplements: 1 on Aug 12, 1900 (CFJ, ECJ).
- 1914 & 1916 Checklists: included 1916.
- 1915–1919 Taylor Journals: 1915–Sep 2 (1); 1916–Sep 4 (1), 10; 1919–Sep 4 (1).
- 1918 Fall Migration Census: Dewis–Sep 7 (1), 8 (1); Wentworth–Oct 9, 16, 17 (several), 23.
- 1939 Summer Census: regular summer resident.
- 1944–1967 Farrell Records: 1948–Dec; 1949–Mar, Apr, Oct, Dec; 1950–Mar, Apr, Nov; 1951–Mar, Apr, May; 1952–Mar, Apr; 1954–Jun; 1955–Aug; 1957–Aug; 1959–Aug; 1960–Apr, Jul, Aug, Sep; 1961–May.
- 1954 & 1955 Summer Records: 1954–included June 19-25; 1955–Aug 30 (1 male).
- 1970 Summer Checklist: marked as known to breed in area.
- Banding: 51 total over five seasons, peak 17 in Fall 1960, max 6 on Oct 7, 1961 & Oct 2, 1962.

Habitat use outside the popular birding areas in town undoubtedly limits reports, especially during breeding season. All max counts occurring in fall may indicate breeding success or an influx of migrating/dispersing inds. from the mainland; movements known to occur during normal migration periods, but poorly understood (Jackson and Ouellet, 2020). Often found along the town roads, especially in apple trees, but likely to be found in deciduous scrub and spruces, as well, and possible anywhere on the island. One of 4 observed on Oct 4, 2020 was seen coming in high off the water (JT, LS, BBy).

Historical/Regional:

- Vickery: notes 1–3 in spring and 1–4 in fall as regular, with status as resident, migrant or both as unclear, slightly higher counts >6 suggestive of some movement (lists two records of 6 inds. and the three max counts of 8 inds. as examples; PDV in Vickery et al., 2020).

HAIRY WOODPECKER
Picoides villosus

Status: Scarce spring and fall visitor/migrant, accidental summer visitor and possible breeder, very rare winter visitor.

Occurrence: Complicated and unclear status for this wandering and partially migratory species, certainly underreported in Apr, Nov, and winter months and probably in the summer. Spring dates span Mar 20–May 31; spring max: 3 on May 16, 2019 (DPJ) & May 16, 2021 (JT, LS, JO), 2 on twelve days over six seasons. Only one documented record during designated summer period: unreported number on Jul 18, 2018 (TRo), although listed as possible in *MABB*, MBA and historic inclusion (see below); notable potential breeding record during trip report May 25–27, 1998 (HB–female "dive-bombed" observer). Fall dates span Aug 8–Nov 21, peak mid Oct–mid Nov; fall max: **6 or 8** on Oct 19, 1918 (BHW), 6 on Oct 22, 1918 (BHW), 5 on Oct 25, 2022 (ShF), 3 on Oct 12, 2009 (JM), Nov 2, 2010 (TMag), Nov 11, 2018 (DH, FK), Nov 9, 2020 (LS, JT), Oct 23, 2022 (JTh, LMo) & Nov 9, 2022 (LS, MWa). Nine winter records over nine years since 1978, all but two associated with CBC period, span Dec 21–Feb 5; winter max: 2 on Dec 22, 1988 (CBC–PDV) & Jan 1, 1992 (CBC–PDV). Ten-Year: SP-7, SU-2, F-10, W-1.

- *MABB*: possible; MBA: possible.
- CBC: 6 years (23%) plus 1 count week, first on Dec 28, 1978, max 2 on Dec 22,1988 & Jan 1, 1992, avg 0.3.
- 1915–1919 Taylor Journals: 1916–Aug 22 (1), Sep 10.
- 1918 Fall Migration Census: Wentworth–Oct 16, 17 (several), 19 (6 or 8), 21, 22 (6), 23, 24 (several), 25 (several).
- 1939 Summer Census: regular summer resident.
- 1944–1967 Farrell Records: 1949–Mar; 1951–Mar, Apr; 1955–Aug; 1959–May; 1960–May, Aug; 1961–Apr.
- 1970 Summer Checklist: has been a summer resident and possible breeder.

A species that is known to wander, particularly southward in the winter, and to show partial migratory tendencies in spring and fall, but not a true migrant, hence the term visitor may be more appropriate. Consistent yearly coverage would surely present a more complete picture of its presence on the island, as indicated by records from early spring 2011 (consistent coverage by TMag) and on a number of CBCs. Historically must have been more regular in summer, based on 1939 Census, 1970 Checklist, and *MABB*; the lack of summer records may be partially due to habitat use outside the normal birding areas in town. Also complicated by possible early breeders/residents considered migrants in late May (note record in late May 1998 as nesting behavior [HB] and MBA status based on an ind. in appropriate habitat on May 27, 2021 [LiM]). Several records in Aug may indicate summering inds., but just as likely to be post-breeding/fledging wanderers and considered such here, based on general breeding period data (Jackson et al., 2020), with the summer period designated as Jun 1–Jul 31. Extremely few details are available for a species of such limited numbers. A male was visiting the Cundy feeders on Feb 5, 2019 and the 3 inds. on Oct 22, 2022 were observed in separate areas: 1 near the Ice Pond, 1 behind the lighthouse and 1 near Lobster Cove (part of an apparent incursion in fall 2022—note high count of 5 on Oct 25). Length of stay on the island is unknown; one ind. noted as continuing Oct 29–31, 2010 near Lobster Cove (MI) and May 23–24, 2013 in the Hitchcox yard near the Ice Pond (DH).

Historical/Regional:

- Vickery: notes 2 as the max count in spring and regular 1–2 inds. in fall (with no higher reports to indicate "marked" fall migration (PDV in Vickery et al., 2020).

Hairy Woodpecker, May 14, 2010. © Geoff Dennis.

NORTHERN FLICKER
Colaptes auratus

Status: Uncommon spring and fairly common to common fall migrant, rare summer visitor and possible breeder, rare winter visitor.

Occurrence: Spring dates span Mar 16–May 31, peak early Apr–early May; spring max: 38 on Apr 21, 2011 (TMag), 34 on Apr 12, 2011 (TMag), 25 on Apr 30 2011 (TMag). Nineteen summer records over thirteen years since 1914 (fourteen records since 2010), scattered throughout the Jun 1–Aug 15 period; summer max: 2 on Aug 4, 2020 (AMo). Fall dates span mid Aug–Nov 21, peak mid Sep–mid Oct; fall max: **240** on Sep 18, 2013 (PDV et al.), 153 on Oct 4, 2020 (JT, LS, BBy), 150 on Oct 1, 1993 (BN), Sep 25, 2005 (TV), Sep 26, 2005 (TV) & Sep 26, 2013 (PDV, SBe), 140 on Sep 22, 2007 (LS) & Sep 30, 2022 (DH). Eleven winter records over nine years since 1939 (all but one since 1988; two records in 2006 & 2010), all singles, span Dec 3–w/e Mar 3. Ten-Year: SP-10, SU-8, F-10, W -3.

- *MABB*: possible; MBA: possible.
- CBC: 4 years (15%) plus one count week, first recorded Dec 22, 1988, max 1 on Dec 22, 1988, Jan 1, 1992, Jan 3, 2015 & Jan 2, 2020, avg 0.2.
- 1900–1908 Reconnaissance & Supplements: included in Jenney supplement as Flicker.
- 1914 & 1916 Checklists: unreported number on Aug 1, 1914; included 1916.
- 1915–1919 Taylor Journals: 1915–Aug 9 (3), Sep 2, 5 (1), 12 (6); 1916–Aug 19, 20, 21 (1), 22, 25, 26, 30, 31, Sep 3, 6, 10; 1917–Aug 4 (2), Sep 5 (3); 1919–Sep 5 (3), 11 (6), 13 (75), 14 (100).
- 1918 Fall Migration Census: Dewis–Sep 4 (1), 10 (2), 11 (8); Wentworth–Sep 29, Oct 1, 4, 7, 8, 9 (usual large numbers), 12 (2), 15 (few), 16, 17 (7–10), 19 (3).
- 1939 Summer Census: regular summer visitor. Listed as Flicker.
- 1944–1967 Farrell Records: 1949–Mar, Apr, Sep, Oct; 1950–Apr, May, Sep, Oct; 1951–Apr, Oct; 1952–Apr; 1953–Aug, Sep; 1954–Jun, Jul; 1955–Aug; 1957–Aug; 1958–Sep, Oct; 1959–Apr, May, Aug; 1960–Apr, May, Aug, Sep; 1961–Apr, May; 1967–Apr 2 (2), 3, 4, 5, 7, 8, 9, 14, 15 (2), 16 (2), 17, 18, 21, 22, 23, 24.
- 1954 & 1955 Summer Records: included June 19–25 & Jun 27–Jul 4; 1955–Aug 28 (1+), 29 (3+), 30 (1). Listed as Flicker.
- 1970 Summer Checklist: has been a summer resident and possible breeder. Listed as Yellow-shafted Flicker.
- Banding: 10 total over three seasons, peak 8 in Fall 1960, max 2 on Sep 22, 1960.

A species that often comes in "waves," during migration, producing notable tallies over multiple days and reported as "everywhere" for the larger flights, especially anywhere there are trees, including Manana; noted as the most abundant migrant on the island several times in Sep. Sometimes difficult to be sure of numbers at a given time, as they are regularly moving around and difficult to determine if staying or leaving. Form loose flocks upwards of 20 inds., noted moving in a uniform direction on occasion in the early morning; 8–10 staging at Lobster Cove as late as noon during the flight of Oct 4, 2020 (JT, LS, BBy). Undoubtedly underreported in Apr, as evidenced by the numbers present in 2011, a year with consistent coverage by TMag; all of the spring max flights occurred this year, along with counts of 24 on Apr 29 and 23 on Apr 14. Fall 2013 was exceptional for two major peaks over Sep 17–21 and Sep 24–28 that included two of the max counts and nine days of at least 25 inds. MBA status of possible based on an ind. in appropriate habitat on Jun 5, 2021 (TF), possibly a late migrant.

While all are expected to be the Yellow-shafted subspecies (C. a. *auratus*), there are two apparent records of the western Red-shafted subspecies (C. a. *cafer*): 1 involving feathers found by TMar on May 4, 2005 and identified as Red-shafted Flicker, 1 on Oct 26, 2013 (JP).

Historical/Regional:

- Vickery: cites the max counts above as high spring counts and 10 on May 6, 1984 (PDV) as reflecting end of spring flight; cites 8 on Sep 6, 1980 (PDV and 9 on Sep 9, 2010 (JSt) as early fall and seven counts >100 (including some of the max counts above) as peak migration late Sep–Oct (PDV in Vickery et al., 2020).

Northern Flicker, Oct 5, 2021. © Jeremiah Trimble.

AMERICAN KESTREL
Falco sparverius

Status: Rare spring and uncommon to fairly common fall migrant, very rare summer visitor and possible breeder, accidental winter visitor.

Occurrence: Forty-one spring records over only seventeen years since 1961 (sixteen records in 2011, three in 2012, two in 2016, four in 2019, two in 2021), span Apr 5–May 27; spring max: 2 on May 6, 1984 (PDV), Apr 24, 2011 (TMag), May 9, 2011 (TMag), May 13, 2016 (EG) & May 18, 2019 (JVW). Six summer records (four in 2020): unreported number during w/e Jul 6, 2005 (fide SP, KG; MARBA), 1 on Jul 19, 2010, 1 on Jun 1–8, 2020 (JT, LS), 1 on Jun 15, 2020 (DH), 1 on Jul 4, 2020 (DH), 1 on Jul 26, 2020 (GBr). Fall dates span Aug 12–Nov 12, peak early Sep–early Oct; fall max: **70** on Sep 17, 2013 (PDV et al.), 40 on Sep 14, 1986 (PDV), 35 on Oct 2, 1994 (LBr), 30 on Sep 16, 1984 (PDV). One winter record: male on Jan 19, 2013 (DC). Ten-Year: SP-5, SU-1, F-10, W-1.

- 1900–1908 Reconnaissance & Supplements: unreported number on Aug 1, 1907 (CFJ, ECJ).
- 1914 & 1916 Checklists: included 1916. Listed as Sparrow Hawk.
- 1915–1919 Taylor Journals: 1916–Sep 10; 1919–Sep 10 (1), 13 (2). Listed as Sparrow Hawk.
- 1918 Fall Migration Census: Dewis–Sep 10 (1), 11 (10); Wentworth–Sep 29, Oct 21. Listed as Sparrow Hawk.
- 1944–1967 Farrell Records: 1960–Aug, Sep; 1961–Apr. Listed as Sparrow Hawk.
- 1970 Summer Checklist: included. Listed as Sparrow Hawk.
- Banding: 2 juveniles in Fall 2010.
- 2010 Fall Hawkwatch: 64 total (58 Lob, 6 Man) over nine days spanning Sep 16–Oct 4, max 26 on Sep 20.

Undoubtedly underreported in Apr, as evidenced by eight of the sixteen records in spring 2011, when more consistent reporting was provided by TMag, and supported by regional timing; possibility of repeat sightings on consecutive days during this period and in general, but no details to support this. Breeding confirmed on Jun 1, 2020 (JT, LS) with an ind. carrying a snake over to Manana, with additional sightings on Jun 2, 3, 4, 7, 8 and possibly the same ind. reported on Jun 15, Jul 4, and Jul 26 (on Manana) but without specific details (not included on MBA). Two documented fall instances of inds. lingering (Oct 28–31, 2010 and Nov 9–12, 2018), both late season cases where a specific ind. is more easily tracked. Possible anywhere on the island as flyovers, but often noted at Lobster Cove, Lighthouse Hill, the eastern cliffs, and over/on Manana; noted as hawking insects and harassing a Peregrine. Seldom documented to sex, with only a handful of records listed as males, including the two lingering fall inds. noted above and the only winter record.

Historical/Regional:

- Vickery: cites 1 on Aug 17, 2004 (WBo) and 1 on Aug 12, 2010 (TMag) as early fall, and 70 on Sep 17, 2003 (TJ, PDV et al.), 25 on Sep 21, 1991 (PDV), 35 on Oct 2, 1994 (LBr) and 40 on Sep 14, 1986 (PDV) as high counts on island (PDV in Vickery et al., 2020).

American Kestrel, Oct 10, 2020. © Jeremiah Trimble.

MERLIN
Falco columbarius

Status: Scarce to uncommon spring and fairly common fall migrant, very rare summer resident, very rare winter visitor.

Occurrence: Spring dates span w/e Mar 8–June 7, peak late Apr–third week of May; spring max: 6 on Apr 27, 2011 (TMag), May 2, 2011 (TMag) & May 17, 2019 (BTn, KL, BP), 4 on May 6, 1985 (PDV), Apr 28, 2011 (TMag), Apr 30, 2011 (TMag), May 18, 2011 (DH), May 19, 2011 (DH), May 20, 2011 (DH) & May 18, 2019 (JVW). Six summer records, all from 2019 & 2020 (five from 2019 are presumed to be the same ind. or part of a breeding pair): 1 on Jun 11–12, 2019 (DH), 1 on Jun 22, 2019 (KD), 1 on Jun 29, 2019 (KL), 1 on Jul 2, 2019 (DH, DL, JL), 1 on Jul 6, 2019 (DH), 2 on Jul 3, 2020 (DH). Fall dates span Aug 24–Nov 22, peak mid Sep–early Oct; fall max: **110** on Sep 25, 1981 (PDV), 70 on Sep 25, 1986 (PDV et al.), 69 on Sep 18, 2010 (FT), 66 on Sep 20, 2010. Five winter records, all associated with CBC period: 1 on Dec 30, 1980 (CBC–PDV), 1 on Dec 29, 1981 (CBC–PDV), 1 on Dec 27, 1982 (CBC–PDV), 1 on Dec 29, 1983 (CBC–PDV), 1 on Jan 2 & 4, 2013 (CBC count week–PDV et al.). Ten-Year: SP-10, SU-2, F-10.

- MBA: confirmed.
- CBC: 4 years (15%) plus 1 count week, first on Dec 30, 1980, max 1 on all four dates, avg 0.2.
- 1900–1908 Reconnaissance & Supplements: included in Jenney supplement as Pigeon Hawk.
- 1914 & 1916 Checklists: included 1916.
- 1915–1919 Taylor Journals: 1916–Sep 10; 1919–Sep 4 (5), 5 (4), 10 (2), 11 (3), 13 (5), 14 (5). Listed as Pigeon Hawk.
- 1918 Fall Migration Census: Dewis–Sep 7, 9; Wentworth–Oct 1, 7. Listed as Pigeon Hawk.
- 1939 Summer Census: uncommon summer visitor. Listed as Pigeon Hawk.
- 1944–1967 Farrell Records: 1949–Aug; 1951–Sep; 1960–Apr, Aug; 1967–Apr 13 (1). Listed as Pigeon Hawk.
- 1970 Summer Checklist: included. Listed as Pigeon Hawk.
- Banding: 6 juveniles in Fall 2010.
- 2010 Fall Hawkwatch: 393 total (247 Lob, 146 Man) over twenty days spanning Sep 15–Oct 17, max 69 on Sep 18.
- DOWTS Surveys 2011–2014: None observed in Control Quadrant; 1 on May 13, 2014 observed in northern end of Test Quadrant and included here.

Significant increase in state since 1970s after decline from pesticides, quickly becoming a common Maine breeder after first confirmation in 1986 (Vickery et al., 2020). Due to its propensity for patrolling the island for prey and returning through the same areas, with activity all day, it is often unclear as to how many inds. are involved, with many reports noted as conservative counts and length of stay is also indeterminable for these reasons. The peak count of 110 recorded "non-

Merlin, Oct 9, 2020. © Jeremiah Trimble.

stop Merlins flying south over the island" (PDV–this report included a ferry crossing, but was included due to the details provided). Most reported as flyovers, occurring regularly at Lobster Cove, Ballfield/Lighthouse, the Meadow, and over Manana (up to 6 in view at once on Oct 7, 2012–LS), possible anywhere on the island, although up to three have been reported in a single tree and noted as perching on Manana and many other locations. Other direct evidence of migration included nearly ninety minutes of inds. coming in off the ocean at White Head on Sep 25, 2013, roughly 1 every five minutes (PB). It is interesting that a male on May 27 & 29, 2014 was noted as possibly nesting (JT). The confirmation of breeding in 2019 (carrying food on Jul 6 [DH], apparently breeding in woods north of the Ice Pond) justifies counting all the summer reports from that year as a single record; also noted as calling along Pebble Beach Trail on Jun 29, 2019 (KL). Possibly the same pair bred in 2020, with sightings of a pair east of the Meadow below the Lighthouse on Jun 7 (JT, LS) and possible begging calls heard on Jul 3 beyond the Ice Pond, the same area as breeding occurred in 2019. Has been observed with prey, including dragonflies, Cedar Waxwing, and an adult male American Redstart coming in off the water (TMag), and chasing/harassing robins, grackles, waxwings, swallows, flickers, and even a kingfisher.

Historical/Regional:

- Vickery: 1–4 inds./day typical in spring, high of 6 on Apr 27, 2011 (TMag); lists five high counts of 50+ in fall, including the top two max counts above (PDV in Vickery et al., 2020).

GYRFALCON
Falco rusticolus

Status: Accidental summer visitor.

Occurrence: One record: 1 white morph on Jun 22–25, 1969 (RCo, LCo et al.; *AFN* 23: 639).

Described as white variant, observed perched and flying. Seen by RCo & LCo on the 22nd and by six observers on the 25th. It is remarkable that the only record for Monhegan would be in summer (possibly the only summer record for all of New England [Vickery et al., 2020]) and that it was a white morph.

Historical/Regional:

- Vickery: cites as Maine's only summer record as remarkable and possibly only one at this season for all of New England (PDV in Vickery et al., 2020).

PEREGRINE FALCON
Falco peregrinus

Status: Scarce to uncommon spring and uncommon to fairly common fall migrant, very rare summer visitor, very rare winter visitor.

Occurrence: Spring dates span Mar 18–Jun 5, peak late Apr–late May; spring max: 2 on eleven days over six years (including the early date on Mar 18, 2022–KL), span Mar 18–May 27. Four summer records, all since 2019: 1 on Jul 26, 2019 (DP), 2 on Aug 4, 2020 (AMo), 1 on Aug 15, 2021 (CEl), adult on Jul 7, 2022 (LS, MWa). Fall dates span Aug 17–Nov 19, peak mid Sep–mid Oct; fall max: **72** on Oct 4, 2020 (JT, LS, BBy), 39 on Oct 11, 2010 (JT), 30 on Sep 30, 2008 (DL et al.), 25+ on Sep 30, 1989 (BN). Ten winter records over eight years since 2008 (two records in 2008 & 2012), six associated with CBC period, two in early Feb and one in early Mar (see below); winter max: 2 on Jan 3, 2013 (CBC–DH, PM), Jan 4, 2015 (DH, WN, FK) & Dec 16, 2021 (DC). Ten-Year: SP-10, SU-4, F-10, W-4.

- CBC: 5 years (19%) plus 1 count week (the six most recent counts), first on Jan 3, 2008, max 2 on Jan 3, 2013, avg 0.3.
- 1914 & 1916 Checklists: included 1916. Listed as Duck Hawk.
- 1944–1967 Farrell Records: 1950–Oct; 1955–Aug; 1957–Aug. Listed as Duck Hawk.
- 1954 & 1955 Summer Records: Aug 29 (1 near White Head, flying west across island). Listed as Duck Hawk.
- Banding: 17 juveniles in Fall 2010.
- 2010 Fall Hawkwatch: 139 total (9 Lob, 130 Man) over 20 days spanning Sep 15–Oct 18, max 31 on Oct 11.

Recent numbers clearly show the recovery of this species in the East since the DDT era (mid 20th century), with first confirmed Maine breeding in 1988, and emphasized by CBC results (only recorded on the six counts since 2008). First known Monhegan record during Aug 16–Sep 16, 1916 (MCG) and not again until Oct 1950 (IF–see 1944–1967 Farrell Records above). Possible anywhere on the island, usually as flyovers, but most often seen along the shore at Lobster Cove, the Harbor, the eastern cliffs (White Head in particular), and over/on Manana. Often seen in loose groups in the fall, when several congregations of 5–7 have been reported. Migration clearly evident some days in fall: most of the 21 on Sep 29, 2007 were seen flying out over the water and 33 of the 39 on Oct 11, 2010 were confirmed leaving the island (this day also lines up with the peak day of 31 for the

2010 Hawkwatch–see below). The max fall count of 72 produced a kettle of 28+ in the early afternoon. As with Merlin, the habit of repeat patrolling of areas can result in uncertain numbers; an extreme is 100+ sightings from White Head on Oct 5, 2009, but only 7 inds. reported (CT)—these 7 immatures were all seen together and unsuccessfully chased a Northern Flicker coming in off the ocean. Certainly lingers on occasion, but details unclear and more obvious outside of migration; in winter 2007–2008, an ind. reported on Feb 10 was noted as arriving in late Jan and may have been the same ind. recorded on the Jan 3 CBC. Additionally, an adult was noted Feb 6–8, 2009 (LS), an immature *F. p. tundrius* (see below) lingered along the east cliffs on Oct 30–31, 2010 (MI), an adult on Mar 6, 2012 (DH) was reported as probably the same ind. as present on the Jan 5, 2012 CBC, and two immatures satellite-tracked during the BRI banding in 2010 spent two subsequent nights on the island before departing southward (DeSorbo et al., 2012). Obvious differences in plumage make immatures easy to distinguish from adults in fall and quite a few reports include this detail, with a mix often noted, but immatures dominating: all 17 banded in 2010 were immatures and only 3 out of the 72 on Oct 4, 2020 were adults, with the rest apparently immatures. Known for chasing prey, including warblers, robins ,gulls, the aforementioned flicker, and most notably capturing a Western Kingbird on Sep 26, 2012 (SB).

The blond/buffy features of immatures of the Arctic subspecies *F. p. tundrius* have led to the identification of five fall records, involving 8 inds..

Both of the juveniles fitted with satellite transmitters mentioned above continued their southward migration along the East Coast after departing from Monhegan (one on Oct 7 and the other on Oct 10). They both spent time in Hatteras, NC before departing southeast over the open ocean for a couple of days, then turned southwest and ultimately ended up in Cuba by late Oct. One ind. spent the winter in Cuba, while the other continued onward to Colombia and spent the winter there. Reception of data from both transmitters stopped in early Mar for unknown reasons (DeSorbo et al., 2012). Two of the four Peregrine Falcons fitted with transmitters at the Naval Support Activity Installation in Cutler, Maine in Fall 2020 passed over or spent time at Monhegan, followed by open water crossings to the Cape Cod, Massachusetts area, illustrating the island's migration stopover importance (Persico et al., 2021).

Historical/Regional:

- Vickery: nearly annual in spring since 2010

(daily counts 1–2), cites 1 chasing Red-necked Phalaropes on May 26, 1984 (JP), 1 on Jun 5, 2001 (WBo) and 2 on May 27, 2017 (mob) as late; 6–8 during late Sep–early Oct 1978 "considered good then" (DF et al.) for fall, considered low by 2000, lists six counts of 11–39 inds. since 1981 (PDV in Vickery et al., 2020).

Peregrine Falcon, Oct 11, 2021. © Bobby Wilcox.

ASH-THROATED FLYCATCHER
Myiarchus cinerascens

Status: Very rare fall vagrant.

Occurrence: Two records: 1 on Oct 23, 2011 (JT et al.), 1 on Oct 21, 2013 (TMz). Sixth and eighth Maine records; accepted as ME-BRC #2011–010 & ME-BRC #2013–018. Ten-Year: F-1.

The Oct 2011 ind. was observed flycatching at the Trailing Yew, where it caught a stinkbug and an earthworm. The Oct 2013 ind. was observed between the school and the library.

Historical/Regional:

- Vickery: cites two records in 2011 & 2013 (PDV in Vickery et al., 2020).
- OLMB: twelve additional state records—eight accepted and four not yet reviewed, earliest in 1971.

Ash-throated Flycatcher, Oct 22, 2011. © Jeremiah Trimble.

GREAT CRESTED FLYCATCHER
Myiarchus crinitus

Status: Rare to scarce spring and rare fall migrant, very rare summer visitor.

Occurrence: Spring dates span Apr 27–mid Jun, peak last ten day of May; spring max: 2 on May 28, 2004 (JVW), May 20, 2013 (JH), May 28, 2013 (KL, DL, JL), Jun 12, 2016 (DFu) & May 15, 2021 (JT, LS, JO). Three summer records: unreported number during Jun 19–25, 1954 (ES, AS), 1 on Jul 20, 2010 (TMag), 1 on Jun 18, 2018 (BEv, TEv). Twenty-seven fall records over twenty years since 1916 (twenty-two over seventeen years since 1978), span Aug 31–Oct 29, peak early–mid Sep; fall max: **3** on Sep 3, 1983 (PDV), 2 on Sep 5, 1987 (PDV). Ten-Year: SP-9, SU-1, F-5.

- MBA: possible.
- 1914 & 1916 Checklists: included 1916. Listed as Crested Flycatcher.
- 1915–1919 Taylor Journals: 1916–Sep 10.
- 1918 Fall Migration Census: Dewis–1 on Sep 11; Wentworth–1 on Oct 12 & Oct 21. Listed as Crested Flycatcher and Crested Fly-catcher.
- 1944–1967 Farrell Records: 1954–Jun; 1955–Aug; 1960–Aug. Listed as Crested Flycatcher.
- 1954 & 1955 Summer Records: 1954–included Jun 29–25; 1955–Sep 2 (1–IW, MLn).
- 1970 Summer Checklist: included.

Has apparently lingered for two–three days on occasion. MBA status based on an ind. in appropriate habitat on May 26, 2021 (BBl), probably a migrant. Most frequent in deciduous habitat, scattered reports from near the Ice Pond, Burnt Head Trail, behind the Monhegan House, the road to Fish Beach, behind the Lighthouse, Lobster Cove and the Trailing Yew. Sometimes located by its call, a distinctive, loud "wheep.".

Historical/Regional:
- Palmer: lists 1918 Wentworth records as late.
- Vickery: cites 1 on Oct 29, 2013 (PDV, JP) as later date (WJS in Vickery et al., 2020).

WESTERN KINGBIRD
Tyrannus verticalis

Status: Very rare spring and rare fall vagrant, accidental summer vagrant.

Occurrence: Forty-four records (4 spring, 1 summer, 39 fall) since 1961. Spring records over three years since 2002: 1 on May 15, 2002 (fide LBr; *G* 32: 26), 1 on Jun 15, 2002 (DAb, DF), 1 on Jun 7, 2008 (fide EH, KG, LS; MARBA), 1 on May 29, 2010 (KL). Summer record: 1 on Jul 7, 2022 (LS, MWa). Fall records over twenty-four years since 1961 (twenty-one years since 1978), scattered throughout extended period Sep 5–Nov 23; fall max: **6** on unknown date during Sep 26–Oct 10, 1970 (TMar et al.; *AFN* 25[1]: 29–30), 3 on Sep 13, 1981 (PDV), 2 on Sep 12, 1981 (PDV), Sep 27, 2011 (DH, SM), Nov 22, 2011 (DH) & Sep 24–26, 2012 (MW, DL et al.). Ten-Year: SU-1, F-6.

- Banding: 3 in Fall 1961 (Oct 5, 6 & 7).

A remarkable number of records for this western vagrant (nearest breeding west of the Mississippi R.), with 15 inds. in fall 1957 and 6 in fall 1970 and at least 3 inds. in 1961 (when banded on three consecutive days), 1981, & 2011 (peak numbers statewide in 1960s & 1970s, but daily totals and observers unknown for Monhegan records–see Vickery, below). The long period of fall presence is highlighted by four records in Nov. Movement around the island makes tracking inds. and ascertaining length of stay complicated, especially when more than one present. Many stays of at least three days or more, with an exceptional stay of "all of Nov" (until the 23rd) in 1988 (WBo); four records in 2021 spanning Sep 14–Dec 5 possibly one ind. but more likely several, with breakdown of records as Sep 14–15, Sep 27 & Oct 2, Oct 22 and Nov 20, 22 & Dec 5 (later dates suggest a long-staying ind.–noted as continuing by DC). The unusual summer record in Jul 2022 was observed at Lobster Cove. Usually seen at town locations, often perched up; a favored location is around the Meadow, where sometimes on the utility wires, also multiple sightings near the Ice Pond, wires along Wharton Ave. and even on Manana. Sometimes associating with Eastern Kingbirds. The 2010 spring ind. perched on a fence at the edge of the Meadow with Eastern Kingbirds (KL). One met its demise in the talons of a Peregrine

Falcon over Burnt Head (Sep 26, 2012–SB). Three fall inds. were noted to age: two adults and one juvenile.

Historical/Regional:

- Vickery: lists three of the four spring records above as the only ones for the state in that season (*does not include Jun 7, 2008*); nearly annual in fall, latest fall record Nov 22, 2011 (DH), cites 2 in Sep 1956 (unknown obs.), 15 during Sep 6–15, 1957 (unknown obs.), the 3 banded in 1961, and 6 during Sep 26–Oct 10, 1970 (*AB* 25: 29) as a period of greater abundance and becoming less numerous but annual by 1980s (1–5/year), with 4 in 1988 (*AB* 44: 58; PDV in Vickery et al., 2020).

Western Kingbird, Oct 2, 2021. © Luke Seitz.

EASTERN KINGBIRD
Tyrannus tyrannus

Status: Uncommon to fairly common spring and uncommon fall migrant, very rare summer visitor.

Occurrence: Spring dates span Apr 27–mid Jun, peak mid–late May; spring max: **31** on May 26, 2014, (JT), 30 on May 25, 1985 (SS) & May 23, 2014, 26 on May 30, 2013 (RL, ML). Nine summer records (mid Jun–end of Jul) over seven years since 1909 (excluding *MABB*), most likely underreported; summer max: 2 on Jun 27, 2011 (TMag). An early fall migrant, dates span early Aug–w/e Oct 28 (only record later than Oct 4), peak mid Aug–mid Sep; fall max: 40 on Sep 4, 1919 (WT), 30 on Sep 5, 1919 (WT) & Sep 3, 1983 (PDV), 25 on Aug 9, 1915 (WT, CFJ), 20 on Sep 3, 1919 (WT), Sep 4, 1983 (PDV) & Sep 6, 1983 (PDV), 18 on Sep 4 & 5, 1982 (PDV), 16 on Sep 7, 1980 (PDV). Ten-Year: SP-10, SU-3, F-10.

- *MABB*: possible; MBA: probable.
- 1899 Checklist: included.
- 1900–1908 Reconnaissance & Supplements: 5 during May 31–Jun 6, 1908 (FA), unreported number during Jul 31–Aug 2, 1908 (WM).
- 1909 Notes: a few seen in the open fields.
- 1914 & 1916 Checklists: unreported number on Aug 1, 1914; included 1916.
- 1915–1919 Taylor Journals: 1915–Aug 9 (25), 11, 16, Sep 12 (1); 1916–Aug 19, 20, 21 (1), 22, 30, 31, Sep 3, 4 (15), 6, 10; 1917–Aug 4 (1), 16 (7); 1918–prior to Aug 4, Aug 28; 1919–Sep 3 (20), 4 (40), 5 (30), 11 (1), 13 (2).
- 1918 Fall Migration Census: Dewis–6 on Sep 7. Listed as Kingbird.
- 1939 Summer Census: regular summer visitor.
- 1944–1967 Farrell Records: 1950–May; 1953–Aug, Sep; 1954–Jun, Jul; 1955–Jun, Jul, Aug; 1956–May; 1958–Aug, Sep; 1959–May, Aug, Sep; 1960–May, Jun, Aug, Sep; 1961–May.
- 1954 & 1955 Summer Records: 1954–included Jun 19–25 & Jun 27–Jul 4; 1955–Aug 22–30, mainly toward south end of island (15 on Aug 23 moving north along edge of spruces facing Lobster Cove Rd.).
- 1970 Summer Checklist: included.
- Banding: 15 total over one season (1981), max 3 on Aug 30, 1981.

It is interesting that spring max counts have remained rather steady, while fall numbers have declined from the highs in the 1980s (significant decline statewide over last fifty years); note that all fall max counts occurred 1983 or earlier. Larger movements tend to be multi-day events, as some birds likely remain on the island for short stays. Spring 2014 was exceptional for 10+ inds. on fourteen of fifteen days May 17–31, including the max counts on the 23rd and 26th. Underreported during summer/early fall, particularly with significant migration taking place in Aug. MBA status based on pair in appropriate habitat on Jun 1, 2021 (RS), possibly migrants. Two during w/e Oct 28, 2006 (fide JWa, KG; MARBA) exceptionally late: over two weeks later than any other record for Monhegan and one of latest for the state. Favored locations are in/around the Meadow, including the wires, and Lobster Cove, where even observed resting on the rocks, but possible anywhere in more open areas. Largest single report/flock was 19 at the Meadow on May 30, 2013 (out of 26 that day–RL, ML), while 9 were seen coming in off the water at Lobster Cove on May 25, 2014 (JT).

Historical/Regional:

- Vickery: cites 1 on Apr 27, 2011 (TMag) as early and lists eleven high spring counts (16–31 inds., includes max counts above); lists six fall high counts (8–30 inds., includes top two max counts above) and four records on Oct 1 & 2 as late (PDV & WJS in Vickery et al., 2020).

Eastern Kingbird, May 18, 2011. © Geoff Dennis.

OLIVE-SIDED FLYCATCHER
Contopus cooperi

Status: Scarce spring and rare to scarce fall migrant, very rare summer visitor (historical).

Occurrence: Spring dates span May 14–Jun 9, peak last ten days of May; spring max: **6** on Jun 4, 2020 (JT, LS), 4 on May 29, 1987 (PDV), May 26, 2016 (JT, JO, JE) & May 27, 2019 (JT et al.), 3 on May 30, 2013 (RL, ML) & May 21, 2022 (JT, LS, MWa). Three historical summer records (excluding 1939 Census): 1 singing during Jul 2–6, 1909 (CJM), 1 during Jun 27–Jul 4, 1954 (FNR, MFNR), 1 during Jun 11–15, 1955 (CFH, MCFH). Fall dates span Aug 7–Oct 7, peak mid Aug–mid Sep; fall max: **6** on Sep 7, 1984 (PDV), 4 on Sep 4, 1982 (PDV) & Sep 7, 1985 (PDV), 3 on Aug 15, 2013 (FH). Ten-Year: SP-10, F-8.

- *MABB*: possible.
- 1908 Summer Reconnaissance: 1 on May 31, 2 on Jun 2, 3 on Jun 4, 1908 (FA).
- 1909 Notes: one singing.
- 1914 & 1916 Checklists: included 1916.
- 1915–1919 Taylor Journals: 1915–Aug 31 (4); 1916–Aug 30; 1917–Aug 19 (1 juvenile); 1919–Sep 14 (1).
- 1918 Fall Migration Census: Dewis–1 on Sep 7.
- 1939 Summer Census: uncommon summer visitor.
- 1944–1967 Farrell Records: 1954–Jun, Jul; 1955–Jun, Aug; 1958–Aug; 1959–Jun; 1960–Aug.
- 1954 & 1955 Summer Records: 1954–included Jun 27–Jul 4; 1955–included Jun 11–15, Aug 23 (1).
- 1970 Summer Checklist: included.

Possibly a breeder, supported by historical records and a juvenile reported in 1919 (see above), but no recent summer records (Jun 11–Jul 31); likely underreported during summer/early fall. Reports scattered around the island, on multiple occasions along the Black Head Trail, back of the Meadow, Ballfield, Lobster Cove Trail, and near the Brewery. Of the 3 reported on May 21, 2022, 2 were singing near Lobster Cove (JT, LS, MWa). The late date of Oct 7 was noted as a juvenile (LBr).

Historical/Regional:

- Vickery: cites 1 juv. on Oct 7, 2000 (LBr) and 1 late Sep–Oct 2, 2005 (JT, DL et al.) as latest (*a Gilsland Farm record erroneously attributed to Monhegan*; WJS in Vickery et al., 2020).

Olive-sided Flycatcher, May 26, 2013. © Luke Seitz.

EASTERN WOOD-PEWEE
Contopus virens

Status: Uncommon to fairly common spring and uncommon fall migrant, accidental summer visitor (historical possible breeder).

Occurrence: A late spring migrant, dates span May 13–Jun 15, peak the second half of May; spring max: **40+** on May 28, 2019 (DL, JL), 22 on May 28, 2019 (LS), 18 on Jun 4, 2020 (JT, LS), 15 on May 30, 1987 (PDV) & May 28, 1995 (SS). Only one summer record despite inclusion as a known breeder on 1970 checklist (excludes *MABB*): unreported number during Jun 19–25, 1954 (ES, AS). Fall dates span Aug 14–Oct 30, peak early–mid Sep; fall max: 12 on Sep 5, 1987 (PDV), 11 on Sep 7, 1985 (PDV), 10 on Sep 20, 2020 (LMu, BBc, JMu), 8 on Sep 3, 1983 (PDV). Ten-Year: SP-10, SU-1, F-10.

- *MABB*: possible.
- 1900–1908 Reconnaissance & Supplements: 2 singing during May 31–Jun 6, 1908 (FA). Listed as Wood Pewee.
- 1914 & 1916 Checklists: included 1916.
- 1915–1919 Taylor Journals: 1915–Aug 27 (1); 1916–Sep 4 (1), 6 (3), 10; 1917–Sep 5 (1). Listed as Pewee.
- 1918 Fall Migration Census: Wentworth–2 on Sep 9. Listed as Wood Pewee.
- 1939 Summer Census: uncommon summer visitor.
- 1944–1967 Farrell Records: 1950–Jun; 1953–Aug; 1954–Jun, Jul; 1955–Jun, Aug; 1959–May, Aug; 1960–Aug, Sep; 1961–May. Listed as Wood Pewee.
- 1954 & 1955 Summer Records: 1954–included Jun 19–25; 1955–included Jun 11–15, Aug 22–29 (1–4 inds. each day). Listed as Wood Pewee.
- 1970 Summer Checklist: marked as known to breed in the area.
- Banding: 4 total over four seasons, 1 each on Oct 4, 1961, Sep 25, 1962, Sep 8, 1981, May 22, 1984.

Experiencing a decline in fall presence since the 1980s, similar to Eastern Kingbird, despite relatively consistent numbers in spring. No recent evidence to support summer presence or breeding, but lack of coverage at this season. Reports are scattered from many town areas and major trails, e.g. Black Head, Burnt Head, Lobster Cove. An odd location was one sitting on rocks in the harbor (May 22, 2013–DH). Eight in view at once on May 28, 2019 (part of the max count–LS). Heard singing or calling on occasion.

Historical/Regional:
- Vickery: lists six high spring counts (8–15 inds.); cites the three max counts above as high counts that only occur in early Sep, 1 on Oct 28–30, 2013 (PDV, JP) as late (WJS in Vickery et al., 2020).

Eastern Wood-Pewee, Sep 17, 2015. © Bill Thompson.

YELLOW-BELLIED FLYCATCHER
Empidonax flaviventris

Status: Scarce to uncommon spring and scarce fall migrant.

Occurrence: A late spring migrant, dates span May 15–Jun 11, peak late May–early Jun; spring max: **28** on May 28, 2014 (JT), 22 on May 30, 2013 (RL, ML), 20 on May 25, 2000 (TV), 12 on May 30, 1987 (PDV). Early fall migrant, dates span Aug 16–Oct 11, peak early Sep but undoubtedly underreported in Aug; fall max: 4 on Sep 3, 1981 (banding), 3 on Sep 20, 2020 (LMu, BBc, JMu), 2 on twenty-two days spanning Aug 16–Oct 5. Ten-Year: SP-10, F-10.

- 1914 & 1916 Checklists: included 1916.
- 1915–1919 Taylor Journals: 1916–Sep 10; 1917–Aug 16 (2), Sep 5 (2); 1919–Sep 11 (1).
- 1918 Fall Migration Census: Dewis–1 on Sep 7.
- 1944–1967 Farrell Records: 1959–Aug; 1960–Aug, Sep.
- Banding: 13 total over 3 seasons, peak 8 in Fall 1981, max 4 on Sep 3, 1981.

Similar to other *Empidonax* flycatchers in migration timing, lack of coverage undoubtedly leads to underreporting in June and Aug. The top two spring max counts were part of major flycatcher fallouts, including the mega-flight on May 30, 2013 (see The *Empidonax* Fallout on page 158). Scattered reports from around the island, include the north end, Black Head, Underhill, and Alder Trails, near Lobster Cove, Fish Beach and other town locations.

Yellow-bellied Flycatcher, May 26, 2013. © Luke Seitz.

ACADIAN FLYCATCHER
Empidonax virescens

Status: Very rare spring and accidental fall vagrant.

Occurrence: Six records (6 spring, 1 fall) since 1984. Spring records over six years since 1984, all singles, span May 19–Jun 6: Jun 6, 1984 (banded–MPl), Jun 3, 2007 (KL), May 22, 2011 (RL), May 25–31, 2013 (LS, DH, mob), May 28, 2019 (DL, JL), 1 on May 19, 2022 (LS, JT; OLMB). Fall record: 1 on Oct 1, 2009 (EO). Ten-Year: SP-2.

- 1944–1967 Farrell Records: 1954–Jun (see 1954 & 1955 Summer Records and discussion below).
- 1954 & 1955 Summer Records: 1954–included on Jun 19–25 checklist, but excluded here (see discussion below.
- Banding: 1 on Jun 6, 1984.

An overshoot by spring migrants of their breeding range to the south (the nearest is in southern New Hampshire). Only three of the recent Monhegan records are listed on the OLMB: May 2013 accepted by ME-BRC #2013–029, May 2011 & May 2022 not yet reviewed. The Jun 2007 ind. was calling. Further details provided only for the 2013 record; although observed on May 25, it was confirmed by vocalization on the 26th at Fish Beach. It was next observed on the 30th and heard calling from the firs at Lobster Cove. The next day, the 31st, it was seen and recorded near the Monhegan House. While it is possible there could have been up to three different inds., especially considering the very large movement of *Empidonax* flycatchers reported on the 30th ("several hundred arriving throughout the day"–RL), it has been considered one record due to the species' rarity. The questionable inclusion on the Jun 19–25, 1954 checklist has been excluded here based on remarks by the 1954 Records compilers doubting this report of "nesting" Acadian Flycatchers, as they are "absent" as breeders in New England; the first Maine record didn't occur until 1960 (see Vickery, below).

Historical/Regional:
- Vickery: cites the 1984, 2011 and 2013 records above for spring (*lists an eBird record of 1 singing on Jul 6, 2011 that does not currently exist in eBird*; PDV in Vickery et al., 2020).
- OLMB: seven additional state records since 2008—three accepted and four not yet reviewed; several reports not listed.

Acadian Flycatcher, May 26, 2013. © Luke Seitz.

ALDER FLYCATCHER
Empidonax alnorum

Status: Uncommon spring and rare to scarce fall migrant, very rare summer visitor and historical breeder.

Occurrence: A late spring migrant, dates span May 13–Jun 16, peak late May–early Jun; spring max: **145** on May 30, 2013 (RL, ML), 17 on May 23, 2013 (SK, JZ), 9 on May 30, 2019 (JT), 8 on May 22, 2013 (SK, JZ). Included on 1939 and 1970 checklists as a breeder, but only six official summer records (five since 2013): unreported number during Jul 1960 (fide IF), 1 on Jun 21, 2013 (JKe), 1 on Jun 23, 2015 (JLa), 1 on Jul 29, 2020 (SRe, TRe), 1 on Jul 19–20, 2021 (HIAC et al.). Early fall migrant, dates span Aug 17–Oct 4, peak late Aug–early Sep; fall max: 6 on Sep 4, 1982 (PDV), 5 on Sep 3, 1982 (PDV), 4 on Sep 5 (PDV). Ten-Year: SP-10, SU-4, F-7.

- MBA: possible.
- 1900–1908 Reconnaissance & Supplements: 1 on Jun 2, 1 on Jun 3, 2 on Jun 4, 4 on Jun 5, 1 on Jun 6, 1908–all singing; "abundant growth of alders should ensure presence as regular summer resident" (FA).
- 1914 & 1916 Checklists: included 1916.
- 1915–1919 Taylor Journals: 1915–Aug 9 (1), 16 (1), Sep 2; 1916–Aug 22 (1), Sep 6 (1), 10.
- 1918 Fall Migration Census: Wentworth–1 on Sep 7 (identified by CFJ); Dewis–mentions

- possibility of confusion with Least Flycatcher.
- 1939 Summer Census: regular summer resident.
- 1944–1967 Farrell Records: 1960–Jul, Aug.
- 1970 Summer Checklist: the combined Traill's Flycatcher is included as known to breed in area (*likely pertains to this species*).
- Banding: combined with Willow Flycatcher as Traill's Flycatcher (see special account below).

Underreported during the Jun and Aug portions of its migrations due to lack of coverage, its confusion with Willow Flycatcher (and other *Empidonaces*) and lumping as Traill's Flycatcher (see account below). THE singular event for this species occurred on May 30, 2013, part of an exceptional season to begin with (note max counts), as an astounding 145 were reported (along with 87 Willow Flycatchers); massive numbers of birds and "largest movement of *Empids* personally witnessed, with hundreds arriving throughout the day" (RL, ML–Red-eyed Vireo and Magnolia Warbler were also numerous). Summer records in late Jun and late Jul are probably late/early migrants (summer period Jun 21–Jul 31 for these purposes); MBA status based on an ind. in appropriate habitat on Jul 19, 2021 (MCu). 1982 produced an exceptional fall movement, with all the max counts and the only days of more than 2 inds. reported. Often located and identification confirmed by singing/calling in the spring, less vocal in the fall; possible anywhere in birding areas around town or along the major trails in deciduous woods and thickets.

Historical/Regional:

- Vickery: cites 1 on May 13, 1997 (PDV et al.) as early; 1 on Oct 12, 2010 (JT–actually entered as Traill's Flycatcher in eBird) as late (WJS in Vickery et al., 2020).

Traill's Flycatcher - Alder/Willow: due to the difficulty of separating these two formerly combined species (separated in 1973), there are actually more non-specific reports than either Alder or Willow Flycatcher, resulting from non-vocalizing inds. Along with the incredible number of Alder and Willow Flycatchers on May 30, 2013, even more were attributed to this category—250, making for a combined total of 482 of these two species on that date (RL, ML)! As with Alder, the more abundant of the two, 2013 was the exceptional year in general, with additional high counts of 30 on May 23, 20 on May 24, 20 on May 25, and 30 on May 26. Another high count of 47 was reported on May 28, 2014, including "10 in view at several spots" (JT). Of note are two records later than either species: 1 on Oct 7, 1989 and 1 on Oct 12, 2010. As expected, sightings from many locations in town; of interest are "lots" on the beaches on May 23, 2013 (DH) and feeding on seaweed-covered rocks on May 27, 2014 (TW).

- Banding: total 64 over three seasons, peak 44 in Fall 1981, max 14 on Jun 6, 1984.

Alder Flycatcher, May 26, 2013. © Luke Seitz.

WILLOW FLYCATCHER
Empidonax traillii

Status: Scarce to uncommon spring and very rare fall migrant.

Occurrence: A late spring migrant, dates span May 15–Jun 30, peak late May–early Jun; spring max: **87** on May 30, 2013 (RL, ML), 6 on May 28, 2016 (JT, JO), 5 on Jun 4, 2011 (TMag). Seven fall records over seven years since 1983, all singles, span Sep 16–27: Sep 25, 1983 (DF et al.), Sep 27, 2000 (JT), Sep 23, 2007 (LS), Sep 20, 2012 (LB), Sep 21, 2017 (DL), Sep 16, 2018 (BTn), Sep 25, 2019 (RHe). Ten-Year: SP-10, F-3.

- MBA: possible.
- 1970 Summer Checklist: the combined Traill's Flycatcher is included as known to breed in area (*likely pertains to Alder Flycatcher*).
- Banding: combined with Willow Flycatcher as Traill's Flycatcher (see special account under Alder Flycatcher).

Much less common than the very similar Alder Flycatcher and likewise probably underreported in Jun and Aug (notably absent during a peak period regionally for this species) due to lack of coverage, its confusion with Alder (and other *Empidonaces*) and lumping as Traill's Flycatcher (see special account under Alder Flycatcher). As in Alder, THE singular event for this species occurred on May 30, 2013, as an astounding 87 were reported (along with 145

Alder), mostly around the Ice Pond, Tribler Rd. and Lobster Cove; massive numbers of birds and "largest movement of *Empids* personally witnessed, with hundreds arriving throughout the day" (RL, ML). MBA status based on a singing ind. on Jun 7, 2020 (DR), likely a migrant. Often located and identification confirmed by singing or calling in the spring and fall; possible anywhere in birding areas around town or along the major trails in deciduous woods and thickets, but around the Meadow is a favorite location.

Historical/Regional:

- Vickery: cites 1 on May 15, 2005 (HN) as early spring and 1 singing on Sep 20, 2012 LB, WR), 1 on Sep 23, 2007 (LS et al.) and 1 on Sep 27, 2000 (JT) as latest fall (WJS in Vickery et al., 2020).

Willow Flycatcher, May 23, 2022. © Bill Thompson.

LEAST FLYCATCHER
Empidonax minimus

Status: Uncommon to fairly common spring and uncommon fall migrant, very rare summer visitor.

Occurrence: Earlier than other *Empidonax* flycatchers in spring, dates span Apr 26–Jun 9, peak last three weeks of May; spring max: **33** on May 30, 2019 (JT), 25 on May 28, 2013 (KL), 21 on May 21, 2022 (JT, LS, MWa), 20 on May 15, 2005 (HN) & May 20, 2015 (DL). Two summer records: unreported number during Jun 27–Jul 4, 1954 (FNR, MFNR), unreported number during Jun 11–15, 1955 (CFH, MCFH). Fall dates span Aug 16–Nov 16, peak early–mid Sep; fall max: 20 on Sep 3, 1983 (PDV) & Sep 8, 1985 (PDV), 15 on Sep 7, 1985 (PDV), Sep 9, 1985 (PDV), & Sep 5, 1987, 12 on Sep 3, 1982 (PDV) & Sep 4, 1983 (PDV). Ten-Year: SP-10, F-10.

- *MABB*: possible.
- 1899 Checklist: included.
- 1900–1908 Reconnaissance & Supplements: 1 on Aug 16, 1900 (CFJ, ECJ).
- 1914 & 1916 Checklists: included 1916.
- 1918 Fall Migration Census: Wentworth–Sep 29, Oct 4, 13, 25.
- 1939 Summer Census: uncommon summer visitor.
- 1944–1967 Farrell Records: 1949–Sep; 1950–Sep; 1954–Jun, Jul; 1955–Jun, Aug; 1957–Aug; 1959–Jun, Aug; 1960–Aug, Sep; 1961–May.
- 1954 & 1955 Summer Records: 1954–included Jun 27–Jul 4; 1955–included Jun 11–15, Aug 25 (1), 28 (1).
- 1970 Summer Checklist: included.

It is interesting that the spring max counts have occurred since 2005, while the fall max counts occurred 1987 and earlier. Large movements often two to four-day events, such as occurred in spring 2013 (12+ inds. four days out of five May 25–30) and fall 1983 and fall 1985. While part of the massive movement of *Empidonaces* on May 30, 2013, the count of 16 Least Flycatchers was not as significant as those of other species. Lingering inds. included late records Oct 7–11, 2012 near the Ice Pond (JT, DH) and Nov 13–16, 2015 near the top of Horn's Hill (DH). Often calling, reported from many town birding locations.

Historical/Regional:

- Vickery: cites Apr 26, 2011 (TMag) as early spring and 25 on May 28, 2013 (KL) and 16 on May 30, 2013 (RL) as large spring counts; 8 on Aug 17, 2006 (PDV) as early fall, lists four large counts (12–20 inds.–included in max counts above), and lists four Oct records as late fall (latest 1 on Oct 29, 2013 (PDV, JP; PDV in Vickery et al., 2020).

Least Flycatcher, May 15, 2011. © Geoff Dennis.

> **The *Empidonax* Fallout of May 30, 2013**
>
> On this date, Robert and Maggie Lambert witnessed a flycatcher fallout of astonishing proportions, with several hundred arriving throughout the day. The end result was 22 Yellow-bellied, 145 Alder, 87 Willow, 250 Alder/Willow (Traill's), 16 Least, and 250 *Empidonax* sp., for an amazing total of 770 flycatchers (a single Acadian Flycatcher was also reported by others on the island)! Part of an overall massive number of birds that day, Red-eyed Vireo and Magnolia Warbler also had single-day island high counts with 345 and 353, respectively. "At one point several hundred birds/minute could be seen flying away from the island" (RL pers. comm.).
>
> This fallout is supported by a morning flight counted by Marshall Iliff on this date at the Vines Landing & Yacht Club at Biddeford Pool, Maine (roughly 55 miles west-southwest of Monhegan). In just over ninety minutes, starting at 7:43 a.m., he tallied over 5,000 passerines heading west to the mainland from offshore, notably including 185 *Empidonaces* (a mix of 26 Yellow-bellied, 10 Alder, 2 Willow, 4 Least, and 143 unidentified flycatchers) and hundreds each of Red-eyed Vireo (245), American Redstart (376) and Magnolia Warbler (336), with many birds left unidentified. MI commented, "I can only imagine the thousands that I missed" early and that the day was "preceeded by a lot of wet and cold weather that bottled up the migration" (eBird, 2023).

GRAY FLYCATCHER
Empidonax wrightii

Status: Accidental fall vagrant.

Occurrence: One record: 1 photographed on Oct 4, 2018 (LS, JT, RDo, DH). First and only Maine record; accepted by ME-BRC #2008–036. Ten-Year: F-1.

First observed at a home above Lobster Cove, then moved towards Lobster Cove and observed at several locations along the slope above the cove.

Historical/Regional:

- Vickery: cites 2018 record above (only four other East Coast records; CDD in Vickery et al., 2020).
- OLMB: no additional state records.

Gray Flycatcher, Oct 4, 2018. © Jeremiah Trimble.

EASTERN PHOEBE
Sayornis phoebe

Status: Uncommon *(presumably fairly common)* spring and uncommon to fairly common fall migrant, rare summer visitor and possible breeder.

Occurrence: Early spring migrant, dates span Mar 19–end of May, peak early–mid Apr; spring max: 16 on Apr 6, 2011 (TMag), 12 on Apr 5, 2011 (TMag), 7 on Apr 8, 2011 (TMag) & Apr 17, 2011 (TMag). Twenty-five summer records (excluding *MABB*) over nineteen years since 1915 (nineteen records since 1991–none between 1960 and 1991), scattered Jun–Aug; summer max: 10 on Aug 4, 2016 (IK), 2 on Aug 28–29, 1955 (EAB), Aug 17, 2006 (PDV) & Aug 27, 2010 (TMag). Late fall migrant, dates span early Sep–Nov 23, peak mid Sep–mid Oct; fall max: **35** on Sep 29, 1998 (JT), 25 on Oct 3, 2020 (LMu, BBc) & Sep 29, 2022 (DH), 23 on Oct 5, 2019 (LS, AO), 19 on Oct 10, 2011 (JM). Ten-Year: SP-10, SU-9, F-10.

- *MABB*: confirmed; MBA: possible.
- 1899 Checklist: included.
- 1914 & 1916 Checklists: included 1916.
- 1915–1919 Taylor Journals: 1915–Aug 10 (1); 1917–Sep 8 (1).
- 1918 Fall Migration Census: Dewis–2 on Sep 11. Listed as Phoebe.
- 1944–1967 Farrell Records: 1950–Mar, Apr; 1951–Apr; 1953–Aug, Sep; 1955–Aug; 1958–Sep; 1959–May, Aug; 1960–Apr, May, Aug, Sep; 1961–Apr, May; 1967–Apr 2 (1), 3, 4 (2), 5, 8, 9, 14 (2), 16 (1), 23, 24 (1).
- 1954 & 1955 Summer Records: 1955–Aug 23 (1), 28 (2), 29 (2+).
- 1970 Summer Checklist: included.
- Banding: 25 total over three seasons, peak 17 in Fall 1960, max 5 on Oct 5, 1960.

Larger movements tend to be two- or three-day

Eastern Phoebe, Sep 26, 2018. © Bill Thompson.

events. Spring 2011 was exceptional, providing all the max counts, a year of more consistent coverage in Apr that illustrates the underreporting in other years. Similarly, the fact that it has been reported nine of the last ten years during summer, a stretch of increased reports on eBird during a very under-covered season, highlights an understated summer status; surprising lack of evidence of breeding after the *MABB*; MBA status based on an ind. in suitable habitat on May 28, 2021, probably too late to be a migrant. A late fall ind. in 2016 apparently worked its way south from the library to the Monhegan House over Nov 4–6 (FK, JF). Found at many of the town birding locations, especially around the Meadow, the Ice Pond, near the library, near the lighthouse, Lobster Cove Rd., Horn's Hill, and around the bridge on Ocean Ave. Two were seen feeding on kelp flies at Fish and Swim Beaches on the early date of Mar 20, 2022 (KL).

Historical/Regional:
- Vickery: cites 16 on Apr 6, 2011 (TMag) as a high spring count; fall numbers >10 Sep 21–Oct 10, lists three high counts (16–35 inds.), 7 on Oct 26, 2010 (TMag) as unusually late, and 1 on Nov 23, 1988 (WBo) as latest (PDV in Vickery et al., 2020).

SAY'S PHOEBE
Sayornis saya

Status: Very rare fall vagrant.

Occurrence: Nine records over nine years since 1974, span Sep 5–Oct 28; all singles: Oct 8, 1974 (DF, WR et al., ph.; first Maine record), Oct 26, 1988 (WBo; *AB* 43[1]: 65), immature on Sep 14–21, 1992 (SMa, TMar, JMar), Sep 14, 1998 (WBo), Oct 8–10, 2000 (MR, MRe, JSl), Sep 5, 2001 (LG, RD et al.), Sep 26, 2007 (JSc, BSc), Sep 24, 2009 (EO, LS, SM), juvenile on Sep 16–17, 2017 (JF, BTn). Ten-Year: F-1.

It is surprising that nine of Maine's sixteen records are from Monhegan/Manana. All listed on the OLMB, the 2007, 2009 & 2017 records have been accepted (#2007–008, #2009–014 [Manana] & #2017–031, respectively), while the others have not yet been reviewed. The Oct 1974 ind. was an immature on the wires between the former general store and the Monhegan House (DF). The Oct 2000 ind. was at Pulpit Rock, the Sep 2009 ind. perched on the house on Manana, and the 2017 ind. was at White Head

Say's Phoebe, Gull Cove, Sep 17, 2017. © Bill Thompson.

on Sep 16 and nearby along the shoreline by Gull Cove on Sep 17. Incredibly, the 2017 ind. landed on someone's head for several minutes at White Head before catching a dragonfly (JF). There are several other records without supporting evidence or with questionable circumstances that have not been included above: an unreported number on an eBird checklist for May 26, 2007 gives no details (*possibly a Sep 26, 2007 report mis-entered?*) and two records in the *Guillemot* (2 on Nov 12, 2000 and 1 on Aug 29, 2001) without any details and with possible data entry issues (two on one day would be exceptional).

Historical/Regional:

- Vickery: cites the nine Monhegan/Manana records listed above (PDV in Vickery et al., 2020).
- OLMB: nine additional state records—three accepted and six not yet reviewed.

WHITE-EYED VIREO
Vireo griseus

Status: Rare to scarce spring and fall vagrant, accidental summer vagrant/breeder.

Occurrence: Spring records over twenty-six years since 1978 (annual since 2006, except 2020), span short period May 13–Jun 5; spring max: 2 on May 23, 2012 (LSt, JTu), May 28, 2017 (DL), May 16, 2022 (LS, MWa) & May 20, 2022 (LS). Anecdotal reports of 2 summering inds. in 2012 (see discussion below), but only one definite record: 1 on Aug 7, 2012 (DL). Fall records over twenty-five years since 1977, span Sep 7–Oct 12; fall max: **3** on Sep 21, 2012 (SM et al.), Sep 24, 2012 (SB et al.) & Sep 26, 2012 (DL), 2 on Oct 11, 2010 (JM), Sep 22, 2011 (MW), Sep 23, 2011 (MW) & Sep 26, 2011 (SB et al.) Ten-Year: SP-9, F-8.

- Banding: 1 adult on May 22, 1984.

Apparent increase in presence over the past fifty years, although closest breeding remains southeast Massachusetts. Its habit of singing/calling during migration allows repeated relocation and a general sense of continuing birds. Many spring records are one- to three-day events, while several recent records involve more extensive stays (May 25–30, 2015, May 21–30, 2017). This pattern is repeated in the fall, with a four-day stay in 2010 (Oct 9–12) and five-day stay in 2014 (Oct 4–9). While the possibility that more inds. are involved may be credible, details are not available to support this, and the rarity of this species makes it unlikely; repeated reports on consecutive/near consecutive days without details have been considered the same bird, and even a gap of a week or more, while considered a separate record without details, may actually involve the same ind.

2012 is a story in itself. Officially considered here as two spring, one summer and two fall records for that year (note max counts, with 2 separate inds. in spring and 3 in fall). The last spring report, a single bird, occurred on May 26 (earliest was May 16); the only summer record was on Aug 7; the earliest fall eBird report from Sep 18 mentions continuing inds., while following reports note inds. in same locations as heard all summer and "apparently pair bred on the island this summer" (MW). No other summer details or reports confirm or refute this possibility, but the presence in the same locations is more than suggestive of lingering and one ind. in fall, while not seen with either of the other two, was noted as an immature—in fact, only one day in spring (May 23) and six days in fall (3 on Sep 21 & 24, 2 on Sep 22, 23, 26, & 27) had multiple inds., never with even two seen together. One spring ind. was a singing male along Lobster Cove Rd. in scrubby growth near the start of Underhill Trail; it is unclear where the second ind. was located, but it was calling. The Aug ind. sang a couple of times (DL). The first fall ind. (identified as an immature on Sep 2 2–CDe) was reported singing along Lobster Cove Trail (later specified as the scrubby area on the east side), while the first report of 3 on Sep 21 noted that two of the inds. were where the apparent summer birds were located, Lobster Cove Rd. and Lobster Cove Trail, with the third ind. (later identified as adult) noted near the Harlow Studio by the Ice Pond. The Lobster Cove Rd. ind. was last clearly reported on Sep 21 (some later reports of 3 inds. lacked details); an ind. was reported along Lighthouse Hill Rd. on the way to the Museum only on Sep 22 and Oct 2. The Ice Pond ind. continued until Oct 6, making it a probable stay of at least sixteen days. It is a confusing situation to say the least and very possibly there were at least four birds on the island in fall 2012.

Most often found in scrubby growth, with multiple sightings (in addition to 2012) around the Ice Pond, Lobster Cove Rd., Lobster Cove Trail, and Burnt Head Trail, but also behind the school, along Lighthouse Hill Rd. and above Christmas Cove. Few additional age/sex details: 2 adults and 3 males (based on singing) in spring and 3 immatures in fall.

Historical/Regional:

- Vickery: regular in spring; summer reports "suggest eventual nesting"; nearly annual during fall, cites 1 on Oct 5, 2011 (HN) as part of a mini-fallout in state (PDV in Vickery et al., 2020).

White-eyed Vireo, May 23, 2018. © Luke Seitz.

Bell's Vireo, May 26, 2015. © Jeremiah Trimble.

BELL'S VIREO
Vireo bellii

Status: Very rare spring and accidental fall vagrant.

Occurrence: Three records (2 spring, 1 fall) since first recorded in 2003, all singles. Spring records: May 20–22, 2003 (RE, HN, GD et al.–first Maine record, accepted as ME-BRC #2003–003), May 26, 2015 (JT, JO, BN et al.–fifth state record, not yet reviewed by ME-BRC). Fall record: Oct 5–6, 2012 (DH, JT–second Maine record, accepted as ME-BRC #2012–006). Ten-Year: SP-1.

Three out of the five Maine records on the OLMB have occurred on Monhegan (a possible first state record, 1 on Oct 23, 1998 [P. Donahue, fide JD; *AB* 53: 33] at Basin Cove, South Harpswell, Cumberland Co. is not presently listed on the OLMB). The May 2003 ind. was seen and photographed by many, accepted by the ME-BRE and on the OLMB as May 20-21, and reported near the school on May 22 (RSm, TMar); appearance consistent with *V. b. bellii*, the eastern subspecies (nearest nesting in Indiana). The Oct 2012 ind. was noted along Underhill Trail both days. The May 2015 ind. was observed in tall shrubs and small trees at the north end of Lobster Cove Trail.

Historical/Regional:
- Vickery: cites the three records above (PDV in Vickery et al., 2020).
- OLMB: two additional state records—both accepted (Oct 7–8, 2012 at Dresden, Lincoln Co. [*just one day after the Oct 5–6, 2012 record on Monhegan*] & Oct 22, 2013 at Harpswell, Cumberland Co.).

YELLOW-THROATED VIREO
Vireo flavifrons

Status: Very rare spring and rare fall migrant.

Occurrence: Forty-six records (9 spring, 36 fall, 1 unknown) since 1916. Spring records over nine years, span May 7–Jun 4, all singles (two unreported number in 2006): May 7, 1984 (PDV), May 28, 1988 (SS), unreported number May 26, 2006 (fide JWa, KG; MARBA), unreported number w/e Jun 2, 2006 (fide JWa, KG; MARBA), Jun 3, 2007 (JSc), May 16, 2012 (SWk), May 24, 2016 (LM), Jun 4, 2020 (JT, LS), May 23, 2021 (SS, RMi, JBl), May 22, 2022 (MWa). Fall records include one each in 1916 & 1917 (see historical checklists and Cruickshank, below) and thirty-four records over twenty-four years since 1977 (three in 2003, two records in eight years), span Aug 20–Oct 14 (possibly as early as Aug 16 [triplist record]); fall max: **3** on Sep 13, 1981 (PDV et al.; *AB* 36[2]: 155) & Sep 19, 2013 (KL), 2 on Oct 1, 2003 (JT) & Sep 19, 2005 (BME et al.). One record from 1966 of unreported number or date (TMar personal notes). Ten-Year: SP-4, F-8.

- 1914 & 1916 Checklists: included 1916.
- 1915–1919 Taylor Journals: 1916–Sep 10; 1917–Aug 20 (1).
- 1970 Summer Checklist: included.

Surprisingly few records for a species that nests in the southwestern part of the state, albeit in very low numbers. It is likely that reports by Gleason & Taylor in 1916 involve the same ind. and are counted as one record here. Probable lingering ind. Sep 16–19, 2014 (possibly through the 24th, but few details available) and Sep 16–21, 2018. Possibly the two records from consecutive weeks in Spring 2006 involved the same ind. (and even possibly on consecutive days, but no way to clarify further). One spring ind. was singing, another was observed with a group of warblers along Trail #1 at the north end of the island, and one was observed along Lobster Cove Trail. Fall inds. were noted twice at the Ice Pond, once at the Hitchcox residence, once feeding in the trees beside Tom Martin's house, once along Lighthouse Hill Rd. and once at the junction of the White Head Trail and 1A.

Historical/Regional:

- Cruickshank: 1 in Sep 1916 (Mrs. Gleason).
- Vickery: six spring reports; 2–3 inds. almost annually in fall, with only two records before Sep 16, lists three max counts of 3 inds. (*the 3 on Sep 21, 2005 is actually 1 on Sep 19 and 2 on Sep 20*) and 1 on Oct 14, 2003 (SM) and 1 on Oct 12, 2010 (DH–latest) as Oct records (PDV in Vickery et al., 2020).

Yellow-throated Vireo, May 18, 2006. © Geoff Dennis.

CASSIN'S VIREO
Vireo cassinii

Status: Accidental fall vagrant.

Occurrence: One record: 1 on Sep 29–30, 2017 (LS, JT). First and only Maine record; accepted by ME-BRC #2017–037 (photos by LS, BTn). Ten-Year: F-1.

Considered a subspecies of Solitary Vireo until 1997. Originally found in the shrubby patch to the north of Wharf Hill Rd., just east and below the crest from the Island Inn. Rediscovered the following day between Tribler Cottage and the Community Garden (behind the library).

Historical/Regional:

- Vickery: cites this as the only state record (BSV in Vickery et al., 2020).
- OLMB: no additional state records.

Cassin's Vireo, Tribler Rd., Sep 30, 2017. © Bill Thompson.

BLUE-HEADED VIREO
Vireo solitarius

Status: Uncommon to fairly common spring and fall migrant, accidental summer visitor.

Occurrence: The earliest vireo to return in spring, dates span Apr 21–Jun 1, peak the middle two weeks of May; spring max: 15 on May 13, 1997 (PDV, DAb), 12 on May 17, 2005 (TV) & May 16, 2022 (LS, MWa), 10 on May 14, 2011 (LS). One summer record, most likely a late spring migrant: 1 on Jun 16, 2011 (CDd, DDd). Fall dates span Aug 24–Nov 9, peak late Sep–late Oct; fall max: **25** on Sep 29, 2008 (DL) & Sep 30, 2019 (JT), 20 on Sep 30, 2003 (JT), 16 on Oct 5, 2019 (LK). Ten-Year: SP-10, F-10.

- 1914 & 1916 Checklists: included 1916.
- 1918 Fall Migration Census: Wentworth–Oct. 7, 21 (1), 23 (1).
- 1944–1967 Farrell Records: 1959–Aug.
- 1970 Summer Checklist: included.
- Banding: 21 total over four seasons, peak 9 in Fall 1962, max 7 on Oct 7, 1961; 1 on Aug 24, 1991 (early date).

Most likely underreported during the early portion of its spring migration (late Apr/early May). Few details have been provided for this species, but it has been reported from the north end of the island, Trail #1, and interior forest, as well as more traditional locations such as Lighthouse Hill, Lobster Cove Rd. and the Ice Pond. Reported singing on two occasions in the fall.

Historical/Regional:

- Vickery: cites 15 on May 13, 1997 (PDV, DAb) as a high spring count and 15 on Sep 21, 2004 (LB) as high fall count (JVW in Vickery et al., 2020).

Blue-headed Vireo, May 14, 2011. © Luke Seitz.

PHILADELPHIA VIREO
Vireo philadelphicus

Status: Uncommon spring and fall migrant.

Occurrence: Spring dates span May 7–w/e Jun 9 (latest definite date Jun 4), peak the last ten days of May; spring max: 7 on May 31, 2019 (JT), 6 on May 24, 2019 (DL), 5 on May 24, 2019 (SS), 4 on May 25, 1985 (SS), May 27, 1989 (SS), May 25, 2000 (TDu), May 22, 2013 (JSs), May 26, 2014 (MZ, DL), May 28, 2014 (JT) & May 22, 2022 (LS). Fall dates span Aug 22–Oct 20, peak early Sep–late Sep; fall max: **9** on Sep 22, 2007 (LS), 8 on Sep 15, 2014 (TV), 7 on Sep 17, 2015 (PDV et al.), 6 on Sep 8, 1986 (PDV), Sep 17, 2013 (PDV, HP), Sep 25, 2000 (JT), Sep 21, 2004 (RQ, LB, DM) & Sep 20, 2018 (DL). Ten-Year: SP-9, F-10.

- 1914 & 1916 Checklists: included 1916.
- 1944–1967 Farrell Records: 1954–Aug, Sep; 1955–Aug; 1956–May; 1958–Sep; 1959–Aug; 1960–Aug.
- 1954 & 1955 Summer Records: 1955–Sep 2 (1).
- 1970 Summer Checklist: included.
- Banding: 5 total over two seasons, peak 3 in Fall 1981, max 2 on May 22, 1984.

A trip report Sep 8–10, 2000 totaled 15, with "large" numbers on the 10th (HN). Reports scattered from town locations and nearby trails, most often in deciduous trees/scrub, including feeding in apple and plum trees, with multiples from Black Head Rd., Wharf Hill Rd., Lobster Cove Trail, and near the Ice Pond. Inds. within a report vary from scattered to up to 3 together; noted with other vireos and in mixed flocks.

Historical/Regional:

- Vickery: cites May 12, 2005 (HN) as early spring and 4 on May 25, 2000 (TDu) and two days of 3 inds. as high counts; cites 6 on Sep 21, 2004 (LB, DM) as a high fall count and 1 on Oct 19, 1999 (WBo) as late (JVW in Vickery et al., 2020).

Philadelphia Vireo, Oct 14, 2019. © Bill Thompson.

WARBLING VIREO
Vireo gilvus

Status: Scarce to uncommon spring and fall migrant, accidental summer visitor.

Occurrence: Spring dates span May 13– Jun 11, peak mid–late May; spring max: **10** on May 28, 1995 (SS), 7 on May 26, 2016 (JT et al.), 5 on May 27, 1995 (SS), May 21, 2013 (JH, MM), May 22, 2013 (JH, MM) & May 25, 2016 (JE). One summer record: 1 on Jul 17, 2013 (JAi, NLo). Fall dates span Aug 22–Oct 13, peak mid–late Sep; fall max: 9 on Sep 18, 2019 (BTn), 6 on Sep 17, 2014 (PDV, TJ, MJ) & Sep 20, 2019 (BTn), 4 on Sep 21, 2004 (LB), Sep 16, 2017 (MW) & Sep 14, 2021 (DD et al.). Ten-Year: SP-9, SU-1, F-10.

- 1914 & 1916 Checklists: included 1916.
- 1915–1919 Taylor Journals: 1915–Sep 2 (1), 12 (1); 1916–Aug 22, Sep 10.
- 1970 Summer Checklist: included.

Few records with details; reported from scattered town/road locations, including the Ice Pond, Tribler Rd., and Lobster Cove Rd.

Historical/Regional:

- Vickery: cites 4 on Sep 21, 2004 (LB) as a high count and 1 on Oct 11, 2014 (mob) as late (JVW in Vickery et al., 2020).

Warbling Vireo, May 22, 2006. © Geoff Dennis.

RED-EYED VIREO
Vireo olivaceus

Status: Fairly common to common spring and fall migrant, rare summer visitor/resident.

Occurrence: Spring dates span May 11–mid Jun, peak the last ten days of May; spring max: **345** on May 30, 2013 (RL, ML), 200 on May 25, 2000 (TV), 100 on May 26, 2016 (PDV, WJS) & May 28, 2016 (BBa), 80 on May 26, 2018 (DL). Twelve summer records, all singles (nine) or unreported number (three) over eight years since 1954, scattered in the Jun 16–Aug 15 period (three records in 2018, two in 2019), suggest the probability of regular breeding, but only one confirmed record: 1 carrying nesting material on Jun 12, 2019 (DH). Fall dates span mid Aug–Nov 3, peak early Sep–early Oct; fall max: 220 on Sep 22, 2007 (LS), 140 on Sep 25, 2009 (LS), 120 on Sep 19, 2014 (TV), 115 on Sep 23, 2007 (LS), 100 on May 27, 2016 (DL, JL). Ten-Year: SP-10, SU-5, F-10.

- *MABB*: possible; MBA: confirmed.
- 1900–1908 Reconnaissance & Supplements: one heard singing on Jun 6, 1908 (FA).
- 1914 & 1916 Checklists: included 1916.
- 1915–1919 Taylor Journals: 1916–Sep 6 (2), 10; 1917–Sep 5 (1); 1919–3 (1), 4 (2), 5 (1), 11 (2), 13 (1).
- 1918 Fall Migration Census: Dewis–Sep 7 (1), 9 (1).
- 1944–1967 Farrell Records: 1953–Aug; 1954–Jun, Jul; 1955–Jun, Aug; 1959–Jul, Aug; 1960–Aug, Sep.
- 1954 & 1955 Summer Records: 1954–included Jun 27–Jul 4; 1955–included Jun 11–15, Aug 22–Sep 2 (10+ on Sep 2, with 6 together in a flock).
- 1970 Summer Checklist: included as marked as known to breed in area.
- Banding: 217 total over eight seasons, peak 174 in Fall 1981, max 33 on Sep 3, 1981.

Notable that all the max counts have occurred since 2000. The spring peak is significantly focused during the short period May 25–30. Large fallouts in spring and fall deposit birds all over the island (sometimes abundant in mixed species flocks) and in "seemingly every tree on island" (JT); otherwise found at all the usual birding locations. Often multi-day events, undoubtedly involving lingering birds, as highlighted by the exceptional flights in Spring 2016 (three consecutive days of 25+, including 100 on May 26 & 28), Fall 2000 (five consecutive days of 20+), Fall 2007 (three consecutive days of 95+, all max counts), and Fall 2009 (eight consecutive days of 20+). Departure sometimes happens dramatically: only 4 reported on Sep 24, 2007 after the three-day event and only 12 the day following the incredible 345 on May 30, 2013. Observed passing over in morning flight, including many among several hundred birds/minute (*of all species*) leaving the island on the max day of May 30, 2013 (RL, ML); ~10 coming in off the water at dawn at Lobster Cove on Sep 25, 2009 (LS). Likely underreported in summer due to lack of coverage, recent records reflect increased reporting; Jun migrants overlap probable resident inds., as illustrated by confirmed breeding on Jun 12, 2019 (DH–carrying nesting material; occurring in the "spring" period for these purposes).

Historical/Regional:

- Vickery: cites 30 on May 25, 1983 (ST et al.) and May 25, 2006 (DL et al.) as high spring counts; lists four high fall counts (50–75 inds.—the 75 on Sep 21, 2005 is a trip total Sep 17–21 with a daily high of 35+ inds.; JVW in Vickery et al., 2020).

Red-eyed Vireo, Sep 21, 2006. © Geoff Dennis.

LOGGERHEAD SHRIKE
Lanius ludovicianus

Status: Accidental spring and very rare fall migrant, accidental summer visitor (historical).

Occurrence: Nine records (1 spring, 1 summer, 7 fall) since first recorded in 1918. Spring record: 1 on May 16, 2001 (TMar). Summer record: 1 on Jul 11, 1954 (EAB, MEAB). Fall records: 1 on Oct 25–26, 1918 (BHW), 1 on Aug 23, 1940 (CBu, JCa, AC), unreported number during Nov 1952 (IF), 1 on Aug 22, 1955 (EAB), 1 on Aug 28, 1955 (EAB), unreported number during Aug 1960, 1 on Sep 12, 1988 (HN).

- 1918 Fall Migration Census: Wentworth–Oct 25, 26.
- 1944-1967 Farrell Records: 1952–Nov; 1954–Jul; 1955–Aug; 1960–Aug.
- 1954 & 1955 Summer Records: 1954–Jul 11 (1 on wires on Manana); 1955–Aug 22 (1), 28 (1).

Formerly a regular breeder in the northeast, it has all but disappeared, with the last Maine breeding in 1975 (last record in 2009) and the last New England nesting taking place in Vermont in 1978; a rapid decline since the mid 1900s, largely due to habitat loss, development and pesticides (Yosef, 2020). Nearest breeding now southern Quebec, but largely in the midwest. Almost no details available for the Monhegan sightings; the 1954 summer ind. was perched on wires on Manana. There is one additional ambiguous report, reliably identified, of an immature during the last few days of Aug sometime in the 1994–1996 period.

Historical/Regional:

- Cruickshank: 1 on Aug 23, 1940.
- Vickery: cites May 2001 as last spring record in the state (PDV in Vickery et al., 2020).

NORTHERN SHRIKE
Lanius borealis

Status: Accidental spring and very rare fall migrant, very rare winter visitor.

Occurrence: Fifteen records (1 spring, 9 fall, 5 winter) since 1940, all singles or unreported number (two records). Spring record: unreported number during Apr 1950 (IF). Fall records over six years since 2010, span Oct 11–Nov 22: Oct 31, 2010 (LS, JT, MI), Oct 23, 2011 (JT, DH), Nov 7, 2011 (DH), Nov 22, 2011 (DH), Oct 11, 2016 (DH), Nov 4–6, 2016 (DH et al.), Nov 12, 2018 (DH, FK), Nov 13, 2020 (LS, JT), Oct 23, 2021 (SJ, CJ). Winter records over five years, all but one centered around CBC period, but certainly underreported throughout winter: Dec 29, 1940 (CBC), unreported number during Feb 1950 (IF), Dec 28, 1978 (CBC–PDV), during Dec 24–30, 1987 (CBC count week–PDV), Jan 3, 2008 (CBC). Ten-Year: F-4.

- CBC: 3 years (12%) plus one count week, first on Dec 29, 1940, max. 1 all three years (also Dec 28, 1978 & Jan 3, 2008), avg 0.1.
- 1944–1967 Farrell Records: 1950–Feb, Apr.

This species' winter range is highly variable from year to year, dependent on severity of weather and availability of prey; prone to irruptions. Undoubtedly underreported late fall to early spring due to lack of coverage; sparsity of reports leaves the possibility of lingering inds. unclear in fall seasons with multiple records (2011, 2016). With lengthy gaps between some records in these two years, they are considered separate records despite rarity. No real sense of winter status or potential length of stay, as reports lacking, even negative, to follow-up inds. noted on the CBCs. The CBC count week ind. from 1987 is erroneously listed in eBird as Dec 27, which was the day of the actual count. The Oct 2010 ind. was an immature observed perched on the wires along the Meadow across from Swim Beach. The Nov 22, 2011 ind.

was an immature hunting the Meadow all morning. The Oct 11, 2016 ind. was an immature hunting around Lobster Cove. The Nov 4–6, 2016 ind. was an immature at the west end of the Ice Pond on the 4th and around the Meadow on the 6th, first in the garden sunflowers and then in a spruce at the south end, where mobbed by chickadees and nuthatches. The Nov 2018 ind. was an immature perched in dead conifers across the road from the Trailing Yew. The Oct 2021 ind. was near the school.

Historical/Regional:

- Vickery: cites 1 on Oct 11, 2016 (DH) as early fall (PDV in Vickery et al., 2020).

Northern Shrike, Oct 31, 2010. © Jeremiah Trimble.

BLUE JAY
Cyanocitta cristata

Status: Uncommon permanent resident, fairly common spring and common fall migrant, irregular uncommon to fairly common winter visitor.

Occurrence: Present in limited numbers throughout the year, supplemented by highly variable migrations and lesser numbers of winter visitors. Spring migration early Mar–mid Jun (overlapping early breeding in late May), peak mid–late May; spring max: 86 on May 25, 2019 (SS), 80 on May 31, 1982 (PDV), 69 on May 27, 2019 (JT, LS, JO), 60 on May 30, 1982 (PDV), May 28, 1988 (SS) & May 26, 1996 (SS). Summer presence/breeding continues into second half of Aug; summer max: 12 on Jun 22, 2019 (KD), 9 on Jun 23, 2019 (KD), 8 on Aug 17, 2006 (PDV) & Aug 15, 2022 (LS, MWa), 7 on Jun 16, 2018 (BEv, TEv). Fall migration late Aug–end Nov, peak mid Sep–mid Oct; fall max: **200** on Sep 27, 1991 (SS), 173 on Sep 30, 2019 (JT, LS, AO), 150 on Oct 7, 1984 (SS) & Sep 18, 2013 (TJ et al.). Variable winter numbers, most records associated with CBC period; winter max: 21 on Jan 1, 1991 (CBC–PDV), 16 on Dec 27, 1984 (CBC–PDV), 14 on Dec 26, 1982 (PDV), 12 on Dec 27, 1982 (CBC–PDV) & Dec 22, 1988 (CBC–PDV). Ten-Year: SP-10, SU-10, F-10, W-6.

- *MABB*: confirmed; MBA: confirmed.
- CBC: 21 years (81%) plus one count week, first on Dec 28, 1978, max 21 on Jan 1, 1991, avg 6.2.
- 1914 & 1916 Checklists: included 1916.
- 1915–1919 Taylor Journals: 1916–1 on Aug 26.
- 1918 Fall Migration Census: Wentworth–Oct 31.
- 1944–1967 Farrell Records: 1949–Oct; 1950–May; 1951–May; 1954–Jul; 1955–Jun, Jul, Aug; 1958–May; 1959–May, Jul, Aug; 1960–May, Aug, Sep; 1961–May; 1967–Apr 2 (2), 3 (2), 4 (1), 5, 7, 8, 9, 14, 17, 21, 22, 24 (1), Jun 1 (2), 2 (2), 3 (2), 4 (3), 5 (12), 7 (10), 8 (14).
- 1954 & 1955 Summer Records: 1955–included Jun 11–15, Aug 23 (2), Sep 1 (1).
- 1970 Summer Checklist: marked as known to breed in area.
- Banding: 5 total over three seasons, peak 2 in Fall 1984 & Spring 1990, max 2 on Oct 3, 1984 & May 29, 1990.

Partial and highly variable migrant, status and details of movements not fully understood, complicating the separation of residents from visitors, especially during winter. In seasons with notable movements, appears in waves over several weeks, although max flights usually concentrated on one day. Spring 2019 exceptional, with seven days (out of eight) of 25+ May 24–31, including high counts of 86 and 69 on May 25 & 27, respectively. Possible anywhere on the island, including many town locations and feeders. Often observed as flyovers during migration, generally in small flocks (<20), and sometimes flying about the island as if determining whether to continue onward; difficult to determine numbers present. Few breeding details available; adults feeding young during Jun 22–25, 2018 (KL) and on Jul 5, 2018 (JSn) and recently fledged young observed on Jul 6, 2019 (DH) and Jul 25, 2020 (TB) account for status on MBA.

Historical/Regional:

- Palmer: fairly common some winters.

AMERICAN CROW
Corvus brachyrhynchos

Status: Uncommon to fairly common permanent resident, fairly common spring and common fall migrant, fairly common winter visitor.

Occurrence: Noticeably present throughout the year, including on adjacent islands; understanding incomplete due to inconsistent reporting, undocumented numbers, and unclear separation of residents from migrants. Spring migration late Feb–end May (overlapping early breeding), extended peak late Mar–late May; spring max: 25 on May 22, 2014 (BBa), 20 on May 5, 2010 (NL), Mar 30, 2011 (TMag), Apr 6, 2011 (TMag), May 19–20, 2015 (BBa) & May 27, 2017 (SK), 18 on May 23, 2015 (RSm) & May 27, 2016 (MO). Breeding underway in May with young present by Jul; summer max: 18 on Jun 1, 2022 (SDa, JMy, VW), 16 on Jun 13, 2021 (JFo), 13 on Jul 27, 2020, 12 on Jun 3, 2008 (JSc). Fall migration spans late Aug–end Nov, peak mid Sep–late Oct; fall max: **50** on Oct 3, 1997 (JT) & Sep 29, 2003 (JT), 42 on Sep 24, 2016 (RH), 40 on Sep 12, 2006 (PDV) & Oct 29, 2010 (JT, LS, MI). Winter numbers highest earlier in season and mostly associated with CBC period, otherwise undoubtedly underreported; winter max: 32 on Jan 5, 2012 (CBC–DH, PM), 31 on Dec 22, 1988 (CBC–PDV), 30 on Dec 29, 1940 (CBC–JAT) & Dec 28, 1978 (CBC). Ten-Year: SP-10, SU-10, F-10, W-6.

- *MABB*: confirmed; MBA: confirmed.
- CBC: 26 years (100%), max 32 on Jan 5, 2012, avg 19.1.
- 1899 Checklist: included.
- 1900–1908 Reconnaissance & Supplements: ~8 inds. seen during May 31–Jun 6, 1908 (FA); unreported number during Jul 31–Aug 2, 1908 (WM).
- 1909 Notes: common; pair have nested on cliffs at northern end for a number of years, but not seen on this trip (CFJ).
- 1914 & 1916 Checklists: unreported number on Aug 1, 1914; included 1916.
- 1915–1919 Taylor Journals: 1915–Aug 9, 16, 31 (20), Sep 2 (1), 5, 12 (10); 1916–Aug 19, 20, 21, 22, 25, 26, 30, 31, Sep 4, 6, 10; 1917–Jul 29, Aug 4, 16, Sep 5, 8; 1918–prior to Aug 4, Aug 28; 1919–Sep 4 (10), 5 (10), 11 (10), 13 (15), 14 (10).
- 1918 Fall Migration Census: Dewis–Sep 7 (9), 8 (6), 9 (1), 10 (6), 11 (7), 12 (8); Wentworth–practically every day, Oct 6 (migrants first noted), 24, 25 (many).
- 1939 Summer Census: regular summer resident.
- 1944–1967 Farrell Records: 1949–Feb, Mar, Apr, May, Sep, Oct, Dec; 1950–Oct, Dec; 1951–Mar; 1952–Nov; 1954–Jun, Jul; 1955–Jun, Aug; 1957–Aug; 1958–Oct; 1959–Apr, May, Jun, Jul, Aug; 1960–Apr, May, Jun, Jul, Aug, Sep; 1961–Apr, May.
- 1954 & 1955 Summer Records: 1954–included all three checklists; 1955–included Jun 11–15 & Aug 22–Sep 2 (up to 12).
- 1970 Summer Checklist: highlighted and marked as known to breed in area.

Understanding American Crow's level of presence is complicated by seasonal underreporting (especially late fall and Jan–Apr after CBC, which comprise portions of the peak migratory periods), mixing of migrants/residents, inclusion on checklists including ferry crossings, many records with an unreported number, and even overlooked due to its commonness. Possible anywhere on the island (particularly as flyovers, when often vocalizing) but also perched on Manana and any of the surrounding small islands. Migration was apparent on Oct 18, 1989 when 12 were observed heading out to sea off Lobster Cove (PDV). Breeding recently confirmed on a number of occasions, most for MBA: adult observed carrying nesting material (grass and twigs) as early as Apr 4, 2014 (DC), adult carrying food on Jul 7, 2018 (RD, PD), May 15, 2019 (DPJ), Jun 4, 2020 (DR) & Jun 2, 2021 (RS), and recently fledged young observed on Jul 3, 2018 (DH), Jul 2, 2021 (DH) & Jul 19, 2021 (HIAC et al.). Largest single flock noted was 40 mobbing something unknown on Oct 29, 2010 (JT, LS, MI); a group (a total of 16 was reported) was observed mobbing a family of ravens on Jun 13, 2021 (JFo).

Historical/Regional:

- Vickery: cites the 40 on Oct 29, 2010 as an offshore observation (Richard V. Joyce in Vickery et al., 2020).

COMMON RAVEN
Corvus corax

Status: Uncommon permanent resident, irregular fall and winter wanderer.

Occurrence: Present in limited numbers throughout the year, with the highest totals recorded in fall and winter; year max: **22** on Oct 3, 2020 (WR), 20 on Jan 1, 1987 (CBC), 18 on Oct 18, 1989 (PDV), 15 on Dec 21, 1989 (CBC–PDV), 12 on Oct 2, 1997 (JT). Ten-Year: 10.

- *MABB*: probable; MBA: confirmed.
- CBC: 26 years (100%), max 20 on Jan 1, 1987, avg 5.2.
- 1900–1908 Reconnaissance & Supplements: one pair with nest and two young Jun 2–5, 1908 (FA–see *Bird-Lore* description below, listed as Northern Raven); unreported number heard during Jul 31–Aug 2, 1908 (WM).
- 1909 Notes: not recorded, but noted by CFJ as having nest on cliffs at the northern end of the island for several years.

- 1914 & 1916 Checklists: included 1916.
- 1915–1919 Taylor Journals: 1915–Aug 20 (1); 1916–Aug 25 (2), 26 (1), 30, Sep 6, 10; 1917–Jul 29 (3), Aug 4, 16, Sep 5; 1918–Aug 4, 28; 1919–Sep 4 (2), 5 (2), 11 (1). Listed as Northern Raven or Raven.
- 1918 Fall Migration Census: Dewis–Sep 8 (2); Wentworth–Oct 6 (~5 harried by crows), 9, 12, 15, 17, 19, 20, 21–25. Listed as Northern Raven.
- 1939 Summer Census: regular summer resident.
- 1944–1967 Farrell Records: 1949–Oct, Nov; 1951–Jan; 1952–Nov; 1954–May, Jun, Jul; 1955–Jun, Aug; 1956–May; 1959–Jun, Jul; 1960–Apr, May, Jun, Jul, Aug, Sep; 1961–Apr, May; 1967–Apr 6, 7, 14, 15, 16, 17, 18, 23, 24.
- 1954 & 1955 Summer Records: 1954–included all three checklists; 1955–included Jun 11–15, Aug 25 (2), 30 (1).
- 1970 Summer Checklist: highlighted and marked as known to breed in area.
- DOWTS Surveys 2011–2014: 1 on Mar 18, 2014 (1.7%)—a flyover at a height of approximately 10m about 1.4 miles from the southern tip of the island.

Generally non-migratory, gathers into local flocks after breeding season, sometimes wandering in fall and winter, with inds./small groups supplementing local populations. Higher numbers on Monhegan in fall and winter likely reflect a combination of reproductive success and visitors. Of the max count of 22 on Oct 3, 2020, 18 were in a flock high over the Ice Pond (possibly migrating–WR, DH), while of the 18 on Oct 18, 1989, 7 were seen migrating south out to sea off Lobster Cove (the same day 12 crows were observed doing the same thing–PDV) and a single flock of 8 were southbound over Burnt Head on Oct 4, 2021 (JT, LS); note single DOWTS sighting above, direction of flight unknown. Breeding details lacking, but likely overlooked due to preference for nesting in remote areas/cliffs, and early breeding season (Apr–May). A descriptive account of a Monhegan raven's nest/family Jun 2–5, 1908 is presented by Allen in *Bird-Lore* (1908b), involving fledging juveniles (left nest June 4) on/around a nest placed halfway up a forty-foot cliff. Recent breeding confirmed on Jun 13, 2021 with a family being mobbed by crows, with the 2 adults chasing off the crows before returning to the 3 vocal, recently fledged young (JFo). Routinely heard/seen anywhere on the island, particularly as a flyover, but more prevalent in forested areas and along the shoreline and cliffs, and often seen over/on Manana and adjacent islands.

BLACK-CAPPED CHICKADEE
Poecile atricapillus

Status: Fairly common to common permanent resident, irregular irruptive fall migrant.

Occurrence: Regularly reported throughout the year, highest numbers consistently in fall and early winter; year max: **108** on Oct 5, 2019 (LK), 93 on Nov 10, 2020 (LS, JT), 75 on Nov 6, 2016 (DH et al.), 70 on Jan 5, 2010 (CBC), 68 on Nov 9, 2020 (LS, JT), 63 on Jan 3, 2013 (CBC), 62 on Dec 29, 1983 (CBC), 61 on Dec 27, 1982 (CBC) & Jan 5, 2016 (CBC). Ten-Year: 10.

- *MABB*: confirmed; MBA: confirmed.
- CBC: 26 years (100%), max 70 on Jan 5, 2010, avg 34.6.
- 1899 Checklist: included as Chickadee.
- 1900–1908 Reconnaissance & Supplements: 7 observed during May 31–Jun 6, 1908 (FA); unreported number during Jul 31–Aug 2, 1908 (WM). Listed as Chickadee.
- 1914 & 1916 Checklists: unreported number on Aug 2, 1914; included as Chickadee 1916.
- 1915–1919 Taylor Journals: 1915–Aug 9 (10), 16 (1), 31 (5), Sep 2, 12 (6); 1916–Aug 20, 22, 26, Sep 6 (2), 10; 1917–Aug 23 (2), Sep 5 (2); 1918–prior to Aug 4; 1919–Sep 4 (3), 5 (1), 11 (1), 13 (1).
- 1918 Fall Migration Census: Dewis–Sep 7 (1), 8 (3), 11 (1); Wentworth–Sep 29, Oct 1, 6, 9, 12, 13, 16, 17 (a few), 19 (one flock), 20 (several), 22 & 23 (one flock), 24 (two flocks), 25 (1), Nov 1.
- 1939 Summer Census: regular summer resident. Listed as Chickadee.
- 1944–1967 Farrell Records: 1948–Dec; 1949–Feb, Mar, Apr, Sep, Dec; 1950–Feb, Mar, Apr, May, Sep, Oct, Nov, Dec; 1951–Jan, Mar, Apr, May, Jun, Sep, Oct, Nov; 1952–Feb, Mar, Apr, Nov; 1954–Jun, Jul; 1955–Jun, Aug; 1957–Aug; 1958–Aug, Oct; 1959–May, Jun, Jul, Aug, Sep; 1960–Apr, May, Jun, Jul, Aug, Sep; 1961–Apr, May; 1967–Apr 2 (2), 3 (2), 4, 5, 7, 8, 9, 14, 15, 16, 17, 18, 23, 24.
- 1954 & 1955 Summer Records: 1954–included all three checklists; 1955–included Jun 11–15 & Aug 22–Sep 2 (up to 15).
- 1970 Summer Checklist: highlighted and marked as known to breed in area.
- Banding: total 30 over nine seasons, peak 12 in Fall 1981, max 4 on Aug 26, 1981.

Highest counts later in year likely result from juveniles added to breeding population, supplemented by irregular irruptions of young birds (occurring only every 2+ years, with no apparent spring return) from farther north due to reproductive success combined with lack of food (Foote et al., 2020). It is difficult to distinguish when irruptive inds. are present, except when exhibiting arrival/departure behavior, such as a flock of 16 on Oct 7, 2016 (out of 33 reported that day) flying up and out over the water 150' off Lobster Cove before returning (LS–flock of 21 moving around the island the next day) and up to 40 (out of 75 reported) gathering and very vocal in the tops of the southernmost conifers at Lobster Cove on Nov 6, 2016, "launching" into the sky over the ocean and returning steeply several times (DH et al.). Resident birds observed in loose, roving feeding flocks outside of the breeding period, when often mixed with nuthatches and kinglets and appearing throughout the island, including in town near houses and at feeders. The max count of 108 on Oct 5, 2019 involved approximately 30 in town, the rest on trails in the woods to north and west. Breeding information includes a nest hole in front of Shining Sails on Jun 13, 2013, with adults constantly bringing food to vocal young (DH), an ind. visiting a probable nest site (inside insulation holes on a house) on May 28, 2018 (NHa, FHo), inds. "shoveling out and building nests all over" on Apr 25, 2020 (DC) and multiple reports confirming breeding from early Jun–mid/late Jul for the MBA (2018–2021) involving adults carrying food, nest w/young and recently fledged young.

Historical/Regional:

- Vickery: typically 10–30 inds. (*lists highest count ever as 60 on Oct 1, 2003*; PDV in Vickery et al., 2020).

Black-capped Chickadee, Oct 9, 2020. © Jeremiah Trimble.

BOREAL CHICKADEE
Poecile hudsonicus

Status: Very rare spring and accidental fall visitor.

Occurrence: Three records (2 spring, 1 fall). Spring records: unreported number on May 19, 1971 (TMar personal notes), 1 on May 25, 2018 (OK–fide KL). Fall record: 1–**3** on Oct 5–8, 1974 (DF, WR et al.). Ten-Year: SP-1.

The Oct 1974 inds. were observed near the south end of the island, with 2 on Oct 5, 1 on Oct 6, 2 on Oct 7 & 3 on Oct 8 (DF) and considered one record here, despite varying numbers, since it was likely a group that arrived at the island together. The May 2018 ind. was with two Black-capped Chickadees on White Head Trail. If encountered again, most likely to occur during late fall to early spring, when this largely non-migratory species is prone to wandering.

HORNED LARK
Eremophila alpestris

Status: Accidental spring and rare to scarce fall migrant, very rare winter visitor.

Occurrence: Forty-two records (1 spring, 34 fall, 7 winter) since 1980. Spring record: 1 on May 27–29, 1994 (SS). Fall records over nineteen years since 1997, span Sep 19–Nov 14, peak late Sep–mid Oct; fall max: **21** on Nov 13, 2020 (LS, JT), 10 on Oct 10, 2014 (JT) & Nov 28, 2014 (DC), 9 on Sep 29, 2007 (BSc), 8 on Sep 29, 2002 (JT) & Oct 3, 2017 (LS). Majority of winter records associated with CBC period: 1 on Dec 30–31, 1980 (CBC on Dec 30–PDV), 1 on Dec 29, 1983 (CBC–PDV), 1 on Dec 27–28, 1987 (CBC on Dec 28–PDV), unreported number during Dec 18–24, 1989 (CBC count week), 2 on Dec 13, 2014 (DC), 1 on Feb 12, 2015 (DC), 2 on Jan 26–Feb 5, 2022 (only 1 after Jan 30–DC). Ten-Year: F-9, W-2.

- CBC: two years (8%) plus one count week, first on Dec 30, 1980, max 1 on Dec 1, 1980 & Dec 27, 1987, avg 0.1.

Possibly underreported in migration periods of early spring and late fall due to lack of coverage. Surprising lack of records before 1980, considering common to abundant coastwise fall status for Maine in Palmer (1949). Inds. have lingered on occasion for multiple days; not clear from many records on consecutive days whether same ind. or not, but same number reports considered the same due to rarity, such as the two-day winter records in 1980 and 1987 and the 2 inds. in the Ballfield for four days, Sep 26–29, 2009 (LS). Most likely to be observed in bare grassy locations, such as the Ballfield, but few details available; other reports include 3 inds. running on the crest of Manana, two calling flyovers, and the max count of 10 in a single flock departing from Lobster Cove. The longest staying inds. were in Jan 2022 in an area cleared of snow with scattered seed at the Cundy residence: 2 were present on the 26th & 27th and returned after a blizzard on the 30th, with only 1 seen daily afterward (the other perhaps the victim of a predator) until at least Feb 5 (DC pers. comm.).

No subspecific identification given for any records, but based on photos (DC) the 2 on Jan 26–27, 2022 appear to be the expected "Northern" Horned Lark—*E. a. alpestris*.

Historical/Regional:

- Vickery: cites 1 on May 29, 1994 (SS) as late spring (PDV in Vickery et al., 2020).

Horned Larks, Jan 27, 2022. © Donna Cundy.

BANK SWALLOW
Riparia riparia

Status: Rare to scarce spring and very rare fall migrant, accidental summer visitor.

Occurrence: Fifty-two records (46 spring, 1 summer, 6 fall) since 1908. Spring records over twenty-six years (all but the 1908 & 1960 records since 1982), span relatively short period May 14–Jun 4; spring max: **10** on May 27, 1985 (JVW), 6 on May 20, 1983 (PDV), 4 on May 21, 1983 (PDV), May 30, 1983 (PDV) & May 19, 2016 (PMo, MS). Summer record: 3 on Jul 9–10, 2018 (JK). Fall records: unreported number during Aug 1959 (fide IF), unreported number during Jul 1960 (IF), 4 on Sep 5, 1982 (PDV), 2 on Sep 5, 1983 (PDV), 1 on Sep 26, 1987 (PDV), 1 on Sep 23, 2022 (SJ). Ten-Year: SP-10, SU-1, F-1.

- 1900–1908 Reconnaissance & Supplements: 3 seen Jun 3, 1908 (FA).
- 1944–1967 Farrell Records: 1959–Aug; 1960–May, Jul.
- 1970 Summer Checklist: included.

Likely overlooked in fall due to lack of coverage during late Jul–Aug, the time of peak movement by this early migrant, most of which are gone by Sep. Possibly certain inds. may have lingered for multiple days, but this is unclear due to gaps in coverage and lack of details; consecutive days of same/declining number have been considered same record for these purposes due to rarity; the two records from 2021 involved 1 on May 17, followed by 2 on May 18–20 with 1 remaining on May 22–23 (potential for 1 ind. to have been present May 17–23). Noted as flying over the Meadow and around the harbor, sometimes with Barn Swallows and Purple Martins. Also observed in the company of Tree Swallows.

Historical/Regional:

- Vickery: cites 1 on Sep 26, 1987 (PDV) and 2 on Sep 13, 2015 (KY) as late (JVW in Vickery et al., 2020).

Bank Swallow, May 17, 2021. © Jeremiah Trimble.

TREE SWALLOW
Tachycineta bicolor

Status: Fairly common spring and scarce to uncommon (*presumably fairly common to common*) fall migrant, uncommon summer resident.

Occurrence: Spring dates span Apr 4–end of May (overlapping with early breeders), peak early–mid May; spring max: 20 on May 7, 1984 (PDV), 15 on May 6, 1984 (PDV), May 29, 1987 (PDV), May 17, 1997 (RSh), May 23, 2021 (DGi) & May 28, 2021 (WBs), 13 on May 24, 2014 (FK). Breeds in limited numbers, principally in nest boxes in town, with nesting activity apparent by late May and extending into Jul with multiple broods; summer max: 6 on Jun

7, 1967 (IF) & Jul 2, 2021 (DH), 5 on Jul 1, 2021 (CEs), 4 on Jun 5, 2008 (DH), Jun 8, 2016 (FK, KLi), Jun 24, 2018 (AD), Jun 8, 2020 (JT, LS), Jun 1, 2021 (GP, KB) & Jun 30, 2021 (CEs). Fall dates span last two-thirds of Jul–Oct 11, peak late Aug–mid Sep, but undoubtedly underreported throughout Jul–Aug; fall max: **50** on Aug 22, 2010 (TMag), 30 on Aug 23, 2010 (TMag), 25 on Aug 27, 2010 (TMag), 20 on Sep 5, 1982 (PDV). Ten-Year: SP-9, SU-10, F-9.

- *MABB*: confirmed; MBA: confirmed.
- 1899 Checklist: included.
- 1900–1908 Reconnaissance & Supplements: four seen during May 31–Jun 6, 1908 (FA); unreported number during Jul 31–Aug 2, 1908 (WM).
- 1909 Notes: a few around the village, none seen breeding; two or three pairs about cliffs at north end. Listed as White-bellied Swallow.
- 1914 & 1916 Checklists: unreported number on Jul 31, 1914; included 1916.
- 1915–1919 Taylor Journals: 1916–Aug 19, 21, 22, Sep 6; 1917–Aug 5; 1918–prior to Aug 4.
- 1939 Summer Census: regular summer visitor.
- 1944–1967 Farrell Records: 1954–Jun, Jul, Aug; 1955–Jun, Jul, Aug; 1956–May; 1958–Sep; 1959–Apr, May, Jun, Jul, Aug; 1960–Apr, May, Jun, Jul, Aug; 1961–Apr, May; 1967–Jun 4 (3), 7 (6).
- 1954 & 1955 Summer Records: 1954–included all three checklists; 1955–included all three checklists (up to 6 Aug 23–29).
- 1970 Summer Checklist: highlighted and marked as known to breed in area.

Extended fall migration begins with dispersal/gathering during Jul and more evident movement during Aug, a time of limited coverage; illustrated by the max counts in fall 2010, a season of regular reporting by TMag and suggesting an elevated status. Few details regarding nesting, although an aerial battle with a Barn Swallow near a nest box was noted on Jun 1, 2018 (BJ); MBA status based on recently fledged young on Jul 2, 2021 (DH). Except when nesting, most often encountered as flyovers around town, particularly over the Meadow.

NORTHERN ROUGH-WINGED SWALLOW
Stelgidopteryx serripennis

Status: Rare spring and very rare fall migrant, very rare summer visitor.

Occurrence: Twenty-five records (18 spring, 2 summer, 5 fall) since 1954. Spring records over fifteen years since 1982 (three in 2022), span May 12–31; spring max: **4** on May 31, 1982 (PDV), 2 on May 21, 2015 (BBa). Summer records: unreported number during Jun 19–25, 1954 (AS, ES), 1 on Jul 5, 1995 (LR). Fall records: unreported number during Aug 1955 (IF), 1 on Oct 4, 1975 (JY et al.; AB 30[1]: 33), 2 on Aug 17, 2006 (PDV), unreported number on Aug 23, 2012 (GA), 1 on Sep 4, 2019 (DHt). Ten-Year: SP-7, F-1.

- 1944–1967 Farrell Records: 1954–Jun; 1955–Aug.
- 1954 & 1955 Summer Records: 1954–included June 19–25.

Slow expansion since the mid 1800s into the Northeast and ultimately into Maine in the mid 1900s, where the northern edge of its breeding range remains (De Jong, 2020). The three records in Spring 2022 (1 on May 17, 19, 22) may have involved a lingering ind., but no details provided to support that. Undoubtedly underreported as a fall migrant due to lack of coverage during the last two-thirds Jul–mid Sep (the regional migration period), especially during the late July–mid Aug peak. Despite rarity, few details provided with sightings; usually observed as flyovers, noted with Tree and Barn Swallows over the Meadow and hunting off north end of Manana.

PURPLE MARTIN
Progne subis

Status: Rare spring and very rare fall migrant.

Occurrence: Thirty-seven records (34 spring, 3 fall) since 1978. Spring records over twenty-one years since 1978, span short period May 12–31; spring max: **10** on May 20, 1978 (PDV), 6 on May 25, 2013 (DH), 4 on May 26, 2013 (FM), 3 on six days. Fall records: 1 on Sep 14, 1980 (PDV), 1 on Sep 6, 2010 (TMag), 2 on Sep 11, 2019 (SBe et al.). Ten-Year: SP-7, F-1.

- 1970 Summer Checklist: included.

Likely overlooked in fall due to lack of coverage during Aug, the peak time of movement by this early migrant species. Certain inds. may have lingered for multiple days (definite instance of a "very wet" female continuing at the Meadow May 24–25, 2013 [FM, DH]), but unclear due to gaps in coverage and lack of details; consecutive days of same/declining number have been considered same record for these purposes due to rarity (days with a gap in between sightings have not). Almost always observed as flyovers, notably over the Meadow, around the Lighthouse, Lobster Cove, and over the harbor, but a couple of records of inds. perched on the wires along the Meadow. Generally multiples are seen together, although the aforementioned female at the Meadow on May 25, 2013 was distant from the group of 5 at Lobster Cove, which is the largest single gathering noted. Observed associating with Chimney Swifts and Bank Swallows. Of those identified to age/sex in the spring, the breakdown is two adult males, 1 immature male, 4 females, and 8 female-types (difficult to distinguish immature males from females).

Historical/Regional:

- Vickery: cites 1 on May 30, 1983 (PDV), 3 on May 30, 2013 (JNo) and 1 on May 29, 2015 (JT, BN) as late and the max spring count above as notable; 1 on Sep 14, 1980 (PDV) and 1 on Sep 6, 2010 (TMag) as late (PDV in Vickery et al., 2020).

BARN SWALLOW
Hirundo rustica

Status: Fairly common spring and uncommon to fairly common fall migrant, rare summer visitor and possible breeder.

Occurrence: Spring dates span Apr 4–mid Jun, peak mid–late May; spring max: 40 on May 24, 1986 (JVW), 30 on May 25, 1990 (JVW), May 18, 2019 (JVW), 25 on May 26, 1985 (JVW). Sixteen summer records over ten years since 1909 (1909 sightings counted as one record and 1954 Records as three; excludes *MABB*); summer max: 6 on Jul 8, 2018 (JK), 4 on Jun 22, 2014 (BTh) & Jul 7, 2018 (RD, PD), 2 on Jun 19, 2011 (TMag) & Jun 16–18, 2021 (TP, RB, AB). Fall dates span last two-thirds of Jul–Oct 11, uncertain peak due to lack of coverage but possibly mid Jul–mid Sep; fall max: **300** on Sep 6, 1985 (PDV), 40 on Sep 7, 1985 (PDV), 30 on Aug 16, 1917 (WT), 20 on Sep 4, 1982 (PDV), Sep 6, 1982 (PDV) & Jul 27, 2010 (TMag), 16 on Jul 18, 2019 (JT). Ten-Year: SP-10, SU-3, F-9.

- *MABB*: confirmed.
- 1899 Checklist: included.
- 1900–1908 Reconnaissance & Supplements: 1 every day during May 31–Jun 6, 1908 (FA); unreported number during Jul 31–Aug 2, 1908 (WM).
- 1909 Notes: a few flying about; none entering buildings.
- 1914 & 1916 Checklists: unreported number on Jul 31, 1914; included 1916.
- 1915–1919 Taylor Journals: 1916–Aug 30, Sep 6, 10; 1917–Aug 4 (3), 16 (30); 1918–prior to Aug 4.
- 1918 Fall Migration Census: Sep 5 (3), 6 (2).
- 1939 Summer Census: regular summer resident.
- 1944–1967 Farrell Records: 1950–May; 1954–Jun, Jul, Aug; 1955–Jun, Jul, Aug; 1957–Aug; 1958–May, Aug; 1959–May, Jun, Jul, Aug; 1960–Apr, May, Jun, Jul, Aug; 1961–Apr, May; 1967–Jun 1 (2), 2 (3), 3 (2), 4 (2), 5 (2), 6 (3), 7 (3).
- 1954 & 1955 Summer Records: 1954–included all three checklists; 1955–included all three checklists (widely distributed during Aug 22–Sep 2).
- 1970 Summer Checklist: highlighted and marked as known to breed in area.
- Banding: 8 total over two seasons, peak 5 in Spring 1984, max 2 on Aug 27, 1981, May 22, 1984 & Jun 6, 1984.

Undoubtedly underreported during spring and fall migration periods due to lack of coverage, especially Apr (only two records: 4th & 30th) and late Jul–Aug; amazing movement in early Sep 1985 (see max counts) suggests of an elevated fall status. Likely underreported in summer as well, but little evidence in limited reports to suggest it is a regular breeder as in the past (see 1970 Summer Checklist and earlier); WT reported it in early Jul 1938 as thriving on the island in great numbers (considered one record for these purposes–Monhegan Press, 1938b). Usually encountered as flyovers, particularly at the Meadow, but also noted at the Ice Pond, Harbor, and over Manana. Known to associate with Tree Swallows.

Historical/Regional:

- Vickery: cites 2 on Apr 4, 2000 (WBo) as early spring (JVW in Vickery et al., 2020).

CLIFF SWALLOW
Petrochelidon pyrrhonota

Status: Rare spring and fall migrant, very rare summer visitor and former breeder.

Occurrence: Spring dates span Apr 14–early Jun, peak second half of May; spring max: 6 on May 31, 1982 (PDV) & May 29, 1983 (PDV), 5 during May 30–Jun 6, 1908 (FA), 4 on May 23, 1987 (SS). Eight summer records (excludes *MABB*) over five years: "in abundance" early Jul, 1938 (WT), **12** (6 pairs) during Jul 2–7, 1909 (CJM), "a few" during Jul 2–7, 1909 (CJM), unreported number during Jun 27–Jul 4, 1954 (FNR, MFNR), unreported number Jul 10–16, 1954 (EAB, MEAB), unreported number during Jun 11–15, 1955 (CFH, MCFH), unreported number during Jun 30–Jul 5, 1955 (MA, MSA), 6 on Jul 19, 1984 (PDV). Fall dates span Jul 29–Sep 26, no apparent peak (only two records since 1987 – see historical checklists below): fall max: **12** on Jul 29, 1917 (WT, CTa), 6 on Sep 6, 1985 (PDV), 4 on Sep 5, 1917 (WT), 3 during Sep 5–6, 1987 (WH) & Sep 5–6, 1918 (JDe). Eight records of unknown date: unreported number during 1899 (MEH) and unreported numbers during Jun & Jul, 1957 (IF), Jun & Jul 1958 (IF), Jul 1959 (IF) and Jun & Jul 1961 (IF). Ten-Year: SP-7, F-1.

- *MABB*: confirmed.
- 1899 Checklist: included.
- 1900–1908 Reconnaissance & Supplements: 5 seen during May 31–Jun 6, 1908 (FA); unreported number during Jul 31–Aug 2, 1908 (WM).
- 1909 Notes: colony of six pairs breeding beneath veranda of village house, nesting on shingles put up for the birds); a few seen about the cliffs at the north end of island and possibly breeding there. Listed as Eave Swallow.
- 1914 & 1916 Checklists: unreported number on Jul 31, 1914 (listed as Eave Swallow); included as Eave Swallow 1916.
- 1915–1919 Taylor Journals: 1915–Aug 9, 16, 28 (1), Sep 1; 1916–Aug 25, Sep 6; 1917–Jul 29 (12), Aug 4, 16, Sep 5 (4); 1918–prior to Aug 4.
- 1918 Fall Migration Census: Dewis–Sep 5 (3), 6 (3), 11 (1).
- 1939 Summer Census: regular summer resident.
- 1944–1967 Farrell Records: 1954–Jun; 1955–Jun, Aug; 1956–May; 1957–Jun, Jul, Aug; 1958–May, Jun, Jul, Aug; 1959–May, Jul, Aug; 1960–May, Jun, Jul, Aug; 1961–May; 1967–Jun 4 (2).
- 1954 & 1955 Summer Records: 1954–included Jun 27–Jul 4 & Jul 10–16; 1955–included Jun 11–15 & Jun 30–Jul 5.

Expanded its range eastward and into Maine in the 1800s until introduction and nest-usurpation by House Sparrows helped cause a slow decline in the Northeast through at least the mid 1900s (and apparently continuing), from which the species has not recovered (Brown et al., 2020). Decline illustrated by all ten records after 1987 being only single birds and historical summer records ending in 1984; likely no longer breeding on the island. Circumstances of breeding in 1909 are particularly interesting (see above); WT indicated in early Jul 1918 that they bred "in abundance, despite the fact they are uncommon inland" (Monhegan Press, 1938b). Also likely overlooked during fall migration, which commences regionally by late Jul and peaks in Aug, due to lack of coverage. The cluster of fall records in the early 1900s, especially those in late Jul/early Aug (including max count of 12 on Jul 29, 1916) were possibly residents lingering on the island, rather than early migrants, but are considered fall records for these purposes by date. The Jun and Jul reports from 1957–1960 (see Farrell Records above) are considered separate records on inds. by month and listed as unknown date rather than being assigned to spring, summer, or fall due to overlapping of designations within months and possibility (likelihood?) of breeding at that time. The Gleason and Taylor reports from 1916 considered two records. Almost always single-day records (excepting uncertain sighting dates of 1909 Notes, Farrell Records and 1954 & 1955 Summer Records), although observed on consecutive days on a couple of occasions—considered the same ind./record for these purposes due to rarity—including an ind. reported on Sep 3 & 5, 1982. Even the max counts have all been single-day events, with none reported the following day. Observed as flyovers, and noted a couple of times each over the Meadow and Harbor.

Historical/Regional:

- Palmer: cites Dewis Sep 11 record as late.
- Cruickshank: cites Dewis Sep 11 record as latest.
- Vickery: cites 1 on Apr 14, 1998 (WBo) as early spring and 1 on Sep 16, 1984 (PDV) as late fall (JVW in Vickery et al., 2020).

CAVE SWALLOW
Petrochelidon fulva

Status: Accidental fall vagrant.

Occurrence: One record: 1 on Oct 31, 2010 (TMag). Fourth Maine record; formerly on the OLMB, now omitted but not listed as unaccepted (see OLMB below).

Observed by the Wyeth house near Lobster Cove.

Historical/Regional:

- Vickery: no mention of the 2010 record (more than twenty recent reports statewide; PDV in Vickery et al., 2020).
- OLMB: six additional state records (noted as 2014+ not reviewed)—all accepted, three over Nov 8–18, 2005, three over Nov 24–25, 2012.

RUBY-CROWNED KINGLET
Regulus calendula

Status: Uncommon to fairly common spring and common fall migrant, very rare summer and winter visitor.

Occurrence: Spring dates span Mar 5–May 31, peak late Apr–mid May; spring max: 50 on May 4, 2010 (NL), 41 on Apr 29, 2011 (TMag), 40 on May

13, 1997 (PDV). Two summer records: unreported number over summer 1907 (CFJ–see Cruickshank, below), unreported number during Jun 11–15, 1955 (CFH, MCFH). Fall dates span during Aug (earliest definite date Sep 2)–end Nov, peak late Sep–mid Oct; fall max: **300** on Oct 7, 1990 (SS), 250 on Oct 7, 1984 (SS) & Oct 1, 1993 (BN), 175 on Oct 7, 1989 (SS). Four winter records: 1 on Jan 23, 2001 (*NAB* 55(2): 149), 1 on Dec 8, 2010 (TMag), 2 on Jan 4–Mar 6, 2012 (including CBC–DH, PM), 1 on Dec 9, 2021 (DC). Ten-Year: SP-10, F-10, W-1.

- *MABB*: possible.
- CBC: one year (4%), 2 on Jan 5, 2012, avg 0.0.
- 1900–1908 Reconnaissance & Supplements: unreported number during summer 1907 (CFJ, ECJ–see Cruickshank, below).
- 1918 Fall Migration Census: Wentworth–Oct 6, 7, 8, 9 ("common everywhere"), 12, 15 (fewer), 16, 17 (many), 19 (many), 20 (several), 21 (1); solitary, no flocks.
- 1944-1967 Farrell Records: 1944–Apr; 1945–May; 1946–Mar; 1950–Apr, May; 1952–Apr; 1955–Jun, Aug; 1956–May; 1959–Aug; 1960–Apr, May, Aug, Sep; 1961–May; 1967–Apr 2 (1), 14 (1).
- 1954 & 1955 Summer Records: 1955–included Jun 11–15, Sep 2 (1).
- 1970 Summer Checklist: marked as known to breed in area.
- Banding: 52 total over five seasons, peak 22 in Fall 1960, max 10 on Oct 10, 1960.

Likely underreported in peak periods of Apr and Oct due to lack of coverage. Fall migration possible by late Aug; reports from Aug in 1955, 1959 & 1960 likely early fall migrants and considered such for these purposes. Large movements often two–three day events. The 100 reported on Oct 12, 2009 were noted as hundreds and "more Ruby-crowned Kinglets than blades of grass" (JM). Reported from throughout the island—town, trails, and woods; more likely in deciduous habitat/away from conifers than Golden-crowned Kinglets, with which it sometimes associates, along with chickadees and nuthatches. Often located when heard calling; sometimes singing in spring. The 2012 winter record involved 2 inds. near Lobster Cove, observed with Golden-crowned Kinglets on Jan 4, recorded on the CBC on Jan 5, refound on Mar 5–6 and possibly the same two inds. relocated near Lobster Cove on Apr 4 (an additional 2 inds. recorded on Mar 5 & 6, 2012 were near Burnt Head–DH). The Dec 2021 ind. was along the road to Fish Beach. A leucistic ind. was found (HN) and photographed on May 14, 2005 (GD).

Historical/Regional:
- Cruickshank: "species spent the summer of 1907" (CFJ).
- Vickery: cites 4 on Mar 6, 2012 (DH) as remarkable, major spring flights occur mid Apr–mid May (lists four records 15–50 inds.) and cites 8 on May 20 1983 (PDV) as a high late count; cites 8 on Sep 13, 1980 (PDV) as early fall, major fall flights of 20–60 inds. Sep 26–mid Oct (lists five records 100–300 inds. as larger flights); cites 2001 record above as one of few later winter reports and attributes apparent overwintering in Jan–Mar 2012 (see above) to a mild winter.

Leucistic Ruby-crowned Kinglet, May 15, 2005. © Geoff Dennis.

GOLDEN-CROWNED KINGLET
Regulus satrapa

Status: Uncommon to fairly common permanent resident, fairly common to common spring and common to abundant fall migrant, uncommon to common winter visitor.

Occurrence: Present in limited numbers throughout the year but likely underreported due to habitat preference (conifers). Spring migration spans early Mar–end of May, peak late Mar–mid Apr; spring max: 80 on Apr 4, 2012 (DH), 63 on Apr 10, 2011 (TMag), 60 on Apr 5, 2012 (DH). Few breeding details available despite historical/*MABB*/MBA status; summer max: 20 on Aug 11, 2013 (KY), 19 on Aug 16, 2021 (NHn), 16 on Jul 29, 2021 (SD) & Aug 15, 2022 (LS, MWa), 9 on Jun 23, 2019 (CEl) & Jul 30, 2020 (GBr). Fall migration spans late Aug–end of Nov, peak late Sep–late Oct; fall max: **800** on Oct 7, 1990 (SS), 200 on Oct 7, 1989 (SS), Oct 10, 2001 (TV), & Sep 25–26, 2005 (TV), 150 on Sep 29, 1989 (BN). Variable winter numbers, mostly associated with CBC period; winter max: 74 on Jan 1, 1992 (CBC–PDV), 62 on Dec 27, 1984 (CBC–PDV), 45 on Dec 31, 1990

(PDV). Ten-Year: SP-9, SU-10, F-10, W-4.

- *MABB*: confirmed; MBA: confirmed.
- CBC: 23 years (88%), first on Dec 22, 1979, max 74 on Jan 1, 1992, avg 11.1.
- 1900–1908 Reconnaissance & Supplements: 3 singing during May 31–Jun 6, 1908 (FA); included in Jenney supplement; unreported number during Jul 31–Aug 2, 1908 (WM).
- 1909 Notes: a few heard singing in the evergreens.
- 1914 & 1916 Checklists: included 1916.
- 1915–1919 Taylor Journals: 1915–Aug 16, 31 (100), Sep 2, 5, 12 (20); 1916–Aug 21, 22, 25, 26 (10), 30, 31, Sep 6, 10; 1917–Jul 29, Aug 4, 16, Sep 5; 1918–prior to Aug 4, Aug 28; 1919–Sep 4 (5), 5 (10), 14 (10).
- 1918 Fall Migration Census: Dewis–Sep 10 (1); Wentworth–Sep 29, Oct 4, 6, 7, 12, 15 (many), 16, 17 (common), 19 (several flocks), 20 (several), 22 & 23 (one flock), 24 (several), Nov 1.
- 1939 Summer Census: regular summer resident.
- 1944–1967 Farrell Records: 1946–Apr; 1949–Mar, Apr, Oct, Dec; 1950–Mar, Apr, May, Nov; 1951–Apr, Nov; 1952–Apr; 1953–Aug; Sep; 1954–Jul; 1955–Aug; 1959–Jul, Aug; 1960–Apr, Jul, Aug; 1961–Apr; 1967–Apr 2 (1).
- 1954 & 1955 Summer Records: 1954–included Jul 10–16; 1955–included Aug 22–Sep 2 (up to 15).
- 1970 Summer Checklist: highlighted and marked as known to breed in area.
- Banding: 11 total over three seasons, peak 6 in Fall 1961, max 3 on Oct 9, 1961 & Oct 2, 1962.

Undoubtedly underreported during summer, winter, and particularly peak migration periods, due to lack of coverage and preference for upper branches of evergreens. Larger movements often three- to five-day events. The 800 recorded on Oct 7, 1990 is exceptional; unfortunately, no reports for the previous or following days. Normally found high in dense spruces dominating the northern portion of the island and consequently often heard and not seen or numbers hard to estimate. In popular places like Black Head Trail and Cathedral Woods, all bets are off when migratory influxes occur, with hungry inds./small flocks of ~10 scattered throughout, including tamely on lawns and even along walls and rocks near Swim Beach, where noted as catching tiny insects–JP. Sometimes associating with roving flocks of chickadees and nuthatches outside of breeding season. Breeding details lacking for reasons stated, except numerous adults singing, with a rare confirmation on Jul 5, 2019 involving adults carrying food (DH).

Historical/Regional:

- Vickery: cites five records from late May as late spring (May 20–29, 6–12 inds.); large flights in fall late Sep–early Oct, lists four records from late Sep and six from early Oct as large flights (80–800 inds.) and 75 on Oct 29, 2013 (JP) as latest (*max counts of 800 and 150 erroneously listed as 1991 (for 1990) and 1995 (for 1989), respectively*; PDV in Vickery et al., 2020).

Golden-crowned Kinglet, Apr 7, 2013. © Doug Hitchcox.

BOHEMIAN WAXWING
Bombycilla garrulus

Status: Accidental spring and very rare fall migrant, very rare winter visitor.

Occurrence: Fifteen records (1 spring, 8 fall, 6 winter) since 1981. Spring record (extremely late): 1 on Jun 9, 1998 (WBo; *FN* 52[4]: 437). Fall records over five years since 2008, span Sep 12–Nov 10: 1 on Sep 12–13, 2008 (fide EH, LS, SWh; MARBA), 1 on Oct 30, 2010 (JT, MI, LS), 3 on Nov 1, 2010 (TMag), 8 on Nov 3, 2010 (TMag), 1 on Oct 27, 2012 (JP), 1 on Nov 5, 2016 (DH et al.), 5 on Nov 8, 2020 (DH), 1 on Nov 10, 2020 (LS, JT). Winter records over six years, all but two associated with CBC period, span Dec 1–Jan 1: **16** on Dec 29, 1981 (CBC–PDV, DF), 1 on Dec 27, 1987 (CBC count week–PDV), 9 on Jan 1, 1991 (CBC–PDV), 12 during w/e Feb 3, 2006 (fide JWa, KG; MARBA), 1 on Dec 1, 2010 (TMag), unreported number ("large group") on Feb 12, 2015 (DC). Ten-Year: F-2, W-1.

- CBC: 2 years (8%) plus one count week: 16 on Dec 29, 1981, 1 on Jan 1, 1991, avg 0.7.

Likely underreported, as there is a lack of coverage during the peak regional period of late fall–early spring; prone to incursions, but never to be expected. Near southern edge of winter range; difficult to distinguish fall migrants from wandering winter visitors (Dec 1 used as beginning of winter period for these purposes). The 16 recorded on the Dec 29, 1981 CBC were feeding on berries just above the waterline on Manana (DF). The ind. in Sep 2008 was noted as being in the same spruce both days. The Feb 2015 report noted the "large group still here," suggesting a continuing presence (DC). The Oct 30, 2010 ind. was noted as seen and heard as it made "laps around the island" (JT), the Oct 27, 2012 ind. accompanied a single Cedar Waxwing at the Murdock House (JP), the Nov 5, 2016 ind., perhaps first seen as a flyover at the Ballfield, was later photographed with a group of Cedar Waxwings over the Hitchcox house (DH et al.) and the 5 on Nov 8, 2020 were mixed with a flock of Cedar Waxwings over the Meadow. Most unusual is the Jun 9 ind. in a flock of Cedar Waxwings (WBo; FN 52[4]: 437). *The report of a single ind. on Dec 27, 1987 shows up as count week for CBC, but an additional report of an ind. on the count day of Dec 28, 1987 is included in eBird but not the CBC data, and omitted here as a possible reporting error.*

Historical/Regional:

- Vickery: cites Jun 9, 1998 (WBo) as latest spring date for the state (PDV in Vickery et al., 2020).

CEDAR WAXWING
Bombycilla cedrorum

Status: Abundant spring and fall migrant, fairly common summer resident, very rare winter visitor.

Occurrence: A late spring migrant, dates span Apr 4–first two thirds of Jun (overlapping with breeding), peak mid May–mid June; spring max: **1,425** on Jun 1, 2020 (JT, LS), 905 on Jun 3, 2020 (JT, LS), 746 on Jun 4, 2020 (JT, LS), 645 on Jun 2, 2020 (JT, LS), 530 on May 30, 2013 (RL, ML), 450 on May 27, 2012 (RL). Breeding underway by mid Jun, extending through Jul into early Aug; summer max: 86 on Jul 7, 2022 (LS, MWa), 50 on Aug 9, 2001 (BH, SHu) & Aug 10, 2010 (TMag), 40 on Jul 25, 2020 (TB), 37 on Jul 27, 2020 (unknown observer) & Jul 29, 2022 (TW). Fall dates span last two thirds of Aug–Nov 16, extended peak late Aug–mid Oct; 800 on Sep 7–10, 1984 (PDV), 600 on Sep 6, 1985, 500 on Sep 10, 2016 (PR, CHy). Six winter records, three associated with CBC period: 1 on Jan 3, 1986 (CBC–PDV), unreported number w/e Jan 13, 2006 (fide JWa, KG; MARBA), unreported number during Jan 1–7, 2007 (CBC count week), unreported number (small flock) during Jan 16–17, 2018 (KL), 1 on Jan 2–3, 2021 (CBC Jan 3–DH), 3 on Mar 20, 2022 (KL). Ten-Year: SP-10, SU-10, F-10, W-3.

- *MABB*: confirmed; MBA: confirmed.
- CBC: 2 years (8%) plus one count week (2007), 1 on Jan 3, 1986 & Jan 3, 2021, avg 0.1.
- 1899 Checklist: included as Cedar Bird.
- 1900–1908 Reconnaissance & Supplements: included in Jenney supplement; unreported number during Jul 31–Aug 2, 1908 (WM).
- 1914 & 1916 Checklists: unreported number on Aug 1, 1914 (listed as Cedar Bird); included as Cedar Bird 1916.
- 1915–1919 Taylor Journals: 1915–Aug 9 (10), 11 (10), 16, 27, 28, Sep 1, 2, 5, 12 (100); 1916–Aug 20, 21, 22, 25, 26, 31 (200), Sep 3, 4, 6, 10; 1917–Jul 29 (10), Aug 16 (10), 19 (20), Sep 5 (30); 1918–prior to Aug 4, Aug 28; 1919–Sep 4 (50), 5 (30), 13 (6), 14 (6).
- 1918 Fall Migration Census: Dewis–Sep 4 (1), 7 (74 [flocks]), 8 (flocks of 5, 15, 18), 10 (6), 10 (very few), 11 (3); Wentworth–Oct 6 (1), 10 (3), 12 (2).
- 1939 Summer Census: regular summer resident.
- 1944–1967 Farrell Records: 1949–Sep; 1953–Sep; 1954–Jun, Jul, Sep; 1955–Jun, Aug; 1957–Aug; 1958–Aug; 1959–Jun, Jul, Aug, Sep; 1960–Jul, Aug, Sep.
- 1954 & 1955 Summer Records: 1954–included all three checklists; 1955–included Jun 11–15 & Aug 22–Sep 2 (abundant, at least 100 in a day).
- 1970 Summer Checklist: highlighted and marked as known to breed in area.
- Banding: 110 total over four seasons, peak 105 in Fall 1981, max 20 on Aug 26, 1981.

Likely underreported throughout Apr and late spring/summer/early fall (Jun–Aug) due to lack of coverage; the only two Apr records both occurred in 2014 (8 on Apr 4 [DC] & unreported number on Apr 9 [WBo]). Large movements are often events of four days or more, whether lingering or new birds, although sometimes significant departure after only one day, such as 600 decreasing to 120 on Sep 6–7, 1985 (PDV) and 530 to 123 on May 30–31, 2013 (RL, ML). Spring 2020 was exceptional, with the max count of 1,425 on Jun 1 (in sight at once–JT, LS) producing follow-up counts of the other highest spring counts of 645, 905, 746 on Jun 2–4, respectively. Notable for fall is the max flight of 800 reported four straight days Sep 7–10, 1984, another indication that birds arrived and lingered. Inds./flocks "everywhere" during large flights, often multiple large flocks moving around the island (typical behavior for this species—"massive flock flying around all day" [RL]), making counting difficult and likely underreported by some conservative observers. Besides the huge flocks

Cedar Waxwing, May 24, 2019. © Jeremiah Trimble.

in Jun 2020, single flocks noted of 100+ on multiple occasions, including a flock of 200+ on May 28, 2014 (out of 385 reported that day–JT); often many small flocks scattered around the island. Possible anywhere, particularly as flyovers and generally easy to locate due to numbers and flight calls, but also prone to perch as a flock in conifer or deciduous trees; noted as feeding on blossoms or apple petals, and abundant berries in the fall. One flock was observed migrating south from White Head over the ocean until out of sight (Sep 24, 2013–CDd). Often pursued by Merlins during migration. Nesting underway by late May/early Jun while migration continues, with Jun 20 the spring cutoff date for these purposes; courting behavior was noted on May 22, 2016 between 2 inds. sliding back and forth on a branch (BBl). Breeding also confirmed for MBA with an ind. carrying nesting material on Jul 6, 2019 (DH) and carrying food on Jul 19, 2021 (HIAC et al.). One brood is likely due to late arrival and/or early departure of many inds., but a second brood is possible on occasion, as evidenced by several large groups of adults feeding recently fledged young (1/2–2/3 full size) on Sep 5, 1987 (out of 200 inds. reported that day, with 50% immatures–PDV), one juv. begging and being fed by an adult on Sep 20, 2012 (one of many juvs.–LB) and recently fledged young on Sep 11, 2021 (CDD).

Although an unreported number, this species was noted as the "most prevalent bird of the day" on Jul 29, 2015 (TR). Post-breeding gathering/movements begin in Aug, with the fall dates beginning Aug 11 for these purposes. Immature birds may make up a large proportion of fall sightings, mixed with adults, such as those noted above and 80% juvs. on Oct 5, 2005 (70 reported–MI, AM), about 25% juvs. on Aug 31, 2014 (250 reported–JP), mostly immatures on Sep 25, 2016 (150 reported–MW), and mostly juvs. on Oct 22, 2017 (150 reported–JP).

Historical/Regional:

- Vickery: largest spring numbers last week of May–early Jun with numerous counts >100 (none >50 after first week of Jun), lists seven records of 120–530 inds. (including max counts above); common late Aug–mid Oct with flocks of 150–400 inds. nearly annual late Sep–Oct, cites 250 on Aug 31, 2014 (JP) as earliest large fall count and 400 on Sep 5, 1980 (PDV), 800 on Sep 7–10, 1984 (PDV) and 400 on Sep 4, 1987 as concentrations (PDV in Vickery et al., 2020).

RED-BREASTED NUTHATCH
Sitta canadensis

Status: Uncommon to fairly common permanent resident, uncommon to fairly common spring and fairly common to abundant fall irruptive migrant, uncommon to fairly common winter visitor.

Occurrence: Present in limited numbers throughout the year, complicated by frequent irruptive migration (pronounced in fall with minimal return in spring) and likely underreported in summer and late winter/early spring. Spring dates span beginning Mar–end May, peak early–late May; spring max: 40 on May 18, 2019 (BTn) & May 21, 2019 (MBu, EG), 37 on May 18, 2021 (JT, LS, JO), 33 on May 19, 2021 (JT, LS, JO), 30 on May 5, 1984 (PDV), May 19, 2019 (KF) & May 20, 2019 (WBr et al.). Breeding underway by late May (overlapping migration) and sometimes continuing into Aug; summer max: 6 on Jun 9, 2018 (TAn), Jul 4, 2018 (DH) & Jun 7, 2021 (JFo), 5 on Jul 17, 2016 (DH), Jun 10, 2018 (TAn) & Jun 30–Jul 1, 2021 (CEs), 4 on Jun 4, 2019 (TW), Jun 22, 2019 (KD), Jun 23, 2019 (CEl) & Jul 4, 2022 (DH, AH). Fall irruptions often underway in Jul and extended fall dates span last third Jul–end Nov, peak mid Sep–mid Oct; fall max: **>500** on Sep 1, 1957 (MMJ; *MFO* 2: 105), ~ 500 on Sep 2, 1961 (SHi; *AFN* 16[1]: 11), 400 on Oct 3, 2020 (WR), 310 on Oct 25, 2022 (ShF), 300 on Oct 7, 1990 (SS) & Sep 19, 2012 (PDV et al.), 248 on Oct 7, 2020 (JT, LS, HS). Winter records scattered throughout season; winter max: 63 on Jan 1, 1992 (CBC–PDV), 51 on Dec 21, 1989 (CBC–PDV), 29 on Jan 3, 2013 (CBC). Ten-Year: SP-10, SU-8, F-10, W-4.

- *MABB*: confirmed; MBA: confirmed.
- CBC: 21 years (80%) plus one count week, first on Dec 22, 1979, max 63 on Jan 1, 1992, avg 12.7.
- 1899 Checklist: included.
- 1900–1908 Reconnaissance & Supplements: included in Jenney supplement.
- 1914 & 1916 Checklists: included 1916.
- 1915–1919 Taylor Journals: 1915–Aug 28, Sep 12 (5); 1916–Aug 19, 20, 22, 26, 30, 31, Sep 3, 4, 6, 10; 1918–Aug 4, 28; 1919–Sep 5 (1), 6 (6), 11 (1), 13 (40), 14 (50).
- 1939 Summer Census: regular summer visitor.
- 1944–1967 Farrell Records: 1949–Apr, Sep, Dec; 1950–Feb, Oct; 1951–Nov; 1953–Aug, Sep; 1954–Jun, Jul, Sep; 1955–Jun, Aug; 1957–Aug; 1959–Aug; 1960–Apr, May, Aug; 1961–Apr, May.
- 1954 & 1955 Summer Records: 1954–included Jun 19–25 & Jul 10–16; 1955–included Jun 11–15 & Aug 22–Sep 2 (up to 6).
- 1970 Summer Checklist: highlighted and marked as known to breed in area.
- Banding: total 14 over two seasons, peak 9 in Fall 1961, max 3 on Oct 7 & 9, 1961.

Regular irruptions (every two–three years) due mainly to food shortages remove much of the northern population, with minimal return flight in spring (Ghalambor and Martin, 2020). Large numbers may appear for extended periods in fall during irruptions, with some remaining through the winter; unclear proportion of residents that remain or are replaced/supplemented by northern visitors in fall through winter. The ~500 on Sep 2, 1961 "completely dominated the scene (18 in one tree) and with thorough coverage the total count might well have exceeded 2,000." Although a count was not given, on Sep 12, 1929 there were "literally hundreds everywhere, on the ground, on the houses, and flying all about" (unknown obs.; *BL* 31[6]: 407). Fall 2012 was exceptional, with nine days of 100+ spanning Sep 19–Oct 8 (including a high count of 300 on Sep 19); largest single group contained at least 60 inds. flying over the Verizon tower clearing behind the lighthouse in twenty minutes on Sep 2, 2016 (JC). Fall 2020 produced five days of 100+ spanning Sep 19–Oct 9 (including a high count of 400 on Oct 3; largely morning flight overhead with multiple groups of 10–20+–WR); 40 were observed streaming by west of Shining Sails 8:30–9:30 a.m. on Oct 1, part of a daily total of 100 (WR). Surprisingly, a notable return flight Spring 2021 produced a count of 23 on May 4 and counts of 23, 21, 18, 37, 33, & 18 on May 16–20, consecutively. Despite being vocally exuberant, likely underreported during much of year due to preference for deep coniferous forest and lack of coverage during non-migration periods. During irruptive influxes, as mentioned above, inds. seem to be "everywhere," noted as constantly calling from spruces (notably red spruces in 2012, but also appearing "on fences, rocks, houses, and driveways"–LS) and in "just about every bush and tree in town" (Oct 7, 2020–JT, LS, HS). Likely anywhere on the island (less so during breeding), as spruces are always near, including at feeders. Sometimes mixes with chickadees and kinglets in roving flocks; in non-irruption years most likely to be encountered in spruce forest among these flocks, and their vocalizations are often the reason the flocks are first detected. Anecdotal report of three being eaten by a house cat at a feeder in town (2012). Few direct breeding details: two were observed coming/going from a nest hole on May 24, 2016 (LM), adults feeding young on Jul 4, 2018 (DH), and a "feeding frenzy" along White Head Trail on Aug 25, 2018 included adults and begging offspring (TR).

Historical/Regional:

- Vickery: typically 1–4/day in spring (larger counts follow fall incursions), lists seven reports >10 (10–30 inds.–only 30 on May 25, 1984 and 18 on May 8, 2011 part of max counts above); avg 22.5/day in fall (1980–2014), high counts 40–100 occurred in eight years 1983–2013, cites max counts above of 200 or more as high counts (only 200 on Sep 27, 1981 included); cites CBC range as 1–63 inds. (PDV in Vickery et al., 2020).

Red-breasted Nuthatch, Oct 7, 2012. © Luke Seitz.

WHITE-BREASTED NUTHATCH
Sitta carolinensis

Status: Uncommon permanent resident, irregular irruptive fall migrant.

Occurrence: Reports scattered throughout the year but likely underreported, highest numbers consistently in fall; year max: **20** on Oct 5, 2003 (WJS), 12 on Sep 26, 1981 (PDV), Oct 2, 1997 (JT) & Oct 5, 2018 (JT, LS), 11 on Oct 9–10, 2010 (JT) & Oct 4, 2021 (JT, LS), 8 on Sep 13, 1981 (PDV), Sep 24, 2001 (JT), Oct 11, 2014 (LS et al.), Sep 22, 2016 (WR), Sep 29, 2020 (DL) & Sep 30, 2022 (DH). Ten-Year: 10.

- *MABB*: possible; MBA: possible.
- CBC: recorded 3 years (12%) plus one count week, first on Jan 1, 1992, max 2 on Jan 1, 1992, avg 0.2.
- 1914 & 1916 Checklists: included 1916.
- 1915–1919 Taylor Journals: 1916–Sep 10; 1917–Sep 5 (1).
- 1918 Fall Migration Census: Wentworth–several seen and others heard on Oct 16.
- 1944–1967 Farrell Records: 1950–Apr, May; 1951–Oct, Nov; 1952–Apr; 1954–Jun, Jul; 1956–May; 1958–May; 1960–Apr, May, Aug; 1967–Apr 6, 7, 8, 9, 14, 15, 16, 17, 18, 19, 20, 21, 22, 23, 24.
- 1954 & 1955 Summer Records: 1954–included Jun 27–Jul 4.
- 1970 Summer Checklist: marked as known to breed in area.
- Banding: total 4 in Fall 1961, max 2 on Oct 7.

Likely underreported throughout year due to preference for forest habitat and lack of coverage except migration periods. Resident status supported by reports in every season and species' largely non-migratory tendency, despite lack of direct breeding evidence; inds. in appropriate habitat on Jun 5, 2021 (TF) and Jul 2, 2021 (DH) provided the basis for status on MBA. Highest counts later in fall likely result of juveniles added to breeding population, supplemented by irregular irruptions from the north; max counts all occurring within Sep 13–Oct 11. Higher numbers sometimes considered influxes, but no apparent pattern, and no apparent spring return. Reports scattered across the island, including deep woods, town locations and feeders.

Historical/Regional:

- Palmer: has nested.
- Vickery: typical spring count 2 or fewer, cites 5 on May 5, 2010 (NL), 4 on Apr 6, 2011 (TMag) and 6 on Apr 27, 2011 (TMag) as probably reflecting migrants; typical fall count 3 or fewer, lists eight high counts as moderate flight years (6–20 inds.), seven of which are listed above as max counts (*8 on Oct 11, 2011 should be 2014*; PDV in Vickery et al., 2020).

White-breasted Nuthatch, Oct 4, 2020. © Luke Seitz.

BROWN CREEPER
Certhia americana

Status: Rare to uncommon spring and uncommon to fairly common fall migrant, very rare summer visitor and possible breeder, very rare winter visitor.

Occurrence: Spring dates span Mar 20–May 31, peak early Apr–early May; spring max: 15 on May 6, 1984 (PDV), 12 on Apr 29, 2011 (TMag), 10 on Apr 6, 2013 (DH). Eight summer records over three years since 2010 (six in 2021): 1 on Jul 12, 2010 (TMag), 1 on Jul 13, 2017 (FMa), 3 on Jun 7, 2021 (JFo), 1 on Jun 29, 2021 (JFo, TFo), 1 on Jul 27, 2021 (TMe), 2 on Jul 30, 2021 (NP), 3 on Aug 3–4, 2021 (LHa, JCe), 2 on Aug 7, 2021 (AMo). Fall dates span Aug 23–Nov 16, peak late Sep–mid Oct; fall max: **50** on Sep 30, 2007 (DL), 30 on Oct 7, 1984 (SS) & Oct 9, 1991 (PMo), 25 on Oct 26–27, 1996 (SA), Oct 1, 2007 (DL) & Oct 4, 2010 (LS). Five winter records, all but one associated with CBC, span Dec 22–Jan 7: 2 on Dec 22, 1979 (CBC–PDV), 1 on Dec 29, 1983 (CBC–PDV), 2 on Jan 1, 1992 (CBC), 1 on Jan 7, 2012 (EH, CHy), 1 on Jan 3, 2013 (CBC–DH, PM). Ten-Year: SP-7, SU-3, F-10.

- *MABB*: possible; MBA: possible.
- CBC: recorded four years (15%), first on Dec 22, 1979, max 2 on Dec 22, 1979 & Jan 1, 1992, avg 0.2.
- 1914 & 1916 Checklists: included 1916.
- 1915–1919 Taylor Journals: 1915–Sep 12 (1); 1916–Sep 10.
- 1918 Fall Migration Census: Wentworth–Sep 29, Oct 1, 6, 7, 8, 9 (common), 12, 15, 16 (fewer), 17 (many), 19 (very many), 20 (several), 22 (several), 23 (1), 24 (1).
- 1939 Summer Census: rare summer visitor.
- 1944–1967 Farrell Records: 1949–Mar, Apr; 1950–Mar, Apr, May, Nov; 1951–Mar, Apr, May, Sep, Oct, Nov; 1952–Apr; 1959–Aug; 1960–Apr, May, Aug, Sep; 1961–Apr, May; 1967–Apr 2 (1), 14 (1), 15 (1), 23 (1).
- 1970 Summer Checklist: marked as known to breed in area.
- Banding: 62 total over four seasons, peak 36 in Fall 1960, max 10 on Oct 5, 1960.

Likely underreported throughout much of year due to its quiet nature and preference for deep woods and during peak migration periods due to lack of coverage (notably Apr and Oct). Larger influxes appear to be mainly one- three-day events. No clear evidence of breeding despite status on 1970 Summer Checklist and inclusion as possible in *MABB* & MBA, but easily overlooked; MBA status based on an ind. in appropriate habitat on May 25, 2021 (BBl), but note 2021 summer records. Most often encountered on coniferous northern trails, notably Black Head Trail, but also in spruces around town at locations such as along Lobster Cove Rd. between the Trailing Yew and the Brewery; 8 noted in apple trees from the Lupine Gallery to the start of Lobster Cove Trail on Oct 2, 2021 (JT, LS).

Historical/Regional:

- Vickery: typical spring count 2–4 inds., lists the three max counts above and 8 on May 7, 1984 (PDV) as higher counts; fall counts >10 typically Sep 25–Oct 11, lists seven reports of 7–50 inds. (including most max counts above), with 25 on Oct 26, 1996 (SA) as notably late (PDV in Vickery et al., 2020).

Brown Creeper, Oct 9, 2021. © Jeremiah Trimble.

BLUE-GRAY GNATCATCHER
Polioptila caerulea

Status: Scarce to uncommon spring and uncommon fall migrant.

Occurrence: Spring dates span Apr 19–Jun 15; peak mid May; spring max: **6** on May 14, 2016 (HN), 5 on May 13, 1997 (PDV) & May 20, 2019 (JLo), 4 on May 18, 2019 (JLo) & Jun 1, 2020 (JT, LS). Fall dates span Aug 20–Oct 27, peak early–late Sep; fall max: 5 on Aug 26, 1972 (BT; *AB* 27[1]: 28) & Sep 25, 1983 (DF et al.), 4 on Sep 27, 2012 (JT, BN), Sep 18, 2016 (DMa) & Sep 29, 2020 (WR), 3 on Sep 6, 1986 (PDV), Sep 29, 2003 (JT), Sep 16, 2007 (JBy), & Sep 20, 2016 (DMa). Ten-Year: SP-10, F-10.

- 1915–1919 Taylor Journals: 1915–Sep 5 (1); 1916–Aug 30 (1); 1919–Sep 1 (1), 3 (1), 4 (1).
- 1918 Fall Migration Census: Dewis–Sep 11 (1), noted as rare; Wentworth–Oct 6 (1 near Kelsey Cottage); previous records include: 1 on Sep 5, 1915 & Aug 30, 1916 (WT), 1 each day in 1917 on Aug 20, 22, Sep 1, 2, 11 (mob).
- 1939 Summer Census: accidental summer visitor.
- 1944–1967 Farrell Records: 1955–Aug; 1959–Aug; 1960–May.
- 1954 & 1955 Summer Records: 1955–Sep 1 (1).
- 1970 Summer Checklist: included.

Breeding range expanded northward during much of 20th century, extending into New England in the 1960s and 70s (Kershner and Ellison, 2020), with first Maine confirmation in 1979; Monhegan is now at the northern limit, with an elevated but still limited status as a migrant over historical accounts. A high total of 9 was reported w/e May 12, 2006 (fide JWa, KG; MARBA) but no specific daily totals provided. Scattered reports from many town locations, a favorite being near/around the Ice Pond, but it is also often found along Main St. and Lobster Cove Rd. Inds. known to linger for several days (1 for three days in same area in lilacs along Wharf Rd. (May 13–15, 2011–LS) and 1 for five days near the church and Black Duck Emporium (Sep 20–24, 2012 (LB, et al). Often located due to its persistent vocalizations.

Historical/Regional:

- Palmer: cites 1915, 1916, 1917, 1918 records as listed by Jenney in 1918 Fall Migration Census.
- Cruickshank: very rare fall visitant; cites same records listed by Jenney in 1918 Fall Migration Census.
- Vickery: annual in fall 2009–2017 (cites 4 on Sep 18, 2016 [DMa] and 2 on Sep 10, 2017 [JVW]), cites 5 on Sep 25, 1983 (DF) and 4 on Sep 27, 2012 (JT, BN) as high counts (PDV in Vickery et al., 2020).

Blue-gray Gnatcatcher, Sep 23, 2019. © Bill Thompson.

HOUSE WREN
Troglodytes aedon

Status: Scarce to uncommon spring and uncommon fall migrant, rare to scarce summer visitor and possible breeder, accidental winter visitor.

Occurrence: Spring dates span during Mar 18–21–end of May, perhaps overlapping with possible breeders, peak mid–late May; spring max: 5 on May 16, 2022 (LS, MWa), 4 on May 14, 2010 (DH, MLe), May 21, 2013 (JH) & May 17, 2022 (LS, MWa), 3 on May 26, 1996 (SS), May 25, 2011 (TMag), May 12, 2012 (RS) & May 20, 2022 (BGr, MGr). Summer records over thirteen years since 1971 (eight in 2010, four each in 2020 & 2021, eleven in 2022), but little evidence of breeding; summer max: **6** on Jul 21, 2008 (SWi), 3 on Jul 3, 2007 (JSc) & Jun 29, 2021 (JFo, TFo), 2 on Jun 1–3, 2008 (JSc), Jul 24, 2010 (TMag), Jul 31, 2010 (TMag), Jun 5, 2011 (TMag), Jun 6, 2022 (NB) & Jul 7, 2022 (LS, MWa). Fall dates span late Aug–Oct 28, peak late Sep–mid Oct; fall max: 4 on Sep 27, 2005 (JT), 3 on Sep 29, 1985 (PDV), Oct 2, 1997 (JT), Oct 13, 2015 (LS), Oct 5, 2017 (JO), Oct 5, 2019 (LK), Sep 28, 2020 (KWo), Oct 3, 2020 (MW) & Oct 9, 2020 (JT, LS, HS). One winter record: 1 on Jan 2, 2020 (CBC–DH). Ten-Year: SP-9, SU-4, F-10, W-1.

- MBA: confirmed.
- CBC: recorded one year (4%), 1 on Jan 2, 2020, avg 0.0.
- 1914 & 1916 Checklists: included as Wren 1916.
- 1970 Summer Checklist: marked as known to breed in area.
- Banding: 1 on Sep 10, 1981.

Although near the northern edge of its breeding range, likely underreported as a summer visitor/breeder due to lack of coverage, supported by increased sightings in summer 2010 with regular reports by TMag. An ind. singing incessantly near the Cundy residence during Mar 18–21, 2022 (triplist report–KL) is over a month earlier than any other (Apr 30). Despite inclusion on 1970 Summer Checklist, only direct evidence of breeding involved a pair at a box in the village on May 16, 2010 (EH) and an adult carrying nesting material on May 16, 2021 (DR–confirmed for MBA), while the max count of 6 on Jul 21, 2008 suggests a possible family group. Reports from scattered town locations and trails, particularly in deciduous brush/scrub, including the north end of the island; sometimes singing in the spring or giving harsh calls throughout much of the year. The only winter record was observed along the edge of the Meadow near the Lupine Gallery, and represents a possible first winter record for Maine (DH).

WINTER WREN
Troglodytes hiemalis

Status: Uncommon spring and uncommon to fairly common fall migrant, scarce to uncommon summer resident, rare winter visitor; possible permanent resident.

Occurrence: Spring dates span Mar 6–end of May, peak mid Apr–mid May; spring max: 6 on May 18, 2021 (JT, LS, JO), 5 on May 13, 1997 (PDV), May 23–24, 2019 (MC, CC) & May 26, 2019 (CMu, GJ), 4 on May 14, 1997 (PDV), May 15, 2005 (HN), May 5, 2010 (NL), Apr 27, 2011 (TMag), May 13, 2011 (TMag), May 22, 2011 (JH), Apr 5, 2012 (DH), May 17, 2021 (JAl, HN, LBl) & May 30, 2022 (MO). Breeding activity likely overlaps spring migrants in late May, likely underreported and continues unobtrusively into Jul; summer max: 5 on Jun 22, 2019 (KD), Jul 27, 2020 (GBr), Jul 29, 2020 (GBr) & Jun 20, 2021 (CEl) & Jul 19, 2022 (WP), 4 on Jun 21, 2019 (KD) & Jul 11, 2022 (RHa, SHa), 3 on nine dates over six years since 2007 (all but one since 2018), span Jun 7–Aug 29. Fall migration underway early Sep–late Nov, peak late Sep–early Nov; fall max: **16** on Nov 10, 2021 (LS, JT) & Nov 12, 2021 (LS, JT), 14 on Oct 30, 2010 (JT, MI, LS), 11 on Nov 11, 2021 (LS, JT), 10 on Oct 2, 1997 (JT), Sep 30, 1998 (JT), Sep 28, 2005 (JT) & Sep 30, 2005 (JT). Twenty-one winter records over fourteen years, many associated with CBC period, span early Dec–Jan 26; winter max: 8 on Jan 4, 2007 (CBC–PDV et al.), 2 on Dec 29, 1983 (CBC–PDV), Dec 27, 1984 (CBC–PDV), Jan 1, 1992 (CBC–PDV), Dec 27, 1994 (CBC–PDV), Dec 27, 2004 (PDV), Jan 26, 2013 (DH) & Jan 2, 2020 (DH). Ten-Year: SP-9, SU-10, F-10, W-2.

- *MABB*: confirmed; MBA: probable.
- CBC: ten years (38%) plus two count weeks, first on Dec 22, 1979, max 8 on Jan 4, 2007, avg 0.9.
- 1939 Summer Census: accidental summer resident (one record).
- 1944–1967 Farrell Records: 1945–Oct; 1954–Jul; 1955–Jun, Jul, Aug; 1959–Jul, Aug; 1960–Jul, Aug; 1961–Apr, May; 1967–Apr 14 (1).
- 1954 & 1955 Summer Records: 1954–included Jul 10–16; 1955–included Jun 11–15 & Jun 30–Jul 5, Aug 22 (2), 29 (1).
- 1970 Summer Checklist: highlighted and marked as known to breed in area.

Remarkably consistent presence throughout much of the year; likely underreported during important portions of spring and fall migration (Apr & Oct) and summer due to lack of coverage, and at all times by secretive nature and preferred habitat (brushy deciduous/downed tree areas of conifer forests). Breeding activity overlooked; MBA status based on a singing ind. present 7+ days on Jun 24, 2018 (KL). Unclear whether winter records involve lingering residents or visitors from the north, likely the latter; inds. possibly pushed out by harsher weather as winter progresses. Reports from Jan & Feb in 2000, 2001, 2003, & 2007 not included in twenty winter records, as date and number of inds. involved not known (see Vickery below). Scattered reports over much of island—town locations during migration include around the Ice Pond, Ocean Ave. and areas along Lobster Cove Rd., but often found along trails, such as Underhill, Burnt Head, Alder and White Head in southern half and many of the trails in the coniferous-dominated northern half (likely breeding areas, but few details are at hand), such as Long Swamp, Black Head, Maple, Red Ribbon, Cathedral Woods and others. Often identified by sound and not seen, whether singing in the spring/summer or repeating its double note: "kit-kit".

Historical/Regional:

- Vickery: cites 1 on Mar 6, 2012 (DH) as early spring; 8 on Jan 4, 2007 as part of a widespread winter event in 2006–2007 and Jan & Feb reports in 2000, 2001, 2003, & 2007 (WBo) and Jan 26, 2013 (DH) and Jan 5, 2016 (mob) as other winter reports (PDV in Vickery et al., 2020).

Winter Wren, Oct 22, 2011. © Jeremiah Trimble.

SEDGE WREN
Cistothorus platensis

Status: Accidental spring and very rare fall migrant, accidental winter visitor.

Occurrence: Ten records (1 spring, 8 fall, 1 winter) since Sep 1970, all singles. Spring record: May 18, 2005 (JWa, SWk, GD et al.). Fall records over eight years since 1970, span Sep 8–Nov 12: Sep 8–9, 1970 (ELK et al.; *AFN* 25[1]: 29–30), Sep 28, 1982 (DF),

Sep 29, 1992 (PDV), Sep 25–27, 1993 (PDV, BN), Sep 29–during Oct 3–5, 2003 (JT et al.), Oct 10, 2014 (JT), Oct 12–13, 2015 (LS), Nov 12, 2020 (JT, LS). Winter record: Jan 5, 2010 (CBC–PDV, DF). Ten-Year: F-3.

- CBC: one year (4%), 1 on Jan 5, 2010, avg. 0.0.

Formerly more common in the state, but always a fairly rare and local breeder at the northeast edge of its range. Six of the recent Monhegan records (since 1992) listed on the OLMB (three accepted—Sep 2003, May 2005, Oct 2015; three not yet reviewed), with four records not included (Sep 1970, Sep 1982, Oct 2014 & Nov 2020). Easily overlooked due to secretive habits and wet marsh or grassland habitat. Few details available, but the Fall 2014 & 2015 and Winter 2010 inds. were located in the wet meadow at Lobster Cove; all three were heard calling, the Oct 2014 ind. incessantly at first (JT) and observed perching up and in short flights. The Nov 2020 ind. was seen and heard calling in the Meadow at dusk.

Historical/Regional:

- Vickery: six fall records since 1970 span Sep 8-Oct 5 (four last week of Sep); cites the Jan 2010 winter record (PDV in Vickery et al., 2020).
- OLMB: thirteen additional state records since 1988 (historically bred and more numerous)—seven accepted and six not yet reviewed.

Sedge Wren, Oct 12, 2015. © Luke Seitz.

MARSH WREN
Cistothorus palustris

Status: Very rare spring and scarce to uncommon fall migrant.

Occurrence: Fifty-seven records (2 spring, 55 fall) since 1981. Spring records: 1 on May 23, 1987 (SS), unreported number on May 23–28, 1999 (TV). Fall records since 1981 span Sep 16–Oct 17, peak late Sep–mid Oct; fall max: **8** on Oct 1, 2010 (DL), 4 on Oct 6, 2017 (LS), 3 on Sep 25, 2000 (JT), Oct 5, 2005 (MI, AM), Oct 5, 2012 (DH) & Oct 2, 2019 (JT, LS, AO), 2 on thirteen days. Ten-Year: F-10.

Although near the northern edge of its breeding range, Marsh Wren is still probably underreported in Oct due to lack of coverage and throughout migrations due to secretive nature. Number of fall records possibly higher; reports of same number on consecutive days considered one record due to rarity, but details and certainty lacking. As expected, most often reported from the Meadow and Lobster Cove marsh/meadow, although single reports from near start of Underhill Trail (west end) and north end of Lobster Cove Trail. Largest group is 3 in the Meadow on Oct 2, 2019 (JT, LS, AO).

Historical/Regional:

- Vickery: not found on surveys Sep 1–10 in 1980s; regular Sep 22–Oct 10 (PDV in Vickery et al., 2020).

Marsh Wren, Oct 6, 2017. © Luke Seitz.

CAROLINA WREN
Thryothorus ludovicianus

Status: Uncommon to fairly common permanent resident.

Occurrence: Reports scattered throughout the year, largely based on coverage, highest in fall and early winter; year max: **20** on Sep 25, 2002 (JT), 18 on Sep 16, 2022 (WR), 15 on May 28, 2021 (KKl), 14 on Jan 3, 2013 (CBC–PDV et al.), 12 on Sep 26, 2002 (JT), 11 on Oct 2, 2013 (BSt) & Sep 8, 2022 (WR), 10 on Sep 26–28, 2001 (JT), Sep 27, 2010 (DL), Oct 8, 2011 (JM), Sep 26, 2013 (BN), Oct 3, 2014 (BBa, JWy), & Sep 7, 2022 (WR). Ten-Year: 10.

- MBA: probable.
- CBC: 8 years (31%), first on Jan 1, 1992, max 14 on Jan 5, 2010, avg 1.4.
- 1944–1967 Farrell Records: 1954–Jul; first known Monhegan record (see 1954 & 1955 Summer Records).
- 1954 & 1955 Summer Records: 1 reported during Jul 10–16, 1954; first known Monhegan record.

Irregular but steady northward expansion over the past century has brought the nonmigratory Carolina Wren into Maine (Haggerty and Morton, 2020); a fairly recent addition to the Monhegan avifauna, with the first known record on Jul 14, 1954 (EAB, MEAB) and fewer than ten records for the island before 1998, after which it became annual and established as a resident. Well-known for proliferating over periods with mild winters and decreasing markedly during or after severe winters; almost absent after early Jan 2015, with only fall records in remaining 2015 and 2016, year-round reports resuming in 2018, and no reports of more than 2 inds. until 2019 (max of 4), with numbers increasing through 2022 (see max counts above). Recorded on six consecutive CBCs 2007–2015 and then lacking in 2016 and 2020 (recorded in 2021). The highest counts later in the year are likely the result of juveniles added to breeding population; the 18 inds. on Sep 16, 2022 involved multiple family groups with well-grown young (WR). Pairs noted throughout much of year and obvious within territories, with singing and calling prevalent; at least six territories recorded on Aug 17, 2006 (PDV). Few breeding details: pair with 3 fledglings on May 19, 2000 (LBr), pair with 3 fledglings in late May 2001 (KL) and one pair with recently fledged young on May 13, 2011 (TMag); MBA status based on a pair in suitable habitat on Jul 20, 2021 (BMu). Reports scattered throughout the island (sometimes referred to as basically everywhere during peak periods), from northern forest to eastern ravines to the village, mainly in thickets; favored locations include around the Ice Pond and Meadow, along Lobster Cove Rd., Ocean Ave. and the Lighthouse/Ballfield area.

Historical/Regional:

- Vickery: cites the 2000 and 2001 breeding records above; likely nested since 1990; cites max count of 20 above as fall record (PDV in Vickery et al., 2020).

Carolina Wren, Oct 23, 2021. © Sebastian Jones.

GRAY CATBIRD
Dumetella carolinensis

Status: Fairly common spring and fall migrant, uncommon to fairly common summer resident, very rare winter visitor.

Occurrence: Spring dates span Apr 5–early Jun (overlapping with breeders), peak last two-thirds of May; spring max: **136** on May 16, 2022 (LS, MWa), 89 on May 17, 2022 (LS, MWa), 46 on May 23, 2014 (BCo), May 21, 2018 (JT, CK) & May 24, 2021 (JT et al.), 42 on May 24, 2018 (JT). Residents in evidence by late May, mingling with migrants (summer dates begin Jun 11), breeding continues with second brood into Aug; summer max: 16 on Jul 18, 2019 (JT), 15 on Aug 17, 2006 (PDV), 12 on Jul 19, 2019 (JT) & Jul 15, 2021 (BTh). Fall migration spans early Sep–w/e Dec 4, peak mid Sep–early Oct; fall max: 21 on Sep 24, 2012 (JT, BN), 20 on Sep 26, 1981 (PDV), 18 on Sep 14, 2021 (JLo), 17 on Sep 22, 2012 (MW) & Sep 26, 2012 (JT, BN). Four winter records since 2012: 1 on Mar 6, 2012 (DH), 1 on Jan 3, 2015 (CBC–DH, FK, WN), 1 on Jan 2, 2020 (CBC–DH), 1 on Mar 18, 2022 (KL). Ten-Year: SP-10, SU-10, F-10, W-2.

- *MABB*: confirmed; MBA: confirmed.
- CBC: 2 years (8%): 1 on Jan 3, 2015, 1 on Jan 2, 2020, avg 0.0.
- 1900–1908 Reconnaissance & Supplements: included in Jenney supplement; unreported number during Jul 31–Aug 2, 1908 (WM).
- 1909 Notes: a few singing in thickets on border of woodlands. Listed as Catbird.
- 1914 & 1916 Checklists: included 1916.
- 1915–1919 Taylor Journals: 1919–Sep 13 (1).
- 1918 Fall Migration Census: Dewis–1 on Sep 12 (Prof. Taylor); Wentworth–Sep 29, Oct 1, 17. Listed as Catbird.
- 1939 Summer Census: uncommon summer visitor.
- 1944–1967 Farrell Records: 1948–May; 1949–Apr; 1950–May; 1951–May; 1954–Jun, Jul; 1955–Jun, Jul, Aug; 1956–May; 1957–Aug; 1958–Sep; 1959–May, Jun, Jul, Aug; 1960–May, Jun, Jul, Aug, Sep; 1961–May; 1967–Jun 1–8 (2 each day).
- 1954 & 1955 Summer Records: 1954–included all three checklists; 1955–included all three checklists (up to 6 Aug 22–Sep 2).
- 1970 Summer Checklist: marked as known to breed in area.
- Banding: 47 total over six seasons, peak 18 in Fall 1981, max 5 on Sep 1, 1981, May 22, 1984 & May 23, 2002.

Increasing in overall presence, note preponderance

of recent max counts. Larger movements often three–five day events; spring 2021 was exceptional, producing twelve consecutive days of 20+ inds. May 14–25, including two max counts (41 and 46 inds.). Inds. on Mar 6, 2012 and Mar 18, 2022 are likely too early to be true migrants, as earliest in Maine usually late Mar/early Apr, and considered winter visitors here (Mar 21 used as beginning of spring period). Late May movements and totals noted as being a mix of residents and migrants on several occasions. Few details for breeding, although many (of 15 inds.) were noted as on territory on the late date of Aug 17, 2006 (PDV–oddly included as early fall migration in Vickery, below). An adult was noted carrying nesting material on May 27, 1989 (JVW) and the MBA status is based on an adult carrying nesting material on May 27, 2021 (BBl) and recently fledged young on Jul 25, 2020 (TB). The "recent arrival from the mainland" in early Jul 1938 of 2 inds. was considered the "rarest bird sight of the year" by WT (Monhegan Press, 1938b). Preference for deciduous scrub, but likely at many town locations, especially the edges of the Meadow, between the Ice Pond and school, edge of the Ballfield, scrubby swale along Ocean Ave., Black Head Rd., Lobster Cove Trail, Alder Trail, Underhill Trail, Burnt Head Trail and White Head Trail.

Historical/Regional:

- Palmer: cites Wentworth Oct 17 record as a late date.
- Cruickshank: cites Wentworth Oct 17 record as late.
- Vickery: counts of 20–30 inds. May 14–31, cites 30 on May 14, 1997 (PDV) and 28 on May 26, 2014 (JT), and 10 on Apr 28, 2011 (TMag) as notable early spring; cites 15 on Aug 17, 2006 (PDV) and 12 on Sep 4, 1983 (PDV) as major early fall flights (>10), 20 on Sep 26, 1981 (PDV) as max and 15 on Oct 8, 2012 (JT) as late (PDV in Vickery et al., 2020).

Gray Catbird, May 16, 2021. © Jeremiah Trimble.

BROWN THRASHER
Toxostoma rufum

Status: Uncommon spring and fall migrant, rare summer resident, accidental winter visitor.

Occurrence: Spring dates span during Mar 22–26– early Jun, peak early–late May; spring max: **9** on May 20, 2021 (JT, LS, MWa), 7 on May 16, 2022 (LS, MWa) & May 27, 2022 (CHi), 6 on Jun 3, 2007 (JSc), May 5, 2010 (NL), May 27, 2016 (BBa), May 19–22, 2021 (JT et al.) & May 21–22, 2022 (JT, LS, MWa), 5 on May 14, 2011 (TMag), May 25, 2015 (JT, BN, JO) & May 23, 2021 (JT et al.). Thirty-one summer records over sixteen years since 1909 (five records in 2021 & 2022, three each in 2006, 2018 & 2019), span Jun 11 (beginning of summer period for these purposes)– late Aug; summer max: 3 on Jun 13, 2020 (DH), 2 on Aug 10, 1915 (CFJ), Aug 18, 1917 (WT, CFJ, MCG), Jun 11, 2018 (EM), Jun 18, 2018 (BEv, TEv), Jun 23, 2019 (CEl) & Jun 12, 2011 (CDo). Fall dates span Sep 2–w/e Nov 11 (Nov 6 latest definite date), peak mid Sep–early Oct; fall max: 4 on Sep 26, 1994 (PDV), Sep 25, 2001 (JT), Sep 27, 2010 (EH, LY, ED), Sep 28, 2012 (JT, BN) & Sep 29, 2019 (MW), 3 on twenty-two dates that span Sep 6–Oct 11. One winter record: 1 on Jan 3, 1986 (CBC–PDV). Ten-Year: SP-10, SU-9, F-10.

- *MABB*: probable; MBA: confirmed.
- CBC: 1 year (4%), 1 on Jan 3, 1986, avg 0.0.
- 1900–1908 Reconnaissance & Supplements: 1 on Jun 3, 1908, giving "smack" call (FA–Monhegan noted as unlikely place).
- 1909 Notes: 2 seen (one singing).
- 1914 & 1916 Checklists: included as Brown Thrush 1916.
- 1915–1919 Taylor Journals: 1915–Aug 10 (2); 1916–Aug 22, Sep 6 (1); 1917–Aug 18 (2).
- 1918 Fall Migration Census: Wentworth–1 each on Oct 12, 13.
- 1944–1967 Farrell Records: 1950–May; 1954–Jun; 1956–May; 1959–May, Jul; 1960–May; 1961–Apr, May; 1967–Jun 1 (1), 7 (1), 8 (1).
- 1954 & 1955 Summer Records: 1954–included Jun 19–25.
- 1970 Summer Checklist: marked as known to breed in area.
- Banding: 4 total over four seasons, peak 1 in Fall 1960, Fall 1961, Spring 1984, Spring 2002, max 1 on four dates.

For a species of such limited status, it is encountered with remarkable consistency. Monhegan being near the northern edge of its breeding range undoubtedly limits the likelihood of migration peaks. Fifteen were recorded during Sep 25–Oct 2, 1962, but no daily totals reported (MWG; *MFN* Oct 1962: 159, *AFN* 17[1]: 11). Noticeably increased presence in Spring 2021, with ten days of 4+ spanning May 15–31. Consistency may be due to lingering inds., which occur on a regular basis for an unknown duration, but certainly for three or more days. Its secretive nature and preference for deciduous thickets lead them to be underreported, but their loud call and song say otherwise. While the 1970 Summer Checklist, *MABB,* and a notation as "taken up residence, hearing daily" on Jun 23, 2014 (DC) are suggestive, the only direct evidence of breeding is a pair noted as recently nesting on Jun 7, 2007 (KL), a pair with nesting material on May 23 or 24, 2014 (KL, PD) and an adult carrying nesting material on May 26, 2021 (PMc-confirmed status for MBA). The 1916 record of unknown specific date by MCG not considered separate from the two records by WT. Favored locations include the swale/bridge area along Ocean Ave., edges of the Ballfield and Meadow, Lobster Cove and Underhill Trails, near the start of the Burnt Head Trail, and between the Ice Pond and school; has been known to visit feeders.

Historical/Regional:

- Palmer: cites Allen (1909 Notes) record as unusual occurrence and Wentworth records as late.
- Cruickshank: cites Wentworth records as latest.
- Vickery: cites 4 on May 13, 1997 (PDV, DAb) and 5 on May 14, 2011 (TMag) for spring; cites 2 on Jun 7, 2007 (KL) as recent nesting; earliest fall Aug 28, 2001 (possibly resident–WBo), Sep 10, 2010 (TMag), Sep 12, 2006 (PDV), and Sep 12, 2016 (HM), 2 noted on Sep 13, 1980 (PDV), and 3 on Sep 18–19, 2016 (WR), with nine+ days of 3–4 inds. Sep 19–29, max of 3 in Oct, and late date of Nov 6, 2001 (WBo; PDV in Vickery et al., 2020).

Brown Thrasher, Oct 8, 2016. © Luke Seitz.

NORTHERN MOCKINGBIRD
Mimus polyglottos

Status: Scarce to uncommon permanent resident, spring and fall migrant of unknown status (*presumably rare to uncommon*).

Occurrence: Scattered but regular reports of 1 or 2 inds. throughout the year, with slightly higher numbers reported in spring and Sep–early Oct; true status as a probable migrant confusing and unclear, surely underreported outside main reporting periods of May & Sep. Spring peak in mid–late May; spring max: 6 on May 27, 1995 (SS) & May 17, 1997 (RSh), 5 on May 27, 2009 (NH), 4 on May 15, 2005 (HN). Twenty-one summer records (Jun 1–Aug 20 period) over thirteen years since 1916 (see 1918 Fall Migration Census below—unreported 1918–2006, four in 2022), with breeding evidence lacking despite *MABB*; summer max: 2 on Jul 31–Aug 1, 2012 (MWi) & Aug 3, 2022 (AMo). Fall peak early Sep–early Oct; fall max: **12** on Sep 14, 1981 (PDV), 8 on Oct 7, 1990 (SS), 7 on Sep 12, 1981 (PDV). Twenty-six winter records (Dec 1–Feb 29 period) over twenty-three years/seasons since 1964, most associated with CBC period; winter max: 4 on Jan 2, 1997 (CBC–PDV), 3 on Dec 29, 1983 (CBC–PDV), Jan 1, 1992 (CBC–PDV), & Jan 4, 2007 (CBC), 2 on Dec 27–28, 1982 (CBC Dec 28–PDV), Dec 21, 1989 (CBC–PDV), Jan 1, 1991 (CBC–PDV), & Jan 4, 2012 (DH, PM). Ten-Year: SP-10, SU-9, F-10, W-3.

- *MABB*: confirmed; MBA: possible.
- CBC: 15 years (58%) plus three count weeks, first on Dec 28, 1978, max 4 on Jan 2, 1997, avg 1.1.
- 1914 & 1916 Checklists: included 1916.
- 1915–1919 Taylor Journals: 1916–Sep 6 (1); 1919–Sep 3 (1), 5 (1).
- 1918 Fall Migration Census: Wentworth–Oct 16, 17 (1 near school, 1 "near farthest pine tree north"), 18, 21 (1 calling in Barstow yard), 23 (1), 24 (1), 25 (1), 26 (1). Reported by Linwood A. Davis on Nov 6. Earlier records cited: 1 on Aug 26–27, 1916, 1 on Aug 20 & 22, 1917, 3 together on Sep 1–2, 1917, 1 on Sep 11, 1917. Listed as Mockingbird.
- 1939 Summer Census: rare summer visitor. Listed as Mockingbird.
- 1944–1967 Farrell Records: 1951–Apr; 1959–May, Jun, Aug; 1960–Apr; 1961–Apr, May.
- 1970 Summer Checklist: included.
- Banding: 2 on Sep 7, 1981.

A general northward expansion of this southern species' range occurred during the late 1800s and much of the 1900s, becoming more apparent in Maine in second half of the century. Its expected presence on the island, despite its uncommonness, results in few details provided with sightings. Lack of coverage throughout much of year complicates understanding of its status, but it is very consistent across seasons/years. Lack of migratory tendencies for species, except partly in northern range, with some limited seasonal movements between territories, makes the presence of supplemental inds. notable and intriguing (Farnsworth et al., 2020). A definite influx of inds. occurred in fall 1981, with 4+ seen on all seven days of reported sightings Sep 11–27. One on Oct 6, 2021 was considered a "new bird" based on shabby, molting plumage (JT, LS). Inds. noted continuing for multiple days in certain areas; but no breeding data available except for confirmation in *MABB* and possible in MBA (singing ind. on Jun 8, 2019 [Cro] and ind. in appropriate habitat on Jul 2, 2021 [DH]) may indicate a non-breeding resident/visitor status; reported as nesting behind the Cundy residence on May 13, 2020 (DC). Noted on Mar 31, 2015 as having been around all winter (DC). Observed at many town locations and once near Burnt Head.

Historical/Regional:

- Palmer: notes three records, cites Wentworth's listing of 3 on Sep 1–2, 1917 as unusual number.
- Cruickshank: cites 1 in late Aug, 2016 (MCG) and Wentworth's listing of 3 on Sep 1–2, 1917.
- Vickery: most fall observations 1–3 inds. late Sep, cites 12 on Sep 14, 1981 (PDV) and 8 on Oct 7, 1990 (SS) as high counts (PDV in Vickery et al., 2020).

Northern Mockingbird, May 25, 2022. © Jessica Bishop.

EUROPEAN STARLING
Sturnus vulgaris

Status: Fairly common to common permanent resident, possible migrant.

Occurrence: Consistently reported throughout the year, highest numbers in fall and early winter (with limited possible movements–see below); year max: **140** on Nov 8, 2020 (FK, DH), 75 on Oct 23, 2017 (JP) & Nov 13, 2020 (LS, JT), 70 on Nov 9–10, 2020 (LS, JT), 65 on Dec 21, 1989 (CBC–PDV), 55 on Jan 1, 1992 (CBC–PDV) & Nov 9, 2018 (DH, FK), 50 on Sep 25, 2018 (SBa). Ten-Year: 10.

- *MABB*: confirmed; MBA: confirmed.
- CBC: 24 years (92%; all except 1941, 2010), first on Dec 28, 1978, max 65 on Dec 21, 1989, avg 23.8.
- 1944–1967 Farrell Records: 1952–Mar, Apr; 1954–Jun, Jul, Aug; 1955–Jun, Aug; 1956–May; 1958–May, Aug; 1959–Apr, May, Jun, Jul; 1960–Apr, May, Jun, Jul, Aug, Sep; 1961–Apr, May; 1967–Apr 2, 3, 4, 5, 7, 8, 9, 14, 15, 16, 17, 18, 23, 24, Jun 2 (1), 3 (2), 4 (1), 5 (1).
- 1954 & 1955 Summer Records: 1954–included all three checklists; 1955–included Jun 11–15 & Aug 22–Sep 2 (up to 15, "pretty well confined to sheep pens on Manana."
- 1970: highlighted and marked as known to breed in area. Listed as Starling.

With its rapid spread in North America after intentional introduction in NYC in 1890, the first known record for Monhegan occurred on Aug 16, 1914 (see Palmer, below). Apparent steady population/numbers over last forty years. Despite its relatively limited numbers on the island, it is commonly overlooked or few details provided due to the perception that it is commonplace and non-native; ~15% of eBird records are of an unreported number (marked X). Residents (adults and recently fledged juveniles) possibly supplemented by post-breeding/fledging dispersal from the mainland in fall/early winter, leading to peak numbers on the island. Species gathers into flocks post-breeding and through winter, with some wandering through spring, but movements poorly understood or unclear with respect to local residents (species is relatively sedentary or of variable migratory tendencies, traveling short distances [Cabe, 2020]). Max count of 140 on Nov 8, 2020 (FK, DH) involved a flock of 110 arriving from the north, settling into town for a short time, then departing; high counts on Nov 9–10 & 13, 2020 suggest a noticeable movement. Year-round preference for town areas, including feeders; small flocks often perched at the top of tall spruces. Breeding underway by early May, with nests sometimes in cavities in buildings, but also in trees. Adults observed carrying food/feeding young as early as May 14; on May 19, 2019 three nests with chicks being fed were observed, one beneath the Monhegan House fire escape and two in "witch's broom" formations in spruce trees (DR). Recently fledged young reported on multiple dates spanning May 23–Jul 19. Only one brood likely, with local gathering becoming noticeable in Jul. An amusing anecdote involved a tourist's comment that a Starling looked like a baby eagle (WJS).

Historical/Regional:
- Palmer: flock of 25–30 on Aug 16, 1914 (Fuller), recorded some winters.
- Vickery: reported on Monhegan (Richard V. Joyce in Vickery et al., 2020).

EASTERN BLUEBIRD
Sialia sialis

Status: Uncommon to fairly common spring and rare to fairly common fall migrant, very rare summer visitor and possible breeder, very rare winter visitor.

Occurrence: Spring dates span Mar 17–end of May, peak mid Apr–mid May; spring max: 10 on May 16, 2014 (REl), 7 on May 20, 2017 (REl) & May 22, 2017 (REl), 6 on Mar 26, 1934 (MJT), 5 on May 12, 2012 (RS). Eight summer records over seven years since 1960 (all but one since 1997): unreported number during Aug 1960 (IF), 1 on Jun 2, 1997 (WBo), 2 on Jun 3, 2008 (JSc), 2 on Jun 9, 2011 (TMag), 1 on Jun 28–29, 2011 (TMag), 1 on Jun 13–14, 2013 (DH), 1 on Jun 17, 2018 (BEv, TEv), 2 on Jun 1, 2022 (DH et al.). Fall dates span Sep 2–Nov 14, peak late Oct–early Nov; fall max: **13** on Nov 12, 2011 (DH, PM), 12 on Oct 26, 2010 (TMag) & Nov 6, 2020 (FK, DH), 11 on Nov 13–14, 2011 (TMag). Four winter records, all from the 2021–22 season and likely involving repeat inds.: 11 on Dec 24, 2021 (DC), 1 on Dec 26, 2021 (DC), 4 on Jan 7, 2022 (DC), 1 on Jan 27, 2022 (DC). Ten-Year: SP-10, SU-3, F-8, W-1.

- *MABB*: probable; MBA: confirmed.
- 1944–1967 Farrell Records: 1949–Mar, Apr; 1950–Apr, May; 1951–Apr; 1952–Mar; 1958–May; 1959–May; 1960–Aug.
- 1970 Summer Checklist: included.

No doubt underreported in peak migration periods during Apr and Oct–Nov. The only clear evidence of breeding was a pair of adults nest building on May 17, 2022 (EG, MBu-confirmed status for MBA). The multiple records during winter 2021–22 probably all originate from the original 11 inds. on Dec 24. Many reports from town locations, including the Meadow, Tribler Rd., and the Monhegan House/church area; also frequently heard calling overhead. Inds. identified to sex have included 6 males & 3 females in spring, 3 males & 2 females in fall, 1 female in summer, 1 male in winter (the latest winter record of Jan 27, 2022, but possibly the same ind. reported Mar 18–20 [KL]).

Historical/Regional:
- Vickery: cites 1 on an outer island on Jun 2, 1997 (WBo) as late spring and 13 on Nov 12, 2011 (PM, DH) as a high fall count (PDV in Vickery et al., 2020).

TOWNSEND'S SOLITAIRE
Myadestes townsendi

Status: Very rare fall vagrant.

Occurrence: Three records: 1 on Oct 27 & 31, 1988 (WBo; *AB* 43[1]: 66). 1 on Oct 2, 2013 (anonymous eBird), 1 on Oct 2–8, 2019 (JT, LS et al.). Ten-Year: F-2.

The Oct 2013 ind. was at the end of the trail past the end of Ice Pond Rd. The Oct 2019 ind. was flushed from the road by the Ice Pond and seen in nearby spruces on Oct 2, and spent the rest of its time on the island near the Brewery and in the yard opposite the Underhill Trail.

Historical/Regional:
- Vickery: cites 1988 and 2013 records (at least ten well-documented records, 23 records listed statewide; PDV in Vickery et al., 2020).

Townsend's Solitaire, Oct 3, 2019. © Jeremiah Trimble.

VEERY
Catharus fuscescens

Status: Scarce to uncommon spring and scarce (*presumably uncommon to fairly common*) fall migrant, very rare summer visitor.

Occurrence: Spring dates span May 5–Jun 3, peak throughout May; spring max: 30 on May 25, 1983 (ST) & May 25, 1990 (JVW), 13 on May 17, 2005 (TV), 8 on May 19, 1983 (PDV) & May 24, 1997 (SS), 7 on May 6, 2017 (DH), May 15, 2017 (JT) & May 21, 2018 (JT, CK). Three summer records: unreported number on Jun 21, 2013 (JKe), 1 on Jul 19, 2018 (MF), 1 on Jul 25, 2020 (TB). Fall dates span Aug 21–w/e Nov 11 (only two records after Oct 8, both in 2006), peak early–mid Sep; fall max: **100** on Sep 26, 1994 (PDV), 60 on Sep 4, 1982 (PDV), 30 on Sep 11, 1983 (PDV). Ten-Year: SP-9, SU-3, F-10.

- *MABB*: possible; MBA: possible.
- 1914 & 1916 Checklists: included as Wilson Thrush 1916.
- 1918 Fall Migration Census: Wentworth–Oct 1, 12, 19.
- 1944–1967 Farrell Records: 1960–Aug; 1961–May; 1967–Jun 2 (1).
- 1970 Summer Checklist: included.
- Banding: 8 total over three seasons, peak 6 in Fall 1981, max 2 on Sep 3 & 4, 1981.

Likely underreported throughout its migration periods due to its skulking behavior typical of thrushes and fondness for wooded areas rather than town locations, and during Aug due to lack of coverage. The two latest fall records may have involved the same ind. w/e Oct 28, 2006 & w/e Nov 11, 2006, along with the latest records for Wood Thrush (fide JWa, KG; MARBA). An obvious nocturnal migrant on occasion in fall, emitting a distinctive flight call when passing overhead, as illustrated by the max counts of 100 on Sep 26, 1994 (a portion of thousands of birds, including many Swainson's and other thrushes that evening–PDV) and 60 on Sep 4, 1982 (mostly heard calling at night–PDV); should be listened for more often. MBA status based on a singing ind. on Jul 25, 2020 (TB), possibly an early fall migrant. Reported several times from Cathedral Woods and other trails, including Alder, Burnt Head, and White Head, but also right along Main St. and Lobster Cove Rd.

Historical/Regional:

- Vickery: cites 30 on May 25, 1983 (ST) as one of few large spring counts; 6 on Sep 28, 2012 (JT) as example of fall count and 30 on Sep 11, 1983 as high diurnal, 60 nocturnal on Sep 4, 1982 (PDV; PDV in Vickery et al., 2020).

Veery, May 18, 2021. © Jeremiah Trimble.

GRAY-CHEEKED THRUSH
Catharus minimus

Status: Very rare spring and rare fall migrant.

Occurrence: Twenty-six records (7 spring, 19 fall) since 1916. Spring records over five years since 2004 (three in 2019–Gray-cheeked/Bicknell's Thrushes reported earlier, see below), span short period May 24–30: 2 on May 28, 2004 (JVW), 1 on May 30, 2013 (RL, ML), 1 on May 27, 2014 (BN), 1 on May 29, 2018 (MGa, HM, TW), 1 on May 24–25, 2019 (AK, KLi), 1 on May 30 2019 (MI, JT, RDo–nocturnal), 1 on May 30, 2019 (JT). Fall records over sixteen years since 1978, span Sep 12 or 13–Oct 8; fall max: **3** on Sep 28, 2012 (JT). Ten-Year: SP-4, F-5.

- 1914 & 1916 Checklists: included 1916. *Possibly Bicknell's Thrush–see below.*
- 1915–1919 Taylor Journals: 1916–Sep 10. *Possibly Bicknell's Thrush–see below.*
- 1918 Fall Migration Census: Wentworth–Oct 19, 24 (?)(*excluded as questionable*). *Possibly Bicknell's Thrushes–see below.*
- 1944–1967 Farrell Records: 1959–May; 1961–May. *Possibly Bicknell's Thrushes–see below.*

Despite rarity, likely underreported or overlooked due to its shy, skulking behavior and fondness for densely wooded areas, instead of town locations. Several records from around the Ice Pond, one from the Underhill Trail and one from the south end of Lobster Cove Rd., but few locations reported. Only one obviously lingering ind., reported at the Ice Pond on Sep 30–Oct 1, 1978 (PDV). Nocturnal flight calls recorded on May 28, 2004 (9:15–10:15 pm–JVW), Sep 24, 2009 (10:30–11:30 pm–LS, EO), the max of 3 on Sep 28, 2012 (midnight–1:30 am–JT), and May 30, 2019; ind. noted singing shortly after sunset (8:30 pm) on May 29, 2018 (MGa, HM, TW).

The splitting of the nominate *C. m. minima* and Bicknell's subspecies (*C. m. bicknelli*) in 1998 elevated the confusion involved in specific identification. Before 1998, inds. not always identified to subspecies; possibility of some pre-1998 records of Gray-cheeked Thrush without details involving Bicknell's and not included in status above (unreported number on Sep 10, 1916 [WT–considered the same record as on the 1916 Checklist by MCG], unreported number on Oct 19, 1918 [BHW], unreported number during May 1959 [IF], unreported number during May 1961 [IF], 18 on May 25, 1983 [ST], 1 on Oct 5, 1985 [JVW], 1 on Sep 26,1986 [PDV], 1 on Sep 23 & 26, 1994 [PDV]). Twenty-one records (9 spring, 12 fall) of Gray-cheeked/Bicknell's Thrushes. Spring records over seven years since 1983, span May 16/20–May 30 (trip report for earliest date); spring max: 2 on May 25, 1990 (AWe, JVW). Fall records over ten years since 1982, span Sep 11–Oct 12; fall max: 150+ on Sep 25, 1994 (no details available–PDV et al.), 2 on Sep 24, 2011 (nocturnal calls–DL).

Historical/Regional:

- Vickery: cites 18 on May 25, 1983 (ST) as fallout (may have included Bicknell's), 1 on May 27 & 30, 2014 as recent spring records; >60% fall records Sep 20–30, latest on Oct 8 in 2000 (LBr) and 2012 (DH, JT); mentions large nocturnal thrush flight of Sep 25, 1994 (see species discussion above) as primarily Gray-cheeked with some Bicknell's (no numbers given for separation; PDV in Vickery et al., 2020).

Gray-cheeked Thrush, Oct 4 2018. © Luke Seitz.

BICKNELL'S THRUSH
Catharus bicknelli

Status: Very rare spring migrant.

Occurrence: Two records: 1 on May 15, 2017 (JT), 1 on May 29, 2019 (JT, LS RDo). Ten-Year: SP-2.

No doubt overlooked as a migrant due to its shyness and densely wooded haunts, and confusion with Gray-cheeked Thrush (see below). The May 2019 ind. was reported near the Fire Station on Lobster Cove Rd. As with other thrushes, should be listened for overhead at night in late spring and fall.

The splitting of the nominate *C. m. minima* and Bicknell's subspecies (*C. m. bicknelli*) in 1998 elevated the difficulty of identifying the two species. Before 1998, inds. were rarely identified to subspecies; possibility of some pre-1998 records of Gray-cheeked Thrush without details involving Bicknell's and not included in status above (unreported number on Sep 10, 1916 [WT–considered the same record as on the 1916 Checklist by MCG], unreported number on Oct 19, 1918 [BHW], unreported number during May 1959 [IF], unreported number during May 1961 [IF], 18 on May 25, 1983 [ST], 1 on Oct 5, 1985 [JVW], 1 on Sep 26,1986 [PDV], 1 on Sep 23 & 26, 1994 [PDV]). There are twenty-one records (9 spring, 12 fall) of Gray-cheeked/Bicknell's Thrushes. Spring records over seven years since 1983, span May 16/20–May 30 (trip report for earliest date); spring max: 2 on May 25, 1990 (AWe, JVW). Fall records over eleven years since 1982, span Sep 11–Oct 12; fall max: 150+ on Sep 25, 1994 (no details available–PDV et al.), 2 on Sep 24, 2011 (nocturnal calls–DL).

Bicknell's Thrush, May 29, 2019. © Jeremiah Trimble.

SWAINSON'S THRUSH
Catharus ustulatus

Status: Fairly common spring and uncommon to fairly common fall migrant, uncommon summer resident.

Occurrence: Spring dates span May 6–mid Jun, peak last two-thirds of May (largest flights May 25–29);

spring max: 200+ on May 25, 1983 (ST; *AB* 37[5]: 845), 75 on May 25, 1990 (JVW), >70 on May 25, 1990 (JVW), 40 on May 29, 1983 (PDV). Summer presence extends mid Jun–mid Aug, undoubtedly underreported; summer max: 7 on Jul 9, 2017 (DH) & Jul 20, 2019 (JT), 6 on Jul 10, 2018 (TAn), 5 on Jul 19, 2019 (JT). Fall dates span mid Aug–Oct 25, peak early–late Sep (largest counts Sep 24–28); fall max: **>800** on Sep 26, 1994 (PDV, VL), 150 on Sep 24, 2009 (LS, EO–also reported as hundreds that night [WR]), 90 on Oct 3, 2020 (DH), 70 on Sep 25, 2009 (LS), 35 on Sep 28, 2012 (JT). Ten-Year: SP-10, SU-9, F-10.

- *MABB*: confirmed; MBA: confirmed.
- 1914 & 1916 Checklists: included 1916. Listed as Olive-backed Thrush.
- 1915–1919 Taylor Journals: 1916–Sep 10; 1917–Sep 5 (1).
- 1918 Fall Migration Census: Dewis–1 on Sep 8; Wentworth–Oct 7, 12, 15 (many), 16 (several), 19, 20 (1), 21 (several), 22 (2), 23 (1), 24 (2). Listed as Olive-backed Thrush.
- 1944–1967 Farrell Records: 1953–Aug, Sep; 1954–Jun, Jul; 1955–Jun, Aug; 1956–May; 1959–Jul, Aug; 1960–Jul, Aug; 1961–May; 1967–Jun 1 (1). Listed as Olive-backed Thrush.
- 1954 & 1955 Summer Records: 1954–included all three checklists; 1955–included Jun 11–15 & Aug 22–Sep 2 (up to 5 or 6). Listed as Olive-backed Thrush.
- 1970 Summer Checklist: highlighted and marked as known to breed in area.
- Banding: 7 total over three seasons, peak 3 in 1960 & 1981, max 1 on seven days.

Likely underreported throughout much of presence due to its secretive behavior and fondness for wooded areas, rather than locations around town; also Jun–Aug due to lack of coverage. An plainly audible nocturnal migrant on occasion in spring and fall with a distinctive overhead flight call; exceptionally illustrated by the max flights of >800 on the evening of Sep 25, 1994 (a portion of thousands of birds calling continually, including many Veeries and other thrushes that evening–PDV) and 150 on Sep 24, 2009 (10:30–11:30 pm) and ~65 pre-dawn the next day (out of 70 reported, with only 5 seen during the day–LS). Unfortunately, there is no record of numbers present on Sep 26, 1994 (*the total reported that day is for the >800 reported the evening before*), after the massive flight, to see how many may have put down and remained on the island. Nocturnal monitoring overlapping May 29–30, 2019 produced 8 on the 29th from 11:32 pm–midnight and the high count of 23 from midnight–12:38 am (JT, RDo, MI); 18 were seen during the day on the 30th (JT), but it is impossible to know if they were in addition to or different from the inds. heard overnight. MBA status based on an adult carrying food on Jul 3, 2021 (DH). Not surprisingly, most often reported from wooded sections of the island, including Black Head, Cathedral Woods, Red Ribbon, White Head, Alder, and Underhill Trails, with song often giving them away in the spring.

Historical/Regional:

- Vickery: cites the max counts above as large spring counts; top two fall max counts as highest counts and 12 on Oct 5, 2003 (WJS) and 7 on Oct 12, 2009 (JM) as late (PDV in Vickery et al., 2020).

HERMIT THRUSH
Catharus guttatus

Status: Scarce to fairly common spring and fairly common (*presumably common*) fall migrant, rare summer visitor and possible breeder, very rare winter visitor.

Occurrence: An early spring migrant, dates span Mar 21–end of May, peak mid–late Apr when undoubtedly underreported; spring max: 36 on Apr 27, 2011 (TMag), 12 on Apr 29, 2011 (TMag), 10 on Apr 22, 2011 (TMag). Twenty-five summer records over eleven years since 1954 (three records in 1954 and 2018, five in 2021 & 2022), but no confirmed breeding; summer max: 2 on Aug 30, 2013 (JHo), Jun 8, 2018 (TAn), Jul 14, 2021 (BTh) & Jul 3, 2022 (WK). A late fall migrant, dates span early Sep–Nov 21, peak mid Oct–early Nov when undoubtedly underreported; fall max: **70** on Oct 12, 2014 (LS et al.), 40 on Oct 10, 2001 (TV), 37 on Nov 2, 2010 (TMag). Seven winter records over six years, almost all associated with CBC period: 1 on Jan 4, 2007 (CBC), 1 on Jan 5, 2010 (CBC–PDV, WJS), 1 on Jan 3, 2013 (CBC–DH, PDV, PM), 1 on Jan 2–4, 2015 (including CBC Jan 3–DH, FK, WN), 3 on Jan 3, 2015 (CBC–DH, FK, WN), 1 on Jan 6, 2016 (CBC count week–DH et al.), 2 during Jan 16–17, 2018 (KL). Ten-Year: SP-8, SU-8, F-10, W-3.

- *MABB*: probable; MBA: possible.
- CBC: four years (15%) plus one count week, first on Jan 4, 2007, max 3 on Jan 3, 2015, avg 0.2.
- 1900–1908 Reconnaissance & Supplements: included in Jenney supplement.
- 1914 & 1916 Checklists: included 1916.
- 1915–1919 Taylor Journals: 1916–Sep 10.

- 1918 Fall Migration Census: Wentworth–Oct 4, 7, 8, 12, many on 15, 16, 17, & 19, 20 (2), several on 21, 22, 23, & 24.
- 1939 Summer Census: rare summer visitor.
- 1944–1967 Farrell Records: 1951–Apr; 1954–Jun, Jul; 1959–May; 1960–Apr; 1961–Apr.
- 1954 & 1955 Summer Records: 1954–included all three checklists (noted as only 1 ind. during Jul 10–16).
- 1970 Summer Checklist: included.

Main migration periods underreported due to lack of coverage, especially highlighted in spring by the max counts all in 2011, a season of consistent reporting by TMag, and likely underreported throughout summer on a limited scale. MBA status based on a singing ind. on May 26, 2021 (BBl), prior to the five summer records that year. Secretive nature and fondness for wooded areas, instead of town locations, also limits numbers reported; multiple reports from Cathedral Woods, Underhill Trail, around the Ice Pond, "most in woods," and "incredible numbers in woods on north end of island" on max. day of 70 (Oct 12, 2014–LS et al.). The 2015 winter records involved a continuing ind. along Lobster Cove Rd. (noted all three days Jan 2–4), with the additional 2 inds. on Jan 3 noted at the edge of the Ice Pond; Jan 2018 ind. near White Head.

Hermit Thrush, Oct 5, 2020. © Luke Seitz.

WOOD THRUSH
(Hylocichla mustelina)

Status: Rare to scarce spring and rare fall migrant, very rare summer visitor.

Occurrence: Spring dates span Apr 28–May 31, peak mid–late May; spring max: **4** on May 13, 1997 (PDV) & May 17, 2005 (TV), 3 on May 25, 2007 (LS), 2 on May 21, 1983 (PDV), May 22, 2018 (JT, CK) & May 26, 2022 (JBi). Two summer records, both in the same year and possibly same ind.: 1 on Jun 18, 2018 (TEv, BEv), 1 on Jul 8, 2018 (JK). Seventeen fall records over fourteen years since 1959 (three in 2006, two in 2022) span during Aug (earliest definite Aug 26)–w/e Nov 11 (only two records after Oct 2, both in 2006); fall max: 2 on Oct 2, 1997 (JT). Ten-Year: SP-8, SU-1, F-3.

- 1944–1967 Farrell Records: 1959–May, Aug; 1961–May
- 1970 Summer Checklist: included.

Most likely in deciduous woodlands, but few details available. Heard on a number of occasions, including singing near the Ballfield (May 25, 2007–LS) and along Burnt Head Trail (May 17, 2015–KL) and heard near the Trailing Yew (May 24, 2016–LM). 1 on Sep 28, 2012 was part of an "incredible night flight" and was heard calling three times (JT). The two latest fall records may have involved the same ind. w/e Oct 28, 2006 & w/e Nov 11, 2006, along with the latest records for Veery (fide JWa, KG; MARBA). The MARBA also contained a questionable report without details of 2 on Dec 4, 2005 that is not included here (there is one Maine record in Jan).

Historical/Regional:

- Vickery: uncommon in fall, with 1–3 inds. unusual; cites 1 on Sep 30, 2017 (DL) as late (PDV in Vickery et al., 2020).

AMERICAN ROBIN
Turdus migratorius

Status: Fairly common to common spring and fall migrant, fairly common summer resident, rare (*presumably uncommon to fairly common*) winter visitor; possible permanent resident.

Occurrence: Spring migration spans late Feb–late May (overlapping breeding period), peak early Mar–mid Apr; spring max: 275 on Apr 5, 2011 (TMag), 100 on Mar 5, 2012 (DH), 80 on Apr 12, 2011 (TMag), 79 on May 15, 2017 (JT). Breeding commences in May, with fledglings present by the end of the month, and continues through Aug with multiple broods; summer max: 39 on Jul 20, 2019 (JT), 35 on Jun 1, 2008 (JSc), 30 on Jul 14–15, 2021 (BTh) & Aug 15, 2022 (LS, MWa), 29 on Jun 9, 2021 (JFo). Fall migration spans dispersal beginning by mid Aug–early Dec, peak mid Oct–mid Nov; fall max: **1600** on Oct 30, 2010 (MI, JT, LS), 300+ on Oct 11, 1987 (JVW), 250 on Oct 29, 2010 (MI, LS, JT) & Oct 31, 2010 (MI, JT, LS), 200 on Oct 7, 1984 (SS). Twenty-six winter records over twenty-two years since 1940, but undoubtedly underreported, most associated with CBC period; winter max: 30 on Feb 7, 2009 (LS), 25 on Feb 8, 2009, 21 on Jan 5, 2010 (CBC–PDV), 16 on Jan 3, 2008 (CBC). Ten-Year: SP-10, SU-10, F-10, W-2.

- *MABB*: confirmed; MBA: confirmed.
- CBC: fifteen years (58%) plus three count weeks, first on Dec 29, 1940, max 21 on Jan 5, 2010, avg 3.8.
- 1899 Checklist: included.
- 1900–1908 Reconnaissance & Supplements: a rover and hard to say how many—not more than six pairs during May 31–Jun 6, 1908 (FA); unreported number during Jul 31–Aug 2, 1908 (WM).
- 1909 Notes: common in fields and somewhat so in woods; still singing, adult seen carrying food (locust larvae).
- 1914 & 1916 Checklists: unreported number on Jul 31, 1914; included as Robin 1916.
- 1915–1919 Taylor Journals: 1915–Aug 9, 11, 16, 28, Sep 5 (1), 12 (2); 1916–Aug 19, 20, 21, 22, 25, 26, 30, Sep 3, 4, 6, 10; 1917–Jul 29, Aug 4, 16, Sep 5; 1918–prior to Aug 4; 1919–Sep 4 (10), 5 (5), 14 (3).
- 1918 Fall Migration Census: Dewis–Sep 8 (4), 9 (1), 11 (2); Wentworth–Sep 29, Oct 4, 7, 8, 9, 12, 13, 15 (very many), 16 & 17 (many), 19, 20 (several), 21 (few), 22 (several), 23 (few), 24 (large flock headed toward mainland), 25 (few). Listed as Robin.
- 1939 Summer Census: regular summer resident. Listed as Robin.
- 1944–1967 Farrell Records: 1946–Mar; 1949–Mar, Apr, Oct; 1950–Mar, Apr, Nov, Dec; 1951–Apr, May, Oct, Nov, Dec; 1952–Mar, Apr, Nov; 1953–Sep; 1954–Jun, Jul; 1955–Jun, Jul, Aug; 1957–Aug; 1958–Aug, Oct; 1959–Apr, May, Jun, Jul, Aug; 1960–Apr, May, Jun, Jul, Aug, Sep; 1961–Apr, May; 1967–Apr 2 (3), 3, 4 (5), 7, 8, 9, 10, 11, 12, 13, 14, 15 (3), 16 (4), 17 (1), 23, 24, Jun 1 (1), 2 (1), 3 (1), 4 (1), 5 (1), 6 (1), 7 (1), 8 (1).
- 1954 & 1955 Summer Records: 1954–included all three checklists; 1955–included all three checklists (up to 6 or 8 Aug 22–Sep 2). Listed as Robin.
- 1970 Summer Checklist: marked as known to breed in area. Listed as Robin.
- Banding: 4 total over three seasons, peak 2 in Fall 1960, max 1 on Oct 8 & 10, 1960, Oct 8, 1961 & May 22, 1984.

While seemingly ever-present in varying numbers, true level of abundance and length of presence are not fully known due to lack of coverage and underreporting during peak migration periods, summer, and winter. It is possible that some breeding inds. remain year-round, but likely that summer residents are replaced by northern visitors for the winter. In 2020, resident Donna Cundy noted spring arrival as Mar 10, the birds having been absent during winter, when usually present. Larger movements are often two- to four-day events. Fall 2010 was exceptional, with eight days of 100+ inds. between Oct 24 and Nov 3, including the max flights noted above; the 250 noted flying south at dusk on Oct 29th were precursors of the mass exodus of 1,600 from the north half of the island at dawn the next day (JT, LS, MI). The 300+ on Oct 11, 1987 involved "many flocks of 50+ flying over" (JVW). Due to early spring and late fall migration peaks, largest seasonal numbers are likely underreported on a regular basis. Seemingly ubiquitous in limited numbers, possible anywhere on the island and even Manana, from settled areas to deep woods, even as breeders Two or even three broods likely through summer; recently fledged birds noted as early as May 25 (2012–SBe) and May 29 (family group with full-sized fledgling in 2010–KL) and into mid Jul (Jul 19, 2021 [HIAC et al.]). Juveniles noted second half of Aug/Sep just as likely to be migrants as residents, as post-breeding dispersal commences.

American Robin, May 22, 2018. © Luke Seitz.

VARIED THRUSH
Ixoreus naevius

Status: Accidental spring vagrant.

Occurrence: One record: 1 apparent male on Mar 15–27, 1939, joined by presumed female ~Mar 22–27, 1939 (MJT). First Maine Record. Account published in *Monhegan Press* 1(47): 1&5 on Apr 28, 1939 (Palmer, 1949).

Numerous winter records scattered throughout the state and nearly annual since 1951 (Vickery et al., 2020). One ind. described as a male was first seen on Mar 15, then joined after about a week by a paler, presumed female, both leaving sometime after Mar 27. In her Mar 17, 1939 correspondence with Mrs. Jenney, Mrs. Townsend noted the first ind. as a new bird, not in any of the books she had, and describing it as a cross between a Robin, Flicker and Meadowlark.

Historical/Regional:

- Palmer: source of 1939 record, including personal observation of and a documentation drawing by MJT; only Maine record.

NORTHERN WHEATEAR
Oenanthe oenanthe

Status: Accidental fall vagrant.

Occurrence: One record: 1 on Sep 16–17, 1976 (RLP et al.; ph.; *AB* 31[2]: 230).

No details available.

HOUSE SPARROW
Passer domesticus

Status: Very rare spring and rare fall visitor.

Occurrence: Twenty-one records (7 spring, 14 fall) since 1959. Spring records over seven years since 1961, span short period May 14–26 (includes trip reports, possibly only May 17–26, unknown date in May 1961): unreported number during May 1961 (fide IF), unreported number on May 26, 1984 (SS), unreported number during May 14–25, 1998 (GD), unreported number during May 19–24, 2002 (TV), unreported number on May 22, 2004 (SH), 2 on May 17, 2007 (GD), unreported number on May 23, 2008 (LBl). Fall records over twelve years since 1959 (two records in 1980 & 2022), span during Aug (earliest definite Sep 6)–Oct 24; fall max: **20** on Oct 7, 2022 (PD et al.), 6 on Oct 8, 2022 (PD), 2 on Sep 29, 2013 (SS, MBa), Oct 12, 2013 (LDi), Oct 15, 2013 (LS, MK) & Oct 20, 2013 (GC et al.). Ten-Year: F-4.

- 1944–1967 Farrell Records: 1959–Aug; 1960–Aug; 1961–May.
- 1970 Summer Checklist: included.

An unfortunate introduction of the late 1800s, which quickly spread across much of the United States and Canada, is now a much-vilified, non-migratory resident of urban and rural habitats, yet however ubiquitous it may be, it is still a surprise to encounter one on Monhegan. As early as 1908, Allen remarked: "glad to see no English Sparrows on Monhegan, as yet," while Vickery's statement "occur on all inhabited islands" isn't necessarily correct for Monhegan (2020: 466). Although single-day sightings seem to be the rule in spring, all but four of the fall records with definite dates involved extended stays: 1 on Sep 28, 1980 (one of only two years with two records, though this may have been the holdover of an ind. reported Sep 6–7–PVD), 1 on Sep 27, 2010 (DL) & 1 on Oct 5, 2021 (calling while circling high over Lobster Cove–JT, LS), 13 of the 20 on Oct 7, 2022 were seen at the Monhegan House (KL) and on a porch at the Black Duck Emporium (PR), with 1 female behind the Lupine Gallery likely part of the same flock; only 6 were noted the following day (PD). The stays longer than two days included 1 on Oct 21–23, 2011 (three days–a female near Tom Martin's), 1 on Oct 9–18, 2014 (nine days–a female frequenting lobster traps in town), 1 on Sep 19–30, 2007 (twelve days), and 1–2 on Sep 25–Oct 24, 2013 (thirty days–a male for the duration, joined by a female Sep 29–Oct 20). The male in was first observed on the veranda of the Island Inn and spent most of its time around lobster traps near the inn or docks in the harbor, together with the female when present; on the 11th one of them (unid. sex) joined a mixed flock of sparrows coming to feeders near the school on the 12th and on lobster traps below the Black Duck Emporium on the 15th. The male was heard singing on the 13th and the final sighting involved the male calling from a shrub behind Shining Sails on the 24th. The only other inds. identified to sex were a male and female in Tom Martin's yard on May 17, 2007 and a male behind Shining Sails on Oct 7–8, 2012.

House Sparrow, Oct 7, 2012. © Jeremiah Trimble.

AMERICAN PIPIT
Anthus rubescens

Status: Rare spring and uncommon to fairly common fall migrant, accidental winter visitor.

Occurrence: Eleven spring records over eleven years since 1996, span short period May 12–28; spring max: 10 on May 22, 2013 (SK, JZ), 9 on May 23, 2013 (MM), 6 on May 24, 2013 (DH). Fall dates span during Aug (earliest definite Sep 8)–Nov 15, peak late Sep–late Oct; fall max: **30** on Oct 4, 1997 (AG), 25 on Sep 28, 2018 (AK), 15 on Oct 3, 1997 (JT), 14 on Oct 11, 2010 (JT). Winter record: 1 on Jan 5, 2007 (CBC count week–DF). Ten-Year: SP-6, F-10.

- CBC: one count week of Jan 4, 2007.
- 1918 Fall Migration Census: Wentworth–Oct 8 (5 in flock on bare ground near house, 1 on seaweed at Lobster Cove), 12 (1), 16 (1).
- 1944–1967 Farrell Records: 1960–Aug. Listed as Water Pipit.

Spring 2013 was exceptional; at least 10 inds. on May 22 (at least 6 feeding in the wrack at Fish Beach and others flying near Lobster Cove) continued at Fish Beach in diminishing numbers through the 27th (only 3 remaining). Few details provided considering number of records; difficult to determine true number of fall records/inds. or length of stay, with variable numbers on consecutive days. Most often reported as calling flyovers, with Lobster Cove the most favored location by far, and sometimes foraging on the beach there (2 were with a mixed flock of sparrows on Oct 12, 2018–TMz). The count of 25 on Sep 28, 2018 involved a tight flock, calling over Monhegan House (AK). Uniquely, an ind. was observed on Smutty Nose on Sep 28, 2019 (CJ, SJ).

Historical/Regional:

- Vickery: cites 1 on Jan 4, 2007 winter report (*listed as count week of the Jan 4 count in CBC records—observed on Jan 5 [DF pers. comm.]*; PDV in Vickery et al., 2020).

American Pipit, May 26, 2013. © Luke Seitz.

COMMON CHAFFINCH
Fringilla coelebs

Status: Accidental fall vagrant.

Occurrence: One record: 1 on Sep 28, 1989 (videotaped by DHr, later identified by PDV; *AB* 44[1]: 60). Second Maine record; not yet reviewed by ME-BRC.

As a possible escapee, the origin of this species in North America is always in question. However, with ~15 eastern records, mainly in New England, Maritime Canada and Newfoundland, a pattern of vagrancy appears established.

Historical/Regional:

- Vickery: cites 1989 record above (PDV in Vickery et al., 2020).
- OLMB: two additional state records—both accepted (Apr 3, 1980 in Lincoln, Penobscot Co. & May 23, 1997 in Camden, Knox Co.)

EVENING GROSBEAK
Coccothraustes vespertinus

Status: Rare spring and rare to uncommon fall migrant, very rare summer and rare (irregularly uncommon to fairly common) winter visitor.

Occurrence: Spring dates span w/e Apr 11–May 31, no clear peak and likely underreported in early spring; spring max: 10 on May 6–7, 1984 (PDV) & May 26–27, 1990 (JVW), 5 on May 30, 1982 (PDV), 4 on May 27, 2017 (JWi). Five summer records: unreported number on Jul 17, 1980 (KZ), 1 on Jun 16, 2014 (JKa), 1 on Jun 12, 2015 (DC), 1 on Jun 8, 2020 (JT, LS), 1 on Jun 14–16, 2021 (JFo, CDd). Fall dates span Aug 28–Nov 26, peak early–late Sep; fall max: 50 on Nov 26, 2018 (AI), 25 on Sep 26, 1981 (PDV), 20 on Sep 27, 1981 (PDV), 16 on Oct 9, 2020 (JT, LS, HS). Thirteen winter records over twelve years since 1978, all associated with CBC period, span Dec 21–Jan 4; winter max: **51** on Dec 28, 1982 (CBC–PDV), 40 on Dec 27, 1982 (PDV), 24 on Dec. 28, 1978 (CBC–PDV), 15 on Dec 21, 1979 (PDV). Ten-Year: SP-6, SU-4, F-7.

- *MABB*: possible.
- CBC: eight years (31%) plus three count weeks (*1990 not included in CBC database*), first on Dec 28, 1978, max 51 on Dec 28, 1982, avg 4.3.
- 1944–1967 Farrell Records: 1956–May; 1959–May; 1960–Apr, May; 1961–May.
- 1970 Summer Checklist: included.

Generally considered an irruptive species in the east on a two-year cycle, resulting from a diminished food supply; Monhegan records irregular and not following a pattern. Few known records before 1978, surprisingly, (highest numbers statewide in mid 1900s [Vickery et al., 2020]), although included on 1970 Summer Checklist; no winter records since 2010. Likely underreported in early spring and late fall/winter due to lack of coverage. Fall peak likely indicates general lack of food to north, while late fall/winter visitors indicate food supplies dwindling (Gillihan and Byers, 2020); max count of 50 in Nov 2018 descended on the island's feeders (AI). Fall 1981 exceptional, with numbers over extended period in Sep; counts of 10+ on five days: Sep 5 (10), 6 (12), 25 (12), 26 (25), 27 (20). Most often encountered as calling flyovers or at feeders; known to linger for three–five days on occasion.

Historical/Regional:

- Vickery: cites 51 on Dec 28, 1982 (PDV et al.) as large CBC count (WJS in Vickery et al., 2020).

Evening Grosbeak, May 15, 2011. © Geoff Dennis.

PINE GROSBEAK
Pinicola enucleator

Status: Accidental spring and very rare fall migrant, very rare summer and winter visitor.

Occurrence: Eighteen records (1 spring, 2 summer, 5 fall, 8 winter, 2 unknown date) since 1899. Spring record: 1 on May 27, 1995 (SS). Summer records: unreported number during Aug 1949 (IF), unreported number during Jun–Jul 1955 (IF). Fall records: unreported number during Oct 1950 (IF), 1 on Nov 8–11, 2020 (FK et al.), 2 on Nov 12, 2020 (JT, LS), 3 on Nov 13, 2020 (LS, JT), 1 on Nov 9, 2022 (LS, MWa). Winter records over eight years since 1939, five associated with CBC period: "flock" during winter 1938–39 (prior to Jan 27–MJT), **75** on Dec 29, 1940 (CBC), unreported number during Feb 1950 (IF), unreported number during Dec 1951 (IF), 4 on Jan 2, 1986 (CBC count week–PDV), 2 on Jan 1, 1987 (CBC), 5 on Dec 21, 1989 (CBC–PDV), 1 during w/e Jan 5, 2007 (fide JWa, KG; MARBA). Unknown dates: unreported number in 1899 (MEH), unreported number prior to Mar 26, 1934 (MJT–winter or early spring). Ten-Year: F-2.

- CBC: three years (12%) plus one count week, first on Dec 29, 1940, max 75 on Dec 29, 1940, avg 3.2.
- 1899 Checklist: included.
- 1944–1967 Farrell Records: 1949–Aug; 1950–Feb, Oct; 1951–Dec; 1955–Jun, Jul.
- 1970 Summer Checklist: included.

Surprisingly, few records for a species prone to incursions; certainly underreported late fall–early spring due to lack of coverage. Inclusion on 1970 Summer Checklist undoubtedly refers to Aug 1949 and Jun–Jul 1955 (considered one record due to rarity) records and involved failed breeders or unpaired inds. (similar to reports in Jul 1938 [Hog Island] and Jul 1951 [Pemaquid] cited by Vickery [2020]; current breeding range within the state limited to northern Maine). It is interesting that Fall 2020 records involved a continuing female discovered calling at the Ice Pond on Nov 8, moving to the southern portion of the island on Nov 9 and apparently being joined by 1 more ind. on Nov 12 and a third on Nov 13.

HOUSE FINCH
Haemorhous mexicanus

Status: Scarce spring and scarce to uncommon fall migrant, accidental summer and very rare winter visitor; has bred.

Occurrence: Spring dates span Mar 20–Jun 20 since 1982, peak last two-thirds of May but underreported earlier in spring; spring max: 8 on May 25, 1984 (JP, LP) & Jun 5, 2021 (TF), 6 on May 28, 1988 (SS), 5 on May 13, 1997 (PDV) & May 17, 1997 (RSh). One summer record: 3 on Jun 30, 2021 (CEs); only known breeding confirmed on Sep 8, 1984 (pair w/ female feeding juv.–PDV), late and dates within the fall period. Fall dates span Aug 15–Nov 13 since 1984, peak early Sep–early Oct; fall max: **25** on Oct 3, 2010 (NH), 15 on Sep 22, 2016 (TM), 8 on Oct 1, 2016 (LSo et al.) & Sep 20, 2022 (CPa). Seven winter records over six years, span Dec 22–Jan 1: 1 on Dec 27–28, 1982 (CBC on Dec 28–PDV), 1 on Dec 22, 1988 (CBC–PDV), 2 on Dec 31, 1990 (CBC count week–PDV), 2 on Jan 1, 1992 (CBC–PDV), 1 on Dec

25, 2010 (TMag), 1 on Dec 29, 2010 (TMag), male on Jan 18, 2022. Ten-Year: SP-9, SU-1, F-10, W-1.

- *MABB*: possible.
- CBC: three years (12%) plus one count week (*not included in CBC database*), first on Dec 28, 1982, max 2 on Jan 1, 1992, avg 0.2.
- 1970 Summer Checklist: included.
- Banding: 1 on May 29, 1990.

Released on Long Island, New York in 1940, the species spread throughout the East, becoming common in Maine in the 1970s; Monhegan remains near the northern edge of its breeding range (Badyaev et al., 2020). Only partially migratory (northern populations), its movements are not fully understood. First appearance on Monhegan unknown, appears on the 1970 Summer Checklist; first known record is 1 on May 30, 1982 (PDV). Underreported in Apr/early May and likely winter due to lack of coverage. Breeding likely to have occurred in addition to 1984 record, but lack of summer reports. Reported from various locations around town, often at feeders. Known to linger multiple days, but few details on specific inds. Records a mix of males and females.

Historical/Regional:

- Vickery: cites 15 on Sep 22, 2016 (TM) as a high count (Tamara Enz in Vickery et al., 2020).

PURPLE FINCH
Haemorhous purpureus

Status: Uncommon to fairly common spring and irruptive uncommon to common fall migrant, rare (*presumably scarce to uncommon*) summer resident, very rare winter visitor.

Occurrence: Spring dates span Mar 18–mid Jun, peak early–late May but certainly underreported in Apr; spring max: 21 on May 30, 1982 (PDV), 20 on May 8, 2011 (JP, NW, PDV), 15 on May 29, 1982 (PDV), May 28, 1987 (PDV) & May 20, 2021 (JT, LS). Twenty-nine summer records over ten years since 1917 (twenty-four records since 1984—three in 2018, four in 2019, five in 2020, seven in 2021, three in 2022); possibly breeds regularly, but few details, despite *MABB* & MBA; summer max: 10 on Jul 7, 2022 (LS, MWa), 6 on Aug 13, 1917 (WT), 4 on Jul 18, 2019 (JT) & Jul 29, 2019 (ER), 3 on Aug 11, 2010 (TMag), Jul 19, 2019 (JT) & Jun 17, 2021 (CDd). Fall migration underway second half of Aug, particularly during irruptions, and continues through Nov, peak early Sep–early Oct; fall max: **300** on Sep 26, 1981 (PDV), 250 on Sep 6, 1985 (PDV), 200 during Sep 7–9, 1965 (HT, RLP, CP et al.; *AFN* 20[1]: 9) & on Sep 11, 1983 (PDV). Eight winter records over seven years (two in 1980) since 1980, span Dec 25–Feb 17; winter max: 4 on Jan 4, 2007 (CBC), 3 on Dec 31, 1980 (CBC count week–PDV). Ten-Year: SP-10, SU-6, F-10, W-1.

- *MABB*: confirmed; MBA: confirmed.
- CBC: four years (15%), first on Dec 30, 1980, max 4 on Jan 4, 2007, avg 0.3.
- 1914 & 1916 Checklists: included 1916.
- 1915–1919 Taylor Journals: 1915–Sep 12 (1); 1916–Aug 26 (4), 30, 31 (25), Sep 3, 4 (50), 6 (30), 10; 1917–Aug 13 (6), 16 (7), 18 (1), Sep 5 (6); 1918–Aug 28; 1919–Sep 6 (2), 14 (1).
- 1918 Fall Migration Census: Dewis–Sep 6 (4), 8 (1), 9 (10), 10 (3), 11 (4), 12 (4); Wentworth–Oct 12, 13, 15, 16 (many on each day), 23 (a few).
- 1939 Summer Census: uncommon summer visitor.
- 1944–1967 Farrell Records: 1950–Apr, May; 1951–Sep; 1955–Aug; 1959–May, Aug; 1960–Apr, May, Jul; 1961–Apr, May; 1967–Apr 23, Jun 1 (6), 3 (3), 4 (2).
- 1954 & 1955 Summer Records: 1955–Aug 28 (5 [2 males]), 29 (1–MLn).
- 1970 Summer Checklist: highlighted and marked as known to breed in area.
- Banding: total 32 over seven seasons, peak 11 in Fall 1961, max 9 on Sep 23, 1985.

Irruptions generally follow biennial pattern; obvious in odd years during 1980s (note max counts), and even years during 2010s; return spring flights not apparent. Lack of coverage in Mar/Apr and Aug adversely affects understanding full breadth of migration. Highest fall counts all in 1980s or earlier illustrates general decline in numbers. Larger fall movements often stretch three days or more, with peak days surrounded by lesser but still significant numbers, with flocks possibly staying for a week or longer. Surprisingly few winter records considering irruptions. Preference for breeding near the top of tall evergreens undoubtedly affects detection during summer period; also underreported due to lack of coverage, although an increase in recent years, perhaps related to MBA efforts, has resulted in an annual presence since 2017 and suggests a heightened species status. Recently fledged young on Jun 3, 2020 (JT) provided the only record of confirmed status for the MBA. Possible throughout the island, usually in small flocks at both forest and town locations; most noticeable when flocks frequent feeders and localities with scattered seed during migration, often for extended periods. When indicated, majority of fall inds. noted as immature/female types, with adult males sometimes completely lacking; no adult males out of 24 and only one out of 18 on Sep 15 & 16, 2018, respectively (BME).

Historical/Regional:

- Vickery: cites top two max counts above as large numbers and 95 on Sep 23, 2007 (LS) and 45 on Sep 22, 2016 (WR) as smaller recent high counts (Paul Dougherty in Vickery et al., 2020).

Purple Finch, May 11, 2013. © Geoff Dennis.

COMMON REDPOLL
Acanthis flammea

Status: Very rare spring and fall migrant, rare winter visitor.

Occurrence: Thirty-two records (8 spring, 5 fall, 19 winter) since 1949. Spring records over eight years since 1949, span early Mar–May 25: unreported number during Mar 1949 (IF), unreported number during Apr 1960 (IF), unreported number on Apr 24, 1967 (?Be, fide IF), 2 on May 25, 1981 (JP, LP), unreported number during May 17–19, 1998 (TV), 6 on Mar 7, 2011 (TMag), 1 on Mar 14, 2011 (TMag), 1 on Apr 9, 2011 (TMag), 2 on May 4, 2019 (DHi). Fall records all in 2020, span Nov 8–13: 2 on Nov 8, 2020 (FK, DH), 9 on Nov 9, 2020 (FK, DH), 21 on Nov 10, 2020 (LS, JT), **29** on Nov 12, 2020 (JT, LS), 3 on Nov 13, 2020 (LS, JT). Winter records over fourteen years since 1949, span during Dec 28–30 (CBC count week)–mid Feb; winter max: 20 on Feb 18, 2011 (TMag), 16 on Jan 3, 2008 (CBC), 6 during w/e Dec 29, 2005 (fide KG, SP; MARBA) & on Jan 4, 2013 (PDV, WN). Ten-Year: SP-2, W-2.

- CBC: six years (23%) plus one count week, first during count week Dec 28–30, 1981, max 16 on Jan 3, 2018, avg 0.8.
- 1944–1967 Farrell Records: 1949–Jan, Mar; 1950–Jan; 1960–Apr; 1967–Apr 24.

Surprisingly few records for an irruptive species that is common on the mainland, undoubtedly underreported during its expected time frame (Nov–Apr) due to lack of coverage; supported by the five winter/early spring records 2010/2011 by TMag and five fall records from 2020 by various observers. Questionable report from Jun/Jul 1955 excluded as unprecedented during summer. Even when reported on consecutive days, numbers have differed (5 and 1 on Dec 31, 1990 & Jan 1, 1991, 1 and 6 on Jan 3 & 4, 2013 and the five fall records listed above). Most likely to appear at feeders, the location noted for four records, including a male in town on Jan 3, 2013 (PDV, WN), apparent female at the Hitchcox feeders on Jan 27, 2013 (DH), an ind. on Jan 14, 2015 (WBo) and 2 at Donna Cundy's on May 4, 2019 (DHi); there is also one record of 2 at the Ice Pond on Nov 8, 2020 (FK, DH).

Common Redpoll, Nov 9, 2020. © Luke Seitz.

RED CROSSBILL
Loxia curvirostra

Status: Irregular nomadic visitor across seasons; rare spring migrant/resident and rare fall migrant/visitor, very rare summer and winter visitor.

Occurrence: Sixty-five records (17 spring, 15 summer, 27 fall, 4 winter, 2 unknown date) since 1899. Spring records over twelve years since 1950 (fourteen since 1982), span Apr 5–mid Jun, peak second half of May, apparent breeding in 2012 & confirmed breeding in 2018 (see below); spring max: 30 on May 25, 2018 (SS, DL), 27 on May 23 & 25, 2021 (HN, JBi), 25 on May 17, 2021 (DH), 24 on May 24, 2021 (SS), 21 on May 30, 2021 (MD). Summer records over nine years since 1908; summer max: "large flocks" during Jul 31–Aug 2, 1908 (WM–

also included as Jul & Aug 1908 by CFJ, ECJ), 30 on Jul 8, 2000 (TBe), 25 on Jul 4, 2022 (DH, AH), 15 on Jul 29, 2020 (GBr), 14 on Aug 6–7, 2012 (DH). Fall records over eleven years since 1917 (all but the 1917 record since 1994), span mid Aug–Nov 12, no obvious peak, apparent breeding in 2012 (see below); fall max: **36** on Oct 23, 2022 (LMo, JTh), 21 on Sep 19, 2012 (PDV et al.), 20 on Sep 21, 2012 (LB) & Nov 12, 2020 (JT, LS), 16 on Sep 23, 2012 (MW). Winter records: 9 on Jan 4, 2007 (CBC), 9 on Jan 3, 2013 (CBC–PDV, WN), 10 on Jan 27, 2013 (DH), 1 on Jan 3, 2021 (CBC–DH). Unknown dates: unreported number in 1899 (MEH), unreported number prior to Mar 26, 1934 (MJT–winter or early spring). Ten-Year: SP-6, SU-3, F-3, W-1.

- MBA: confirmed.
- CBC: three years (12%), 9 on Jan 4, 2007 & Jan 3, 2013, 1 on Jan 3, 2021, avg 3.2.
- 1899 Checklist: included as American Crossbill.
- 1900–1908 Reconnaissance & Supplements: in large flocks Jul & Aug 1908 (CFJ, ECJ–listed as American Crossbill); in large flocks during Jul 31–Aug 2, 1908 (WM–listed as American Cross Bill).
- 1914 & 1916 Checklists: unreported number on Aug 3, 1914. Listed as American Crossbill.
- 1915–1919 Taylor Journals: 1917–Aug 20 (1).
- 1939 Summer Census: uncommon summer visitor. Listed as American Crossbill.
- 1944–1967 Farrell Records: 1950–Mar, Apr, May; 1955–Aug.
- 1970 Summer Checklist: marked as known to breed in area, irregular or erratic, dependent on abundance of spruce cones.

A nomadic wanderer that doesn't conform to standard seasonal movements or breeding, with two main breeding periods: late winter/early spring and late summer/early fall, dictated largely by its food supply of conifer seeds (Benkman and Young, 2020); its status on Monhegan is variable and confusing. All records (seventeen) one-day events except those in 2012, 2016, 2018, 2020, 2021 & 2022, and apparently 1908 and 1950. In 1908, large flocks were reported as present in both Jul and Aug but considered one record here (along with more specific Jul 31–Aug 2 [WM]; it is notable that none were reported during May 31–Jun 6, 1908 [FA]), while the monthly reports in Apr and May 1950 were likely a lingering group (breeding?) and considered one record here. Possible anywhere on the island as flyovers (often calling), but notably present feeding on cone seeds in the upper reaches of conifers and likely underreported from the northern portion of the island. 2012 records (total 10) involved inds. reported twenty days Apr 5–Oct 8 (and recorded in Jan 2013–see subspecies below), with notable gaps May 29–Aug 5 & Aug 8–Sep 11 likely due to lack of coverage (smaller gaps and variable numbers divide other reports into separate records, although likely involving the same inds.); numbers varied from 1 to 21 at various locations, first found (4 inds.) in Cathedral Woods; breeding apparent as a family group including 3 juveniles was present on May 21 (PW) along Lobster Cove Rd. near the Trailing Yew, becoming a mixed flock of 20 adults (males and females) and juveniles on May 28; continued in the southern half through the fall, from the Ice Pond to Lobster Cove and along Underhill Trail, with small flocks noted as flyovers or in spruces and firs; a flock (13) of adult males, females and juveniles eating red spruce seeds on Sep 21, 2012 (CDe) may indicate further breeding. 2016 reports all considered one record, involving 1–7 inds. over six of seven days May 24–30 (all but May 29); adults and juvs. feeding in spruces in Cathedral Woods and apple trees near the library, possibly indicating breeding and a single family group (adult male & female, 5 juvs.). Four 2018 records less clear, with reports involving 2–30 inds. over twelve days May 17–31, centered around the Ice Pond, including confirmed breeding (adult female feeding juv. on May 17–TMo); 12 on Jun 24 were located along the Cathedral Woods Trail near the cliffs, a single ind. was noted on Oct 8, and 7 and 2 inds. were reported on Nov 11 & 12, respectively, the former calling along Trail #1 and the latter calling over Tribler Rd. Eight 2020 records were scattered, with 2–6 inds. over seven days Jun 1–14 (one record), 4–15 inds. on Jul 4, 6 & 15 (two records), and 1–20 inds. over nine days Sep 20–Nov 12 (five records); 14 on Nov 12, 2020 (out of a total of 20) were observed coming in off the water from the south (JT, LS) after only 3 inds. reported the previous day. 2021 reports all considered one record (except Jan 3), involving 2–27 inds. over eighteen days May 14–Jun 1 (all but May 18), with reports of a roaming flock from the dock area, center of the island, and the north end of Lobster Cove Trail. Fifteen 2022 records scattered May 22–Nov 10, with 1–3 inds. over two days May 22 & Jun 9, 2–25 inds. over eight days Jul 4–Aug 15 (six records), 1–6 inds. over twenty-eight days Aug 26–Oct 11, and 2–36 inds. over five days Oct 23–Nov 10.

Three subspecies (types) of Red Crossbill have been confirmed by calls recorded on Monhegan (audio analysis by Matt Young and Tim Spahr). Sitka Spruce (Type 10) were the most prevalent (the most frequently encountered statewide [Vickery et al.,

2020]) and noted in 2012 on Apr 5 (4) & 19 (3), Aug 6–7 (14), and Sep 18 (2), in 2016 on May 25 (6), in 2018 on May 21 (1), 22 (13), & 23 (1), in 2020 on Jun 1 (6), 2 (5), 3 (4), 4 (6), 7 (4), 12 (2), 14 (4), Nov 10 (2), 12 (1), in 2021 on May 15 (12), 20 (5), 23 (21), 24 (1), and in 2022 on Oct 23 (36). Western Hemlock (Type 3) were noted on Sep 21, 2012 (1), Oct 8, 2012 (1), Jan 27, 2013 (10–suggesting the possibility that the inds. reported Oct 7–8, 2012 & Jan 3 & 27, 2013 were new arrivals to the island, as earlier 2012 inds. were identified as Type 10) & Nov 12, 2020 (1, in addition to Type 10). Appalachian (Type 1) were noted on May 21 (1), 23 (1), 26 (2), & 27 (4), 2018 (in addition to Type 10 on May 21 & 23) & May 24, 2021 (1, in addition to Type 10); two subspecies have been reported on the same day only three times.

Historical/Regional:

- Vickery: many Sep 12–Oct 7, 2012, high of 21 on Sep 19, 2012 (PDV et al.; Paul Dougherty in Vickery et al., 2020).

Red Crossbill, May 28, 2021. © Bill Thompson.

WHITE-WINGED CROSSBILL

Loxia leucoptera

Status: Irregular nomadic resident/visitor across seasons; fairly common to common spring resident/visitor and uncommon to common fall migrant/visitor, rare summer and winter visitor.

Occurrence: Spring records span early Mar–mid Jun, no apparent peak, with breeding confirmed in 2018; spring max: 60 on May 6–7, 1985 (PDV), 50 on Mar 6, 2012 (DH), 40 on May 26, 1995 (SS), Apr 4, 2008 (DH) & Apr 5, 2012 (DH). Fifteen summer records over fourteen years since 1908 (nine since 1984, two in 2000), nine records of unreported number; summer max: 200+ on Jul 18, 2008 (CA), "hundreds" on Jul 28, 1989 (JN; *AB* 43[5]: 1291), "large flocks" during Jul 31–Aug (WM) and Jul & Aug 1908 (CFJ, ECJ), 8 on Jul 19, 1984 (PDV), 6 on Jul 25, 2012 (AJ). Fall records span early Sep–Nov 19, peak late Oct–early Nov; fall max: **553** on Nov 12, 2020 (JT, LS), 227 on Nov 13, 2020 (LS, JT), ~200 on Sep 2, 1961 (SHi; *AFN* 16[1]: 11), 150 on Oct 25, 2008 (JP) & Oct 26, 2012 (JP), 120 on Oct 25, 2012 (JP). Twenty-one winter records over fifteen years since 1979, span Dec 21–late Feb (extending into spring in 2007, 2012 & 2013), most associated with CBC period; winter max: 300 on Dec 30, 1981 (PDV), 251 on Dec 27–28, 1987 (CBC Dec. 28–PDV), 110 on Dec 29, 1981 (PDV), 93 on Dec 21, 1989 (CBC–PDV). Ten-Year: SP-5, F-6, W-2.

- *MABB*: confirmed; MBA: confirmed.
- CBC: twelve years (46%) plus one count week, first on Dec 22, 1979, max 251 on Dec 28, 1987, avg 33.9.
- 1899 Checklist: included.
- 1900–1908 Reconnaissance & Supplements: in large flocks Jul & Aug 1908 (CFJ, ECJ); in large flocks during Jul 31–Aug 2, 1908 (WM–listed as White-winged Cross Bill).
- 1914 & 1916 Checklists: included 1916.
- 1915–1919 Taylor Journals: 1918–Aug 4.
- 1939 Summer Census: uncommon summer visitor.
- 1944–1967 Farrell Records: 1949–Sep; 1950–Mar; 1953–Aug, Sep; 1954–Jun; 1955–Aug; 1958–Aug.
- 1954 & 1955 Summer Records: 1954–included June 19–25.
- 1970 Summer Checklist: marked as known to breed in area, irregular or erratic, dependent on abundance of spruce cones.
- Banding: 1 on Aug 27, 1981.

Similar to Red Crossbill, a nomadic wanderer that doesn't conform to standard seasonal movements or breeding—indeed, it may breed any time of the year, even winter—dictated largely by its food supply of conifer seeds; prone to late fall irruptions that supplement frequent movements (Benkman 2020), supported by max counts in late fall/early winter, but note Jul high counts. While more common on Monhegan than Red Crossbill, the two species are sometimes seen together and under similar conditions—particularly in 2012, 2016, 2018. Its status is variable and confusing, apparently lingering or residing for extended periods when the food supply is sufficient. Undoubtedly underreported, especially during these periods, in all but typical migration months of May and Sep/early Oct due to lack of coverage. While gaps between reports and variable numbers may be considered separate records (Jul & Aug 1908 and Jul 31–Aug 2, 1908 reports of large flocks considered one record here), likely involve the same inds./flocks in some instances. 1916 checklist report, occurring during Aug 16–Sep 16, probably either a late summer or early fall record, or both (not included in summer for these purposes). Possible anywhere on the island as flyovers but more often concentrated in coniferous areas in the northern half, particularly spruces, where often calling continually. 1981 was exceptional for numbers, with five days of 60+ (including fall and winter high counts) Sep 5–Dec 30, with likely no coverage Oct–Dec 28 or Jan 1982 to determine true level of presence/length of stay (next report on island in Sep 1982). Present as early as w/e Feb 2 in 2007, reports continued into early Jun (none in Apr but lack of coverage), with a max of 24 feeding on spruce cones during w/e Mar 3, 2007 (fide JWa, KG; MARBA). Even more prevalent than Red Crossbill in 2012, presence apparently extended fall 2011–spring 2013 (reports Nov 8, 2011 [possibly as early as Sep 26]–May 31, 2013), with notable gaps during underbirded periods of mid/late winter & summer (one report on July 25) and the first Sep report on the 27th (while Red Crossbills were present/reported most of the month), possibly indicating a departure/return. The high counts during late Oct 2012 (75, 120, 150, and 45 on Oct 24–27, respectively) indicate a supplemental irruption, with flocks noted everywhere on the island and "rarely out of earshot" (calling flyover groups of 5–15 inds. and in trees in all spruce areas, sometimes 5–10 in a single tree–JP). Similarly, the exceptional movements of fall/winter 2021 (present in small numbers through Jun 2021) involved a huge flight on Nov 12 (moving southeast to northwest over the island 8:30–noon, with groups approaching 100 inds.–JT, LS) after reports of 60–90 inds. every day Nov 7–11; a follow-up flight of 227 on Nov 13 (LS, JT) was moving off the island to the southwest and 200 were present on the CBC on Jan 3, 2021 (DH). Many reports indicating a mix of males and females, with first-year immatures sometimes present. Despite reports of first-year inds., the only clear evidence of breeding is the *MABB* status, a report of "many feeding young" during May 16–26, 2001 (GD) and recently fledged young on Jun 1, 2018 (TW–providing the confirmed status for the MBA). Likely overlooked due to lack of coverage (early spring and late fall, but possible any season) and preference for upper reaches of coniferous forest; reports of males singing in Jan & Mar, 2012 and a "family (adult male, adult female, two immature) seen foraging overhead" on May 20, 2012 (PW) apparently indicate additional breeding.

Historical/Regional:

- Vickery: cites 40 on Apr 4, 2008 (WJS) as high coastal spring count, 150 on Oct 25, 2008 (JP) as high fall count, and the top two max counts above and 85 on Jan 4, 2008 CBC (DH et al.) as high winter counts (Paul Dougherty in Vickery et al., 2020).

White-winged Crossbill, May 28, 2021. © Bill Thompson.

PINE SISKIN
Spinus pinus

Status: Uncommon to common spring and irruptive uncommon to abundant fall migrant, very rare summer and rare winter visitor; has possibly bred.

Occurrence: Spring dates span Mar 5–Jun 8, with no apparent peak; spring max: 100 on Mar 5–6, 2012 (DH), 80 on May 25, 2012 (SBe), 75 on Apr 4–5, 2012 (DH). Three summer records: unreported number during Aug 1960 (fide IF), unreported number during Aug 30–31, 1965 (HT, RLP, CP et al.; *AFN* 20[1]: 9, 1 on Jul 2, 2019 (DL, JL). Fall dates span Sep 5–end Nov, peak late Sep–mid Oct; fall max: **1,880** on Oct 9, 2020 (JT, LS, HS), 1,000 on Sep 28, 1989 (BN), 874 on Oct 11, 2014 (JT), 417 on Oct 10, 2014 (JT), 386 on Oct 8, 2020 (JT, LS), 350 on Sep 28, 2012 (JT, BN). Fifteen winter records over thirteen years since 1939, span early Dec–w/e Feb 3 (most associated with CBC period); winter maxima: 421 on Jan 1, 1987 (CBC), 30 on Dec 29, 1983 (CBC–PDV), 25 on Dec 29, 1940 (CBC). Ten-Year: SP-8, SU-1, F-10, W-1.

- *MABB*: possible.
- CBC: five years (19%) plus two count weeks, first on Dec 29, 1940, max 421 on Jan 1, 1987, avg 18.5.
- 1899 Checklist: included.
- 1900–1908 Reconnaissance & Supplements: 1 on Jun 1 & 3, 1908 (FA).
- 1914 & 1916 Checklists: included 1916.
- 1918 Fall Migration Census: Wentworth–many on Oct 17 & 19, small flocks on 23 & 24.
- 1939 Summer Census: uncommon summer visitor.
- 1944–1967 Farrell Records: 1949–Jan, Mar; 1950–Jan; 1960–Aug.
- 1970 Summer Checklist: irregular or erratic summer breeder.
- Banding: total 16 over one season (Spring 1984), max 7 on May 22, 1984.

Prone to unpredictable movements based on food supply, with fall irruptions on a general two-year basis (spring numbers don't necessarily follow fall pattern); illustrated throughout the 2010s, with large movements in the even years (see max counts) and generally only minor reports in odd years. Fall 2014 was exceptional, with four days of 140+ during Oct 6–12, with counts of 176 on Oct 6 and 140 on Oct 12 adding to the max counts listed above, along with 150 on Sep 27. Spring 2012 was also exceptional, with counts of 75+ in early Mar, early Apr, and late May, suggesting breadth of movement and extent of underreporting in seasons lacking coverage, notably late Oct–late Apr. Fall 2020 outdid them all, producing the highest max count of 1,880 on Oct 9 and eleven days of 100+ spanning Oct 4–Nov 12, centered around the peak day with a secondary movement in early Nov. 1916 record possibly a summer or earliest fall record, occurring during Aug 16–Sep 16; likewise, Aug 30–31, 1965 record is likely an early fall migrant, but considered summer for these purposes. Lack of any late winter reports may indicate early winter inds. were a continuation of the fall movements/irruption and departed; there were "quite a few" still present as of Jan 27, 1939 and the 3 inds. reported on Jan 3, 2015 were observed flying in off the water in the morning (DH, FK, WN). Large movements are often three- to five-day events and sometimes longer, with flocks moving around the island; possible anywhere, particularly in upper branches in coniferous areas, such as Cathedral Woods, and often frequenting/lingering at feeders around town. Roving small to large flocks make determining the number present on island problematic. Largest flocks reported involve hundreds, with two flocks of 300+ as part of 874 on Oct 11, 2014, 200+ around the Trailing Yew on Sep 28, 2012, and others of 100+. The max count of Oct 9, 2020 included flocks of 300+, with flocks of 75–100 flying out over the ocean at dawn and flocks of 25–75 lingering through early afternoon, when many settled to drink at the Ice Pond and Meadow, where raptors chased and preyed on a few (JT, LS, HS). Exuberantly vocal, with flocks described as "deafening" in Cathedral Woods on Mar 6, 2012 (DH). Adults were observed feeding juveniles on May 25, 2012, perhaps indicating that breeding took place on the island; no other breeding evidence except inclusion on *MABB*.

Historical/Regional:

- Vickery: cites 1,000 on Sep 28, 1989, 169 on Oct 23, 2006 (TMag), 350 on Sep 27, 2008 (JT) and at least 874 on Oct 10, 2010 (JT) as fall irruption high counts (PDV in Vickery et al., 2020).

Pine Siskin, Oct 6, 2014. © Jeremiah Trimble.

AMERICAN GOLDFINCH
Spinus tristis

Status: Fairly common spring and common fall migrant, fairly common summer resident, rare winter visitor.

Occurrence: Spring dates Mar 5–mid Jun, peak early–late May; spring max: 100 on May 25, 1986 (JVW), 87 on May 16, 2021 (JT, LS, JO), 60 on May 24, 1986 (PDV, SS), 59 on May 18, 2021 (JT, LS, JO), 56 on May 17, 2021 (JT, LS, JO), 50 on May 26, 1986 (JVW) & May 24, 2013 (DH). Limited breeding occurs Jun–early Sep (overlapping early migrants); summer max: 30 on Aug 17, 2006 (PDV), 26 on Jul 7, 2022 (LS, MWa), 20 on Jul 30, 2021 (NP), 17 on Aug 31, 2010 (TMag) & Jul 17, 2018 (RD, PD). Fall dates span early Sep–early Dec, peak late Sep–mid Nov; fall max: **377** on Nov 12, 2020 (JT, LS), 250 on Sep 27, 2010 (EH), 200 on Oct 2, 1997 (JT), 150 on Nov 15, 2015 (DH). Eleven winter records over ten years since 1940 (all but the one in 1940 since 1989, two in 2015), span Dec 21–Jan 7, most associated with CBC period; winter max: 45 on Jan 4, 2007 (CBC), 19 on Jan 7, 2012 (EH, CHy), 18 on Jan 5, 2016 (DH et al.). Ten-Year: SP-10, SU-10, F-10, W-2.

- *MABB*: possible; MBA: confirmed.
- CBC: seven years (27%), first on Dec 29, 1941, max 45 on Jan 4, 2007, avg 3.7.
- 1899 Checklist: included.
- 1900–1908 Reconnaissance & Supplements: one pair during May 31–Jun 6, 1908 (FA); also included in Jenney supplement.
- 1914 & 1916 Checklists: included 1916.
- 1915–1919 Taylor Journals: 1916–Aug 26 (2), Sep 10; 1919–Sep 13 (1).
- 1918 Fall Migration Census: Dewis–Sep 8 (1), 9 (1), 11 (1); Wentworth–Oct 8, 9, 12 (50), 15, 16, 17 (many), 22 & 23 (small flocks).
- 1939 Summer Census: uncommon summer visitor.
- 1944–1967 Farrell Records: 1950–May, Jun; 1951–Oct, Nov; 1954–Jun, Jul; 1955–Jun, Aug; 1957–May; 1958–May; 1959–May, Jun, Jul, Aug; 1960–May, Aug.
- 1954 & 1955 Summer Records: 1954–included Jun 19–25 & Jun 27–Jul 4; 1955–included Jun 11–15.
- 1970 Summer Checklist: highlighted and marked as known to breed in area.
- Banding: total 96 over seven seasons, peak 58 in Fall 1960, max 18 on Sep 23, 1960.

Movements often three- to five-day events; lingering inds./flocks often frequenting feeders. Undoubtedly underreported during much of peak late fall period and into early winter; lack of mid–late winter reports also likely due to departure as harsh weather sets in. As is the case with Pine Siskin, exact numbers present are often difficult to determine, as flocks move around the island; flocks of 75+ noted on Nov 13, 2020 (LS, JT) and 50+ on Nov 14, 2015 (DH). Possible anywhere on the island as flyovers, especially during migration, and present in coniferous and deciduous habitat, as well as town locations, particularly gardens, the edge of the Meadow, and around the Ballfield; most noticeable at feeders. Unusually late breeding, correlated to thistle bloom, begins by late Jun: courtship noted on Jul 5, 2018 (JSn) & Jul 6, 2019 (DH), carrying nesting material noted on Jul 16, 2018 (WBs) & Jun 26, 2021 (KL), and recently fledged young observed on Jul 19, 2021 (HIAC et al.), and can extend into Sep (1 adult feeding non-fledged young on Sep 1, 2014 [PDV] and adults feeding fledged young on Sep 15, 1984 [PDV]).

American Goldfinch, Oct 29, 2010. © Luke Seitz.

LAPLAND LONGSPUR
Calcarius lapponicus

Status: Rare fall migrant, accidental winter visitor.

Occurrence: Fourteen records (13 fall, 1 winter). Fall records over nine years since 2003 (two records in 2009, 2010, 2012, 2021), span short period Sep 25–Oct 10; fall max: **2** on Sep 26, 2009 (DH et al.), Oct 10, 2014 (JT) & Oct 9, 2021 (JT, LS). Winter record: 1 on Dec 30, 1980 (CBC–PDV). Ten-Year: F-3.

- CBC: 1 year (4%): 1 on Dec 30, 1980, avg 0.0.

It is surprising that all the fall records have occurred since 2003. Unclear if a dead ind. on Sep 26, 2009 (PL) was one of the two reported by DH et al. that day, while only one was reported on Oct 1, 2009 (WR et al.). Consecutive-day sightings without details on Sep 29–30, 2005 and Sep 25–26, 2011 have each been considered as single records and are the only reports involving multiple days. Six of the fall records have been flyovers, three calling, including one at Lobster Cove on Oct 3, 2021 (JT, LS); the Oct 10, 2014 ind. was a flyover near the school. Exceptions were the Sep 25, 2011 ind. eating grass seeds at Lobster Cove (AW) and the Oct 9, 2012 ind. with a Clay-colored Sparrow at a bird feeder near the post office (DH).

Lapland Longspur, Oct 9, 2012. © Doug Hitchcox.

SNOW BUNTING
Plectrophenax nivalis

Status: Very rare spring and rare fall migrant, very rare winter visitor.

Occurrence: Thirty-nine records (5 spring, 25 fall, 9 winter) since 1940. A very early spring migrant, dates span Feb 17–Apr 11, almost all records from one year with Feb/Mar coverage: 1 on Feb 17–18, 2011 (TMag), 1 on Feb 26, 2011 (TMag), 10 on Mar 7, 2011 (TMag), 1 on Apr 11, 2018 (DC), 1 on Apr 11, 2019 (DC). A late fall migrant, records over nine years since 1989, dates span Oct 12–Nov 15, peak late Oct–early Nov, but likely underreported; fall max: 25 on Nov 10, 2018 (DH, FK), 6 on Oct 24, 2021 (SJ, CJ), 5 on Nov 3, 2010 (TMag) & Nov 5, 2016 (DH, FK, JF), 4 on Nov 13, 2020 (LS, JT) & Nov 10, 2022 (LS, MWa). Winter records over eight years since 1951 (two in 2010), almost all associated with CBC period and undoubtedly underreported throughout winter, span Dec 27–Jan 10; winter max: **50** on Jan 5, 2010 (CBC–PDV), 15 on Dec 30, 1980 (CBC–PDV), 6 on Dec 27, 1987 (CBC–PDV) & Dec 28, 1987 (PDV). Ten-Year: SP-2, F-8, W-1.

- CBC: six years (23%), first on Dec 29, 1940, max 50 on Jan 5, 2010, avg 3.0.
- 1944–1967 Farrell Records: 1951–Jan.

It is surprising that all the fall records have occurred since 1989. Underreported throughout much of its occurrence due to lack of coverage, particularly late fall through early spring (excepting CBC counts); illustrated by most spring records in a year that TMag provided consistent reports. Several instances of varying counts on consecutive fall days suggest movement, instead of lingering, although reports of a single ind. Oct 27–30, 2013, 2 on Nov 9–11, 2020 (part of a movement that produced 1 on Nov 8, 3 on Nov 12 & 4 on Nov 13), and 4 on Nov 10, 2022 followed by 3 on Nov 9, and 2 on Nov 11, 12, & 13 have been considered one record, without any details to suggest otherwise. Several flyovers, including one by Black Head, one over the White Head Trail near the Ballfield, and one flying into the cemetery; exceptions were a "confiding bird at Lobster Cove" (MI) and on the lawn of the Island Inn (DC).

Snow Bunting, Nov 5, 2016. © Louis Bevier.

GRASSHOPPER SPARROW
Ammodramus savannarum

Status: Very rare spring and rare fall migrant.

Occurrence: Twenty records (8 spring, 12 fall) since 1962, all singles. Spring records over eight years since 1983, span May 11–29: May 29, 1983 (PDV), May 1984 (TMar), May 15–17, 1989 (banded on the 16th–MPl, PDV), May 27, 1990 (AW, JVW), May 18, 2002 (GD), May 14–w/e May 25, 2004 (GD, WBo), May 27–28, 2014 (JT, BN, TW), May 18, 2015 (DL, JL). Fall records over eleven years since 1962 (two banded in 1962), span Sep 27–Oct 19. Ten-Year: SP-2, F-5.

- 1970 Summer Checklist: included.
- Banding: 3 total over two seasons, peak 2 in 1962, max 1 on Oct 5, 1962, Oct 10, 1962, & May 16, 1989.

The May 1990 ind. was observed at Lobster Cove. Sep 27, 2009 ind. was in the marshy meadow at Lobster Cove (DL). Oct 29, 2010 ind. was in the damp area just south of Fish Beach Lane (JT, LS, MI). May 2014 ind. was observed on the ground along Monhegan Ave. (Main St.) north of Swim Beach. Oct 2014 ind. was at Lobster Cove on the 6th, at one point in a small spruce with a Seaside Sparrow (JT et al.); the next report was from Burnt Head on the 9th (assumed to be the same ind. due to rarity–JT). May 15, 2015 ind. was near the Verizon tower. Oct 8, 2016 ind. was at the east end of Mooring Chain Rd. (DH). Oct 15, 2017 ind. was in a tomato garden in town center (assumed to be the garden to the southwest of the Horn's Hill/Lobster Cove Rd. intersection–DH). Oct 6, 2019 ind. was by Horn's Hill (LK). The presumed same ind. in May 2004 was first reported on May 11 and then as w/e reports for May 18 & 25; without details and due to rarity considered one record here. Oct 8, 2021 ind. was in the shorter grass uphill from Lobster Cove (CHi).

Historical/Regional:

- Vickery: cites four of the records above for spring and six for fall (PDV in Vickery et al., 2020).

Grasshopper Sparrow, Oct 10, 2020. © Luke Seitz.

BLACK-THROATED SPARROW

Amphispiza bilineata

Status: Accidental spring vagrant.

Occurrence: One record: 1 on Apr 29–May 3, 1983 (various observers [fide PDV]). First Maine record; not yet reviewed by ME-BRC (OLMB dates Apr 29–30). "Well described" but lacking official documentation (*AB* 37[5]: 849).

Located directly across Wharf Rd. from the entrance to the Island Inn (DF pers. comm.).

Historical/Regional:

- Vickery: cites above record (PDV in Vickery et al., 2020).
- OLMB: one additional state record—accepted (1 on Jan 1–Mar 17, 2016 at Winter Harbor, Hancock Co.).

LARK SPARROW

Chondestes grammacus

Status: Very rare spring and scarce fall vagrant.

Occurrence: Nine spring records over nine years since 1986, span Apr 21–May 25 (only one before May 11), all singles. Fall dates span Aug 14–Nov 6 since first recorded on Aug 25, 1913 (RFC–first Maine record), peak early Sep–mid Oct; fall max: **4** on Sep 23–24, 2001 (JT, LBr, TV), Oct 1, 2003 (JT) & Oct 5, 2003 (WJS), 3 on Oct 2, 2003 (JT), Oct 4, 2003 (KE), Oct 7, 2003 (WJS), Sep 23, 2007 (LS), Oct 6, 2008 (BP), Sep 6, 2010 (TMag), Oct 1, 2011 (BM), Oct 5, 2011 (DH) & Sep 21, 2014 (CDe). Ten-Year: SP-3, F-10.

- 1914 & 1916 Checklists: included 1916.
- 1915–1919 Taylor Journals: 1916–Aug 20 (1), 22 (1).
- 1918 Fall Migration Census: Dewis–1 on Sep 9–10 near Swim Beach and noted as tame, gives another name as Western Song Sparrow and "one of the few rare birds."
- 1939 Summer Census: uncommon summer visitor.
- 1944–1967 Farrell Records: 1958–Sep; 1960–Sep.
- 1970 Summer Checklist: included.

Despite the number/regularity of records for this species, the distance and direction to the nearest sustained breeding population (western Ohio) and standard route to wintering grounds argue for its status as a vagrant. The majority of records for Maine are from Monhegan, including the first for the state on Aug 25, 1913, followed by 1 on Aug 20–22, 1916 (WT) and 2 or 3 seen Aug 16–29, 1917 (RFC; Forbush, 1929). Since it is known to linger, possibly up to several weeks, particularly when frequenting a feeder or where seed has been regularly scattered, it is no surprise that many of the max counts occur consecutively or within a short stretch of days. Hard to determine exact length of stay with shifting locations and possibility of inds. arriving/departing. Seen at many town birding locations, including in/on lobster traps or at spots where seed has been scattered along Ocean Ave. south of the scrubby swale, the Cundy and Hitchcox feeders, or formerly at Tom Martin's feeders near Fish Beach, where multiples would gather and four were seen at one time on Sep 23–24, 2001 (LBr, TV). Only one spring ind. was aged—an adult. Another spring ind. was singing on May 19 & 24, 2002 (GD, TV). While there have been a number of adults in fall, the majority identified have been immatures; due to the difficulty of distinguishing the age of certain inds., some records have indicated uncertain age despite careful observation.

Historical/Regional:

- Palmer: 1 (*erroneously listed as 2 or 3*) on Aug 25, 1913 (first Maine record–RFC), 2 or 3 on Aug 16–29, 1917 (RFC), Dewis records from 1918 (see above), 1 on Aug 14, 1938 (MAC et al.).
- Cruickshank: cites records from Palmer plus 1 in late Aug 1916 (Gleason).
- Vickery: lists six spring records; usually single in fall, but 3–4 inds. have been recorded on same day (PDV in Vickery et al., 2020).

Lark Sparrow, May 14, 2014. © Geoff Dennis.

LARK BUNTING
Calamospiza melanocorys

Status: Accidental summer and very rare fall vagrant.

Occurrence: Five records (1 summer, 4 fall) since 1976, all singles. Summer record: male on Jun 23, 1983 (CWo). Fall records: female-type on Sep 18–19, 1976 (RLP, PDV et al., ph.; *AB* 31[2]: 230), female on Sep 30–Oct 6, 1978 (DF, PDV et al.; *AB* 33[2]: 158), Sep 11, 1979 (HT et al.; *AB* 34[2]: 141), immature female on Sep 14–17, 2010 (BP, WR et al.).

The 1978 record was accepted by the ME-BRC (#1978–003) as Oct 4–6, while there is an additional record on the OLMB of Sep 30–Oct 3 that hasn't yet been reviewed, considered one record here; the other five records have not yet been reviewed. The Sep 1976 ind. was associating with a number of Brown-headed Cowbirds. The Sep/Oct 1978 ind. was coming to seed scattered on the "horseshoe lawn" at the Trailing Yew on at least Oct 5–6 (DF). The Sep 2010 ind. was foraging around the rocks at White Head.

Historical/Regional:

- Vickery: cites 1978 record as first confirmed female in state (PDV in Vickery et al., 2020).

- OLMB: ten additional state records (first in Aug 1950)—two accepted and eight prior to the species' placement on the review list in 2014.

CHIPPING SPARROW
Spizella passerina

Status: Uncommon to fairly common spring and uncommon to common fall migrant, rare summer visitor and possible breeder, accidental winter visitor.

Occurrence: Spring migration spans during Mar (earliest definite Apr 3)–mid Jun, peak late Apr–first three weeks of May; spring max: 60 on May 5–7, 1985 (PDV), 40 on May 19–21 (PDV), 30 on May 20, 2011 (DL), 21 on May 15, 2011 (TMag). Twenty-six summer records (excludes *MABB*) over eighteen years since 1908 (three records in 1954) during mid Jun–mid Aug period, when undoubtedly underreported; summer max: 6 on Jul 19, 1984 (PDV) & Jul 19, 2018 (MF), 5 on Aug 11, 1915 (WT), 3 on Jun 30, 2021 (CEs). Fall migration spans mid Aug–Nov 22, peak late Sep–late Oct; fall max: **125** on Oct 2, 1998 (JT), 120 on Sep 30, 1983 (PDV), 115 on Oct 9, 2020 (JT, LS, HS), 100 on Oct 11–12, 1987 (JVW). One winter record: 1 on Jan 3, 2013 (CBC–PDV, WN). Ten-Year: SP-10, SU-9, F-10.

- *MABB*: confirmed; MBA: probable.
- CBC: one year (4%), 1 on Jan 3, 2013, avg 0.0.
- 1899 Checklist: included.
- 1900–1908 Reconnaissance & Supplements: included in Jenney supplement; unreported number during Jul 31–Aug 2, 1908 (WM).
- 1914 & 1916 Checklists: unreported number on Jul 31, 1914; included 1916.
- 1915–1919 Taylor Journals: 1915–Aug 11 (5), 16, 31 (6), Sep 2, 5, 12 (3); 1916–Aug 19, 21, 22, 26, 30, Sep 6, 10; 1917–Jul 29, Aug 4 (1), 18 (1); 1918–prior to Aug 4; 1919–Sep 3 (1), 4 (2), 5 (1), 13 (2).
- 1918 Fall Migration Census: Dewis–1 on Sep 7 & 8, 8 on Sep 11; Wentworth–several on each day Sep 29, Oct 7, 8, 9, 12, 13, 15, 16, 17 (many), 19 (many), 20 (many), 22, 23, 24.
- 1939 Summer Census: regular summer resident.
- 1944–1967 Farrell Records: 1949–Mar; 1950–Apr, May; 1951–May; 1954–Jun; 1955–Aug; 1958–May; 1959 May, Aug; 1960–Apr, May, Aug; 1961–Apr, May; 1967–Apr 3, Jun 2 (1).
- 1954 & 1955 Summer Records: 1954–included all three checklists.
- 1970 Summer Checklist: included.
- Banding: 59 total over ten seasons, peak 15 in Fall 1962, max 9 on May 21, 1984.

It is noteworthy that the spring max counts of 60 and 40 were both three-day events with consistent numbers, a clear sign of a tendency to linger during some large movements. Certainly underreported during Apr, Oct, & summer months due to lack of coverage. The status/presence given in 1939, 1954, and *MABB* (see above) supports its status as a breeder, as does the comment "apparently only one to two territories seems odd" by PDV in Aug 2006. The lack of this designation on the 1970 Summer Checklist and only probable on MBA (based on a pair in suitable habitat on Jun 5, 2021 [TF]) supports a more cautious designation; further summer observations would help to clarify this status. Probable overlap of migrants and residents in Jun and Aug also confuses the situation. Its widespread and common status for many birders engenders only casual observation and there is a scarcity of details provided with reports. Possible anywhere on the island, but certainly most consistent at feeders and the more or less established scattered seed locations, e.g. Ocean Ave., Wharton Rd., and the Ballfield; a count of 61 on Oct 13, 2014 (out of 80 reported on the island) at the south end of Wharton Rd. is a good example (LS et al.). The only winter record was observed at a feeder on Horn's Hill.

Historical/Regional:

- Vickery: 15–30 inds. May 5–15, 5–10 inds. May 25–30, lists four Apr records as early (earliest Apr 6); 6–15 summer residents; small flocks arrive in fall Sep 8–15, migrant waves 20–40 inds. in late Sep–Oct, lists three high counts (>40–>80 ind.) as high counts and 1 on Nov 22, 2011 (DH) as late (PDV in Vickery et al., 2020).

Chipping Sparrow (top) and Clay-colored Sparrow (bottom), Oct 3, 2018. © Jeremiah Trimble.

CLAY-COLORED SPARROW
Spizella pallida

Status: Rare spring and scarce to uncommon fall migrant.

Occurrence: Thirty-four +/- spring records over twenty-seven years since 1968, span short period May 13–Jun 2; spring max: 2 on May 15, 1977 (WR). Fall dates span Sep 5–Nov 12 since 1964, peak late Sep–mid Oct; fall max: **13** on Oct 6, 2012 (JT), 8 on Oct 1, 2009 (WR et al.), Oct 7, 2012 (JT) & Oct 4, 2021 (JT, LS), 6 on w/e Oct 9, 2001 (PMo), Oct 3, 2021 (JT, LS) & Oct 5, 2021 (JT, LS), 5 on Oct 3, 2009 (SS), Oct 3, 2011 (DH), Oct 8, 2012 (DH), Oct 12, 2012 (DH), Oct 14, 2012 (DH), Oct 5, 2017 (JO) & Oct 2, 2021 (LMu, BBc). Ten-Year: SP-6, F-10.

- Banding: 1 on Oct 25, 1989.

An plainly apparent expansion of breeding grounds from the midwest to the east has occurred in the last 70 years (since 1950; Grant and Knapton, 2020), resulting in its initial and quickly expanding presence in Maine (first state record in fall 1958 and annual since 1968, first spring record in 1966 and regular since 1974 [Vickery et al., 2020]) and on Monhegan. Although generally migrating west of the Mississippi, it is now expected on Monhegan most years in spring and multiples every fall. The second state record was on Monhegan Sep 5, 1964 (HT; *AFN* 19: 8) and the first spring record for the island was on May 21–23, 1968 (in the back yard of the parsonage–TMar personal notes, IM); a photo of the latter bird made the cover of Audubon Field Notes (Vol. 22, No 4–Aug 1968; see below). This was just the beginning, as the species returned in spring 1969 and was recorded for the next nine years (not noted if these were spring or fall records, but included May 17, 1977–TMar personal notes). Unknown if the total of 15+ reported by TMar et al. during Sep 26–Oct 10, 1970 (*AFN* 25(1): 31) were clearly separate inds.; possibly some repeat inds. given the species' tendency to linger. Fall 2012 & 2021 were exceptional, with many of the max counts (5–8 inds. Oct 2–5, 2021), undoubtedly involving some lingering inds.; 2012 included a flock of 7 on Oct 6, noted at the south end (cul-de-sac) of Wharton Ave and 2021 included a flock of 6 at the same location Oct 4–5 (a group of 8 together on Oct 1, 2009 [WR et al.] is the largest gathering). Inds. often linger for multiple days, sometimes for a week or more, especially when coming to bird feeders or consistently scattered seed; shifting of locations, especially movement from one feeding area to another occurs, making number of inds. present unclear, both daily and seasonally. For many years, the feeders of TMar & JMar were the most consistent place to find them, with at least 3 there on Oct 8, 2011 (JM). Other attractive feeding locations include the edge of the Ballfield, the cul-de-sac at the southern end of Wharton Ave., Ocean Ave. south of the scrubby swale, and the Hitchcox feeders. Other reports scattered around town and nearby, especially across the road from the Trailing Yew, Lobster Cove Trail, and near the marsh by the cove itself. Often associates with other sparrows, including Chipping, Song, and Lark. Noted singing in spring on a number of occasions. Aged inds. have been almost equally split, with one adult and one immature each for spring and four adults and three immatures in fall.

Historical/Regional:

- Vickery: lists 2 on May 15, 1977 (WR) as first spring record (see discussion above), 1–4 inds. nearly annual since 1977 (*must refer to yearly, as these numbers not supported by known spring records*), lists three recent records; cites fall 1964 record as second for state, fall peak late Sep–Oct, with max 3–4 inds., 1 on Oct 2, 2017 (LS et al.) as recent record (PDV in Vickery et al., 2020).

Audubon Field Notes journal cover from Aug 1968, including the photo of a Clay-colored Sparrow, taken on May 22, 1968 by Tom Martin. Cover image by permission of Audubon; bird image courtesy Monhegan Historical and Cultural Museum Association.

FIELD SPARROW
Spizella pusilla

Status: Scarce to uncommon spring and rare to uncommon fall migrant, very rare summer visitor (historical).

Occurrence: Spring dates span Apr 5–Jun 7, peak early–late May; spring max: **6** on May 6, 1985 (PDV), 4 on May 26, 2017 (SSs), 3 on Apr 23, 1967 (IF) & May 27, 2008 (MW). Three summer records: unreported number on Aug 2, 1914 (WF), unreported number during Jul 1954 (IF), unreported number during Jun 30–Jul 5, 1955 (MA, MSA). Fall dates span Sep 4–Nov 9, peak early–late Oct; fall max: 4 on Oct 9, 2010 (JT), Oct 10, 2010 (JT), Oct 31, 2010 (MI, JT, LS) & Oct 10, 2014 (JT), 3 on Oct 17, 1986 (PDV), Oct 18, 1989 (PDV), Oct 11, 2010 (DH). Ten-Year: SP-10, F-9.

- 1900–1908 Reconnaissance & Supplements: one singing on Jun 5, 1908 (FA).
- 1914 & 1916 Checklists: unreported number on Aug 2, 1914; included 1916.
- 1915–1919 Taylor Journals: 1919–Sep 4 (1).
- 1918 Fall Migration Census: Wentworth–Oct 12, 15, 17, 19 (a few).
- 1944–1967 Farrell Records: 1950–May; 1954–Jul; 1955–Jun, Jul; 1958–May; 1959–May; 1960–May; 1961–Apr, May; 1967–Apr 23 (3).
- 1954 & 1955 Summer Records: 1955–included Jun 30–Jul 5.
- 1970 Summer Checklist: included.
- Banding: 1 on May 16, 1989.

Likely underreported most years in Apr/early May due to lack of coverage. Observed at many of the typical town locations and trails, including around the Meadow, Lobster Cove and Lobster Cove Trail, Burnt Head Trail, and feeders; typically found in bushy habitat. Sometimes associates with other sparrow species. Spring inds. noted as singing on occasion.

Historical/Regional:

- Palmer: cites Jun 5, 1908 Allen record, Wentworth records of 1918, and a late date of week of Oct 22, 1939 involving several birds (MJT).

BREWER'S SPARROW
Spizella breweri

Status: Accidental spring vagrant.

Occurrence: One record: 1 on May 25–29, 2014 (LBr, JT et al.). First Maine record; accepted by ME-BRC #2014–006 (photos and audio). Ten-Year: SP-1.

This was the seventh record for the entire East Coast and first in spring (LB, eBird). First located by LBr in the path near the Ice Pond, later moving to the Hitchcox yard along Black Head Rd., feeding on dandelion seed heads, which it continued to do throughout its stay. Relocated to the community garden at the north end of the Meadow (behind the library) on the 26th, the grassy area near the Wharton Ave. cul-de-sac on the 27th, and across from the Trailing Yew at Donna Cundy's on the 28th (mob). Associating with Savannah Sparrows on the 27th & 28th and heard singing on the 25th & 28th.

Historical/Regional:

- Vickery: cites record above as only one for state (BSV in Vickery et al., 2020).
- OLMB: one additional state record—accepted (Sep 4, 2020 at Steuben, Washington Co.)

Brewer's Sparrow, May 27, 2014. © Jeremiah Trimble.

FOX SPARROW
Passerella iliaca

Status: Rare spring and fall migrant (*presumably scarce in both seasons*), very rare winter visitor.

Occurrence: Forty-seven records (24 spring, 15 fall, 6 winter, 2 unknown date) since first recorded in 1899. An early spring migrant and undoubtedly underreported, dates span Mar 6–Apr 23, all from 1939, 1949–1967 & 2006–2022 periods (two records in 1949, two in 1950, three in 1967, six in 2011); spring max: **10** on Apr 7, 2011 (TMag), 2 on Mar 22, 2011 (TMag), Apr 10–11, 2011 (TMag), Mar 6, 2012 (DH) & Apr 6, 2013 (DH). Late fall migrant and certainly underreported, records over only eight years since 1918 (four records in 1918, three in 2010, two in 2011 & 2021; nine records after 1954, all since 2004), dates span during Sep (earliest definite Sep 30)–Nov 22; fall max: 3 on Nov 5, 2016 (DH et al.) & Nov 9, 2020 (LS, JT), 2 on Oct 17, 1986 (PDV), Oct 30–31, 2010 (MI, JT, LS), Nov 22, 2011 (DH) & Nov 8, 2020 (FK, DH). Winter records almost all associated with CBC period, likely underreported in other years and remainder of season: 1 on Dec 23, 1939 (MJT), 2 on Dec 29, 1980 (PDV), 3 on Dec 30, 1980 (CBC–PDV), 1 on Jan 1, 1987 (CBC), 1 on Jan 4, 2007 (CBC), 1 on Jan 3, 2008 (CBC), 1 on Jan 4–5, 2016 (CBC Jan 5–DH et al.). Unknown dates: unreported number in 1899 (MEH), unreported number prior to Mar 26, 1934 (MJT). Ten-Year: SP-3, F-2, W-1.

- CBC: five years (19%), first on Dec 30, 1980, max 3 on Dec 30, 1980, avg 0.3.
- 1899 Checklist: included.
- 1918 Fall Migration Census: Wentworth–Oct 17 (many), 19 (several flocks), 21 (1), 22 (1), 23 (1), 24 (several).
- 1944–1967 Farrell Records: 1949–Mar, Apr; 1950–Mar, Apr; 1951–Apr; 1952–Apr, Nov; 1954–Sep; 1960–Apr; 1967–Apr 2, 3, 9, 14 (1), 15 (1).
- 1970 Summer Checklist: included.

Due to lack of coverage, this species is underreported and likely deserves a status of uncommon or common during migration and rare to scarce in winter; this is especially highlighted by the concentration of records in spring 2011, during a year of consistent coverage by TMag, and historically in the fall of 1918 with concerted Oct birding. Unclear why it would be included on the 1970 Summer Checklist, given the distribution of records. Prefers scrubby habitat, with several reports from the Burnt Head Trail area and the edge of the Ballfield; also noted along Lighthouse Rd., near the Trailing Yew, the Ice Pond and feeders. The 1934 report of unknown date was noted as a "winter bird" in correspondence dated Mar 26, so possibly a winter or early spring record; likely coming in to feeders. Consecutive-day reports may indicate lingering birds in some cases and are treated as such when the same number of inds. involved or fewer on the second or third day, such as the 2 inds. along Burnt Head Trail on Oct 30, 2010 and near the Trailing Yew on Oct 31 and the ind. noted on top of Horn's Hill on Jan 4–5, 2016. Several reports of calling and/or singing inds. in the fall.

Most records have been identified as Red Fox Sparrow (*P. i. iliaca*), the subspecies native to Eastern North America.

Historical/Regional:

- Palmer: 1 on Dec 23, 1939 as latest fall sighting (MJT).
- Vickery: cites 1 on Sep 30, 2004 (SWh) and 1 on Oct 14, 2010 (TMag) as early fall records (PDV in Vickery et al., 2020).

AMERICAN TREE SPARROW
Spizelloides arborea

Status: Rare spring and fall migrant, rare winter visitor.

Occurrence: Sixty-six records (23 spring, 20 fall, 23 winter) since 1906, undoubtedly underreported throughout. Spring records over only ten years since 1949 (the only records after 1967 being one in 2010, nine in 2011, one in 2013), span Mar 17–May 23; spring max: 3 on Mar 22, 2011 (TMag), 2 on Apr 7, 1967 (IF) & Apr 12, 2011 (TMag). Fall records over fourteen years since 1906, definite dates span Oct 14–Nov 19; fall max: 19 on Nov 8, 2020 (FK, DH), 4 on Nov 10, 2020 (FK, DH), 2 on Oct 18, 1989 (PDV), Nov 15, 2015 (DH), Nov 5, 2016 (LB et al.) & Nov 9, 2022 (LS, MWa). Winter records over eighteen years since 1939, definite dates span Dec 21–w/e Feb 16, most recent records (since 1980) associated with CBC period; winter max: **24** on Dec 27, 1984 (CBC–PDV), 9 on Jan 3, 2013 (CBC–DH, PM), 7 on Jan 4, 2013 (PDV, WN). Ten-Year: SP-1, F-5.

- CBC: 10 years (38%), first on Dec 30, 1980, max 24 on Dec 27, 1984, avg 2.2.
- 1900–1908 Reconnaissance & Supplements: unreported number Oct 14–15, 1906 (CFJ, ECJ).
- 1918 Fall Migration Census: Wentworth–Oct 17 (1), 19 (a few), 23 (1), 24 (several). Listed as Tree Sparrow.
- 1944–1967 Farrell Records: 1949–Mar, Apr; 1950–Feb, Mar, Apr, May, Nov, Dec; 1951–Jan, Mar, Nov, Dec; 1952–Feb, Mar, Nov; 1958–May; 1960–Apr; 1967–Apr 2 (1), 7 (2), 14, 15, 16. Listed as Tree Sparrow.

Lack of coverage throughout this species' migration periods and winter undoubtedly leads to underreporting and lack of status clarity; presumably scarce to fairly common in early spring (especially late Mar–early Apr; supported by the nine records in 2011, a season of consistent reports by TMag, and possibly involving lingering inds.), late fall, and throughout winter. Monthly reports from the 1944–1967 Farrell Records treated as separate records for these purposes, adding a significant number to the overall species status, highlighting the lack of recent reports. Max fall count of 19 on Nov 8, 2020 followed by 4 & 1 on Nov 9 & 10, respectively, and considered one record involving lingering birds here. Few details available. Two inds. arriving on Jan 8, 1939 continued at feeders through at least Jan 27 (MJT). There are single spring reports from Tribler Cottage and a feeder near the Monhegan House, a fall report from Burnt Head and presumably the same ind. at Lobster Cove the next day, and a winter report from Horn's Hill.

Historical/Regional:

- Vickery: cites 1 on May 23, 2013 (FM) as a recent late spring report (PDV in Vickery et al., 2020).

American Tree Sparrow, Nov 9, 2020. © Luke Seitz.

DARK-EYED JUNCO
Junco hyemalis

Status: Uncommon to fairly common (*presumably common*) spring and common to abundant fall migrant, rare summer visitor and possible breeder, uncommon to fairly common winter visitor, possible permanent resident.

Occurrence: Spring migration spans early Mar–late May, peak Apr (undoubtedly greatly underreported in late Mar/Apr); spring max: 100 on Apr 12, 2011 (TMag), 90 on Apr 29, 2011 (TMag), 80 on Apr 21, 2011 (TMag). Seventeen summer records over thirteen years since 1908 (only eight since 1918 and occurring after 2010, annual 2018–2022–see historical checklists below); summer max: 20 on Aug 4, 1917 (WT, BHW), 6 on Jul 29, 1917 (WT, CTa), 2 on Aug 11, 2010 (TMag) & Jun 21, 2019 (KD). Fall migration spans late Aug-late Nov; extended peak late Sep–early Nov; fall max: **5,000–10,000** over Oct 8–13, 1997 (SS; *FN* 52[1]: 32), 710 on Oct 12, 2014 (BBy et al.), 600 on Oct 9, 2001 (TV), 500 on Oct 30, 2010 (MI, LS, JT). Most winter records associated with CBC period; winter max: 57 on Dec 27, 1984 (CBC–PDV), 50+ on Jan 16, 2018 (KL), 48 on Jan 4, 2007 (CBC), 46 on Jan 2, 1997 (CBC–PDV). Ten-Year: SP-10, SU-5, F-10, W-5.

- *MABB*: confirmed.
- CBC: 22 years (85%), first on Dec 29, 1940, max 57 on Dec 27, 1984, avg 12.8; includes 1

"Oregon Junco" on Jan 2, 1997.
- 1899 Checklist: included as Junco.
- 1900–1908 Reconnaissance & Supplements: probably six or eight pairs on the island during May 31–Jun 6, 1908 (FA–listed as Slate-colored Junco); unreported number during Jul 31–Aug 2, 1908 (WM).
- 1909 Notes: very common in the woods; singing. Listed as Junco.
- 1914 & 1916 Checklists: unreported number on Aug 1, 1914; included as Junco 1916.
- 1915–1919 Taylor Journals: 1915–Aug 28 (1), 31 (50), Sep 2, 5, 12 (50); 1916–Aug 19, 20, 21, 22, 25, 26, 30, 31, Sep 3, 4, 6, 10; 1917–Jul 29 (6), Aug 4 (20), 16, Sep 5; 1918–prior to Aug 4; 1919–Sep 4 (10), 5 (6), 13 (1), 14 (2).
- 1918 Fall Migration Census: Dewis–Sep 4 (4), 8 (1), 10 (1), 11 (2), 12 (1); Wentworth–recorded eighteen days Oct 1–25, with very many on Oct 15, 16, 17, 19, many on 20, 22, 23, 24, and few on 21 & 25. Listed as Slate-colored Junco.
- 1944–1967 Farrell Records: 1949–Mar, Apr, Oct; 1950–Mar, Apr, May, Oct, Nov; 1951–Mar, Apr, Oct, Nov; 1952–Mar, Apr, Nov; 1958–May; 1959–May, Aug; 1960–Apr, May, Aug, Sep; 1961–Apr, May; 1967–Apr 2, 3, 5, 7, 8, 9, 14, 15 (2). Listed as Slate-colored Junco.
- 1970 Summer Checklist: marked as known to breed in area.
- Banding: 347 total over four seasons, peak 225 in Fall 1960, max 58 on Oct 9, 1960.

The true picture of this species' status is unclear, and complicated by the lack of coverage during peak times of its spring and fall migrations, as well as in the summer and winter. While possibly a permanent resident, there is no recent tangible evidence to support this, with no summer records after 1918 until 2010 (despite inclusion on 1970 Summer Checklist) and only one summer record each year 2018–2022, with no breeding reports in the MBA; all clear evidence seems to be from the *MABB* and prior. The lack of inclusion on the 1939 Summer Census and 1954 & 1955 Records may imply sporadic breeding on the island; its preference for nesting sites in coniferous forest may limit observations by birders concentrating on town and main trail locations. Inds. reported in late May/early Jun may refer to possible breeders or migrants (Jun 1 is considered the start of summer records for this purpose). Large movements are often two- or three-day events; however, the max count of 710 was preceded by 39 and followed by 10. The significant spring max counts all occurred in the one season with consistent coverage by TMag throughout, suggesting that eleveating the status to common is warranted at a minimum. While Monhegan is more heavily birded in late fall than early spring, coverage is nonetheless lacking and abundant counts may be more regular; the max count in 1997 is remarkable, but unclear as to a daily max and was part of a larger sparrow movement that included thousands of White-crowned Sparrows. A high count of 492 on Nov 9, 2020 (LS, JT) included an amazing 270+ on the lawn at The Mooring

Dark-eyed Junco, Oct 4, 2022. © Jeremiah Trimble.

Chain at the start of Mooring Chain Rd. (apparently mostly adult males), part of a four-day movement with counts of 320, 335, and 238 on Nov 8, 10 & 11, respectively (140+ still on the lawn at Mooring Chain–JT, LS). Undoubtedly underreported in winter after CBCs due to lack of coverage; onset of severe weather may reduce/eliminate winter presence (noted as new arrivals at feeders on Mar 8, 2019 [DC]). Possible anywhere on the island, particularly in the northern undeveloped areas and wherever there are stands of conifers; other notable reports include several hundred flying past the school at dawn and hundreds in the north wood during the max count on Oct 12, 2014 (BBy et al.) and 100+ on Black Head Rd. towards Cathedral Woods on Oct 11, 2010 (JM).

As expected, the majority of inds. have been identified as Slate-colored Junco (*J. h. hyemalis/carolinensis*). There have been three records of Oregon Junco (a western grouping of eight subspecies): 1 during third week of Feb 1984 (fide BT; *G* 13[2]: 19), bright female with Slate-coloreds on Jan 2, 1997 (CBC–PDV, DM), male on May 15, 2021 at The Mooring Chain (JT, LS, JO; ph.).

There is one record of Dark-eyed Junco x White-throated Sparrow hybrid: 1 on Apr 22, 2011 (TMag; ph.) along Lobster Cove Rd. near the Brewery.

Historical/Regional:

- Vickery: cites 90 on Apr 29, 2011 (TMag) as high spring count and lists six high fall counts (40–10,000 inds., includes top two max counts above); cites 46 on Jan 2, 1997 (PDV, DM) and 35 on Jan 5, 2016 (DH et al.) as high early-winter counts (PDV in Vickery et al., 2020).

Oregon Junco, The Mooring Chain, May 15, 2021. © Luke Seitz.

WHITE-CROWNED SPARROW
Zonotrichia leucophrys

Status: Uncommon to fairly common spring and fall migrant, accidental winter visitor.

Occurrence: Spring dates span May 4–Jun 16, peak middle two weeks of May; spring max: 80 on May 17, 2005 (TV), 75 on May 20, 2011 (DL), 45 on May 15, 2011 (LS), 40 on May 14, 2011 (TMag, LS) & May 21, 2011 (DL), 30 on May 13, 1997 (PDV). Fall dates span Sep 5–Nov 13, peak late Sep–late Oct; fall max: **3,000–5,000** over Oct 8–13,1997 (SS; *FN* 52[1]: 32), 200 on Oct 10, 2001 (TV), 175 on Sep 30, 2007 (DL), 108 on Nov 9, 2020 (JT, LS, HS), 100 on Oct 1, 2007 (DL). One winter record: 1 on Jan 5, 2010 (PDV). Ten-Year: SP-10, F-10.

- CBC: one year (4%), 1 on Jan 5, 2010, avg 0.0.
- 1918 Fall Migration Census: Wentworth–Oct 4, 7, 8 (two flocks about 6 each), 12, 13, 15, 16 (many), 17 (many), 19 (few), 20 (many), 21 (several), 23 (1), 24 (several).
- 1944–1967 Farrell Records: 1950–May, Oct; 1951–May; 1952–Oct; 1958–May; 1959–May; 1960–May; 1961–May; 1967–Jun 2 (1).
- 1970 Summer Checklist: included, with the subspecies Gambel's Sparrow (*Z. l. gambelii*) also listed as a separate species (likely included due to spring records–see discussion below).
- Banding: total 58 over nine seasons, peak 24 in Fall 1960, max 14 on Oct 10, 1960.

Large movements are often two- or three-day events; note consecutive-day high counts in the spring and fall maxima above. Spring 2011 was exceptional with eight consecutive days of 20+ inds. (May 14–21), including the max counts of 75, 45 & 40. The incredible max count from Oct 1997 was part of a massive sparrow movement that also involved thousands of Dark-eyed Juncos. Possible anywhere on the island and seen at many town locations, especially grassy areas, feeders, and spots with scattered seed. The 175 reported on Sep 30, 2007 involved most patches of lawn with at least a few feeders with 25+; seemingly an equal mix of adults and immatures (DL). Such a mix of adults and immatures is typical for the island in the fall, although 13 on Oct 4, 2020 were all immature (JT, LS, BBy) and there were "only a few adults" out of the 108 tallied on Oct 9, 2020 (JT, LS, HS). Inds. noted singing in both spring and fall.

As expected, the majority of inds. have been identified as *Z. l. leucophrys*. There have been four records (three spring, one fall) of the western race, Gambel's White-crowned Sparrow (*Z. l. gambelii*): 1

on Oct 4, 1976 (DF, WR; *AB* 31[2]: 231), 1 on May 15, 1977 (PDV, BCa; *AB* 31[5]: 976), 1 adult on May 5–6, 1984 (PDV, BSV, CDD; *AB* 38[5]: 887) & 1 on May 15–18, 2003 (PDV). An unknown spring or fall record is likely the reason for its inclusion on the 1970 Summer Checklist (despite being outside the stated Jul–Aug period). While Vickery states that *Z. l. gambelii* is "rare but regular on Monhegan in fall," records are provided (Vickery et al., 2020: 497).

Historical/Regional:

- Vickery: cites May 7, 1961 as an early spring report, lists four reports (12–45 inds.) as rare spring counts >8 inds. and three Jun records as late (latest 2 on Jun 13–16, 2006 (WBo); cites 3 on Sep 17, 2013 (PDV et al.) as representative of mid Sep, 175 on Sep 30, 2007 as a max count for late Sep (see discussion above) and three records of 8 inds. as more typical of late Sep, >60 on Oct 3, 1988 (PDV) illustrating that year as a flight year, 1 on Nov 18, 2003 (WBo) and 1 on Nov 16, 2005 (WBo) as late, and the max count of 3,000–5,000 from Oct 1997 as far exceeding any other known concentration (PDV in Vickery et al., 2020).

White-crowned Sparrow, Oct 14, 2019. © Bill Thompson.

HARRIS'S SPARROW
Zonotrichia querula

Status: Accidental spring and fall vagrant.

Occurrence: Spring record: 1 on Mar 24–May 8, 2012 (JB, DH, mob). Fall record: 1 in Oct 1970 (TMar personal notes). The 1970 record is the second for Maine (not yet reviewed by ME-BRC), the 2012 record is the ninth (accepted by ME-BRC #2012-012).

- 1970 Summer Checklist: included, noted as rare, casual, or accidental visitor.

The Oct 1970 ind. was seen in the backyard of the parsonage with Clay-colored and Lark Sparrows (TMar); the species' inclusion on the 1970 Summer Checklist may relate to this record, though it is outside the stated Jul–Aug period. The spring 2012 ind. was discovered near Deadman's Cove where it frequented the feeders at the Boegel residence throughout its stay, calling on occasion.

Historical/Regional:

- Vickery: cites 2012 record for spring (*Oct 1970 record not included*; PDV in Vickery et al., 2020).
- OLMB: ten additional state records—three accepted and seven not yet reviewed, earliest in 1965.

Harris's Sparrow, Apr 19, 2012. © Doug Hitchcox.

WHITE-THROATED SPARROW
Zonotrichia albicollis

Status: Fairly common to common (sometimes abundant) spring and common to abundant fall migrant, rare summer visitor and possible breeder, uncommon to fairly common winter visitor.

Occurrence: Spring migration spans late Mar–late May, peak late Apr–mid May; spring max: **600** on May 17, 2005 (TV), 150 on May 7, 1985 (PDV), 130 on Apr 29, 2011 (TMag). Thirty-nine summer records over twenty-one years since 1914 (twenty-three records since 1984), established breeding uncertain despite being confirmed for *MABB*, undoubtedly underreported throughout season; summer max: 6 on Aug 19, 1917 (WT) & Jul 19, 1984 (PDV), 5 on Jun 1, 2022 (DH et al.), 3 on Aug 4, 1917 (WT, BHW) & Jun 24, 2018 (KL), 2 on Aug 31, 1915 (WT), Aug 9, 2001 (SHu, BH), Aug 7, 2012 (DH), July 2, 2017 (LMa) & July 29, 2020 (GBr). Fall migration spans early Sep–late Nov, peak late Sep–late Oct; fall max: **600** on Oct 9, 2001 (TV), 400 on Oct 1, 1993 (BN), 315 on Oct 12, 2014 (BBy et al.). Winter reports scattered early

Dec–third week Mar, although most associated with CBC period and underreported throughout.; winter max: 26 on Dec 27, 1984 (CBC), 25 on Jan 16, 2018 (KL), 21 on Dec 27, 1984 (CBC), 20 on Jan 4, 2007 (CBC). Ten-Year: SP-10, SU-7, F-10, W-5.

- *MABB*: confirmed; MBA: possible.
- CBC: 23 years (88%), first on Dec 28, 1978, max 26 on Dec 27, 1984, avg 6.0.
- 1900–1908 Reconnaissance & Supplements: 1 on Oct 14, 1906 (CFJ, ECJ).
- 1914 & 1916 Checklists: unreported number on Aug 1, 1914; included 1916.
- 1915–1919 Taylor Journals: 1915–Aug 28, 31 (2), Sep 2, 5, 12 (100); 1916–Aug 20, 21, 22, Sep 10; 1917–Jul 29, Aug 4 (3), 18 (1), 19 (6), Sep 5 (3); 1919–Sep 13 (5), 14 (5).
- 1918 Fall Migration Census: Dewis–Sep 6 (1), 8 (3), 10 (1), 11 (2); Wentworth–Sep 29, Oct 1, 4, 6, 7, 8, 9, 12, 13, many on 15, 16, 17, 19, & 20, several on 21, 22, & 23, many on 24.
- 1944–1967 Farrell Records: 1949–Apr, May, Sep, Oct; 1950–Apr, May, Oct, Nov; 1951–Apr, May, Oct; 1952–Nov; 1954–Jun, Jul; 1955–Jun, Jul, Aug; 1958–Oct; 1959–May, Jun, Jul, Aug; 1960–Apr, May, Jul, Aug, Sep; 1961–Apr, May; 1967–Apr 23, 24 (1).
- 1954 & 1955 Summer Records: 1954–included all three checklists; 1955–included Jun 11–15 & Jun 30–Jul 5.
- 1970 Summer Checklist: highlighted (*possibly marked as known to breed in area–likely typo of : instead of **).
- Banding: 125 total over nine seasons, peak 53 in Fall 1960, max 21 on Oct 8, 1961.

Largest numbers often arrive in a wave, becoming ubiquitous and sometimes remaining three days or more. The high count of 315 on Oct 12, 2014 included many in the woods at the north end of the island (BBa et al.), while a count of 264 on Oct 4, 2020 involved "amazing numbers, even in dense forest covering the ground and all over town and seeded areas, 30–40 together in groups" (JT, LS, BBy). Better coverage throughout the year would provide a more complete picture of status, including more high counts in Apr and Oct. As almost all populations are migratory, it is unlikely that any possible Monhegan breeders remain as permanent residents, but are instead replaced by northern migrants in winter. One pair on Aug 7, 2012 was considered aggressive (DH–*possibly defending a second brood?*) A singing ind. on Jun 24, 2018 (KL) provided the basis for its status on the MBA. May be similar to Dark-eyed Junco in apparent intermittent breeding, evidenced by lack of inclusion on 1939 Census and appearance on all checklists in 1954 Records. Likely to be found at feeders during the winter.

There is one record of Dark-eyed Junco x White-throated Sparrow hybrid: 1 on Apr 22, 2011 (TMag; ph.) at a feeder along Lobster Cove Rd. near the Brewery.

Historical/Regional:

- Vickery: cites 10 on Mar 15, 2011 (TMag) as early spring, counts of 35 on May 6, 2017 (DH), 80 on May 13, 1997 (PDV, DAb) and 48 on May 17, 2013 (KL) as expected in south coastal ME, and 10 on May 26, 1983 as notable for lateness; lists five high fall counts 50–315 (*only the 315 ind. day included in max counts above*), and 53 on Nov 2, 2010 (TMag) as a flock in early Nov (PDV in Vickery et al., 2020).

White-throated Sparrow x Dark-eyed Junco hybrid, Lobster Cover Rd., Apr 22, 2011. © Tom Magarian.

VESPER SPARROW
Pooecetes gramineus

Status: Very rare spring and rare fall migrant, very rare summer visitor and possible former breeder (historical).

Occurrence: Thirty-nine records (6 spring, 4 summer, 28 fall, 1 unknown date) since first recorded in 1899. Spring records: unreported number during May 1951 (IF), unreported number during Apr 1960 (IF), 1 on May 6–7, 1985 (PDV), 1 on May 28, 1987 (PDV, JS), 2 on May 8, 2011 (TMag), 1 on May 17–22, 2019 (BP et al.). Four summer records: unreported number during Jul 31–Aug 2, 1908 (WM), unreported number on Aug 1, 1914, unreported number during Jun 1959 (IF), unreported number during Aug 1959 (IF). Fall records over eighteen years since 1918 (five records in 1918), span Sep 6–week of Dec 3; fall max: **3** on Oct 14, 1982 (PDV), 2 on Oct 13, 1982 (PDV), Oct 9–10, 1983 (JVW), Oct 17, 1986 (PDV) & Oct 8,

2011 (JM); note "a few" Oct 19–20, 1918 (see below). Unknown date: unreported number in 1899 (MEH). Ten-Year: SP-1, F-6.

- 1899 Checklist: included.
- 1900–1908 Reconnaissance & Supplements: unreported number during Jul 31–Aug 2, 1908 (WM).
- 1914 & 1916 Checklists: unreported number on Aug 1, 1914 (WF).
- 1918 Fall Migration Census: Dewis–Sep 6 (1), 11 (1); Wentworth–Oct 8, 17, 19 (a few), 20 (a few), 21 (1).
- 1944–1967 Farrell Records: 1951–May; 1959–Jun, Aug; 1960–Apr.
- 1970 Summer Checklist: included.
- Banding: 5 in Fall 1960, max 3 on Oct 10, 1960 (2 on Oct 9).

Declined in numbers through much of the 1900s, supported by the records from the early 1900s, especially 1918 (considered five records for this purpose, with those Oct 19–21 grouped as one); possibly bred at that time, suggested by the two summer records and more appropriate habitat (agricultural and cleared lands). Undoubtedly underreported in late fall. Lingers on occasion, such as inds. coming to seed at the end of Wharton Ave Oct 11–13, 2014 & Oct 1–3, 2018 and an ind. visiting the pumpkin garden along the edge of the Meadow on May 17–22, 2019. Other locations have included the grass at the edge of the Ballfield, Lobster Cove, the open area at the top of Horn's Hill and associating with a flock of Dark-eyed Juncos near the Ice Pond.

Historical/Regional:

- Palmer: lists a late date of week of Dec 3, 1939 (MJT).
- Vickery: cites 1 on Dec 3, 1939 (MJAT–*actually listed in Palmer as week of Dec 3*) as late (PDV in Vickery et al., 2020).

Vesper Sparrow, Oct 2, 2021. © Jeremiah Trimble.

LECONTE'S SPARROW
Ammospiza leconteii

Status: Very rare fall migrant.

Occurrence: Three records: 1 on Oct 1974 (DF et al.; ph.; Vickery, 1978: 20), 1 on Oct 8, 2007 (DF [personal comm.], DAb, BAk), adult on Oct 7, 2012 (LBr et al.). Second, fourth, and sixth Maine records; 2012 record accepted by ME-BRC #2012–030, 1974 record not yet reviewed, 2007 record not listed on OLMB.

The Oct 1974 ind. was observed at the end of the path by Squeaker Cove (DF). The Oct 2007 ind. was observed along the Underhill Trail. The Oct 2012 ind. continued throughout the day at the Lobster Cove meadow.

Historical/Regional:

- Vickery: cites the 1974 and 2012 records above (PDV in Vickery et al., 2020).
- OLMB: seven additional state records—four accepted and three not yet reviewed, earliest in 1968.

SEASIDE SPARROW
Ammospiza maritima

Status: Very rare fall migrant.

Occurrence: Four records: 1 on Aug 18, 1975 (AKe; *AB* 30[1]: 35), 1 on Sep 14, 1981 (PDV), 1 in early Oct, 1997 (SS; *AB* 52[1]: 33), 1 juvenile on Oct 6–10, 2014 (JT et al.). Ten-Year: F-1.

The Sep 1981 ind. was in the Lobster Cove meadow. The Oct 2014 ind. was also at Lobster Cove, observed on the 6th and the 10th.

Historical/Regional:

- Vickery: cites the latter three records above for fall (PDV in Vickery et al., 2020).

NELSON'S SPARROW
Ammospiza nelsoni

Status: Very rare spring and rare fall migrant.

Occurrence: Twenty-three records (8 spring, 15 fall) since 1982. Spring records over seven years since 1995, span May 21–Jun 7: 1 on May 21, 1995 (WJS), 2 on Jun 3, 2007 (JSc), 2 on May 29, 2011 (TMag), 1 on May 24, 2015 (JT, JO, BN), 1 on May 29, 2016 (DL, JL), 1 on May 23, 2019 (MC, CC), 1 on May 28, 2019 (JT, JO, MI), 1 on Jun 7, 2020 (JT, LS). Fall records over twelve years since 1982, span Sep 23–Oct 12;

LeConte's Sparrow, meadow at Lobster Cove, Oct 7, 2012. © Jeremiah Trimble.

fall max: **7** on Oct 4, 2020 (JT, LS, BBy), 3 on Sep 28, 1984 (PDV), Sep 28, 2013 (SS, JG) & Oct 12, 2014 (BVD et al.), 2 on Sep 23, 1983 (JSm), Oct 1, 2005 (JT), Sep 28, 2013 (JG) & Sep 30, 2022 (DH). Ten-Year: SP-4, F-5.

- 1914 & 1916 Checklists: included as Sharp-tailed Sparrow 1916 (former combined species with Saltmarsh Sparrow–see below).
- 1939 Summer Census: rare summer visitor; included as Sharp-tailed Sparrow (former combined species with Saltmarsh Sparrow–see below).

Eight of the records (including two in spring) occurred at Lobster Cove, probably all in the wet meadow (only three explicitly say so), including two of the fall max counts of three inds.; the only other record to mention location is the fall max count of 7, with 1 at the Brewery, 1 along the shore of the inner harbor and 5 at the Meadow (including a mix of subspecies–see below). The longest-staying ind. appears to be Oct 5–7, 2012, and it may have been the same ind. reported on Sep 29; 1 on Oct 5, 2020 (DL, JL) and 1 on Oct 8, 2020 (JT, LS, CHi) likely a lingering ind. or inds. from the 7 on Oct 4 (the Oct 8 ind. considered a separate record due to gap in days). All other records were single-day events, except probably the single ind. on Oct 11, 2014 remaining to be part of the three reported the next day.

The taxonomy of Nelson's Sparrow and Saltmarsh Sparrow is complicated and intertwined, as Sharp-tailed Sparrow, until split into current status in 1998. Seven records of Sharp-tailed Sparrow (unreported number during Aug 16–Sep 16 (MCG), 1 on Sep 13, 1919, unreported number during Aug 1955, May 1959, Aug 1959 & May 1960 and 1 during May 29–31, 1993) cannot be separated for certain, but were most likely Nelson's Sparrows; one eBird record of Saltmarsh Sparrow, 1 on Oct 6, 1990, is now considered inconclusive and possibly a Nelson's Sparrow.

Two subspecific groups of Nelson's Sparrow have been reported on a regular basis: the duller plumaged, maritime Atlantic Nelson's Sparrow (*A. n. subvirgata*, which breeds in small numbers in the coastal marshes of Maine) and the brighter-plumaged Interior Nelson's Sparrow (includes nominate *A. n. nelsoni* and *A. n. altera*, which breed in the northern midwest and along Hudson and James Bays, respectively). There have been two spring (involving two inds.) and nine fall records (involving 15 inds.) of Atlantic and five fall records of Interior (involving 8 inds., including all three on Sep 28, 1984). Notably, there are three occasions when both subspecies occurred together (1 each on Sep 26, 1986, 2 Atlantic and 1 Interior on Oct 12, 2014 and 4 Atlantic and 1 Interior on Oct 4, 2021 [two other separate Atlantic inds. that day]) and one other occurrence of both reported on the same day (1 Atlantic and 2 Interior on Sep 28, 2013).

Historical/Regional:

- Vickery: cites fall 2013 and 2014 records of *A. n. nelsoni/altera* (PDV in Vickery et al., 2020).

Nelson's Sparrow (Atlantic), meadow at Lobster Cove, Oct 11, 2014. © Jeremiah Trimble.

Nelson's Sparrow (Interior), meadow at Lobster Cove, Oct 5, 2020. © Luke Seitz.

HENSLOW'S SPARROW
Centronyx henslowii

Status: Very rare spring and fall migrant.

Occurrence: Four records (2 spring, 2 fall) span 1983–2003, all singles. Spring records: May 20, 1983 (PDV, CDD; *AB* 37[6]: 969), adult on May 25–28, 1984 (JP, EP, SS; *AB* 38[5]: 887). Fall records: Oct 1–6, 1997 (JT, BN, mob; *FN* 52: 32), Oct 3, 2003 (JT). The 1983 and 2003 records accepted by ME-BRC (#1983–001 & #2003–004, respectively), 1984 not yet reviewed, 1997 (listed only for Oct 3) not accepted due to lack of any documentation, but included here.

Declining since the mid 1900s in the Northeast; nearest breeding now in NY (Herkert et al., 2020), but never documented in Maine. Interesting that the only spring records occurred in consecutive years—same ind.? The May 1983 ind. was observed in the brush near the Meadow behind the Monhegan House. The Oct 1997 ind. was observed for many hours at the start of the Underhill Trail along Lobster Cove Rd. There is one other possible record for Monhegan with an unclear date and no details: Sep 21 in 2005 or 2006 (fide MAS–listed on OLMB as not yet reviewed).

Historical/Regional:

- Vickery: cites four records above (PDV in Vickery et al., 2020).
- OLMB: seven additional state records – two accepted, five not yet reviewed, earliest in 1969.

SAVANNAH SPARROW
Passerculus sandwichensis

Status: Fairly common to common spring and fall migrant, rare summer visitor and possible breeder, accidental winter visitor.

Occurrence: Spring dates span Mar 20–early Jun, peak late Apr–mid May; spring max: 175 on May 14, 2011 (LS), 143 on May 14, 2021 (JT, LS, JO), 112 on Apr 27, 2011 (TMag), 100 on Apr 30, 2011 (TMag) & May 13, 2011 (DH). Twenty-seven summer records over only sixteen years since 1908, with only four since 2001 (1954 accounting for four records, 1917 & 1955 three each, 1908, 1916, 1959 & 1960 two each [many of unreported number], excludes *MABB*–see below), historical breeder; summer max: 25 on Aug 9, 1915 (WT, CFJ), 13 on May 31, 1908 (FA) & Jun 2, 1908 (FA), 3 on Aug 9, 2001 (BH, SHu), 2 on Aug 16, 2015 (PBm). Fall dates span early Sep–Nov 10, peak late Sep–mid Oct; fall max: **800** on Oct 4, 2012

(DH), 500 on Sep 20, 1964 (RLP; *AFN* 19[1]: 15), 275 on Sep 24, 2009 (LS), 200 on Sep 25, 2009 (LS). One winter record: 1 on Dec 28, 1982 (CBC–PDV). Ten-Year: SP-10, SU-2, F-10.

- *MABB*: confirmed.
- CBC: recorded 1 year (4%), 1 on Dec 28, 1982, avg 0.0.
- 1900–1908 Reconnaissance & Supplements: commonest land bird on the island during May 31–Jun 6, 1908 (FA)—11 singing and one pair engaged in courtship on May 31, 13 seen (9 singing) on Jun 2, other days fewer, but undoubtedly more pairs on island than these numbers indicate; unreported number during Jul 31–Aug 2, 1908 (WM–listed as Savanna Sparrow).
- 1909 Notes: common in the fields, males singing.
- 1914 & 1916 Checklists: unreported number on Aug 1, 1914 (listed as Savanna Sparrow); included as Savanna Sparrow 1916.
- 1915–1919 Taylor Journals: 1915–Aug 9 (25); 1916–Aug 19, 20, 21, 22, 31, Sep 3, 6, 10; 1917–Jul 29, Aug 5, 16, Sep 8 (5); 1918–Aug 28; 1919–Sep 3 (4), 4 (1), 5 (2), 13 (3). Listed as Savanna Sparrow.
- 1918 Fall Migration Census: Dewis–Sep 6 (1), 10 (1); Wentworth–Sep 29, Oct 8, 9, 12, 17 (many), 19 (few), 21 (1), 24 (3).
- 1939 Summer Census: regular summer resident.
- 1944–1967 Farrell Records: 1950–May; 1954–Jun, Jul, Aug; 1955–Jun, Jul, Aug; 1957–Aug; 1958–May; 1959–May, Jul, Aug; 1960–Apr, May, Jul, Aug, Sep; 1961–Apr, May; 1967–Apr 2 (1 Ipswich), 23 (1).
- 1954 & 1955 Summer Records: 1954–included all three checklists; 1955–included Jun 11–15 & Jun 30–Jul 5.
- 1970 Summer Checklist: highlighted and marked as known to breed in area.
- Banding: total 494 over 9 seasons, peak 223 in Fall 1962, max 56 on Oct 5, 1962.

Undoubtedly underreported in Apr and Oct due to lack of coverage. The earliest spring record on Mar 20, 2022 at Pebble Beach (KL) was an "Ipswich" Savannah Sparrow (see below); the next earliest record is Apr 6. Large movements are often multi-day events. Spring 2011 was exceptional, with the max counts occurring in two pulses. Conversely, after 800 on Oct 4, 2012, only 61 were reported the next day. The 275 and 200 on Sep 24 & 25, 2009 were actually one movement, with nocturnal listening from 10:30–11:30 p.m. yielding the entire count on the 24th (LS, WR, EO–sparrows and many thrushes) and predawn listening combined with extensive coverage of the southern half of the island yielding the count of the 25th (LS–~80 predawn, remaining scattered, including ~20 at Lobster Cove, ~20 at the Ballfield, ~15 at TMar's feeders, ~30 behind the school). While often reported from many town birding locations, including feeders and road edges, the most reliable locations are the wet meadow at Lobster Cove and the Meadow edges. The incredible 800 on Oct 4, 2012 were "everywhere", with 60+ in the Hitchcock yard, a few hundred through town, notably along the Meadow and behind post office, and 100+ around Lobster Cove (DH). Part of the 196 on Sep 30, 2019 involved 50–75 moving across the Meadow (JT, LS, AO). Five were recorded on Eastern Duck Rock on Sep 8, 1917 (WT, CTa). While a decline in summer numbers is to be expected from the early 1900s, when much of the island had been cleared of trees and fields for livestock undoubtedly provided more suitable breeding habitat, the sparsity of recent summer records and no clear breeding evidence since the *MABB* is a surprise (despite inadequate coverage); this abundance of sightings from the early 1900s–1950s is evident in the historical checklists above.

While many records have been identified as the expected subspecies (*P. s. sandwichensis* group), there are fifteen records (5 spring, 10 fall) of the distinctive subspecies "Ipswich Sparrow" (*P. s. princeps*), which breeds on Sable Island, Nova Scotia and has a separate migration and wintering distribution. Spring records: 1 on Apr 2, 1967 (IF), unreported number w/e May 22, 2001 (WBo, TV), 1 on Apr 6, 2013 (DH–feeding in the wrack at Swim Beach), 1 on Apr 6, 2018 (DC–in yard), 1 on Mar 20, 2022 (KL–Pebble Beach). Fall records over nine years since 1929 (all but one since 2001), span Sep 12–Nov 10; max: 3 on Nov 9, 2020 (LS, JT), 2 on Oct 6, 2005 (MI, AM–Lobster Cove) & Oct 2, 2010 (NH). Reports of 1 on Oct 3, 2010 and an unreported number on Oct 4, 2010 are considered the same record (lingering ind.) and the only one involving multiple days. Fall locations include Lobster Cove (four records), Fish Beach, Burnt Head and the yard at the Mooring Chain. This subspecies is likely underreported due to lack of coverage during its most expected period of mid fall–mid spring.

Historical/Regional:

- Palmer: "Ipswich Sparrow" listed as separate species: one of four spring Maine records listed was on Monhegan in 1940 (MJT).
- Vickery: cites >30 Savannah Sparrows on May 12, 1997, >25 on May 13, 1997 (PDV, DAb) and 37 on May 15, 2011 (TMag) as high spring

counts and 30 on Sep 25, 1983 and 12 on Oct 21, 2017 (JP) as typical; cites 1 on Sep 22, 2008 (JM) and Sep 30, 2007 (DL) as early for "Ipswich" Savannah Sparrow (PDV in Vickery et al., 2020).

Ipswich Savannah Sparrow, Oct 9, 2021. © Luke Seitz.

Savannah Sparrow, May 25, 2019. © Jeremiah Trimble.

SONG SPARROW
Melospiza melodia

Status: Fairly common permanent resident, fairly common spring and fairly common to common fall migrant.

Occurrence: Noticeably present in limited but fairly consistent numbers throughout the year (lowest in winter), supplemented and complicated by migrants; surely underreported in summer and late fall to early spring due to lack of coverage. Spring migration early Mar–end May (transitioning to breeding/residents), peak late Mar–late Apr; spring max: 75 on Apr 5 & 6, 2011 (TMag), 50 on Apr 9, 2011 (TMag), 46 on Apr 12, 2011 (TMag), 40 on May 25, 2021 (BTh) & May 16, 2022 (LS, MWa). Breeding occurs May–Aug (nest-building by late May); summer max: 50 on Jul 15, 2021 (BTh), 35 on Jul 12, 2021 (BTh), 31 on Jun 9, 2021 (JFo), 30 on Aug 17, 2006 (PDV), 29 on Jun 12, 2018 (DH). Fall migration early Sep–early Dec, peak late Sep–late Oct; fall max: **254** on Nov 9, 2020 (LS, JT), 180 on Oct 9, 2020 (JT, LS, HS), 120 on Nov 8, 2020 (FK, DH), 114 on Nov 10, 2020 (LS, JT), 92 on Oct 12, 2014 (BBy et al.), 67 on Oct 10, 1960 (banded). Winter numbers possibly affected by severity of weather conditions; winter max: 34 on Jan 4, 2007 (CBC), 24 on Dec 27, 1994 (CBC–PDV) & Dec 27, 2004 (PDV), 13 on Dec 28, 1987 (PDV). Ten-Year: SP-10, SU-10, F-10, W-6.

- *MABB*: confirmed; MBA: confirmed.
- CBC: 26 years (100%), max 34 on Jan 4, 2007, avg 7.2.
- 1899 Checklist: included.
- 1900–1908 Reconnaissance & Supplements: six or fewer singing males on any one day during May 31–Jun 6, 1908, but probably a higher number of pairs (FA); unreported number during Jul 31–Aug 2, 1908 (WM).
- 1909 Notes: common on margins of fields, singing.
- 1914 & 1916 Checklists: unreported number Jul 31, 1914; included 1916.
- 1915–1919 Taylor Journals: 1915–Aug 9 (10), 16, 31 (1), Sep 2 (1), 12 (1); 1916–Aug 19, 20, 21, 22, 25, 26, 31, Sep 3, 4, 6, 10; 1917–Jul 29, Aug 4, 16, Sep 5; 1918–prior to Aug 4, Aug 28; 1919–Sep 3 (6), 4 (5), 5 (2), 11 (1), 13 (2), 14 (4).
- 1918 Fall Migration Census: Dewis–Sep 4 (4), 5 (1), 6 (1), 7 (2), 8 (4), 10 (2), 11 (2), 12 (2); Wentworth–Sep 29, Oct 6, 7, 8, 9, 12, very many on 13, 15, 16, 17, & 19, 20 (many), 21 (few), many on 22, 23, 24, 25 (few), Nov 1.
- 1939 Summer Census: regular summer resident.
- 1944–1967 Farrell Records: 1949–Mar, Apr, Sep; 1950–Mar, Apr, May, Oct, Nov; 1951–Mar, Apr, May, Sep, Oct, Nov; 1952–Mar, Apr, Nov; 1954–Jun, Jul; 1955–Jun, Jul, Aug; 1957–Aug; 1958–May, Jun, Aug, Oct; 1959–Mar, May, Jun, Jul, Aug; 1960–Apr, May, Jun, Jul, Aug, Sep; 1961–Apr, May; 1967–Apr 2, 3, 4, 5, 7, 8, 9, 10, 11, 12, 13, 14, 15, 16, 17, 18, 24, Jun 1 (2), 3 (1), 5 (2), 6 (1), 7 (1), 8 (1).
- 1954 & 1955 Summer Records: 1954–included all three checklists; 1955–included Jun 11–15 & Jun 30–Jul 5.
- 1970 Summer Checklist: highlighted and marked as known to breed in area.
- Banding: 503 over eleven seasons, peak 244 in Fall 1960, max 67 on Oct 10, 1960.

While present year-round, particularly in scrub habitat and around feeders/scattered seed, it is unclear whether inds. present in winter are lingering breeders or northern visitors. Predominance of winter sightings centered around CBC period, with few later season reports of lesser numbers, possibly indicating departure of inds. due to harsh conditions. MJT reports a "very tame" ind. present at the feeder all winter (1933–1934), attempting song all day long ("a few squabbles now and then") on Mar 20 and in full song on Mar 21; on Jan 26, 1939 an ind. sang at the "top of his voice" for three others nearby (MJT). The early spring and late fall timing of migration leads to underreporting, supported by the max spring counts all occurring in 2011 (a season with consistent reporting by TMag) and exceptional movement in fall 2020, providing max counts much higher than other years. Larger movements, spring and fall, are sometimes multi-day events; Fall 2020 movement concentrated Oct 9-10 & Nov 8–12. Few details of breeding outside MBA, but consistent presence through the years; carrying nesting material noted as early as May 25, 2019 (collecting dog hair at Donna Cundy's–GP), carrying food and feeding young reports span May 30–Jul 2 and recently fledged young reported Jun 11–Jul 19. While possible anywhere with deciduous scrub and even mixed woodlands, and everywhere during large movements, favored locations include feeders, spots near/at scattered seed (Ballfield, Wharton Ave., scrubby swale along Ocean Ave., Meadow edges (including pump house area and behind Monhegan House), and the Lobster Cove meadow; groups of 5–10 with mixed flocks of White-throated Sparrow, White-crowned Sparrow, and Chipping Sparrow and in all areas of the island on Oct 9, 2020 (JT, LS, HS– counts of 60+ on Mooring Chain lawn), 40 at the Wharton Rd. cul-de-sac and 42 on Swim Beach as part of the 254 reported on Nov 9, 2020 (LS, JT). Noted singing spring–fall.

Song Sparrow, May 21, 2007. © Geoff Dennis.

LINCOLN'S SPARROW
Melospiza lincolnii

Status: Uncommon to fairly common spring and fall migrant, accidental winter visitor.

Occurrence: Spring dates span May 7–Jun 7, peak mid–late May; spring max: **40+** on May 25, 1983 (ST; *AB* 37[5]: 845), 25 on May 25, 1990 (JVW), 12 on May 24, 1997 (LBr). Fall dates span Aug 30–Nov 10, peak mid Sep–mid Oct; fall max: 36 on Oct 3, 2020 (JT, LS), 32 on Sep 10, 1964 (RLP; *AFN* 19[1]: 15), >25 on Sep 16, 1982 (observer unknown), 25 on Sep 20, 1964 (RLP; *AFN* 19[1]: 15), 20 on Sep 26, 2002 (JT) & Sep 22, 2004 (MI). Winter record: 1 on Dec 27, 1984 (CBC–PDV). Ten-Year: SP-9, F-10.

- CBC: one year (4%), Dec 27, 1984, avg 0.0.
- 1915–1919 Taylor Journals: 1919–Sep 13 (1).
- 1918 Fall Migration Census: Dewis–Sep 6 (1), noted as "one of the three most important birds seen"; Wentworth–Sep 29, Oct 17 (several).
- 1970 Summer Checklist: included.
- Banding: 26 over seven seasons, peak 13 in Fall 1962, max 8 on Oct 3, 1962.

Reported from many town birding locations, often in deciduous scrub, notably the edge of the Meadow and the wet meadow near Lobster Cove, also scattered seed and feeders, the Ballfield and Verizon Tower, along Lobster Cove Rd. and behind the school, among other places; the max count on Oct 3, 2020 involved birds throughout town, including groups of 3–5, and even a few in spruce woods (JT, LS). The unexpected winter record was along the edge of the Meadow near Tribler Rd (PDV). Many were heard singing on May 14, 2021 (total 11 reported that day– JT, LS, JO).

Historical/Regional:

- Palmer: cites Wentworth Oct 17, 1918 record as the late date.
- Vickery: cites three of the spring max counts above (including top two) as concentrations on outer islands and 1 on Jun 7, 2005 (WBo) as latest spring record, and top two fall max counts as large concentrations on outer islands and 1 on Nov 5, 2016 (DH, LB, FK) as late; cites winter record above (PDV in Vickery et al., 2020).

Lincoln's Sparrow, Oct 8, 2016. © Luke Seitz.

SWAMP SPARROW
Melospiza georgiana

Status: Uncommon spring and fairly common fall migrant, very rare summer visitor and possible breeder, rare winter visitor.

Occurrence: Spring migration spans Mar 21–end of May, peak late Apr–mid May; spring max: 65 on May 19, 2003 (TV), 38 on May 16, 2022 (LS, MWa), 23 on May 17, 2022 (LS, MWa), 15 on May 7, 1985 (PDV) & May 25, 1990 (JVW). Eight summer records over seven years since 1984 (excludes *MABB*, note 1939 Census): 1 on Jul 19, 1984 (PDV), 1 on Aug 2, 1999 (GS), 1 on Jun 3, 2008 (JSc), unreported number on Jul 8, 2008 (DB), 1 on Aug 29, 2014 (GMa), 1 on Jun 8, 2016 (FK, KLi), 1 on Jun 4, 2020 (DR), 1 on Aug 14, 2022 (LS, MWa). Fall migration early Sep–late Nov, peak late Sep–late Oct; fall max: **>100** on Oct 1, 1993 (BN), 50 on Sep 25, 1994 (PDV), Sep 26, 2002 (JT) & Oct 4, 2012 (DH), 40 on Oct 1, 1983 (PDV). Thirteen winter records over thirteen years since 1980, all associated with the CBC period or similar timing, span only Dec 27–Jan 5; winter max: 7 on Jan 4, 2007 (CBC), 4 on Jan 2, 2020 (CBC–DH), 2 on Dec 27, 1984 (CBC–PDV) & Jan 1, 1992 (CBC–PDV). Ten-Year: SP-9, SU-4, F-10, W-3.

- *MABB*: possible.
- CBC: 11 years (42%) plus one count week, first on Dec 30, 1980, max 7 on Jan 4, 2007, avg 0.9.
- 1915–1919 Taylor Journals: 1916–Sep 6 (2).
- 1918 Fall Migration Census: Wentworth–Oct 17 (several), 19 (few), 23 (1), 24 (many), 25 (few).
- 1939 Summer Census: regular summer resident.
- 1944–1967 Farrell Records: 1950–May; 1960–May.
- 1970 Summer Checklist: included.
- Banding: 106 total over eleven seasons, peak 31 in Fall 1961 & Fall 1962, max 10 on Oct 8, 1961 & Oct 5, 1962.

Larger movements are often two- to four-day events, whether new arrivals or lingering inds.; undoubtedly underreported in later fall (Oct–Nov). Winter visitors may be "pushed" out by harsh weather, as there are no records after Jan 5, but possibly underreported. Most often found in thickets and wet areas, especially the edge of the Meadow, including 12 in view at once on Oct 11, 2014 (JT), and the wet meadow at Lobster Cove, but also reported from feeders, along Trail #1, behind the school, the swale on Ocean Dr. and other scattered town locations. Nocturnal listening from 10:30–11:30 p.m. on Sep 24, 2009 yielded 3 as part of a large movement of sparrows and thrushes (LS, WR, EO); 30 were around the island the next day (LS).

Historical/Regional:
- Vickery: cites 2 on Mar 21, 2012 (TMag) as early spring and >10 on May 13, 1997 (DAb, PDV), 5 on May 26, 1983 (ST), and 5 on Apr 28–29, 2011 (TMag) as unusual concentrations; cites five records as early (earliest Sep 2) and six records as "many birds noted by late Sep" (15–100+ inds. spanning Sep 24–Oct 1–*only the top max count above is included*); present on eight CBCs, max 7 inds. (PDV in Vickery et al., 2020).

Swamp Sparrow, Sep 21, 2020. © Bill Thompson.

EASTERN TOWHEE
Pipilo erythrophthalmus

Status: Scarce to uncommon spring and fall migrant, very rare summer visitor and possible breeder, very rare winter visitor.

Occurrence: Spring dates span Apr 13–early Jun, peak late Apr–mid May; spring max: **12** on May 6, 1985 (PDV) & May 13–14, 1997 (PDV), 5 on May 17, 1997 (RSh), 4 on May 19, 2021 (RG). Six summer records over six years since 1954 (excludes *MABB*): unreported number during Jun 27–Jul 4, 1954 (FNR, MFNR), 1 on Jul 19, 1984 (PDV), 1 singing male during Jun 27–29, 2005 (DL, JL), 1 on Jul 1, 2014 (DSk), 1 on Jun 18, 2018 (TEv), 1 on Jun 13, 2020 (DH). Fall dates span Sep 4–Nov 21, peak late Sep–mid Oct; fall max: 8 on Oct 7, 2010 (SS), 6 on Oct 14, 1982 (PDV), 5 on Oct 7, 2014 (BN et al.). Three winter records, all associated with CBC period: 1 on Dec 28, 1983 (CBC count week–PDV), 1 during Dec 24–30, 1984 (CBC count week), 1 on Jan 1, 1991 (CBC–PDV). Ten-Year: S-9, SU-3, F-10.

- *MABB*: possible; MBA: possible.
- CBC: 1 year (4%) plus two count weeks (1984, 1985), 1 on Jan 1, 1991, avg 0.0.
- 1944–1967 Farrell Records: 1951–May, Oct; 1954–Jun, Jul; 1955–Aug; 1959–May, Jul, Aug; 1960–Apr, May; 1961–Apr, May.

- 1954 & 1955 Summer Records: 1954–included Jun 27–Jul 4.
- 1970 Summer Checklist: included as Rufous-sided Towhee and marked as known to breed in area.
- Banding: total 2 in Fall 1962; 1 on Oct 5, 1960 & Oct 9, 1960.

Doubtless underreported in Apr and Oct due to lack of coverage. No clear evidence for breeding, despite inclusion as possible in *MABB* & *MBA* and designation on 1970 Checklist; MBA status based on an ind. singing on Jun 4, 2019, but may involve a very late migrant. Inds. known to linger for at least a couple of days. Reported from scrub habitat at many typical town birding locations, such as near the Ice Pond, Lobster Cove Rd., Ocean Ave., Underhill Trail, and near White Head; also at Donna Cundy's feeders (Apr & May). Often heard calling.

Historical/Regional:

- Vickery: 1–2 inds. regular Sep 28–Oct 17, but not annual in fall; cites 1 on Nov 4, 1988 (WBo) as notable (PDV in Vickery et al., 2020).

Eastern Towhee, Oct 14, 2019. © Bill Thompson.

YELLOW-BREASTED CHAT
Icteria virens

Status: Very rare spring and scarce fall vagrant, very rare winter vagrant.

Occurrence: Four spring records, all single birds spanning May 16–25: May 25, 1981 (JP, EP), May 23, 1987 (SS), May 21, 2010 (EG), May 16, 2017 (RM). Fall dates span Aug 22–Nov 21, peak mid Sep–mid Oct; fall max: **4** on Oct 9, 1960 (banded), Sep 25–26, 2002 (JT) & Sep 20, 2016 (RH), 3 on four dates. Two winter records: 1 on Dec 18, 2009 (fide EH, SWh, MARBA), 1 on Jan 2, 2020 (CBC–DH). Ten-Year: SP-1, F-9, W-1.

- CBC: 1 year (4%), 1 on Jan 2, 2020, avg 0.0.
- 1944–1967 Farrell Records: 1953–Aug; 1955–Aug; 1960–Aug.
- 1954 & 1955 Summer Records: 1955–Aug 22 (1), 30 (1), Sep 2 (MLn, MEAB); noted as possibly involving only one ind. and the first Monhegan records (1 east of "town pump" and 1 at White Head–*first known record actually occurred in 1953*)
- 1970 Summer Checklist: included.
- Banding: 10 over four seasons, peak 5 in Fall 1960, max 4 on Oct 9, 1960.

It is surprising to note that historically Yellow-breasted Chat was noted mostly in Jun/summer in Maine, as the species has now largely retreated from breeding in southern New England. On Sep 20, 2016, one of the max days, the number was probably higher, as a single observer of 4 reported that others had seen additional chats that day. Although there are reports of inds. seen together, in most instances on days of multiple inds. the birds are in separate locations. Often reported over multiple days (usually two–three) or noted as a continuing ind. A shy or skulking species that is normally found in dense tangles or thick, scrubby vegetation in areas around town or along nearby trails, such as behind the schoolhouse, Burnt Head Trail, near the Trailing Yew, Underhill Trail, Lobster Cove Trail, and the scrubby swale along Ocean Ave. (the bridge here is known as the chat bridge); easily heard and identified if singing/calling, but difficult to locate. The CBC ind. in 2020 was found at the west end of Sterling Cove Rd. Unusual reports include an ind. that stayed several days and "found great interest in frozen baked beans put out for the doves" (likely late fall/early winter 1938–1939 but date unknown–MJT), an ind. missing an eye and a deceased bird in a cat's possession (specimen recovered) both on the same day (Oct 2, 2016–JT), and one chat chasing away another (LS, JT).

Historical/Regional:

- Vickery: cites 2010 and 2017 spring records; nearly annual Sep 7–Oct 29 2000–2017 (JVW in Vickery et al., 2020).

Yellow-breasted Chat, Oct 2, 2021. © Jeremiah Trimble.

YELLOW-HEADED BLACKBIRD
Xanthocephalus xanthocephalus

Status: Accidental spring and rare fall vagrant, very rare summer vagrant.

Occurrence: Twenty-one records (1 spring, 2 summer, 18 fall) since first recorded on Sep 11, 1925 (adult female; second Maine record; *MN* 6[1]: 46). Spring record: 1 first-year male on May 25, 2008 (MZ, KL, PD). Summer records: 1 male w/e Jun 18, 2002 (WBo), 1 first-year male on Jun 19, 2019 (DC). Fall records over sixteen years since 1925, span Aug 19–Oct 7; fall max: **3** during mid Sep 1975 (AKe; *AB* 30[1]: 35), 2 on Sep 19–23, 1975 (AKe et al.; *AB* 30[1]: 35) & Sep 25–Oct 2, 1990 (BN, MAS), Sep 20, 1995 (LBr, TMar) & Sep 14, 2001 (HN). Ten-Year: SU-1, F-4.

- 1939 Summer Census: accidental summer visitor.
- 1944–1967 Farrell Records: seen several times in May and between Aug/Sep (cited as Edison– presumably Ann, *fide Richard Farrell pers. comm.*), but noted with a question mark and *excluded here*.
- 1970 Summer Checklist: not included in the species list, but mentioned in the categories of presence as a rare, casual, or accidental visitor.

A regular vagrant along the East Coast, the nearest consistent breeding of this western species is in Ohio and southwestern Ontario. Despite some gaps between reports within a season, inds. considered same record due to rarity, a tendency to linger, and ind. plumage; 1975 is an exception, when 3 inds. were noted mid Sep after 2 inds. reported in Aug (see above), although it may have involved the same ind(s). Eight of the records have been multi-day events, with the longest twenty days (Sep 5–24, 1983). The Sep 11,1925 ind., collected by Warren Taylor (*Auk* 1926: 241) may be the source of inclusion on the 1939 Summer Census, as he was the compiler. Most often seen over or in the Meadow, but inds. have moved around to locations like the Trailing Yew and the Wharf, and once an ind. was reported flying past Smutty Nose. Single reports have also occurred at the Martin and Cundy feeders and on Nigh Duck. Sometimes observed in the company of other species, such as the Sep 22–28, 2014 ind. with up to four Rusty Blackbirds and a European Starling, and the Sep 13, 2016 ind. with four Common Grackles. The two summer records were identified as a male and an immature male, while seven of the fall records were identified as 5 immature males and 2 females. The Sep 2014 ind. illustrates the difficulty of separating some immature males and females, as it was identified by different observers as immature male (five times), female (four times), immature type (once), and either immature male or female (once) over the course of its seven-day stay; some wondered if there might have been two inds. involved, but this seems unlikely.

Historical/Regional:

- Palmer: cites adult female collected by Taylor on Sep 11, 1925.
- Cruickshank: cites Taylor 1925 as only Lincoln Co. record.
- Vickery: cites 1 male week of Jun 18, 2002 (WBo, fide KG) as summer record; of more than 40 fall records for the state, more than one third are from Monhegan (Richard V. Joyce in Vickery et al., 2020).

Yellow-headed Blackbird, Sep 26, 2014. © Bill Thompson.

BOBOLINK
Dolichonyx oryzivorus

Status: Fairly common spring and fairly common to common fall migrant.

Occurrence: Spring dates span May 5–June 9, peak mid–late May; spring max: 50 on May 25, 1986 (JVW) & May 14, 2011 (TMag), 43 on May 26, 2016 (JT, JO, BN), 40 on May 24, 1986 (JVW) & May 15, 2020 (DC), 35 on May 22, 2013 (DH). An early fall migrant, dates span Jul 27–Nov 6, peak late Aug–late Sep; fall max: **240** on Sep 6, 1985 (PDV), 200 on Sep 11, 1983 (PDV), 140 on Sep 4, 1982 (PDV). Ten-Year: SP-10, F-10.

- *MABB*: probable.
- 1915–1919 Taylor Journals: 1916–Sep 6 (15); 1918–Aug 28; 1919–Sep 13 (1).
- 1918 Fall Migration Census: Dewis–Sep 7 (14), 8 (3), 9 (1), 10 (1), 11 (1).
- 1944–1967 Farrell Records: 1950–May; 1951– May; 1955–Aug; 1958–May, Sep; 1959–May, Jun; 1960–May, Jun, Aug, Sep; 1961–May.
- 1954 & 1955 Summer Records: 1955–Aug 22– Sep 2 (up to 20+).

- 1970 Summer Checklist: included.
- Banding: 92 total over six seasons, peak 71 in Fall 1981, max 41 on Aug 29, 1981.

Curiously, max spring counts are all since 2011 while fall max counts are all from the 1980s. Post-breeding dispersal starts in Jul and is likely underreported in Aug due to lack of coverage. It is often difficult to be sure of numbers on the island at a given time, as they frequently circle around and one can't determine if they are staying/leaving. Most often reported as flyovers calling "bink". Birds on the ground are usually seen in the Meadow, but also reported at the Lobster Cove meadow.

Historical/Regional:

- Vickery: cites 15 on Oct 11, 2010 (JT) as notable (CDD in Vickery et al., 2020).

Bobolink, Sep 26, 2012. © Jeremiah Trimble.

EASTERN MEADOWLARK
Sturnella magna

Status: Very rare spring and fall migrant, very rare winter visitor.

Occurrence: Twelve records (7 spring, 3 fall, 2 winter) since 1956, all singles or unreported number (four records). Spring records: unreported number during May 1956 (IF), unreported number during May 1959 (IF), unreported number during Apr 1960 (IF), unreported number during Apr–May 1961 (IF), 1 on Apr 7–15, 1967 (IF), 1 on May 26, 2016 (BBa), 1 on May 22, 2019 (WBr et al.). Fall records: 1 on Oct 15, 1982 (PDV), 1 on Oct 7, 1989 (SS), 1 on Sep 27, 2017 (JT). Winter records: 1 on Dec 27, 1994 (CBC–PDV), 1 on Dec 27, 2004 (PDV). Ten-Year: SP-2.

- CBC: 1 year (4%), 1 on Dec 27, 1994, avg 0.0.
- 1944–1967 Farrell Records: 1956–May; 1959–May; 1960–Apr; 1961–Apr, May; 1967–Apr 7 (1), 8, 9, 14 (1), 15 (1).

Due to rarity, the Apr & May 1961 reports considered one record, as are the multiple reports from Apr 1967. Few details provided for any of the records; the May 2016 ind. was noted disappearing into the grass of the Meadow.

Historical/Regional:

- Vickery: cites 1 on May 26, 2016 (BBa) and both fall and both winter records (Richard V. Joyce in Vickery et al., 2020).

Eastern Meadowlark, Sep 27, 2017. © Jeremiah Trimble.

ORCHARD ORIOLE
Icterus spurius

Status: Scarce to uncommon spring and rare fall migrant.

Occurrence: Spring dates span Apr 30–Jun 13, peak early–late May; spring max: **15** on May 15, 1983 (TMar et al.), 11 on May 13, 1988 (AWe, JVW), 10 during May 21–23, 1984 (BBo). Eighteen fall records over twelve years since 1957 (all but one since 1981), span Aug 24–Oct 5; fall max: 3 on Sep 21, 2016 (WR), 2 on Sep 24, 2016 (RH). Ten-Year: SP-10, F-1.

- 1970 Summer Checklist: included.
- Banding: 10 total over three seasons, peak 7 in Spring 1984, max 4 on May 22, 1984.

Inds. are known to linger for several days, particularly in town and coming to feeders. A favored location in spring of recent years (since at least 2015) is Donna Cundy's yard with its feeders offering oranges, where multiple inds. sometimes gather alongside Baltimore Orioles. Other reports have occurred at scattered town locations. Of 64 inds. positively identified to age/sex in the spring, there were 32 immature males, 7 adult males, 21 females, and 4 identified only as males. In the fall, 1 was identified as a female, while 4 were only designated as female/immature types.

Historical/Regional:

- Vickery: cites 1 on Apr 30, 2011 (TMag) as early spring and lists seven high spring counts of 4–15 inds. (including max counts above); cites five fall records as late, spanning Sep 16–Oct 5 (latest fall record for state; PDV in Vickery et al., 2020).

Orchard Oriole, May 16, 2007. © Geoff Dennis.

BULLOCK'S ORIOLE
Icterus bullockii

Status: Accidental fall vagrant.

Occurrence: One record: immature male on Nov 11–13, 2017 (AI, DH et al.). Accepted by the ME-BRC #2017–049. Ten-Year: F-1.

First discovered by AI at her feeders on the top of Horn's Hill; also reported as continuing in the same area on Nov 13 (DH, LB, AV). Noted coming to a variety of feeders that offered fresh oranges, suet, and a platform feeder with seed; the bird also frequented a nearby multiflora rose (DH, LB).

Historical/Regional:

- Vickery: cites Nov 2017 record above (PDV in Vickery et al., 2020).
- OLMB: eleven additional state records—seven accepted and four not yet reviewed, earliest in 1889.

Bullock's Oriole, Nov 13, 2017. © Louis Bevier.

BALTIMORE ORIOLE
Icterus galbula

Status: Fairly common spring and fall migrant, very rare summer visitor.

Occurrence: Spring dates span Apr 27–Jun 15, peak middle two weeks of May; spring max: **60** on May 13, 1997 (PDV) & May 14, 1997 (PDV), 50 on May 20, 2002 (TV), 40 on May 19, 1983 (PDV), May 21, 1997 (SS). Four summer records: 2 on Jun 22, 2014 (BTh), 1 on Jul 7, 2015 (JFi), immature male on Jun 27, 2021 (DC), 1 on Jun 18, 2022 (MY). Early fall migrant and likely underreported in Aug, dates span Jul 22–Nov 16, two apparent peaks—early Sep and late Sep–early Oct, fall max: 50 on Sep 27, 2011 (DH), 40 on Sep 6, 1985 (PDV), Sep 22, 2003 (SS), Oct 2, 2003 (JT), Oct 1, 2009 (SS), Oct 1, 2020 (WR) & Sep 27, 2021 (JP), 35 on Sep 6, 1980 (PDV), Sep 21, 2003 (SS) & Sep 14, 2022 (EH et al.). Ten-Year: SP-10, SU-3, F-10.

- *MABB*: possible.
- 1914 & 1916 Checklists: included 1916.
- 1915–1919 Taylor Journals: 1915–Sep 5 (1); 1916–Aug 30 (1), Sep 6 (1), 10; 1919–Sep 5 (1), 14 (2).
- 1918 Fall Migration Census: Dewis–Sep 7 (4), 8 (1 male).
- 1944–1967 Farrell Records: 1950–May; 1955–Aug; 1956–May; 1958–May, Sep; 1959–May, Jun, Aug; 1960–May, Sep; 1961–May; 1967–Jun 1 (4), 2 (4), 3 (4), 4 (2), 5 (1).
- 1954 & 1955 Summer Records: 1955–Aug 22 (1), 27 (1), 29 (1), 30 (1), Sep 2 (2–IW, MLn).
- 1970 Summer Checklist: marked as known to breed in the area.
- Banding: 33 total over eight seasons, peak 12 in Fall 1981, max 10 on Aug 24, 1981.

Larger movements often multi-day events (two–three days; note several max counts above). Often seen in small flocks moving around the island; the largest single flocks reported include the 35 on Sep 14, 2022 "loosely associating" as they crossed the Meadow (EH et al.), 17 "streaming by" on Oct 1, 2020 (part of a total of 40–WR) and 16 on Oct 6, 2014 (JT), while 21 were present at one time at the Cundy feeders on May 13, 2015 (GD). No clear evidence of breeding, despite inclusion on *MABB* and designation on 1970 Summer Checklist; these were likely based on singing migrants in late spring or early fall migrants. Lack of summer/early fall coverage complicates understanding of status. For unknown reasons, there appear to be two peaks in fall migration, and undoubtedly underreported in Aug, as many begin fall migration at the end of Jul/beginning of Aug.

Known to linger for several days, sometimes in small flocks, especially in the spring when coming to fresh oranges at feeders (e.g. those of Donna Cundy). Reported from many town locations, especially feeding on apple blossoms in the spring and wild or cultivated grapes in the fall (e.g. at the big grape arbor at Tribler Cottage). Inds. identified to age/sex have been a mix in both spring and fall, with difficulties in separating some age/sex classes leading to unclear identifications.

Historical/Regional:
- Palmer: cites Dewis records as late.
- Vickery: cites 60 on May 14, 1997 (PDV) as high spring count, 1 on Jul 22, 2008 (PF) and 1 on Jul 7, 2015 (JFi) as summer records, 25 on Sep 26, 1994 (PDV) as a peak year on offshore islands, and three of the max counts above (including the top two) as high counts (Richard V. Joyce in Vickery et al., 2020).

Baltimore Oriole, May 26, 2018. © Scott Surner.

RED-WINGED BLACKBIRD
Agelaius phoeniceus

Status: Fairly common spring and fall migrant, fairly common summer resident, rare winter visitor.

Occurrence: Spring migration spans Feb 28–early Jun, overlapping with summer residents, peak early–late May, but underreported in early spring (particularly Apr); spring max: 78 on May 26, 2016 (JT, BN, JE), 75 on May 29, 2017 (JT, LS, CL), 70 on May 26, 2014 (JT). Breeding under way by end of May and continuing into Jul; summer max: 35 on Jun 23, 2019 (KD), 25 on Jun 12, 2019 (DH), 24 on Jul 2, 2021 (DH), 22 on Jun 11, 2019 (DH), 18 on Jun 13, 2013 (DH). Post-breeding dispersal underway by late Jul with migration continuing until early Dec, peak late Oct–mid Nov; fall max: **96** on Nov 13, 2020 (LS, JT), 72 on Nov 9, 2022 (LS, MWa), 45 on Nov 9, 2018 (FK, DH), 35 on Nov 5, 2016 (DH et al.). Twelve winter records over twelve years since 1979, all associated with the CBC period, span Dec 21–Jan 5; winter max: 3 on Dec 29, 1980 (CBC–PDV) & Dec 28–30, 1983 (CBC Dec 29–PDV), 2 on Dec 30–31, 1980 (PDV), Dec 21, 1989 (CBC–PDV) & Dec 27, 1994 (CBC–PDV). Ten-Year: SP-10, SU-10, F-10.

- *MABB*: confirmed; MBA: confirmed.
- CBC: eleven years (42%) plus one count week, first on Dec 22, 1979, max 3 on Dec 29, 1983, avg 0.6.
- 1900–1908 Reconnaissance & Supplements: unreported number during summer 1907 (CFJ, ECJ).
- 1914 & 1916 Checklists: unreported number on Aug 1, 1914; included 1916.
- 1915–1919 Taylor Journals: 1916–Sep 3, 10; 1917–Aug 18 (1).
- 1918 Fall Migration Census: Wentworth–Oct 16 (1), 25 (1), 31 (1).
- 1939 Summer Census: regular summer visitor.
- 1944–1967 Farrell Records: 1949–Mar, Apr; 1950–Mar, Apr, May; 1951–Apr, May; 1952–Apr; 1954–Jun, Jul; 1955–Jun, Jul, Aug; 1957–Aug; 1958–May, Aug; 1959–Apr, May, Jun, Jul, Aug; 1960–Apr, May, Jun, Jul, Aug, Sep; 1961–Apr, May; 1967–Apr 2, 3, 4, 5, 7, 8, 9, 10, 11, 12, 13, 14, 15, 16, 17, 18, 23, 24, Jun 1 (4), 2 (5), 3 (4), 4 (4), 5 (4), 6 (5), 7 (5), 8 (4).
- 1954 & 1955 Summer Records: 1954–included all three checklists; 1955–included all three checklists (up to 4–6 during Aug 22–Sep).
- 1970 Summer Checklist: highlighted and marked as known to breed in area.
- Banding: 8 total over five seasons; peak 4 in Spring 1984, max 2 on May 10, 1984.

Larger numbers are often prolonged events (three+ days), as inds./flocks undoubtedly linger. Underreported in early spring, summer, and late fall due to lack of coverage; mixing of migrants/residents also confuses status. Most often reported in/around the Meadow and also frequent feeders, where spring arrivals are often first encountered. Few breeding details available, but the Meadow and wet meadow area by Lobster Cove are the most likely locations for nesting; MBA status based on carrying food on Jul 2, 2021 (DH), nest with young on Jun 11, 2019 (DH) and recently fledged young on Jul 4, 2018 (DH).

Historical/Regional:

- Palmer: cites Nov 14, 1939 record as latest (MJT).

Red-winged Blackbird, Nov 3, 2010. © Geoff Dennis.

SHINY COWBIRD
Molothrus bonariensis

Status: Accidental spring vagrant.

Occurrence: One record: male on May 24–26, 1991 (LBr, JVW, mob; *AB* 34[2]: 141). First and only Maine record; accepted by ME-BRC #1991–001 (photos by CMa).

Normally a bird of the West Indies and South America and first reported in the U.S. in 1985 (Florida), it has now occurred from Texas to the Carolinas; this was the first record for the entire Northeast (SS; *MBN* 5[1]: 1–2), and 745 miles farther north than any previous record (Post et al., 1993). First located by LBr and JVW at Tom Martin's feeder and singing from a nearby spruce. The next day (May 25), it was observed by many observers at the feeders, then at the Monhegan House, and later at a platform feeder near the start of Burnt Head Trail, where it was once again heard singing.

Historical/Regional:

- Vickery: cites 1991 record above as only Maine record (PDV in Vickery et al., 2020).
- OLMB: no additional state records.

BROWN-HEADED COWBIRD
Molothrus ater

Status: Scarce to fairly common spring and scarce to uncommon fall migrant, very rare summer visitor and possible breeder, very rare winter visitor.

Occurrence: Spring dates span Mar 21–May 31, peak early–mid Apr; spring max: **70** on Apr 12, 2011 (TMag), 40 on Apr 10, 2011 (TMag) & Apr 5, 2013 (DH), 25 on Apr 9, 2011 (TMag), Apr 6, 2013 (DH) & Apr 7, 2013 (DH). Five summer records: unreported number during Jun 27–Jul 4, 1954 (FNR, MFNR), 1 on Jun 14, 2013 (DH), 1 on Jun 20, 2021 (CEl), 1 on Jul 5, 2021 (AL, EL), 3 on Jul 7, 2022 (LS, MWa). Extensive fall dates span Jul 17–Nov 8, peak early–late Sep; fall max: 40 on Sep 5, 1982 (PDV), 30 on Sep 6–8, 1980 (PDV), Sep 4, 1982 (PDV) & Sep 6, 1982 (PDV), 20 on Sep 3, 1982 (PDV), Sep 10–13, 1982 (PDV) & Oct 2, 2016 (HE). Nine winter records over nine years since 1978, all associated with CBC period: winter max: 12 on Dec 28–30, 1983 (CBC Dec 29–PDV), 5 on Dec 27, 1984 (CBC–PDV), 4 on Dec 29–30, 1980 (CBC Dec 30–PDV). Ten-Year: SP-9, SU-3, F-10.

- *MABB*: possible; MBA: confirmed.
- CBC: nine years (35%), first on Dec 28, 1978, max 12 on Dec 29, 1983, avg 1.2.
- 1914 & 1916 Checklists: unreported number on Aug 1, 1914, included as Cowbird 1916.
- 1915–1919 Taylor Journals: 1917–Aug 20 (1); 1918–prior to Aug 4; 1919–Sep 4 (2), 5 (2), 13 (1).
- 1918 Fall Migration Census: Dewis–Sep 7 (3); Wentworth–Sep 29, Oct 4. Listed as Cowbird.
- 1944–1967 Farrell Records: 1949–Mar; 1950–Apr; 1951–Apr; 1954–Jun, Jul; 1955–Aug; 1958–May, Aug, Sep; 1959–May, Jun, Jul, Aug; 1960–Apr, May, Jun, Jul, Aug, Sep; 1961–Apr, May; 1967–Apr 2, 3, 4, 5, 7, 8, 9, 10, 11, 12, 13, 14, 15, 16, 17, 18, 23, 24, Jun 1 (8), 2 (6), 3 (6), 4 (5), 5, 6, 7, 8 (6).
- 1954 & 1955 Summer Records: 1954–included Jun 27–Jul 4; 1955–Aug 30 (3).
- 1970 Summer Checklist: highlighted and marked as known to breed in area.
- Banding: 14 total over four seasons, peak 8 in Fall 1960, max 7 on Sep 23, 1960.

Larger numbers are often two- to four-day events, as inds./flocks undoubtedly linger; note both spring/fall migration and winter max counts, with spring of 2011 and 2013 and fall of 1980 and 1982 being exceptional. Undoubtedly underreported in early spring (late Mar/Apr), highlighted by the exceptional years above, when there was some coverage at this time; also likely more abundant in late fall/early winter than reported. With lingering spring migrants (late May/early Jun) and early post-breeding dispersal (Jul), inds. during these periods could be breeders/summer residents, but no clear evidence of such, despite status given on 1970 Summer Checklist and MBA (2 juveniles at Lobster Cove on Jul 20, 2021 were likely dispersing inds. from elsewhere); Jun and Jul reports from 1954, 1959 and 1960 possibly additional summer records, but considered spring and fall migrants for these purposes (not included as summer visitors). Both inds. on Jul 20, 2021 were juveniles and possibly post-fledging dispersals instead of resident young. Scattered sightings at town locations, including feeders and in/around the Meadow, sometimes with other blackbirds or starlings. It is interesting that only 1 out of 40 observed on Apr 5, 2013 and 3 out of 25 on Apr 6, 2013 were female (DH); a clear example of males migrating north earlier than females.

Historical/Regional:

- Vickery: peak first half of Sep (Richard V. Joyce in Vickery et al., 2020).

RUSTY BLACKBIRD
Euphagus carolinus

Status: Rare spring and fairly common fall migrant, very rare winter visitor.

Occurrence: Twenty-four spring records over twenty-one years since 1949 (two records in 2007, three in 2021), span during Mar (earliest definite Apr 29)–May 29; spring max: 5 on May 7, 2007 (KW) & May 5, 2010 (NL), 3 on May 25, 1996 (SS), 2 on May 15, 2021 (JT, LS, JO). Fall dates span during Aug (earliest definite Sep 2)–Nov 22, peak late Sep–mid Oct; fall max: **50** on Oct 2, 1997 (JT), 40 on Sep 30, 1982 (PDV) & Sep 25, 2005 (LS et al.), 32 on Oct 4, 2021 (JT, LS), 30 on Sep 29, 1998 (JT). Four winter records, almost all associated with CBC period: 1 on Jan 3, 1986 (CBC–PDV), 1 on Dec 27–28, 1987 (CBC Dec 27–PDV), 1 on Jan 3, 2008 (CBC), 1 on Feb 24, 2022 (JCh). Ten-Year: SP-3, F-10, W-1.

- CBC: three years (12%), 1 on Jan 3, 1986, 1 on Dec 27, 1987, 1 on Jan 3, 2008, avg 0.1.
- 1914 & 1916 Checklists: included 1916.
- 1915–1919 Taylor Journals: 1916–Sep 10.
- 1918 Fall Migration Census: Wentworth: Sep 29, Oct 4 (not as many), 15 (2), 17, 25 (1).
- 1944–1967 Farrell Records: 1949–Mar; 1950–Mar, Oct; 1958–May; 1959–Aug; 1960–May, Aug.
- Banding: total 15 over four seasons, peak 9 in Fall 1962, max 3 on Sep 24, 1962.

Population and range significantly declining in Maine since 1970 (Vickery et al., 2020). Likely underreported on Monhegan in Apr and Oct/early Nov. Almost all spring records are one-day sightings, with single inds. occurring May 13–14, 1997 and Apr 29–May 4, 2011. Inds./small flocks known to linger in fall; an ind. with a broken leg was noted at least Nov 6–8, 2020 (DH, FK). Largest known flock of 17 on Oct 4, 2021 (out of a total 32 that day–JT, LS), but details not provided for almost all of the max counts. Most often seen around/over the Meadow or at the Ice Pond, and also frequents feeders (Tom Martin's were especially attractive) or perched in nearby treetops; noted several times on the lawn at Monhegan House and at other town locations. Sometimes associates with Common Grackles or European Starlings.

Historical/Regional:

- Vickery: cites 40 on Sep 25, 2005 (LS et al.) as a peak count and 1 on Nov 6, 2016 (LB, mob) as late (Richard V. Joyce in Vickery et al., 2020).

Rusty Blackbird, Oct 5, 2020. © Luke Seitz.

BREWER'S BLACKBIRD
Euphagus cyanocephalus

Status: Accidental fall vagrant.

Occurrence: One record: male on Sep 24–25, 1985 (KJo; *AB* 40[2]: 259). Third Maine record, accepted by ME-BRC #1985–004.

Historical/Regional:

- Vickery: cites 1985 record above (PDV in Vickery et al., 2020).
- OLMB: three other state records: Oct 2, 1977 in Phippsburg (Sagadahoc Co.), Oct 1981 in Mount Desert (Hancock Co.), Nov 25, 1987 in East Pittston (Kennebec Co.); none of these records reviewed by the ME-BRC.

Brewer's Blackbird, Sep 24, 1985. © Kyle Jones.

COMMON GRACKLE
Quiscalus quiscula

Status: Common spring and fairly common to common fall migrant, fairly common to common summer resident, rare winter visitor.

Occurrence: Spring dates span Mar 11–early Jun, overlapping with summer residents, peak early–late May, but underreported in Mar–Apr; spring max: 135 on May 26, 2015 (JT, JO, BN), 100 on May 24, 2015 (JT, JO, BN), 98 on May 15, 2017 (JT). Breeding under way by mid May and continues into Jul; summer max: 109 on Jun 1, 2020 (JT, LS), 54 on Jun 4, 2020 (JT, LS), 52 on Jul 2, 2021 (DH), 47 on Jun 3, 2020 (JT, LS), 42 on Jun 12, 2018 (DH). Post-breeding dispersal under way by late Jul with migration continuing until early Dec, peak late Oct–mid Nov; fall max: **278** on Oct 19, 1918 (BHW), 213 on Nov 9, 2022 (LS, MWa), 200 on Oct 25, 2012 (JP), 150 on Oct 24, 1918 (BHW), 120 on Oct 31, 2010 (MI, JT, LS). Twenty-one winter records over twenty years (two in 1982) since winter 1938–39 (all but the winters of 1938–39 and 1939–40 [see Palmer, below] and Dec 1940 CBC records since 1978), almost all associated with CBC period (one record Feb 7–8, 2009); winter max: 9 on Jan 2–4, 1986 (CBC Dec 3–PDV), 6 on Dec 28, 1978 (CBC–PDV), 5 on Dec 29, 1940 (CBC–JAT) & Jan 3, 2008 (CBC). Ten-Year: SP-10, SU-10, F-10, W-3.

- *MABB*: confirmed; MBA: confirmed.
- CBC: fourteen years (54%), first on Dec 29, 1940, max 9 on Jan 3, 1986, avg 1.5.
- 1918 Fall Migration Census: Dewis–Sep 11 (1), 12 (2); Wentworth–Oct 15 (1), 19 (three flocks: 78, 100, 100), 23 (10), 24 (2 flocks: 50, 100). Listed as Bronzed Grackle.
- 1944–1967 Farrell Records: 1949–Mar; 1951–Apr; 1952–Nov; 1956–May; 1959–May, Jun, Jul, Aug; 1960–Apr, May, Jul; 1961–Apr, May; 1967–Apr 2, 3, 4, 5, 7, 8, 9, 10, 11, 12, 12, 14, 15, 16, 17, 18, 23, 24, Jun 1 (4), 2 (2), 3 (4).
- 1970 Summer Checklist: highlighted and marked as known to breed in area.
- Banding: 3 total over two seasons, peak 2 in Spring 1984, max 1 on May 9, 1984, May 21, 1984 & May 17, 1985.

Undoubtedly underreported in Apr and Oct–Nov due to lack of coverage. Late spring migrants pass through while summer residents are already nesting; breeding evident in many parts of the island into Jul. Inds. noted carrying nest material May 15–Jun 7, carrying food or feeding young May 15–Jul 6, and recently fledged young observed May 30–Jul 17. In the report of the max summer count of 109 on Jun 1, 2020, the species was common throughout the island (JT, LS). Dispersal starts by the end of Jul, with southward migration starting in earnest in Sep. Large movements are often multi-day events as inds./flocks linger. Spring 2005 was noteworthy, with counts of 80, 100, 88, and 135 on May 23–26. Single flocks have contained as many as 175 on Oct 25, 2012 (out of 200 reported–JP), 120 newly arrived on Oct 31, 2010 (MI, JT, LS), 103 flying around Manana on Nov 21, 2011 (DH), and several flocks of 100 in Oct 1918 (see Wentworth, below). Possible anywhere on the island, with flocks roaming, but often reported around the Meadow, at the Ice Pond, or at feeders (the only Feb record was a bird that spent both days at a feeder on Horn's Hill–LS); breeding around the village and in the forest.

Many records identified as the expected northern subspecies Bronzed Grackle (*Q. q. versicolor*). Only one report of the southern Purple Grackle (*Q. q. stonei*), which breeds as close as Massachusetts and New York; this report involved 1 ind. associating with 1 Bronzed Grackle during winter 1938–39 (departed some time prior to Jan 27, 1939–MJT).

Historical/Regional:

- Palmer: 3 overwintered in 1939–40 (MJT). Listed as Bronzed Grackle.

OVENBIRD
Seiurus aurocapilla

Status: Uncommon spring and scarce to uncommon fall migrant, very rare summer visitor and possible resident.

Occurrence: Spring dates span Apr 28–Jun 8, peak mid May; spring max: **40** on May 23, 1987 (HBC–unusually high), 19 on May 16, 2022 (LS, MWa), 17 on May 14, 2011 (TMag), 16 on May 18, 2005 (TV).

Two summer records in addition to the *MABB*: 1 on Jun 17, 2018 (BEv, TEv), 1 singing on Jul 5, 2018 (JSn). Fall dates span Aug 14–Oct 31, with fairly even distribution of reports throughout the season (banding and Farrell records accounted for all records before Sep 3); fall max: 8 on Sep 10, 1964 (RLP; *AFN* 19[1]: 15), 5 on Sep 20, 1964 (RLP; *AFN* 19[1]: 15), 4 on Sep 30, 1978 (PDV), Sep 4 & 6, 1983 (PDV–part of a multi-day event), 3 on Sep 3 & 5, 1983 (PDV), Oct 4, 2012 (DH). Ten-Year: SP-10, SU-1, F-7.

- *MABB*: possible; MBA: possible.
- 1914 & 1916 Checklists: included as Oven Bird 1916.
- 1915–1919 Taylor Journals: 1919–Sep 13 (1).
- 1944–1967 Farrell Records: 1949–Sep; 1959–Aug; 1960–Aug, Sep. Listed as Oven-bird.
- 1970 Summer Checklist: included.
- Banding: 17 total over 5 seasons; peak 10 in Fall 1991, max 3 on Aug 14, 1991.

The most abundant breeding warbler in Maine (Vickery et al., 2020), but fall numbers on Monhegan lower than spring, despite supplement of juvenile birds. MBA status based on single singing inds. on Jul 5, 2018 (JSn), Jun 8, 2019 (MW) & Jun 5, 2021 (FT); the final two reports falling within the spring migration period used here and possible migrants. Most likely underreported in Aug/early Sep due to lack of coverage; note that most of the fall max counts occurred prior to 1985; Sep 1964 and four-day event Sep 3–6, 1983 responsible for majority of them. Scattered reports at many locations across island; most often seen near the Ice Pond or between the Trailing Yew and Lobster Cove.

Ovenbird, May 14, 2011. © Geoff Dennis.

WORM-EATING WARBLER
Helmitheros vermivorum

Status: Very rare spring and fall vagrant.

Occurrence: Eight records (3 spring, 5 fall) since first recorded Sep 26, 1985 (MAS; *G* 14[5]: 49), all singles. Spring dates: May 12, 199? (TMar), May 30, 2003 (LBr), May 22, 2019 (HN). Fall dates: Sep 26–27, 1985 (MAS, CDD), Sep 21, 2005 (DL, JL), Oct 7, 2007 (LBr, fide DF), Oct 8, 2010 (TMag), Oct 9, 2011 (JM). Ten-Year: SP-1.

- 1944–1967 Farrell Records: 1954 –Jun, Jul (*excluded*–see discussion below).
- 1954 & 1955 Summer Records: included in the Jun 27–Jul 4 checklist (*excluded*–see discussion below).

Only four sightings reported location: the Oct 2007 ind. was at Tribler Cottage, the Oct 2010 ind. was along Lobster Cove Rd. south of the Trailing Yew (TMag), the Oct 2011 ind. was seen in thick shrubs "below" the Ice Pond, northeast of the school (JM), and the May 2019 ind. was in the apple trees on the north side of Wharf Hill Rd. west of Winter Works (HN). An unsubstantiated summer report from the week of Jun 27–Jul 4, 1954, as listed in the Farrell Records and 1954 & 1955 Summer Records, is not included here; there were no observer comments and the report was considered of doubtful certainty by the compiler ("does not nest in New England north of central Conn., and stragglers are generally in late April").

Historical/Regional:

- Vickery: cites 1 on May 30, 2003 (LBr) as latest spring and 1 on Oct 8, 2010 (TMag) and 1 on Oct 9, 2011 (JM) as recent fall (PDV in Vickery et al., 2020).

LOUISIANA WATERTHRUSH
Parkesia motacilla

Status: Very rare spring and accidental fall migrant.

Occurrence: Seven records (6 spring, 1 fall) since 1982, all singles. Spring records: May 6, 1984 (PDV), third week of May 1989 (JS), May 26, 1997 (LBr; *FN* 51[4]: 847), May 15, 2001 (WBo), during May 11–20, 2005 (GD), Jun 2, 2020 (JT, LS). Fall record: Sep 5, 1982 (PDV; *AB* 37[2]: 158). Ten-Year: SP-1.

- 1970 Summer Checklist: included.

Little or no pattern to these few sightings; the May 1997 eBird and Sep 1982 records were noted as late, as this species, that only breeds in the southwestern portion of the state, is an early fall migrant and usually gone by late Aug (little to no coverage in many years during the peak time period, no doubt adding to the sparsity of sightings). Questionable why this species was included on the 1970 Summer Checklist. Only two sightings reported location: the May 1984 & Jun 2020 inds. were at the Ice Pond; the 1984 ind. first noticed when heard giving a call note" (PDV).

Historical/Regional:

- Vickery: cites 1 on May 15, 2001 (WBo) and 1 on May 26, 1997 (LBr) as late spring and 1 on Sep 5, 1982 as a fall migrant (JVW in Vickery et al., 2020).

Louisiana Waterthrush, Ice Pond, Jun 2, 2020. © Jeremiah Trimble.

NORTHERN WATERTHRUSH
Parkesia noveboracensis

Status: Fairly common spring and fall migrant.

Occurrence: Spring dates span Apr 27–Jun 6, peak occurring mid–late May; spring max: 25 on May 25, 1983 (ST) & May 14, 2011 (LS), 20 on May 16, 2004 (TV), 19 on May 26, 2016 (BN, JT, JO) & May 21, 2018 (LS). Listed on the *MABB*, but only one other "summer" report at the end of July (1 on July 29, 2015–TR), most likely an early migrant, as is inclusion on the 1939 census and 1970 checklist. Its early and prolonged fall migrantion, dates span Jul 29–Nov 10, peak mid Aug–mid Sep; fall max: **36** on Sep 10, 1964 (RLP; *AFN* 19[1]: 15), 28 on May 22, 2022 (LS), 18 on Sep 7, 1964 (HT, RLP, CP; *AFN* 19[1]: 15), Sep 4, 1983 (PDV) & Sep 6, 1983 (PDV), 15 on Sep 12, 1982 (PDV) & Sep 7, 1985 (PDV), 14 on Sep 3, 1983 (PDV). Ten-Year: SP-9, F-10.

- *MABB*: possible.
- 1914 & 1916 Checklists: included 1916. Listed as Water Thrush.
- 1915–1919 Taylor Journals: 1915–Sep 1 (1), 2, 12 (3); 1916–Aug 21 (1), 26 (1), Sep 10; 1917–Aug 13 (1), 19 (2), Sep 5 (3); 1918–Aug 4, 28; 1919–Sep 3 (4), 4 (5), 5 (3).
- 1918 Fall Migration Census: Dewis–Sep 11 (1). Listed as Water-thrush.
- 1939 Summer Census: uncommon.
- 1944–1967 Farrell Records: 1953–Aug, Sep; 1955–Aug; 1956–May; 1958–Sep; 1959–May, Aug; 1960–May, Aug, Sep; 1961–May; 1967–Jun 1 (1).
- 1954 & 1955 Summer Records: 1955–Aug 22 (6), 23 (4+), 24 (1), 25 (1), 27 (2), Sep 2 (1–IW).
- 1970 Summer Checklist: included.
- Banding: 62 total over 6 seasons; peak 41 in Fall 1981, max 10 on Sep 3, 1981 (banded every day Aug 24–Sep 1).

Notable that almost all the fall max counts occurred in 1985 or earlier. Listed on the *MABB*, but no other "summer" records. A late high count of 11 was reported on Oct 4, 2020 (JT, LS, BBy). Typically found on/near the ground in thicker vegetation along the main roads and trails during periods of heavier movement, but also present in sloughs and wet areas scattered across the island; an ind. lingered at the Ice Pond Oct 4–8, 2020 (TMz); often located by its distinctive call note or when singing in the spring.

Historical/Regional:

- Vickery: cites 25 on May 25, 1983 (ST) as unusual spring concentration and 8 on Aug 18, 2006 (PDV) numerous along coast Sep 15–Oct 15 (PDV & JVW in Vickery et al., 2020).

Northern Waterthrush, May 13, 2011. © Geoff Dennis.

GOLDEN-WINGED WARBLER
Vermivora chrysoptera

Status: Very rare spring and fall migrant.

Occurrence: Sixteen records (9 spring, 7 fall) since Sep 1958. Spring records over seven years 1981–2014, all within the short span of May 17–30: 1 on May 24, 1987 (WH; *AB* 41[3]: 403), male on May 28–30, 1988 (WH et al., fide BT; *G* 17[3]: 28), 1 on May 18, 1997 (WBo, fide BT; *G* 27[3]: 28), male on May 19–20, 1998 (GD et al.), 1 on May 22, 1999 (GD, HN), 1 on May 25, 2002 (CDD, fide BT; *G* 32[3]: 28), 1 on May 17, 2003 (fide BT; *G* 33[3]: 28), **2** males on May 19, 2003 (TV, SW, GD), female on May 18, 2014 (KL). Fall records span Sep 13–Nov 10 (only one later than Oct 1): unreported number during Sep 1958 (IF), 1 on Sep 13, 1981 (PDV; *AB* 36[2]: 155), 1 during w/e Sep 30, 2003 (WBo), 1 on Oct 1, 2008 (BP), 1 on Sep 21, 2009 (CM), 1 on Sep. 23–26, 2012 (PM, mob), 1 on Nov 9–10, 2020 (LS, JT). Ten-Year: SP-1, F-1.

- 1944–1967 Farrell Records: 1958–Sep.

The Sep 2012 bird was the longest-lingering ind. at four consecutive days (two occasions of two-day reports in spring, one in fall). It was first found on the morning of Sep 23 along Black Head Rd. near Treetops (a residence east of Ice Pond Rd.), then moved to the Ice Pond area, where it continued on subsequent days; the first day it was associating with Black-capped Chickadees and a Red-eyed Vireo, later a White-eyed Vireo (DH). The Oct 2008 ind. was near the lighthouse. The May 1999 ind. was found in lilacs near Tom Martin's House near Fish Beach (HN). The May 2014 ind. was in the thicket just south of Donna Cundy's feeders along Lobster Cove Rd. The Nov 2020 ind., a hatch-year female, was over a month later than the previous latest record (Oct 1, 2008); it was present at the north end of Lobster Cove Trail on Nov 9 and at the Hill Studio (Ocean Ave.) on Nov 10. Few other reports regarding age/sex: 5 males, 1 female in spring (including the multiple bird day) and two adult males in fall (1981 and 2012). A report of a female on Sep 14, 1982 (*AB* 37[2]: 158) is not included here, the observer being unknown.

Two records of Brewster's Warbler (typical hybrid Golden-winged x Blue-winged): 1 on Sep 9, 1969 (RLP; *AFN* 24[1]: 19), 1 on May 21, 2017 (BP, KL, JVW), an ind. with "more" yellow on underparts. Two records of Lawrence's Warbler (hybrid *Vermivora chrysoptera x cyanoptera* F2 backcross—a variable backcross between a hybrid Golden-winged Warbler x Blue-winged Warbler [Brewster's Warbler] and either species, but typically a Golden-winged [Stephenson and Whittle, 2015]): 1 in Oct 1988 (TMar personal notes–no exact date), 1 on May 21, 2018 near Winter Works (LB, mob; many photos; possibly a female or second-year male).

Lawrence's Warbler, May 21, 2018. © Luke Seitz.

Historical/Regional:
- Vickery: at least eight spring reports and six fall reports (notes 4 during 1981–1986 and cites the Oct 2008, Sep 2009 & Sep 2012 records listed above; PDV & JVW in Vickery et al., 2020).

Golden-winged Warbler, Nov 9, 2020. © Luke Seitz.

BLUE-WINGED WARBLER
Vermivora cyanoptera

Status: Rare spring and fall migrant, very rare summer visitor.

Occurrence: Forty-seven records (16 spring, 2 summer, 29 fall) since Aug 1960 (IF). Spring records over fourteen years since 1994 (three records in 2011 [4 inds.], only year with multiple reports), dates span Apr 27–May 25 (one trip report May 21–26 period), with only the earliest record before May 15; spring max: 2 on Apr 27–28, 2011 (TMag). Two summer records: 1 on Jul 17, 2013 (JAi, NLo), unreported number on Jun 30, 2014 (MP). Fall records over eighteen years since 1960, span during Aug (earliest definite Aug 29)–w/e Oct 9 (last definite date Oct 1); fall max: **2** males on Sep 9, 1984 (PDV) only multiple bird day in fall and part of 4 distinct reports (5 birds or repeats?). Ten-Year: SP-4, SU-2, F-2.

- 1944–1967 Farrell Records: 1960–Aug.
- 1970 Summer Checklist: included.
- Banding: 1 on Aug 29, 1981.

The summer records notable, especially considering lack of historical presence, but without supporting details. Reports involving birds lingering over two days on several occasions both seasons (none confirmed for three days). Potential for repeat sightings where gaps exist between reports of one or several days; the fall max count (2 on Sep 9, 1984) was one of four records that season, with singles on Sep 6, 17, 19— unclear actual number of inds. involved; 2–3 inds. reported during Aug 29–Sep 8, 1970 (HT, ELK et al.; *AFN* 25[1]: 30), but exact dates or daily max unclear. Usually seen in areas in or near town, such as the Ice Pond, Tribler Rd., or Lobster Cove Rd. Unusual report of an ind. along Trail #1, in a steep stream crossing just before reaching Black Head (NL). Very few reports identified to age/sex class; two spring males and 4 fall males (one adult).

See Golden-winged Warbler for hybrid discussion.

Historical/Regional:

- Vickery: cites May 24, 1997 (LBr) and May 24, 2006 (WBo) records as late spring and ~Oct 9, 2001 (WBo) as late fall.

Blue-winged Warbler, May 14, 2011. © Geoff Dennis.

BLACK-AND-WHITE WARBLER
Mniotilta varia

Status: Fairly common spring and fall migrant, accidental summer visitor or possible breeder.

Occurrence: Spring dates span during Apr (earliest definite Apr 26)–Jun 9, peak early–late May; spring max: **138** on May 16, 2022 (LS, MWa), 127 on May 21, 2018 (JT, CK), 125 on May 14, 2011 (LS), 100 on May 13, 2011 (LS) & May 16, 2004 (TV). Although designated probable in *MABB*, only one summer record: 1 during Jun 22–25, 2018 (KL). Extended fall dates span Aug 11–Nov 8, peak late Aug–early Oct; fall max: 80 on Sep 25, 2009 (LS), 50 on Sep 26, 2013 (PDV, LS), 30 on Sep 10, 1964 (RLP; *AFN* 19[1]: 15) & Sep 22, 2004 (MI). Ten-Year: SP-10, SU-1, F-10.

- *MABB*: probable; MBA: possible.
- 1899 Checklist: included as Black-and-white Creeping Warbler.
- 1914 & 1916 Checklists: included 1916.
- 1915–1919 Taylor Journals: 1915–Sep 2 (1); 1916–Sep 6 (2), 10; 1917–Sep 5 (3); 1919–Sep 13 (1).
- 1918 Fall Migration Census: Dewis–Sep 8 (1), 10 (1); Wentworth–Sep 29, Oct 7, 8, 9.
- 1944–1967 Farrell Records: 1950 – Sep; 1951 – May; 1953–Aug; 1955–Aug; 1959–May, Aug; 1960–May, Aug, Sep; 1961–Apr.
- 1954 & 1955 Summer Records: 1955–Aug 22 (3), 23 (3), 24 (1), 29 (3).
- 1970 Summer Checklist: known to breed in the area.
- Banding: 18 over six seasons, peak 10 in Fall 1981, max 5 on Sep 8, 1981.

Large fallouts in spring and fall deposit Black-and-white Warblers all over the island. The significant flight of 127 on May 21, 2018 involved a careful count on the western side of the island, with 7–8 at many stops (follow-up count of 61 the next day). MBA status based on a singing ind. on Jun 7, 2021 (CDD, LBl), possibly a late migrant. Likely underreported as a migrant in Aug (and possibly late Jul) due to lack of coverage. They are particularly drawn to the apple trees in town and along the roads; reports of 10 in a single tree (SBe, PDV) and every apple tree seeming to have one or two (LS); at least 10 were present in a grove of firs on Sep 20, 2020 (RG); also noted as hopping on rocks and in the road (LS). Birds identified to age/sex in the third week of May (six reports involving 15 inds.) have indicated adult males and females present in almost equal numbers. In late fall, the several records noted were all females (three reports involving 5 inds. Oct 4–Oct 11).

Historical/Regional:

- Palmer: notes Oct 9 date in Wentworth in 1918 Fall Migration Census as late date.
- Cruickshank: also notes Wentworth as late date.
- Vickery: cites 125 on May 14, 2011 (LS) as a max spring count and 30 on Sep 22, 2004 (MI) and 25 on Sep 26, 2003 (SM) as high fall counts (JVW in Vickery et al., 2020).

Black-and-white Warbler, May 14, 2011. © Geoff Dennis.

PROTHONOTARY WARBLER
Protonotaria citrea

Status: Rare spring and very rare fall vagrant.

Occurrence: Twenty records (12 spring, 8 fall) since Aug 1959, all single birds or unreported number (two records). Spring records over ten years since 1960, span Apr 21–May 26; all but two Apr records (Apr 23, 1988 & Apr 21, 2015) occurring May 13 or later. Fall dates over seven years since 1959, span during Aug (earliest definite Sep 13)–Oct 3 (possibly as late as Oct 5 as report was from a three-day visit): unreported number during Aug 1959 (ERo, fide IF), Sep 13 or 15, 1986 (fide BT; *G* 15[5]: 47, *AG* 41[1]: 60), Sep 27, 1998 (BSc), Sep 26, 2000 (JT), Sep 28–29, 2003 (WBo, TV, JT), during Oct 3–5, 2003 (DAb, DF), Sep 21 & 23, 2011 (JT, LS), Sep 25, 2021 (DL, KL et al.). Ten-Year: SP-4, F-1.

- 1944–1967 Farrell Records: 1959–Aug; 1960–May.

Surprising number of records for a species breeding no closer than Connecticut and New York. Often reported over multiple days by numerous observers, the longest staying ind. was present for eleven days (May 15–25, 1986). Although some birds have been identified to age/sex, helping to separate inds., the lack of details on some reports makes it hard to be sure of the actual number present. Birds reported as male and female in May 2000 (GD, HN et al.) provided the only definite occurrence of two birds in one season. Reports of an adult female and a young male on May 26, 2016 *may* have referred to the same ind.—this day saw "thousands of birds moving north at dawn" (PDV). An report of one found "this summer" in Jul or Aug 2004 (*G* 34[4]: 39) was unsubstantiated. Usually reported at locations around the northern part of town, most notably the Ice Pond area, but also Wharf Hill Rd., Tribler Rd., the pump house, Main St. near the Lupine Gallery, the Meadow, and the scrubby swale on Ocean Ave. near the "chat" bridge. One report of a bird singing in the Meadow (May 24, 2008–PMo). Anecdotal notes also mention "hunting insects around greenhouse in garden, taking shelter from rain under boards (May 14, 2017–JT) and "feeding on apple blossoms" (May 26, 2016–PDV).

Prothonotary Warbler, May 24, 2018. © Luke Seitz.

TENNESSEE WARBLER
Leiothlypis peregrina

Status: Uncommon spring and fall migrant (formerly fairly common in fall), very rare summer visitor.

Occurrence: One of the latest spring warbler migrants, spring dates span May 6–Jun 13, with the peak occurring the last week of May; spring max: **70+** on May 25, 1983 (ST; *AB* 37[5]: 845), 40 on May 24, 2019 (DL), 26 on May 29, 2014 (JT), 25 on May 25, 2019, (DL), 21 on May 24, 2019 (JT et al.). Three summer records: singing male on Jul 7, 2018 (RD, PD), 1 on Jul 2, 2019 (DL, JL), 1 on Jul 19, 2019 (JT). Fall dates span Aug 26–Nov 6, peak early–late Sep; fall max: 45 on Sep 6, 1983 (PDV), 40 on Aug 19, 1975 (AKe; *AB* 30[1]: 34), 20 on Sep 7, 1980 (PDV) & Sep 8, 1984 (PDV), 18 on Sep 25, 1981 (PDV). Ten-Year: SP-10, SU-2, F-10.

- 1915–1919 Taylor Journals: 1918—Aug 28; 1919–Sep 4 (3).

- 1918 Fall Migration Census: Dewis–Sep 7 (1), Wentworth–Oct 7.
- 1944–1967 Farrell Records: 1955–Aug.
- 1954 & 1955 Summer Records: 1955–Aug 27 (1), 28 (2), 29 (1), 30 (4–EAB, IW).
- 1970 Summer Checklist: included.
- Banding: 19 total over 4 seasons; peak 14 in Fall 1981, max 5 on Sep 11, 1981.

A boreal breeder whose population fluctuations apparently coincide with Spruce Budworm outbreaks; last significant outbreak in late 1960s/early 1970s (Vickery et al., 2020). Similar to many other warbler species that pass through in significant numbers, the largest totals are often part of multiple day events, sometimes lasting three or more days. Although generally less common in the spring, the majority and the highest of the max counts occurred in May; the nineteen highest fall counts (8 per day or more) all took place in the 1980s and prior to Sep 13, while high counts in recent years have all occurred after Sep 15 (7 on Oct 5 in 2019), indicating an apparent trend toward later migration. Reports are most often from town locations but also from trails; 9 in one apple tree on May 30, 2019 (out of 19 that day–JT) and two late inds. together in the apple trees at the north end of Lobster Cove Trail on Nov 6, 2020 (FK, DH). The three summer records all involved a singing male in 2018 and 2019—twice in the southern portion of the island and once near the school (Jul 2, 2019); *possibly a returning ind.(?).*

Historical/Regional:

- Palmer: cites 1918 Fall Migration sightings.
- Cruickshank: cites Wentworth Oct 7, 1918 record as latest for county.

Tennessee Warbler, Oct 5, 2018. © Jeremiah Trimble.

ORANGE-CROWNED WARBLER
Leiothlypis celata

Status: Rare spring and scarce fall migrant, accidental winter visitor.

Occurrence: Twenty-two spring records over sixteen years since 1946 (three records in 1997, two in 2000, two in 2008 & 2019), all single birds or unreported number (three records), span during Apr–w/e Jun 6, peak second half of May. One of the latest fall warbler migrants, dates span Sep 8–Nov 22, peak early–late Oct; fall max: **10** on Nov 10, 2020 (LS, JT), 7 on Nov 9, 2020 (LS, JT), 4 on Sep 30, 1978 (DF), Oct 13, 1982 (PDV), Oct 29, 2010 (MI, LS, JT), Oct 11, 2014 (NG, MZ), Oct 7, 2016 (LS, JT) & Nov 8, 2020 (FK, DH). Winter record: 1 on Jan 1, 1992 (CBC–PDV, et al.). Ten-Year: SP-4, F-10.

- CBC: 1 year (4%), 1 on Jan 1, 1992, avg 0.0.
- 1944–1967 Farrell Records: 1946–Apr; 1948–May.
- Banding: 1 on Sep 21, 1960.

Regular occurrence, especially in fall, may indicate an increased presence over historical status. Inds. often encountered over two, or rarely, three days). Fall 2020 was exceptional, with nine records spanning Sep 21–Nov 12, including three of the max counts listed above. On four fall occasions, two inds. were seen together; on the max count of 10 on Nov 10, 2020, 4+ were noted in the short distance between the Brewery and the start of Lobster Cove Trail and 2 in the area of the Fire Station and the Trailing Yew (LS, JT–others at Lobster Cove Trail, Burnt Head and White Head that day), but there is no indication that they were associating with each other. This species is also noted as associating with Nashville and Tennessee Warblers. Other reports scattered throughout town, often in apple trees and lilacs along the roads, while the most reported location is the brushy Lobster Cove Trail; on Sep. 25, 2009 (LS), one was observed coming in off the water at Lobster Cove and alighting in a spruce (one of many warblers to do so that morning). What was presumed to be a continuing ind. was behind the lighthouse on May 21, 2018 and behind the pump house the following day.

Only two records (Oct 29, 2010–PDV et al., Nov 5, 2016–JF et al.) included information relating to subspecific identification, indicating that all 5 inds. (4 and 1, respectively) were consistent with *V. c. celata*, the expected subspecies across the eastern U.S. (breeds throughout much of the boreal forests of Canada and westward into Alaska).

Historical/Regional:

- Vickery: seven+ spring records, 3 inds. in 1997 (PDV); cites 4 on Sep 30, 1978 (DF) and 4 on Oct 13, 1982 (PDV–11 inds. seen Oct 13–15 [*should actually be 10 inds., as 3 were reported each day Oct 14 & 15*]) and Nov 22, 2011 (DH) as latest fall (PDV in Vickery et al., 2020).

Orange-crowned Warbler, Oct 13, 2019. © Bill Thompson

NASHVILLE WARBLER
Leiothlypis ruficapilla

Status: Uncommon to fairly common spring and fall migrant, rare summer visitor and possible breeder.

Occurrence: Spring dates span May 4–early Jun, peak early–late May; spring max: 20 on May 13, 2011 (LS), 18 on May 14, 2011 (LS), 16 on May 15, 2011 (RS), 15 on May 17, 2005 (TV). Lack of breeding information, despite inclusion on historical summer checklists (including all three checklists in 1954) and MBA; sixteen summer records over twelve years since 1909 (only six recent, all since 1999; eight of unreported number); summer max: 7+ during Jun 27–29, 2005 (DL, JL), 4 on Aug 9, 1915 (WT, CFJ), 2 on Aug 5, 1917 (WT) & Jul 27, 2020 (eBird). Fall migration spans Aug 13–Nov 7, extended peak mid Sep–first third of Oct; fall max: 35 on Sep 25, 2009 (LS), 20 on Sep 28, 2000 (JT), 18 on four dates. Ten-Year: SP-10, SU-2, F-10.

- MBA: possible.
- 1900–1908 Reconnaissance & Supplements: 1 on Jun 4, 3 on Jun 5, 2 on Jun 6, 1908 (all heard singing–FA).
- 1909 Notes: most common warbler on island, singing full song in open woodland glades in.
- 1914 & 1916 Checklists: included 1916.
- 1915–1919 Taylor Journals: 1915–Aug 9 (4), Sep 12 (1); 1916–Aug 22; 1917–Jul 29 (1), Aug 5 (2); 1918–prior to Aug 4; 1919–Sep 4 (1), 13 (1).
- 1918 Migration Census: Wentworth–Oct 7.
- 1944–1967 Farrell Records: 1954–Jun, Jul, Aug; 1955–Jun, Aug; 1959–Jul, Aug; 1960–Jul, Aug, Sep.
- 1954 & 1955 Summer Records: 1954–included all three checklists; 1955–included Aug 11–15, 22 (1), 23 (4+), 25 (1), 28 (2), 30 (1).
- 1970 Summer Checklist: known to breed in area.
- Banding: 20 over 5 seasons, peak 5 in Fall 1960, Fall 1962 & Fall 1981, max 3 on Oct 3, 1960, Sep 11, 1981 & Sep 24, 1984).

Likely overlooked in late Apr and underreported in Oct due to lack of coverage. As indicated by the spring maxima, 2011 saw a major movement of Nashville Warbler, with reports of this species for thirteen straight days (May 13–25), and five days with 11 or more inds. The fall max of 35 was part of a day that found "birds everywhere," with Nashville Warblers a major component of mixed flocks (LS). Also of note, a two-day total of 50 was recorded Sep. 16 & 17, 2000, when Nashville Warbler was the most numerous warbler species (HN). As with other species, these big movements find birds in many of the apple trees and lilacs along the town roads—scattered from the Ice Pond to Lobster Cove, sometimes reported from deciduous areas along trails. As suggested by the lack of Jul records since 1960, some of the summer reports from mid June and early Aug could pertain to unusually late/early migrants, rather than indicate breeding; the summer max of 7+ during Jun 27–29, 2005 noted as singing males, however, is almost certainly indicative of breeding; MBA status based on a singing ind. on Jun 24, 2018 (KL). Note that in Jul 1909 it was noted as the most common warbler on the island (Maynard–see above; considered one record due to lack of details); no doubt adversely affected by the maturing and expansion of forested areas on the island.

Historical/Regional:

- Palmer: Wentworth report (1918) mentioned as a late record.
- Vickery: cites 15 on May 17, 2005 as an unusual concentration and May 30, 2006 (WBo) as late spring; 1–4 /day typical in Sep, cites Aug 29, 2006 (WBo) as early fall and 6 on Sep 12, 1982 (PDV) and 8 on Oct 3, 2003 (WJS) as high fall counts (PDV & JVW in Vickery et al., 2020).

Nashville Warbler, Oct 12, 2020. © Bill Thompson.

VIRGINIA'S WARBLER
Leiothlypis virginiae

Status: Very rare spring and fall vagrant.

Occurrence: Four records (2 spring, 2 fall) since 1998, all single birds. Spring records: May 21, 1998 (GD; ph.; first Maine record; *MBN* 11[1]: 18–19, *FN* 52[3]: 307), May 29–30, 2014 (GW, mob; ph., audio recordings of song and call). Fall records: Sep 28–30, 2006 (VL et al.), Nov. 8, 2011 (DH; ph.). Only records for Maine; 2006, 2011 & 2014 records accepted by ME-BRC (#2006–010, #2011–011 & #2014–007, respectively), 1998 not yet reviewed. Ten-Year: SP-1.

These four inds. represent the only records for Maine. A western bird that breeds on brushy mountain slopes from CO and NM westward, this species is truly a long-distance vagrant. All four birds occurred on the southern half of the island; three of them were located in the same general area: the May 1998 ind. was in an apple tree by the Cundy property along the road to Lobster Cove, the Sep 2006 ind. was across from the Trailing Yew along Lobster Cove Rd., the May 2014 ind. was first discovered in the apple trees on the east side at the head of Lobster Cove Trail, and relocated the next day near the Trailing Yew. The only outlier occurred in 2011, when a bird was seen for only eight seconds (and photographed) near Burnt Head. The May 1998 ind. was an adult male, the Nov 2011 ind. was identified as a first-year bird (probably female based on lack of yellow on throat), while the May 2014 ind. was identified by some as a male.

Interestingly, the identification of the May 1998 ind., the first of the four and one of <10 records for Eastern North America., was not confirmed until more than a week later when photographs were finally developed and viewed. It was initially thought to be an oddly plumaged Nashville Warbler, as Virginia's Warbler was not even mentioned in eastern field guides. It remained long enough for twelve images to be taken before it flew off to the east (GD).

Historical/Regional:
- Vickery: cites four records above as the only ones for Maine (JVW in Vickery et al., 2020).
- OLMB: no additional state records.

Virginia's Warbler, May 29, 2014. © Jeremiah Trimble.

CONNECTICUT WARBLER
Oporornis agilis

Status: Very rare spring and rare fall migrant.

Occurrence: Twenty-seven records (4 spring, 22 fall, 1 unknown) since earliest known record of a bird banded on Oct 9, 1960, all single birds or unreported number (five records). Spring records over four years during 1997–2003: w/e May 20, 1997 (WBo), May 25, 1997 (fide WT; *G* 27[3]: 28), w/e May 25, 1999 (WBo), May 17, 2003 (RE). Fall records over sixteen years, with all but the 1960 record since 1981, span Sep 4–Oct 8; three reports in 2003 (possibly 1–3 inds.) and two in 2001 & 2011 are only years of multiple sightings. Unknown date: 1966 (TMar personal notes). Ten-Year: F-4.

- 1970 Summer Checklist: included.
- Banding: 2 total over two seasons–Oct 9, 1960, Sep 18, 1991.

Only one multiple-day sighting: Sep 20–21, 2016 in the swale along the trail past the Ice Pond (DL). The other five records giving location (all in fall) occurred in the southern half of the island—edge of the beach at Lobster Cove, start of the Lobster Cove Trail, start of the Underhill Trail, bird bath at the Cundy feeders (right next to Underhill Trail), Horn's Hill half of the Gull Cove Trail and a garden near the church. Only three records identified to age, all immature: Sep 26, 1993 (PDV), Oct 5, 2016 (LS, JT), Sep 28, 2017 (BBa).

Historical/Regional:

- Vickery: cites three of the four spring records above (*all except w/e May 20, 1997*); lists six recent fall reports of singles 2001–2017, span Sep 7–Oct 5 and 1 on Oct 5–8, 2001 (WBo) as late fall (PDV in Vickery et al., 2020).

Connecticut Warbler, Oct 3, 2021. © Jeremiah Trimble.

MACGILLIVRAY'S WARBLER
Geothlypis tolmiei

Status: Accidental fall vagrant.

Occurrence: One record: 1 on Sep 17, 2020 (LMu, BBc, JMu et al.). Fifth Maine record; accepted by ME-BRC #2020–032. Ten-Year: F-1.

Observed in shrubs by the Sterling Harbor House (across Wharf Rd. from the Island Inn) at ~2 p.m., the same area that the island's first Black-throated Gray Warbler had been seen that morning.

Historical/Regional:

- OLMB: five additional state records—all accepted (2009, two in 2010, 2015, 2021).

MacGillivray's Warbler, Sep 17, 2020. © Lukas Musher.

MOURNING WARBLER
Geothlypis philadelphia

Status: Scarce spring and fall migrant.

Occurrence: A late spring migrant with a narrow window of movement, dates span May 19–Jun 7 (May 1945 & May and Jun 1959 records of unreported date), peak last week of May; spring max: 5 on May 30, 2013 (RL, ML), 3 on May 29, 1987 (PDV), May 28, 1988 (SS) & May 27, 2016 (DL, JL). Fall dates span Aug 22–Oct 21 (possibly as early as Aug 16 [checklist]), peak early Sep–early Oct; fall max: **10** on Sep 16, 1982 (DF), 5 on Sep 9, 1985 (PDV), 4 on Sep 5, 1983 (PDV), 3 on five dates. Ten-Year: SP-8, F-8.

- 1914 & 1916 Checklists: included 1916.
- 1915–1919 Taylor Journals: 1916–Sep 10.
- 1918 Migration Census: Wentworth–Oct 15, 20 (2), 21 (1).
- 1944–1967 Farrell Records: 1945–May; 1955–Aug; 1959–May, June; 1960–Aug.
- 1954 & 1955 Summer Records: 1955–Aug 22 (1–EAB et al.).
- 1970 Summer Checklist: included.
- Banding: 16 total over three seasons, peak 8 in Fall 1981, max 3 on Sep 9, 1981; late movement in 1984 highlighted by 2 on Jun 5 & 6.

Despite increased coverage, all but two of the max counts occurred 1988 or earlier, possibly indicating a decline in population. This species is often found in thickets and brushy areas, with reports scattered all around town; the area near the Ice Pond, past the Ice Pond along Black Head Rd., east end of Wharf Hill Rd., Lobster Cove Trail, and the start of the Underhill Trail (3 on May 30, 2013) and nearby intersection are all favored locations. Lobster traps are another spot to check, as Mourning and other warblers were formerly occasional in those around the Martin feeders). Many inds. in spring identified as males and adult males, and sometimes singing; only one report of a first-year male and two of females (one adult). In fall, all of the aged birds have been immatures, including the 4 seen on Sep 5, 1983 (PDV) and the 3 seen on Sep 11, 1982 (PDV), with one identification of a hatch-year male; two birds photographed in fall 2018 appear to be immature females (Sep 20 & Oct 2).

Historical/Regional:

- Palmer: cites Wentworth 1918 records.
- Cruickshank: cites Wentworth 1918 records.
- Vickery: cites 1 on June 7, 2005 (WBo) as late spring and 10 on Sep 16, 1982 (DF) as exceptional fall count, lists seven Oct records as late (including 1918 records above as latest; PDV in Vickery et al., 2020).

Mourning Warbler, May 20, 2019. © Bill Thompson.

Kentucky Warbler, May 15, 2005. © Geoff Dennis.

KENTUCKY WARBLER
Geothlypis formosus

Status: Very rare spring and fall vagrant.

Occurrence: Twelve records (10 spring, 2 fall) since May 1956. Spring records all single birds (one unreported number) within the dates May 6–25: unreported number during May 1956 (IF), May 22, 1984 (BBo), May 21, 1988 (MBe, NF), May 19, 1991 (AT), May 1995 (TMar–unknown date), 3rd week May 1996 (JS, TMar, "seen by all"), May 25, 1997 (LBr), May 15, 2005 (GD), May 6–7, 2011 (TMag), May 15, 2019 (DPJ). Fall records: 1 on Sep 18–19, 1964 (RLP; *AFN* 19[1]: 8 & 15), 1 on Sep 5, 1970 (ELK et al.; *AFN* 25[1]: 30). Only the May 15, 2019 record listed and accepted on the OLMB (ME-BRC #2019–016). Ten-Year: SP-1.

- 1944–1967 Farrell Records: 1956–May.

First Maine record in 1952, since then ~60 records statewide and in roughly equal numbers spring and fall (Vickery et al., 2020). It is interesting to note that the May 2011 ind. involved the only multiple-day stay and was also eight days earlier than any other record. The May 15, 2019 ind. was a male along Black Head Rd. just north of the Fire Dept. The May 2005 ind. was photographed both alive and dead that day, most likely the victim of a cat (GD).

Historical/Regional:

- Vickery: cites 1 on May 6–7, 2011 (TMag) as early May (*does not give location as Monhegan*; PDV in Vickery et al., 2020).
- OLMB: seventeen additional state records listed (many historical records not listed)—sixteen accepted, one not yet reviewed; one Monhegan record on May 21, 2019 listed as not accepted.

COMMON YELLOWTHROAT
Geothlypis trichas

Status: Fairly common to common spring and fall migrant, fairly common summer resident.

Occurrence: Spring migration Apr 30–mid Jun (overlapping with residents), peak mid May–early Jun; spring max: **200** on May 16, 2004 (TV), 146 on May 16, 2022 (LS, MWa), 100+ on May 19, 2005 (TV), 100 on May 25, 1990 (JVW), 96 on May 22, 2022 (LS). Residents prevalent by mid Jun and augmented by juveniles in Jul; summer max: 26 on Jul 15, 2021 (BTh), 16 on Jul 12, 2021 (BTh) & Jun 30, 2022 (MaB), 14 on Jul 7, 2018 (PD, RD). Extended fall dates span early Aug–Nov 12, peak early Sep–mid Oct; fall max: 80 on Oct 1, 2016 (MB et al.), 60 on Oct 4, 2012 (DH) & Sep 26, 2013 (PB), 48 on Sep 10, 1964 (RLP; *AFN* 19[1]: 15), 45 on Sep 20, 2020 (EJ). Ten-Year: SP-10, SU-10, F-10.

- *MABB*: confirmed; MBA: confirmed.
- 1899 Checklist: included as Maryland Yellowthroat.
- 1900–1908 Reconnaissance & Supplements: 2 (one male, one female) during May 31–Jun 6, 1908 (FA). Listed as Maryland Yellow-Throat.
- 1909 Notes: fairly common, singing. Listed as Northern Yellow-throat.
- 1914 & 1916 Checklists: included as Maryland Yellow-throat 1916.
- 1915–1919 Taylor Journals: 1915–Aug 31 (2), Sep 2, 5 (1); 1916–Aug 26, Sep 6 (10), 10; 1917–Aug 18 (1), Sep 5 (2); 1918–Aug 4, 28; 1919–Sep 1 (1), 3 (10), 4 (4), 5 (2), 11 (3), 13 (3), 14 (1).
- 1918 Fall Migration Census: Dewis–Sep 7 (2), 11 (1), 12 (1); Wentworth–Sep 29, Oct 8 (~12), 13, 17 (2), 19 (2–one in "spring male plumage"), 23, 24 (3). Listed as Maryland Yellow-Throat.
- 1939 Summer Census: regular summer resident.

- 1944–1967 Farrell Records: 1948–May; 1951–May; 1953–Aug, Sep; 1954–Jun, Jul; 1955–Jun, Jul, Aug; 1956–May; 1957–Aug; 1959–May, Jun, Jul, Aug; 1960–May, Jun, Jul, Aug, Sep; 1961–May; 1967–Jun 1 (2), 2 (1), 3 (2), 4 (1).
- 1954 & 1955 Summer Records: 1954–included all three checklists; 1955–included all three checklists (up to 6 or 8 Aug 22–Sep 2). Listed as Yellowthroat Warbler.
- 1970 Summer Checklist: highlighted and marked as known to breed in area. Listed as Yellowthroat.
- Banding: 131 total over twelve seasons, peak 60 in Fall 1981, max 27 on May, 20 1985.

Second-most common summer resident warbler in the state (Vickery et al., 2020). Large movements often events of five+ days, especially in spring, when the birds occur all over the island, preferring brushy/grassy areas; a favored spot in migration is the edge of the Meadow. The large count of 60 on Sep 26, 2013 was mostly seen/heard in shrubby thickets on the east side of the island. In addition to persistent singing in summer and territorial defense on Jun 11, 2019 (DH), breeding was confirmed for the MBA based on reports of adults carrying food spanning Jun 24–Jul 3, feeding young on Jul 19, 2021 (MCu), and recently fledged young on Jul 19, 2021 (HIAC et al.). Most notable age/sex data refers to the count of 60 on Oct 4, 2012—"mostly juvenile looking birds" (DH), otherwise scattered reports of all classes.

Historical/Regional:

- Palmer: cites Dewis and Wentworth records.
- Cruickshank: cites Wentworth Oct 24 record as late.
- Vickery: cites >20 on May 29, 1983 (ST) as late May migration and 20 on Sep 25, 1983 (DF, 25 on Sep 26, 1994 (PDV) and 25 on Sep 22, 2004 (MI) as past peak. (JVW in Vickery et al., 2020).

Common Yellowthroat, May 22, 2018. © Luke Seitz.

HOODED WARBLER
Wilsonia citrina

Status: Rare spring and fall vagrant.

Occurrence: Thirty-seven records (25 spring, 12 fall) since first recorded Sep 1970. Spring records over nineteen years since 1979 (three records in 2004), span limited period of May 13–w/e Jun 6; Spring maxima: 2 on May 28, 1994 (HN), May 17–21, 2005 (GD, RSm, et al.), May 17, 2019 (BP et al.) & May 21, 2019 (KS). Fall records over eleven years since 1970 (two records in 2014), span Aug 28–Oct 10; fall max: **3** on Sep 8–9, 1970 (ELK et al.; *AFN* 25[1]: 30). Ten-Year: SP-2, F-3.

- 1970 Summer Checklist: included.

A regular vagrant from the south whose breeding range extends into New York, Connecticut, and Rhode Island; increasing statewide since the 1950s (only four records before 1953) with now ~60 all-time Maine records, with roughly equal numbers occurring in spring and fall (Vickery et al., 2020). Sometimes lingering for multiple days, the longest-staying inds. involved two birds together for five days in 2005 (male and female May 17–21), with the male present for eight days (first reported on May 14–GD et al.) and a single bird for five days in 2015 (May 16–20). It is possible that the max count of 3 in Sep 1970 involved a lesser count on either/both days, but it is still the only fall record involving more than 1 ind. The report of 2 inds. from fall 1998 (*NAB* 53:34–as part of a larger influx in Northeast/Canada) may refer to separate reports of an unreported number during Sep 25–28 (JWa et al.) and unreported number w/e Sep 28, and without further clarification may refer to two reports of the same ind. (considered such for these purposes; included in Vickery, below). Reported from typical locations with thickets around town, including the Ice Pond, Wharf Hill Rd., Tribler Rd., Lobster Cove Rd. (Trailing Yew, the Brewery), Ocean Ave. (Hill Studio) and even on the rocks near a beach; one ind. was found about one hundred yards into dense cover at west end of Alder Trail. Often first located by its distinctive metallic "chip". Many of the inds. were identified to age/sex, involving all classes. Three distinct birds in 2005 (adult male, adult female, first-year female) helped to separate records, while the three records from 2004 cannot be eliminated as a continuing ind. over a ten-day period. The two distinct fall reports in 2014 involved a male and an adult female. A male and female reported on May 17, 2019 (BP et al.) may be the two inds. reported on May 21, 2019 (1 female, 1 unknown–KS).

Historical/Regional:

- Vickery: cites 1 on May 31–Jun 6, 2000 (WBo–*reported as w/e Jun 6*) as latest spring; 2 inds. reported fall 1998 (*NAB* 52:34 [*should be volume 53*]) part of a wider influx and 1 on Sep 23, 2011 (JT, LS), 1 on Sep 24, 2012 (mob) and 1 on Sep 19, 2016 (WR, RH, BTn; PDV in Vickery et al., 2020).

Hooded Warbler, May 15, 2005. © Geoff Dennis.

AMERICAN REDSTART
Setophaga ruticilla

Status: Common spring and fairly common fall migrant, uncommon summer resident.

Occurrence: Spring dates span May 5–mid Jun (overlapping with breeding), peak mid–end May; spring max: **250** on May 23, 2013 (FM), 163 on May 24, 2019 (JT, CL, TJe), 160 on May 26, 2016 (PDV), 134 on May 22, 2022 (LS), 130 on May 30, 2013 (RL, ML). Present in low numbers throughout summer, with breeding under way Jun–Jul; summer max: 6 on Jul 12, 2021 (BTh), 5 on Jun 21, 2019 (KD), 4 on Jun 17, 2019 (ASa), Jul 14, 2021 (BTh), Jul 5, 2022 (DH) & Jul 7, 2022 (LS, MWa). Fall dates span early Aug–Oct 22, peak late Aug–mid Sep; fall max: 45 on Sep 21, 2004 (LB) & Sep 20, 2020 (LMu, BBc, JMu), 36 on Sep 7, 1964 (HT, CP, RLP; *AFN* 19[1]: 15) & Sep 10, 1964 (RLP; *AFN* 19[1]: 15), 30 on Sep 15, 1964 (RLP; *AFN* 19[1]: 15) & Sep 7, 1980 (PDV) & Sep 7, 1986 (PDV), 25 on Sep 19, 2020 (DH, EJ), 21 on Sep 12, 2020 (BMa). Ten-Year: SP-10, SU-8, F-10.

- *MABB*: possible; MBA: confirmed.
- 1899 Checklist: included as Redstart.
- 1900–1908 Reconnaissance & Supplements: 10 on Jun 5, 1908—heard as many as 8 and saw one pair; commonest warbler, along with Black-throated Green (FA); unreported number during Jul 31–Aug 2, 1908 (WM).
- 1909 Notes: quite common and singing in woodlands. Listed as Redstart.
- 1914 & 1916 Checklists: unreported number on Aug 1, 1914; included as Redstart 1916.
- 1915–1919 Taylor Journals: 1915–Aug 9 (2), 15, 16, 28, Sep 12 (1); 1916–Aug 19, 21 (1), 26, Sep 6 (20), 10; 1917–Aug 4 (7), 16 (6), 18 (5), 19 (4); 1919–Sep 3 (2), 4 (6), 5 (1), 13 (1).
- 1918 Fall Migration Census: Dewis–Sep 4 (2), 7 (1), 8 (1), 9 (1), 11 (1), 12 (1); Wentworth–Oct 8, 9. Listed as Redstart.
- 1939 Summer Census: true summer resident. Listed as Redstart.
- 1944–1967 Farrell Records: 1948–May, 1949–Sep; 1950–Sep; 1951–May; 1953–Aug, Sep; 1954–Jun, Jul; 1955–Jun, Jul, Aug; 1956–May; 1957–Aug; 1959–May, Jun, Jul, Aug; 1960–May, Jul, Aug, Sep; 1961–May; 1967–Jun 1 (1).
- 1954 & 1955 Summer Records: 1954–included all three checklists; 1955–included all three checklists (up to 6 Aug 22–Sep 2). Listed as Redstart.
- 1970 Summer Checklist: highlighted and marked as known to breed in the area.
- Banding: 55 total over ten seasons, peak 23 in Fall 1981, max 9 on May 20, 1985 & May 29, 1990.

It is interesting that almost all of the spring max counts occurred in the 2010s; noted as commonest warbler in 1908 (see above). Although the summer max counts all occurred in 2019, 2021 & 2022, there are several days of 3 inds. and many of 2 inds. in other years, and likely underreported due to lack of coverage, as is the case with fall migration in Aug. Largest movements the last week of May often extend over several days. Occasionally, fallouts involving thousands of birds of many species, deposit redstarts "everywhere and in town," and have even included many of them feeding on sand fleas at the town beaches, referred to as the "redstart invasion at the beach" in 2013 (DH). Likewise, in fall, redstarts are found in all the well-known birding locations around town and along the main trails. Breeding evident as early as late May (although not counted as "summer" record until Jun 16) and continuing until migration starts in early Aug; confirmed as early as May 29 in 2018 (carrying nesting material five times–HIAC) and also carrying food on Jul 4, 2019 (DH) & Jul 19, 2021 (HIAC et al.). The largest flights near the end of May are composed mostly of females and second-year males—sometimes the majority are second-year males (adult males migrate earlier).

Historical/Regional:

- Palmer: cites 1918 Wentworth records (see above), listed as late occurrences.
- Vickery: cites 250 on May 23, 2013 (FM) as high spring number at coastal site and 45 on Sep 21, 2004 (LB) and 12 on Sep 25, 1982 (DF) as high fall counts (JVW in Vickery et al., 2020).

American Redstart, May 12, 2014. © Geoff Dennis.

CAPE MAY WARBLER
Setophaga tigrina

Status: Scarce to uncommon spring and uncommon to fairly common fall migrant.

Occurrence: Spring dates span May 13–w/e Jun 12, peak the second half of May; spring max: 31 on May 24–25, 2019 (JT), 11 on May 21, 2018 (JT, CK), 9 on May 23, 2019 (SS), May 26–27, 2019 (JT, LS, JO) & May 20, 2022 (LS, MWa), 8 on May 24, 2018 (LS). Fall dates span Aug 14–Oct 22, peak early Sep–mid Oct; fall max: **95** on Aug 19,1975 (AKe; *AB* 30[1]: 34), 50 on Aug 31, 1962 (SHi; *AFN* 17[1]: 10), 32 on Sep 30, 2019 (JT, LS, AO), 30 on Sep 6, 1916 (WT, CTa) & Sep 23, 1983 (DF et al.). Ten-Year: SP-10, F-10.

- 1914 & 1916 Checklists: included 1916.
- 1915–1919 Taylor Journals: 1915–Aug 27, 31 (1), Sep 1 (2), 2, 12 (2); 1916–Aug 22, 25, 26, 30, 31, Sep 3, 4, 6 (30), 10; 1917–Sep 5 (25); 1919–Sep 1 (2), 3 (3), 4 (10), 5 (2), 14 (4).
- 1918 Fall Migration Census: Dewis–Sep 7 (3), 8 (1), 11 (1).
- 1944–1967 Farrell Records: 1953–Aug; 1955–Aug; 1959–Aug; 1960–Aug, Sep.
- 1954 & 1955 Summer records: 1955–Aug 22 (1), 24 (3), 26 (2), 27 (1), 28 (2), 30 (1), Sep 1 (2–IW), 2 (1).
- 1970 Summer Checklist: included.
- Banding: 8 total over four seasons, peak 5 in Fall 1981, max 2 on Sep 11, 1981.

Numbers fluctuate greatly from year to year, apparently tied to spruce budworm infestations on the breeding grounds (last significant outbreak in late 1960s/early 1970s [Vickery et al., 2020]); note max fall count in Aug 1975 (also notable for its early timing). A total lack of summer non-migrant sightings is surprising. Spring 2018 was exceptional for a movement May 19–25, with counts of 4+ each day and including the two max reports listed above. Spring 2019 was also exceptional, with 5+ reported eight of the ten days May 19–28, including the five days of max counts noted above. Likely underreported in Oct due to lack of coverage. Most often reported in spruces (especially in their higher branches) at many locations around town; favored areas include Lobster Cove Rd., especially the Trailing Yew area and southward, and the spruces along the upper portion of Lobster Cove Trail (undoubtedly present, as well, in stands of spruce in less-travelled areas of the island). An interesting report involves the high count of 17 on Sep 25, 2016, when the majority were counted as they came ashore in rapid succession at Lobster Cove (MW); 8 were also noted together in the spruces around the power station on Sep 17, 2019 (HIAC). Notable age/sex data relate to reports on Aug 17, 2006—2 males and 1 female in full alternate plumage among 7+ birds (PDV), Sep 17, 2013—all young, both males and females (21 birds, TJ et al.) and Sep. 27, 2013—mostly drab young females (5 birds, SM); otherwise, scattered reports of all age/sex classes.

Historical/Regional:

- Palmer: common on the island Aug 17–28, 1914, when 5–20 were repeatedly seen on single outings (Fuller, 1914).
- Vickery: cites 4 on May 20, 2009 (EH) as a max spring count and highest fall state counts of 30 on Sep 23–24, 1983 (DF), 17 on Sep 23, 2013 (KL) and 12 on Sep 28, 1989 (BN; JVW in Vickery et al., 2020).

Cape May Warbler, May 24, 2019. Jeremiah Trimble.

CERULEAN WARBLER
Setophaga cerulea

Status: Very rare spring and fall vagrant.

Occurrence: Fourteen records (8 spring, 6 fall) since Sep 1965. Spring records over seven years, span May 15–30: 1 during spring 1977 (fide JCa; *AB* 31[5]: 976), immature male on May 15–25, 1986 (CDD, JS, mob), 1 on May 23, 1987 (SS), 1 on May 25–26, 1996 (SS, TMar, mob), 1 on May 30, 2004 (fide BT), male on May 23, 2016 (PMo) & female on May 23, 2016 (LM, BMo–separate records providing spring max of **2**), 1 on May 21, 2017 (KL). Fall records, all singles over six years, span Aug 17–Sep 28: Sep 1, 1965 (HT, NR; *AFN* 20[1]: 10), Sep 10, 1988 (MAS), Sep 19, 1989 (fide BT), immature on Sep 28, 1995 (JSo, BN), Aug 17, 1999 (EO), female on Sep 17, 2014 (PDV, TJ et al.). Only seven records are listed on the OLMB: three accepted (two in May 2016 and May 2017—ME-BRC #2016–010, #2016–011 & #2017–012, respectively) and four not yet reviewed (May 1986, May 1987, May 1996 & Sep 2014). Ten-Year: SP-2, F-1.

Note that two separate records occurred on Sep 23, 2016, a male and female reported by different observers. The May 1986 ind. was the longest-staying by far, as the only other multiple-day record was two days in May 1996. The 1986 ind. spent at least three of its later days at Swim Beach, while the Sep 1995 and Sep 2014 inds. were found at the Ice Pond, the latter foraging in the alders and a white birch. The Sep 1965 was approached almost close enough to touch (*AFN* 20[1]: 10).

Historical/Regional:

- Vickery: notes four spring records and cites unknown number on May 21, 2017 (DL–*actually 1 ind., observer KL*) as recent; notes six fall records with 1 on Sep 17, 2014 the only one included in eBird (PDV in Vickery et al., 2020).
- OLMB: seventeen additional state records listed (some historical reports not listed)—seven accepted and ten not yet reviewed.

Cerulean Warbler, May 1986. © Scott Surner.

NORTHERN PARULA
Setophaga americana

Status: Common spring and fairly common fall migrant, uncommon summer resident.

Occurrence: Spring dates span Apr 27–mid Jun, peak early May–early Jun; spring max data complicated: **244** on May 21, 2018 (JT), 225 on May 14, 2011 (LS), 187 on May 22, 2022 (LS), 166 on May 16, 2022 (LS, MWa), 150 on May 16, 2004 (TV), hundreds on May 24, 1998 (TV), hundreds on May 20, 2002 (600–800 listed as total for May 19–24–TV). Small numbers present as breeders in coniferous forest, where the nest is made in usnea lichen; summer max: 5 on Jul 15, 2021 (BTh), 4 on Jul 9, 2018 (JK), Jun 22, 2019 (KD), Jun 29, 2022 (NE) & Jul 4, 2022 (DH, AH), 3 on Jul 4, 2018 (DH), Jun 17, 2019 (ASa) & Aug 14–15, 2022 (LS, MWa). Fall migration mid Aug–Nov 4, peak early Sep–early Oct; fall max: 180 on Sep 25, 2009 (LS–unusually high fall total), 70 on Sep 25, 2009 (WR), 60 on Sep 20, 1964 (RLP; *AFN* 19[1]: 15), 50 on Sep 19, 2020 (LMu, BBc, JMu). Ten-Year: SP-10, SU-7, F-10.

- *MABB*: confirmed; MBA: confirmed.
- 1909 Notes: a few singing in evergreen woods containing usnea lichen. Listed as Blue Yellow-backed Warbler.
- 1914 & 1916 Checklists: unreported number on Aug 2, 1914 (listed as Parula Warbler); included as Parula Warbler 1916.
- 1915–1919 Taylor Journals: 1915–Sep 12 (1); 1916–Sep 6 (1), 10; 1917–Aug 16 (1), 18 (1), 19 (1), 23 (2); 1919–Sep 1 (2), 3 (1), 4 (1), 13 (2).
- 1918 Fall Migration Census: Dewis–Sep 8 (1); Wentworth–Sep 29, Oct. 4, 6, 7, 8, 9, 20 (1). Listed as Northern Parula Warbler.
- 1944–1967 Farrell Records: 1948–May; 1955–Jun, Aug; 1959–May, Jul, Aug; 1960–May, Jul, Aug, Sep; 1961–May. Listed as Parula Warbler.
- 1954 & 1955 Summer Records: 1955–included Jun 11–15, Aug 23 (1), 24 (1).
- 1970 Summer Checklist: highlighted and marked as known to breed in area. Listed as Parula Warbler.
- Banding: 11 total over seven seasons, peak 4 in Spring 1985, max 3 on May 20, 1985.

Large fallouts are often two- or three-day events, with birds occurring everywhere on the island. The impressive count of 225 on May 14, 2011 involved 10–12 inds. in a single apple tree and 25 in a stand of spruces (LS). The unprecedented fall total of 180 on Sep 25, 2009 far exceeds any other fall total and was a one-day wonder; it involved ~15 heard pre-dawn and

~10 coming ashore at Lobster Cove at dawn; third commonest warbler that day after Yellow-rumped and Palm (LS). MBA status based on an adult feeding young on Jul 4, 2019 (DH) and 2 recently fledged young in an apple tree by the Trailing Yew on Jul 15, 2021 (BTh); historical breeding supported by a pair feeding three young on Aug 23, 1960 (*AFN* 14[5]: 432). Age/sex data, noted on days of numerous inds. in mid May over several years, indicates an almost even split of adult males and adult females.

Historical/Regional:

- Palmer: cites 1918 Wentworth records and includes Monhegan among islands with breeders.
- Cruickshank: lists Wentworth Oct 20, 1918 record as late date. Listed as Parula Warbler.
- Vickery: cites hundreds during May 19–24, 2002 (TV) and 225 on May 14, 2011 (LS) as exceptional and 40 on May 26, 1983 (ST) and 40 on May 13, 1997 (DAb, PDV) as typical high spring counts; cites 70 on Sep 25, 2009 (WR) as max fall count (JVW in Vickery et al., 2020).

Northern Parula, May 21, 2018. © Luke Seitz.

MAGNOLIA WARBLER
Setophaga magnolia

Status: Common spring and fairly common fall migrant, uncommon summer resident.

Occurrence: Spring dates span May 3–mid Jun, peak the second half of May; spring max: **353** on May 30, 2013 (RL, ML), 180 on May 26, 2016 (PDV), 120 on May 21, 2014 (BBa), 109 on May 22, 2022 (LS), 100 on May 20, 2002 (TV) & May 20, 2005 (TV). Small numbers present throughout summer as breeders; summer max: 6 on Jul 19, 1984 (PDV), 2 on Jun 16, 2011 (CDd), Jul 4, 2019 (DH) & Jul 10, 2019 (DH). Fall migration dates span mid Aug–Oct 22, peak early Sep–early Oct; fall max: unusually high 150 on Sep 25, 2009 (LS), 30 on Sep 19, 1964 (RLP; *AFN* 19[1]: 15) & Sep 21, 2004 (LB et al.), 22 on Sep 30, 2019 (JT, LS, AO), 20 on Sep 7, 1964 (HT, CP, RLP; AFN 19[1]: 15), 18 on Oct 5, 2012 (WN) & Sep 26, 2013 (SM). Ten-Year: SP-10, SU-3, F-10.

- *MABB*: probable; MBA: confirmed.
- 1900–1908 Reconnaissance & Supplements: 3 singing during May 31–Jun 6, 1908 (FA).
- 1914 & 1916 Checklists: included 1916.
- 1915–1919 Taylor Journals: 1915–Aug 28, 31 (2); 1916–Aug 22, 25, Sep 10; 1917–Sep 13.
- 1918 Fall Migration Census: Dewis–Sep 10 (1), 11(1); Wentworth–Oct 7, 8.
- 1944–1967 Farrell Records: 1948–May, 1951–May; 1954–Jun, Jul; 1955–Jun, Aug; 1959–May, Aug; 1960–May, Aug, Sep; 1961–May.
- 1954 & 1955 Summer Records: 1954–included all three checklists; 1955–included Jun 11–15, Aug 24–Sep 2 (up to 12).
- 1970 Summer Checklist: highlighted and marked as known to breed in area.
- Banding: 14 over seven seasons, peak 3 in Spring 1985 & Spring 2002, max 2 on May 19, 1985 & May 22, 2002.

Highly variable totals from year to year; spring movement is noticeably larger than fall, despite the 150 reported in Sep 2009. Largest numbers tend to be part of massive multi-species fallouts, with Magnolia Warbler one of the most numerous. Remarkable stretches of abundance in some recent springs, with 10+ reported daily May 18–31, 2014 (fourteen days), and May 20–29, 2017 (ten days); 2013 was an incredible year May 17–30 (fourteen days), culminating in the largest count ever (only 4 reported the following day). Reported as "everywhere" during major flights and regularly reported from town or main trail locations, with notable concentrations in spruces; observations include ~20 coming in off the water at Lobster Cove on Sep 25, 2009 (LS), many along Red Ribbon Trail on May 23, 2013 (DH), part of a flight of hundreds of birds/minute flying away from the island on May 30, 2013 (RL, ML), and 60 "falling out of the sky" onto the rocks and bordering trees as they arrived at the island on May 24, 2019 (MC, CC). Another anecdotal observation includes many flycatching from spruces on the still afternoon of May 16, 2019 (DPJ). Few details of breeding beyond singing males; confirmed for MBA on Jul 4, 2019 with a pair carrying food near Burnt Head (DH). Among scattered age/sex data, 19 reported

Magnolia Warbler, May 24, 2019. © Jeremiah Trimble.

May 18–20, 2012 were all adult males.

Historical/Regional:

- Palmer: Wentworth dates cited as latest for state.
- Cruickshank: cites Wentworth records as latest.
- Vickery: cites hundreds during May 19–24, 2002 (TV) and 20 on May 28, 1983 (ST) as high spring counts and 30 on Sep 21, 2004 (LB et al.) as max fall count (JVW in Vickery et al., 2020).

BAY-BREASTED WARBLER
Setophaga castanea

Status: Uncommon spring and fall migrant, accidental summer visitor (historical).

Occurrence: Spring dates span May 13–Jun 5, peak the second half of May; spring max: **14** on May 25, 1985 (SS), 12 on May 26, 1984 (SS), May 24, 2019 (SS) & May 22, 2022 (LS), 11 on May 20, 2018 (JT) & May 20, 2021 (JT, LS). Summer record: unreported number prior to Aug 4, 1918 (WT). Fall dates span Aug 19–Oct 11, peak early Sep–early Oct; fall max: 10 on Aug 19, 1975 (AKe; *AB* 30[1]: 34) & Sep 5, 1981 (PDV), 9 on Sep 11, 1982 (PDV), 8 on Sep 6, 1981 (PDV). Ten-Year: SP-10, F-10.

- 1914 & 1916 Checklists: included 1916.
- 1915–1919 Taylor Journals: 1915–Aug 27 (1); 1918–prior to Aug 4.
- 1918 Fall Migration Census: Dewis–Sep 9 (1), 11 (1); Wentworth–Oct 1, 4, 6.
- 1944–1967 Farrell Records: 1955–Aug; 1959–May, Aug; 1960–May, Aug.
- 1954 & 1955 Summer Records: 1955–Aug 22 (3), 24 (1), 28 (2).
- 1970 Summer Checklist: listed as a summer resident in the past and possible breeder.
- Banding: 8 total over four seasons, peak 5 in Fall 1981, all singles. Banding records provided both the late spring and early fall dates.

High daily numbers of this species do not seem to correlate with the largest overall movements of warblers. The early fall max count on Aug 19, 1975 does, however, correspond with the max fall count of Cape May Warblers that same day. Reports scattered throughout town, without any obvious concentration point.

Historical/Regional:

- Palmer: includes Dewis and Wentworth (latest) records.
- Vickery: cites 1 on Oct 8, 2000 (LBr) as late (JVW in Vickery et al., 2020).

Bay-breasted Warbler, May 24, 2019. © Scott Surner.

BLACKBURNIAN WARBLER
Setophaga fusca

Status: Fairly common spring and scarce to uncommon fall migrant, very rare summer visitor and possible resident.

Occurrence: Spring dates span May 9–mid Jun, peak the second half of May; spring max: **50** on May 23, 1999 (WBo), 35 on May 24, 2019 (MC, CC), 30 on May 26, 2016 (PDV, WJS) & May 27, 2016 (PDV, WJS), 21 on May 20, 2018 (JT). Only four summer records scattered over four years since 1954 (excludes the *MABB* for which there is no date or details): 1 during Jun 19–25, 1954 (ES, AS), 1 on Jul 19, 1984 (PDV), 1 on Jun 20, 2001 (WW), 1 on Aug 10–11, 2010 (TMag). Fall dates span mid Aug–Oct 14, peak early–late Sep; fall max: 6 on Sep 6, 1985 (PDV), Sep 19, 2020 (LMu, BBc, JMu) & Oct 3, 2020 (WR), 4 on Sep 5, 1983 (PDV), Sep 7, 1984 (PDV) & Sep 25, 2009 (WR). Ten-Year: SP-10, F-10.

- *MABB*: possible; MBA: possible.
- 1899 Checklist: included.
- 1915–1919 Taylor Journals: 1916–Sep 10; 1919–Sep 3 (1), 4 (2).
- 1918 Fall Migration Census: Dewis–Sep 7 (1).
- 1944–1967 Farrell Records: 1949–Sep; 1955–Jun, Aug; 1959–May, Aug; 1960–Aug, Sep; 1961–May.
- 1954 & 1955 Summer Records: 1954–included Jun 19–25; 1955–included Jun 11–15, Aug 29 (1).
- 1970 Summer Checklist: listed as a summer resident in the past and possible breeder.
- Banding: 1 on Aug 25, 1981.

Spring of 2016 was exceptional for this species, highlighted by two of the highest single-day counts as part of an eight-day movement (including additional high counts of 18 on May 23 and 14 on May 28). On the other hand, the two max counts in 2019 were the result of just a two-day movement, with numbers tapering off dramatically. Reports scattered from the town birding locations, including Fish Beach and the Ice Pond, and more often from the southern end towards Lobster Cove; also noted in mixed hardwood/fir forest. One large flight was noted as mostly in spruces (LS). MBA status based on a report of a singing ind. on Jun 1, 2021 (RS et al.), possibly a late spring migrant.

Historical/Regional:

- Vickery: cites 50 on May 23, 1999 (WBo) and 12 on May 27, 2006 (LS) as max spring counts and 1 on Oct 14, 2003 (SM et al.) as late fall (JVW in Vickery et al., 2020).

Blackburnian Warbler, May 19, 2019. © Bill Thompson.

YELLOW WARBLER
Setophaga petechia

Status: Common spring and fairly common fall migrant, fairly common summer resident.

Occurrence: Spring dates span Apr 26–early Jun (later migrants mixing with summer residents by late May), peak second half of May; spring max: **"hundreds"** on May 24, 1998 (TV), 180 on May 26, 2016 (PDV, LJ, WJS), 150 on May 14, 2011 (LS), 116 on May 26, 2016 (BN, JO, JT). Multiple inds. regularly reported throughout summer period; summer max: 10 on Jul 8, 2017 (DH), 9 on Jun 12, 2018 (DH), 6 on Jun 12, 2019 (DH). Fall migration is early, extended and complicated, with early migrants mixing with residents by mid–late Jul–Oct 23, peak mid Aug–late Sep; fall max: 33 on Sep 28, 2000 (JT), 27 on Sep 10, 1964 (RLP; *AFN* 19[1]: 15), 25 on Sep 8, 1984 (PDV) & Sep 9, 1985 (PDV), 24 on Jul 20, 2019 (JT). Ten-Year: SP-10, SU-10, F-10.

- *MABB*: confirmed; MBA: confirmed.
- 1899 Checklist: included.
- 1900–1908 Reconnaissance & Supplements: 2 singing during May 31–Jun 6, 1908 (FA); unreported number during Jul 31–Aug 2, 1908 (WM–listed as Summer Yellow Warbler).
- 1914 & 1916 Checklists: unreported number on Aug 1, 1914 (listed as Summer Warbler); included 1916.
- 1915–1919 Taylor Journals: 1915–Aug 9 (5), Sep 2 (1); 1916–Sep 6 (8), 10; 1917–Aug 16 (3), 18 (3), Sep 5 (1); 1918–Aug 4; 1919–Sep 4 (3), 5 (2).
- 1918 Fall Migration Census: Dewis–Sep 4 (3), 6 (2), 7 (3), and 9 (1).
- 1939 Summer Census: regular summer resident.
- 1944–1967 Farrell Records: 1953–Sep; 1954–Jun, Jul; 1955–Jun, Aug; 1956–May; 1957–Aug; 1958–Aug, Sep; 1959–May, Jun, Jul, Aug; 1960–May, Jun, Jul, Aug, Sep; 1961–May.
- 1954 & 1955 Summer Records: 1954–included all three checklists; 1955–included Jun 11–15, Aug 22 (1), Sep 2 (1).
- 1970 Summer Checklist: highlighted and marked as known to breed in area.
- Banding: 89 over 8 seasons, peak 41 in Fall 1981, max 18 on May 20, 1985.

Spring 2011 was exceptional for the early timing and abundance, with 20 occurring on Apr 27 and peaks of 70 on May 13 and 150 on May 14, while Spring 2016 and Spring 2018 were distinctly later with seven out of eight days May 21–28 totaling 20+ (including 116 on May 26) in 2016 and seven straight days of 25+ (May 19–25), including 86 on May 21 and 71 on May 22 in 2018. While some of the largest spring counts occur the last week of May, multiple observers have commented that it already occurs as a common breeder in addition to notable movement during this period, complicating the migration picture in late spring; a similar overlap occurs in early fall. Despite this regular summer presence and certain breeding, few details have been noted; nest building observed on May 30, 2018 (HIAC), adult carrying food on May 26, 2018 (NHa) & Jun 11, 2019 (DH), recently fledged young on Jul 19, 2021 (HIAC et al.). The fall counts of 11 on Jul 18, 2019 (JT) and high count of 24 on Jul 20, 2019 (JT), while falling in the "fall" period (summer parameters Jun 11–Jul 15), are likely a mix of early migrants and remaining breeders. Also of note for early fall were 8 recorded on Jul 29, 2015 as "everywhere above Pebble Beach" (TR). Historical/regional observations (mostly from the mainland) do not even mention the notable presence along the coast/islands in late Sep, while the largest fall Monhegan total occurred on Sep. 28. Late fall birds (Oct) involve scattered reports around town (two identified to sex have been drab females). Of anecdotal interest were many streaming south off the island on the morning of Sep 4, 2016 (DH) and "found in most flowering trees" on May 26, 2016 (WJS–one of the largest spring flights). The 150 on May 14, 2011 were nonetheless fewer than Northern Parulas. Consistently found throughout the fall in lilacs and apple trees along town roads.

The Yellow Warbler picture is further complicated by the probable presence of more than one subspecies. While *S. p. aestiva* is the most widespread in eastern North America, and the subspecies that breeds throughout Maine, darker *S. p. amnicola* breeds just to the north from maritime Canada to the western provinces, and undoubtedly passes through Maine in undetermined numbers. The difficulty of separating subspecies in the field leads to speculation with respect to presence/identification (e.g. "several darker *amnicola*-like birds" among others on May 28, 2017 [LB], one "*amnicola-like*" bird on Sep 29, 2019 [LB], and the separate listing as Newfoundland Yellow Warbler by Palmer [see below]).

Historical/Regional:

- Palmer: cites Dewis records from 1918 as later dates (but not latest).
- Cruickshank: cites Dewis Sep 9, 1918 record as latest.
- Vickery: cites 50 on May 25, 1990 (JVW, AW), 40 on May 25, 1983 (ST) and 25 on May 25–26, 2006 (DL) as state max spring counts and 15 on Sep 25, 1983 (DF) as a max fall count and 1 on Oct 13 & 18, 1998 (WBo) as late (JVW in Vickery et al., 2020).

Yellow Warbler, May 18, 2011. © Geoff Dennis.

CHESTNUT-SIDED WARBLER
Setophaga pensylvanica

Status: Fairly common spring and uncommon fall migrant, very rare summer visitor and possible breeder.

Occurrence: Spring dates span May 9–mid Jun, peak second half of May; spring max: **32** on May 22, 2022 (LS), 25 on May 26, 2019 (DL), 24 on May 30, 2013 (RL, ML), 20 on May 27 & 28, 1995 (SS), May 25, 2014 (DL), May 23, 2016 (BN, JO, JT) & May 25, 2019 (DL). Only three summer records (Jun 16–Aug 15 period): 1 during Jun 27–29, 2005 (DL, JL), 1 on Jul 12, 2010 (TMag), 2 on Jun 16, 2011 (CDd), but included as possible on *MABB* (no details) and MBA. Fall dates span Aug 16–Oct 24, peak last three weeks of Sep; fall max: 18 on Sep 25, 2009 (KFe, SFe), 14 on Sep 12, 1981 (PDV), 10 on Sep 22 & 23, 2004 (MI). Ten-Year: SP-10, F-10.

Chestnut-sided Warbler, Sep 22, 2020. © Bill Thompson.

- *MABB*: possible; MBA: probable.
- 1900–1908 Reconnaissance & Supplements: included in Jenney supplement.
- 1909 Notes: a few in thickets singing late summer song.
- 1915–1919 Taylor Journals: 1915–Aug 16.
- 1944–1967 Farrell Records: 1955–Aug; 1959–May; 1961–May.
- 1954 & 1955 Summer Records: 1955–Aug 22 (1).
- 1970 Summer Checklist: included.
- Banding: 7 over five seasons, peak 3 in Fall 1981, max 3 on Sep 10, 1981.

Spring max counts have all occurred since 1995, with all but one since 2013. MBA status based on a pair in appropriate habitat on Jun 1, 2021 (RS), possibly late migrants; the Jun 29, 2005 report involved a singing male. Few location details provided, but usually reported in/around town. Of 12 inds. reported and identified to sex during a three-day period in 2012 (May 18–20), 11 were adult males and 1 an adult female (DHe, et al.). Four late fall inds. (all in Oct) were identified as juvenile, hatch-year, and 2 female/immature, with the late fall reports occurring at scattered town road locations.

Historical/Regional:

- Vickery: cites 1 on Oct 13, 2013 (KL) as late fall (JVW in Vickery et al., 2020).

BLACKPOLL WARBLER
Setophaga striata

Status: Common spring and fairly common fall migrant, very rare summer visitor and possible former breeder (historical).

Occurrence: One of the later-arriving warbler migrants, spring dates span May 10–Jun 13, peak the second half of May; spring max: **200** on May 25, 1985 (SS), "hundreds" on May 29, 2007 (KL), 160 on May 26, 2016 (WJS), 150 on May 16, 2004 (TV), 142 on May 22, 2022 (LS), 100 on May 26, 1985 (JVW), May 25, 1996 (SS) & May 26, 2010 (TD). Three summer records: 1 singing male during Jun 27–29, 2005 (DL, JL), 1 singing male on Jun 23, 2019 (CEl), unreported number on Jul 28, 2020 (SRe). Fall dates span Aug 10–Nov 9, peak mid Sep–mid Oct; fall max: **200+** on Sep 25, 2011 (DL), 100+ on Sep 29, 2008 (DL), 80 on Sep 25, 2009 (WR), 65 on Sep 17, 2014 (TJ, PDV, MJ), 55 on Sep 24, 2022 (BME). Ten-Year: SP-10, SU-2, F-10.

- 1900–1908 Reconnaissance & Supplements: 10 reports over five days (5 of singing males, 4 females) during May 31–Jun 6, 1908 (FA); perhaps all migrating, although a male singing in one place for several days considered a possible summer resident. Listed as Black-poll Warbler.
- 1909 Notes: a male, singing a song different from that heard in spring, was on top of a low spruce (MCFJ, CFJ, CJM), possibly indicating breeding and "the most southern summer record" on the Atlantic seaboard. Listed as Black-polled Warbler.
- 1915–1919 Taylor Journals: 1915–Aug 15; 1917–Sep 5 (1); 1919–Sep 13 (3).
- 1918 Fall Migration Census: Dewis–Sep 11 (1), Wentworth–Oct 7.

- 1944–1967 Farrell Records: 1955–Aug; 1959–May, Aug; 1960–Aug. Listed as Black-poll Warbler.
- 1954 & 1955 Summer Records: 1955–Aug 22 (3), 23 (2), 24 (1), 29 (1), 30 (1). Listed as Black-poll Warbler.
- 1970 Summer Checklist: included.
- Banding: 82 over five seasons, peak 53 in Fall 1960, max 37 on Oct 1, 1960.

Inds. occur all over the island during major flights, often the most abundant warbler on peak days, with song audible from all directions in spring. The high count on May 26, 2010 involved "many groups of a dozen or more" (EH). Spring 2018 was consistent with ten straight days of 13+ reported (May 21–30), including 75 on May 26. While not included as a breeder in the *MABB* or MBA, former breeding is suggested by historical accounts (see above) and a statement in 1959 by Sewall Pettingill that Monhegan has nesting pairs. Blackpolls are easily sexed in spring, but seldom reported as such—males reported more often than females (possibly due to their loud singing); of 9 inds. reported and identified to sex during a three-day period in 2012 (May 18–20), 8 were adult males and 1 an adult female (DHe, et al.).

Historical/Regional:

- Palmer: reported after mid Jun on islands as far west as Monhegan.
- Vickery: cites "hundreds" on May 29, 2007 (KL) as high count, 8 on Jun 3, 2007 (JSc) as a coastal high summer count (*considered spring migration for these purposes*), and occasional fall reports of numbers greater than the routine 5–20 inds. (JVW in Vickery et al., 2020).

Blackpoll Warbler, Sep 20, 2020. © Bill Thompson.

BLACK-THROATED BLUE WARBLER
Setophaga caerulescens

Status: Uncommon spring and scarce to uncommon fall migrant, very rare summer visitor.

Occurrence: Spring dates span Apr 27–Jun 8, peak middle two weeks of May; spring max: **40** on May 14, 2011 (LS), 29 on May 16, 2022 (LS, MWa), 20 on May 15, 2011 (TMag) & May 20, 2018 (JT), 19 on May 22, 2022 (LS). Seven summer records over six years since 1954: unreported number during Jun 19–25, 1954 (ES, AS), unreported number w/e Jun 16, 2006 (fide JWa, KG; MARBA), unreported number on Jun 21, 2013 (JKe), 2 on Jul 17, 2013 (JAi, NLo), 1 on Jul 27, 2020 (GBr), 1 on Jul 20, 2021 (MRo), 1 on Jul 29, 2021 (SD); Fall migration more protracted, dates span during Aug (earliest definite Aug 23)–Nov 9; fall max: 20 on Sep 20, 2020 (LMu, BBc, JMu), 18 on Sep 23, 2003 (SS), 17 on Oct 7, 2012 (JT), 15 on Sep 25, 2009 (WR). Ten-Year: SP-10, SU-3, F-10.

- 1918 Fall Migration Census: Wentworth–Oct 6 (1).
- 1944-1967 Farrell Records: 1948–May; 1950–May; 1951–May; 1953–Aug; 1954–Jun; 1955–Aug; 1959–May; 1960–May, Aug, Sep; 1961–May.
- 1954 & 1955 Summer Records: 1954–included Jun 19–25; 1955–Aug 23 (1 male), Sep 1 (1 male).
- 1970 Summer Checklist: included.
- Banding: 13 total over four seasons, peak 5 in Fall 1981, max 4 on Sep 11, 1981.

Several instances of multi-day movements or lingering birds: Fall 2012 saw four straight days of 10+ (Oct 5–8), with significant counts of 14, 14, 13, & 13; likewise, Spring 2018 produced counts of 20, 15, & 10 on May 20–22. On peak migration days, can often be found in the lilacs and apple trees along the town roads, or even feeding in the wrack on the beaches. Six in view at one time have been reported on several occasions, including one unusual instance when they were coming in to feed on orange halves in the spring. Outside of the major fallouts, they are seen in small numbers, often in thickets or dense shrubs around the Ice Pond, Alder Trail, or Underhill Trail. An eBird report of 7 on Aug 15, 2013 has been omitted due to questionable location; it is unclear if any/all of them were on Monhegan, as the distance recorded indicates birding other than on the island—intriguing if correct.

Black-throated Blue Warbler, Oct 13, 2019. © Bill Thompson.

Historical/Regional:

- Palmer: "apparently only a few occur"; a late fall record on Oct 29, 1939 (Mrs. J. Townsend).
- Vickery: cites 1 on Apr 27, 2001 (WBo) and 1 on Apr 27, 2011 (TMag) as early spring and 40 on May 14, 2011 (LS) as max spring and 15 on Sep 25, 2009 (WR) and 14 on Oct 3, 1997 (BN) as high fall counts (JVW in Vickery et al., 2020).

PALM WARBLER
Setophaga palmarum

Status: Scarce to fairly common spring and common fall migrant, very rare summer visitor (historical).

Occurrence: One of the earliest warblers to arrive, spring dates span Apr 6–May 28, peak mid Apr–early May; spring max: 25 on Apr 27, 2011 (TMag), 18 on Apr 21, 2011 (TMag), 16 on Apr 28 & 29, 2011 (TMag). Four summer records from 1954–1960 but possibly migrants (see below): unreported number during Aug 1954 (IF), unreported number during Aug 1955 (IF), unreported number during Aug 1959 (IF), unreported number during Aug 1960 (IF). Fall migration protracted and late, dates span late Aug (earliest definite during Aug 30–31)–Dec 10, peak mid Sep–late Oct; fall max: **350** on Oct 4, 2012 (DH), 275 on Sep 25, 2009 (LS), 270 on Sep 24, 1994 (PDV). Ten-Year: SP-9, F-10.

- 1914 & 1916 Checklists: included 1916.
- 1915–1919 Taylor Journals: Sep 13 (1).
- 1918 Fall Migration Census: Wentworth– recorded seventeen days Sep 29–Oct 25, including every day Oct 17–25; most noteworthy were many on Oct 19 and fairly common on Oct 24. Listed as Yellow-palm Warbler.
- 1944–1967 Farrell Records: 1950–Apr, May, Oct; 1951–Apr, May, Nov; 1954–Aug, Sep, 1955– Aug; 1959–May, Aug; 1960–Apr, May, Aug, Sep; 1961–Apr, May.
- 1970 Summer Checklist: included.
- Banding: 92 total over 5 seasons (recorded as Western Palm Warbler and Yellow Palm Warbler), peak 45 in Fall 1960 (all Western), max 21 on Oct. 1, 1960; 26 banded in 1962 were all Yellow (max 6 on Sep 24); overall 30 Yellow, 62 Western.

Lack of coverage in Apr affects the extent and understanding of the spring migration, as evidenced by max counts all from 2011 (a year with almost daily reporting from TMag); likely underreported in late fall for the same reason. Aug reports from 1954–1960 (see Farrell Records above) lack specific dates and could be from late in the month and therefore would likely be early fall migrants instead of wandering non-breeders; species does breed around sphagnum bogs and blueberry barrens just to the north and east, including large islands, so included as summer records here. Sightings on Monhegan are widespread—major fallouts involve birds "everywhere", including numbers in the wrack on the beach and rocks at Lobster Cove, town beaches, in trees and on lawns.

There are two subspecies that are distinguishable in the field: "Yellow" *D. p. hypochrysea* and "Western" *D. p. palmarum*. Yellow Palms are the subspecies that breeds in portions of Maine and are the expected spring migrant; almost all of the records since Spring 2011 have been identified to subspecies (40+ records), including 31 of 35 inds. in 2011 (the only Apr with extensive coverage), and several others dating back to 1984—all have been Yellows, except in 2015, when three reports of singles were all Western Palms (one unidentified report). There are many Westerns that follow a coastal path in the fall that includes Monhegan, to the extent that either subspecies can be present or predominate throughout the season (Western considered more common than Yellow by Vickery et al., 2020); subspecific identification has increased with the use of eBird, and roughly half of all reports since 2011 indicate subspecies, most often with both present on the same day; it should be noted, however, that on twelve of the fourteen days with 50+ identified, Yellows dominate by a large margin (including the max of 350 [40 were Yellow and 10 Western], 200–300 on Sep 25, 2009 (WR–"mostly Yellow"), 165 on Oct 7, 2012 [LS, DL, KL–"almost all Yellow"], and 100 on Oct 11, 2011 (DH–75 Yellow, 25 Western)—also note banding results below. Subspecies max: Yellow–270 on Sep 24, 1994 (PDV), Western–60 on Sep 30, 1985 (PDV). It is remarkable that the acceptance of Westerns is a fairly recent phenomenon, as that was not the case as recently as Palmer in 1949.

Historical/Regional:

- Cruickshank: *D. p. hypochrysea*–early fall record of Sep 4, 1936 (RTP, AC); *no mention of spring migration or Western, D. p. palmarum.* Listed as Yellow Palm Warbler.
- Vickery: cites 25 on Apr 27, 2011 (TMag) as high spring count and four high fall counts of "Western" Palm Warblers: 300 on Oct 4, 2012 (*actually 350 reported with 40 Yellow and 10 Western*), 165 on Oct 7, 2012 (DL, KL, LS–*noted as "almost all Yellow"*), 100 on Sep 28, 2013 (SS) and 75 on Oct 11, 2011 (DH–*actually 100 reported with 75 Yellow and 25 Western*; JVW in Vickery et al., 2020).

Palm Warbler, Sep 22, 2020. © Bill Thompson.

PINE WARBLER
Setophaga pinus

Status: Rare to scarce spring and uncommon fall migrant, very rare summer and accidental winter visitor.

Occurrence: An early spring warbler migrant, dates span Apr 5–May 31; spring max: 5 on May 13, 2022 (LS, MWa), 3 on May 16, 2022 (LS, MWa), 2 on Apr 5, 2011 (TMag), May 21, 2011 (NH), May 20–21, 2017 (DHe, LC), May 14, 2022 (LS, MWa) & May 22, 2022 (DTu). Five summer records: 1 on Aug 11, 1915 (WT), unreported number on Aug 19, 1916 (WT, CTa), pair on June 23, 2012 (RC), 2 on Jul 27, 2020 (eBird), 1 on Jul 3, 2022 (WK). Protracted fall dates span Aug 22–Nov 12, peak mid Sep–early Nov; fall max: **11** on Oct 12, 2015 (LS), 10 on Oct 2, 2009 (BC), 9 on Oct 1, 2003 (JT). An amazing record of 4 on Feb 7 & 15, 1995 is the only winter report (fide SP, KG; *FN* 49[2]: 129). Ten-Year: SP-7, SU-3, F-10.

- 1914 & 1916 Checklists: included 1916.
- 1915–1919 Taylor Journals: 1915–Aug 11 (1), Sep 1 (1), 2; 1916–Aug 19, 22, 25, 26, Sep 10; Sep 5 (5); 1919–Sep 3 (3).
- 1918 Fall Migration Census: Dewis–Sep 6 (1), Sep 9 (1), Wentworth–Oct 1.
- 1944–1967 Farrell Records: 1959–Aug; 1960–Aug.
- 1970 Summer Checklist: included.

As one of the earlier warblers to arrive in spring, it is undoubtedly underreported due to the lack of coverage before May; it is surprising that all of the spring records have occurred since 1997. In fall, all of the highest counts (7+) have occurred since 2003 and fall between the dates Sep 30–Oct 12. In fact, there are few fall records before 2000 and all of single inds., except for historical records by WT in 1916 and 1919; the extended seasonal peak is largely due to a late push in 2016, with 5 inds. each on Oct 23 & 24 and the last fall date of Nov 5. Better late-season fall reporting may explain the increase in numbers over the season/years and bears further investigation. The summer and winter records also seem lacking, based on broader range or occurrence considerations; the Aug 1959 and 1960 reports are possible summer visitors, but considered early fall migrants for these purposes. Despite small numbers, inds. often located together in areas around town, e.g., 7 or 8 in trees near Island Inn (out of 10 birds reported), 3 in spruces west of the church (out of 8), 5 in trees near the Library/school (out of 7), "all 3 together", etc.; other locations include the town side of the Meadow and the Lobster Cove area. Continuing birds are likely the source of reports on subsequent days, particularly noticeable in spring, when it appears there are a number of two-day records and one three-day record. Very few assigned to age/sex (all in fall): 4 males, 2 females on Oct 10, 2014 (JT), adult males on a couple of occasions, and only one hatch-year male—multiple reports only touch on brightness of yellow or gray, illustrating a probable range.

Historical/Regional:

- Vickery: cites Feb 1995 records above as remarkable in winter (JVW in Vickery et al., 2020).

Pine Warbler, May 13, 2022. © Luke Seitz.

YELLOW-RUMPED WARBLER
Setophaga coronata

Status: Common spring and abundant fall migrant, scarce summer visitor and probable breeder, very rare winter visitor.

Occurrence: Spring migration spans Apr 4–early Jun, extended peak mid–late Apr–end of May (undoubtedly underreported in Apr); spring max: 104 on Apr 27, 2011 (TMag), 80 on May 12, 1997 (PDV), 70 on Apr 29, 2011 (TMag). Probable breeder, with scattered reports of singles or pairs during the summer months, but direct evidence lacking; summer max: 7 on Jul 2, 2019 (DL, JL), 6 on Aug 11, 1915 (WT), 4 on Jun 21, 2019 (KD), 3 on Jul 27, 2020 (GBr) & Jun 25, 2022 (KL). Apparent fall migrants arrive the last week of Aug–early Dec, peak second week Sep–late Oct; fall max: **1,900** on Oct 12, 2014 (LS et al.), 1,000 on Sep 28, 1983 (PDV), Oct 7, 1989 (SS), Oct 7, 1990 (SS) & Sep. 29, 1992 (PDV), 825 on Oct 4, 2020 (JT, LS, BBy), 687 on Oct 5, 2015 (JT, JO). Eight winter records, all but one from the CBC period (1 on Feb 7, 2009–TMag), highlighting the lack of coverage during this season; winter max: 14 on Jan 4, 2007 (CBC–PDV, et al.), 7 on Dec 22, 1988 (CBC–PDV), 3 on Jan 3, 2015 (CBC–DH, et al.). Ten-Year: SP-10, SU-10, F-10, W-1.

- *MABB*: possible; MBA: possible.
- CBC: 6 years (23%) plus one count week, first on Dec 22, 1988, max 14 on Jan 4, 2007, avg 1.2.
- 1900–1908 Reconnaissance & Supplements: one male observed on Jun 5, 1908 (FA).
- 1909 Notes: a few heard singing in the woods.
- 1914 & 1916 Checklists: included 1916.
- 1915–1919 Taylor Journals: 1915–Aug 11 (6), 15, 27, 28, 31 (6), Sep 1, 2, 5, 12 (1); 1916–Aug 21, 22, 25, 26, 31 (1), Sep 3, 4, 6; 1919–Sep 1 (3), 3 (15), 4 (10), 5 (3). Listed as Myrtle Warbler.
- 1918 Fall Migration Census: Dewis–Sep 7 (1), 9 (1), 10 (1), 11 (1), one noted as feeding on the sand near the fish house; Wentworth–Oct 4, 6, 7, 8, 9, 12, 15, 16, 17 (a few), 18, 19 (fairly many), 20 (several), 21 (many), 23 (many), 24, (common), 25 (3). Listed as Myrtle Warbler.
- 1944–1967 Farrell Records: 1948–May; 1949–Sep; 1950–Apr, Oct; 1951–Oct; 1953–Aug; 1954–Jun, Jul; 1955–Jun, Jul, Aug; 1956–May; 1957–Aug; 1958–Sep; 1959–May, Jul, Aug; 1960–Apr, May, Aug, Sep; 1961–May.
- 1954 & 1955 Summer Records: 1954–included Jun 27–Jul 4 & Jul 10–16; 1955–included all three checklists (up to 6 or 8 Aug 22–Sep 2). Listed as Myrtle Warbler.

- 1970 Summer Checklist: included, marked as known to breed in area.
- Banding: 520 total over six seasons (most common species banded), peak 261 in Fall 1961, max 104 on Oct 9.

Easily the most abundant warbler species encountered on Monhegan during migration (and eastern North America as a whole). Seen everywhere on the island during fallouts, including descriptions such as "bundles." Notable flights described from numerous locations during the fall: as part of the record 1,900 on Oct 12, 2014, 1,100 were seen after dawn behind the school, with many departing from the island and hundreds present the rest of the day, especially at the north end (LS et al.); many at dawn over Lobster Cove and heading west toward the mainland on Sep 30, 2007 (DL); most abundant warbler on island Sep 25, 2009 with 50+ coming in off the water at Lobster Cove at dawn and hundreds streaming over the Murdock House afterwards (LS); flocks of 20+ flying overhead most of morning on Oct 22, 2011 (MI et al.); "masses seen from the ferry" on Oct 7, 2012 (LS). As in the case of other early arriving species, lack of coverage in April affects the extent and understanding of the spring migration, not to mention the lack of late fall and winter reporting. Fall 2015, 2020 & 2021 were exceptional for large movements over extended periods: 2015–100+ recorded ten straight days (Oct 4–13), including high counts of 687 on the 5th and 478 on the 6th; 2020–100+ on seven straight days (Oct 3-9, 100 on Oct 11), including high counts of 825 on the 4th and 500 on the 3rd; 2021–100+ on nine straight days (Sep 30–Oct 8), including a high of 321 on the 3rd. While not included in the fall max, a significant combined total of 4,000 was reported for the period Oct 8–13, 1997 (SS). Numbers can fluctuate markedly from day to day, with only 75 present the day after the record flight of 1,900 in 2014 (375 the day before). Of note regarding breeding, one first-year bird (out of 2 inds.) was reported Aug 6, 2013 (TR) and 3 juveniles were reported Aug 21, 2013 (BW)—the possibility of post-fledging dispersal or early migration cannot be ruled out. Possible status on MBA due to a singing male on Jun 4, 2019 & Jun 4, 2020 (DR), both possibly late migrants. Other age/sex data has been largely absent. One ind. banded as part of Operation Recovery on Oct 9, 1961 was recovered in Mississippi on Mar 15, 1962.

While "Myrtle" is the expected subspecies (*S. c. coronata*), no records of the western "Audubon's" subspecies (*S. c. auduboni*) have been recorded on Monhegan, despite their casual status in most eastern states and provinces. Roughly half of all reports over the past ten years have indicated the subspecies as "Myrtle."

Historical/Regional:
- Palmer: although nests on inshore islands, not yet reported as a breeder on Monhegan.
- Vickery: cites 400 on Sep 26, 1994 (PDV) as max fall count and 180 on Oct 2, 2017 (LS) as a recent high count (JVW in Vickery et al., 2020).

Yellow-rumped Warbler, Oct 12, 2019. © Bill Thompson.

YELLOW-THROATED WARBLER
Setophaga dominica

Status: Very rare spring and rare fall vagrant.

Occurrence: Twenty records (9 spring, 11 fall) since Oct 1989. Spring records over eight years since 1999 (two in 2017), span May 6–29: 1 during w/e May 11, 1999 (WBo; *NAB* 53]1]: 260), one on May 21–25, 2000 (WH, GE et al.), 1 on May 17–21, 2001 (GD, WBo; *NAB* 55[3]: 277), unreported number w/e May 30, 2008 (fide KG, LS, BHa; MARBA), unreported number May 5–6, 2009 (fide EH; MARBA), 1 on May 21, 2010 (GD), 1 on May 6–16, 2017 (TDo et al.), 1 on May 16, 2017 (RM–a second ind. joining the long-staying previous record), 1 on May 29, 2018 (PMo, MS). Fall records over ten years since 1989, span Sep 13–Nov 2: 1 on Oct 7–8, 1989 (SS, MBe), 1 on Sep 27, 1991 (SS), unreported number w/e Sep 29, 1998 (WBo; *NAB* 53[1]: 33), unreported number on Sep 13 *or* 14–w/e Sep 30, 2003 (WBo; *G* 33[4]: 38, *G* 33[4]: 48), 1 on Sep 22, 2004 (MI), 1 on Sep 27–28, 2010 (DH, EH et al.), 1 on Oct 17–26, 2010 (TMag.), 1 on Oct 7, 2011 (LD), 1 on Sep 13, 2016 (PDV, HM, EL), **3** on Oct 28–30, 2017 with 1 resighted on Nov 2, (KL, PD), 1 on Nov 2, 2017 (DC), 1 on Sep 30, 2022 (KFe). Ten-Year: SP-2, F-3.

This southeastern species has experienced a limited northward expansion since the 1940s and now breeds as close as New York and New Jersey (McKay and Hall, 2020); first recorded in Maine in 1948, accidental until 1970 but >40 records statewide since then (Vickery et al., 2020). Seven of the Monhegan records involve multiple-day stays, sometimes over extended periods containing days without sightings (presumed same ind. based on rarity, but not definite): Oct. 7–8, 1989, three days over May 21–25, 2000, two days over May 17–21, 2001, three days of an undetermined period Sep 13–w/e Sep 30, 2003, two days Sep 27–28, 2010 (reported as present already for a few days on Sep 27), five days over Oct 17–26, 2010, five days over May 7–16, 2017, and the max count of 3 each day Oct 28–30, 2017, with 1 apparently continuing until Nov 2. The May 2010 ind. was seen on the railing of the "chat" bridge on Ocean Ave. (GD). The Sep 27, 2010 ind. was reported in the spruces at Tom Martin's and later feeding on plums near the dock (DH). The long-staying spring 2017 ind. was seen at Travis Dow's suet and orange feeders on the top of Horn's Hill on May 6–7, near the Monhegan House on May 14, and in town and then near the library on May 15 (DH, JT); the next day 2 inds. were simultaneously seen in adjacent spruces (location unknown). The 3 in Oct 2017 were flycatching together at the Fish Beach breakwater on the 28th and on Swim Beach (on the beach wrack and from the rocks) on the 29th (one was behind the parsonage earlier), and one spent much of the day on the 30th feeding in the seaweed-mulched garden near the church (the other two were seen near Hill Studio earlier); the Nov 2, 2017 ind. was undoubtedly one of three from days previous, still feeding in the church garden (DC). The May 2018 ind. was observed in an apple tree. The Sep 2022 ind. was in a spruce tree north of the Brewery.

Two historically recognized subspecies were possible in Maine: *S. d. dominica* (eastern) and *S. d. albilora* (western). Only one Monhegan record was officially identified to subspecies—the "white-lored" *S. d. albilora* (*mistakenly listed as "white-lored" dominica in report*) on Sep 22, 2004 (MI; *G* 34[4] :48). While the fall 2010 record appeared to be all white (EH) and the spring 2017 record had a tinge of yellow in the lores (DH), recent studies have shown this trait to be clinal, so subspecies are no longer recognized (PDV in Vickery et al., 2020).

Historical/Regional:

- Vickery: cites 1 on May 7, 2017 (DH) as early spring and 1 on Sep 13, 2016 (PDV, EL, HM), 1 *S. d. albilora* on Sep 22, 2004 (MI), and 1 intermittently Oct 17–26, 2010 (TMag) as fall records (PDV in Vickery et al., 2020).

Yellow-throated Warbler, May 12, 2010. © Geoff Dennis.

PRAIRIE WARBLER
Setophaga discolor

Status: Scarce spring and scarce to uncommon fall migrant.

Occurrence: Spring dates span May 6–Jun 8, peak mid–late May; spring max: 2 on May 15, 2011 (RS), May 15, 2021 (JT, LS, JO) & May 22, 2022 (JT et al.). Fall dates span Aug 9–Nov 4, peak mid Sep–early Oct; fall max: **7** on Sep 27, 1997 (JWa), 6 on Sep 27, 1997 (JMa), 4 on Sep 25, 2000 (JT), 3 on fourteen days spanning Sep 21–Oct 5. Ten-Year: SP-9, F-10.

- 1944–1967 Farrell Records: 1959–Aug; 1960–Aug; 1961–May.
- 1970 Summer Checklist: included.
- Banding: 3 total over three seasons, 1 on Oct 4, 1960 (*first record for the island?*), May 20, 1985, & Sep 23, 1985.

Sightings reported at many of the town locations, often occurring in shrubs, thickets, or apple trees, but also in spruces. Inds. will often continue for two–three days or even longer, and, when multiple inds. are present they are sometimes seen together, such as 3 inds. at the end of Sep 2017. Only 3 spring inds. identified to age/sex, all females (although 1 singing bird was doubtless an adult male), while 6 juveniles (including both inds. on Oct 9, 2011) and 2 adult females (with one juvenile on Sep 28, 2017) were identified in the fall. The earliest fall ind. on Aug 9, 2022 was a female found at White Head with other warblers (LZ).

Historical/Regional:

- Vickery: cites 7 on Sep 22, 2003 (JWa) and 6 on Sep 27, 1997 (JMa) as high fall counts (JVW in Vickery et al., 2020).

Prairie Warbler, Sep 26, 2021. © Bill Thompson

BLACK-THROATED GRAY WARBLER

Setophaga nigrescens

Status: Accidental fall vagrant.

Occurrence: One record: 1 on Sep 17, 2020 (DR et al.). Sixth Maine record; accepted by ME-BRC #2020–030. Ten-Year: F-1.

Observed feeding in the lower limbs of a spruce tree by the Sterling Harbor House (across Wharf Rd. from the Island Inn) at ~8:30 a.m. Remarkably, this is the same area in which the island's first MacGillivray's Warbler was seen that afternoon.

Black-throated Gray Warbler, Wharf Rd., Sep 17, 2020. © Don Reimer.

Historical/Regional:

- Vickery: mentions three additional Maine sight records in 1952, 2007, & 2015 to go along with the other state records on the OLMB (PDV in Vickery et al., 2020).
- OLMB: six additional state records—four accepted and two not yet reviewed; earliest in 1936.

TOWNSEND'S WARBLER

Setophaga townsendi

Status: Accidental spring and very rare fall vagrant.

Occurrence: Three records (1 spring, 2 fall). Spring record: second-year on May 23, 2022 (MWa et al.; ph.). Fall records: adult male on Sep 13, 1993 (JSu, MSu, HT [ph.], TMar; *MBN* 7[1], *AB* 48[1]: 89), juvenile male on Sep 13–21, 1999 (HN, TMar). First, third and sixth Maine records; 2022 record accepted by ME-BRC #2022–013, 1993 & 1999 records not yet reviewed. Ten-Year: SP-1.

The May 2022 ind. was in spruces and a flowering pear tree at the nouth end of Lobster Cove Trail.

Historical/Regional:

- Vickery: cites two records above (PDV in Vickery et al., 2020).

- OLMB: three additional state records—two accepted (Nov 28, 2012–Jan 19, 2013 in Winterport, Waldo Co. and Jan 8–27, 2022 in Cape Elizabeth, Cumberland Co.) and one not yet reviewed (Dec 15, 1993–Jan 5, 1994 in Portland, Cumberland Co.).

Townsend's Warbler, May 26, 2022. © Luke Seitz.

HERMIT WARBLER

Setophaga occidentalis

Status: Accidental fall vagrant.

Occurrence: One record: immature male on Sep 28–Oct 1, 2008 (SS, VM et al.). First Maine record; accepted by ME-BRC #2008–006 (photos by BM).

Historical/Regional:

- Vickery: cites 2008 record above (PDV in Vickery et al., 2020).
- OLMB: one additional state record—accepted (Nov 18–Dec 13, 2013 at Harpswell, Cumberland Co.).

BLACK-THROATED GREEN WARBLER

Setophaga virens

Status: Fairly common spring and fall migrant, uncommon summer resident.

Occurrence: Spring dates span May 5–early Jun, peak the second half of May; spring max: 35 on May 21, 2018 (JT), 30 on May 29, 2016 (DL, JL), 29 on May 26, 2016 (JT, BN, JO), 28 on May 26, 2013 (KL, DL, JL). Breeds in small numbers; summer max: 13 on Jun 22, 2019 (KD), 11 on Jun 23, 2019 (CEl), 10 on Jul 17, 2016 (DH), Jun 21, 2019 (KD) & Jul 15, 2021 (GBr). Fall migration spans mid–late Aug–Nov 13, peak early Sep–mid Oct; fall max: **85** on Sep 25, 2009 (LS), 55 on Sep 21, 2004 (LB), 50 on Oct 1, 2003 (JT), 36 on Sep 21, 2007 (LS). Ten-Year: SP-10, SU-10, F-10.

- *MABB*: confirmed; MBA: confirmed.
- 1900–1908 Reconnaissance & Supplements: 7 singing on Jun 5, 1908, not so many other days (FA).
- 1909 Notes: rather common in evergreen woods singing late-summer song.
- 1914 & 1916 Checklists: unreported number on Aug 2, 1914; included 1916.
- 1915–1919 Taylor Journals: 1916–Aug 20, 22, 26 (1), 30 (1), Sep 4 (1), 6 (10), 10; 1917–Jul 29 (3), Aug 4 (4), 23 (4); 1918–prior to Aug 4; 1919–Sep 1 (4), 3 (5), 4 (3), 5 (1).
- 1918 Fall Migration Census: Dewis–Sep 7 (1), 9 (1), 11 (1); Wentworth–Sep 29, Oct 1, 4, 7, 8, 9, 12, 13, 19 (1), 21 (1).
- 1939 Summer Census: regular summer resident.
- 1944–1967 Farrell Records: 1954–Jun, Jul; 1955–Jun, Aug; 1959–Jul, Aug; 1960–May, Jul, Aug; 1961–May.
- 1954 & 1955 Summer Records: 1954–included all three checklists; 1955–included Jun 11–15 & Aug 22–Sep 2 (up to 10, some apparently still in family groups).
- 1970 Summer Checklist: highlighted and marked as known to breed in area.
- Banding: 9 total over four seasons, peak 4 in Fall 1960, max 3 on Oct 5.

More abundant breeder in Maine than any other state (Vickery et al., 2020). Significant movement in Spring 2018, with 10+ May 18–22, including the max total of 35. Likely to be found anywhere on the island in migration, often in spruces or other evergreens, but also in apple and other deciduous trees, and even seen foraging on the ground. Prefers pines and other evergreens in mixed woodlands for breeding; possible nesting near the north fire station on Jun 13, 2013 (DH) and along the Pebble Beach Trail (aggressive adult male and female responding to "pishing") as late as Aug 7, 2012 (DH). Confirmed breeding on Aug 14, 1964 (adult feeding fully fledged young–AMB; *AFN* 18[5]: 498), Jul 4, 2018 (carrying food–DH) and Jun 22, 2019 (recently fledged young–KD).

Historical/Regional:

- Palmer: cites Wentworth record as a late date.
- Cruickshank: cites Wentworth record as latest date.
- Vickery: cites 55 on Sep 21, 2004 (LB) and 30 on Sep 29, 1995 (BN) as high fall counts and 1 on Nov 7, 2011 as late (JVW in Vickery et al., 2020).

Black-throated Green Warbler, May 21, 2018. © Luke Seitz.

CANADA WARBLER
Cardellina canadensis

Status: Uncommon spring and rare to scarce fall migrant.

Occurrence: One of the later arriving spring warblers, dates span May 14–during Jun 11–15, peak the last two weeks of May (especially numerous May 25–30); spring max: **40** on May 29, 1987 (PDV), 28 on May 26, 2013 (LS), 27 on May 26, 2016 (JT, BN, JO). Fall dates span Aug 9–Oct 6, peak early–late Sep; fall max: 3 on Aug 23, 1955 (EAB), Sep 4, 1981 (PDV), Sep 26, 1981 (PDV), Sep 11, 1982 (PDV), Sep 8, 1984 (PDV) & Sep 9, 1985 (PDV). Ten-Year: SP-10, F-8.

- *MABB*: possible.
- 1899 Checklist: included as Canadian Warbler.
- 1944–1967 Farrell Records: 1955–Jun, Aug; 1959–May, Jun, Aug; 1960–Aug; 1961–May; 1967–Jun 1 (2).
- 1954 & 1955 Summer Records: 1955–included Jun 11–15 (noted as a pair), Aug 23 (3), 24 (1+), 29 (2).
- 1970 Summer Checklist: marked as known to breed in the area.
- Banding: 11 total over three seasons, peak 5 in Spring 1984, max 3 on Jun 6, 1984.

Inclusion on *MABB* and 1970 Summer Checklist possibly due to late spring/early fall migrants, although a "pair" was noted during Jun 11–15, 1955 (CFH, MCFH). Spring 2013 was an extremely productive season, with counts of 8+ on seven of nine days May 22–30, including 28 on the 26th and 20 on the 27th. Noted at the usual birding locations around town and once along the Alder Trail; in one instance it was observed flycatching by a brush pile (near the Brewery), indicating the possible origin of one of its historical names—Canadian Flycatching Warbler (Knight, 1908). Very few records indicate age/sex, but the 13 recorded on May 24, 2013 were "males and females all over town" (FM).

Historical/Regional:
- Vickery: cites 18 on May 29, 1983 (ST) and 40 on May 29, 1987 (PDV et al.) as major spring flights and 1 on Sep 29, 1982 (DF) and 1 on Oct 1–5, 2012 (AV, mob) as late fall (JVW in Vickery et al., 2020).

Canada Warbler, May 23, 2007. © Geoff Dennis.

WILSON'S WARBLER
Cardellina pusilla

Status: Uncommon spring and fall migrant.

Occurrence: Another late-season migrant, spring dates span Apr 25–Jun 16, peak the second half of May; spring max: 37 on May 22, 2018 (JT), 25 on May 25, 1990 (JVW) & May 30, 2013 (RL, ML), 22 on May 20, 1985 (banded). Fall migration dates span Aug 22–Oct 29, peak early/mid Sep–end Sep; fall max: **80** on Sep 7, 1964 (HT, CP, RLP; *AFN* 19[1]: 15), 75 on Sep 11, 1981 (PDV), 60 on Sep 12, 1981 (PDV), 26 on Sep 13, 1981 (PDV), 14 on Sep 7, 1980 (PDV). Ten-Year: SP-10, F-10.

- *MABB*: possible.
- 1914 & 1916 Checklists: included 1916.
- 1915–1919 Taylor Journals: 1917–Sep 5 (5).
- 1918 Fall Migration Census: Dewis–Sep. 9 (1). Listed as Wilson's Black-cap Warbler.
- 1944–1967 Farrell Records: 1948–May; 1949–Sep; 1954–Aug; 1955–Aug; 1956–May; 1959–May, Aug; 1960–Aug, Sep.
- 1954 & 1955 Summer Records: 1955–Aug 22 (1 male).
- 1970 Summer Checklist: included.
- Banding: 99 total over eight seasons, peak 49 in

Fall 1981, max 22 on May 20, 1985, 20 on Sep. 11, 1981 (max fall date).

The Apr 25, 2018 record (DC) is the only one before May 11 and, however unlikely at this date, is supported by a photo. Note that three of the top four fall max counts are consecutive days in 1981 that far outnumber any other fall movement except the 80 inds. on Sep 7, 1964. In addition to the incredible fall movement of 1981 mentioned above, there were notable spring fallouts May 29–31, 1982 (15, 16, 10 reported, respectively), an extensive one May 21–30, 2013 (six days of 10+ reported, concluding with a high count of 25—this fallout also brought many Canada Warblers) and a significant flight May 21–23, 2018 (21, 37, 18 reported, respectively); this latter record contains notes of "covering the western side of the island, including deciduous swales" on May 21 (JT) and an overnight influx on May 22 (JT). Unusually, Wilson's was reported to be one of the most numerous warblers observed on Sep 22, 2008 (unfortunately, total not provided). Inclusion on the *MABB* is possibly based on a late spring/early fall migrant. Most often encountered in brush or scrubby deciduous habitat, including the apple trees and lilacs along many of the town roads and trails such as Underhill. Males and females are readily separable in the field, but age is not. Almost all spring inds. identified to sex were males (20+) and included singing birds on several occasions (the only report indicating females was of 12 inds. that were "almost all males;" twenty-four fall inds. were split—13 male, 11 female.

Historical/Regional:

- Vickery: cites 1 on Jun 13 & 16, 2006 (WBo) as late spring and 10 on Sep 10, 2004 (LBr) as unusual fall count (JVW in Vickery et al., 2020).

Wilson's Warbler, Sep 14, 2021. © Brett M. Ewald.

SUMMER TANAGER
Piranga rubra

Status: Rare to scarce spring and rare fall vagrant.

Occurrence: Fifty-six records (44 spring, 12 fall) since first recorded Oct 20, 1918 (BHW). Spring records over twenty-eight years since 1946 (four in 2019, three each in 1987, 2018 & 2022), span during Apr (earliest definite May 2)–Jun 8; spring max: **3** on May 24, 1987 (DF), 2 on nine days. Fall records over twelve years (eleven years since 1982), span Sep 6 or 7–Oct 21; fall max: 2 on Oct 11, 2010 (JT) & Sep 18, 2015 (BTn, AK). Ten-Year: SP-7, F-3.

- 1918 Fall Migration Census: Wentworth—two records (molting male on Oct 20 and female on Oct 21).
- 1944–1967 Farrell Records: 1946–Apr; 1959–May.
- 1970 Summer Checklist: included.

Spring overshoots and post-breeding dispersal account for the surprising number of records of this "southern" species, which breeds no closer than northern New Jersey; almost annual in spring since late 1990s. Due to its distinguishable plumages during molting and between sexes, tracking of inds. often possible, providing clarity of records and length of stay. Although only 2 were reported on any single day in May 2014 (14th, 18th, 21st), at least 4 inds. (1 male, 3 females) were present during May 19–23 (CB) and 6 for the whole spring (DH; MARBA). Spring inds. are known to linger more often and have remained for much longer periods than fall, the longest being twenty-two days in 2001 (May 9–30); their attraction to oranges at feeders may provide some explanation. Almost all fall records involve single-day reports, except for one two-day (2014) and one three-day (2015). The presence of two inds. on a certain day sometimes permitted simultaneous sightings, but more often these were at different locales. The aforementioned feeders, located at Donna Cundy's and the back of the Meadow are favored recent locations, and inds. have even shown up at seed spread behind the lighthouse. Other sightings have been reported in both seasons at scattered locations throughout the town and once each in the wrack at Lobster Cove and on Fish Beach. Of those identified to age/sex, twelve spring records involved 2 adult males, 8 immature males and seven females. The six fall records identified were all immature/female types.

Historical/Regional:

- Palmer: cites Wentworth records.
- Cruickshank: cites Wentworth records.

- Vickery: cites 3 on May 24, 1987 (DF et al.) as max and 1 on May 27, 2017 (DL) as recent spring, 1 on Jun 3, 2017 (obs. unk.—*observer was MJe*) as summer (*counted as spring for these purposes*; PDV in Vickery et al., 2020).

Summer Tanager, May 16, 2022. © Luke Seitz.

SCARLET TANAGER
Piranga olivacea

Status: Uncommon spring and scarce fall migrant.

Occurrence: Spring dates span Apr 8–Jun 13 (only two records prior to May 3), peak early–late May; spring max: **31** on May 18, 2021 (JT, LS, JO), 15 on May 25, 1983 (ST), 11 on May 20, 2019 (HN), 9 on May 22, 2018 (JT), May 24, 2019 (JT, TJe, CL), May 19, 2021 (JT, LS, JO) & May 23, 2021 (JT et al.). Fall dates span Aug 17–Nov 6, peak mid Sep–early Oct; fall max: 12 on Sep 9, 1983 (PDV), 10 on Sep 12, 1983 (PDV), 8 on Sep 10, 1983 (PDV) & Sep 11, 1983 (PDV). Ten-Year: SP-10, F-10.

- 1900–1908 Reconnaissance & Supplements: unreported number May 1908 (CFJ, ECJ).
- 1914 & 1916 Checklists: included 1916.
- 1915–1919 Taylor Journals: 1916–Sep 10.
- 1918 Fall Migration Census: Wentworth–Oct 1, 6.
- 1944–1967 Farrell Records: 1949–May, Sep; 1950–May; 1955–Aug; 1956–May; 1959–May; 1960–May; 1961–May; 1967–Jun 3 (1), 4 (3).
- 1954 & 1955 Summer Records: 1955–Aug 28 (1).
- 1970 Summer Checklist: included.
- Banding: 4 total over two seasons, peak 2 in Fall 1960 & Spring 1985, max 2 on May 19, 1985.

Exceptional seasons spring of 2019 & 2021 and fall of 1983 resulted in many of the max counts, undoubtedly as inds. lingered over multiple days; 6 at Donna Cundy's feeders (5 male, 1 female) on May 24, 2019 (KL, PDo). Reports from many locations scattered around the island, including the Ice Pond, town roads, White Head Trail, Underhill Trail, and often feeders in spring. Reports of males/females split fairly evenly, with males sometimes singing in the spring. An unusual orange variant male was noted on May 21, 2014 (CB).

Historical/Regional:
- Palmer: cites Wentworth records.
- Cruickshank: cites Wentworth record as late.
- Vickery: cites Apr 8 1990 (KK) and Apr 12, 2005 (WBo) as early spring, Jun 13, 2000 (obs. unk.), Jun 8, 2004 (WBo), and Jun 6, 2011 (TMag) as late spring, 15 on May 25, 1983 (ST) as large spring fallout and a female on Oct 22, 2011 (PM) and 1 on Nov 6, 1988 (*AB* 43: 67) as late fall (PDV in Vickery et al., 2020).

Scarlet Tanager, May 17, 2007. © Geoff Dennis.

WESTERN TANAGER
Piranga ludoviciana

Status: Very rare fall vagrant, accidental winter visitor.

Occurrence: Four records (3 fall, 1 winter). Fall records: 1 on Aug 27, 1968 (PAB, FGB; *AFN* 23[3]: 457), immature female on Sep 29–Oct 6, 2001 ((DF et al., PMo), 1 on Sep 28, 2022 (KFe, SFe). Winter record: 1 on Jan 3–4, 2007 (CBC Jan 4–DF et al.). Ten-Year: F-1.

- CBC: 1 year (4%): 1 on Jan 4, 2007.
- 1970 Summer Checklist: included, noted as rare, casual, or accidental visitor.

There are now ~30 state records since 1949, at

which time only an 1889 record was known, with a concentration in fall and winter (Vickery et al., 2020). The 2001 ind. was located along the slope just below the lighthouse on Sep 29, first seen from Lighthouse Hill Rd. and then from the top of the hill; it was not reported again until Oct 6 (no details). The Jan 2007 ind. was observed in the spruces across from the general store (in front of Tom Martin's) and in the area just to the south, sometimes feeding on bittersweet berries, last seen flying across the Meadow on Jan 4; seen by all members of the CBC count (DF personal comm.). The 2022 ind. was perched along Lobster Cove Rd. near the Brewery.

Western Tanager, Sep 28 2022. © Ken Feustel

NORTHERN CARDINAL
Cardinalis cardinalis

Status: Uncommon to fairly common permanent resident.

Occurrence: Reports scattered throughout the year since 1977, with only one previous record in May 1960 (fide IF), generally fewest in summer; year max: **43** on Nov 9, 2020 (LS, JT), 37 on Nov 12, 2020 (LS, JT), 34 on Nov 10, 2020 (LS, JT) & Nov 13, 2020 (LS, JT), 28 on Nov 9, 2022 (LS, MWa), 25 on May 28, 2016 (BBa), 24 on Nov 11, 2020 (LS, JT), 23 on Nov 13, 2022 (LS, MWa), 20 on Sep 18, 2016 (WR), Sep 19, 2016 (WR, RH), Sep 23, 2016 (BBn, PBn), May 26, 2017 (BBa) & Nov 11, 2022 (LS, MWa). Ten-Year: 10.

- *MABB*: confirmed; MBA: confirmed.
- CBC: 25 years (96%; all but 1941), first on Dec 28, 1978, max 22 on Jan 3, 2013, avg 8.1.
- 1944–1967 Farrell Records: 1960–May.

This formerly southern breeder has established itself as a regular resident, with numbers slowly increasing from the 1970s to the present (considered by Palmer a rare Maine visitor with fewer than ten records as late as 1949 ["most escaped captives"] and breeding first confirmed in 1969); all max counts since 2013 and no report of 10 or more before 1997. No details or specific date provided for the first known Monhegan record in May 1960 (fide IF), but 2 inds. present for the second record on Sep 18, 1977 (PDV). Possible anywhere on the island and sometimes in family groups, most frequent around town and often present at feeders. Breeding noted as early as 1983, with an adult pair with 1 fledged juv. on May 26 (JP, EP) and an adult feeding a fully grown juv. on Sep 18, 1983 (JVW). Recent breeding confirmation includes recently fledged young on Jul 3 & 4, 2018 (DH) & Jul 2, 2021 (DH), an adult feeding two young on Sep 23, 2019 (DR) and an adult female feeding a nearly full-grown juvenile as late as Sep 29, 2020 (WR). The period Nov 9–13, 2020 was exceptional and unexpected, providing max counts (24–43 inds.) and suggests an influx of visitors from the mainland (all other reports in fall 2020 <14); the high of 43 on Nov 9 involved a "concentration at feeders and thickets," with ~12 behind the Monhegan House and Nov 12 produced pockets of up to 11 inds. (LS, JT).

Historical/Regional:
- Vickery: pair with fledged young on May 26, 1984 (JP; PDV in Vickery et al., 2020).

Northern Cardinal, Oct 11, 2020. ©Bill Thompson.

ROSE-BREASTED GROSBEAK
Pheucticus ludovicianus

Status: Uncommon to fairly common spring and uncommon fall migrant, very rare summer visitor and possible breeder.

Occurrence: Spring dates span Apr 15–Jun 4, peak

mid–late May; spring max: **225** on May 25, 1983 (ST; *AB* 37[5]: 845), 100 on May 28, 1983 (PDV) & May 24, 2002 (TV), 80 on May 30, 1983 (PDV). Seven summer records, most in very recent years in Jul (although noted as a possible breeder in *MABB*): unreported number during summer 1907 (CFJ, ECJ– possibly a late spring or early fall migrant), unreported number during Jul 1960 (IF), 1 on Jul 10, 2018 (BPa), 1 on Jul 19, 2018 (MF), 1 on Jul 31, 2018 (JMa), 1 on Jul 18, 2019 (JT), 1 on Jul 18, 2021 (MMe). Fall dates span Aug 24–Nov 5, peak early–late Sep; fall max: 150 on Sep 26, 1981 (PDV), 40 on Sep 9, 1983 (PDV), 30 on Sep 5, 1982 (PDV). Ten-Year: SP-10, SU-3, F-10.

- *MABB*: possible; MBA: possible.
- 1900–1908 Reconnaissance & Supplements: unreported number summer 1907 (CFJ, ECJ), unreported number May 1908 (CFJ, ECJ).
- 1915–1919 Taylor Journals: 1916–Sep 10; 1917– Sep 5 (1); 1919–Sep 13 (1).
- 1944–1967 Farrell Records: 1948–May; 1956– May; 1959–May, Aug; 1960–May, Jul, Aug; 1961– May; 1967–Jun 1 (10), 2 (7), 3 (2), 4 (2).
- 1970 Summer Checklist: included.
- Banding: 48 total over six seasons, peak 24 in Fall 1981, max 8 on May 19,1985.

All max counts took place in the early 1980s, with exceptional numbers in Sep 1981 and May 1983; The mass movement of 1983 extended May 19–30, all seven report days of 25+, including all the top tallies. Abundance has decreased since the 1980s, with no counts over 20 since Sep 2003. The three summer records of 2018 may have involved the same ind., but no details provided and there is a substantial interval between reports; Aug reports in 1959 & 1960 considered early fall migrants for these purposes. MBA status based on singing inds. in two separate locations on Jun 4, 2020 (DR), possibly late migrants. Possible anywhere on the island with deciduous scrub and frequently reported from near the Ice Pond, behind the school, Lighthouse Hill, and Lobster Cove Trail, and at the Cundy feeders in the spring. Scattered reports over the years have indicated a mix of age and sex, with no discernible pattern.

Historical/Regional:

- Vickery: cites 1 on Apr 27, 2011 (TMag) as early, ~225 on May 25, 1983 (ST) and 100+ on May 24, 2002 (TV) as spring fallouts and 20 on May 13, 1997 (DAb, PDV) as unusual spring (PDV in Vickery et al., 2020).

Rose-breasted Grosbeak, May 17, 2013. © Geoff Dennis.

BLACK-HEADED GROSBEAK
Pheucticus melanocephalus

Status: Accidental spring and very rare fall vagrant.

Occurrence: Three records (1 spring, 2 fall), all single birds. Spring record: first-spring male on May 14–15, 2014 (MBu, EG, GD, DC). Fall records: w/e Sep 25, 2001 (VL, fide WBo), immature on Oct 3, 2003 (DAb, MBo, DF). The 2014 record accepted by ME-BRC #2014–004, 2001 & 2003 records not yet reviewed. Ten-Year: SP-1.

No details available for the 2001 report. The Oct 2003 immature ind. was found in the apple tree at the northeast corner of the Lupine Gallery, later moving to near the Tribler Cottage on Tribler Rd (DF). The May 2014 ind. was observed at Donna Cundy's feeders; there are conflicting descriptions of this bird as an adult and immature (pictures indicate a first-spring male)—the ME-BRC's fifth report actually calls it both and eBird has it as an adult.

Historical/Regional:

- Vickery: cites three records above (PDV in Vickery et al., 2020).
- OLMB: fourteen additional state record—four accepted and ten not yet reviewed, earliest 1958.

Black-headed Grosbeak, May 14, 2014. © Geoff Dennis.

BLUE GROSBEAK
Passerina caerulea

Status: Rare spring and scarce fall vagrant, accidental winter vagrant.

Occurrence: Thirty-one spring records over twenty-two years since 1958 (three records in 2012 & 2022), span Apr 12–Jun 13, peak mid–late May; spring max: 3 during w/e May 16, 2000 (WBo), 2 on May 22, 2009 (fide EH; MARBA), Apr 24, 2012 (JB), May 28, 2013 (RL), May 29, 2014 (PMo, MS), May 18–25, 2021 (JT et al., mob). Fall dates span Sep 6–mid Nov, first recorded in Sep 1959 (?Ba, fide IF), peak last third of Sep–early Oct; fall max: **7** on Oct 5, 2011 (DH), 6 on Oct 10, 2011 (DH), 5 on Oct 8, 2011 (JM). Winter record: 1 on Dec 27, 1982 (CBC–PDV). Ten-Year: SP-8, F-8.

- CBC: 1 year (4%), 1 on Dec 27, 1982, avg 0.0.
- 1944–1967 Farrell Records: 1958–May; 1959–Sep.
- 1970 Summer Checklist: included.
- Banding: 1 on Sep 26, 1962.

Surprising number of records for a vagrant; the nearest breeding occurs in northern New Jersey. The max counts, all occurring since 2000, are indicative of an increased presence, supported by extensive records in other parts of Maine, predominantly along the coast, and in sharp contrast to historical accounts (only one record and several questionable reports included by Palmer in 1949). Fall 2011 was exceptional, with the 7 recorded on Oct 5 translating into five days of 3 or more Oct 5–11. Many records have involved stays of one–three days; two spring inds. (immature male & female) apparently lingered for ten days (May 18–27) along Lobster Cove Rd., with at least one present until May 31, while several fall inds. were seen for five days or more; multiple inds. and scattered reports make tracking specific inds. difficult. The phenomenal 1982 CBC ind.—the only CBC record in the U.S. or Canada that year—was apparently present for two weeks or more prior, according to the owner of the feeder it was visiting; heard on several occasions giving its "chink" call. Spring records were sometimes at feeders, but also noted near the Ice Pond on several occasions. Fall reports also occurred at feeders (Tom Martin's in the past and Donna Cundy's or others in recent times) and many other locations around town, including the Meadow, the community garden along Tribler Rd., near the Monhegan House, Lobster Cove Trail and the Ice Pond; the only records away from town occurred at the ravine on the trail approaching Black Head and 1 flying to Manana. In Fall 2011, up to 4 were seen at Tom Martin's feeders at one time, while 5 were seen together on Wharton Ave. The only winter record, an immature, was observed at Rita Wilson's feeders opposite the entrance to the Island Inn. Sixteen of the spring inds. were identified to some stage of age/sex; 4 adult male, 5 immature male, 3

Blue Grosbeak, Oct 3, 2019. © Luke Seitz.

adult female, 1 immature female, 1 female type and 2 immature. Over twenty fall inds. were categorized as female, immature, or female type, along with one blue-headed male; the similarity in plumages makes separation confusing.

Historical/Regional:

- Vickery: cites 1 on May 26, 1984 (SS), 1 on May 28, 1988 (SS), 1 on May 21 & 23–24, 1997 (SS), and 1 on May 29–30, 1982 (PDV) as spring records, 1 on Jun 13, 2011 (TMag) as summer (*counted as spring for these purposes*), 3–5 inds. each fall (DF), and an immature on the Dec 27, 1982 CBC (PDV; PDV in Vickery et al., 2020).

LAZULI BUNTING
Passerina amoena

Status: Accidental fall vagrant.

Occurrence: One record: immature on Oct 4–6, 1978 (DF, TMar, PDV; *AB* 33[2]: 158). Second Maine and entire Northeast record (first confirmed); accepted by ME-BRC #1978–003 (photo by TMar).

First observed coming to seed scattered on the lawn at the Trailing Yew; noted there in the company of a Lark Sparrow and other sparrows on Oct 5 (PDV). Also observed at several localities just to the north of the Trailing Yew towards Tom Martin's place (DF).

Known to hybridize with Indigo Bunting on the western Great Plains where the ranges overlap; a possible hybrid was reported on May 29, 2014 (JT), showing some characteristics of Lazuli Bunting.

Historical/Regional:

- Vickery: cites 1978 record above (PDV in Vickery et al., 2020).
- OLMB: two additional state records—one accepted (Jun 13, 2010 at St. George, Knox Co.) and one not yet reviewed (Oct 1974 on Mount Desert Island, Hancock Co.); there is an unaccepted record for Monhegan on May 25, 2010.

INDIGO BUNTING
Passerina cyanea

Status: Uncommon spring and fall migrant, very rare summer visitor.

Occurrence: Spring dates span Apr 22–w/e Jun 12 (latest definite date Jun 9), peak mid–late May; spring max: >18 on May 25, 1983 (ST), 15 on May 23, 2009 (DS et al.), 9 on May 25, 2015 (JT, BN, JO), 8 on May 29, 1983 (PDV), May 30, 1983 (PDV), May 14, 1997 (PDV), May 31, 2011 (DH) & May 25, 2014 (JT). Four summer records: 2 or 3 during July 2–7, 1909 (CJM–see below), 1 on Jul 16, 1991 (banded), unreported number on Jul 22, 2008, 1 on Jun 18, 2018 (BEv, BEt). Fall dates span during Aug (earliest definite Aug 28)–Nov 14, peak late Sep–mid Oct; fall max: **23** on Sep 24, 2012 (JT, BN), 17 on Oct 2, 2021 (JT, LS), 11 on Sep 26, 1986 (PDV), Oct 6, 2014 (JT et al.), Oct 7, 2020 (JT, LS, BBy) & Oct 3, 2021 (JT, LS). Ten-Year: SP-10, SU-1, F-10.

- 1909 Notes: two or three were seen. Listed as Indigo Bird.
- 1944–1967 Farrell Records: 1958–May; 1959–Jun, Aug; 1960–Apr, May; 1961–May.
- Banding: 8 total over five seasons, peak 3 in Fall 1962, max 2 on Oct 1, 1962.

Known to linger on occasion for several days. The largest flock contained 7 inds., part of the total of 11 on Sep 26, 1986. Reported from many areas around town, but most often from Lobster Cove Rd., also near the Hitchcox House and its feeders, the back of the Meadow, near the lighthouse, and the Cundy feeders in the spring. Of the 20+ spring records indicating age/sex details, the split is roughly 50% male/female, most noted as adult with only 1 first-spring male and 4 indicating female type. Adult males are absent from the twenty relevant fall records, with 1 immature male, 5 adult female, 3 female, 3 immature and 8 immature/female type (highlighting the difficulty in separating the different age/sex groups).

Historical/Regional:

- Palmer: probable female on Oct 22, 1939 (MJT).
- Cruickshank: cites Oct 22, 1939 (MJT) record as latest.
- Vickery: major flight in 1988, cites >18 on May 25, 1983 (ST) and 8 on May 14, 1997 (DAb, PDV) as high spring counts (PDV in Vickery et al., 2020).

Indigo Bunting, May 19, 2021. © Jeremiah Trimble.

PAINTED BUNTING
Passerina ciris

Status: Very rare spring and fall vagrant.

Occurrence: Five records (2 spring, 3 fall) since 1983, all singles. Spring records: male on Apr 27–May 6, 1983 (unknown, fide BT, ph.; *AB* 37[5]: 848), adult male on May 12–14, 2014 (DC, EG, GD). Fall records: immature on Sep 6–8, 1985 (PDV; *AB* 40[2]: 259), adult male on Nov 1, 2010 (TMag), immature on Sep 16–17, 2017 (MW et al., mob). Ten-Year: SP-1, F-1.

After the first Maine record involved a "clearly escaped" adult male in 1904 (Knight, 1908), the second wasn't reported until 1951, after which there are >30 state records, most in spring (Vickery et al., 2020). The Nov 2010 Monhegan ind. was observed at Mattie Thompson's house along Tribler Rd. (near the back of the Meadow). The May 2014 ind. frequented Donna Cundy's feeders off and on all day on May 12 & 14 (no mention of the 13th); a photo by GD also shows the Black-headed Grosbeak! The Sep 2017 ind. was observed foraging on the ground along Ocean Ave. at the south end of the scrubby swale, where seed is often scattered, with two Chipping Sparrows and a Clay-colored Sparrow; observed at the nearby "chat" bridge on the 17th.

Historical/Regional:
- Vickery: cites the five records listed above (PDV in Vickery et al., 2020).

Painted Bunting, May 12, 2014. © Geoff Dennis.

DICKCISSEL
Spiza americana

Status: Rare spring and uncommon fall migrant, accidental summer and very rare winter visitor.

Occurrence: Fifteen spring records over twelve years since 1983 (three records in 2008 & two in 2014), span Apr 22–w/e Jun 2 (latest definite date May 30), all but the Apr 26, 1983 (CL) and Apr 22, 2011 records (TMag) occurring May 14–w/e Jun 2; spring max: 2 on May 16, 2008 (fide EH, SWh, KG; MARBA). One summer record: 1 on Jul 17, 2011 (TMag). Fall dates span Aug 11–Nov 4, peak mid Sep–mid Oct; fall max: **15–35** during Aug 1963 ("almost every day"–JY fide TMar; *AFN* 18[1]: 12), 15–20 on Oct 4, 1963 (TMar; *AFN* 18[1]: 12), 12 on Sep 24, 1995 (PDV, VL et al.), 9 on Sep 1, 1957 (VL et al.) & Oct 3, 2006 (PDV, DM), 8 on Sep 24, 2012 (JT, BN), Oct 10, 2014 (JT), Oct 8, 2016 (LS, JT) & Sep 25, 2021 (DL, ID). Two winter records: 1 on Dec 27, 1994 (CBC–PDV), 1 on Dec 27, 2004 (PDV, CDD). Ten-Year: SP-3, F-10.

- CBC: 1 year (4%), 1 on Dec 27, 1994, avg 0.0.
- 1944–1967 Farrell Records: 1959–Sep.
- 1970 Summer Checklist: included.
- Banding: 13 over three seasons, peak 7 in Fall 1962, max 4 on Sep 26, 1962.

Unclear whether Dickcissel should be considered a true migrant or a regularly occurring vagrant, as the nearest breeding occurs rarely in Pennsylvania, western New York, and south-central Ontario, with the main breeding range occupying the eastern Great Plains. Definite increase in presence over historical accounts; noted as "increasing rapidly" during 1946–1957 along Atlantic seaboard, including the 9 reported on Sep 1, 1957 on Monhegan (Baird et al., 1958). Fall 1963 was exceptional, with a flock of 15–35 reported as "almost every day" in August, dropping to 1–2 almost daily in the first half of Sep (RLP, fide TMar), and a flock of 15–20 on Oct 4. Other large single flocks of 8 noted on Sep 24, 1995 (out of 12 that day) and Sep 25, 2021 (with 2 Clay-colored Sparrows near Meadow behind Monhegan House–DL, ID); despite these flocks, inds. often scattered when multiple birds around. Several other fall records listed as "small flocks" in Vickery (see below) involve multiple days (even a month) without daily totals or discussion regarding repeat sightings: 7 inds. in Sep 1956 (VL et al.), 6 inds. during Sep 25–Oct 2, 1962 (VL et al.) and 18 inds. during Sep 6–10, 1970 (VL et al.). Monhegan records do not appear to reflect as strong a statewide decline since 1980 as indicated by Vickery (2020). Heard as a flyover giving its distinctive call note much more often than it is seen, let alone perched. Reported from many locations all around town; favored sites include behind the school, near the lighthouse, edge of the Meadow (particularly near community garden behind library), and Lobster Cove (4 seen departing the island together early on Oct 10, 2014–JT), but possible anywhere. Noted at feeders on numerous occasions (sometimes multiples at one time—TMar's in the past and DC's recently), as well as at seed scattered along Ocean Ave. and Wharton Ave.; reported in the company of Purple Finches and Song, Chipping, and Clay-colored Sparrows. Known to linger for two–four days, but tracking specific inds. difficult due to roaming nature. Spring records all single day events, except adult male at Donna Cundy's feeders May 14–18, 2014; a calling flyover on May 26 may have been the same ind., but included here as a separate record. The three records in Spring 2008 may have involved the same inds. but the reports following the 2 inds. on May 16 only provide unreported number w/e May 23 and unreported number w/e May 30. Of the spring records, 4 were identified as adult males (including one singing w/e Jun 2, 2006) and 1 as a female type. The only summer record was an immature, indicating a post-fledging dispersal. Immatures (20+) represented two-thirds of the fall records indicating age/sex (2 as immature male, 1 as immature female), while only 2 were positively noted as adults (1 adult male, 1 adult type); 6 were noted only as female, 3 male.

Historical/Regional:

- Palmer: 1 the week of Oct 29, 1939 (MJT–Palmer suggests the possibility of being the same ind. collected on Nov 20, 1939 in Bar Harbor).
- Vickery: ten+ records of singles Apr 26, 1983 (CL)–May 30, 2017 (LS, JT), one summer record on Jul 17, 2011 (TMag), lists seven "small flocks" from Sep 1956–Oct 2005 (VL et al.), 1 intermittently Aug 11–27, 2010 (TMag) and on Sep 29 & Oct 1, 2010 (DL) as more recent, and one occurrence on CBC (PDV in Vickery et al., 2020).

Dickcissel, Oct 1, 2018. © Jeremiah Trimble.

Chimney Swift, May 14, 2022. © Luke Seitz.

HYPOTHETICALS

The following nineteen species have been reported on/from Monhegan or within the Monhegan Island Lobster Conservation Area. While possibly correct, they lack adequate documentation or clarity of location, or the documentation does not completely support the record. Further details supporting any of these records or acceptance by the ME-BRC may change the status as presented here.

Cackling Goose (*Branta hutchinsii*) - a single-day sighting of 1 during Oct 1989 (prior to specific split from Canada Goose–SS); although supported by photos, the origin of this banded individual is unclear.

Lesser Scaup (*Aythya affinis*) - Tom Martin's personal checklist without date or details.

Gray Partridge (*Perdix perdix*) - unestablished escape/release; Tom Martin's personal checklist without date or details.

Spruce Grouse (*Falcipennis canadensis*) - Tom Martin's personal checklist without date or details, except marked as dead remains (feathers preserved).

Western Grebe (*Aechmophorus occidentalis*) - Tom Martin's personal checklist without date or details.

Western Sandpiper (*Calidris mauri*) - inclusion on 1914 checklist only report (MCG).

Stilt Sandpiper (*Calidris himantopus*) - inclusion in 1944–1967 Farrell Records in Aug 1960 only report (fide IF).

South Polar Skua (*Stercorarius maccormicki*) - incidental sighting of 1 on Aug 6, 2012 while assisting DOWTS survey only report (DL); presence likely within MILCA but not certain.

Long-tailed Jaeger (*Stercorarius longicaudus*) - 1 "off Monhegan" on May 29, 2019 without details (Jennifer Eston).

Masked Booby (*Sula dactylatra*) - 1 distant over water with feeding group of Northern Gannets on Oct 9, 2021 (JT), the same day as the only other report and first accepted record for Maine (ME-BRC #2021–027) at Mount Desert Rock, Hancock Co. (Nathan Dubrow); not included on OLMB.

Long-eared Owl (*Asio otus*) - inclusion in 1944–1967 Farrell Records in Nov 1949 only report (IF).

Pileated Woodpecker (*Dryocopus pileatus*) - inclusion in 1944–1967 Farrell Records in Aug 1959 only report (?Bu & ERo, fide IF).

Western Wood-Pewee (*Contopus sordidulus*) - 1 at the edge of the cemetery on Oct 5, 2021, no vocalization (LS, JT–ph.); included on the OLMB, but not yet reviewed by ME-BRC (one other state record).

Fish Crow (*Corvus ossifragus*) - four questionable reports: unreported number on Aug 1, 1914 was followed by a '?' (WF), 3 reported on Dec 29, 1940 (CBC with 30 American Crows and likely misidentified), included on Jun 19–25, 1954 checklist without details, and an anonymous report from eBird of 1 on May 23, 2012 without details. Fish Crow was officially added to state list in 1978.

Bewick's Wren (*Thryomanes bewickii*) - reported as questionable by Wentworth in 1918, listed on Tom Martin's personal checklist and noted as a Peter Vickery sighting (*not included in his records*).

Saltmarsh Sparrow (*Ammospiza caudacuta*) - 1 identified and reported as such on Oct 6, 1990, now considered inconclusive by the observer.

Boat-tailed Grackle (*Quiscalus major*) - report of 1 vocalizing female at the northern end of the Meadow on Sep 26, 2010 (Gerard Therrien, CA); not accepted by ME-BRC due to lack of confirming details.

Swainson's Warbler (*Limnothlypis swainsonii*) - Tom Martin's personal checklist without date or details.

Kirtland's Warbler (*Setophaga kirtlandii*) - 1 adult male on May 21, 2010 along Lobster Cove Rd. (TV, Gloria Hoag); not accepted by ME-BRC due to lack of confirming details.

Purple Finch, Nov 3, 2010. © Geoff Dennis.

REFERENCES

Adamus, P. R. 1987. *Atlas of Breeding Birds in Maine, 1978–1983*. Augusta, ME: Maine Department of Inland Fisheries and Wildlife. 366 pp.

Allen, F. H. 1908a. An Ornithological Reconnaissance of Monhegan Island. *The Journal of the Maine Ornithological Society* 10(4): 94–99.

Allen, F. H. 1908b. A Raven's Nest. *Bird-Lore* 10(5): 195–197.

Audubon, J. J. 1839. *Ornithological Biography* 34. 664 pp.

Badyaev, A. V., V. Belloni, and G. E. Hill. 2020. House Finch (*Haemorhous mexicanus*), version 1.0. In Birds of the World (A. F. Poole, Editor). Cornell Lab of Ornithology, Ithaca, NY, USA. https://doi.org/10.2173/bow.houfin.01.

Baird, J., Robbins, C., Bagg, A., and Dennis, J. 1958. "Operation Recovery" - The Atlantic Coastal Netting Project. *Bird-Banding* 29(3): 137–168.

Benkman, C. W.. 2020. White-winged Crossbill (*Loxia leucoptera*), version 1.0. In Birds of the World (S. M. Billerman, Editor). Cornell Lab of Ornithology, Ithaca, NY, USA. https://doi.org/10.2173/bow.whwcro.01.

Benkman, C. W. and M. A. Young. 2020. Red Crossbill (*Loxia curvirostra*), version 1.0. In Birds of the World (S. M. Billerman, B. K. Keeney, P. G. Rodewald, and T. S. Schulenberg, Editors). Cornell Lab of Ornithology, Ithaca, NY, USA. https://doi.org/10.2173/bow.redcro.01.

Bergstrom, E. A. 1961. Operation Recovery at Monhegan Island, Maine, 1960. *Bird-Banding* 32: 231.

Bergstrom, E. A. 1964. Three Years of Operation Recovery at Monhegan. *Bird-Banding* 35: 207.

Bird Observer. 1994. *A Birder's Guide to Eastern Massachusetts*. American Birding Association. 292 pp.

Boyle, W. J. 2011. *The Birds of New Jersey: Status and Distribution*. Princeton, NJ: Princeton University Press. 308 pp.

Brown, C. R., M. B. Brown, P. Pyle, and M. A. Patten (2020). Cliff Swallow (*Petrochelidon pyrrhonota*), version 1.0. In Birds of the World (P. G. Rodewald, Editor). Cornell Lab of Ornithology, Ithaca, NY, USA. https://doi.org/10.2173/bow.cliswa.01

Burger, J. 2020. Laughing Gull (*Leucophaeus atricilla*), version 1.0. In Birds of the World (P. G. Rodewald, Editor). Cornell Lab of Ornithology, Ithaca, NY, USA. https://doi.org/10.2173/bow.laugul.01.

Cabe, P. R. 2020. European Starling (*Sturnus vulgaris*), version 1.0. In Birds of the World (S. M. Billerman, Editor). Cornell Lab of Ornithology, Ithaca, NY, USA. https://doi.org/10.2173/bow.eursta.01.

Chesser, R. T., S. M. Billerman, K. J. Burns, C. Cicero, J. L. Dunn, B. E. Hernandez-Banos, A. W. Kratter, I. J. Lovette, N. A. Mason, P. C. Rasmussen, J. V. Remsen, Jr., D. F. Stotz, and K. Winker. 2020. *Check-list of North American Birds* (online). American Ornithological Society. http://checklist.aou.org/taxa.

Cook, M. P. 1901. A List of Plants Seen on the Island of Monhegan, Maine, June 20–25, 1900. *Rhodora* 3: 187–190.

Cooke, M. T. 1942. Returns From Banded Birds: Some Longevity Records of Wild Birds. *Bird-Banding* 13: 70.

Cooper, L. 1981. *The Wildflowers of Monhegan, Maine, Including Nearby Islets*. Monhegan Associates, Inc. Monhegan Historical and Cultural Museum Association. 11 pp.

Cruickshank, A. D. 1938. Observations at Muscongus Bay, Maine. *Auk* 55: 550–552.

Cruickshank, A. D. 1950. *Summer Birds of Lincoln County, Maine*. New York: National Audubon Society. 55 pp.

Cundy, D. 2023. My Life On Monhegan (Online). Available: https://www.facebook.com/groups/371244494621 (February 23, 2023).

De Jong, M. J. 2020. Northern Rough-winged Swallow (*Stelgidopteryx serripennis*), version 1.0. In Birds of the World (A. F. Poole and F. B. Gill, Editors). Cornell Lab of Ornithology, Ithaca, NY, USA. https://doi.org/10.2173/bow.nrwswa.01.

DeSorbo, C. R., K. G. Wright, I. Johnson and R. Gray. 2012. Bird migration stopover sites: ecology of nocturnal and diurnal raptors at Monhegan Island. Report BRI 2012-08 submitted to the Maine Outdoor Heritage Fund, Pittston, Maine, and the Davis Conservation Foundation, Yarmouth, Maine. Biodiversity Research Institute, Gorham, Maine. 43 pp. plus appendices.

Dewis, J. W., M.D. 1909. A Visit to Monhegan Island, Maine, September 1918. *Records of Walks and Talks with Nature Conducted by C. J. Maynard* 11: 21–32.

Dunn, J. L. and J. Alderfer. 2011. *Field Guide to the Birds of North America*. Washington, D.C.: National Geographic. 575 pp.

Drury, W. H. 1974. Population Changes in New England Seabirds. *Bird Banding* 45(1): 1–15.

eBird: An online database of bird distribution and abundance [web application]. 2021. eBird, Cornell Lab of Ornithology, Ithaca, New York. Available: http://www.ebird.org. (Accessed May 31, 2021).

eBird: An online database of bird distribution and abundance [web application]. 2023. eBird, Cornell Lab of Ornithology, Ithaca, New York. Available: http://www.ebird.org. (Accessed February 23, 2023).

eBird Basic Dataset. 2017. Version: EBD_relNov-2017. Cornell Lab of Ornithology, Ithaca, New York. Nov 2017.

eBird Maine Bird Atlas. 2023. eBird, Cornell Lab of Ornithology, Ithaca, New York. Available: https://www.ebird.org/atlasme/home. (Accessed Jun 12, 2023).

Edison, T. 1976. Ted Edison's Story: Notes on the Background and Early History of Monhegan Associates, Inc., Monhegan Associates, Inc., https//monheganassociates.org/who-we-are/ted-edisons-story/, accessed May 5, 2021.

Ellsworth, W. W. 1912. *Monhegan Island, Maine*. Hartford Press: The Case, Lockwood & Brainard Co. 13 pp.

Farnsworth, G., G. A. Londono, J. U. Martin, K. C. Derrickson, and R. Breitwisch. 2020. Northern Mockingbird (*Mimus polyglottos*), version 1.0. In Birds of the World (A. F. Poole, Editor). Cornell Lab of Ornithology, Ithaca, NY, USA. https://doi.org/10.2173/bow.normoc.01.

Faller, A. J. 2003. *The Weather and Climate of Monhegan*. Mainstay Publications. 141 pp.

Faller, R. G. 2001. *Monhegan, Her Houses and Her People*. Mainstay Publications. 122 pp.

Finch, D. W., W. C. Russell, and E. V. Thompson. 1978. Pelagic Birds of the Gulf of Maine. *American Birds* 32: 140–155 and 32: 281–294.

Foerster, A. 1936. Worm-eating Warbler in Maine. *Auk* 53: 88–89.

Foote, J. R., D. J. Mennill, L. M. Ratcliffe, and S. M. Smith. 2020. Black-capped Chickadee (*Poecile atricapillus*), version 1.0. In Birds of the World (A. F. Poole, Editor). Cornell Lab of Ornithology, Ithaca, NY, USA. https://doi.org/10.2173/bow.bkcchi.01.

Forbush, E. H. 1925. *The Birds of Massachusetts and other New England States: Part I. Water Birds, Marsh Birds, and Shore Birds*. Norwood, Massachusetts. Department of Agriculture.

Forbush, E. H. 1929. *The Birds of Massachusetts and other New England States: Part III. Land Birds from Sparrows to Thrushes*. Norwood, MA: Massachusetts Department of Agriculture.

Fuller, W. 1914. The Starling in Maine. *Bird-Lore* 16: 446.

Ghalambor, C. K. and T. E. Martin. 2020. Red-breasted Nuthatch (*Sitta canadensis*), version 1.0. In Birds of the World (A. F. Poole and F. B. Gill, Editors). Cornell Lab of Ornithology, Ithaca, NY, USA. https://doi.org/10.2173/bow.rebnut.01.

Gillihan, S. W. and B. E. Byers. 2020. Evening Grosbeak (*Coccothraustes vespertinus*), version 1.0. In Birds of the World (A. F. Poole and F. B. Gill, Editors). Cornell Lab of Ornithology, Ithaca, NY, USA. https://doi.org/10.2173/bow.evegro.01.

Grant, T. A. and R. W. Knapton. 2020. Clay-colored Sparrow (*Spizella pallida*), version 1.0. In Birds of the World (A. F. Poole, Editor). Cornell Lab of Ornithology, Ithaca, NY, USA. https://doi.org/10.2173/bow.clcspa.01.

Gross, A. O. 1947. Cyclic invasions of the Snowy Owl and the migration of 1945–46. *Auk* 64: 584–601.

Haggerty, T. M. and E. S. Morton. 2020. Carolina Wren (*Thryothorus ludovicianus*), version 1.0. In Birds of the World (A. F. Poole, Editor). Cornell Lab of Ornithology, Ithaca, NY, USA. https://doi.org/10.2173/bow.carwre.01.

Harris, L. 2014–15. *Monhegan Nature Guide, Natural history and guided hikes on one of Maine's wildest offshore islands.* Monhegan Associates, Inc. 118 pp.

Hatch, S. A., G. J. Robertson, and P. H. Baird. 2020. Black-legged Kittiwake (*Rissa tridactyla*), version 1.0. In Birds of the World (S. M. Billerman, Editor). Cornell Lab of Ornithology, Ithaca, NY, USA. https://doi.org/10.2173/bow.bklkit.01.

Herkert, J. R., P. D. Vickery, and D. E. Kroodsma. 2020. Henslow's Sparrow (*Centronyx henslowii*), version 1.0. In Birds of the World (P. G. Rodewald, Editor). Cornell Lab of Ornithology, Ithaca, NY, USA. https://doi.org/10.2173/bow.henspa.01.

Hitchcock, C. H. 1862. Catalogue of the Birds of Maine. *Proceedings of the Portland Society of Natural History* 1: 66–71.

Hitchcox, D. P., T. Aversa, L. R. Bevier, and T. B. Persons. 2020. Ninth Report of the Maine Bird Records Committee. *Bird Observer* 48(2):96–105.

Holberton, R. L. and Wright, W. A. 2012. *Results of Abbreviated Passive Acoustic Monitoring of Nocturnal Bird Migration Conducted Near the University of Maine Deepwater Test Site at Monhegan Island During Fall Migration, 2011; a report submitted to the University of Maine and DeepC Wind Consortium.*

Hughes, J. M. 2020a. Yellow-billed Cuckoo (*Coccyzus americanus*), version 1.0. In Birds of the World (P. G. Rodewald, Editor). Cornell Lab of Ornithology, Ithaca, NY, USA. https://doi.org/10.2173/bow.yebcuc.01.

Hughes, J. M. 2020b. Black-billed Cuckoo (*Coccyzus erythropthalmus*), version 1.0. In Birds of the World (P. G. Rodewald, Editor). Cornell Lab of Ornithology, Ithaca, NY, USA. https://doi.org/10.2173/bow.bkbcuc.01.

Jackson, J. A. and H. R. Ouellet. 2020. Downy Woodpecker (*Dryobates pubescens*), version 1.0. In Birds of the World (P. G. Rodewald, Editor). Cornell Lab of Ornithology, Ithaca, NY, USA. https://doi.org/10.2173/bow.dowwoo.01.

Jackson, J. A., H. R. Ouellet, and B. J. Jackson, 2020. Hairy Woodpecker (*Dryobates villosus),* version 1.0. In Birds of the World (P. G. Rodewald, Editor). Cornell Lab of Ornithology, Ithaca, NY, USA. https://doi.org/10.2173/bow.haiwoo.01

Jenney, C. F. 1919. The Fall Migration of 1918 at Monhegan Island, Maine, from Letters of Bertrand H. Wentworth of Gardiner, Maine, Compiled by Charles F. Jenney. *Records of Walks and Talks with Nature Conducted by C. J. Maynard* 11: 33–41.

Jenney. C. F. 1922. *The Fortunate Island of Monhegan.* The Davis Press. 78 pp.

Jonkel, G. M. & Pettingill, O. S. 1974. Retraction of a longevity record for a 36-year-old Herring Gull. *Auk* 91(2): 432.

Kennedy, L. & Holberton, R.L. 2012. Visual Observations for Birds, Turtles, and Marine Mammals at the University of Maine Test Site off Monhegan Island, a report submitted to the Maine State Planning Office and University of Maine.

Kennedy, L. 2012b. Visual Observations for Birds, Turtles, and Marine Mammals at the University of Maine

Test Site near Monhegan, Maine; June–August 2012. A report submitted to the University of Maine's Advanced Structures and Composites Center.

Kennedy, L. 2013a. Visual Observations for Birds, Turtles, and Marine Mammals at the University of Maine Test Site near Monhegan, Maine; July 2013. A report submitted to the University of Maine's Advanced Structures and Composites Center.

Kennedy, L. 2013c. Visual Observations for Birds, Turtles, and Marine Mammals at the University of Maine Test Site near Monhegan, Maine; July–December 2013. A report submitted to the University of Maine's Advanced Structures and Composites Center.

Kennedy, L. 2014a. Visual Observations for Birds, Turtles, and Marine Mammals at the University of Maine Test Site near Monhegan, Maine; December–May 2014. A report submitted to the University of Maine's Advanced Structures and Composites Center.

Kershner, E. L. and W. G. Ellison. 2020. Blue-gray Gnatcatcher (*Polioptila caerulea*), version 1.0. In Birds of the World (A. F. Poole, Editor). Cornell Lab of Ornithology, Ithaca, NY, USA. https://doi.org/10.2173/bow.buggna.01.

Knight, O. W. 1908. *Birds of Maine*. Bangor, ME: C. H. Glass and Company. 693 pp.

Korschgen, C. E. 1979. *Coastal Waterbird Colonies: Maine*. U.S. Fish and Wildlife Service, Biological Services Program, FWS/OBS-79/09. 83 pp.

Lavers, J., J. M. Hipfner, and G. Chapdelaine. 2020. Razorbill (*Alca torda*), version 1.0. In Birds of the World (S. M. Billerman, Editor). Cornell Lab of Ornithology, Ithaca, NY, USA. https://doi.org/10.2173/bow.razorb.01.

Levine, E. 1998. *Bull's Birds of New York State*. Ithaca and London: Cornell University Press. 622 pp.

Livingston, W. H. and R. W. Dyer. 2003. Land-use History and Vegetation Composition of Monhegan Island. Presentation to Monhegan Associates, Inc. University of Maine. Available online: http://www2.umaine.edu/fes/FES/Monhegan_2003_files/v3_document.htm (accessed Aug 10, 2021).

Lovitch, D. 2020. Maine Birding Field Notes (Online). Available: https://mebirdingfieldnotes.blog/?s=Monhegan (Nov 19, 2020).

Maine Bird Records Committee. 2022. Official List of Maine Birds (Online). Available https://sites.google.com/site/mainebirdrecordscommittee/official-list-of-maine-birds (February 23, 2023).

Maynard, C. J. 1909. Notes on Birds, Butterflies, Etc., Observed on Monhegan Island, Maine. *Records of Walks and Talks with Nature Conducted by C. J. Maynard* 2: 116–120.

McKay, B. and G. A. Hall. 2020. Yellow-throated Warbler (*Setophaga dominica*), version 1.0. In Birds of the World (A. F. Poole, Editor). Cornell Lab of Ornithology, Ithaca, NY, USA. https://doi.org/10.2173/bow.yetwar.01.

Miller, L. T. 2014. *Warner Taylor, Photographing Monhegan, 1912–1958*. Yellow House Studio. 120 pages.

Miller, M. 2005. *Monhegan Forest, Stewardship Management Plan*. Report prepared for Monhegan Associates, Inc. 29 pp.

Mizrahi, D., A. Leppold, R. Fogg, and T. Magarian. 2013. *Radar Monitoring of Bird and Bat Movement Patterns on Monhegan Island, Maine and Its Coastal Waters*. Final report submitted University of Maine and DeepC Wind Consortium. 210 pp.

Monhegan Museum. 1970. *Birds of Monhegan Island, Maine; Also Manana, Nearby Islets, and Surrounding Waters. July and August Observations*. Monhegan Historical and Cultural Museum Association. 8 pp.

Monhegan Press. 1938a. State Requests Aid of Summer Visitors in Protecting Birds. Monhegan Press 1 (4). Information accessed through the archives of the Monhegan Historical and Cultural Museum Association.

Monhegan Press. 1938b. Monhegan Bird Life Varied, Mr. Taylor Informs the Press. Monhegan Press 1 (5). Information accessed through the archives of the Monhegan Historical and Cultural Museum Association.

Morey, D. C. 2005. The Voyage of Archangell. Gardiner, Maine. Tilbury House Publishers.

National Audubon Society. 2018. The Christmas Bird Count Historical Results (Online). Available http://www.chrismasbirdcount.org (Nov 11, 2018).

National Audubon Society. 2020. The Christmas Bird Count Historical Results (Online). Available http://www.chrismasbirdcount.org (Jan 18 2021).

National Audubon Society. 2021a. Audubon Project Puffin (Online). Available https://projectpuffin.audubon.org/conservation/eastern-egg-rock (Feb 7, 2021).

National Audubon Society. 2021b. Hog Island Audubon Camp (Online). https://hogisland.audubon.org/about/ornithology-hog-island (Jun 20, 2021).

Norton, A. H. 1916. Notes on some Maine Birds. *Auk* 33: 376.

Palmer, R. S. 1949. *Maine Birds*. Cambridge, MA: Museum of Comparative Zoology. 656 pp.

Paynter, Jr., R. A. 1949. Report of the Field Director - 1948. *The Ninth Annual Report of the Bowdoin Scientific Station, Bulletin No. 11*. Bowdoin College, Brunswick, ME.

Persico, C. P., C. R. DeSorbo, D. E. Meattey, and M. E. H. Burton. 2021. Migrant raptor research at the Naval Support Activity Installation, Cutler, Maine: Fall 2020. Report # 2021-05. Submitted to: Naval Facilities Engineering Command (NAFAC) PWD-ME, Portsmouth, New Hampshire. Biodiversity Research Institute, Portland, Maine. 15 pp.

Persons, T. B., L. R. Bevier, D. Hitchcox, and T. Aversa. 2021. Tenth Report of the Maine Bird Records Committee. *Bird Observer* 49(2): 118–131.

Persons, T. B., T. Aversa, K. A. Lima, M. Weber, and L. R. Bevier. 2022. Eleventh Report of the Maine Bird Records Committee. *Bird Observer* 50: 87–96.

Pettingill, S. 1959. Bird Finding with Sewall Pettingill. *Audubon Magazine* 61(3): 128–129.

Pope, F. A. 1916. Preliminary Examination of Monhegan Harbor, ME. A letter from the Secretary of War to the House of Representatives Committee on Rivers and Harbors, Document No. 536. 7 pp.

Post, W., A. Cruz, and D. B. McNair. 1993. The North American Invasion Pattern of the Shiny Cowbird. *Journal of Field Ornithology* 64(1): 32–41.

Proper, I. S. 1930. *Monhegan, the Cradle of New England*. Portland, ME. The Southworth Press.

Rosenberg, K. V. et al. 2019. Decline of the North American Avifauna. Science 365(6461). doi: 10.1126/science.aaw1313.

Rosier, J. 1887. [Reprint of] *Rosier's Relation of Waymouth's Voyage to the Coast of Maine, 1605, with an introduction and notes*. By H. S. Burrage, D.D. Printed for Gorges Society. Portland ME. 176 pp.

Schnitzer, A. 1962. The 1961 Fall Migration at Monhegan, Maine. *EBBA News* 25(3): 105–106.

Schnitzer, A. 1963. Three Years of Operation Recovery at Monhegan. *EBBA News* 26(4): 129–137.

Schutsky, R. M. and J. Pushcock. 2016. *A Checklist of the Birds of Monhegan Island and Nearby Mainland Maine*. Bird Treks. 9 pp.

Shetterly, S. H. 2005. Really Seeing. *Island Journal* 21: 38–43.

Sibley, D. A. 2000. *The Sibley Guide to Birds*. New York: National Audubon Society. 544 pp.

Spiess, A. 2004. Letter from the Maine Historic Preservation Commission to Mark Miller, Conservation Forestry.

Stephenson, T. and S. Whittle. 2015. *The Warbler Guide*. Princeton University Press. 560 pp.

Sylvester, H. M. 1909. *Olde Pemaquid*. Boston, Massachusetts. W. B. Clarke Co.

Taylor, W. 1939. Monhegan Bird Census Lists 91 Species Observed Here During Summer. *Monhegan Press* 2(8). Information accessed through the archives of the Monhegan Historical and Cultural Museum Association.

Townsend, J. A. 1941. Audubon Magazine's Forty-first Christmas Bird Census. *Audubon Magazine supplement*. January–February 1941: 77.

U.S. Geological Survey Bird Banding Laboratory. 2005. North American bird banding and band encounter data set. Patuxent Wildlife Research Center, Laurel, MD. Dec 29, 2005.

Verrill, A. E. 1862. Catalogue of the Birds Found at Norway, Oxford County, Maine. *Proceedings of the Essex Institute* 3: 136–160.

Vickery, P. D. 1978. *Annotated Checklist of Maine Birds*. Maine Audubon Society. 20 pp.

Vickery, P. D. 2013. *The Birds of Monhegan Island Checklist*. Freeport, ME. Freeport Wild Bird Supply.

Vickery, Peter D., C. D. Duncan, W. J. Sheehan, and J. V. Wells. 2020. *Birds of Maine*. Edited by Barbara S. Vickery and Scott Weidensaul, Princeton University Press.

Weather Underground. 2021. Owls Head, ME Weather History. Retrieved Jun 12, 2021 from https://www.wunderground.com/history/daily/us/me/owls-head/KRKD.

West, J. D. and J. M. Speirs. 1959. The 1956–1957 Invasion of Three-toed Woodpeckers. *Wilson Bulletin* 71: 348–363.

Wikipedia contributors. 2021. Monhegan, Maine. In Wikipedia, The Free Encyclopedia. Retrieved Apr 26, 2021 from https://en.wikipedia.org/w/index.php?title=Monhegan,_Maine&oldid=1026088952.

Wynne-Edwards, V. C. 1935. On the habits and distribution of birds on the North Atlantic. *Proc. Boston Soc. Nat. Hist.* 40: 233–346.

Yosef, R. (2020). Loggerhead Shrike (*Lanius ludovicianus*), version 1.0. In Birds of the World (A. F. Poole and F. B. Gill, Editors). Cornell Lab of Ornithology, Ithaca, NY, USA. https://doi.org/10.2173/bow.logshr.01.

Bay-breasted Warbler, Oct 6, 2018. © Jeremiah Trimble.

ANNOTATED CHECKLIST OF MONHEGAN BIRDS

This checklist contains all 336 species recorded on Monhegan and is intended as a general but concise portrayal of each species' abundance by season (spring = SP, summer = SU, fall = FA, winter = WI) and indicates if a species is a permanent resident (PERM). It may not portray an historical status, such as a species which formerly bred but no longer does so; that information can be found in the specific species account.

STATUS KEY

ABUNDANCE

AB = Abundant (100+ per day)
C = Common (25–100 per day)
FC = Fairly Common (5–25 per day)
U = Uncommon (1–5 per day)
S = Scarce (1–5 per season)
R = Rare (more than 10 historical records, but not annual)
VR = Very Rare (2–10 historical records)
AC = Accidental (1 record ever)

SUPERSCRIPTS

^{B} = Breeds
^{I} = Irruptive
$^+$ = Sometimes far exceeds the expected numbers, but not following an irruptive pattern
$^?$ = Possible migrant in spring or fall (in addition to permanent residents), or possible breeder in summer, but lacks definite evidence, possibly due to lack of coverage
^{P} = Presumably more common than the status indicated due to lack of coverage

	SPECIES	SP	SU	FA	WI	PERM
☐	Snow Goose	AC	-	R	VR	-
☐	Brant	VR	-	VR	-	-
☐	Canada Goose	U	R	FC-C	R	-
☐	Wood Duck	R-S	VR	S	AC	-
☐	Blue-winged Teal	R	VR	R	-	-
☐	Northern Shoveler	AC	-	AC	-	-
☐	Gadwall	-	-	AC	-	-
☐	Eurasian Wigeon	-	-	VR	-	-
☐	American Wigeon	AC	-	VR	-	-
☐	Mallard	U	FC^B	FC	FC	FC
☐	American Black Duck	U	U$^?$	U-FC	FC	?
☐	Northern Pintail	-	-	VR	AC	-
☐	Green-winged Teal	R	-	S-U	VR	-
☐	Redhead	-	-	AC	-	-
☐	Ring-necked Duck	VR	-	VR	-	-
☐	Greater Scaup	AC	-	VR	AC	-
☐	King Eider	AC	-	VR	VR	-
☐	Common Eider	C	C^B	AB	AB	C
☐	Harlequin Duck	VR	-	R	VR	-

SPECIES	SP	SU	FA	WI	PERM
☐ Surf Scoter	R-S	VR	U-FC	R-S	-
☐ White-winged Scoter	S-U	AC	U-FC	S^P	-
☐ Black Scoter	S-FC	VR	U-FC	R-S	-
☐ Long-tailed Duck	U-FC	-	U-FC	FC	-
☐ Bufflehead	AC	-	AC	R-FC	-
☐ Common Goldeneye	VR	-	AC	S	-
☐ Barrow's Goldeneye	-	-	-	VR	-
☐ Hooded Merganser	VR	-	-	-	-
☐ Common Merganser	VR	-	VR	VR	-
☐ Red-breasted Merganser	U	-	U	U-FC	-
☐ Ruffed Grouse	-	-	VR	-	-
☐ Ring-necked Pheasant	U	U^B	U	U	U
☐ Pied-billed Grebe	AC	-	R	-	-
☐ Horned Grebe	AC	-	VR	R	-
☐ Red-necked Grebe	R-S	AC	S	R-S^P	-
☐ Rock Pigeon	VR	VR	VR	VR	-
☐ Band-tailed Pigeon	-	-	VR	-	-
☐ Eurasian Collared-Dove	-	AC	-	-	-
☐ White-winged Dove	VR	-	VR	-	-
☐ Mourning Dove	FC$^?$	FC^B	FC$^?$	FC	FC
☐ Yellow-billed Cuckoo	R	VR	S	-	-
☐ Black-billed Cuckoo	S	R$^?$	S	-	-
☐ Common Nighthawk	S	-	R-S$^+$	-	-
☐ Chuck-will's-widow	VR	-	-	-	-
☐ Eastern Whip-poor-will	VR	-	AC	-	-
☐ Chimney Swift	S-U	VR	R	-	-
☐ Ruby-throated Hummingbird	U	R$^?$	U	-	-
☐ Calliope Hummingbird	-	-	AC	-	-
☐ Rufous Hummingbird	-	-	AC	-	-
☐ Virginia Rail	R	VR$^?$	R	-	-
☐ Corn Crake	-	-	AC	-	-
☐ Sora	R-S	VR	R-S	-	-
☐ Common Gallinule	AC	-	VR	-	-
☐ American Coot	AC	-	VR	-	-
☐ Sandhill Crane	VR	-	-	-	-
☐ American Oystercatcher	VR	AC	AC	-	-
☐ Black-bellied Plover	R	-	S	-	-
☐ American Golden-Plover	-	-	R	-	-
☐ Killdeer	R	VR$^?$	R-S	VR	-
☐ Semipalmated Plover	VR	-	S	-	-
☐ Upland Sandpiper	VR	-	VR	-	-
☐ Whimbrel	AC	-	R	-	-
☐ Hudsonian Godwit	-	-	AC	-	-
☐ Ruddy Turnstone	VR	-	R	-	-
☐ Red Knot	AC	-	AC	-	-
☐ Sanderling	-	-	R	-	-

SPECIES	SP	SU	FA	WI	PERM
☐ Dunlin	AC	-	VR	-	-
☐ Purple Sandpiper	R[P]	AC	VR[P]	R[P]	-
☐ Baird's Sandpiper	-	-	VR	-	-
☐ Least Sandpiper	R	-	S	-	-
☐ White-rumped Sandpiper	-	-	VR	-	-
☐ Pectoral Sandpiper	AC	-	R	-	-
☐ Semipalmated Sandpiper	VR	-	R-S	-	-
☐ Short-billed Dowitcher	R	-	VR	-	-
☐ American Woodcock	R	S[B]	R-S	-	-
☐ Wilson's Snipe	R	-	S-U	VR	-
☐ Spotted Sandpiper	S-U	AC[?]	S-U	-	-
☐ Solitary Sandpiper	R	-	S	-	-
☐ Lesser Yellowlegs	VR	-	R-S	-	-
☐ Willet	R	-	VR	-	-
☐ Greater Yellowlegs	S-U	-	S-U	-	-
☐ Wilson's Phalarope	-	-	AC	-	-
☐ Red-necked Phalarope	R[+]	-	R[+]	-	-
☐ Red Phalarope	VR	-	VR	-	-
☐ Pomarine Jaeger	-	AC	R	AC	-
☐ Parasitic Jaeger	VR	VR	R	-	-
☐ Dovekie	VR	AC	VR	R	-
☐ Common Murre	VR	R	VR	VR	-
☐ Thick-billed Murre	VR	-	-	VR	-
☐ Razorbill	VR[P]	U	R[P]	VR	-
☐ Black Guillemot	FC-C	FC-C[B]	FC-C	FC-C	FC-C
☐ Atlantic Puffin	-	R-S[P]	R	VR	-
☐ Black-legged Kittiwake	R	-	S-FC[P]	C-AB[P]	-
☐ Ivory Gull	AC	-	-	AC	-
☐ Bonaparte's Gull	R	-	S	VR	-
☐ Black-headed Gull	-	-	AC	VR	-
☐ Little Gull	-	-	AC	-	-
☐ Laughing Gull	U-FC	U-FC	U-FC	-	-
☐ Ring-billed Gull	S-U	VR	U	R-S[P]	-
☐ Herring Gull	C-AB	C-AB[B]	AB	AB	C-AB
☐ Iceland Gull	R	-	VR	R-S	-
☐ Lesser Black-backed Gull	VR	-	S	AC	-
☐ Glaucous Gull	VR	-	VR	R	-
☐ Great Black-backed Gull	FC-C	FC[B]	C-AB	C-AB	FC
☐ Bridled Tern	-	AC	-	-	-
☐ Caspian Tern	VR	-	R	-	-
☐ Roseate Tern	VR	VR	VR	-	-
☐ Common Tern	U-FC	R	U	-	-
☐ Arctic Tern	VR	VR	VR	-	-
☐ Royal Tern	-	-	AC	-	-
☐ Black Skimmer	AC	-	VR	-	-
☐ Red-throated Loon	S-U	AC	S-U	VR	-

	SPECIES	SP	SU	FA	WI	PERM
☐	Pacific Loon	AC	-	VR	VR	-
☐	Common Loon	FC	S	FC	U-FC	-
☐	Wilson's Storm-Petrel	-	R-U⁺	-	-	-
☐	Leach's Storm-Petrel	AC	VR	VR	-	-
☐	Northern Fulmar	AC	AC	R	-	-
☐	Cory's Shearwater	-	R-S	R-S	-	-
☐	Sooty Shearwater	-	R-S⁺	R-S⁺	-	-
☐	Great Shearwater	-	U-C⁺	U-C⁺	-	-
☐	Manx Shearwater	-	R-S	R-S	-	-
☐	Magnificent Frigatebird	AC	-	AC	-	-
☐	Northern Gannet	U-FC	U	C-AB	VRᴾ	-
☐	Great Cormorant	U	VR	FC	FC-C	-
☐	Double-crested Cormorant	C-AB	Cᴮ	AB	VR	-
☐	American Bittern	R	-	R	-	-
☐	Least Bittern	VR	-	-	-	-
☐	Great Blue Heron	S-U	R-S?	U	VR	-
☐	Great Egret	VR	VR	VR	-	-
☐	Snowy Egret	VR	-	AC	-	-
☐	Little Blue Heron	VR	VR	VR	-	-
☐	Tricolored Heron	VR	-	-	-	-
☐	Cattle Egret	VR	-	-	-	-
☐	Green Heron	S	-	VR	-	-
☐	Black-crowned Night-Heron	VR	VR	S	-	-
☐	Yellow-crowned Night-Heron	VR	VR	R-S	-	-
☐	Glossy Ibis	VR	-	-	-	-
☐	Black Vulture	-	AC	-	-	-
☐	Turkey Vulture	VR	VR	AC	-	-
☐	Osprey	S-U	R	U	-	-
☐	Swallow-tailed Kite	AC	-	-	-	-
☐	Golden Eagle	-	-	-	AC	-
☐	Northern Harrier	S	-	U-FC	VR	-
☐	Sharp-shinned Hawk	S	VR	U-FC	VR	-
☐	Cooper's Hawk	R	-	S	AC	-
☐	Northern Goshawk	-	-	VR	VR	-
☐	Bald Eagle	S-U	R	U	R	-
☐	Red-shouldered Hawk	AC	-	VR	-	-
☐	Broad-winged Hawk	VR	-	R	-	-
☐	Red-tailed Hawk	AC	AC	VR	-	-
☐	Rough-legged Hawk	-	-	-	VR	-
☐	Great Horned Owl	VR?	-	VR	AC	-
☐	Snowy Owl	-	-	-	R	-
☐	Barred Owl	VR	-	-	-	-
☐	Short-eared Owl	-	-	VR	AC	-
☐	Boreal Owl	-	-	AC	-	-
☐	Northern Saw-whet Owl	AC	-	Rᴾ	-	-
☐	Belted Kingfisher	S	-	U	-	-

SPECIES	SP	SU	FA	WI	PERM
☐ Red-headed Woodpecker	VR	-	R	-	-
☐ Red-bellied Woodpecker	R-S	AC	R-S	VR	-
☐ Yellow-bellied Sapsucker	R-S	-	FC-C	-	-
☐ American Three-toed Woodpecker	-	-	AC	-	-
☐ Black-backed Woodpecker	-	-	VR	AC	-
☐ Downy Woodpecker	U	U^B	U$^?$	U	U
☐ Hairy Woodpecker	S$^?$	AC$^?$	S$^?$	VR$^?$	-
☐ Northern Flicker	U	R$^?$	FC-C	R	-
☐ American Kestrel	R	VR	U-FC	AC	-
☐ Merlin	S-U	VR^B	FC	VR	-
☐ Gyrfalcon	-	AC	-	-	-
☐ Peregrine Falcon	S-U	VR	U-FC	VR	-
☐ Ash-throated Flycatcher	-	-	VR	-	-
☐ Great Crested Flycatcher	R-S	VR	R	-	-
☐ Western Kingbird	VR	AC	R	-	-
☐ Eastern Kingbird	U-FC	VR	U	-	-
☐ Olive-sided Flycatcher	S	VR	R-S	-	-
☐ Eastern Wood-Pewee	U-FC	AC	U	-	-
☐ Yellow-bellied Flycatcher	S-U	-	S	-	-
☐ Acadian Flycatcher	VR	-	AC	-	-
☐ Alder Flycatcher	U	VR	R-S	-	-
☐ Willow Flycatcher	S-U	-	VR	-	-
☐ Least Flycatcher	U-FC	VR	U	-	-
☐ Gray Flycatcher	-	-	AC	-	-
☐ Eastern Phoebe	U^P	R$^?$	U-FC	-	-
☐ Say's Phoebe	-	-	VR	-	-
☐ White-eyed Vireo	R-S	AC	R-S	-	-
☐ Bell's Vireo	VR	-	AC	-	-
☐ Yellow-throated Vireo	VR	-	R	-	-
☐ Cassin's Vireo	-	-	AC	-	-
☐ Blue-headed Vireo	U-FC	AC	U-FC	-	-
☐ Philadelphia Vireo	U	-	U	-	-
☐ Warbling Vireo	S-U	AC	S-U	-	-
☐ Red-eyed Vireo	FC-C	R^B	FC-C	-	-
☐ Loggerhead Shrike	AC	AC	VR	-	-
☐ Northern Shrike	AC	-	VR	VR	-
☐ Blue Jay	FC	U^B	C	U-FC	U
☐ American Crow	FC	U-FC^B	C	FC	U-FC
☐ Common Raven	U	U^B	U$^?$	U$^?$	U
☐ Black-capped Chickadee	FC-C	FC-C	FC-C^I	FC-C	FC-C
☐ Boreal Chickadee	VR	-	AC	-	-
☐ Horned Lark	AC	-	R-S	VR	-
☐ Bank Swallow	R-S	AC	VR	-	-
☐ Tree Swallow	FC	U^B	S-U^P	-	-
☐ Northern Rough-winged Swallow	R	VR	VR	-	-
☐ Purple Martin	R	-	VR	-	-

SPECIES	SP	SU	FA	WI	PERM
☐ Barn Swallow	FC	R²	U-FC	-	-
☐ Cliff Swallow	R	VR	VR	-	-
☐ Cave Swallow	-	-	AC	-	-
☐ Ruby-crowned Kinglet	U-FC	VR	C	VR	-
☐ Golden-crowned Kinglet	FC-C	U-FC^B	C-AB	UN-C	U-FC
☐ Bohemian Waxwing	AC	-	VR	VR	-
☐ Cedar Waxwing	AB	FC^B	AB	VR	-
☐ Red-breasted Nuthatch	U-FC	U-FC^B	FC-AB^I	U-FC	U-FC
☐ White-breasted Nuthatch	U	U^B	U^I	U	U
☐ Brown Creeper	R-U	VR	U-FC	VR	-
☐ Blue-gray Gnatcatcher	S-U	-	U	-	-
☐ House Wren	S-U	R-S²	U	AC	-
☐ Winter Wren	U	S-U^B	U-FC	R	?
☐ Sedge Wren	AC	-	VR	AC	-
☐ Marsh Wren	VR	-	S-U	-	-
☐ Carolina Wren	U-FC	U-FC^B	U-FC	U-FC	U-FC
☐ Gray Catbird	FC	U-FC^B	FC	VR	-
☐ Brown Thrasher	U	R^B	U	AC	-
☐ Northern Mockingbird	S-U²	S-U^B	S-U²	S-U	S-U
☐ European Starling	FC-C²	FC-C^B	FC-C²	FC-C	FC-C
☐ Eastern Bluebird	U-FC	VR²	R-FC	VR	-
☐ Townsend's Solitaire	-	-	VR	-	-
☐ Veery	S-U	VR	S^P	-	-
☐ Gray-cheeked Thrush	VR	-	R	-	-
☐ Bicknell's Thrush	VR	-	-	-	-
☐ Swainson's Thrush	FC	U^B	U-FC	-	-
☐ Hermit Thrush	S-FC	R²	FC^P	VR	-
☐ Wood Thrush	R-S	VR	R	-	-
☐ American Robin	FC-C	FC^B	FC-C	R^P	?
☐ Varied Thrush	AC	-	-	-	-
☐ Northern Wheatear	-	-	AC	-	-
☐ House Sparrow	VR	-	R	-	-
☐ American Pipit	R	-	U-FC	AC	-
☐ Common Chaffinch	-	-	AC	-	-
☐ Evening Grosbeak	R	VR	R-U	R^I	-
☐ Pine Grosbeak	AC	VR	VR	VR	-
☐ House Finch	S	AC	S-U	VR	-
☐ Purple Finch	U-FC	R$^{P?}$	U-C^I	VR	-
☐ Common Redpoll	VR	-	VR	R	-
☐ Red Crossbill	R^{IB}	R^I	R^I	VR^I	-
☐ White-winged Crossbill	FC-C^I	R^I	U-C^I	R^I	-
☐ Pine Siskin	U-C	VR	U-AB^I	R	-
☐ American Goldfinch	FC	FC^B	C	R	-
☐ Lapland Longspur	-	-	R	AC	-
☐ Snow Bunting	VR	-	R	VR	-
☐ Grasshopper Sparrow	VR	-	R	-	-

	SPECIES	SP	SU	FA	WI	PERM
☐	Black-throated Sparrow	AC	-	-	-	-
☐	Lark Sparrow	VR	-	S	-	-
☐	Lark Bunting	-	AC	VR	-	-
☐	Chipping Sparrow	U-FC	R?	U-C	AC	-
☐	Clay-colored Sparrow	R	-	S-U	-	-
☐	Field Sparrow	S-U	VR	R-U	-	-
☐	Brewer's Sparrow	AC	-	-	-	-
☐	Fox Sparrow	R^P	-	R^P	VR	-
☐	American Tree Sparrow	R	-	R	R	-
☐	Dark-eyed Junco	U-FC^P	R^B	C-AB	U-FC	?
☐	White-crowned Sparrow	U-FC	-	U-FC	AC	-
☐	Harris's Sparrow	AC	-	AC	-	-
☐	White-throated Sparrow	FC-C$^+$	R?	C-AB	U-FC	-
☐	Vesper Sparrow	VR	VR	R	-	-
☐	LeConte's Sparrow	-	-	VR	-	-
☐	Seaside Sparrow	-	-	VR	-	-
☐	Nelson's Sparrow	VR	-	R	-	-
☐	Henslow's Sparrow	VR	-	VR	-	-
☐	Savannah Sparrow	FC-C	R?	FC-C	AC	-
☐	Song Sparrow	FC	FC^B	FC-C	FC	FC
☐	Lincoln's Sparrow	U-FC	-	U-FC	AC	-
☐	Swamp Sparrow	U	VR?	FC	R	-
☐	Eastern Towhee	S-U	VR?	S-U	VR	-
☐	Yellow-breasted Chat	VR	-	S	VR	-
☐	Yellow-headed Blackbird	AC	VR	R	-	-
☐	Bobolink	FC	-	FC-C	-	-
☐	Eastern Meadowlark	VR	-	VR	VR	-
☐	Orchard Oriole	S-U	-	R	-	-
☐	Bullock's Oriole	-	-	AC	-	-
☐	Baltimore Oriole	FC	VR	FC	-	-
☐	Red-winged Blackbird	FC	FC^B	FC	R	-
☐	Shiny Cowbird	AC	-	-	-	-
☐	Brown-headed Cowbird	S-FC	VR?	S-U	VR	-
☐	Rusty Blackbird	R	-	FC	VR	-
☐	Brewer's Blackbird	-	-	AC	-	-
☐	Common Grackle	C	FC-C^B	FC-C	R	-
☐	Ovenbird	U	VR?	S-U	-	-
☐	Worm-eating Warbler	VR	-	VR	-	-
☐	Louisiana Waterthrush	VR	-	AC	-	-
☐	Northern Waterthrush	FC	-	FC	-	-
☐	Golden-winged Warbler	VR	-	VR	-	-
☐	Blue-winged Warbler	R	VR	R	-	-
☐	Black-and-white Warbler	FC	AC?	FC	-	-
☐	Prothonotary Warbler	R	-	VR	-	-
☐	Tennessee Warbler	U	VR	U	-	-
☐	Orange-crowned Warbler	R	-	S	AC	-

	SPECIES	SP	SU	FA	WI	PERM
☐	Nashville Warbler	U-FC	R?	U-FC	-	-
☐	Virginia's Warbler	VR	-	VR	-	-
☐	Connecticut Warbler	VR	-	R	-	-
☐	MacGillivray's Warbler	-	-	AC	-	-
☐	Mourning Warbler	S	-	S	-	-
☐	Kentucky Warbler	VR	-	VR	-	-
☐	Common Yellowthroat	FC-C	FC^B	FC-C	-	-
☐	Hooded Warbler	R	-	R	-	-
☐	American Redstart	C	U^B	FC	-	-
☐	Cape May Warbler	S-U	-	U-FC	-	-
☐	Cerulean Warbler	VR	-	VR	-	-
☐	Northern Parula	C	U^B	FC	-	-
☐	Magnolia Warbler	C	U^B	FC	-	-
☐	Bay-breasted Warbler	U	AC	U	-	-
☐	Blackburnian Warbler	FC	VR?	S-U	-	-
☐	Yellow Warbler	C	FC^B	FC	-	-
☐	Chestnut-sided Warbler	FC	VR?	U	-	-
☐	Blackpoll Warbler	C	VR	FC	-	-
☐	Black-throated Blue Warbler	U	VR	S-U	-	-
☐	Palm Warbler	S-FC	VR	C	-	-
☐	Pine Warbler	R-S	VR	U	AC	-
☐	Yellow-rumped Warbler	C	S?	AB	VR	-
☐	Yellow-throated Warbler	VR	-	R	-	-
☐	Prairie Warbler	S	-	S-U	-	-
☐	Black-throated Gray Warbler	-	-	AC	-	-
☐	Townsend's Warbler	AC	-	VR	-	-
☐	Hermit Warbler	-	-	AC	-	-
☐	Black-throated Green Warbler	FC	U^B	FC	-	-
☐	Canada Warbler	U	-	R-S	-	-
☐	Wilson's Warbler	U	-	U	-	-
☐	Summer Tanager	R-S	-	R	-	-
☐	Scarlet Tanager	U	-	S	-	-
☐	Western Tanager	-	-	VR	AC	-
☐	Northern Cardinal	U-FC	U-FC^B	U-FC	U-FC	U-FC
☐	Rose-breasted Grosbeak	U-FC	VR?	U	-	-
☐	Black-headed Grosbeak	AC	-	VR	-	-
☐	Blue Grosbeak	R	-	S	AC	-
☐	Lazuli Bunting	-	-	AC	-	-
☐	Indigo Bunting	U	VR	U	-	-
☐	Painted Bunting	VR	-	VR	-	-
☐	Dickcissel	R	AC	U	VR	-

BIRD SPECIES INDEX BY COMMON NAME

The Species Account or Hypotheticals listing for each species is noted in **bold**, followed by the Annotated Checklist.

Bittern, American - **126**, 278
    Least - **126–127**, 278
Blackbird, Brewer's - **228–229**, 281
    Red-winged - **226–227**, 281
    Rusty - **228**, 281
    Yellow-headed - **223**, 281
Bluebird, Eastern - **188**, 280
Bobolink - **223–224**, 281
Booby, Masked - **267**
Brant - **65**, 275
Bufflehead - **76**, 276
Bunting, Indigo - **263**, 282
    Lark - **206**, 281
    Lazuli - **263**, 282
    Painted - **264**, 282
    Snow - **204**, 280
Cardinal, Northern - **260**, 282
Catbird, Gray - **184–185**, 280
Chaffinch, Common - **195**, 280
Chat, Yellow-breasted - **222**, 281
Chickadee, Black-capped - **168–169**, 279
    Boreal - **169**, 279
Chuck-will's-widow - **84**, 276
Collared-Dove, Eurasian - **80**, 276
Coot, American - **89**, 276
Cormorant, Double-crested - **124–125**, 278
    Great - **124**, 278
Cowbird, Brown-headed - **227–228**, 281
    Shiny - **227**, 281
Crake, Corn - **87–88**, 276
Crane, Sandhill - **89–90**, 276
Creeper, Brown - **180**, 280
Crossbill, Red - **198–200**, 280
    White-winged - **200–201**, 280
Crow, American - **166–167**, 279
    Fish - **267**
Cuckoo, Black-billed - **82–83**, 276
    Yellow-billed - **82**, 276
Dickcissel - **264–265**, 282
Dove, Mourning - **81–82**, 276
    White-winged - **80–81**, 276
Dovekie - **103**, 277
Dowitcher, Short-billed - **96**, 277
Duck, American Black - **69–70**, 275
    Harlequin - **73–74**, 275
    Long-tailed - **75–76**, 276
    Ring-necked - **71**, 275
    Wood - **66–67**, 275
Dunlin - **93**, 277
Eagle, Bald - **136–137**, 278
    Golden - **134**, 278
Egret, Cattle - **129–130**, 278
    Great - **127–128**, 278
    Snowy - **128**, 278
Eider, Common - **72–73**, 275
    King - **72**, 275
Falcon, Peregrine - **149–150**, 279
Finch, House - **196–197**, 280
    Purple - **197–198**, 280
Flicker, Northern - **146–147**, 279
Flycatcher, Acadian - **155**, 279
    Alder - **155–156**, 279
    Ash-throated - **150–151**, 279
    Gray - **158**, 279
    Great Crested - **151**, 279
    Least - **157**, 279
    Olive-sided - **153**, 279
    Willow - **156–157**, 279
    Yellow-bellied - **154–155**, 279
Frigatebird, Magnificent - **122–123**, 278
Fulmar, Northern - **120**, 278
Gadwall - **68**, 275
Gallinule, Common - **89**, 276
Gannet, Northern - **123**, 278
Gnatcatcher, Blue-gray - **180–181**, 280
Godwit, Hudsonian - **92**, 276
Goldeneye, Barrow's - **76**, 276
    Common - **76**, 276
Golden-Plover, American - **90–91**, 276
Goldfinch, American - **203**, 280

Goose, Cackling - **267**
    Canada - **66**, 275
    Snow - **65**, 275
Goshawk, Northern - **136**, 278
Grackle, Boat-tailed - **268**
    Common - **229**, 281
Grebe, Horned - **79**, 276
    Pied-billed - **78–79**, 276
    Red-necked - **79**, 276
    Western - **267**
Grosbeak, Black-headed - **261**, 282
    Blue - **262–263**, 282
    Evening - **195–196**, 280
    Pine - **196**, 280
    Rose-breasted - **260–261**, 282
Grouse, Ruffed - **77**, 276
    Spruce - **267**
Guillemot, Black - **105–106**, 277
Gull, Black-headed - **108**, 277
    Bonaparte's - **108**, 277
    Glaucous - **113–114**, 277
    Great Black-backed - **114–115**, 277
    Herring - **110–111**, 277
    Iceland - **112**, 277
    Ivory - **107**, 277
    Laughing - **108–109**, 277
    Lesser Black-backed - **113**, 277
    Little - **108**, 277
    Ring-billed - **109**, 277
Gyrfalcon - **149**, 279
Harrier, Northern - **134**, 278
Hawk, Broad-winged - **137–138**, 278
    Cooper's - **135–136**, 278
    Red-shouldered - **137**, 278
    Red-tailed - **138**, 278
    Rough-legged - **138**, 278
    Sharp-shinned - **134–135**, 278
Heron, Great Blue - **127**, 278
    Green - **130**, 278
    Little Blue - **128–129**, 278
    Tricolored - **129**, 278
Hummingbird, Calliope - **86**, 276
    Ruby-throated - **85–86**, 276
    Rufous - **86**, 276
Ibis, Glossy - **132**, 278
Jaeger, Long-tailed - **267**
    Parasitic - **102**, 277
    Pomarine - **102**, 277
Jay, Blue - **166**, 279
Junco, Dark-eyed - **210–212**, 281
Kestrel, American - **147–148**, 279
Killdeer - **91**, 276
Kingbird, Eastern - **152–153**, 279
    Western - **151–152**, 279
Kingfisher, Belted - **141**, 279
Kinglet, Golden-crowned - **174–175**, 280
    Ruby-crowned - **173–174**, 280
Kite, Swallow-tailed - **133**, 278
Kittiwake, Black-legged - **107**, 277
Knot, Red - **93**, 276
Lark, Horned - **169–170**, 279
Longspur, Lapland - **203–204**, 280
Loon, Common - **118–119**, 278
    Pacific - **118**, 278
    Red-throated - **117–118**, 278
Mallard - **68–69**, 275
Martin, Purple - **171–172**, 280
Meadowlark, Eastern - **224**, 281
Merganser, Common - **77**, 276
    Hooded - **77**, 276
    Red-breasted - **77**, 276
Merlin - **148–149**, 279
Mockingbird, Northern - **186–187**, 280
Murre, Common - **103–104**, 277
    Thick-billed - **104**, 277
Nighthawk, Common - **83–84**, 276
Night-Heron, Black-crowned - **130–131**, 278
    Yellow-crowned - **131–132**, 278
Nuthatch, Red-breasted - **178–179**, 280
    White-breasted - **179**, 280
Oriole, Baltimore - **225–226**, 281
    Bullock's - **225**, 281
    Orchard - **224–225**, 281
Osprey - **133**, 278
Ovenbird - **229–230**, 281
Owl, Barred - **140**, 278
    Boreal - **140**, 278
    Great Horned - **138–139**, 278
    Long-eared - **267**
    Northern Saw-whet - **140–141**, 278
    Short-eared - **140**, 278
    Snowy - **139**, 278
Oystercatcher, American - **90**, 276
Partridge, Gray - **267**
Parula, Northern - **243–244**, 282
Phalarope, Red - **101–102**, 277
    Red-necked - **101**, 277
    Wilson's - **101**, 277
Pheasant, Ring-necked - **78**, 276
Phoebe, Eastern - **158–159**, 279
    Say's - **159–160**, 279
Pigeon, Band-tailed - **80**, 276
    Rock - **79–80**, 276
Pintail, Northern - **70**, 275
Pipit, American - **195**, 280
Plover, Black-bellied - **90**, 276

Semipalmated - **91–92**, 276
Puffin, Atlantic - **106–107**, 277
Rail, Virginia - **86–87**, 276
Raven, Common - **167–168**, 279
Razorbill - **104–105**, 277
Redhead - **71**, 275
Redpoll, Common - **198**, 280
Redstart, American - **241–242**, 282
Robin, American - **192–193**, 280
Sanderling - **93**, 277
Sandpiper, Baird's - **94**, 277
    Least - **94–95**, 277
    Pectoral - **95**, 277
    Purple - **93–94**, 277
    Semipalmated - **95–96**, 277
    Solitary - **99**, 277
    Spotted - **98–99**, 277
    Stilt - **267**
    Upland - **92**, 276
    Western - **267**
    White-rumped - **95**, 277
Sapsucker, Yellow-bellied - **143**, 279
Scaup, Greater - **71**, 275
    Lesser - **267**
Scoter, Black - **75**, 276
    Surf **74**, 276
    White-winged - **74–75**, 276
Shearwater, Cory's - **120–121**, 278
    Great - **121–122**, 278
    Manx - **122**, 278
    Sooty - **121**, 278
Shoveler, Northern - **67**, 275
Shrike, Loggerhead - **165**, 279
    Northern - **165–166**, 279
Siskin, Pine - **202**, 280
Skimmer, Black - **117**, 277
Skua, South Polar - **267**
Snipe, Wilson's - **97–98**, 277
Solitaire, Townsend's - **188**, 280
Sora - **88**, 276
Sparrow, American Tree - **210**, 281
    Black-throated - **205**, 281
    Brewer's - **208–209**, 281
    Chipping - **206–207**, 281
    Clay-colored - **207–208**, 281
    Field - **208**, 281
    Fox - **209**, 281
    Grasshopper - **204–205**, 281
    Harris's - **213**, 281
    Henslow's - **217**, 281
    House - **194**, 280
    Lark - **205–206**, 281
    LeConte's - **215–216**, 281

Lincoln's - **220**, 281
Nelson's - **215–217**, 281
Saltmarsh - **267**
Savannah - **217–218**, 281
Seaside - **215**, 281
Song - **219–220**, 281
Swamp - **221**, 281
Vesper - **214–215**, 281
White-crowned - **212–213**, 281
White-throated - **213–214**, 281
Starling, European - **187–188**, 280
Storm-Petrel, Leach's - **120**, 278
    Wilson's - **119**, 278
Swallow, Bank - **170**, 279
    Barn - **172**, 280
    Cave - **173**, 280
    Cliff - **172–173**, 280
    Northern Rough-winged - **171**, 279
    Tree - **170–171**, 279
Swift, Chimney - **85**, 276
Tanager, Scarlet - **259**, 282
    Summer - **258–259**, 282
    Western - **259–260**, 282
Teal, Blue-winged - **67**, 275
    Green-winged - **70–71**, 275
Tern, Arctic - **116–117**, 277
    Bridled - **115**, 277
    Caspian - **115**, 277
    Common - **116**, 277
    Roseate - **115–116**, 277
    Royal - **117**, 277
Thrasher, Brown - **185–186**, 280
Thrush, Bicknell's - **190**, 280
    Gray-cheeked - **189–190**, 280
    Hermit - **191-192**, 280
    Swainson's - **190–191**, 280
    Varied - **193–194**, 280
    Wood - **192**, 280
Towhee, Eastern - **221–222**, 281
Turnstone, Ruddy - **92–93**, 276
Veery - **189**, 280
Vireo, Bell's - **161**, 279
    Blue-headed - **162–163**, 279
    Cassin's - **162**, 279
    Philadelphia - **163**, 279
    Red-eyed - **164–165**, 279
    Warbling - **164**, 279
    White-eyed - **160–161**, 279
    Yellow-throated - **161–162**, 279
Vulture, Black - **132**, 278
    Turkey - **132–133**, 278
Warbler, Bay-breasted - **245–246**, 282
    Black-and-white - **233–234**, 281

Black-throated Blue - **249–250**, 282
Black-throated Gray - **255**, 282
Black-throated Green - **256–257**, 282
Blackburnian - **246**, 282
Blackpoll - **248–249**, 282
Blue-winged - **232–233**, 281
Canada - **257**, 282
Cape May - **242**, 282
Cerulean - **243**, 282
Chestnut-sided - **248**, 282
Connecticut - **237–238**, 282
Golden-winged - **232**, 281
Hermit - **256**, 282
Hooded - **240–241**, 282
Kentucky - **239**, 282
Kirtland's - **268**
MacGillivray's - **238**, 282
Magnolia - **244–245**, 282
Mourning - **238–239**, 282
Nashville - **236–237**, 282
Orange-crowned - **235–236**, 282
Palm - **250–251**, 282
Pine - **251–252**, 282
Prairie - **254–255**, 282
Prothonotary - **234**, 281
Swainson's - **268**
Tennessee - **234–235**, 281
Townsend's - **255–256**, 282
Virginia's - **237**, 282
Wilson's - **257–258**, 282
Worm-eating - **230**, 281
Yellow - **246–247**, 282
Yellow-rumped - **252–253**, 282
Yellow-throated - **253–254**, 282
Waterthrush, Louisiana - **230–231**, 281
    Northern - **231**, 281
Waxwing, Bohemian - **175–176**, 280
    Cedar - **176–177**, 280
Wheatear, Northern - **194**, 280
Whimbrel - **92**, 276
Whip-poor-will, Eastern - **84**, 276
Wigeon, American - **68**, 275
    Eurasian - **68**, 275
Willet - **100**, 277
Woodcock, American - **96–97**, 277
Woodpecker, American Three-toed - **144**, 279
    Black-backed - **144**, 279
    Downy - **144–145**, 279
    Hairy - **145**, 279
    Pileated - **267**
    Red-bellied - **142–143**, 279
    Red-headed - **141–142**, 279
Wood-Pewee, Eastern - **154**, 279

Western - **267**
Wren, Bewick's - **267**
    Carolina - **183–184**, 280
    House - **181**, 280
    Marsh - **183**, 280
    Sedge - **182–183**, 280
    Winter - **182**, 280
Yellowlegs, Greater - **100**, 277
    Lesser - **99**, 277
Yellowthroat, Common - **239–240**, 282

"The scenic splendors of Monhegan grow on one, so that a month there passes only too quickly, and one truly regrets to see the high island growing fainter in the distance as he leaves for home."

Wolcott W. Ellsworth
Monhegan Island, Maine, 1912

ABOUT THE AUTHOR

Brett Ewald has been studying and enjoying birds and nature for over 40 years, specializing in migration and distribution patterns. He spent ten years conducting migration research for Braddock Bay Raptor Research along the shores of Lake Ontario, including directing the Hamlin Beach Lakewatch and co-authoring a monograph on waterbird movements. He was the guide and owner of Lakeshore Nature Tours, sharing the joys of birding at premier locations throughout North America including, of course, Monhegan Island. Brett is currently the Director of New Jersey Audubon's Cape May Bird Observatory and shares his favorite moments with his wife, Sheryl, and Neah Bay, a Treeing Walker Coonhound.